Macromedia
Flash MX

Matthew Pizzi, et al.

SAMS

Unleashed

Flash MX Unleashed

Copyright © 2003 by Sams Publishing

All rights reserved. No part of this book shall be reproduced, stored in a retrieval system, or transmitted by any means, electronic, mechanical, photocopying, recording, or otherwise, without written permission from the publisher. No patent liability is assumed with respect to the use of the information contained herein. Although every precaution has been taken in the preparation of this book, the publisher and author assume no responsibility for errors or omissions. Nor is any liability assumed for damages resulting from the use of the information contained herein.

International Standard Book Number: 0-672-32401-6

Library of Congress Catalog Card Number: 2002100052

Printed in the United States of America

First Printing: July 2002

05 04 03 02   4 3 2 1

Trademarks

All terms mentioned in this book that are known to be trademarks or service marks have been appropriately capitalized. Sams Publishing cannot attest to the accuracy of this information. Use of a term in this book should not be regarded as affecting the validity of any trademark or service mark.

Flash MX is a registered trademark of Macromedia, Inc. Windows is a registered trademark of Microsoft Corporation. Mac and OS X are registered trademarks of Apple Computers, Inc. SWiSH is a registered trademark of SWiSHzone.com Pty Ltd. FlashKit and FLASH*typer* are copyrighted by INT Media Group, Inc.

Warning and Disclaimer

Every effort has been made to make this book as complete and as accurate as possible, but no warranty or fitness is implied. The information provided is on an "as is" basis. The authors and the publisher shall have neither liability nor responsibility to any person or entity with respect to any loss or damages arising from the information contained in this book or from the use of the Web site or programs accompanying it.

EXECUTIVE EDITOR
Michael Stephens

ACQUISITIONS EDITOR
Kim Spilker

DEVELOPMENT EDITOR
Brian Proffitt

MANAGING EDITOR
Charlotte Clapp

PROJECT EDITOR
George E. Nedeff

COPY EDITOR
Bart Reed

INDEXER
Ginny Bess

PROOFREADER
Andrea Dugan

TECHNICAL EDITOR
George Gordon

TEAM COORDINATOR
Lynne Williams

MULTIMEDIA DEVELOPER
Dan Scherf

INTERIOR DESIGNER
Gary Adair

COVER DESIGNER
Aren Howell

PAGE LAYOUT
Michelle Mitchell
Rebecca Harmon

Contents at a Glance

Table of Contents

About the Authors

Matthew Pizzi is the Training Director at Train Simple, a software training company specializing in multimedia products, located in Santa Monica, California. Matthew has been teaching fulltime for five years and is the author of multiple training CDs, including his "Up to Speed" series, offering computer-based training in Flash, Dreamweaver, Final Cut Pro, and Photoshop. For more information on classes or training CDs, visit www.trainsimple.com.

Dennis Baldwin is the lead developer for Eternal-Media, a Web/multimedia firm providing technology solutions for ministries and nonprofit organizations (www.eternal-media.com). He also maintains a couple of online resources for Flash and ColdFusion developers at www.flashcfm.com and www.devmx.com.

Todd Coulson joined Haley Productions, a company specializing in multimedia, film-video, and the Internet, in late 1999. Todd's knowledge and creativity with Flash and Director has continued to expand with the growing multimedia industry at large. Due to the increased creativity of employees such as Todd, Haley Productions is enjoying its most profitable year to date. Todd earned his Associate Degree in Multimedia and Web Design from the Art Institute of Philadelphia in 1999. Prior to attending the Art Institute, Todd got his B.S. in Business Administration from Marist College.

George G. Gordon has a Bachelor of Science in Business Administration from Indiana University and has more than 20 years of experience in Information Services. He has designed, implemented, supported, assisted, or served in every aspect of business enterprise. He has also managed, developed, implemented, and maintained a number of Web sites. He currently manages seminars, workshops, and symposiums and has his own project-management consulting firm. He lives in Indianapolis, Indiana with his wonderful and supportive wife of 28 years, Margaret, and their two cats, Bonnie and Clyde.

Brian Hoard is an illustrator and animator, and has been accused of being a cartoon himself. He has spent the better part of his life in front of computers, where he has created Web sites using Flash and has been recognized for his development of user-friendly Flash sites. He has helped countless newbies through his advice on Flash, including technical issues through posts on the Macromedia Flash newsgroups. Through his addiction to video gaming, he has saved the Earth from near destruction almost daily. He runs BHH Studio Art & Animation at www.bhhstudio.com, where he provides original artwork, graphics consulting, and animation products in exchange for food. Brian can be contacted via e-mail at bhoard@bhhstudio.com.

Randy Osborne started using Flash in 1998 for interface design mockups in a large network management company. When Flash 4 was released, he quickly jumped into using ActionScript for making small games for Web sites. In 1999, Randy started working at Icebox as Lead Flash Programmer, creating games and interactive elements on the Web site to support the shows being produced there. Currently he works at the Game Show Network as Lead Flash Programmer, developing games and interactive content for the Web site as well as developing the next generation of interactive television games. He can be contacted at `randyunleashed@hotmail.com`.

James Smith graduated with a degree in Mathematics from Cambridge in 1994. After a brief career as a ship broker, he gave up city life in favor of starting a company with university friends, writing software for digital satellite receivers. He learned his trade working for David Braben, the co-author of *Elite*. He now works as a freelance contractor and lives in south London.

David Vogeleer is the Administrative Coordinator at a Virginia-based technology company. Among his many marketing responsibilities, he has been instrumental in designing and developing Flash-based multimedia Web sites, presentations, and marketing materials. He is an avid poster to ActionScript.org as well as flashmagazine.com. David is also a fulltime student at Old Dominion University, where he will be graduating this fall with a Bachelors degree in Marketing. In addition of all this, David manages his own personal site for Flash experiments and news at `www.evolutionar-e.com`.

Dan Waters is a 19-year-old Computer Science major at the University of Texas at Arlington. An all-around Web enthusiast, Dan spends a substantial amount of time developing Flash applications, designing data interfaces, and programming. If he isn't found on the computer, he can be found behind a drum set or a guitar. His company, Catapultic Web Solutions, provides business intelligence services to corporate clients across the country.

Dedication

I would like to dedicate this book to John and Catherine Pizzi.

Acknowledgments

Matthew Pizzi. As a long-time developer and trainer using Macromedia products, it's truly an honor to share my knowledge with the world through the means of this text. It is of an equal privilege to work with some of the finest people in the Flash community, and I can't thank my coauthors enough for their invaluable input and contributions to this book. Everyone involved with this project has shown a tremendous amount of passion and craftsmanship, yielding what I think is one of the finest Flash books in print.

I would especially like to thank, in no specific order, Kim Spilker, Brian Proffitt, Todd Coulson, David Vogeleer, George Gordon, and Bart Reed for all their contributions to this book. I am also grateful for Ronnie Pirovino's willingness to offer his knowledge and expertise whenever I needed it.

Finally, I would like to thank Katy for all her patience and support throughout the development of this book.

Dennis Baldwin. I would like to thank my amazing wife, Jamie, for her understanding and support through all the late nights. Also, thanks to my friends and family, who helped take my mind off things by interrupting me with door knocks, phone calls, e-mails, and Xbox. You've all been a great stress reliever! To Kim Spilker, who contacted me out of the blue for this project. A special thanks goes out to everyone in the FlashCFM community—you guys and gals have been a great group to converse with. And last but not least, I thank God for giving me the passion for these technologies and the willingness to learn.

Todd Coulson would like to thank most of all his family, including his mother Hilary, his father D. Robert, his sister Ann, and his grandmother Dorothy, for always encouraging him to outdo himself. He would like to thank the staff at Haley Productions, including Bill Haley, Luke Krill, Pete Bretz, Meei Ling Ng, Lisa Kruczek, Travis Longwell, and Brennan Lindeen, for allowing him to work on this book and for giving him the opportunity to grow as a person and as a multimedia developer. Also, he would like to thank all his friends, too numerous to mention by name, but who have stuck with him through the years of endless work. They have been there through all the ups and downs in his career and in his life, and he thanks them endlessly for that. Finally, he would like to thank the staff of Sams Publishing and the crew who collaborated to make this book possible.

James Smith. Thanks to Jonathan Roach, possibly the only man in this industry who has ever managed to teach me anything.

Dan Waters. I'd like to thank my parents for fostering my interests and putting up with my late-night gaming, my brother Steve for providing me with the necessary resources, Jasmine Nacua for her continued support, Dr. Carter Tiernan for clearing up many, many programming questions, Kim Spilker at Sams Publishing for the great opportunity, 2Advanced Studios for the bottomless lake of influence, and Brian Proffitt, George Nedeff, George Gordon, and Bart Reed for their unmatched editorial skills.

David Vogeleer. I want to start out by thanking my parents. They are the best. Thanks to Kevin for all the encouragement and advice; to Caroline for closing my laptop when it was obvious I needed a break; to Cathy for helping me out all those times; to Mountain Dew for their great product; AMP for helping me through countless sleepless nights; and to all my friends and family for their overwhelming support. Also, thanks to the Sams Publishing team, especially George Nedeff, Bart Reed, Brian Proffitt, and George Gordon for their great work in creating this book. A special thanks to Kim Spilker for this great opportunity, and of course, the Peeps. Finally, thanks to God for never letting me accept less than what I'm capable of.

We Want to Hear from You!

As the reader of this book, *you* are our most important critic and commentator. We value your opinion and want to know what we're doing right, what we could do better, what areas you'd like to see us publish in, and any other words of wisdom you're willing to pass our way.

As an executive editor for Sams Publishing, I welcome your comments. You can e-mail or write me directly to let me know what you did or didn't like about this book—as well as what we can do to make our books better.

Please note that I cannot help you with technical problems related to the *topic* of this book. We do have a User Services group, however, where I will forward specific technical questions related to the book.

When you write, please be sure to include this book's title and author as well as your name, e-mail address, and phone number. I will carefully review your comments and share them with the author and editors who worked on the book.

E-mail: feedback@samspublishing.com

Mail: Michael Stephens
               Executive Editor
               Sams Publishing
               201 West 103rd Street
               Indianapolis, IN 46290 USA

For more information about this book or another Sams publishing title, visit our Web site at www.samspublishing.com. Type the ISBN (excluding hyphens) or the title of a book in the Search field to find the page you're looking for.

Introduction

Flash MX, Macromedia's latest effort for its leading Web animation program, is not only an upgrade, but a generational change. Macromedia's new MX strategy caters to a more sophisticated and elegant Web-development process as well as integration among various software applications. Many argue the significance Flash will have on the Web. I for one find it obvious that the majority of Web content in the future will be viewed through the Flash player, regardless of current setbacks.

Flash MX offers some exciting advancements, particularly in the areas of middleware and server communication. Digital video (DV), now able to play natively in the Flash 6 player, pushes the envelope for richer, more interactive experiences. This book covers in tremendous detail how to interact with middleware and how to use DV appropriately.

Flash content can be found everywhere, from PCs, PlayStation consoles, ATMs, and handheld devices. As digital convergence becomes a hotter and debatable topic, one thing is for sure: The Flash player will be found as a key component to the growth of digital information.

This book is designed to help current Web developers create engaging Web sites through the use of Flash. A very large portion of this book is dedicated to the development of Flash Web applications through the integration of ActionScript and middleware such as PHP and ColdFusion. This text can be used by Flash novices, but it does assume Web-development experience. The first couple chapters discuss some Flash basics but move quickly into ActionScript and application development. You'll fine many hands-on exercises as well as a wealth of Flash information on the companion Web site, `http://www.flashmxunleashed.com`, to help you learn Flash and get the most out of this book. As a trainer, I wanted to make this book just as much a learning tool as it is a reference.

Flash MX Unleashed is designed to help you succeed in your Flash development. Please feel free to share your stories by e-mailing me at `mpz@trainsimple.com`. If you have training needs, visit my training company's Web site at `http://www.trainsimple.com`.

What's New in Flash MX?

By Matt Pizzi

This chapter is designed to get existing Flash designers and developers up to speed in the latest Flash MX technology. If you are new to Flash, you may want to skip this chapter and refer back to it once you feel comfortable with the basics. Chapter 2, "Introducing Flash MX," is an appropriate starting place for a beginner or someone less comfortable with Flash, because this chapter hits the ground running and assumes prior Flash experience.

The most obvious change in Flash MX is the redesigned interface. The interface has new dockable panels and a Properties Inspector, which provides a quick way to access vital information about a selected item. The interface is deconstructed in Chapter 2. To avoid redundancy, we'll move on to other features. This chapter is a quick-and-dirty rundown of what I consider the top features of Flash MX. Enjoy!

The New Timeline

Yes, for the third straight release of Flash, Macromedia has changed the timeline's frame-drawing and selection style. This can be seen as good news for some, bad for others. It's good for those of you who insist on changing Flash 5's preferences to have the timeline mimic the Flash 4 drawing and selection style; it's bad for those of you who have the mentality of "out with old, in with new," like I do, because Macromedia has changed the timeline to behave a lot more like the Flash 4 timeline.

As shown in Figure 1.1, the timeline draws blank keyframes with hollow circles again. To move a frame, you must click it once to highlight it and then click it again to move it. To highlight certain frames, you simply click and drag.

FIGURE 1.1

The Flash MX timeline.

Of course, there are also new layer folders for sorting out content and managing the size of the timeline. These can be extremely convenient in large projects because working with numerous layers can become unwieldy.

One of my favorite new features is having the ability to move more than one frame at once. By holding down the Cmd (Mac) or Ctrl (Windows) key and clicking a frame, you then get access to a two-way arrow, allowing you to move more than one frame at a time. This is a huge timesaver (see Figure 1.2). As you can see, this book will cover features for both the Macintosh and Windows operating systems and differences will be pointed out accordingly. The figures in this book also display both the Mac and Windows machines.

FIGURE 1.2

Editing more than one frame at a time.

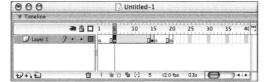

Distribute to Layers

Distribute to Layers is an awesome feature, especially if you're into text effects. Yes, other great programs are out there, such as SWiSH and SWfx, but if you only use text effects once in a while, this is a cheaper solution.

This book contains many exercises. Most exercises are numbered in different steps. Each step explains what is to be done, and the result of that step will follow in a separate sentence.

Distribute Text to Layers

Here are the steps to follow to distribute text to layers:

1. If the Tools panel is not visible, choose Window, Tools. This command makes the tools visible on the left side of the stage. In the Tools panel, click the Type tool to select it (T is the keyboard shortcut). Notice your cursor changes to an I-beam to allow you to place an insertion point for typing. Click anywhere on the stage to place the insertion point and type the word **TEXT**.

2. With the text selected, drag your cursor over the text to highlight it. Then choose Modify, Break Apart. This will separate the letters into individual items, as shown in Figure 1.3.

   Notice that when you choose Break Apart, each letter is separated into its own editable text item. This behavior is new in Flash MX. In Flash 5, Break Apart would turn the text into a primitive shape. That's still possible in MX. To do that, select all the separate layers by clicking each one with the Shift key depressed (or drag a marquee with the Arrow tool) and then simply choose Modify, Break Apart for a second time. This will turn the letters into primitive shapes.

3. Now that the letters are all separate items, choose Modify, Distribute to Layers. Notice, as shown in Figure 1.4, that all the letters show up on their own independent layers, all appropriately named. Also, all the content on the original layer (layer 1) has been moved and replaced accordingly.

FIGURE 1.3
The word TEXT
*after it has been
broken apart.*

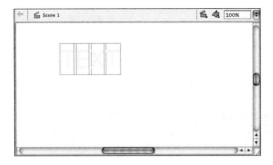

FIGURE 1.4
The word TEXT
*distributed to
layers.*

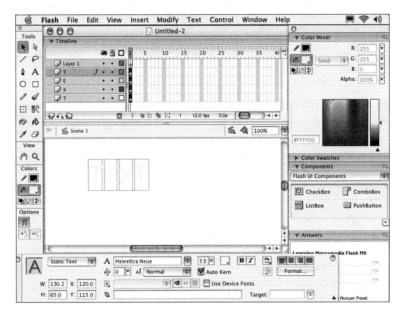

Named Anchors

Most sites designed completely in Flash currently have a tendency to open up in a JavaScript pop-out window, with no buttons or location bar. This is done on purpose, because if standard Web browser navigation is left visible, it could be detrimental to the usability and functionality of the site. Each SWF file is embedded into an HTML document. Therefore, you can think of the entire Flash site as one HTML page, because most likely, new content is getting loaded into the existing SWF file, thus staying in the same HTML page. Flash MX offers a new feature called *named anchors*, which allow the browser navigation to communicate with the anchors, much like it would communicate with named anchors in a standard HTML document. You can place a named anchor on a frame. These named anchors are compliant with standard browser navigation buttons. Furthermore, you can also bookmark a named anchor. All this gives standard Web browsers the ability to communicate with the Flash movie, and vice versa. Let's take a look at how to build a Flash movie that uses named anchors.

Using Named Anchors

From this book's companion Web site, `http://www.flashmxunleashed.com`, download the tutorial file called `anchors.fla`. In this document you'll notice four different frames, and each frame contains different content. You'll also notice `stop` actions on each of the frames. The buttons also have actions—when they are clicked, they move to the appropriate frame. In this exercise, we're going to add named anchors so that the browser's buttons have the functionality of moving backward and forward through the Flash movie. Here are the steps to follow:

1. Open the movie you downloaded, `anchors.fla`. Create a new layer by clicking the Add Layer button. Then name this layer **anchors**. To rename a layer, simply double-click the layer to highlight it and type a new name.

2. You need to create and name the anchor in this step. Therefore, make sure your playhead is on frame 1 and that the anchors layer is the active layer. If your Properties Inspector is not open, choose Window, Properties. In the Properties Inspector, name the frame and choose the Named Anchor option, as shown in Figure 1.5. The name of the frame will act as the anchor name. Notice the small anchor icon that appears on the frame, as shown in Figure 1.6.

   Note that in Edit, Preferences, under the General tab, you can choose to have the first frame in each scene to be a named anchor automatically.

3. Insert a blank keyframe in frame 2 of the anchors layer. Note that you can only name keyframes. Name the frame in the Properties Inspector and choose Named Anchor.

   Note that to remove a named anchor, you can simply uncheck the option in the Properties Inspector.

4. Continue to add blank keyframes and name them just as you did in step 2, until all four frames are finished.

5. This step is very important in getting the functionality of the browser's buttons to work properly. Choose File, Publish Settings. This will launch the Publishing Settings dialog box, as shown in Figure 1.7.

6. Be sure to check the HTML box under the Formats tab. This will activate the HTML tab. Click the HTML tab to view the HTML options.

7. In the Template drop-down menu, choose Flash with Named Anchors. You'll notice that some JavaScript is written when published as an HTML document, activating the browser's navigation buttons. Without this, the buttons will appear gray and are not functional. Notice in Figure 1.8 the buttons' navigation is active as a result of choosing this template.

   It is important to know that the additional HTML and JavaScript Flash writes, when exported, is not part of the SWF file. If the end goal is to place this Flash movie into Dreamweaver or GoLive, at the time of this writing, you must open the HTML document Flash generates through one of those programs by choosing File, Open in that program. Otherwise, you will have to copy the HTML and paste it into an existing HTML document or rewrite the code.

8. You're now ready to check out your work. Choose File, Publish Preview, HTML. Notice, at first, that the navigation buttons in the browser are inactive. Click one of the buttons in the Flash movie to advance it to another frame. The Back button is now active and will work, as shown in Figure 1.8.

FIGURE 1.5

Naming the frame and choosing Named Anchor in the Properties Inspector.

FIGURE 1.6

Anchor icon on the frame.

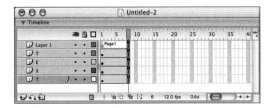

FIGURE 1.7
*The Publish
Settings dialog
box.*

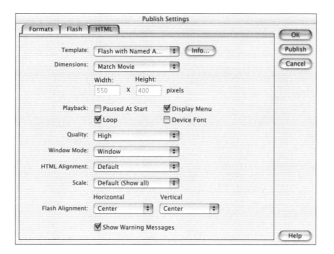

FIGURE 1.8
*The browser's
navigation is
active.*

Quick Start Templates

Quick Start templates provide yet another great timesaving feature in Flash MX. They allow you to create a document and save it as a template. By saving a document as a template, you start every new movie at that point. Some stock templates are available for you to use, but what's even more powerful is the fact that you can create your own. To create your own template is simple. All you have to do is open the file you want saved as a template. With that file open (or if you've done some work in Flash and you want that to be a template), under the File menu choose Save As Template. This will launch the Save As Template dialog box, as shown in Figure 1.9. Here are the options available in this dialog box:

- **Name**. Here, you can name your template. Name it something that makes sense so that it's easy to find when you need to access that template.
- **Category**. Choose a category in this drop-down menu where you want to store your template. If you don't like the categories Macromedia has set up, create your own by typing in the text field.
- **Description**. Use this area to briefly describe the template. This can be useful if you're working on a large project that stores many templates. A description may make it easier to select or find a particular template.

FIGURE 1.9

The Save As Template dialog box.

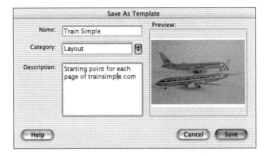

Now that you've saved your template, how do you access it? Simple—under the File menu, choose New from Template. This will open a new window with all the contents of the template.

> **Note**
>
> To update or change a template, you must open that file. When you save a document as a template, it gets stored in the Templates folder in the Applications folder. Typically to find that folder, you must go into the Flash MX folder and then choose the First Run folder, to find the Templates folder. In the Templates folder are the different categories, all divided into separate folders. Choose the folder for the category you saved your template under. In that folder you should be able to find the file. If you update the file, you will not be updating files based on the template.

Backward Compatibility

Even though you were brave enough to buy Flash MX, it doesn't mean the rest of the world was. You can still share files with other team members or clients who are using Flash 5. Once you're done with a project, choose File, Save As. This will launch the dialog box shown in Figure 1.10. In the Format (Mac) or Save as Type (Win) drop-down menu, choose Flash 5. Flash will automatically alert you if there are incompatible features in the document as you save it to Flash 5.

FIGURE **1.10**

The Save As dialog box.

Prebuilt Components

The prebuilt components comprise a great new feature in Flash and are covered in detail in Chapter 16, "Components," which also covers building your own components. The ability to use these components is one of the reasons to upgrade to Flash MX. Flash MX components simplify the creation of complex interactions. In Flash 5, it was pretty easy to make dynamic text scrollable, but it's even easier (and cooler) in Flash MX. The process is a simple one, so let's take a look.

Building a Scrollbar with Prebuilt Components

To follow along with this exercise, visit the Unleashed companion Web site and download the file `precomp.fla`. This file consists of several layers, but the one we'll discuss here is the component layer. In this case, we have a text field that's a bit long; in fact, it covers some of our artwork. To fix this, we are going to use the scrollbar prebuilt component. Here are the steps to follow:

1. Open the file `precomp.fla`, which you downloaded from the Web site.

2. Make sure the component layer is selected. If it's not, you can select it by clicking it. If the other layers are not already locked, you may want to lock them by clicking the bullet under the padlock column of the Layers panel.

3. Click the block of text to select it. In the Properties Inspector, you'll notice that it's set to static text. You cannot apply the scrollbar component to a static text box. In the drop-down menu, choose Dynamic Text, as shown in Figure 1.11.

4. It's very important to name the text field. Go ahead and name yours **text**.
5. Another key factor in making the component work is changing the line type from single to multiline. Use the Line Type drop-down menu in the Properties Inspector, as shown in Figure 1.12.
6. Now select the Text tool. With the Text tool, click inside the block of text, as if you were going to do some editing. As displayed in Figure 1.13, hold down the Shift key on the keyboard and double-click the resize handle of the text box. You'll notice that it becomes solid. This will allow you to resize the text field to a smaller size, hiding any excess text. The hidden text is not harmed or deleted; it's just not visible within the viewable area of the text box. When resizing, make sure to leave room for the scrollbar.
7. Make sure the Components panel is open. If it's not, choose Window, Components. In this panel, simply choose the scrollbar component and drag it into the text field, as displayed in Figure 1.14.
8. Test the movie to see how it works. Under the Control menu, choose Test Movie. Wasn't that simple?

Static Text
Dynamic Text
Input Text
Helvetica Neue
53
Normal
Auto Kern
Format...
Use Device Fonts
Target:

FIGURE 1.11
Choose Dynamic Text in the Text Type drop-down menu.

Dynamic Text
<Instance Name>
Helvetica Neue
53
Normal
Auto Kern
Format...
Single Line
Multiline
Multiline no wrap
Var:
Character...
Target:

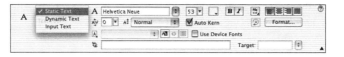

FIGURE 1.12
The Line Type drop-down menu in the Properties Inspector.

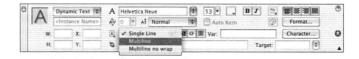

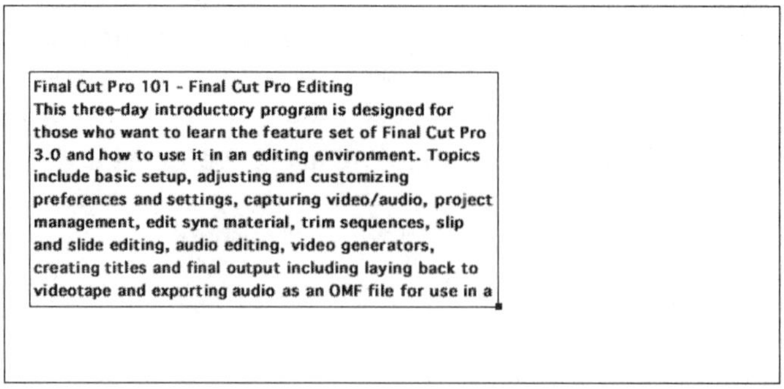
Final Cut Pro 101 - Final Cut Pro Editing
This three-day introductory program is designed for those who want to learn the feature set of Final Cut Pro 3.0 and how to use it in an editing environment. Topics include basic setup, adjusting and customizing preferences and settings, capturing video/audio, project management, edit sync material, trim sequences, slip and slide editing, audio editing, video generators, creating titles and final output including laying back to videotape and exporting audio as an OMF file for use in a

FIGURE 1.13
Notice that the resize handle is solid. This will allow the text box to be resized, regardless of the amount of text within it.

FIGURE **1.14**

When placing the scrollbar, be sure to place it inside the dynamic text field.

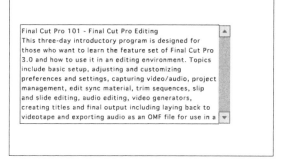

```
Final Cut Pro 101 - Final Cut Pro Editing
This three-day introductory program is designed for
those who want to learn the feature set of Final Cut Pro
3.0 and how to use it in an editing environment. Topics
include basic setup, adjusting and customizing
preferences and settings, capturing video/audio, project
management, edit sync material, trim sequences, slip
and slide editing, audio editing, video generators,
creating titles and final output including laying back to
videotape and exporting audio as an OMF file for use in a
```

As you can see, using prebuilt components is fun. We'll be using each of these components in Chapter 16. The possibilities are endless.

Product Integration

Updating graphics has never been easier. If you are a Dreamweaver user and you've been using the Fireworks Edit feature, you'll now find that same functionality in Flash MX. For those of you who don't use Dreamweaver or the Fireworks Edit feature, you're in for a nice surprise. However, it is important that you own Fireworks and have it installed on your system. Figure 1.15 shows a bitmap graphic in the Library. If for some reason something about the graphic has to change (maybe its background color), instead of opening the source file and making the adjustments (either reimporting the file or updating it through the Library properties), all you have to do is access the Library options menu and then choose Edit With to launch the Select External Editor dialog box. From there, choose Fireworks, as shown in Figure 1.16.

> **Note**
>
> You can also choose other applications, such as Adobe Photoshop and ImageReady.

This will automatically launch Fireworks, which in turn launches a dialog box and prompts you to choose a different source for the image. Choose Yes to find a native equivalent PNG file for the image or No to use the GIF or JPG format used in Flash. If you're just making a minor adjustment, choose No. In the bottom section of the dialog box, you can choose to bypass this dialog box in the future, as shown in Figure 1.17.

FIGURE 1.15

The Library contains graphics.

FIGURE 1.16

The Select External Editor dialog box.

FIGURE 1.17

The Find Source for Editing dialog box.

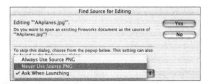

Once you've made the necessary adjustments, click the Done button in the top-left corner of the window, as shown in Figure 1.18. This will close Fireworks and bring you back into Flash with an updated file.

Now, as displayed in Figure 1.19, the image in Flash reflects the changes made in Fireworks. If you do not own Fireworks, you can use another application, such as Adobe Photoshop, to make these changes. In the Library options menu, choose Edit With, which will launch a dialog box asking you to select an editor.

FIGURE 1.18

Click the Done button to save the file's changes and to automatically update the file in Flash.

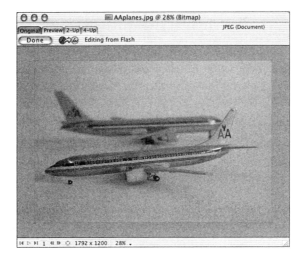

FIGURE 1.19

The image has been automatically updated by the changes made in Fireworks.

Dynamic Media

Flash MX provides the ability to create dynamic JPEG and MP3 files. This means you can load JPEG and MP3 files in runtime, which saves time during the initial download, and create a more interactive experience. For many years this could only be achieved using an application such as Macromedia's Generator. Many Generator faithful probably have already noticed that Generator isn't even supported by Flash MX. However, Macromedia built Generator's number-one feature standard with Flash MX—loading dynamic assets. The following exercise will get you comfortable with creating random dynamic graphics.

Loading in Random Dynamic Bitmaps

This exercise is a simple example of how you can go about creating random images in your Flash movie that load in dynamically. In order to follow along with this exercise, it's best to download all the supporting files located at `http://www.flashmxunleashed.com`. Here are the steps to follow:

1. Open a new document. Save this document as `dynamicImages.fla` in a new folder on your desktop called `media`.

2. After downloading the six images from the companion Web site, be sure to save each in the `media` folder on your desktop. Also note the names of the images, which are `image0.jpg`, `image1.jpg`, `image2.jpg`, `image3.jpg`, `image4.jpg`, and `image5.jpg`.

3. Inside the new document, choose Insert, New Symbol to launch the New Symbol dialog box. Choose the Movie Clip behavior radio button and name your symbol **imageHolder**.

4. Click OK. You will now be placed in the movie clip symbol editing mode. Notice under the timeline the Scene 1 tab and the imageHolder tab. Click the Scene 1 tab to go to the main document.

5. Notice that the stage is empty. Choose Window, Library to open this movie's Library. In the Library, drag out an instance of the imageHolder movie clip and place it anywhere on the stage. Notice the movie clip is nothing more than a crosshair because it currently contains no content.

6. Select the movie clip on the stage. In the Properties Inspector, give it an instance name of **holder**. (If the Properties Inspector is not visible, choose Window, Properties Inspector.)

7. Save this movie in the `media` folder on your desktop.

8. Highlight frame 1 and press F9 on your keyboard to open the Actions panel. In the Actions panel, make sure you are in expert mode. You can enter expert mode by pressing Shift+Cmd+E (Mac) or Shift+Ctrl+E (Windows). Type the following action:

   `_root.holder.loadMovie("image"+random(5)+".jpg");`

   The first part of this script targets the movie clip instance, holder. The `loadMovie` action calls the URL or location of the images. If the images were located in a subdirectory or a directory different from the Flash file, they would have to be sourced accordingly. The name of the image is in quotes, and a random number is concatenated to the literal name of the file to get the number of the image. This is then concatenated to the file extension. Therefore, each image is named `image0.jpg`, `image1.jpg`, and so on.

9. Test the movie by choosing Control, Test Movie. Notice that an image file is loaded into the document. If you continue to test the movie, the images will load in randomly and dynamically.

New ActionScript Editor

Flash MX hosts a series of features that make coding easier and more concise. Code hinting, for example, gives you a pop-out scroll menu in which to choose different conditions when you're scripting. See Figure 1.20 for an example of typing an on() action.

FIGURE 1.20

Code hinting in the ActionScript Editor.

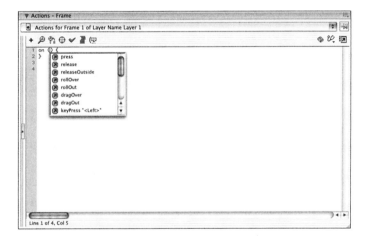

You can change the delay, in seconds, for when the pop-out hint will be activated. You can also choose your own color code to better suit your workflow. In the ActionScript Editor's Options menu, located in the top-right corner of the panel, choose Preferences, as shown in Figure 1.21.

Another wonderful feature of the ActionScript Editor is automatic formatting. This is a nice way to make sure all your code is formatted properly. It comes in handy when you forget to indent, for example, or come across some other formatting issue. By keeping your code formatted properly, it's a lot easier to debug later when you're testing your movies.

The Reference panel has also been revised. If you highlight any piece of your code and click the Reference button, as shown in Figure 1.22, it will launch the newly redesigned Reference panel. This new panel is easier to read and navigate through for additional information.

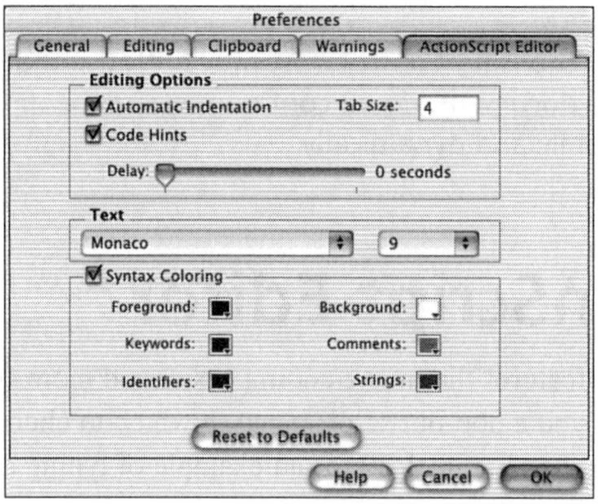

FIGURE 1.21

The ActionScript Editor's Options Menu.

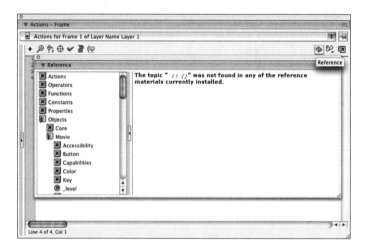

FIGURE 1.22

The newly redesigned Reference panel.

Dynamic Masks

New in Flash MX is the ability to create a dynamic mask. This means any movie clip symbol can be used to mask out another movie clip symbol using the setMask method. The advantage to this is that your Frames panel is not unnecessarily cluttered with mask and mask slave layers.

Possibly one of the most significant enhancements with dynamic masking is the ability to effortlessly create draggable masks (which was never easy in earlier versions of Flash). The addition of draggable masks opens up a whole world of possibilities. For more information on this topic, refer to Chapter 21, "Advanced Interactivity."

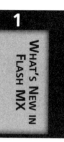

Video Support

Flash MX offers some interesting new features for working with digital video. Many of the hardcore features will be covered in Chapter 9, "Animation Techniques and Digital Video." This section is just a quick overview of what's in store later on. As always, you can import video into Flash and export it out to a QuickTime movie. Now, some new additions can be found in MX. You can embed any QuickTime or Windows Media Player-compatible file format into the Flash movie. The video also becomes an object that you can scale, skew, rotate, and mask. You can even make the video object more interactive using scripting.

Video is supported natively in the Flash MX player with the addition of the Sorenson Spark codec.

Accessibility

With the addition of Flash MX, your Web site can now provide accessible information to people with a variety of disabilities. By doing this, you increase your Web site's marketability to a broader audience. This topic is covered in greater detail on the companion Web site `http://www.flashmxunleashed.com`.

Introducing Flash MX

By Matt Pizzi

IN THIS CHAPTER

- Flash Is Vector Based
- Interface
- Flash MX Preferences
- Keyboard Shortcuts
- Changing the Workspace with the View Menu

Macromedia Flash is a vector-based animation program. However, it is not just limited to animation in the traditional sense. Flash animation is the basis for all things cool on the Web. Going way beyond just traditional animation, Flash gives Web developers the ability to visually communicate and interact with their audiences like never before. The restrictions of HTML are hardly a factor, allowing your imagination to run wild.

Macromedia Flash has become a standard on the Web. Many companies use Flash to impact a greater number of people on the Web, and their messages are more engaging due to the media-rich environment Flash provides.

Flash isn't just limited to nifty graphics and snazzy sounds; it's a hard-core Web-development application—especially with the latest release of Flash MX. Macromedia has decided to switch its naming convention to mark not just a new version of Flash, but also a new generation of the application. This new generation offers you the ability to interact with middleware and other technologies to bring true dynamic content and application development to the Flash platform. Flash's ActionScript is a scripting language built on the ECMAScript standard and closely resembles JavaScript. This is a huge advantage for many; if you know JavaScript, you'll feel comfortable in the ActionScript language because the structures will be familiar to you. However, if this is your first exposure to object-oriented scripting, you'll find that once you get comfortable with ActionScript, learning other types of object-orientated scripting and/or programming languages is a lot easier, because the fundamentals of ActionScript are the same as all object-oriented programming (OOP) languages.

Flash Is Vector Based

Macromedia Flash is a vector-based Web development tool. When graphics are created in Flash, they're constructed of a series of vector points and are connected through math. You gain several advantages when developing content with vector artwork, especially for motion graphics on the Web. Take a look at Figure 2.1. Notice the nice, smooth, crisp lines of the vector graphic on the left and the jagged, low-quality lines of the bitmap on the right.

Vector graphics are especially useful in animation. Oftentimes throughout an animation sequence there will come a point in time when the graphic needs to be scaled up. If a bitmap is being used, the pixels have to be interpolated to account for the new space of the larger image size. When this interpolation occurs, the program will guess as to what the new pixels should look like in terms of color (thus degrading the sharpness) and quality of the original content. If this same scaling animation occurs with a piece of vector artwork, during the scaling sequence the vector points will change position and the math will be recalculated. The change in the mathematics of the vector points does nothing to degrade the quality of the image.

FIGURE 2.1

Vector graphics versus bitmap graphics.

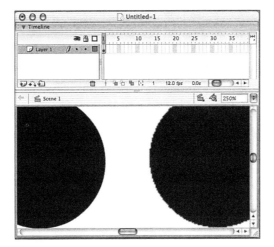

Interface

The new Flash MX interface has many areas to explore. In order to see the many features of this interface, we'll sometimes have to interact with different Flash objects. To do that, I've created a library of artwork that we'll use throughout this book's many lessons. It is located on this book's Web site, www.flashmxunleashed.com.

Installing the Unleashed Common Library

Here are the steps you need to take in order to install the Unleashed common library:

1. Navigate to http:// www.flashmxunleashed.com/library.html using your favorite Web browser and download the Unleashed.fla file.

2. Locate the Macromedia Flash MX program folder on your hard drive.

3. Open the \First Run folder, found within the Flash MX program folder.

4. Open the libraries folder and move the Unleashed.fla file inside of it. You will also notice the other common libraries that are used by Flash, such as the buttons, sounds, and the learning interactions.

5. You can now access the Unleashed library in Flash by selecting the Windows, Common Libraries, Unleashed.fla menu command. This will launch the Unleashed library, as shown in Figure 2.2.

A QuickTime movie can be found on the Web site that shows the installation process of the Unleashed library.

FIGURE 2.2

The Unleashed library.

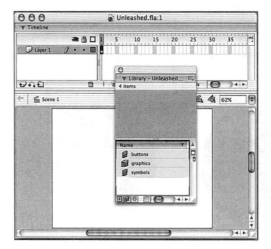

Flash MX sports a brand-new interface that provides a clean style to maximize productivity. Most notable are the new dockable panels and the Properties Inspector. Also, the Layers panel now offers the ability to create subfolders for better organization. Refer to Figures 2.3 and 2.4 to see the Flash MX interface on Macintosh and Windows.

FIGURE 2.3

The new Flash MX interface on the Macintosh. Flash MX in OS X remains true to the Aqua interface.

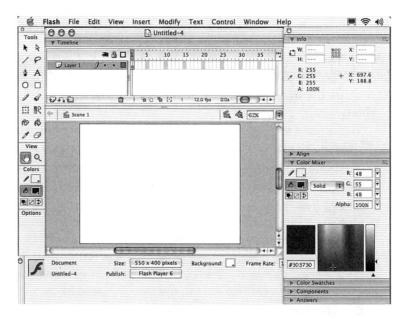

FIGURE **2.4**

The new Flash MX interface on Windows. Notice the nice dockable panels.

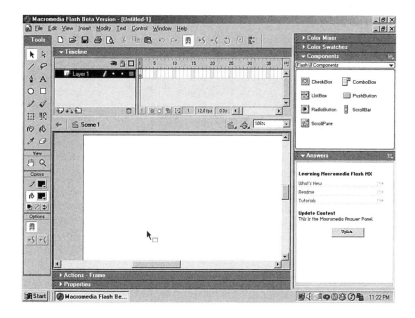

2

INTRODUCING FLASH MX

Let's look a bit closer at what the interface has to offer. First of all, every Flash document has a stage. The stage's size and color can be modified to your specifications. You can alter the properties via the Document Properties dialog box, which can be accessed several ways:

- Click the Modify, Document menu command, which will launch the Document Properties dialog box.

- With the Pointer tool selected in the Tools panel, notice that the Properties Inspector returns basic feedback about the document's properties. If the Properties Inspector is not open, choose Window, Properties. Inside the Properties Inspector, click the Size button, which will also launch the Document Properties dialog box.

- Another way to activate the Document Properties dialog box is to double-click the Frame Rate box at the bottom of the Timeline panel. The Document Properties dialog box is displayed in Figure 2.5.

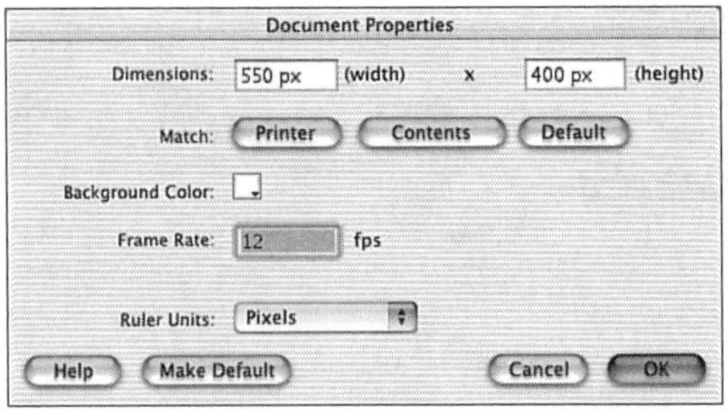

FIGURE 2.5
*Document
Properties dialog
box.*

Document Properties		
Dimensions:	550 px (width) x	400 px (height)
Match:	Printer Contents Default	
Background Color:		
Frame Rate:	12 fps	
Ruler Units:	Pixels	
Help Make Default	Cancel OK	

Let's review the different options in this dialog box so that you have a better understanding of what they mean and how you can use them in your development:

- **Dimensions**. Type in a value for the width and height to set the size of your stage. The minimum size is 1 px by 1 px (pixel), and the maximum size is 2880 px by 2880 px.

- **Match Printer**. Sets the stage size to the maximum available print area, as determined by the paper size minus any margins associated with it in the Page Setup dialog box.

- **Match Contents**. Sets the stage size to fit all objects, with an equal amount of space on all sides.

- **Default**. Sets the stage size to the default of 550 px by 400 px. This option also sets the color to white and the frame rate to 12.

- **Background Color**. Click the ink well to open a swatch of Web-safe colors with their corresponding hexadecimal codes. When you move the cursor out of the swatch area, it will turn into an eyedropper, allowing you to select any color on your monitor.

- **Frame Rate**. Determines how many frames per second to play in the timeline.

- **Ruler Units**. Choose the dimension units to be used: pixels, inches, points, millimeters, or centimeters. Anytime your document refers to *dimensions*—whether in a ruler or the Info panel—it will use the units specified here. For the Web, it's best to leave this setting at pixels.

- **Make Default**. After changing the dimensions, color, frame rate, and/or ruler units, you can use these new characteristics and make them the defaults for any new document created in Flash. This can be a real timesaver!

Setting up the document to suit your work habits and project needs is an essential component of Flash design. In the next section, we're going to explore a crucial part of the interface—using the settings and properties of the different elements within your Flash movie.

The Properties Inspector

The Properties Inspector is a unique panel that gives you feedback on many different objects inside of Flash. If you're coming from Dreamweaver, you will be already familiar with the nature of this panel. Many call the Properties Inspector "context sensitive," meaning that the context of the Inspector will change based on what is selected in the document.

As you can see in Figures 2.6, 2.7, and 2.8, the face of the Properties Inspector isn't constant. There are many different items to work with inside of Flash, and the Properties Inspector helps the interface stay uncluttered. As you begin to work and develop in Flash, you'll see many different characteristics of the Inspector.

FIGURE 2.6

Properties Inspector with the Arrow tool selected.

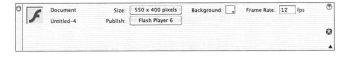

FIGURE 2.7

Properties Inspector with the Pencil tool selected.

FIGURE 2.8

Properties Inspector with a keyframe selected.

Panels

Along with the Properties Inspector, Flash offers many floating panels for more options and information about items. With the new user interface, the panels have a useful way of docking. Instead of panels floating all over the work environment, they can be stored in one central location. To do this, simply drag the top-left corner of the panel to the location of the panel you're looking to dock it to. Of course, if you like the panels scattered all about, you still have that option as well. My favorite part of the new UI is the fact that I can collapse one panel and expand another. This can actually speed up production because you never really need to fully close any of the panels. Notice in Figure 2.9 that all the panels are collapsed but docked in one location. If you're collapsing them on a Mac, you may see the desktop in the background. This is not the case for Windows. In Windows, other panels may shift around and utilize the new unused space. Notice that the "flippy" triangles can expand or collapse a panel, as shown in Figure 2.10.

FIGURE 2.9

Seven docked panels collapsed.

FIGURE 2.10

Seven docked panels with one expanded.

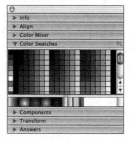

With all theses different panels available for use, organization can become a huge issue. Fortunately for us, the fine folks at Macromedia have already solved this problem by creating several different panel sets. A *panel set* provides a way of sorting the many panels into a manageable configuration, which can be saved for the developer. Macromedia actually saved several different configurations tailored to different monitor sizes. To see an example of this, select the Window, Panel Sets, Default Layout menu command. The panel set will shift to the factory default setting, as shown in Figure 2.11.

FIGURE 2.11

Default panel layout.

Of course, you may have your own workflow and system that works best for you. If you find yourself fooling with panels every time you open Flash to sort them the way you want, instead you can just do it once and then save the layout.

Saving Your Own Panel Layout

Here are the steps to follow to save your panel layout:

1. Configure the panels by moving and resizing them in a way that will best suit your work habits.
2. Select the Window, Save Panel Layout menu command. This will launch the Save As dialog box.
3. Name the panel set anything you want in the text field. Choose OK.
4. To access this new layout, look in the Window, Panel Sets menu to view it in the list of layouts.

2

INTRODUCING
FLASH MX

Let's take a deeper look at the more important panels, and we'll review the minor ones as we use them in different exercises throughout the book. To avoid redundancy, however, we won't go into any great detail for some of these panels, such as the Color Mixer panel, because we'll be reviewing them in Chapter 3, "Creating Graphics in Flash."

Align Panel

The Align panel has five different areas for controlling Flash objects: Align, Distribute, Match Size, Space, and To Stage. The icons on the buttons are fairly accurate indications of their functionality. Click the Window, Align menu command to open the Align panel, shown in Figure 2.12.

FIGURE 2.12

The Align panel.

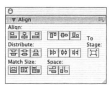

The sets of parameters in the Align panel are detailed here:

- **Align**. The first three buttons are for horizontal alignment, and the last three are for vertical alignment. These buttons are used to align two or more objects.

- **Distribute**. The set of six buttons are for vertical and horizontal distribution. These buttons are commonly used for spacing three or more items. The spacing between the objects is calculated based on the distance of the objects in their original locations, which is then divided evenly.

- **Match Size**. These buttons force two or more objects to be equally sized. They are best used for artwork drawn freehand.

- **Space**. These buttons work much like the Distribute alignment, in the sense that they're used for spacing items evenly. However, if you use Distribute for items or objects different in size, you may find it difficult to get an exact spacing. Distribute spaces the objects from a general reference point of top, middle, or bottom. Therefore, if objects are different sizes, the point of reference may not be 100-percent accurate. Space ensures that all objects are spaced exactly the same amount of pixels from one another.

- **To Stage**. This button factors in the stage for all the alignment commands.

The Align Panel in Action

Using the Align panel is a straightforward operation, as shown in this set of steps:

1. Open the Unleashed library by selecting the Window, Common Libraries, Unleashed menu command.
2. Drag out three copies of the logo file. Place them on the stage randomly.
3. Click one of the instances of the logo, hold down the Shift key, and then click the remaining two. All three logos will be selected.
4. In the Align panel, click the Align Vertical Center button. The logos will be vertically centered (see Figure 2.13).
5. Click the Distribute Horizontal Center button. The logos will now be spaced horizontally (see Figure 2.14).

Figure 2.13
Three instances of the logo on the stage with the Align panel open.

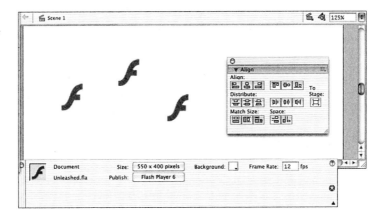

Figure 2.14
Three instances aligned evenly with an equal amount of space between them.

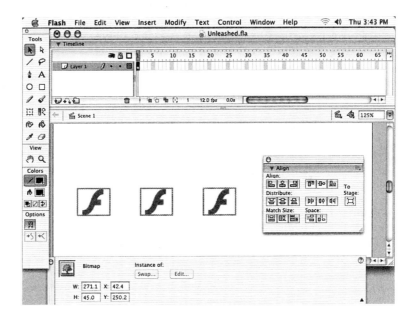

Info Panel

The Info panel provides you with a great deal of information and is useful for positioning and scaling Flash artwork. You can also access the RGB color values of an item as well as the x, y coordinates of the cursor. To view the Info panel, click the Window, Info menu command (see Figure 2.15).

2

INTRODUCING
FLASH MX

FIGURE 2.15

The Info panel.

Transform Panel

The Transform panel is an area designated for the changing of an object's appearance. To access the Transform panel, select the Window, Transform menu command.

The top portion of the panel has options for changing an object's height and width, based on percentage. To change the width and height equally, check the box next to Constrain. This maintains the object's proportions. Here are some other points to keep in mind when using the Transform panel:

- If you choose the Rotate radio button, you must type in a positive or negative numeric value in the text box to rotate the object.
- If you choose the Skew radio button, you must type in a positive or negative numeric value to skew the item.
- After you type in any values, you must press Return (Mac) or Enter (Windows) to apply the transformation.
- The Copy and Apply Transform button (the left button in lower-right corner of the panel, as shown in Figure 2.16) will apply the transformation, if you didn't hit the Enter/Return key first, to an exact duplicate of the item.
- The Reset button (the right button in the lower-right corner of the panel, also shown in Figure 2.16) will reset the altered selected item.

FIGURE 2.16

The Transform panel.

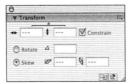

Flash MX Preferences

The preferences in Flash MX contain features for customizing the interface to enhance your workflow. The preferences differ slightly between the Macintosh and Windows platforms—for example, there are a few more options in the General category in

Windows to account for the slight differences between the two operating systems. To access the Preferences dialog box (shown in Figure 2.17), click the Edit, Preferences menu command.

FIGURE 2.17

The Preferences dialog box in Windows.

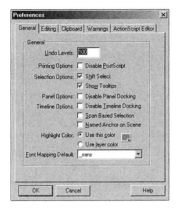

2

INTRODUCING
FLASH MX

General Tab

We're going to deconstruct the Preferences dialog box. We'll start off with the General tab for the Mac, as shown in Figure 2.18, and we'll move on to the other tabs, taking a look at some the differences between the Macintosh and Windows platform:

FIGURE 2.18

The General tab (Macintosh).

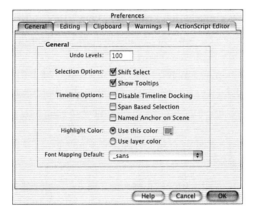

- **Undo Levels**. This number represents the amount of steps stored in the system memory. The higher the number, the more RAM the machine will need to perform common tasks in the application. The default is 100, and with advanced operating systems such as Mac OS X and Windows XP, this remains a reasonable level.

However, you may feel that this setting is a bit high, depending on the age of your machine. Therefore, you can decrease this level—in fact, all the way to 0. A setting of 200 is the maximum amount of undo levels.

- **Printing Options (Windows Only)**. This feature allows you to disable the PostScript output when printing to a PostScript printer, which will decrease printing performance. By default, this option is checked.

- **Selection Options**. Shift Select is checked by default. With this option checked, the way to select more than one object is to click the first item and hold down the Shift key while clicking the second item. If Shift Select is unchecked, you can select multiple items just by clicking them, just like if the Shift key were being pressed.

  Show Tooltips is checked by default as well. This serves as an aid to help point out the names of interface elements as you pause over them briefly.

- **Panel Options (Windows Only)**. Check the Disable Panel Docking option if you want the panels to be free floating.

- **Timeline Options**. By choosing Disable Timeline Docking, the timeline will act as a floating panel.

  Span Based Selection is a fancy term for the Flash 5 frame-selection style. Flash 5 offered the choice of having a Flash 4 selection style. If you're a previous user of both versions, you'll find that Flash MX behaves more like Flash 4 than Flash 5. If you are coming from Flash 5 and are more comfortable with the way frames behaved in that version, you're going to want to check this option.

  Named Anchor on Scene is a new feature in Flash MX. When this option is checked, a named anchor is placed on the first frame of every scene in your movie. When the scenes have named anchors, the forward and back buttons on a browser can be used to move back and forth between scenes, landing on those first frames.

- **Highlight Color**. When a symbol or grouped object is selected, a blue border appears around the item by default. You can change this color by using the swatch. The Use Layer Color option will apply a border using the color in which the outlines for that layer appear.

- **Font Mapping Default**. Many times in production the project file will be moved from one machine to another. In order for certain typefaces to display, those fonts must be installed on the developer's machine. If the developer does not have these fonts, the typefaces cannot be displayed. If this is the case, you can choose what typeface you want to use in place of the missing font. This is called font mapping. When substituting a typeface, you are not replacing it; it's only acting as a placeholder.

Editing Tab

This section covers the different preferences for the items under the Editing tab:

- **Pen Tool**. This section of the Preferences dialog box gives specific information and options for drawing with the Pen tool. See Chapter 3 for more information.

- **Vertical Text**. The Vertical Text area is for setting the default text to type vertically. Check the Right to Left Text Flow box to have the type move to the right when the Return (Mac) or Enter (Windows) key is pressed. Check the No Kerning box to disable kerning features.

- **Drawing Settings**. This area hosts a series of choices to alter the default settings for the drawing tool's ability to recognize shapes. In Chapter 3 we'll discuss how lines or strokes compare to the solid fill colors of a particular shape. These settings aid in the drawing of different objects. For example, if the goal is to draw a perfect circle, Flash will analyze the line and shape of the drawn object and then make adjustments, where necessary, to help achieve the desired effect. These settings determine how sensitive Flash is when analyzing lines and shapes.

- **Connect Lines**. This option determines how close two lines have to be, horizontally and vertically, before they connect together when Snap to Objects is turned on. The choices are Must Be Close, Normal, and Can Be Distant.

- **Smooth Curves**. This choice applies to the Pencil tool. When you're drawing with the Pencil tool and the Straighten or Smooth option is selected, this option determines how much to smooth on curved lines.

- **Recognize Lines**. This option evaluates how straight a line needs to be before Flash will make it a perfect line. The choices are Off, Strict, Normal, and Tolerant. If Off is selected, Flash will not convert a line drawn into a straight line.

- **Recognize Shape**. This option determines how accurately circles, ovals, squares, rectangles, 90-and 180-degree arcs must be drawn before Flash converts them to perfect shapes. The choices are Off, Strict, Normal, and Tolerant.

- **Click Accuracy**. This choice determines how close the pointer must be to a piece of artwork before Flash recognizes it as an item.

Clipboard Tab

Now click the Clipboard tab to reveal the preferences shown in Figure 2.19.

FIGURE 2.19

The Clipboard tab
(Windows).

The Bitmaps area of the Clipboard tab is used to specify the quality and size of the copied content stored in the clipboard. Here are the options available:

- **Color Depth**. Match Screen is the default setting for this option, which will use whatever color bit necessary to match the screen exactly. The other settings include ways to manually increase or decrease the bit depth.

- **Resolution**. Determines what dpi (dots per inch) setting to copy a graphic at.

- **Size Limit**. Type in a value to determine the amount of RAM to allocate to the clipboard. The more installed memory the machine has, the higher this value can be. If the machine has limited system resources, set this to its lowest value (20). Note that the maximum value is 5000.

The Gradients area of the Clipboard tab contains just a single option, Quality, which has to do with setting the quality of the gradient when it is copied in Flash and pasted outside the application.

Let's look at this same tab on the Macintosh platform. Notice in Figure 2.20 that some subtle differences exist.

The PICT Settings area (Macintosh only) is also used to specify the quality and size of copied material stored in the clipboard. Here are the options available:

- **Type**. Objects will preserve vector artwork as it is pasted to the clipboard. To convert copied content, choose a bitmap format in the drop-down menu.

- **Resolution**. Determines what the copied graphic's dpi will be stored at. To include PostScript data, check this option under the Resolution text box.

- **Gradients**. Use this drop-down menu to determine the quality of PICT the gradient will be copied at for pasting in external applications.

FIGURE 2.20

The Clipboard tab (Macintosh).

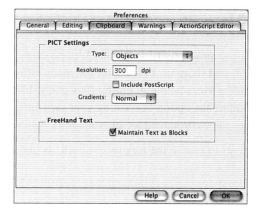

The FreeHand Text area contains a single option, Maintain Text as Blocks. With this box selected, you may preserve the edit ability of FreeHand text files in Flash.

Warnings Tab

The warnings in the Warnings tab are all checked by default and are pretty self-explanatory (see Figure 2.21).

FIGURE 2.21

Warnings tab (Macintosh).

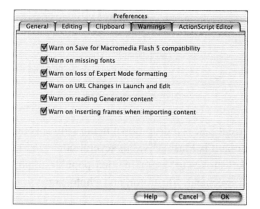

ActionScript Editor

The last tab is ActionScript Editor. This section was created for modifying the ActionScript Editor window. Many of these options are based on personal preferences. This section of the Preferences dialog box is discussed in detail in Chapter 10, " Approaching ActionScript."

Keyboard Shortcuts

Keyboard shortcuts can speed up productivity. For many Web developers and graphic designers, the amount of keyboard shortcuts to learn for the many different applications used throughout a project can be overwhelming. Flash offers many different keyboard shortcut configurations, including the option of creating your own custom set, thus giving you more options to tailor the environment to suit your work habits.

Select Edit, Keyboard Shortcuts to launch the Keyboard Shortcuts dialog box (see Figure 2.22).

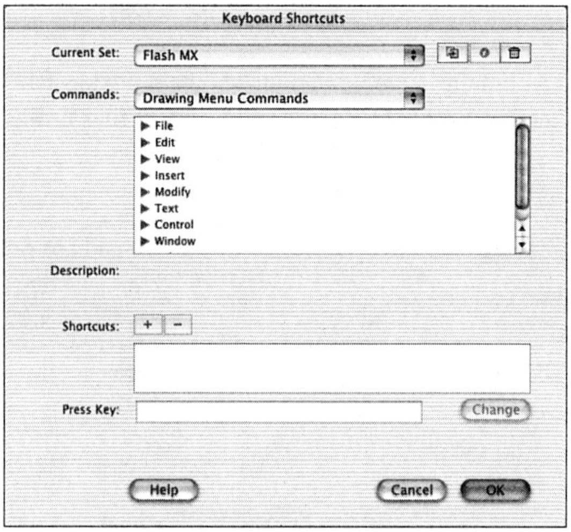

FIGURE 2.22

Keyboard Shortcuts dialog box.

The top portion, labeled Current Set, is a drop-down menu with several predefined configurations. Of course, the default is Flash MX, but several other options are available to alter the keyboard shortcut keystrokes to resemble other popular graphic applications. This list includes Fireworks, Freehand, Illustrator, and Photoshop.

The middle portion of the dialog box offers options for editing certain commands throughout this application. The most commonly customized are the drawing menu commands. The drawing menu commands are the functions performed under one of the menus in Flash.

Choices for customizing the toolbar are also available. In most graphics programs, a single key can be used to switch the active tool. You may be more comfortable with the shortcuts in Photoshop, or you may just want to create your own. In Figure 2.23 you can see the default keyboard shortcuts for the tools in the toolbar.

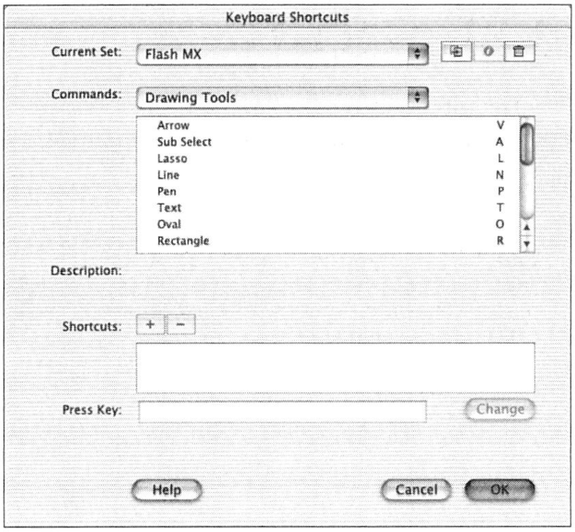

2

INTRODUCING
FLASH MX

FIGURE 2.23

Tool keyboard shortcuts.

The next option in the drop-down menu is Test Movie Menu Commands. The Test Movie menu commands change the keyboard shortcuts within the menus of the Test Movie window. When you test a Flash movie, a new window will open displaying the tested movie. This new window has a series of menus that are different from the actual windows in the Flash authoring environment.

The final choice in the drop-down menu is Actions Panel Commands. These commands are found in the ActionScript window and assist in code development. The keyboard shortcuts access these commands stored in the menus.

Creating Custom Keyboard Shortcuts

The process for creating custom keyboard shortcuts works the same for whatever set you're looking to customize—drawing menu commands, drawing tools, Test Movie commands, or Actions panel commands. The steps are virtually the same:

1. From the Current Set drop-down menu, choose Macromedia Standard.
2. Under the Commands drop-down menu, choose Drawing Tools. Notice that the window underneath changes to provide options for the drawing tools.
3. Click the Duplicate Set button in the top-right corner of the dialog box. This will open a dialog box where you can name the set.
4. Name the duplicate set in the text field **Flash MX Unleashed** and choose OK.

If you decide to change the name of the shortcut set, or if you simply made a mistake in the naming of the set, making this change is quite simple. In the top portion of the Keyboard Shortcuts dialog box, click the center button in between the Duplicate Set button and the trashcan. This will open a small dialog box where you rename the set you're working on.

At this point, all you have to do is decide what you want the new shortcuts to be, or if you want to delete them altogether, you can create brand new ones. Here are the steps:

1. Highlight the Arrow keyboard shortcut by clicking the word *arrow* in the window.

2. Add a new shortcut by clicking the plus sign button. Notice another line has been created in the window, and the word <empty> appears in the Press Key text field.

3. Press the W key on your keyboard to add it to the list of shortcuts for this tool. Then click the Change button.

   While creating your shortcuts, be sure not to use a shortcut already in use for a different command. If a duplicate shortcut is chosen and change is made, a dialog box will appear in which you'll have the option of reassigning the shortcut to the command selected. If Reassign is chosen, the keyboard shortcut will be removed from the original command.

4. To remove the V key from the list of shortcuts, highlight it in the window.

5. Press the Delete or Backspace key on your keyboard. The letter V is removed and will no longer access the Arrow tool.

6. Change any other commands to shortcuts better suited to you by repeating these steps for each shortcut you'd like to modify.

7. Once you're finished, click OK. Try using some of the new keyboard shortcuts you have established by pressing them on your keyboard.

Changing the Workspace with the View Menu

Flash offers many different document views to choose from, most of which are located under the View menu. Some of these options can make certain graphics easier to draw and others a bit more difficult to draw. During development, you'll probably turn on certain options while turning off others. Notice the different options in the View menu, as shown in Figure 2.24.

FIGURE 2.24

The View menu.

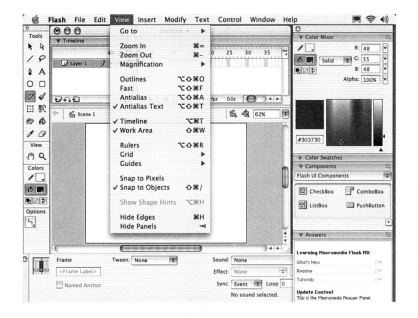

Here is a quick rundown of the different options in the View menu:

- **Go To**. This option produces a pop-out menu offering choices to move to the first, previous, next, and last scenes. The bottom of this menu offers quick jumps to scene names.

- **Zoom In**. This option doubles the document's magnification.

- **Zoom Out**. This option decreases the document's current magnification by half.

- **Magnification**. Choosing this option will also trigger a pop-out menu. In this pop-out menu, you may choose from different magnifications, ranging from 25% to 800%. Note that Ctrl+1 (Windows) and Cmd+1 (Mac) will return you to 100% magnification.

  Show Frame adjusts the screen to display everything within the frame boundary. See the document properties to determine the frame size.

  Show All adjusts the screen size to display everything in the selected frame. If the selected frame is empty, the entire work area will be displayed.

  The next three options on the pop-out menu allow you to toggle between the different views. These three views determine the quality of the graphic. Keep in mind that the higher the quality, the more processor intensive the animation will be for the development machine.

> **Tip**
>
> These toggle options only determine the quality of your content in the Flash MX authoring environment. They have nothing to do with the final published piece.

- **Outlines**. Choose this option to change all artwork in the document to display as outlines. If the artwork isn't a solid object with a fill, the stroke will display thinner than normal. This option is good for precise placement of content and previsualization of complicated animations.
- **Fast**. This option will not antialias your graphics. An advantage of this is improved performance for the animation. I generally use this as my authoring setting.
- **Antialias**. This option softens the edges of your artwork, making them look less jagged. This option works best with a fast processor and a powerful video card.
- **Antialias Text**. Choose this option to antialias text only. If you are working with a good amount of text, beware, because this option can really bog down the system's performance.
- **Timeline**. Toggle this option to hide or show the timeline.
- **Work Area**. Choose this option to display the larger gray area around the stage. This can be useful for content animating into a scene or out of a scene. Sometimes it's even easier to draw in this gray space and then move the artwork into place on the stage.
- **Rulers**. Oftentimes during development, you'll find yourself trying to space objects out for aesthetics or for timing in an animation. Choose the Rulers option to view rulers on the horizontal and vertical axes. The increments the rulers display are determined by what type of ruler units you have chosen in the Document Properties dialog box. To access the Document Properties dialog box, choose Modify, Document.
- **Grid**. By choosing Grid, you will activate a pop-out menu. The pop-out menu has three choices.

    Show Grid obviously displays the grid within the document.

    Snap to Grid is used when you're drawing graphics or moving artwork to snap them to the different grid quadrants. Even if the grid is not visible when you're drawing or moving objects, they will still snap to it.

    Edit Grid has its own dialog box, which is shown in Figure 2.25. Here are the options available:

FIGURE 2.25

The Grid dialog box.

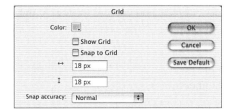

- **Color**. Opens the swatch for you to choose a color for the grid lines.
- **Show Grid**. Displays the grid. This is the same command as choosing Show Grid directly from the View menu.
- **Snap to Grid**. Causes objects and drawings to snap to the grid. This is also the same command located in the View menu
- **Width**. Type in a value to determine the width of the grid boxes. The ruler units selected in the Document Properties dialog box determine in what increments you can input values.
- **Height**. Type in a value to determine the height of the grid boxes. The ruler units selected in the Document Properties dialog box determine in what increments you can input values.

- **Guides**. Making guides visible allows you to drag them from the rulers. Therefore, in order to gain access to guides, be sure to have the rulers visible.

  Lock Guides hold the guides in place, thus avoiding any accidental selections and guide movement.

  Snap to Guides enable objects to snap to the desired guide location.

  Edit Guides has its own dialog box, shown in Figure 2.26, with the following options:

FIGURE 2.26

The Guides dialog box.

- **Color**. Use this swatch to select a color for your guides. This option is handy when the default guide color competes with the foreground artwork.
- **Show Guides**. Displays the guides on the document. This is the same as choosing Show Guides from the View menu.

- **Snap to Guides**. Causes objects and content to snap to the placed guides in the document. Again, this option is the same as choosing Snap to Guides in the View menu.
- **Lock Guides**. Locks the guides down in their current position. This command is also available under the View menu.
- **Snap Accuracy**. This option determine how close or how far the object needs to be from the guide before it snaps.
- **Snap to Pixels**. This command is new to Flash MX. If Snap to Pixels is selected, a pixel grid will appear when zoomed in at 400% or higher. When the document is magnified at such high percentages, it allows for precise placement of objects. When the pixel grid is visible, the objects will snap to the grid.

Tip

You can turn pixel snapping on and off temporarily by pressing the C key. Pressing the X key will hide the pixel grid. When the X key is released, the pixel grid will reappear.

- **Snap to Objects**. When you're moving around artwork or content in Flash with this option chosen, the artwork or content will snap to existing content already on the stage. The snapping will occur when the center of the object being dragged intersects another piece of artwork.
- **Show Shape Hints**. This option turns on or off the visibility of shape hints. Choosing Off does not disable the hints. Shape hints are used when applying a morphing shape tween. For more information on shape hints, see Chapter 4 "Flash Animation."
- **Hide Edges**. Choose Hide Edges to temporarily disable the selection highlights of objects on the stage. The selection highlights will appear the next time you select an object.
- **Hide Panels**. Oftentimes during development, despite the vast improvements in the new interface, you'll find that the panels are cluttering your work area. Choose Hide Panels to remove them from your screen. This option is a toggle, so if you choose it again, the panels reappear where they where before. The Tab key is the handy keyboard shortcut.

Summary

This chapter was written to get you familiar with the Flash MX workspace and the options to customize it. Many of these panels will be revisited as we begin to work a bit more in depth with Flash. Customizing your panel sets, adjusting the preferences, and tinkering with the different views can really speed up your production time.

Macromedia did a wonderful job in developing an interface that is well organized and seemingly less cluttered than most robust applications. Of course, some interface differences exist between Mac and Windows machines, but these differences seem to be necessary for Flash to flow with the experience that each operating system delivers.

Creating Graphics in Flash

By Matt Pizzi

Flash has a unique drawing style associated with it. If you are familiar with other drawing applications, such as Adobe Illustrator and Macromedia FreeHand, you'll find definite similarities and some unexpected differences. Flash offers several drawing tools that allow you to create the graphics for your Flash projects that may seem familiar to you based upon some of those programs. Flash differs from those other applications by the way it handles graphics. Flash will join two items of the same color value if the two graphics intersect. The line or stroke of an item is also considered a separate element. As you will see in this chapter, these differences can be problematic; they can also work in your favor. It's just a matter of getting use to them.

The Tools

As just mentioned, the drawing and handling of graphics in Flash takes a little getting used to, and that's what this portion of the chapter is for. It exposes you to the tools in Flash MX, and even though they may look very similar to those in other programs, this is a different user experience.

All the tools will be reviewed in this chapter, so let's take a look at what these tools look like. Figure 3.1 shows the Flash MX toolbar and highlights each tool found in this powerful toolset.

FIGURE 3.1

The Flash MX tools.

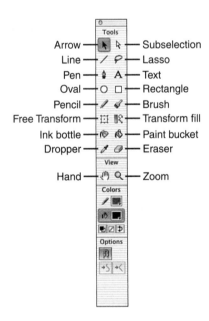

The Arrow Tool

The Arrow tool is Flash's selection tool. If you want to move an item, select and drag it with this tool. Of course, you can always use the arrow keys on your keyboard to move the item for more precise placement.

Toward the end of the chapter, once we get into actually creating artwork in Flash, you'll see how this tool can also be an aid in drawing. The Arrow tool does have one option: Snap to Objects.

Use Snap to Objects to have artwork snap to the grid. This option will also cause objects to snap to one another when you're placing the graphics, depending on how close the objects are horizontally and vertically.

The Subselection Tool

The Arrow tool has a counterpart—the Subselection tool (also known as the *white arrow*). Remember that Flash is vector based, and the main job of the Subselection tool is to select actual vector points of an item. Again, we'll discuss this later in the chapter as we begin creating and working with our own artwork using the Pen tool.

The Line Tool

When drawing with the Line tool, you have the ability to create straight lines in any direction from the starting point. To start drawing a line, choose the Line tool in the Tools panel, click anywhere on the stage, drag the line towards the desired endpoint, and release the mouse. The Line tool has no options. However, the size and style of the stroke will determine the appearance of the line. The stroke's properties can be changed in the Properties Inspector when the Line tool is selected in the Tools panel.

Notice in Figure 3.2 that you can draw several line segments to make a shape.

To change the appearance of the stroke, you can select a color and size from the Properties Inspector. You also have a choice of styles—solid, dashed, dotted, ragged, stipple, and hatched—as well as options to customize each of these styles. Simply click the Custom button in the Properties Inspector with a drawing tool selected. Here's an explanation of each style option:

FIGURE 3.2

The Line tool can be used to draw a triangle by connecting three different lines. Notice the Properties Inspector's options for changing the line's appearance.

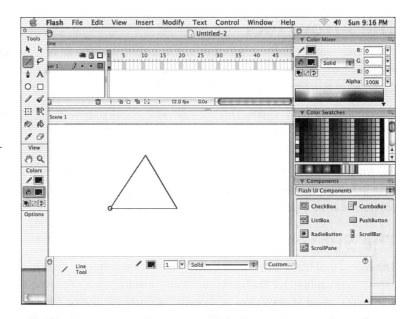

Note

Flash does not offer a way to save custom style settings. Also, all units for spacing and sizing options are in points. You can access the Stroke Style dialog box by clicking the Custom button in the Properties Inspector. Once you click the button, the dialog box will appear, as shown in Figure 3.3.

FIGURE 3.3

The Stroke Style dialog box.

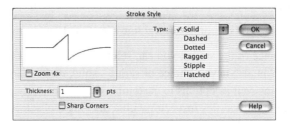

- **Hairline**. This stroke style draws one-pixel-wide strokes and remains one pixel, regardless of magnification or zoom. Oftentimes, when a document gets scaled, the vector lines will scale with it to preserve the proportions of the artwork. This is not an option in the dialog box but is available through the pop-out menu in the Properties Inspector.

- **Solid**. This option is for drawing solid lines and strokes. The only adjustable attributes are the thickness, color, and sharp corners of the stroke.

- **Dashed**. This choice generates a stroke with dashed breaks within the line. To change the length of the dash and the gap space between dashes, enter in numeric values in the respective text fields. Color, thickness, and sharp corners are also adjustable attributes.

- **Dotted**. Choose the dotted style if the desired effect is to have a stroke with evenly spaced dots along the line. This style has an option for changing the distance between the dots. Color, thickness, and sharp corners are also adjustable attributes.

- **Ragged**. The ragged style creates random wavy lines with dotted separations. The Stroke Styles dialog box offers options to change the pattern, wave height, and wave length. Color, thickness, and sharp corners are also adjustable attributes. Use a combination of all these styles for unlimited possibilities.

- **Stipple**. This choice creates a stroke style to resemble that of an artist's hand-stippling technique. Dot size, dot variation, and density are options for changing the appearance of the stippling effect. Color, thickness, and sharp corners are also adjustable attributes.

- **Hatched**. The hatched line style resembles an artist's hatched-line technique. The Thickness attribute determines the thickness of the hatch line, which is independent of the global thickness setting. You also have options for spacing, jiggle, rotate, curve, and the length of the hatched lines. Of course, there are additional choices for global thickness, color, and sharp corners.

The Ink Bottle Tool

The Ink Bottle tool is designed to change the color, style, and thickness of strokes. If you use the Dropper tool to sample the stroke appearance of any art in Flash, after the sample has been made, the Dropper tool will automatically take on all the characteristics of the sampled stroke. The Ink Bottle does not have any options, but you can choose the color, thickness, and style of the stroke using the Properties Inspector in conjunction with one of the vector drawing tools.

The Dropper Tool

Use the Dropper tool to select color values on the screen. If you are drawing a new object and prefer for the fill or stroke color to appear the same as any other value on the screen, simply use the Dropper tool to sample that color value. Once you click the color value, it's automatically stored in the appropriate Ink Well tool in the Tools panel. If you choose a stroke color, all attributes of that stroke (including size, color, and style) will be sampled. If you are using the Dropper tool from the Tools panel, you are limited to sampling within the confines of the stage. If you are using the Dropper tool built in to the Swatches panel, you can sample a color from any source on the computer screen.

The Pencil Tool

When drawing with the Pencil tool, you'll notice it uses a stroke color opposed to a fill color. You may also change its stroke appearance by choosing a stroke style in the Properties Inspector. The Pencil tool has some interesting options that can aid in the final outcome of a drawing. These options are detailed in the following list and displayed in Figure 3.4:

FIGURE 3.4

Pencil tool options.

- **Straighten**. Choose this option if your goal is to draw a perfect circle, oval, square, rectangle, or arc. The sensitivity of how Flash determines a shape is set in the Preferences dialog box. You can access these preferences by choosing Edit, Preferences. For more information on preferences, refer to Chapter 2, "Introducing Flash MX." Check out Figure 3.5 to see an example of drawing with Straighten turned on.

FIGURE 3.5

A circle before and after the release of the mouse.

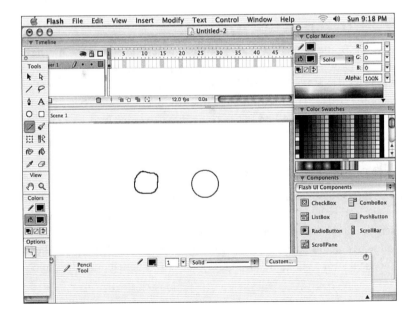

- **Smooth**. Generally this option will smooth out any curvy lines.
- **Ink**. This choice is for freehand drawing without Flash making adjustments to the lines.

Tip

When you're drawing with the Ink option selected, it may look like some modification is happening to your lines when the mouse is released. Flash isn't making any adjustments to the curviness or straightness of the line; rather, it's antialiasing the edges of the line.

After the line has been drawn, you may feel that it needs to be smoother or straighter. This not only may aid in the visual appearance of the stroke, but you may actually reduce file size by reducing the complexity of the stroke. To make a line straighter, follow these steps:

1. Click the line with the Arrow tool. The line will be selected.
2. With the line selected, in the Options portion of the toolbar, as shown in Figure 3.6, choose the Straighten button.
3. Click the Straighten button as many times as needed to get the desired effect.

The same method will work when smoothing a line.

FIGURE 3.6

The Arrow tool's options.

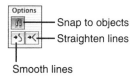

— Snap to objects
— Straighten lines
— Smooth lines

The Rectangle Tool

Rectangle tool is used to create squares and rectangles. To create a perfect square, hold down the Shift key to constrain the drawn object's proportions to that of a square. One option the Rectangle tool has involves setting the corner radius to make rounded edges. If you click the Corner Radius button, a dialog box will appear. In the text field, type in a numeric value between 0 and 999 that represents the corner radius.

Drawing and Coloring Rectangle Shapes

Here are the steps to follow to draw and color a rectangle shape:

1. Choose the Rectangle tool from the Tools panel.

2. In the Color portion of the Tools panel, choose a stroke color. If no stroke is desired, choose the first box in the top-right corner of the swatches, as shown in Figure 3.7.

3. If you would prefer to use a custom color, something other than a web safe color, click the button to the right of the No Stroke button to bring up the Color Picker. Inside the Color Picker are many different ways to view color in terms of organization.

4. Choose a fill color. All the same techniques in terms of color selection used for the stroke apply to the fill as well.

5. To create rounded edges, click the Round Rectangle Radius button in the Options section of the Tools panel.

6. Place the cursor in the stage; then click and drag until the rectangle is the desired size. If the goal is to create a perfect square, hold down the Shift key.

FIGURE 3.7

Choosing the No stroke option.

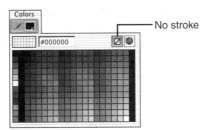

No stroke

Note

If you choose View, Snap to Objects when you draw a rectangle, you'll notice you have a perfect square because your cursor will snap to a large circle around your cursor, as shown in Figure 3.8.

Caution

The higher the value entered in the Round Rectangle Radius dialog box, the more round the corners become. Avoid very large numbers, especially for smaller rectangles. If you do use a large number, you run the risk of turning your rectangle into a circle.

3

CREATING
GRAPHICS
IN FLASH

FIGURE 3.8

*Drawing a square
with Snap to
Objects selected.*

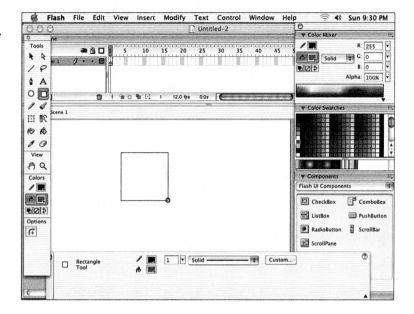

When using the Rectangle tool, you may notice some unusual behavior when it comes to moving objects. This is discussed in detail in the "Tips for Creating Graphics in Flash" section, later in this chapter.

The Oval Tool

The Oval tool is used to create circles and ovals. To create a perfect circle, hold down the Shift key. This will constrain the drawn object's proportions to that of a circle. If Snap to Objects is selected when drawing an oval, the shape will snap to a perfect circle when dragged at a 45-degree angle.

The Oval tool has no options.

The Paint Bucket Tool

The Paint Bucket is used to fill an item with a color or gradient. To choose a color or gradient, click the Ink Well tool of the fill swatch in the Tools panel or in the Properties Inspector.

Once the fill color has been selected, move the Paint Bucket tool over an object and click it to change its fill color to the new fill color.

In the Options area of the Tools panel, notice that the Paint Bucket tool has a Gap Size option as displayed in Figure 3.9.

FIGURE 3.9
The Paint Bucket options.

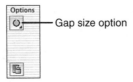 —— Gap size option

Select the first choice, Don't Close Gaps, if there are certain areas in your artwork that shouldn't be filled.

The Close Small, Medium, and Large Gaps options all work in the same way. If you have complex drawings that need to be filled, you may want to choose one of these options. If you have Close Large Gaps selected and it doesn't seem like it's working, either the gap is too large or there are too many gaps in your art.

The last option in the Tools panel is Lock Fill, which allows you to apply a gradient or bitmap fill consistently across multiple items.

Using Lock Fill to Apply a Gradient Across Multiple Objects

Here are the steps to follow to use Lock Fill to apply a gradient across multiple objects:

1. Draw four squares on the stage and align them using the Align panel. Space them out so that the entire stage is being used, edge to edge.

2. Choose the Paint Bucket tool in the Tools panel and be sure to choose the rainbow linear gradient in the fill swatch.

3. Click the Lock Fill button in the Options portion of the Tools panel.

4. Fill the first square, then the second, third, and fourth. You'll notice that the gradient is being applied as if the four squares are one continuous shape.

5. To see the different squares, fill each one with a gradient without the Lock Fill option selected.

   To apply a gradient across multiple items without using Lock Fill, simply choose all the items by drawing an invisible marquee with the Arrow tool or by Shift-clicking each object. Then click one of the items. You'll notice the gradient has applied color across more than one item. The effect, however, looks a bit different when compared to the Lock Fill effect.

6. If you want to fill the squares with a bitmap, choose File, Import and search for the image on your computer. Once the image is in Flash, highlight it and choose the Modify, Break Apart menu command. For more information on importing bitmap graphics, see the "Working with the Color Mixer" section, later in this chapter.

Creating Custom Colors and Gradients

Conveniently, Macromedia has incorporated the Web-safe color palette into the swatches in Flash. Oftentimes, however, you may need to use a color located on a different swatch, or you may want to create gradients using your own color choices.

Therefore, we'll take a look at a couple new panels in Flash. The first is the Color Swatches panel; the second is the Color Mixer panel. Each can be used to select different colors; however, the Mixer panel gives you precise control over certain color properties.

Color Swatches

In the Color Swatches panel, shown in Figure 3.10, you can sort colors, load different swatch sets, and even load bitmap graphics. To import different swatch sets, click in top-right corner of the Color Swatches panel to access the drop-down menu. Choose Add Colors, find a Flash color set file (typically located in your Flash MX program folder), and select it. This will add any additional swatch sets to the panel. However, if you choose Replace Swatches, all existing swatches will be replaced with the new loaded set.

FIGURE 3.10

The Color Swatches panel.

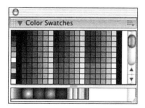

If you've added and arranged this panel in a way in which you feel very comfortable, consider making it the default. In the submenu, choose Save as Default so that every time you open Flash, these color swatches will be loaded in the panel.

However, if you feel like the swatch set that you've customized is good only for certain occasions, you can simply save that swatch set as a swatch. In the submenu, choose Save Colors, which will launch the Export Color Swatch window. Name the color set and save it in an easily accessible location, such as in the Flash program folder under First Run, Color Sets.

Color Mixer

The Color Mixer panel is a bit more robust in comparison to the Color Swatches panel. Notice how much the Color Mixer panel offers in Figure 3.11.

FIGURE 3.11
*The Color Mixer
panel.*

The Color Swatches panel is best for accessing stored colors. The Color Mixer panel, on the other hand, is used in customizing colors and gradients. Once you've created these custom colors, you can store them in the Color Swatches panel. Therefore, these two panels work well together.

At first glance, you'll notice that the Color Mixer panel has a nice color ramp from which you can choose colors. As you take a closer look, you should also notice the many different ways to come up with certain colors.

By default, you can type in numbers for the red, green, and blue values. This can be useful, especially if you're working with a graphics application such as Fireworks or Photoshop to create artwork. If you need to match a certain color element in that graphic, you can get an RGB or HSB readout in the other program and type in those here in this swatch. You can easily change the RGB values to display hue, saturation, and brightness by choosing the appropriate option in the Color Mixer's submenu.

Accessing Custom Colors Using the Color Picker

Here are the steps to follow to access custom colors using the Color Picker:

1. Open the fill swatch and choose the color wheel in the top-right corner of the palette. This will open the Color Picker dialog box. In Windows, the Color Picker dialog box looks like an overgrown Color Mixer panel. You have the color ramp, where you can select a custom color and even add that custom color to a custom swatch within the dialog box. The Mac, however, is quite different. (Notice on the Mac that if you move the dropper away from the color swatches, you can sample any color on your computer screen.) You can see the Mac RGB Color Picker in Figure 3.12.

2. By default, the RGB Color Picker will appear. In this dialog box, you can choose a color by moving the percentage sliders from left to right. Moving them to the right will increase the amounts of the corresponding colors to higher percentages.

3. Move the Red slider to 100%.

4. Move the Green slider to 0%

5. Move the Blue slider to 0%. Notice the color difference between the original color and the new color. The end result is a pure red. Oftentimes you'll need to refer to some numbers generated during content development so that you can match certain pieces or areas of artwork.

   Figure 3.13 shows the Name Color Picker window on Macintosh.

6. Move the slider next to the color ramp to reveal a section of colors.

7. Choose the desired color. Notice that all these colors have a corresponding hexadecimal value. These hexadecimal values are Web-safe colors. A Web-safe color is a color commonly shared between a Macintosh and a Windows machine if you drop them down to their lowest 256, 8-bit color display. There are only 216 Web-safe colors.

   Figure 3.14 shows the HSV Color Picker window on the Macintosh.

8. Enter a value for the hue in the Hue Angle field.

9. In the Saturation field, type in a percentage for saturation.

10. Type in a number to represent the brightness percentage of the desired color in the Value field. (Value behaves the same as brightness.)

FIGURE 3.12

The RGB Color Picker on the Macintosh.

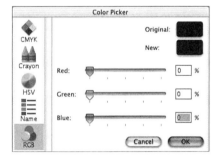

FIGURE 3.13

The Name Color Picker on the Macintosh.

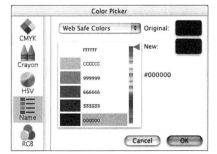

FIGURE 3.14

*The Hue,
Saturation, and
Value (HSV)
Color Picker on
the Macintosh.*

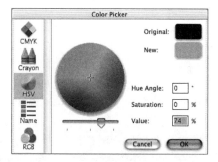

Caution

If you are new to Web development, be aware that even though 216 colors are commonly shared between the Mac and Windows operating systems, a Mac's colors are generally brighter, and the Windows colors are commonly darker. However, Using Web-safe colors seems to be less and less an issue with modern-day machines displaying well over a million colors.

The slider underneath the color wheel will adjust the value. Moving the crosshairs around in the color wheel will adjust the hue angle as well as the percentage of the saturation.

The Crayon Color Picker allows you to choose a color with a specific name. These colors are not necessarily Web-safe colors. The Crayon Color Picker offers an assortment of nicely organized, easy-to-find colors as shown in Figure 3.15.

FIGURE 3.15

*The Crayon Color
Picker on the
Macintosh.*

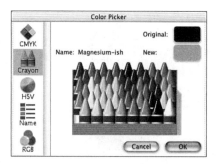

The CMYK section is a color mixer that uses the common four-color print process of cyan, magenta, yellow, and black. As mentioned earlier, Web-safe colors are becoming less of an issue. However, you could find yourself in a situation in which your company wants a CMYK color to be used throughout its Web site. Commonly, this happens with logos. To keep in line with company standards, you may choose to use the exact colors printed in the logo. Ultimately, this will result in a consistent look throughout the Web site. Refer to Figure 3.16 for the CMYK Color Picker.

FIGURE 3.16

The CMYK Color Picker on the Macintosh.

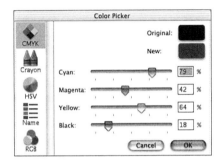

Changing a Color's Alpha

A great feature of Flash is the ability to change the alpha of a color. The Alpha setting controls how opaque or how transparent a color will be. The default is set to 100% but can be lowered all the way down to 0%. This can be useful in animations—perhaps you'd like for an object to fade in or out, or you may want an item to cross over another item, in which case you may want to see the item underneath.

To change a color's alpha, choose the desired color in the fill swatch. Next, use the slider to the right of the Alpha field to lower the percentage of the alpha. You may also type in a value in the Alpha field. The lower the alpha percentage, the more transparent the color will become.

Once the color has been set, you can use this new transparent color just as you would any other color. In fact, you can even save it in the swatch set.

Saving a Color to a Swatch

It's quite simple to save any custom color you've created or selected. With the custom color in the fill or stroke swatch selected, move your cursor into the Color Swatches panel. When your cursor is in an empty area of the swatch, notice that it turns into a Paint Bucket tool. Click an empty area and notice that the color has been added to fill the empty area with the selected fill color. You can also add a color by choosing a color in the Color Mixer panel, by activating the submenu and choosing Add Swatch.

> ### Tip
>
> With all these options in the Color Mixer, you may find yourself with many custom colors. After you've added these colors to the Color Swatches panel, it maybe a good idea to save them as a swatch.

Modifying and Creating a Gradients

The Color Mixer panel is an area where you can modify existing gradient colors by changing, adding, or deleting the colors that make up any given gradient. When you have a gradient selected in the fill swatch, notice the new options in the Color Mixer panel.

Notice in Figure 3.17 that the drop-down menu contains choices for a radial gradient and a linear gradient. Also, take note at the new color ramp for the gradient. Each triangle marker in the ramp is a color that will be represented in the gradient. If you're working with a simple two-color gradient (for example, from white to black), these two colors will gradually intersect one another.

FIGURE 3.17

The Color Mixer panel with a gradient as the active fill.

> ### Modifying a Gradient
>
> Here are the steps to follow in order to modify a gradient:
>
> 1. Draw a circle with no stroke and a radial gradient selected for the fill.
> 2. To change the gradient's colors, highlight one of the makers in the gradient ramp located in the Color Mixer panel.
> 3. With the triangle selected, open the Ink Well tool above the ramp in the Color Mixer panel and choose a new color. Notice that the gradient is automatically updated.
> 4. Select the other marker and change its color as well.

5. To edit this gradient further, you can add even more color by adding additional markers to the gradient ramp. To create a new midrange color in the gradient, simply click in an empty area just underneath the gradient ramp. Notice the new marker with a midrange color.

6. Change the new marker's color by using the Ink Well tool in the Color Mixer panel.

7. You can add as many new markers as necessary to achieve the desired effect. To remove any unnecessary markers, click and drag them down and away from the color ramp.

8. Once the gradient is complete and you feel you might use the new gradient color later down the road, you may want to save it in your Color Swatches panel. Select the submenu in the Color Mixer panel and choose Add Swatch.

Note

Be sure to check out the instructional QuickTime movie on how to create custom gradients located on this book's companion Web site, `http://www.flashmx-unleashed.com`.

The Transform Fill Tool

The Transform Fill tool is designed to change the appearance of an applied gradient or bitmap fill. This tool gives you the ability to make adjustments to the direction, size, center point, and rotation of the gradient or bitmap fill.

Depending on the type of fill—radial gradient, linear gradient, or a bitmap fill—the type of alterations that can be performed vary slightly. After you get some practice using the Transform Fill tool, it will be something you'll use quite often. In the next exercise, you learn how to go about modifying a radial gradient. These same principles apply to transforming a linear gradient. Note that you'll save the bitmap fill for later in the chapter in the "Import Bitmap" section.

Working with the Transform Fill Tool

Here are the steps to follow for this exercise:

1. Draw a circle using the Oval tool (remember, to draw a perfect circle, hold down the Shift key on your keyboard). When choosing a fill color for the circle, choose one of the default radial gradients.

2. With the circle on the stage, select the Transform Fill tool in the toolbar. Notice your cursor has changed into a white arrow with a small gradient icon to the bottom left.

3. Click in the center of the circle. This will activate the bounding transform handles, shown in Figure 3.18.

4. The top square handle will skew the gradient. Therefore, drag the skew handle out just a few pixels.

5. The center handle will change the radius of the gradient (radial gradient only). Drag this center handle out about 40 pixels.

6. The bottom handle will change the rotation of the gradient. There is no need at this point to rotate the gradient.

7. Drag the center circle handle toward the top-left corner of your shape. This will change the center point of the gradient.

8. Click outside of the gradient bounding box to deactivate it. Notice our circle now looks like a 3-D sphere.

FIGURE 3.18

Transform Fill bounding handles.

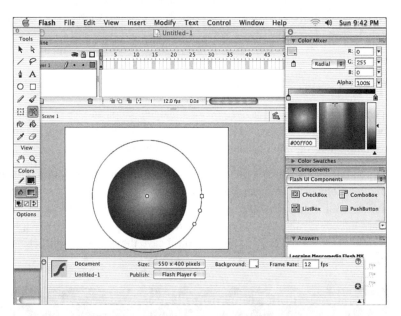

Note

Be sure to check out the instructional QuickTime movie on how to transform fills, located on this book's companion Web site, http://www.flashmxun-leahsed.com.

The Brush Tool

The Brush tool is a painting tool in Flash that offers several options for painting. It's important to note that the Brush tool uses a fill, as opposed to a stroke, like the other tools we've just looked at. The Brush tool can use solid colors, gradients, and even bitmaps to paint. Notice the options in the Tools panel for the Brush tool, as shown in Figure 3.19. The following list details these options:

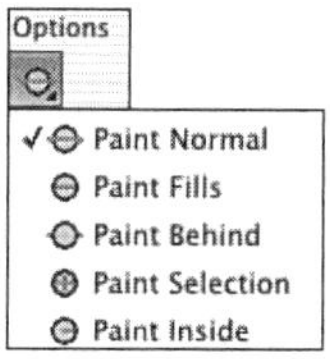

FIGURE 3.19

The different brush modes for the Brush tool.

- **Paint Normal**. Use this option to paint the fill color anywhere you move the Brush tool with the mouse button pressed.

- **Paint Fills**. This option allows you to paint only fill colors (although it really should be called Preserve Strokes). Paint Fills can be a bit confusing, because it will paint empty parts of the stage. However, what it won't do is alter any stroke colors.

- **Paint Behind**. Choose this option if you only want to paint an area underneath art-work already placed on the stage.

- **Paint Selection**. This option allows the Brush tool to paint only in areas that have been selected.

- **Paint Inside**. This option allows the brush to paint only in the interior section of the artwork. It will not paint or alter stroke colors. When using this option, be sure to start in the interior of the item; otherwise, the Brush tool will think the stage is the item to paint inside.

You can also change the size of the brush by using the Brush Size drop-down menu, shown in Figure 3.20. When choosing a brush size, be aware that they are always relative to the magnification of the document. For example, if you have a document magnified at 400 percent, and you select a certain brush size and then zoom out of the document to 100 percent, that same brush will appear smaller at the 100-percent document size than it did at 400-percent magnification.

In the Brush Shape drop-down menu, shown in Figure 3.21, you can select a brush shape or style. It consists of squares, ovals, rectangles, and many different angle brushes. When selecting a brush shape, keep in mind that the size of the brush will also play a big role in the final appearance the brush mark.

FIGURE 3.20
The Brush Size drop-down menu.

FIGURE 3.21
Brush Shape drop-down menu.

The last option for the Brush tool is Lock Fill. We discussed this option in detail in the section "The Paint Bucket Tool," earlier in this chapter. This instance of Lock Fill works the same way. Of course, to get certain effects, you will need to use this option with a combination of brush modes.

Finally, note that the Brush tool offers a Pressure option when a Wacom tablet is used. See the Wacom Technology Company's Web page at www.wacom.com for more information. A Wacom tablet is a pressure-sensitive drawing pad that gives the mouse a behavior like a tradition art pad and pencil.

The Eraser Tool

The Eraser tool is, funny enough, used for erasing. It's a handy tip to keep in mind. If you double-click the Eraser tool in the Tools panel, you'll see that it does in fact have some options:

- **Erase Normal**. This option is the standard way of erasing content. It works exactly as you would expect: If you move the eraser over a fill or stroke color, it will be erased.

- **Erase Fills**. This option only erases the fill color of objects, without harming the stroke color.

- **Erase Lines**. Erase Lines only erases stroke colors and does not alter fills.
- **Erase Selected Fills**. This option only erases items with fills that have been selected. Any fills not selected will not be harmed.
- **Erase Inside**. Erase Inside only erases the interior color of the object you start erasing in initially. This option will not erase anything outside the interior parameter of that object.

The Eraser's Faucet Option

Personally, I think the Faucet tool is great—it's just a poor naming choice by Macromedia. The Faucet tool literally sucks the color out of a fill or stroke.

Finally, you can choose an eraser size and shape, such as a circle or square.

The Pen Tool

The Pen tool was new to in version 5. This tool allows you to define straight lines and smooth curves. To draw with the Pen tool, move the mouse and click successively. Each new point will connect with the previous point to create a line segment. To create a curved line segment, when clicking the mouse drag the point in the direction you want the curve. The length of the tangent will determine the arc of the curve.

The Pen tool has some preference that needs to be set in the Preferences dialog box. To access this dialog box, choose Edit, Preferences. Inside this dialog box, select the Editing tab. Here are the options you'll find:

- **Show Pen Preview**. This option offers a preview of what the line segment will look like once an anchor is placed. If you're new to the Pen tool, you should note that this is a great option to have checked because it helps beginners get more comfortable with the behaviors of the Pen tool.
- **Show Solid Points**. With this option, the appearance of the selected vector points will appear hollow, and the unselected points will appear solid. By default, this option is not selected, giving the opposite appearance (solid indicates selected points and hollow refers to unselected points).
- **Show Precise**. There are two different views for the Pen tool. When using the Pen tool, you can either view the standard pen icon or choose Precise, which will display crosshairs. Checking this box will only change the default appearance of the Pen tool to Precise. This option is pretty useless, seeing that you can toggle between the two different views using the Caps Lock key.

The Pen tool also has several different options in terms of changing, adding, deleting, and transforming points. When these options are available, there is a slight difference in the appearance of the Pen tool's icon. The following list explains these differences:

- **Cursor 1**. Notice that this cursor icon displays a small minus sign (-). This means that if you were to click a vector point, it would be deleted.

- **Cursor 2**. This cursor icon displays a caret sign (^), which means that if you click a vector point, it will turn into a right angle.

- **Cursor 3**. This cursor icon (+) adds a vector point to the existing line segment.

- **Cursor 4**. Notice that this cursor displays a small x. This icon indicates there's no line segment present to edit. To avoid seeing this icon, be sure to have the mouse positioned directly over a line segment.

- **Cursor 5**. When the Pen tool is over the first vector point placed, you'll see the small "o" icon, indicating that this will close the path or shape.

- **Cursor 6**. When the Shift key is held down, the cursor icon changes into an arrow with a solid box. This indicates that you are moving the mouse over a line.

- **Cursor 7**. When the Shift key is held down, the cursor icon changes into an arrow with a hollow box. This indicates that you are moving the mouse over a vector point.

After drawing a path with the Pen tool, you can edit the path using any of the pen icon cursor changes just explained, or you can use the Subselection tool. The Subselection tool allows you to change selected vector points and tangent lines. Remember that tangent lines change the degrees of the arc and the direction of the curve Refer to Figure 3.22 to see an example of tangent handles.

FIGURE 3.22

Tangent handles.

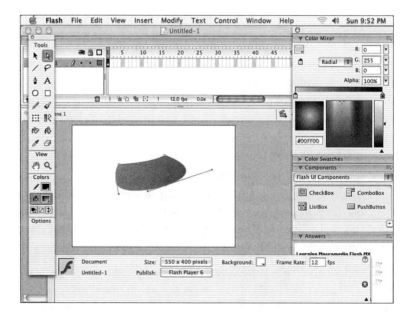

The Free Transform Tool

The Free Transform tool is a new tool in Flash MX. This tool has several options for distorting, skewing, scaling, and rotating items in Flash.

With an item selected on the stage, choose the Free Transform tool in the Tools panel. Notice the bounding box around the item. If there isn't an item selected on the stage when the Free Transform tool is chosen, you will not see this bounding box. However, if you click an item with this tool selected, you'll notice the bounding box will appear around that object.

The handles on the bounding box allow you to make all sorts of modifications to the object. The handles in the corner scale down the item, and holding down the Shift key will constrain the item's proportions. Using the handles on the side will scale it horizontally and vertically. Moving the cursor between handles will allow you to skew and distort the item.

Notice that the Free Transform tool also has several options in the Tools panel (see Figure 3.23). These options are discussed in the following list:

FIGURE 3.23

The Free Transform options.

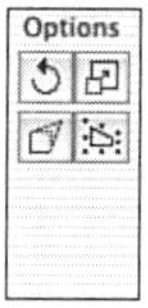

3

CREATING GRAPHICS IN FLASH

- **Rotate**. This option rotates the item around the center point. Notice that you can move the center point to change the axis of rotation.

- **Scale**. This option automatically constrains the proportions of the item when you're using the corner handles. You can also scale the object horizontally and vertically.

- **Distort**. This option moves the corner or edge points to distort the item by realigning the adjoining edges. If you drag a corner handle and hold down the Shift key on your keyboard, the edge will taper. Tapering moves the opposing corner in the opposite direction at an equal distance.

- **Envelope**. This option offers the ultimate control in transforming an item. You adjust the points, and tangent handles modify the item. This option works with one or more selected items.

> **Warning**
>
> The final two options of the Free Transform tool—Distort and Envelope—only work with primitive items. If the artwork is a symbol, a grouped object, a video object, or text, it will be deactivated. In order to use these options, the artwork must be broken apart by choosing Modify, Break Apart.

To flip an item horizontally or vertically, it's best to use the options under the Modify menu. To flip an object, be sure it's selected and then choose Modify, Transform, Flip Horizontal or Vertical.

The Text Tool

Using text in Flash is in some cases as simple as using text in a word processing application. In other cases, it's about as difficult to use as HTML text. Remember, in order for text to be displayed on an end-user's machine, the proper font must be present on that user's system. We're going to take a look at some obstacles to using text and how to remedy any potential problems. We are also going to review the editing features Flash MX has to offer.

Text can be used for many different tasks in Flash—from something as basic as having a word spelled out on a page, all the way to being a container for variable information. This is why our discussion of the Text tool is broken into sections. Let's start at the editing features.

Text Tool Editing Features

Select the Text tool in the Tools panel. You'll notice that the Text tool has no options. However, if you take a look at the Properties Inspector, you'll see that it's loaded with goodies for changing the appearance of your text, as shown in Figure 3.24.

Figure 3.24

Text tool's properties.

The most obvious option in the Properties Inspector is the one for changing the typeface. In the drop-down menu, you'll see a list of the available fonts installed on your system. Along with this option is the ability to change the font size. To change the font's point size, either type in a value or use the slider to increase or decrease the size. To change the color of the text, use the Ink Well tool to the right of the Font Size field. Of course, you also have the options for making the text bold (Ctrl/Cmd+Shift+B) and italic (Ctrl/Cmd+Shift+I).

To begin typing in Flash, choose the Text tool and click where you want the text to appear on the stage. As you type, the text box will resize to accommodate all the text.

The other option, when the Text tool is first selected, is to click and drag a bounding text box on the stage. This will create a text block that will not permit any text to resize its dimensions. As you type, the text will automatically wrap and make beaks whenever and wherever necessary to fit inside the defined text box. You can always resize the text box by grabbing the handle in the top-right corner and dragging to the new desired size (see Figure 3.25).

FIGURE 3.25

Resizing a text box.

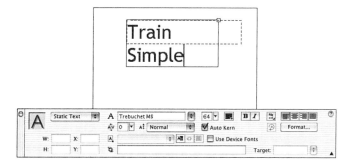

Tracking and kerning options are also available. See Figure 3.26. What you may find tricky, however, is the fact that both options are accessed under the same slider. To adjust the tracking of the text, make sure either the entire word is highlighted in black or the text has been selected with Arrow tool and a blue box is visible around the type.

You can type in a value, where positive numbers increase the space between the letters and negative values decrease the space. When this is done on an individual basis, such as to adjust the space between the letters *A* and *V* instead of a whole word, it's known as *kerning*.

FIGURE 3.26

Adjusting the tracking.

To adjust the kerning between two characters, have both characters highlighted and use the same text box or slider to input a positive or negative value, as shown in Figure 3.27. Many times when you're typing this value, it is beneficial to have the Auto Kern check box selected. This gives you a good chance of returning some acceptable results—and at the very least, it offers a good starting place.

FIGURE 3.27

Adjusting the kerning.

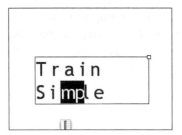

Here are some important shortcuts for adjusting the kerning and/or tracking:

- **Decrease spacing by half a pixel**. Cmd+Option+left arrow (Mac) and Ctrl+Alt+left arrow (Windows)
- **Decrease spacing by two pixels**. Cmd+Shift+Option+left arrow (Mac) and Ctrl+Shift+Alt+left arrow (Windows)
- **Increase spacing by half a pixel**. Cmd+Option+right arrow (Mac) and Ctrl+Alt+right arrow (Windows)
- **Increase spacing by two a pixels**. Cmd+Shift+Option+right arrow (Mac) and Ctrl+Shift+Alt+right arrow (Windows)

The Properties Inspector also has options for using subscripts and superscripts. You use subscripts to type something such as "H_2O," where the small character is just below the baseline, and you use superscripts for something such as "T^i," where the small character is just above the baseline.

Setting Alignment and Margins

With the Text tool selected, inside the Properties Inspector, just to the right of the Italic button is another button that gives you the ability to change the direction of the text. The two choices are Vertical Left to Right and Vertical Right to Left. Also available is the Rotate option, to rotate the text once the direction has been changed from horizontal. Depending on the direction of the text, the next four buttons provide options for justifying the text.

The alignment options include top/left justification, center, right justification, and full justification. These options predetermine the text if a justification option is chosen before the text is entered. If the text has already been entered, highlight the desired text block and then apply the desired justification.

Click the Format button for the following additional formatting options (see Figure 3.28):

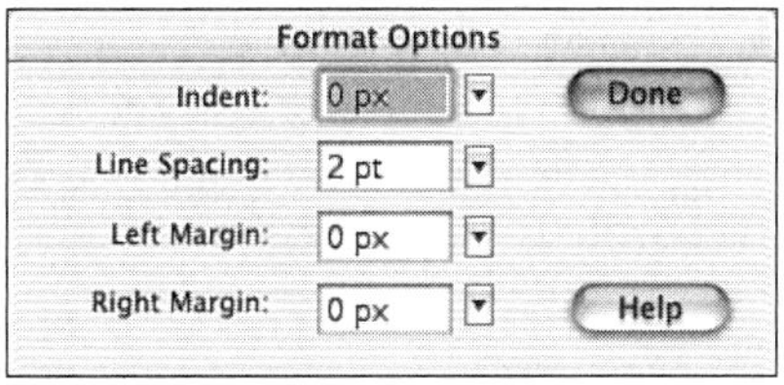

FIGURE 3.28

Format options.

Format Options	
Indent:	0 px ▾ **Done**
Line Spacing:	2 pt ▾
Left Margin:	0 px ▾
Right Margin:	0 px ▾ **Help**

- **Indent**. Enter a value to determine how much the first line of every paragraph should be indented. This option only works with predefined text blocks.
- **Line Spacing**. This option controls the space between lines in text blocks (this is known as *leading*). Positive numbers increase the amount of space between lines; negative numbers decrease the space.
- **Left Margin**. This option creates a margin or space on the left side of a text block.
- **Right Margin**. This option creates a margin or space on the right side of a text block.

Device and Embedded Fonts

In Flash you can use device fonts. If you decide to use a device font, you can save a good amount of file size in your final SWF file. Included in the file when Use Device Fonts is enabled are items such as the name of the typeface, the family of the type, and some other information to help Flash Player evaluate whether the end user has the font. To enable Use Device Fonts, make sure the text field is set to Static and, in the Properties Inspector, check the Use Device Fonts box.

If the end user does not have the typeface installed on his or her system, the Flash Player will know to replace it with a serif or san serif typeface. Device fonts are best used with smaller text and very common typefaces. Device fonts will not antialias, so they tend to look better at smaller sizes. If the text is large, the best bet is to break apart the text so that it becomes a shape.

It also important to note that if you have a text block and you wish to scale, skew, distort, or apply any type of transformation, the editability of the text is preserved.

3

CREATING GRAPHICS IN FLASH

The final options in the bottom portion of the Properties Inspector include making the text selectable and creating hyperlinks. Sometimes in Flash you may want important information on a Web site to be selectable so that the end user can copy that information. You may also want some text to be hyperlinked to additional HTML documents. You can create a hyperlink by typing in a link in the Hyperlink text box at the bottom of the Properties Inspector.

So far, all we have explored is static text. You'll notice in the drop-down menu toward the top-right corner of the Properties Inspector a couple of other choices. These choices—Dynamic and Input Text—are discussed in great detail in Chapter 9, "Animation Techniques and Digital Video."

The Zoom Tool

The Zoom tool allows you to zoom in to a subject as much as 2000 percent. This helps when you're performing precise work. When you click the Zoom tool, it always zooms in twice as much as the magnification you're currently at. To zoom out, hold down the Option (Mac) or Alt (Windows) key and click the mouse.

Double-clicking the Zoom tool will reset the magnification to 100 percent. Here are some keyboard shortcuts you may want to keep in mind:

- To zoom in, use Cmd (Mac) or Ctrl (Windows) with the plus key.
- To zoom out, hold down Cmd (Mac) or Ctrl (Windows) and the hyphen key (-) at the same time.

Remember, there is also the Zoom drop-down menu docked just below the timeline.

The Hand Tool

The Hand tool is used to move around the stage. When zoomed in to a particular part of the Flash movie, you may find it difficult to navigate to different areas of the movie. This is where the Hand tool comes in, well, handy. You can literally move the stage: Just click with the Hand tool and drag until you see the desired location in which you want to work.

> **Tip**
>
> The spacebar acts as a toggle to turn the Hand tool on no matter what tool you are currently using.

Tips for Creating Graphics in Flash

You may have noticed by now that using the drawing tools in Flash has several advantages and some disadvantages. Let's take a look at the behavior of the graphics we've created once we have them placed on the stage.

Drawing and Moving Primitive Items

Here are the steps to follow in this exercise:

1. In the Tools panel, choose the Rectangle tool. In the Options portion of the Tools panel, click the Round Rectangle Radius option.

2. In the Round Rectangle Radius pop-up box, type in a value of 5. This value will add just a small rounded effect on the corners.

3. In the Colors section of the Tools panel, choose a stroke color and a fill color.

4. Draw a rectangle somewhere on the stage.

5. After drawing the rectangle, choose the arrow tool and click the center of the square and drag the object to a new location.

6. Notice after you move the item that a stroke is left behind. To avoid this, you must double-click the item (you'll notice the fill and stroke are both selected) and then click it one more time to move it.

Flash's primitive objects will separate strokes from fills. This, of course, can cause all sorts of problems, but there is a bright side. Although this issue can be sometimes annoying, it does provide for the ultimate control of your primitive items. For example, use the Line tool to draw a star. If you try to trace an outline of a star, it may seem rather difficult. However, if you draw the star in the same way you'd draw it on paper without ever picking up the pencil, then you can remove the interior lines to make the perfect star as shown in Figure 3.29.

FIGURE 3.29

This star was drawn using the Line tool, and the interior lines being selected with Arrow tool are to be deleted.

Tip

Refer to the QuickTime video located on this book's companion Web site for further explanation on how colors and strokes separate.

Flash has some additional issues we need to look at when it comes to creating graphics. Flash will also combine two items with the same fill color, or it will punch a hole in a underlying primitive object. See the next exercise for an example.

Placing Primitive Items on Top of One Another

Here are the steps to follow for this exercise:

1. In the Tools panel, choose the Oval tool. When choosing the Oval tool, be sure to specify a fill color and a stroke color.

2. Draw an oval somewhere on the stage.

3. In the Tools panel, select the Rectangle tool. Again, be sure to select a stroke color, but this time choose a different fill color.

4. Draw a rectangle and cover a portion of the oval.

5. Click away from both objects, somewhere in the white space of the stage.

6. Notice that the rectangle looks like it is on top. This is because it was drawn after the oval.

7. Click once on the rectangle and move to another location on the stage.

8. The oval, which was located underneath the rectangle, now as a square cut out of it.

This is normal behavior for Flash. It is of the utmost importance to keep this in mind when you're developing content in the Flash environment. Small accidents can cause huge problems, and thankfully Flash has a wonderful feature called *Undo* (type Cmd+Z or Ctrl+Z or choose Edit, Undo). These drawing styles are just as much setbacks as they are features. Although this may be a different way to build artwork, it is one that can open up more possibilities. One great feature is the ability to adjust lines. If you move your cursor over a line, you'll notice that you can grab and bend that line. If your mouse cursor shows a small picture of a right angle, you can adjust the placement of that angle by clicking the angle and dragging it around.

Just keep in mind how line and fill colors can separate while changing their position.

You can avoid these problems by grouping your artwork. This may seem somewhat bizarre at first, because ultimately you are grouping an object with itself. The advantage of this is that the object is no longer a primitive and the selection style changes. Take a look at Figure 3.30 to see the differences between a grouped object and a primitive object.

Tip

Refer to this book's companion Web site for further explanation on how colors and strokes separate.

FIGURE 3.30
On the left is a primitive item, and on the right is a grouped one.

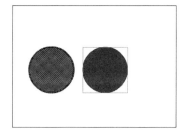

Notice that the grouped object has a blue bounding box as opposed to the primitive object's speckled pattern. Without the speckles, items cannot merge or punch holes in one another.

Grouping an Item

Here are the steps to follow to group an item:

1. Choose the Rectangle tool with a stroke color and a fill color.
2. Draw a rectangle somewhere on the stage.
3. After drawing the object, choose the Arrow tool and double-click it. By double-clicking you are selecting not only the fill but also the stroke.
4. Choose Modify, Group. This will group the object. Notice the different selection style with the bounding box.
5. Choose the Oval tool with a different fill and stroke color.
6. Draw an oval or circle on top of the grouped rectangle. You'll notice that the item you've just drawn automatically appears behind the grouped rectangle.
7. Move the grouped rectangle away from the circle. Notice that the rectangle does not punch a hole in the oval.

Changing the Stacking Order Between Grouped Objects

Here are the steps to follow to change the stacking order between grouped objects:

1. Still working with the last file and with Arrow tool selected, double-click the oval to select the stroke and the fill.
2. Choose Modify, Group.
3. Move the oval on top of the grouped rectangle.

Notice that the rectangle is now underneath the oval. This is because the oval was the last grouped object; therefore, it appears in front of any items grouped previously. In Flash, you have two different ways to change the stacking order of grouped objects: either arrange them on separate layers or change their stacking order within the one layer.

Changing the Stacking Order of Grouped Objects on One Layer

Here are the steps to follow to change the stacking order of grouped objects in one layer:

1. With the oval and rectangle grouped items already on the stage from the previous exercises, draw a new shape. Choose a different fill and stroke color for this shape.
2. Choose the Arrow tool and select the new shape by double-clicking it. After the item is selected, choose Modify, Group. Notice now that the new shape is on top.
3. With the new shape selected, choose Modify, Arrange, Send to Back. The new shape now appears below the other two grouped items.

Here are the options in the Modify, Arrange menu (note that you must have a grouped object selected to get these options):

- **Bring to Front**. This option moves the selected item in front of all other items.
- **Bring Forward**. This option moves the selected item in front of the item it is currently underneath. In other words, it brings the item forward one step.
- **Send Backward**. This option moves the selected item behind the item it is currently in front of. In other words, it sends the item backward one step.
- **Send to Back**. This option moves the selected item behind all other items.

You can also change the stacking order of items using layers. Each time you create a new graphic, place it on a new layer. You can create a new layer by clicking the Add Layer button in the Layers panels, as shown in Figure 3.31.

FIGURE 3.31
The Add Layer button.

To change the stacking order of a layer, simply click and drag it either above or below the desired location of the other layers. For additional information on the Layers panel, refer to Chapter 4, "Flash Animation."

Graphic Techniques

I'd like to point out some of the cool, but small features in Flash you can use to make your Flash graphics look a bit more interesting. Oftentimes, shadow effects are created using bitmap graphics. This largely has to do with the tonal range a raster graphic can provide. Flash, as we all know, is vector based, and vectors cannot offer that same tonal range. Therefore, Flash has a few workarounds, but keep in mind that using them will increase the file size of your final document. Also, these effects, especially when animated, will require the end user to have a more powerful machine. The features that offer these effects can be found under the Modify, Shape menu:

3

CREATING GRAPHICS IN FLASH

- **Convert Lines to Fills**. Oftentimes to create 3D-looking graphics, your artwork must have a large stroke, and that stroke must be filled with tonal colors. To get the tonal values, a gradient must be applied. You may have noticed that there are no gradients in the stroke swatch. This is the main reason for converting the strokes into fill colors. Once that adjustment has been made, you cannot fill the line color with a gradient.
- **Expand Fill**. Use this option to change the size of the fill. In the Expand Fill dialog box, choose how many pixels you'd like the fill to expand or inset. Expand will make the fill appear larger, and Inset will make the fill smaller.
- **Soften Fill Edges**. Inside the Soften Fill Edges dialog box, choose how many steps you'd like to take and indicate whether you'd like to expand or inset the fill. If you choose to expand the fill, it will have additional strokes applied around it in the number of steps that you have designated, and each of these strokes will gradually have less opacity. Inset works the same, but the additional strokes will cut into the size of the fill.

> **Tip**
>
> Refer to the QuickTime video included on this book's companion Web site for further explanation on how to use the Shape menu.

Importing Bitmap Graphics

Even though Flash is a vector-based application, you can still import and work with bitmap graphics. Once a graphic is inside Flash, it becomes an element that is editable. You can animate the bitmap, skew it, scale it, distort it, break it apart, and even convert it into vectors. It's very common in development to combine artwork created in Flash with other vector programs, such as Illustrator or FreeHand, but also with bitmap applications, such as Photoshop or Fireworks. The process of importing a bitmap on a Mac looks a bit different than it does on a Windows machine, so be sure to take a good look at the following figures so you can see the differences.

> **Importing a Bitmap Graphic**
>
> Here are the steps to follow to import a bitmap graphic:
> 1. Choose File, Import to open the Import dialog box.
> 2. Download the file from this book's companion Web site and in the Chapter 3 section find the file `gato.jpg`.
> 3. On Mac OS 9, click the Add button and then the Import button. The advantage of this dialog box is that if you have more than one item to import, you choose the different files and import them all in under one command.
> 4. On Windows and Mac OS X, highlight the file and click the Open button.

The bitmap will now show up on the stage. At this point, you can manipulate the graphic in any way. There are a few different things we can do with this graphic. In the next excise, we're going to take steps to use this bitmap as a fill color, and we're also going to select portions of the image and delete them. To select these different portions, we're going to use the Lasso tool.

The Lasso Tool

The Lasso tool is a selection tool, and it makes the most sense to use this tool with bitmaps. Use the Lasso tool just as you would any drawing tool. To make a clean, precise selection, try to close the path the lasso makes. Otherwise, the results can be less than predictable. The Lasso tool has some options at the bottom of the Tools panel. The first is the Magic Wand tool, shown in Figure 3.32. The Magic Wand tool selects an area or value of pixels based on its set tolerance. You can set the tolerance by clicking the button to the right of the Magic Wand tool. The higher the tolerance, the more values the selection will consider to be the same.

FIGURE 3.32

The Magic Wand settings.

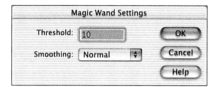

The Smoothing option is for determining how smooth the selected edge should become. Here are the choices:

- **Smooth**. Rounds the selection edges.
- **Pixels**. The selection is wrapped around the rectangular edge of similar color pixels.
- **Rough**. The selection becomes even more angular than with Pixels.
- **Normal**. Creates a selection that is a bit softer than Pixels but not as soft as Smooth.

The last option is the Polygon Lasso tool. Use this tool for angular or geometric type shapes. See Figure 3.33 for the Lasso's options.

FIGURE 3.33

The Lasso tool's options.

Working with Bitmaps

In this section you'll learn more about using bitmapped graphics as individual elements. For instance, you can very easily use a bitmap as a fill color for another graphic.

Breaking Apart a Bitmap and Using It as a Fill Color

Here are the steps to follow to break apart a bitmap and use it as a fill color:

1. zWith a bitmap graphic selected, choose Modify, Break Apart. Notice that the bitmap now look more like a primitive object.

2. Choose the Dropper tool in the Tools panel.

3. Notice that the fill swatch has a small icon representing the bitmap.

4. Choose the Rectangle tool and draw a square on the stage. Notice that it's filled with the bitmap!

5. Now you have the option of transforming the fill using the Transform Fill tool.

Trace Bitmap

Another great feature of Flash MX is having the ability to turn your bitmap graphics into vectors. This can save file size, if the bitmap doesn't have a great deal of detail. It's also an advantage if you plan to animate the graphic and have it scale up. It's important not to break apart the bitmap. If you do, Flash will only recognize it as a primitive and not as a bitmap. If you have the bitmap selected on the stage, select the Modify, Trace Bitmap menu command. Here are the options you'll find in the dialog box that appears in Figure 3.34:

FIGURE 3.34

The Trace Bitmap dialog box.

- **Color Threshold**. This option compares adjacent pixels. If the RGB color values between the two pixels are less than the Color Threshold value, these color values will be considered the same. You can set the Color Threshold value between 1 and 500.

- **Minimum Area**. This option's value determines how many pixels to evaluate when setting the color of a pixel. You can set a value between 1 and 1000.

- **Curve Fit**. This option determines how smooth the vector lines are drawn after the trace has been performed.

• **Corner Threshold**. In this drop-down menu, choose either Many Corners, Few Corners, or Normal. If Few Corners is chosen, corners will be smoothed out in the image. If Many Corners is selected, many of the corners in the image will be preserved. Normal is between Many and Few Corners.

If you want the graphic to look more accurate, choose Many Corners, with lower Color Threshold and Minimum Area values (see Figure 3.35). However, this will probably increase the file size and will bog down animation playback. If you chose higher values, the image may be less accurate and offer a more stylized look, but it will be more functional in a Flash animation.

FIGURE 3.35

A bitmap before and after the Trace Bitmap command. Notice the stylized look on the left.

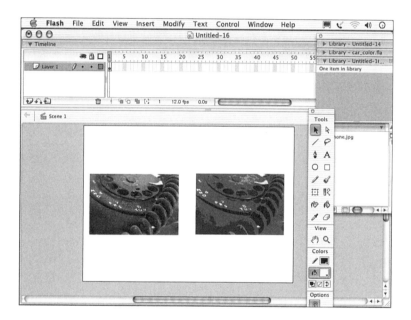

Swap Bitmap

Swap Bitmap is a new feature in Flash MX. This feature allows you to swap out a bitmap on the stage with any other imported bitmap in the document. With the bitmap selected on the stage, choose Modify, Swap Bitmap to launch the Swap Bitmap dialog box. In this dialog box, choose the new bitmap that will replace the existing bitmap on the stage.

Flash Animation

By Matt Pizzi

CHAPTER 4

I notice in many of the classes I teach that the concept of time in Flash seems to be a bit more difficult to grasp than other concepts. For example, in the previous chapters, we discussed the interface and drawing tools. If you are a seasoned graphic or Web designer, these topics are probably well within your comfort zone. What we've reviewed in Flash so far is similar to applications such as Illustrator, FreeHand, and Photoshop. If you haven't used an animation program before, such as After Effects or Director, the dimension and concept of time is something completely new to you. To understand how animation works, and more specifically how Flash animation works, you must understand a whole new world of terminology.

If you are familiar with After Effects or Director, consider yourself slightly ahead of the game. Fully comprehending this chapter is the first step toward mastering Flash. We'll begin with deconstructing the timeline; we'll look at each of its components and how these components can speed up your productivity and enhance your animations.

The Timeline

The timeline is a panel that contains layers, frames, and a play head. In this section, we'll dissect each component of the timeline. With all the timeline's attributes revealed and explained, we'll then start animating. Refer to Figure 4.1 to see the timeline's structure.

Do you remember those old-fashioned animation flipbooks, where you would flip the pages to see the animation play? Flash is very similar in concept. Think of a frame in the timeline as a page in an animation flipbook.

FIGURE 4.1

The timeline.

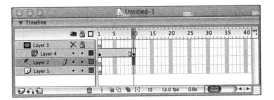

I want to deconstruct certain elements of the timeline. I'll refer to these different components throughout the book, so it's important that you're familiar with these different items, which add functionality to your animation in some way:

- **Keyframe**. A keyframe represents a major change within the animation. Referring back to the flipbook concept, a keyframe is the same as each animated page in the flipbook. To insert a keyframe, press F6 or select Insert, Keyframe.

- **Frame**. A frame simply adds time to an animation. Usually frames don't have any sophisticated movement; they just carry over content from the previous frames. Again, referring back to the flipbook concept, if the characters in the animation have to pause for a moment, without any movement, the exact same page would need to be duplicated as many times as necessary to create the duration of the pause. In Flash, to accomplish this same effect, you would simply add a frame, which in turn adds time to the timeline. To insert a frame, press F5 or choose Insert, Frame.

- **Blank Keyframe**. A blank keyframe does in fact represent a major change within the animation; however, the major change is that it creates a blank area on the layer. To insert a blank keyframe, press the F7 key or choose Insert, Blank Keyframe.

- **Unpopulated Frame**. An unpopulated frame is generally the same concept as a frame, but it contains no data. Unpopulated frames are generally preceded by a blank keyframe.

- **Play Head**. The play head is the red rectangle and line that moves across the timeline, and it indicates what frame is currently being displayed on the stage. You can click and drag the play head along the timeline to view the other frames. This is called *scrubbing*. You may also use the keyboard shortcuts, which are the "<" key to move left and the ">" key to move right.

- **Insert Layer**. This button creates a new layer in the Layers panel. By default, the new layer will be created above the currently selected layer. To rename the layer, double-click its name to get the blinking cursor.

- **Add Motion Guide**. This button creates a new layer above the currently selected layer. However, this layer has a guide property, meaning that whatever is placed on it will not appear in the Flash player. If a line or stroke is drawn on this layer, symbols and grouped objects that are motion-tweened can be attached to the guide layer and can follow the stroke during the animation.

- **Insert Layer Folder**. This is a new Flash MX feature that offers controlled layer management. To keep the Layers panel organized, you can create subcategories within the stacking order of the layers. By moving or changing the stacking order of the layer folder, you change the stacking order of every layer within that folder.

- **Delete Layer**. This removes or deletes the selected layer, layer folder, or guide layer. Of course, if only one layer is left, you cannot delete it.

- **Show/Hide All Layers**. This turns on or off the visibility of layers. Click the eye icon to toggle between the layers being on and off. To turn on or off the visibility of just one layer, click the bullet underneath the eye icon column.

4

FLASH ANIMATION

- **Lock/Unlock All Layers**. The behavior of this icon button and its column bullets act exactly like the Show/Hide All Layers button and its column bullets. However, this option locks the contents of the layer on the stage. This way, any unwanted editing of these items will be avoided. It is important to understand that this will only protect the artwork on the stage from being edited and will not prevent this layer's timeline from being edited.

- **Show All Layers as Outlines**. This option is also a toggle. To view artwork as outlines, click either the bullet for any given layer or the actual icon to affect all layers. This view converts all artwork on the layer to an outline view. This comes in handy for precise placement and animation tweaking.

- **Center Frame**. This option positions the timeline so that the selected or current frame will appear in the center of the timeline view.

- **Onion Skin**. This option allows you to view previous or future frames in the time-line. Onion Skin is best described as a tracing-paper feature. You can adjust the bracket that surrounds the play head to adjust how many frames are visible before and after the current frame.

- **Onion Skin Outlines**. This option allows you to see the outlines of multiple frames.

- **Edit Multiple Frames**. Even if you are viewing your animation with the Onion Skin feature, when you make a change, it will only affect the currently selected frame. Edit Multiple Frames allows you to make a change across all onion-skinned frames.

- **Modify Onion Markers**. Aside from moving the Onion Skin bracket around the play head, this drop-down menu offers other specific choices (see Figure 4.2):

FIGURE 4.2

The Modify Onion Markers menu.

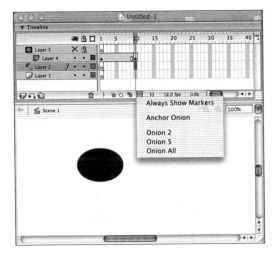

- **Always Show Markers**. This option is pretty self-explanatory. It always displays the Onion Skin bracket around the play head.

- **Anchor Onion**. This option leaves the Onion Skin bracket in the same place, regardless of the play head's position.

- **Onion 2**. This option will onion-skin two frames in front and two frames behind the play head.

- **Onion 5**. This option will onion-skin five frames in front and two frames behind the play head.

- **Onion All**. Choose this option to onion-skin the entire duration of the timeline.

- **Current Frame**. This is an indicator revealing what frame is currently being displayed on the stage.

- **Frame Rate**. This small box refers to the frame rate of the movie. The default frame rate is 12 fps. To give you a point of reference, film plays at 24 fps and digital video plays at 29.97 fps. The higher the frame rate, the more realistic your animation will look. However, this animation will only play at its true frame rate if the end user's computer and Internet connection are fast enough. Therefore, keep in mind the target audience of your Web site when choosing a frame rate. To change the frame rate of your movie, choose Modify, Document or just double-click this small box.

- **Elapsed Time**. This box indicates the amount of time elapsed from the first frame to the currently selected frame, based on the frame rate of the movie.

- **Frame View Options**. This drop-down menu offers a variety of views for the timeline frames. We'll review each of these options later in this chapter, in a section titled "Changing Timeline Views," after we've worked with the timeline a bit.

Creating Animation in Flash

You have several different ways to create animation in Flash, including the following:

- Frame-by-frame animation
- Shape tweening
- Motion tweening

We'll first discuss frame-by-frame animation. I think frame-by-frame animation is the easiest to understand, because you physically create the animation yourself without any help from Flash. Keep in mind that when you create a frame-by-frame animation, every frame within the animation is a keyframe. Recall that a keyframe represents a major

4

FLASH ANIMATION

change within the animation, so on each keyframe your subject can be doing something different. Going back to the flipbook analogy, every page in the book is different, whether the character or whatever the subject may be is making subtle movements or more obvious ones. In order to create the effect of movement, the artwork has to be different on each page; otherwise, there would be no animation—just an object or character in the same place on each page. Think of a keyframe as a page in a flipbook. In the next exercise, we'll create a frame-by-frame animation.

Creating Frame-by-Frame Animation

In this exercise, we are going to create an animation of the sun with rays shooting out from its center. This will truly be a portfolio piece.

Referring to Figure 4.1, click the New Layer button. You will notice a new layer named "layer 2" that appears above layer 1. Now follow these steps:

1. Double-click layer 1 to highlight the text. With the text highlighted, rename the layer "center."

2. Double-click layer 2 and rename this layer "rays."

3. Be sure to have the center layer selected by clicking it. Choose the Oval tool with your choice of fill and stroke colors.

4. Hold down the Shift key and in the center of the stage drag out a small circle.

   Notice that the hollow circle that once occupied the frame has turned into a solid circle, as shown in Figure 4.3. This displays the difference between a blank keyframe () and a keyframe on the rays layer.

   We want our animation to last half a second. The default frame rate is 12 fps. Simple math tells us that we need six frames in order for this animation to last half a second when the animation is playing 12 frames every second.

5. To make the animation lasts half a second, we need more frames on the center layer. In fact, we need five more frames to extend the time to six frames. To do this, click inside frame 6 on layer 1. Notice that frame 6 is now black, indicating that it has been selected.

6. Choose Insert, Frame or press F5 on your keyboard. Notice that all frames between 1 and 6 are now gray, as shown in Figure 4.3, which means they are filled with some content (in this case, a circle representing the sun).

7. Lock the center layer by clicking the black bullet under the pad lock column in the Layers panel. We can no longer edit the stage for this layer.

8. Be sure to highlight the rays layer. Choose the Paint Brush tool with any size, style, and fill color you like.

9. Draw about five small rays around the center of the sun. Notice that these rays have been placed on a new layer. To double-check this, click the black bullet under the eye column in the Layers panel. This will temporarily turn off the visibility of the layer and acts as a toggle. To turn the visibility back on, click the red × under the eye column.

   We now want the animation to continue with the rays growing and bursting out over time.

10. With the play head positioned at frame 1, choose Insert, Blank Keyframe or press F7 on your keyboard. Notice that the ray on the previous frame is no longer on frame 2. (Remember, a blank keyframe is like a new blank page in a flipbook.)

    We're now ready to draw the ray, but this time larger. Let's have ray to grow from the same location as the last ray. That's where Onion Skin comes in.

11. Click the Onion Skin button. Notice the brackets around the play head. Also notice a faded impression of the artwork on the previous frame (in this case, the first ray).

12. Draw new rays but this time extend them a bit further, as shown in Figure 4.4. You'll now have two different frames, 1 and 2, that contain two different sets of rays.

13. Now that we have another set of rays on frame 2, we're ready to draw frames on frame 3, extending our animation. With the play head on frame 2 and the rays layer selected, press F7 on the keyboard or choose Insert, Frame. This will insert a blank keyframe on frame 3.

14. Notice that the Onion Skin markers move with the play head. Extend out the rays by drawing a new set on frame 3.

15. Repeat steps 13 and 14 so that the animation will have the rays growing and bursting out over time.

    Toward the end of the animation, we want the rays to look like they are burning out. The next step will trick our eyes into thinking that the rays are actually growing over time and then suddenly burn out.

16. Insert a blank keyframe for frame 5 by pressing F7 on your keyboard. In frame 5, draw a small dot at the end of each ray. This will make the rays look like they are running out of steam.

17. Insert a blank keyframe on the sixth and final frame. By leaving this frame blank, it will appear in the animation that the rays have burst out from the center of the sun and toward the end of the burst run out of energy and disappear.

18. Under the Window menu choose Toolbars, Controller and click the play button to watch the animation. To see the animation loop (that is, to play it over and over again), choose Control, Loop Play Back and then click the play button again.

FIGURE 4.3

Notice the difference between a keyframe and a blank keyframe.

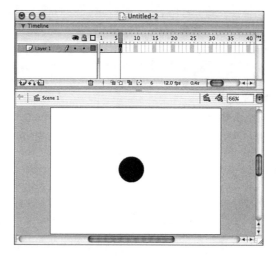

FIGURE 4.4

The new rays are being drawn and their locations are based on Onion Skin.

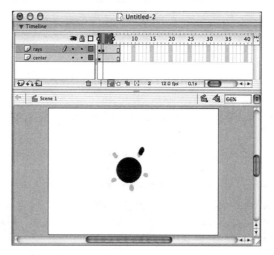

This is frame-by-frame animation. Typically frame-by-frame animation is used in character animation. By drawing on each frame, you're able to achieve more fluid, life-like animation. This is especially true when used in conjunction with a Wacom or pressure-sensitive palette.

Shape Tweening

After creating the sun animation, you can really appreciate the hard work that goes into creating a feature-based animation film. However, feature animation films are truly an art form; you probably don't have a few years to complete your projects. Let's take the Walt Disney Company for example. Disney will typically have an artist painting key cells within an animated sequence. If a character is at bat in a baseball game, for instance, this artist would paint the character waiting for the pitch and then probably another cell after the character takes a swing. To complete the animation, a team of "in-betweeners" would paint all the cells in between the first and last key cells.

Flash has this functionality built in. You can set two keyframes, much like the artist painting those key cells, and let Flash build the animation in between, just like the team of in-betweeners. This process is known as *tweening*. To add to the confusion, there are two different types of tweening in Flash: shape tweening and motion tweening. The differences aren't exactly black and white, at least at this point in the book. Once you've finished Chapter 5, "Symbols and the Library," the differences will be very apparent. Each have very strict rules. For example, the biggest rule for shape tweening is that the item must be a primitive object; it cannot be a grouped object or a symbol.

Creating an Animation with Shape Tween

The point of this exercise is to get you more familiar with creating a shape tween animation. We're going to start by doing something simple—moving a square across the stage. Here are the steps to follow:

1. Draw a square on the stage using the Rectangle tool. Select a fill color but no stroke color. Position the square in the top-left corner of the stage.

2. Click inside of frame 20, not on the play head, but rather physically in the open frame space, as shown in Figure 4.5. Choose Insert, Frame or press F5 on your keyboard.

   Notice that frame 20 and all the frames from 1 through 20 become populated. This means that the square is visible for 20 seconds. It is, however, in the same location, and we want an animation.

3. With the play head set to 20, using the Arrow tool, click and drag the square to the opposite side of the stage. Notice that you may have left a stroke behind if you didn't double-click the square when you selected it to move it. That's okay; just delete the stroke left behind.

4. Select frame 1 by clicking it. Notice that the frame becomes highlighted in black. In the Properties Inspector, use the Tween drop-down menu and choose Shape. Notice the frames have turned green with an arrow pointing from frame 1 to frame 20.

5. Click the play button on Window, Toolbars, Controller or press the Return (Mac) or Enter (Windows) key to play the animation. See the square move its position over time.

   One of the great things about shape tweening is the ability to morph objects. We could actually make this square morph into a circle while it's moving to its new position! All we have to do is modify our previous animation, slightly.

6. Move the play head to frame 20. Highlight the square on the stage with the Arrow tool. Once the square is highlighted, press the Delete or Backspace key on your keyboard. Notice that the square has disappeared on that frame but is still present on all the other preceding frames. The arrow has also turned into a dashed line, indicating a broken tween, as noted in Figure 4.6.

7. With the play head still on frame 20, choose the Oval tool in the Tools panel. This time pick a different fill color while still leaving the stroke color empty. Draw a circle anywhere on the stage that's a good distance from the square.

   Once the circle has been drawn on frame 20, notice the dashed lines have turned back into an arrow.

8. Click the play button in Window, Toolbars, Controller or press the Return (Mac) or Enter (Windows) key on your keyboard. Your animation has already been updated, and the square slowly morphs into a circle and changes color!

FIGURE 4.5

Frame 20 is selected by clicking the empty cell.

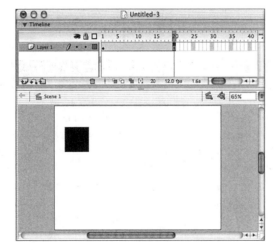

FIGURE 4.6

Notice the dashed line indicating a broken tween.

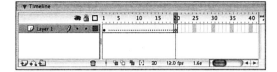

You may want to save this file in a handy location because we'll refer to it later. It will be used as a starting point for other animation we're going to create in this chapter.

Controlling Your Tweens

Now that you understand the basics of shape tweening, we can move on to how to manipulate tweens. The first thing we can do is control the speed of the animation from the beginning and at the end. This can really help in the visual mood you are trying to set. For example, suppose you have a small drawing of a car, and you want to animate that car taking off from a stop light. Unless you are one of the few people who own a Ferrari F-50, the car will take off from the stop light at a slower speed than what it will cruise at. To achieve this effect in Flash, you would use *easing*. You can either ease into an animation or ease out of it. In the case of your car animation, you'd choose to ease in, which means Flash will slowly start the animation before brining it up to full speed. Of course, I don't have a Ferrari, so I will use a square as an example. With the slider in the Properties Inspector, you can make the adjustments. The lower the number's value, the more dramatic (or slow) the ease in will be. Just the opposite applies for easing out: The greater the value, the slower the animation will get towards the end of the animation.

Another important option is to have either angular or distributive tweening. Angular is best used with objects that contain a lot of corners, whereas distributive provides a smoother tween among items. Distributive is the default because it generally yields better results for most tweens.

Making a Shape Tween Animation Fade Away

A common question I get is, how do I make my object fade away in the shape tween? The answer may not be that obvious, but keep in mind we are working with primitive shapes, so there is only one logical way. Open the animation you created earlier with the square morphing into the circle and then follow these steps:

1. Move your play head to the last frame in the animation, which should be frame 20.

2. With the Arrow tool selected, click the circle to select it.

3. If your Color Mixer panel is not open, select Window, Color Mixer. Notice the fill swatch is the same color as the selected circle.

4. If the fill swatch is not selected in the Color Mixer panel, click the Paint Bucket icon just to the right of the swatch in the Color Mixer panel.

5. In the Alpha text box, type in **0** or choose 0 with the slider box (see to Figure 4.7). At first it may look like nothing has happened, but as soon as you click away from the circle, the circle will become invisible.

6. In the controller, click the play button to see the animation. Notice that towards the end of the animation, the square not only turns into a circle and a different color, but it also fades away!

FIGURE 4.7

The Alpha slider bar in the color swatches.

Shape Hinting

So you can change the shape, color, and transparency of your items during tweening, but what if you want more control? Well, more control is on the way. In fact, you can even dictate how an item's corners and points will morph into the other item's corner and points.

This wonderful feature is called *shape hinting*. When you shape-hint, you have more control of the object's morphing appearance by placing anchors. This anchors a point in item A to a point in item B. To further illustrate this, let's do one more exercise.

Shape-Hinting Your Shape Tween

In this exercise, you need to access the Unleashed library, which you turned into a common library in Chapter 2, "Introducing Flash MX." We are going to be using a symbol (a star) and a letter in this lesson. These objects are not primitive objects. You can tell when you select them because they don't get the dotted specks; instead, they have blue borders.

By default, text has the characteristics of a grouped object. The star is a symbol. We need to make both objects primitive object in order to apply a shape tween. Here are the steps for this exercise:

1. Under the Window menu, choose Common Libraries, Unleashed.fla. Notice that the Unleashed library becomes active.

2. In the Unleashed library, drag out an instance of the star graphic. Place the graphic anywhere on the stage.

3. With the star selected, choose Modify, Break Apart. Now the star has a speckled selection, as shown in Figure 4.8, instead of the blue bounding box. This indicates that it's a primitive item.

4. Select frame 15 by clicking in the empty slot. Choose Insert, Blank Keyframe or press F7 on your keyboard. Notice that the frame becomes white and that frames 2 through 19 become populated.

5. On this frame, type the letter A with the Type tool in the same general location as where the star was. If you forget where the star is located, turn on Onion Skin. Use a sans-serif typeface and a larger size (for example, Trebuchet at a size of 200).

6. With the letter A selected, choose Modify, Break Apart to convert the A to a primitive item. This letter is no longer editable with the Type tool. Flash now considers this letter a shape and not a typed letter.

7. Select frame 1 and in the Properties Inspector choose Shape Tween. Play the animation.

   Notice how the star almost disappears before morphing into the letter A, as in Figure 4.9. We're going to fix the appearance of this tween using shape hinting.

8. With the play head set back to frame 1, choose Modify, Shape, Add Shape Hint. Notice the little red circle that appears with the letter A. This is the shape hint anchor.

9. Place the anchor on the top point of the star, as shown in Figure 4.10.

10. Move the play head to frame 15. Notice the same little anchor. Drag the anchor to the top on the letter A. Notice that the color changes to green.

If the color does not change to green, click away from the anchor point. At this point, we have essentially mapped these two points together. The top of the star will join to the top of the A.

11. Play the animation. Notice that the morph is already solid and looks more natural, as shown in Figure 4.11.

12. We'll add one more hint. Move the play head back to frame 1. Under the Modify menu, choose Shape, Add Shape Hint. Notice the new anchor point that appears on the stage.

13. Drag the new anchor point to the bottom part of the middle line of the star.

14. Move the play head to frame 15 and place the anchor point at the bottom part of the middle line of the A. Notice that the anchor changes color.

15. Play the animation to see how smooth it is.

Figure 4.8

The star symbol after it has been broken apart.

Figure 4.9

Unpredictable morphing effects without shape hinting.

Figure 4.10

Placing the shape hint anchor on top of the star.

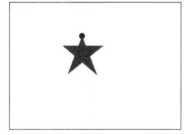

Figure 4.11

Animation after a shape hint has been applied.

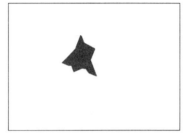

Finally, suppose you like the shape hints, but you think they're a lot of work to use. For many animations, there is no other way to change the blending appearance of the morph. However, in this situation, where the star is turning invisible before turning into the letter A, there is a quick fix. One of the biggest issues with this type of tween is that one object has a hole and the other doesn't. The center portion of the A is hollow, and there is nothing in the star to compensate for it—unless, of course, if we do something to fix that.

If you want to remove a shape hint, you can right-click (Windows) or Control-click (Mac) on the hint. In the contextual menu, choose Remove Hint. In our case, we are going to choose Remove All Hints to bring us back to square one in our tweened animation.

To fix the problem at this point, all we have to do is insert a keyframe on frame 2. Here are the steps to follow:

1. Move the play head to frame 2 and press F6 on your keyboard or choose Insert, Frame.

2. Select the Eraser tool in the Tools panel and choose the smallest brush.

3. With the play head still on frame 2, erase a small circle in the center of the star, as shown in Figure 4.12. The animation now looks normal (see Figure 4.13).

4

Flash Animation

FIGURE 4.12
Erase a small hole in the star.

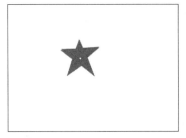

FIGURE 4.13
Perfect tweened animation!

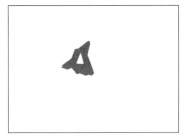

That's shape tweening in a nutshell. In the next chapter, we'll look at motion tweening. You'll see that in many ways motion tweening is a bit more conducive to Web animation.

Changing Timeline Views

For most people, the standard timeline view is the best for most projects. However, Flash offers flexibility in terms of how you can view the timeline. In some cases, you may want a preview of what your animation is going to look like over time, and in others you may want the frames to appear very small so you can fit more on your screen. Whatever the case may be, the ability to change frame styles is an nice option to have, so let's review what each style looks like and the advantages and disadvantages of those styles.

As shown in Figure 4.14, you have options for changing the size, color, and style of the frames. Generally these different views are used for cartoon animators, to get a preview of what their animation will actually look like. You may also scale down the size of the frames to allow more viewable timeline space.

The top choices are for modifying the size options, as detailed in the following list:

FIGURE 4.14

The frame view options menu.

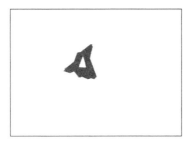

- **Tiny, Small, Normal, Medium, and Large**. These options are for adjusting the width of the frames.

- **Short**. This option changes the height of the frames to afford more room to view more layers within the same Timeline panel size.

- **Tinted Frames**. This option turns the tint of the frames on or off. If this option is turned on, populated frames are indicated by a gray fill, blank or unpopulated frames are indicated by a white fill, and motion and shape tweens display blue and green, respectively. The Tinted Frames option is on by default. Otherwise, when it's turned off, frames will display white, unless they're tweened, in which case they'll show a gray checkered background.

- **Preview**. This view displays a thumbnail preview of the animated subject for each frame, as shown in Figure 4.15.

- **Preview in Context**. This view still offers a thumbnail preview of each frame; however, it does not just focus on the animated subject. Instead, this view displays the subject in context to the placement on the stage, as shown in Figure 4.16.

FIGURE 4.15

Timeline displaying an animation in Preview view.

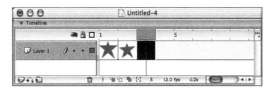

FIGURE 4.16

Timeline displaying an animation in Preview in Context view.

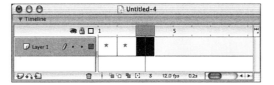

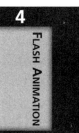

4

FLASH ANIMATION

Symbols and the Library

By Matt Pizzi

IN THIS CHAPTER

- An Overview of Graphic Symbols
- An Overview of Button Symbols
- Motion Tweening
- Creating Interactivity with Buttons
- The Movie Clip
- Nested and Compound Animation
- The Library

As we progress through this book, each topic, and therefore each chapter, becomes more and more important. This chapter is no exception. In fact, this chapter is the building block for the more advanced topics we discuss later. The library and furthermore symbols are what make Flash successful on the Web. By creating a library item, you are really creating a reusable item that's stored in the library. Once the library has been downloaded to the end-user machine, that library item or symbol is available for use at any point within the movie. If you have more than one instance of the library item on the stage, even if it's 50 or more instances, all the complexity and size of the file is stored in the one library item, and each instance is linked to that library item.

An *instance* is a item on the stage that linked to a library item or symbol. Anytime a library item is placed on the stage, it is called an *instance*, and that instance points and refers back to the symbol in the library. A wonderful benefit of using an instance of a symbol is that you can adjust the appearance of the item. You can change the instance's scale, alpha, and color, giving it a very different appearance from the actual library item while maintaining its link to the original symbol. This saves file size, because the complexity of the graphic is actually stored within the library. Flash only needs to render the differences between the instance and the symbol, as opposed to the entire graphic.

With this link between the instance and the library item, you can also save a lot of time updating or changing your movie by simply changing the library item. If you do, in fact, have 50 instances of the same library item, and a change needs to be made, you can simply change or edit the library item, and all instances within that movie will be updated.

Of course, all this may be a bit much to swallow all at once, so let's deconstruct the way we create and use symbols. First, we're going to be looking at how you'd go about creating a symbol and what types of behaviors you can use and why you would use them. Then we'll look at some of the different elements of the library.

An Overview of Graphic Symbols

Up to this point, we've worked with primitive items and grouped objects. The drawback to working with primitive items, especially in an animation sequence, is file size. Every time a primitive item is displayed, Flash has to draw and calculate its color and shape. If you use an item on frame 1 and then use that same item again on frame 20, Flash has to create and render the item twice. It's not cached; once the frame leaves the primitive data leaves, and there is no way to recall it. Grouped items are essentially the same, only a grouped item contains a group of primitive graphics for Flash to calculate.

This is where graphic symbols come in. They behave differently from primitive items in that animated primitive items are calculated for each keyframe for Flash to render the contents. Graphic symbols are simply calling the library item and asking the library to draw the contents of the symbol in any given region on the stage based on the animation.

Therefore, graphic symbols are better than primitive graphics for static and animated content. However, in the world of Flash, graphics symbols are best suited for static use because, when a graphic symbol is animated, Flash must continually point the instance to the library item on every single frame. Needless to say, this statement becomes rather long and complex. The best choice for behaviors when it comes to animated symbols is a movie clip, which we'll review later in this chapter in the section "The Movie Clip."

Creating Graphic Symbols

Let's take a look at some of the many ways to create symbols in Flash--and more specifically how to create graphic symbols. Follow these steps to create a graphic symbol:

1. Choose Insert, New Symbol. This will launch the Create New Symbol dialog box, as shown in Figure 5.1.

2. In this dialog box is a whole series of choices. For now, click the Basic button to switch the dialog box to the basic view. Notice that the additional options are now hidden.

3. Select the Graphic radio button to give the new symbol the graphic symbol behavior.

4. Name the graphic by typing **circle** in the Name text field.

5. Click OK. Notice that the screen changes to a new view. You can also tell by looking at the tabs at the bottom of the timeline, indicating that you are now inside the graphic symbol, as shown in Figure 5.2.

6. The crosshair in the center of the stage, as shown in Figure 5.3, represents the center point of the symbol.

7. Draw a circle over the crosshair, thus placing the circle in the center of the symbol.

   Note that the center of the symbol is important to locate for many reasons. This point defines the center for the axis of any rotation animation. It's also considered when scaling numerically and is used to return feedback about the symbol's placement on the stage.

8. Once you're happy with the appearance of the artwork, you're done editing this symbol. Let's go back to scene 1, also known as the *main timeline*, by clicking the scene 1 tab (refer to Figure 5.2 if you forget where the tabs are).

9. Now that we're back in scene 1, you'll notice that the circle has disappeared...or so it seems. Remember, we've created a symbol, so all our artwork is stored in the library under a symbol named "circle." If your library isn't already open, like it is in Figure 5.4, choose Window, Library. The Library is now visible.

10. Click the symbol in the Library panel and drag it anywhere on the stage. This is an *instance* of our circle symbol.

FIGURE 5.1

The Create New Symbol dialog box.

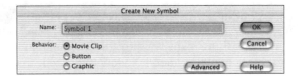

FIGURE 5.2

The graphic symbol's tab.

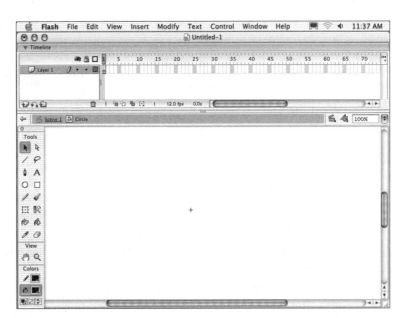

FIGURE 5.3

The crosshair in the stage represents the center of the symbol.

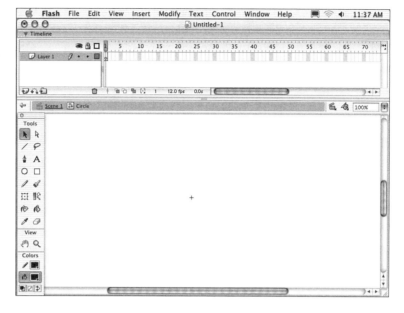

FIGURE 5.4

The Library panel with the circle graphic symbol.

This exercise discusses how you go about creating a new symbol from scratch. However, there is a good chance you may want some existing artwork on the stage to also become a symbol. To deal with that, all you have to do is select the artwork on the stage and under the Insert menu choose Convert to Symbol. This will launch a dialog box, called Convert to Symbol, that's similar to the Create New Symbol dialog box. The one exception is displayed in Figure 5.5--you have a choice as to where you want the center point to be on the new symbol. Just click one of the small squares in the Registration icon to select the center point. Oftentimes you'll want to choose the center box as the center point, unless you have certain requirements that dictate otherwise. An example of choosing a box other than the center box would be if you intend to create a rotating animation and you want the axis point to be something other than the center of the object.

FIGURE 5.5

Use the Registration icon to choose the center point of the symbol.

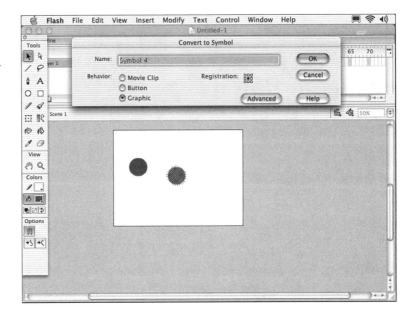

An Overview of Button Symbols

The button symbol is the least complex symbol in terms of understanding its purpose. It is designed for creating buttons! This symbol's timeline has predefined states for making it easier to design and develop a button. Buttons are important symbols when it comes to creating interactivity between a Web site and a user.

Building a Button Symbol

Here are the steps to follow to build a button symbol:

1. Draw a shape anywhere on the stage.
2. Choose the Arrow tool and double-click the shape to select it.
3. With the shape now selected, choose Insert, Convert to Symbol. The Convert to Symbol dialog box pops up.
4. Select the Button radio button to give the symbol the button behavior. Also choose a center point for the symbol in the Registration icon.

5. Click OK. Notice the shape no longer has a speckled selection but rather a blue box with a crosshair for the center point.

6. Double-click the new symbol. Notice that you are brought into button symbol editing mode. Also notice that the first four frames are predefined button states, as shown in Figure 5.6.

   The four states include Up, Over, Down, and Hit. Up is the state the button will have when the movie loads. Over is what the button will change to when the end user moves the mouse over the button. Down is the state the button will refer to when the button is being clicked by the end user by pressing the mouse's button down. Finally, Hit defines the active area of the button. It's typically best to have a Hit state at least the size of the button. If the button is text, be sure to draw a solid box over the text in the Hit state. The Hit state is invisible, but if text is the subject for the end user to click, this could cause some buggy problems for the user. Remember that many characters have "holes" in them, such as the letter *O*, for example. The mouse could, in theory, be clicked in that empty area of the *O*, without ever clicking the Hit state of the button. If you draw a solid box over your text, the Hit state problem is solved.

7. Because we've converted an existing shape to a symbol, we automatically have content in frame 1, also known as the Up state. If you want, you can modify any part of the shape to better suit your liking.

8. Choose Insert, Keyframe or press F6 to insert a keyframe to move to the Over state. Notice a keyframe has been inserted into the Over state, carrying over the attributes of the previous frame.

9. Now that we're in the Over state, all we're going to do is change the fill color of the shape. Select the shape using the Arrow tool and choose a different color in the fill swatch of the Tools panel.

10. Press F6 to insert another keyframe. Make some similar modifications to the artwork in the Over state.

11. Press F6 one last time to insert a keyframe on the Hit state. Remember, the Hit state is invisible; it just defines the active area of the button. Simple shape you can pretty much just leave it alone; however, if the shapes has a hole in it, like the letter *O*, draw a solid shape over it.

12. Come back to scene 1 by clicking the Scene 1 tab, or you can use the Scene Select drop-down menu, as shown in Figure 5.7.

FIGURE 5.6

Button symbol timeline.

FIGURE 5.7

Select a scene by using the Scene Select drop-down menu.

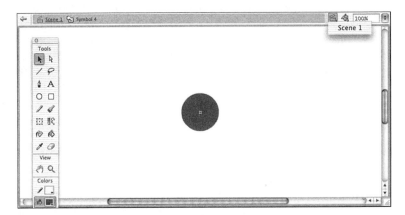

Note

Check out the QuickTime movie on this book's companion Web site on how to build buttons.

You can preview the button you just built within the Flash authoring environment. Choose Control, Enable Simple Buttons. Move your mouse over the button on the stage and click it to see the previews. To turn it off, choose Control, Enable Simple Buttons again.

The real power of buttons is having the ability to communicate with the timeline and other objects. For example, if we had an animation, we could create play and stop buttons to control the animation. Furthermore, we haven't discussed motion tweening. Now that you know how to create a graphic symbol, we can animate it on our main timeline and have it follow a motion guide. The use of motion guides is one of the advantages of motion tweening. In the next few exercises, you'll learn how to create a motion tween, and we'll look at the advantages of motion tweening as well as controlling the timeline with buttons.

Motion Tweening

Creating a Motion Tween

In this exercise, we are going to create an animation of a circle moving from one side of the stage to the other. During this animation, the circle will fade out toward the end of the sequence and follow a motion guide during the tween. For the first time, we are going to be using motion tweening instead of a shape. Remember, the key difference is that when you motion-tween, you are tweening a symbol as opposed to a primitive shape. Here are the steps to follow for this exercise:

1. Double-click layer 1 to rename it. Name it **animation**. Draw a circle on the stage with a fill and stroke color of your choice. With the Arrow tool, double-click the circle to select its fill and stroke.

2. Under the Insert menu, choose Convert to Symbol. Be sure to give this symbol a graphic behavior and name it **circle**. Notice the new symbol, called circle, in the library.

3. Select frame 20 and press F6 to insert a keyframe. With the playhead on frame 20, select the circle and drag it down to the bottom-right corner of the stage. At this point, in frames 1 through 19, the circle is in the top corner, but on frame 20, it jumps down to the bottom-right corner.

4. To have this movement happen over time, select the first frame; then, in the Properties Inspector, choose Motion from the Tween drop-down menu. Notice the frames turn blue with an arrow pointing from the first frame to the last. You've just created a motion tween!

    Now that you have a motion tween, you can add a motion guide. This way, the animation will now follow a path that you draw, as opposed to the circle just plainly moving from one side to the other.

5. To add a motion guide, click the Add Motion Guide button, as shown in Figure 5.8. Notice the new guide layer added above the animation layer. Also notice that the animation layer is indented, illustrating that this layer is now a slave to the motion guide layer.

6. With a new guide layer selected and the playhead moved to frame 1, choose the Pencil tool. With the Pencil tool, draw a curvy line across the stage, being sure not to intersect the line at any point, because this could confuse the animated item. With frame 1 in the animation layer selected, in the Properties Inspector, make sure the Snap check box is selected (see Figure 5.9). Once Snap is checked, notice how the circle "snaps" to the beginning of the guide.

If you play your animation and it does not follow the guide, it's because the item is falling off the guide before it gets to the last frame. To fix this problem, move the playhead to the last frame. Click the center of the circle and drag it to the end of the guide. Once you have the circle in snapping range, the symbol center of the circle increases in size. This size increase is an indication that the circle will snap to the guide in that location.

To make the circle disappear over time, you need to apply a color effect. We have already done something similar with shape tweening, but the process is a bit different for motion tweening. In shape tweening, we took down the alpha of the fill color. We can't do that to a symbol, and if we edited the symbol to apply a lower alpha fill, we would be applying it to the entire symbol, thus causing the circle to appear invisible the whole time. Therefore, we'll apply a color effect to the symbol instead.

7. With the playhead on the last frame of the animation, select the instance of the circle on the stage. In the Properties Inspector, use the Color drop-down menu and choose Alpha. Drag the Alpha slider down to 0, as shown in Figure 5.10.

8. Play your animation. Notice the circle moving across the stage, following the guide and fading out over time.

9. Save this file as `mtween.fla`. We will refer to it later.

FIGURE **5.8**

The Add Motion Guide button.

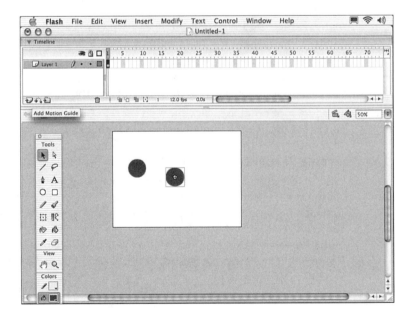

FIGURE 5.9

The guide layer and the Snap option are checked in the Properties Inspector.

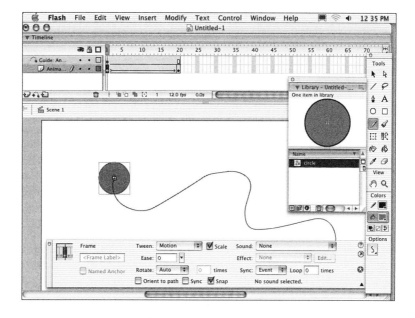

FIGURE 5.10

The color effect-- alpha.

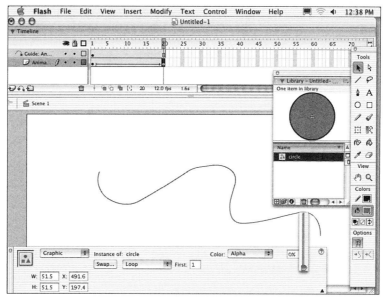

Some additional options are available in the Properties Inspector for motion tweening, as shown in Figure 5.11. Orient to Path, for example, not only makes the object follow the path, but it causes the baseline of the symbol to orient itself to the path.

5

SYMBOLS AND THE LIBRARY

You can also set how many times you'd like the instance to rotate during your animation--either clockwise or counterclockwise.

FIGURE 5.11

Motion tween options in the Properties Inspector.

Also, a shortcut is available for creating a motion tween. Draw a primitive item on the stage and insert a frame (F5) in a later frame. Right-click (Windows) or Ctrl-click (Mac) and, in the pop-up menu, choose Create Motion Tween. Notice that the frames turn blue. The series of dotted lines indicate a broken tween. To fix the tween, simply move the playhead to the last frame, select the item on the stage, and drag it somewhere else on the stage. The frame will turn into a keyframe, and the dotted lines will change into a solid arrow. Scrub the playhead to see the animation. Flash will also put the item into your library, naming it tween1.

Combining Motion and Shape Tweens

In development, you may find it necessary to have a morphing animation, but at the same time you may need the animation to follow a guide. In this exercise, we are going to take a look at how we can use both of these techniques to complete the desired effect. This will also reinforce the concept of keyframes.

We are going to create an animation of five squares, animating them across the stage. As they animate, they will follow a path. After following the path, they will proceed to morph in to the letters *F, L, A, S, H*, respectively. Here are the steps to follow:

1. Draw a square at the top-left corner of the stage without a stroke color but with a fill color of your choice. Convert it to a symbol by selecting it and pressing F8 on your keyboard. Give it a graphic behavior and name it **square**.

2. Insert a keyframe in frame 15. With the playhead on frame 15, move the square to the bottom-right corner. Highlight keyframe 1 and, in the Properties Inspector, choose Motion Tween. This will create an arrow from

frame 1 to 15, and the frames will turn blue. Scrub the playhead to see the animation. Be sure to check Snap, because we are going to create a motion guide in the next step.

3. Name layer 1 **F**. Click the Add Motion Guide button to create a new guide layer. Notice the new guide layer above the F layer. With the Pencil tool, draw a guide in the shape of a half square, as shown in Figure 5.12.

4. Scrub the playhead (that is, drag it back and forth through the frames) to make sure the square is snapped to the motion guide. If not, be sure to fix the last frame, just as you did in the previous exercise.

   Now that you have the motion tween working, you have the first part of your animation. In the next part, we want the square to morph into the letter *F*. To do this, you need to break apart the symbol. However, if you break apart the symbol in frame 15, you will break the motion tween. Remember, a tween is from keyframe to keyframe. In order to have a motion tween, you need the same symbol in two different keyframes. Therefore, you cannot break apart the symbol in frame 15. You can, however, insert a new keyframe in frame 16. A keyframe represents a major change within an animation. In this case, on frame 16 the major change is that the item is no longer a symbol but rather a primitive item.

5. In frame 16, insert a keyframe by pressing F6 on your keyboard. In this new keyframe, highlight the square by clicking it. Under the Modify menu, choose Break Apart. Notice that the symbol changes into a primitive item. Primitive items can be morphed.

6. In frame 20, insert a blank keyframe (F7). This will clear the layer of all its contents.

7. With the Type tool selected, type **F** using a sans-serif typeface. Editable text behaves much like a grouped item. You cannot morph grouped items, so the letter *F* also needs to be broken apart.

8. If you are happy with the style and size of the type, under the Modify menu, choose Break Apart. The letter is no longer editable text and is a primitive shape (see Figure 5.13).

9. Highlight keyframe 16 and, in the Properties Inspector, choose Shape Tween. This completes the first letter of the animation. With the controller, push the play button or press Return (Mac) or Enter (Windows) to see the animation. The next step is to copy this layer and animation.

Instead of going through all these steps again, you can just copy your work onto a new layer and modify the last frame to change the letter that the square morphs into.

10. Click the Add New Layer button to create a new layer. Click the name of the F layer to highlight all the frames. You'll notice that they're all highlighted in black, indicating that all frames in that layer are selected. Hold down the Option (Mac) or Alt (Windows) key and then click and drag the layer up to layer 2 and stagger the layer over four frames. Notice the little plus sign next to your cursor as you drag, as shown in Figure 5.14. This indicates that you are in fact copying the layers and not just moving them.

11. Rename layer 2 **L**. In frame 20 of the L layer, delete the *F* and, with the Type tool, type **L**. This shape tween will not work because the letter *L* is still editable and is not a primitive shape. With the letter *L* selected, choose Modify, Break Apart. Now the shape tween will work.

12. In the F layer, insert a frame (F5) in frame 20 so that the letter *F* lasts throughout the animation, as displayed in Figure 5.15.

13. Repeat steps 10 through 12 until the word *FLASH* is spelled out.

    Once the animation is complete with all the squares flying across the stage and then morphing into their respective letters to spell FLASH, there is still one problem. The *A* turns hollow in the animation because there is a hole in the *A* (note that I could have said this backwards--that there is an *A*... well, you get the point). Therefore, you need to fix this by putting a hole in the square.

14. On frame 25 of the A layer, you need to insert a keyframe by pressing F6. On this new keyframe, choose the Eraser tool with the smallest eraser size. Erase a small hole in the center of the square. Problem solved!

FIGURE 5.12
A half-square motion guide.

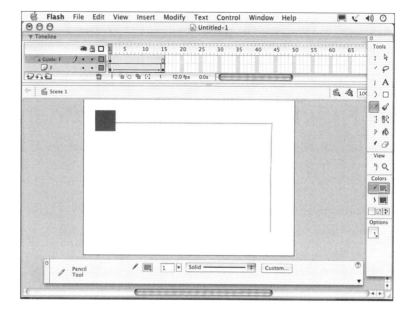

FIGURE 5.13
An animation with a guide layer and text that has been broken apart.

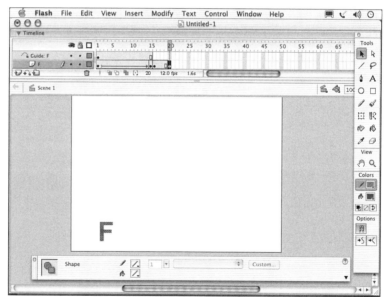

FIGURE 5.14
Duplicating a layer.

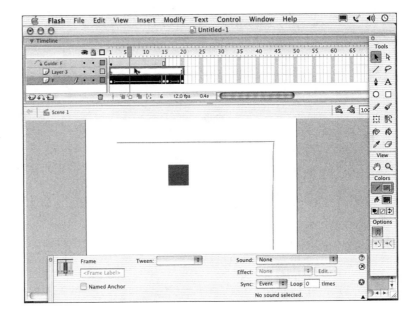

FIGURE 5.15
Extending the timeline for the bottom layer.

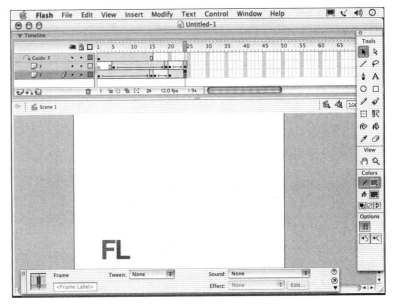

> **Note**
>
> Refer to this book's companion Web site to see the QuickTime movie reviewing this exercise, step by step.

Again, this exercise further illustrates the importance of proper keyframing. It also shows what will be a very common technique in development--combining the shape and motion tweens.

Creating Interactivity with Buttons

For true interactivity, the end user must have some input as to how the Flash movie or animation will unfold. The easiest way to do this is with buttons. Buttons can control certain elements in a Flash movie. For example, a button can play or stop an animation. Buttons can also trigger other events, such as opening up a browser window, setting volume for a sound, or even controlling a space ship in a video game. Understanding how buttons work and how buttons interact with different Flash objects is fundamental to interactive Web design.

> **Controlling the Animation with Buttons**
>
> When you're adding interactivity, it is important to allow the end user to control how an animation is played. Here are the steps to follow to control an animation with buttons:
>
> 1. Open `mtween.fla`, the file you created earlier in this chapter. Create a new layer and name it **Button**. Lock the animation layer so that you don't edit it by accident. Create a new button symbol by choosing Insert, New Symbol. Make sure to choose Button for the behavior and name the symbol **button**. Then add keyframes to all the button's states.
>
> 2. If the Library isn't already open, choose Window, Library or press Cmd+L (Mac) or Ctrl+L (Windows) to open it. Drag out two instances of button and place them anywhere on the stage on the Button layer.
>
> 3. With the Type tool, type **Play** over the first button and **Stop** over the second.

4. With the Play button selected (be sure to have the button selected and not the text *Play*), select Window, Actions. This will bring up the Actions panel, as shown in Figure 5.16. Be sure this panel is labeled Actions – Button and not Actions – Frame (if it does read "Actions – Frame," that means you have the frame selected instead of the button). To fix this, just move the Actions panel off to the side and click the button to select it. This will set the panel to Actions – Button.

5. In the Actions panel, open the Actions book. Inside that book, open the Movie Control book and double-click Play. Notice on the right that some code is typed for you. This is ActionScript. The script should read as follows:

```
on (release) {
    play();
}
```

The event handler `on (release)` can be changed. At this point, the release of the mouse will trigger the event (in this case, `play`). If you want to change this to `press` or some other event, simply click to highlight the line of code for `on (release)`. Notice, as shown in Figure 5.17, all the other options for events. Feel free to choose a different one.

Before we test the script, the animation will automatically start playing. All movies in Flash will play and loop by default. Therefore, you need to fix this so that the Play button will actually serve a purpose.

6. Highlight frame 1 in either layer and under the Window menu choose Actions. Notice that the Actions panel reads "Actions – Frame." Inside the Actions book, open the Movie Control book. Inside the Movie Control book, double-click Stop. This will stop the movie from playing automatically.

7. Under the Control menu, choose Test Movie. Notice that the animation does not start playing by default. Click the Play button. Your animation should now be playing!

8. Watch the entire animation.

This animation looks okay; however, the movie will stop playing, even though we didn't ask it to. The reason why it has stopped is because the playhead is looping. *Looping* simply means that once the playhead reaches the end of the animation, it will come back to the beginning. In our case, the first frame has a `stop` action causing the animation to stop.

Therefore, we need to come up with a workaround for this problem. We can't remove the `stop` action from the first frame because it is stopping the animation from playing automatically.

9. Highlight the last frame in your animation. With it highlighted, open the Actions panel. In the Actions panel, choose Actions, Movie Control, gotoAndPlay (2). This will fix the problem, because once the playhead hits the last frame, the playhead will read the script and send it back to frame 2, thus avoiding frame 1 altogether.

It's important to point out that when you're dealing with ActionScript, you should test your movies often. From this one example, you can see the benefit of testing frequently. It is easier to build upon good scripts and make minor adjustments where needed, as opposed to debugging longer ActionScript code.

10. All you need to do now is add functionality to the Stop button. This task is a bit easier. Highlight the button with the Arrow tool. With the Stop button selected, choose Window, Actions. In the Actions book, choose Movie Control and then Stop. Notice that all the code is typed for you. Feel free to change the event handler as you see fit.

11. Test your movie! See how easy that was?

12. Save this movie as `control1.fla`.

FIGURE 5.16

The Actions – Button panel, with the Movie Control book open.

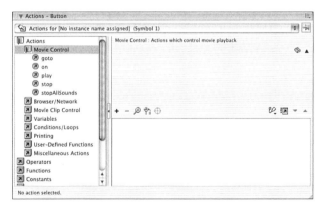

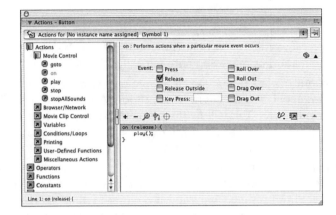

FIGURE 5.17

Additional events in the Actions panel.

This exercise illustrates the first step in creating interactivity between your site and an end user. Much of what we'll cover in the rest of this book builds on these basic principles.

The Movie Clip

The movie clip symbol is by far the most important symbol in Flash. When we get into advanced ActionScript, we'll refer to the movie clip as an object. For now, we'll review the differences between a movie clip and a graphic symbol.

You create a movie clip symbol the same way as you create a graphic or button symbol. To create one from scratch, you simply choose Insert, New Symbol. In the Create New Symbol dialog box, select Movie Clip for the behavior. Of course, if you have some artwork already drawn on the stage, you can convert it to a movie clip symbol. Once you've created a new movie clip symbol, you'll be placed in movie clip symbol editing mode. The crosshair in the center of the stage indicates the center of the symbol.

However, the most compelling thing about the movie clip is that it has its own timeline, just like the button symbol and the graphic symbol, but the key difference is that this timeline will play independently of the main timeline. This offers huge advantages in Flash development. For instance, the main timeline doesn't get clogged with all sorts of animations. Instead, animations can reside inside movie clips. Also, your buttons can communicate with the movie clips, with some additional syntax.

Looking at Nesting Symbols and Controlling a Movie Clip with Buttons.

Here, like in the last exercise, we are going to control the playhead, telling it when to stop and when to play. The biggest difference in this exercise, however, is that we need to communicate with the movie clip's playhead and not the main timeline's. Therefore, our syntax will change slightly.

Also, in this exercise you are going to take your first step in nesting symbols. *Nesting a symbol* simply means placing one symbol inside of another symbol. Nesting has many advantages, but for our purposes, the advantage is that inside the movie clip will be a graphic symbol that's animated, as opposed to a primitive shape. Remember, during an animation with a primitive shape, each keyframe must be redrawn. With a graphic symbol, the keyframe simply points to the Library when it needs graphical information. Here are the steps to follow for this exercise:

1. Choose Insert, New Symbol. Be sure to give the new symbol a graphic behavior. Name this symbol **square_graphic** and click OK. You'll then be placed inside the graphic symbol.

2. Draw a square in the center of the symbol. Choose a fill and stroke color.

3. Click back to scene 1 to get to the main timeline. Notice that the square is not on the stage. Open the Library by choosing Window, Library. Drag out an instance of square_graphic and place it anywhere on the stage.

4. Highlight square_graphic and press F8 to convert it to a symbol. Yes, it already is a symbol; however, by converting to a symbol, you are placing the existing square_graphic symbol inside of this new symbol you're defining. Name this symbol **square_mc** and give it the movie clip behavior. Click OK.

5. You're now placed inside the movie clip. Create a small motion tween of the square moving from one side of the stage to the other. Remember, you are in the movie clip, which means that this is an animated symbol.

6. After creating the motion tween, come back to scene 1. You'll notice that the main timeline has only one frame. If you press Enter (Windows) or Return (Mac), the animation will not play, even though your movie clip has an animation. In order to see animated movie clips, you must test the movie. Choose Control, Test Movie, and the animation should start playing.

7. Close the test window. Then highlight the instance of the movie clip. In the Properties Inspector, name the movie clip **anim** in the Instance Name text field.

We now want to create some buttons to stop and play this animation. Remember that animation will play and loop by default. To fix this problem, you need to place a `stop` action on the first frame and a `gotoAndPlay frame 2` action on the last frame. This will keep the animation from playing automatically and from stopping once it tries to loop. Refer to the exercise in this chapter titled "Controlling the Animation with Buttons."

8. Create a new layer and name it **buttons**.

9. Choose Library, Common Library, Buttons to open the Buttons common library. Drag out two instances of your favorite button.

10. With one of the buttons selected, open the Actions Panel. This time, instead of choosing Play like we did in the last exercise, you need to make sure your button is talking to the movie clip instead of the main timeline. Open the Actions book and then open the Variables book. In the Variables book, double-click `with`. Notice the code written for you in the Actions window, as shown in Figure 5.18.

11. Highlight the `with` line and place a blinking cursor in the Object text field. Notice that the Insert a Target Path icon is activated, as shown in Figure 5.19.

12. Click the Insert a Target Path button to choose what movie clip you'd like to target. Once you click the button, the Insert Target Path dialog box is displayed, as shown in Figure 5.20.

13. Click the Relative option button for the Mode field. Also, choose the Dots option button for the Notation field. We will review these concepts in Chapter 10, "Approaching ActionScript." Click the anim path, as shown in Figure 5.20. Click OK and notice how the `with` statement has been completed for you.

14. At this point, you have successfully targeted the movie clip; however, you haven't yet told it to do anything. Therefore, with the `with` statement still highlighted, choose Actions Book, Movie Control, Play. This will tell the movie clip you've targeted to play.

15. Test the move by pressing Cmd+Return (Mac) or Ctrl+Enter (Windows) or choosing Control, Test Movie.

16. To apply a `stop` action to the next button, follow steps 10 through 15 again, except use a `stop` action instead of a `play` action.

FIGURE 5.18

The ActionScript panel showing the with *statement.*

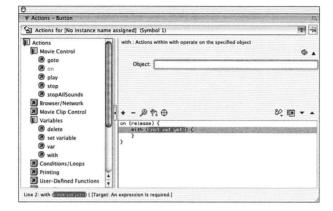

FIGURE 5.19

The Insert a Target Path icon.

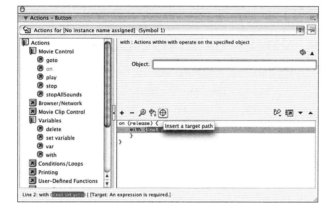

FIGURE 5.20

The Insert Target Path dialog box.

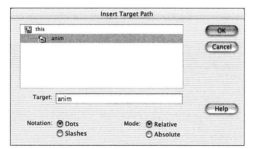

The ability to control and communicate with movie clips is the basis for ActionScript. The more you practice and understand the concepts in this section, the easier writing ActionScript will be. Although the code in the preceding exercise is proper, it might not be the most efficient. In Chapter 10, we'll discuss how objects work and what objects are. The movie clip is an object, and with that comes an easier syntax structure. The way to find this syntax is a bit more difficult because it's nested so deep. You can choose Objects, Movie, MovieClips, Methods, gotoAndPlay. Then all you would have to do is target the movie clip before the syntax so that it reads `anim.gototandPlay(1)`. This results in cleaner, more efficient code. Right now, though, don't worry about all this, because it will soon make more sense as we start to deconstruct the ActionScript language.

> **Note**
>
> Refer to the companion Web site to see a QuickTime movie demonstrating the `movie` object to control playback.

Nested and Compound Animation

We've covered how to take a symbol and place it inside another symbol, thus creating a nested symbol. One of the real powers of nesting symbols is the ability to create compound animation, which means, in not so many words, animating an animated symbol. In the previous exercise, we nested a graphic symbol inside a movie clip. When you tested the movie, the movie clip actually animated, even though the main timeline was only one frame long, because the movie clip was made up of an animation. In the next exercise, we have a movie clip on the main timeline that doesn't animate unless we test the movie. The main timeline contains only one frame, but we'll add more. By inserting a keyframe and tween into that frame and then testing the movie, you'll notice you have animated your animation!

> **Creating an Animated Button**
>
> You can nest movie clips within buttons, and vice versa. By nesting a movie clip within a button, you can create an animated button. In this exercise, we are going to take a look at how to animate a button as the end user moves a mouse over it. Here are the steps to follow:
>
> 1. Open a new document by choosing File, New. In the new document, create a new button symbol by choosing Insert, New Symbol. Give the symbol a button behavior and name it **button**. Click OK to be placed in button symbol editing mode.
> 2. Draw a circle filled with any color of your choice. Add keyframes in the Over, Down, and Hit states. Change the color slightly on each keyframe.

3. Name the layer **button layer** and click the Add Layer button. Name this new layer **glow**.

4. Insert a keyframe in the Over state of the glow layer. If, at this point, you add content to this frame, you would then populate the Down and Hit states as well, and we don't want that. To avoid this, insert a blank keyframe (F7) in the Down state, thus clearing anything on the frames before it.

5. Drag the glow layer underneath the button layer so that the glow layer is on the bottom, as shown in Figure 5.21.

6. On the glow layer, draw a small yellow circle without a stroke underneath the button. Once you let go of the mouse to finish drawing the circle, it will look like nothing has happened, because the circle you just drew is hidden under the button. To see the circle, turn on the visibility of the button layer by clicking the bullet under the eye column, as shown in Figure 5.22.

7. Highlight the circle and convert it to a movie clip symbol by pressing F8. Name this symbol **glow_mc**.

8. Click OK. Double-click the small yellow circle to go into movie clip symbol editing mode.

9. Highlight the circle by clicking it and open the Color Mixer, if it isn't already open. To open the Color Mixer, choose Window, Color Mixer. In the Color Mixer, choose the fill swatch and bring the Alpha setting down to 0%. This will make the circle invisible once you deselect it by clicking away from it (see Figure 5.23).

10. Move the playhead to frame 7. Insert a keyframe on frames 7 and 14 by pressing F6. Notice that the black circle representing the keyframe appears in both frames.

11. Move the playhead back to frame 7. In frame 7, select the circle and then choose Modify, Transform, Scale and Rotate. In the dialog box that appears, you can scale the item numerically. Scale the circle up 400%.

12. With the circle still selected in frame 7, open the Color Mixer. Bring the fill's Alpha setting back up to 100%.

It is important to remember that movie clips play and loop by default. Therefore, the glow movie clip will always be playing. However, glow will only be visible in the Over state of the button. Therefore, only when an end user moves the mouse over the button will he or she see the animated glow.

13. Click the Scene 1 tab to come back to the main timeline. Open up the Library and drag out an instance of the button symbol. By dragging out an instance of button, you are also dragging out an instance of glow, because glow is nested inside of button.

14. Choose Control, Test Movie. This will launch a Flash player. In the Flash player, move your mouse over the button to see the animation play (see Figure 5.24).

FIGURE 5.21
The glow layer underneath the button layer.

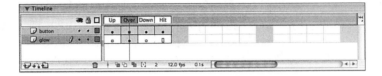

FIGURE 5.22
This figure illustrates how to turn off a layer's visibility.

FIGURE 5.23
In the Color Mixer, you can fill a symbol with a color that has an Alpha setting of 0%, thus filling it with an invisible color.

FIGURE 5.24

An animated button symbol.

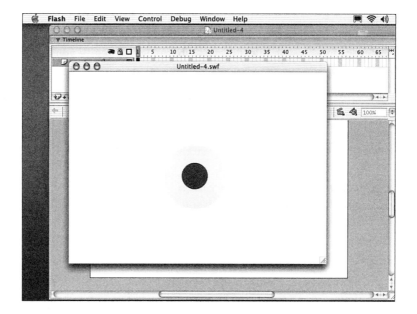

The Library

So far, we've been adding items to the Library. Now we'll dive deeper into organizing and managing the Library. We're going to be looking at some of the more advanced techniques in handling symbols. The Library, as displayed in Figure 5.25, is an area for organizing, storing, and accessing your symbols.

FIGURE 5.25

The Library panel.

Each movie contains a library. Every symbol, movie, sound, and bitmap image in that file becomes a part of that movie's library. You can open different Flash files in the form of a library by choosing File, Open as Library. This will give you full access to that file's library in the movie or file you're currently working with. A library is made up of these basic components:

- **Item Preview**. This area of the Library gives you a thumbnail of the artwork in the Library. If it is a sound, you will see a waveform. Movie clips and sounds have play and stop buttons so that you can preview the animation or sound within the Library!

- **Sort Order**. Sorts the Library items in either ascending or descending order, depending upon which column you have selected (Name, Kind, Use Count, or Linkage).

- **Wide State**. Use this option to set the visibility of the Library in its wide state, maximizing the Library to view all its contents horizontally.

- **Narrow State**. This is the more common state, taking less screen real estate. It's a slimmed-down version of the wide state that just shows the essentials.

- **Delete Item**. This button deletes an item or folder from the Library. Use it only if you are sure you want to remove the contents for the Library (this action is not undoable).

- **Item Properties**. This button launches a dialog box that gives you specific feedback about a particular item. If you get item properties for a bitmap, for example, the dialog box returns information such as the path, dimensions, the date the file was created, and compression options. The properties change depending on the type of item you've selected.

- **New Folder**. This button creates a new folder in the Library for organizational purposes.

- **New Symbol**. This button creates a new symbol and launches the Create New Symbol dialog box. This is the equivalent to choosing Insert, New Symbol.

You may also manage and organize your library by using folders. This can maximize your efficiency and workflow when using Flash assets.

For example, you could create a Graphic Symbols folder, a Buttons folder, and a Movie Clips folder. This would allow you quicker access to the symbols you're looking for. To create a new folder, just click the New Folder button at the bottom of the Library and then type in a name for the folder in the highlighted area. If the Name area is not highlighted, just click it like you would to rename a layer. You can also sort the stacking order, just like layers. Click and drag the folder up that you want to have on top. To move files into the folder, just drag the icon of the Library item on top of the folder icon and drop it. You'll be able to notice the difference between an empty folder and folder that has items in it by their appearance--an empty folder appears "skinnier" than a filled folder.

Once a folder has content in it, you can collapse or open the folder by double-clicking the folder's icon. Alternatively, you can choose Expand or Collapse Folder from the Library Options menu.

You can also easily find content within the Library that is not be used in the movie. For organizational purposes, you should delete this data. It is important to note, however, that Flash will not export any data not used in the movie. Therefore, removing unused items from the Library does nothing to conserve file size. To select or find unused items, use one of the following methods:

- Under the Library Options menu, choose Select Unused Items, as shown in Figure 5.26. This will highlight all the unused Library items in dark blue. With the items highlighted, click the trash can button to remove them all.

- Sort the items by use counts. If the Use Counts column is not active, under the Options menu, choose Update Use Counts Now. If you would like the use counts to continually update, choose Keep Use Counts Updated.

FIGURE 5.26

Choose the Select Unused Items option in the Library Options menu.

Working with Sound in Flash

By Matt Pizzi

IN THIS CHAPTER

- Adding Sound to Your Movie

Adding sounds to your Flash movie can often make or break it. For example, I tend to caution people about using hip-hop and techno music, unless their Web sites cater to an audience for which this type of music is appropriate. As another immediate piece of advice when it comes to sound, in a professional development situation, *never* use the stock sounds. Yes, some are nice, but people recognize these sounds and know they're built in to the program, which ultimately makes you a lame-o for using them. Be creative. Create your own sounds and music; if that's not reasonable, use a Flash resource on the Web, such as Flashkit.com, which offers tons of free sounds and music for you to use in your projects—all royalty free.

You can import three different sound file types: WAV format (most commonly found on Windows), AIF (a Macintosh format), and last but not least, MP3. The sounds can be either 8 bit or 16 bit and have sample rates of 11 KHz to 44 KHz.

This chapter is based on the fundamental concepts of sound in Flash. If you're looking to create advanced jukeboxes and volume and balance sliders, you're in the wrong chapter! You need to be in Chapter 18, "ActionScript's Built-in Objects in Action." ActionScript is object oriented, and within the ActionScript model, there's actually a Sound object you can use to do a lot of cool stuff, such as changing the volume, and so on. If you do want to know how to do that stuff but you've never worked with sound before, then stay right here. You need to understand how the basics of sound in Flash work before you can move into these more advanced topics.

Adding Sound to Your Movie

The first thing you need to know is that sounds must be attached to a keyframe. Whether you're dealing with a keyframe in a timeline or a keyframe in a button state, the sounds must be placed on a keyframe. With that established, let's get in and get our hands dirty.

Adding Sound to a Button

The point of this exercise is to get you more familiar with how sounds work and where you put them in your movie. In this exercise we will add a sound to button so that when the end user clicks the button, a small jingle will play. This does two things: First, it's an aural indicator to end users that they successfully clicked the button. Second, if used properly, it will create an experience for the end users that makes them believe the button has physical qualities and actually makes that noise when clicked! This is the ultimate goal in Flash development—making the end users forget for a moment that they are actually sitting at their desks, believing that they're in the space you created. Sound can play a huge role in creating this illusion.

To add sound to a button, follow these steps:

1. Create a new document. Save this file as `loud button`.

2. You can either create your own button or use a stock one from the common libraries. Choose Window, Common Libraries, Buttons. Choose any button you like and drag out an instance of it onto the stage.

3. After giving you a speech about not using stock Flash sounds, that's exactly what we're going to do here! However, I am not recommending that you publish this project either. It's simply a learning tool.

4. Choose Window, Common Libraries, Sounds to open up the Sounds common library. Notice that you can preview the sound by clicking the Play button in the Preview window of the library, as shown in Figure 6.1. Preview the various sounds until you find the one you like.

5. Double-click the button to go inside the button symbol's editing mode. Inside the button, create a new layer and name it **sound**.

6. Insert a keyframe in the Down state on the sound layer. Notice the hollow circle in the frame, which indicates that there is no content in this frame and on this layer. This is the frame we're going to use to add the sound.

7. With the sound layer still active and the playhead on the Down state, drag the sound from the library and drop it on the stage. Notice the small waveform inside the Down state, as shown in Figure 6.2, indicating that there is a sound on that frame. If you have the frame selected, notice that the Properties Inspector offers some sound options.

8. Come back to scene 1 and test the movie by choosing Control, Test Movie.

9. Click the button to hear the sound. Not bad, huh?

Stop

FIGURE 6.1

Preview sounds by clicking the Play button. Stop them by clicking the Stop button.

Play

FIGURE 6.2

The waveform indicates that there is indeed a sound on the frame.

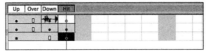

The Sound Sync Menu

You may have noticed in the Properties Inspector some options for synching sound. If you do not see these options, be sure to select the frame holding that sound. In the drop-down menu are four different settings, and each of these settings will make the sound behave in a different way. Let's go ahead and take a look at what these settings are and when would be the right time choose one over the other:

- **Event**. The most important concept to learn here is that once the sound has been triggered, it will play independently of the timeline. On our button, we have a short sound, probably about half a second in length. Now suppose the sound was three seconds long. You can probably click the button about 10 times within a span of three seconds. Because this is set to an event, the sound will play each time the event happens (in this case, pressing down on the mouse button). Therefore, the three-second sound will overlap and play on top of itself. The moral of this story is, don't use a sound of any real length for an event sound.

- **Start**. The great thing about Start is that the second instance of the sound cannot begin playing until the first instance has finished. Therefore, if you do need to use a longer sound for an event situation, such as for a button, this is the solution.

- **Stop**. This simply stops the indicated sound.

- **Stream**. This is the sync setting to use if you are doing character animation or any type of animation that has to be synchronized with sound. Stream literally forces the movie to keep pace with the sound. If, for some reason, it can't (for example, the end user has a slow machine or low bandwidth), Flash will drop frames or skip them. If Flash skips an animation frame, it will also drop or not play the corresponding sound for that frame. This way, everything stays synced. The sound is dependent on the timeline, so if you stop the animation, the sound will stop as well. Stream also has its advantages during the development process. You can scrub the playhead and hear the sound as you scrub. Stream is the only sync option that adds this functionality.

Sound Effects

Also in the Properties Inspector are some options for effects you can apply to your sound, as shown in Figure 6.3. Here's a list of these options:

FIGURE 6.3

Effect options for sound in the Properties Inspector.

- **Left Channel**. This effect will only play the sound in the left speaker if the end user's computer has stereo sound.

- **Right Channel**. This effect will only play the sound in the right speaker if the end user's computer has stereo sound.

- **Fade Left to Right**. With this effect selected, the sound will gradually fade out in the left speaker and gradually fade in on the right speaker. Of course, the end user must have stereo speakers in order to benefit from this option.

- **Fade Right to Left**. With this effect selected, the sound will gradually fade out in the right speaker and gradually fade in on the left speaker. This effect will only be heard on stereo systems.

- **Fade In**. This effect will gradually fade the sound up at the beginning of the sound.

- **Fade Out**. This effect will gradually fade the sound out toward the end of the sound.

- **Custom**. This option allows you to edit the sound envelope manually. Once you modify the sound, the Effect drop-down menu will still display Custom, because it's a custom configuration that you set up.

- **None**. This option disables any sound. No sound will be selected when the None option is chosen.

To open the Edit Envelope dialog box, you can choose Custom in the Effect drop-down menu or you can click the Edit button to the right of the drop-down menu. Go ahead and click Edit to open the Edit Envelope dialog box, as displayed in Figure 6.4.

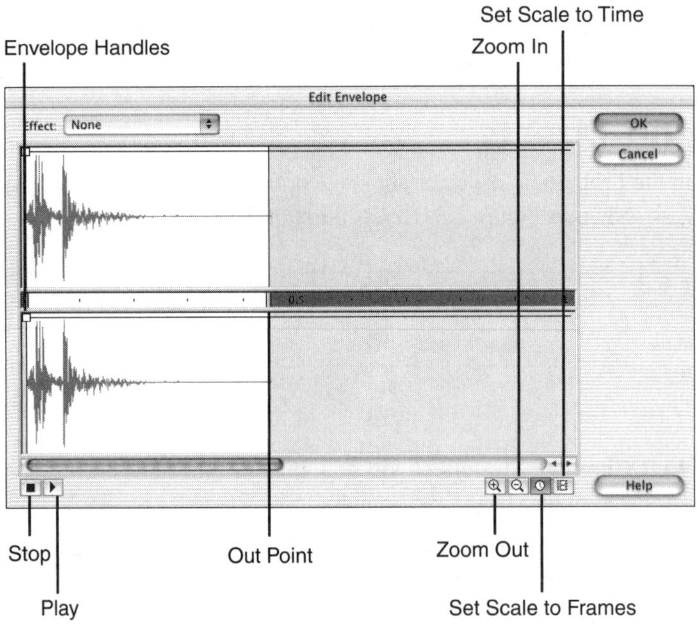

FIGURE 6.4

The sound editing envelope.

Let's go ahead and deconstruct the interface of the Edit Envelope dialog box so that you know what all the buttons stand for.

The four small buttons at the bottom-right corner of the window, from left to right, are as follows:

- **Set Scale to Frames**. This will scale the waveform's length size to the amount of frames used in the animation.

- **Set Scale to Time**. This will scale the waveform's length size to the amount of time used in the animation.

- **Zoom Out**. Choose this button to decrease the amount of time that spans the waveform in the visible area of the dialog box.

- **Zoom In**. Choose this button to increase the amount of time that spans the waveform in the visible area of the dialog box.

- **Play**. This button allows you to preview the custom effect.

- **Stop**. This button stops the preview.

The small bars shown in Figure 6.5 are for setting the in and out points. An *in point* is the start point for the sound. Therefore, if you didn't like the first couple of chords, you can cut them off! The small hollow boxes are handles, as shown in Figure 6.6, for the volume control bars. You add a new handle by clicking a space in the volume bar that isn't already occupied by a handle. A new handle will just appear.

In and Out Point Sliders

FIGURE 6.5

To adjust the in and out points, move the slider bars back and forth.

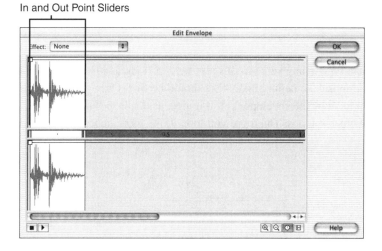

Volume Handles

FIGURE 6.6

You can use these handles to adjust the volume for the area of the waveform.

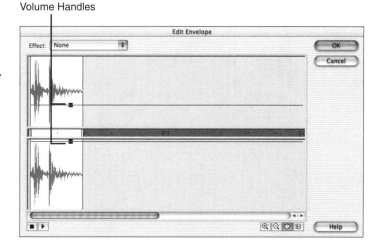

Looping Music

Looping music simply means to play it over and over again. In fact, most music you hear on Web sites are loops. The sound is probably under three seconds, just played over and over again. This is why techno and hip-hop music are so big, because they consist of small, simple loops. The longer the sound you try loop, the larger the file size. Not to imply that looping adds file size, because it doesn't. The longer the sound itself is, however, the more the file size will ultimately be bumped up.

How do you loop music? Simple. As shown in Figure 6.7, you type in a value in the Loop text field.

FIGURE 6.7

The Loop text field for sound in the Properties Inspector.

Loop   Text Field

You can type in any value in this text field, as long as it is a whole number. For background music, something like 9999 should be fine. Once you type a value, click the Edit button to show the envelope. You'll notice, as displayed in Figure 6.8, you can tell how many times it loops. The more you loop it, the more necessary it may be to zoom out a bit.

FIGURE 6.8

Notice how the appearance of the edit envelope changes when you loop the sound.

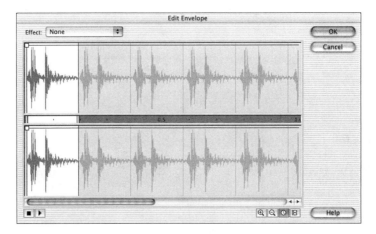

Compression

When Flash exports your movie, it compresses the sound. Four different compression methods are available: Raw, ADPCM, MP3, and Speech. You can compress each sound individually, or you can apply a global compression to any sound you do not compress manually. I highly recommend compressing each sound, especially if it's a looping song, manually. This will ensure optimum file size and fidelity.

Let's first look at how you can optimize each sound manually. First, you must download a looping sound file. You can download a file at `Flashkit.com` or the Unleashed companion Web site. The best file format to download is MP3; however, WAV and AIFF files will work as well. Once you download the file, import it into Flash by choosing File, Import. When the file is imported, it should be visible in the Library. Highlight the sound in the Library and click the Layer Properties icon in the bottom-left corner of the panel (or in the Library Options menu, choose Properties). This will launch the Sound Properties dialog box, as shown in Figure 6.9.

FIGURE 6.9

The Sound Properties dialog box.

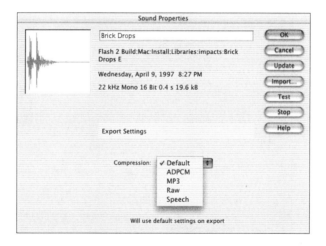

In the Compression drop-down menu, you have five choices:

- **Default**. This option uses whatever compression settings have been set in the Publish Settings dialog box.

- **Raw**. This option resamples at the specified rate. However, no compression will be applied, thus yielding a larger file size than what's appropriate for the Web. However, the sound quality is very high and maybe used for CD-ROM development.

- **ADPCM (Advanced Differential Pulse Code Modulation)**. This compression is used for 8-bit and 16-bit sound data. ADPCM is not as optimal as MP3; however, if for some reason you need to cater to the Flash 3 player, this would be your choice. The Flash 3 player cannot read MP3 files. Otherwise, MP3 would be a better choice than ADPCM.

- **MP3**. This compression method can be heard by the Flash 4, 5, and 6 players. MP3 yields the best compression at the highest sound fidelity. In most cases, you will be using MP3.

- **Speech**. New to Flash MX, Speech may offer a smaller size than MP3 for voiceovers and straight speech without any music.

A nice feature in the Sound Properties dialog box is the ability to test the compression, to make sure the audio quality is still acceptable after the compression. When you choose a compression method, Flash gives a small readout about the end file size and how the file size compares to the original, as shown in Figure 6.10.

FIGURE 6.10

*Compression feed-
back within the
Sound Properties
dialog box.*

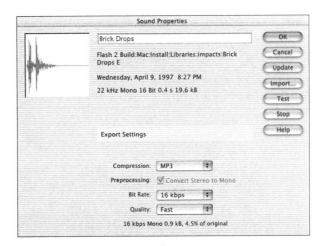

Setting Compression in the Publish Settings Dialog Box

Although I don't recommend using this feature, you can set a global compression for sound files that you don't individually compress. Choose File, Publish Settings, which will open the Publish Settings dialog box, as shown in Figure 6.11.

Click the Flash tab to set the sound compression. When you select the Flash tab, the dialog box will change to give you options for the SWF file, as shown in Figure 6.12.

FIGURE 6.11

*The Publish
Settings dialog
box.*

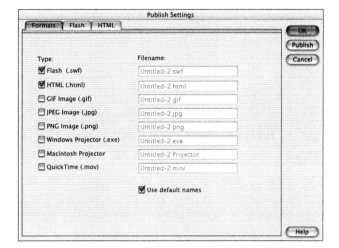

FIGURE 6.12

*The Flash tab in
the Publish
Settings dialog
box.*

Notice toward the bottom portion of the dialog box the options for setting the stream and event sounds. Click the Set button to launch the Sound Settings dialog box, as displayed in Figure 6.13.

Choose File>Publish Setting to open the Publish Settings Dialog Box. This dialog box gives all the options we had in the Sound Properties dialog box that we accessed off the Library. Also notice the Override Sound Settings check box. This option ignores all the settings we defined in the dialog box we accessed off the Library.

FIGURE **6.13**

The Sound
Settings dialog
box.

Updating a Music File in the Sound Properties Dialog Box

You can easily update or replace a sound file in the Library. If you've used instances of that sound file, they'll automatically be updated. If you're not still inside the Sound Properties dialog box, select the sound in the Library and click the little blue properties button to launch the dialog box again. Click the Import button. This will launch the Import Sound dialog box, as shown in Figure 6.14.

FIGURE **6.14**

The Import Sound
dialog box, for
replacing an exist-
ing sound in a
Flash movie's
timeline.

Search for a file to replace the current one with and then choose Import (Mac) or Open (Windows). You can also automatically bring in a newer version of the sound by choosing the Update button. This is good, for example, if you decide to tweak the sound in a third-party sound-editing program. Instead of having to import it again and delete the original file, you can just update it.

Importable File Formats

You can import a few different file formats into Flash MX for sound. Regardless of what they come in as, they must be exported using one of these compressions types:

- **MP3 (MPEG-1 Audio Layer 3)**. MP3 can improve workflow between different developers on different platforms. The other advantage is, of course, all the available MP3 files. Over the past couple years, MP3 has become the standard for storing digital music.

- **WAV**. WAV files are most commonly used in the Windows world. What's great about being able to import WAV files is that you can bring in audio created in third-party sound-editing/creation programs such as SoundForge, Rebirth, and Acid. WAV files are not normally compatible with Macs; however, with the help of QuickTime 4 or 5, Flash on the Mac can import WAV files.

- **AIFF (Audio Interchange File Format)**. This is the WAV equivalent for the Mac. Therefore, sounds created or edited with applications such as Rebirth, Peak, or Deck can be completely imported into Flash MX. Normally, Windows machines cannot read AIFF files, but again with the help of QuickTime 4 or 5, it's not a problem.

Creating a Music On/Off Button

We're going to create a simple button that adds the functionality of turning music on or off. Again, this topic gets far more complex in the ActionScript section of the book. This is an easy, quick-and-dirty way to create a button of this type, which is a must-have on a Web site. You do not want your end users to have to listen to your sound loop all the time, no matter how cool you think it is. Many times Flash sites have dramatic intros with crazy sounds. Remember, as a Flash developer (and more importantly as a Web developer), your number-one job is not to inspire but to deliver content in way that makes finding information easy. With that said, let's create the on/off button. Here are the steps to follow:

1. Open a new file. Save it as `onoff.fla`.

2. Import a sound file that will sound good when looped. If you don't have one on your computer, download one from `Flashkit.com` or the Unleashed companion Web site. Notice that the sound is now visible in this movie's library.

3. Choose Insert, New Symbol. Give the new symbol a Movie Clip behavior and name it **noisy button.**

4. Choose Window, Common Libraries, Unleashed. If you do not have the Unleashed common library, refer to Chapter 2, "Introducing Flash MX," for installation instructions.

5. In the `buttons` folder, choose the button called speaker. Drag an instance out onto the stage. Double-click the layer to rename it **button**.

6. On frame 10, insert a keyframe by pressing F6 or choosing Insert, Keyframe. This will help the structure of our code later in the exercise.

7. Create a new layer and name it **sound**, as shown in Figure 6.15.

8. With the new sound layer selected, drag out an instance of your sound file. Notice the waveform in the frames, as shown in Figure 6.15.

9. With frame 1 of the sound layer selected, in the Properties Inspector type in **999** for the amount of loops you want. Also, choose Start for the Sync option.

10. With frame 1 still selected in the Properties Inspector, label the frame **on**, as displayed in Figure 6.16.

11. With frame 1 still selected, in the Actions panel (if it's not open, choose Window, Actions), open the Actions book and then open the Movie Control book. Then double-click action `stop`. This will stop the playhead from playing automatically.

12. Select frame 10 in the sound layer.

13. Label frame 10 **off** in the Properties Inspector. By labeling frames, we can move to them in our ActionScript.

14. Highlight frame 10 of the sounds layer. Open the Actions panel. Open the Actions book and then open the Movie Control book. Then double-click the action `stopallsounds`. This will stop any sounds playing in the Flash movie.

15. Move the playhead back to frame 1 and select the button. With the button selected, open the Actions panel. When the end user clicks the button, we want the sound to stop playing. Therefore, we need to move the playhead to frame 10. Open the Actions book, open the Movie Control book, and then double-click the `goto` action.

16. After clicking `goto`, choose a frame label in the drop-down menu and then use the Frame Label drop-down menu to select "off." Also make sure that the gotoAndStop radio button is selected, as shown in Figure 6.17.

17. Move the playhead to frame 10 and select the button. Open the Actions panel again. Then open the Actions book, open the Movie Control book, and then double-click the goto action.

18. After clicking goto, choose a frame label in the drop-down menu and then use the Frame Label drop-down menu to select "on."

19. Still on frame 10, with the Line tool, draw a line through the speaker button, as shown in Figure 6.18.

20. Come back to scene 1 and drag out an instance of noisy button.

21. Test the movie by choosing Control, Test Movie.

FIGURE 6.15

The top of the two layers is named sound.

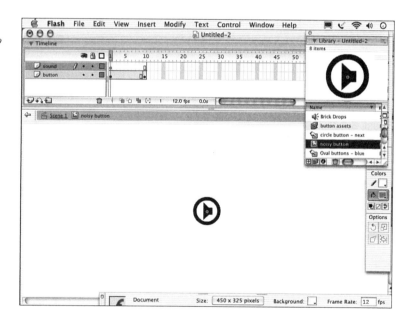

FIGURE 6.16
Label the frame in the Properties Inspector.

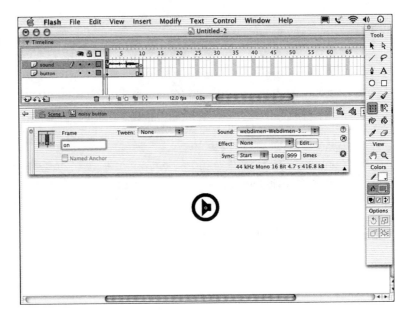

FIGURE 6.17
The Actions panel with a gotoAndStop action applied.

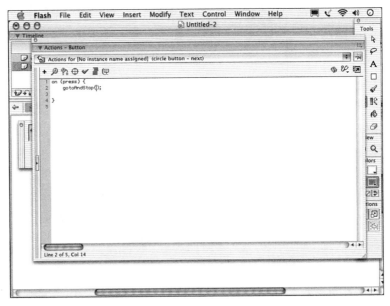

FIGURE 6.18

The speaker button with a line drawn through it.

This is just a basic way of creating an on/off button. With ActionScript, you can do much more with sound—from dynamically fading it, to adjusting the volume and balance.

Development Techniques

By Matt Pizzi

CHAPTER 7

IN THIS CHAPTER

- Masking Techniques
- Loading a Movie
- Preloaders

At this point in the book, you're more than capable of creating an interactive Web site with sound. Of course, you may have some questions as to how you can tie together everything you've learned so far. That's what we'll be doing in the next two chapters. After these two chapters, you really can produce a Web site. However, the door to your Flash learning has just opened. In fact, you can use Flash on two very different levels. You can use Flash as a designer or as a developer. A designer's job is to make things look pretty, whereas a developer makes things work. Coupling these two different qualities can really make you stand out. If you have a good portfolio and great technical skills, you are in a better position than most in the Flash world.

In this chapter, we'll be looking at some interesting masking techniques as well as some crucial concepts for Web site functionality, such as loading a movie and creating preloaders. These techniques form the Web structure around what you've already learned. We're first going to be looking at masking techniques.

Masking Techniques

A *mask* is a layer that defines what will and what will not be visible in the layer below it. Just about anything can be used as a mask, except for strokes and lines. Of course, you can create animated masks, and now in Flash MX you can create dynamic masks as well as masks you can drag. The only downside of masks in Flash is that you can't create soft-edged masks. The mask can't have levels of transparency; it is either on or off. However, some workarounds are available that we'll look at later in this chapter. We'll start off by looking at static masks.

Creating a Static Mask

Here are the steps to follow for this exercise:

1. Open the Unleashed library you downloaded earlier in Chapter 2, "Introducing Flash MX," by choosing Window, Common Libraries, Unleashed. Under the File menu, choose Open as Library and then find the unleashed.fla file on your computer. Notice that the library opens, as shown in Figure 7.1.

2. Inside the Unleashed library, open the Graphics folder. Inside the Graphics folder, find the graphic symbol Gato1. Drag out an instance of Gato1 and place it anywhere on the stage.

3. Double-click layer 1 to get an insertion point. Rename this layer **Gato Jobs**.

4. Create a new layer by clicking the New Layer button at the bottom of the Layers panel. Rename this layer **Mask**.

5. With the Mask layer selected, choose the Oval tool in the Tools panel and, without a stroke, draw a small circle over Gato's face. You're not using a stroke because lines will not mask. By choosing None for the stroke, you'll see an accurate representation of what the mask will look like because the shape will be true to what it will mask. A stroke would make the shape look a bit larger than the area it would actually mask.

6. Double-click the Layer Properties icon to the left of the layer's name, **Mask** to bring up the Layer Properties dialog box, as shown in Figure 7.2.

7. Click the Mask radio button to give this layer a mask behavior. Click OK. Notice the icon in the Mask layer, as displayed in Figure 7.3. This icon indicates that this layer is a mask layer.

    In order for the Mask layer to mask out portions of the layer beneath it, you must make the layer beneath it a slave to the Mask layer. If the layer under the Mask layer is not a slave to the Mask layer, nothing will be masked. This is a must!

8. Double-click the Layer Properties icon in the Gato Jobs layer. This brings up the Layer Properties dialog box again. In this dialog box, choose Masked for the type, which will make this layer a slave to the Mask layer. Click OK.

9. Notice that the layer is indented and has a new icon, as shown in Figure 7.4.

10. The only way you can see whether the mask is working is to lock both the "mask" layer and the "masked" layer. By locking them, you'll see what the mask looks like, as shown in Figure 7.5. You may also test the movie to see the results of the mask.

11. Save your file as `gato_mask.fla`. We'll be using it in the next exercise.

FIGURE 7.1

The Unleashed library.

FIGURE 7.2

*The Layer Prop-
erties dialog box.*

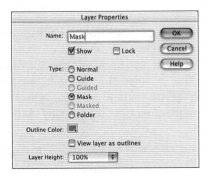

FIGURE 7.3

*The Layer icon
for the Mask
layer.*

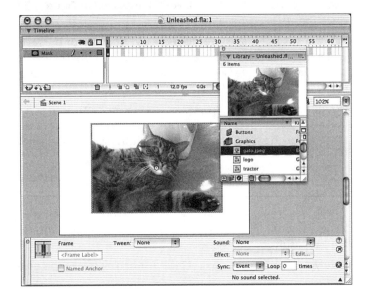

FIGURE 7.4

The Layer icon for a layer that is a slave to a mask.

Slave layer

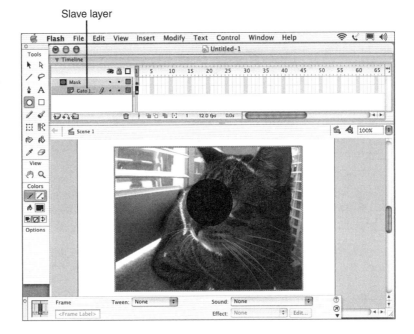

FIGURE 7.5

The mask in the authoring environment with both layers locked.

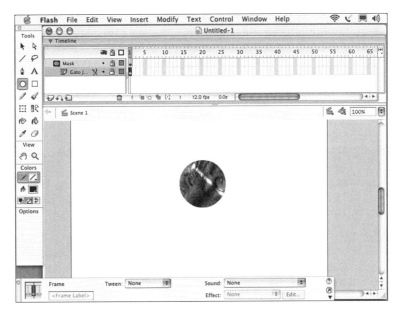

Well, that was fun—and pretty easy to boot. Now, how about making the mask animate? Making an animated mask is just as easy, but the possibilities of what you can do with an animated mask are endless. The procedure is almost the same as before; however, instead of having a static graphic or shape on the Mask layer, you'll use an animated graphic or shape.

Creating an Animated Mask

Here are the steps to follow for this exercise:

1. Open the file gato_mask.fla again. We are going to use this same file to create an animated mask.

2. On the Gato Jobs layer, insert a frame by pressing the F5 key in frame 30. Notice that the timeline has been extended.

3. On the Mask layer, insert a blank keyframe by pressing the F7 key on frame 15. Notice that the timeline on the Mask layer is now extended to frame 15.

4. On frame 15 of the Mask layer, draw a square to cover the entire picture, as shown in Figure 7.6.

5. Move the playhead back to frame 1. Click the keyframe in frame 1 on the Mask layer. In the Properties Inspector, choose Shape for the Tweening option. Notice that the frames become green with an arrow. If you lock the two layers, you can scrub the playhead back and forth from frames 1 to 15 to see the animated mask. Notice that if you scrub beyond frame 15, nothing is visible because we don't have any content on the Mask layer. Therefore, there's nothing to be revealed. Let's fix that in the next step.

6. Insert a blank keyframe in frame 30 of the Mask layer. The timeline will get extended to frame 29, with a blank frame in 30.

7. In frame 30, draw a small star with the Line tool. Yes, I know, lines do not mask, but you're going to use the Line tool to draw the initial shape. Then, after you fill the shape, you'll delete the lines. The best way to draw a star is to cross the lines and draw it like your teacher did when you got a good grade on a paper (which wasn't often for me). Figure 7.7 shows an example of this.

8. After the shape is drawn, fill it with any color. As you discovered in the last example, fill colors do not matter. They don't matter because you'll never see them in the player—the fill area of the shape reveals the layer underneath it.

9. Move the playhead back to frame 15. Highlight frame 15 of the Mask layer. In the Properties Inspector, choose Shape for the Tweening option.

FIGURE 7.6

The square on the Mask layer covers the entire picture on the Gato Jobs layer.

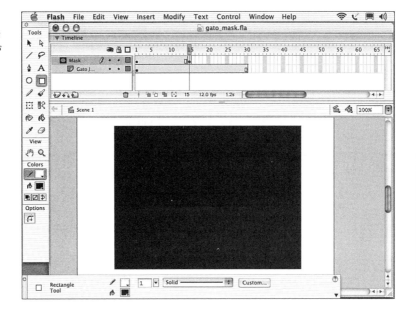

FIGURE 7.7

A star drawn with overlapping lines using the Line tool.

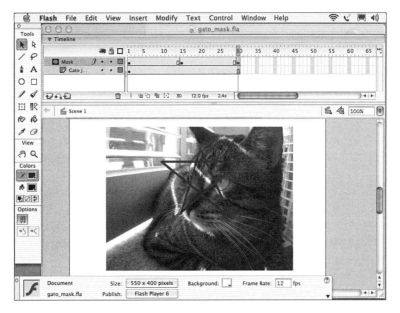

As you can see, creating animated masks in Flash is actually quite simple. In fact, they're just as easy to create as static masks. Think of the possibilities you have by animating masks. You can use this approach to pull off special techniques, such as type hitting the screen, mimicking a typewriter. We'll look at how you can create this effect next. To get a preview of what we're going to create in the following example, visit the companion Web site and look for the Chapter 7 section. You can view the movie on the Web, and you can even download the FLA file so that you can deconstruct it in Flash.

Making a Typewriter Type Effect Using an Animated Mask

This effect is used often in digital video production. In fact, it's a stock effect in many DV editors, such as iMovie from Apple. In this exercise, we're going to spell out the words *Train Simple*. Here are the steps to follow:

1. Create a new document. In this new document, create three layers, named sound, mask, and text, respectively. Make sure the sound layer is on top and the text layer is on the bottom, as shown in Figure 7.8.

   In this animation, we want each letter to appear in a sequential order. Therefore, first we'll see the letter *T*. After a very brief pause, the letter *r* will appear, and this will continue until "Train Simple" is spelled out. As these letters appear, we want a sound to play that's similar to the sound of a typewriter typing. Let's set up the text first.

2. On the text layer, select frame 2 and press F7 to insert a blank keyframe. In frame 2 of the type layer, type **Train Simple** by using the Text tool. You entered a blank keyframe on frame 2 so that a slight delay occurs before the animation starts playing, because frame 1 has no content (see Figure 7.9).

3. In the mask layer, do the same by inserting a blank keyframe on frame 2 by pressing F7 to give it some space. In this new blank keyframe, draw a box, without a stroke, covering only the letter *T*, as shown in Figure 7.9.

   When drawing this box, if you're getting some unpredictable movement, it's because you have Snap to Objects turned on. To turn this feature off, choose View, Snap to Objects.

4. Still on the mask layer, insert two frames by pressing F5 twice. Then move the playhead to the last frame in the mask layer and insert a keyframe by pressing F6, which will convert the second frame you inserted into a keyframe. This adds some time before the appearance of the next letter. On this keyframe, highlight the blue box. With the blue box selected, choose the Free Transform tool and scale the box to cover the letter *r* as well, as shown in Figure 7.10. Highlight frame 40 of the text layer and insert a frame by pressing F5 to extend out the timeline on that layer.

5. Repeat step 4 until all of "Train Simple" is covered by the blue box.

To check your work, you may want to convert the layer properties of the mask and text layers. Double-click the Layer Properties icon in the mask layer. In the Layer Properties dialog box, choose Mask. Do the same for the text layer, except choose Masked for the layer type. Once these properties have been changed, lock both the mask layer and the type layer so that you can preview your work by scrubbing the playhead through the completed frames.

6. As you test your movie, the words "Train Simple" should appear one letter at a time! However, this isn't quite as effective without any sound. Because we covered sound in Chapter 6, "Working with Sound in Flash," let's go ahead and add some.

    Remember in Chapter 6 when I recommended that you not use stock sounds in your Flash movies? Well, there's always an exception to any rule. In this case, we are going to use a stock sound. However, by modifying its in and out points, we can effectively change this stock Flash sound. Let's take a peek at what all this entails.

7. First things first: You need a place on your timeline to store the sound. You also have to consider when you want the sound to play. In this case, we want to hear the sound as each letter appears, thus producing the full effect of a typewriter. Therefore, you need to insert keyframes on the sound layer in the same location as the keyframes in the mask layer. Refer to Figure 7.11 to see the placement. Remember, you can insert keyframes by pressing F6 on your keyboard. We are using keyframes because keyframes represent major changes within an animation. The major change in this case would be the sound playing again. A normal frame would just loop the sound throughout the animation and not play it in sync with the letters appearing.

8. Under the Window menu, choose Common Libraries, Sound. This will open the Sound common libraries. The sound for the typewriter effect is Keyboard Type Sngl. Once you find this sound, make sure to have the keyframe selected on the "sound," which appears above the first square in the mask layer, and drag out an instance and drop it anywhere on the stage. Notice the sound waveforms in the frames.

9. The only problem with this sound is that it's just a bit too long. We can fix this. With the keyframe selected in the timeline that contains the sound, in the Properties Inspector click the Edit button to launch the Edit Envelope dialog box, as shown in Figure 7.12.

10. Move the out point to the end of the waveform, again displayed in Figure 7.12. Click the Play button to preview it. Sounds good!

11. You must apply this sound every time a letter becomes visible. Make sure for every keyframe in the mask layer that there's a keyframe in the sound layer. If there aren't enough keyframes, insert them by pressing F6, just as you did in step 7.

12. Instead of dragging out more instances of this sound for each keyframe in the sound layer, here's a far more efficient technique you can use: Highlight the next keyframe in the sound layer. In the Properties Inspector, you'll see a drop-down menu for sound. Currently it is set to None. If you use that drop-down menu, you'll see your Keyboard Type Sngl sound as an option. Choose it. If you click the Edit button, you can then set your out point.

13. Apply the Keyboard Type Sngl sound to the remaining keyframes in the sound layer.

14. Test the movie!

FIGURE **7.8**

Notice the stacking order of the layers (from top to bottom): sound, mask, and text.

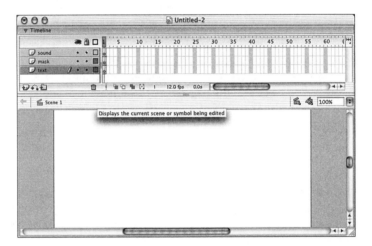

FIGURE 7.9

The square on the mask layer just covers the letter T.

FIGURE 7.10

The box is scaled in the second keyframe of the animation to cover both the letter T *and the letter* r.

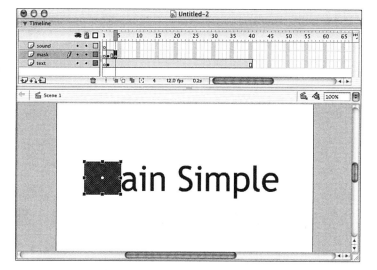

Figure 7.11
Note the placement of the keyframes on the sound layer.

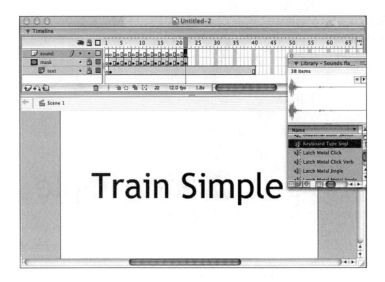

Figure 7.12
The Edit Envelope dialog box. Notice that the endpoint marker moved closer to the end of the waveform.

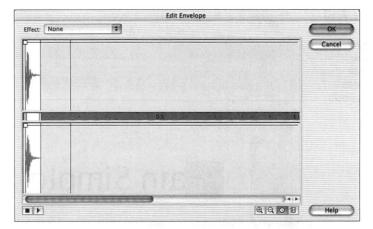

This is just one of many things you can do with animated masks. In the Chapter 7 section of the companion Web site is a series of FLA files you can download that will give you additional ideas for masking.

Earlier I mentioned that one of the problems with masking is not being able to create soft edges or transparency in a mask. Although this is 100-percent true, there are some ways to trick the eye into believing it sees these effects. The trick discussed in the following exercise works best with solid-color backgrounds. Again, you can find a finished example of this technique on the companion Web site under the Chapter 7 section. The link is called Faux Masks.

Faking Soft Edges with Faux Masks

Here are the steps to follow for this exercise:

1. Create a new document. Make sure the movie has a white stage background color. In the Unleashed library you'll find the `movieclip` folder. Inside the `movieclip` folder is a movie clip called "paragraph." Drag an instance of paragraph out onto the stage. Name layer 1 **paragraph**.

2. Insert a frame on frame 20 of the paragraph layer by pressing F5 on your keyboard.

3. Create a new layer and name it **faux_mask**.

   You're going to create a box that is filled with a gradient. This gradient is going to gradually change from a transparent white color to a solid white color. The first thing you need to do is create your own custom gradient.

4. Choose the Rectangle tool in the Tools panel. For the fill color, choose the black and white linear gradient found in the lower-left corner of the Color Swatches panel.

5. Make sure the Mixer panel is open. If it is not open choose, Window, Mixer. Notice in the Mixer panel the gradient slider with the two arrows. If you don't remember how to modify gradients, refer to Chapter 3, "Creating Graphics in Flash." Highlight the black arrow and change its color to white. Of course, you don't want a solid white color for one side of the gradient and a solid white color on the other side because you wouldn't see anything. What you want is a solid white color fading into a transparent value.

6. With the arrow still selected, bring the alpha down to zero. This will make the white color have 0% solidity on this side of the gradient.

7. On the faux_mask layer, draw a rectangle over the text, as shown in Figure 7.13.

8. The only thing you have to fix is the direction of the gradient. Therefore, in the Tools panel, choose the Fill Transform tool. Click the rectangle to get the transform handles, as pictured in Figure 7.14.

9. Drag the rotate handle 90 degrees. Hold down the Shift key to constrain it to 45 degree increments. You may also want to scale the fill so that the top of the transform handle appears flush to the top of the text block, as pictured in Figure 7.15.

10. Insert a keyframe on Frame 20 of the faux_mask layer by pressing F6 on your keyboard. On this new frame, move the rectangle down underneath the text block, as shown in Figure 7.16.

11. In frame 1 of the faux_mask layer, in the Properties Inspector, change Tweening to Shape Tweening. This will animate the box so that slowly, over time, the box will move down, and as it does so it will reveal more and more of the text.

FIGURE 7.13

The rectangle has a gradient that appears to be gradually fading out.

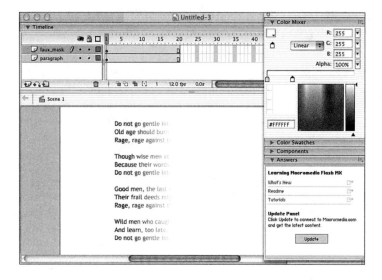

FIGURE 7.14

The transform handles appear when a transform fill is used.

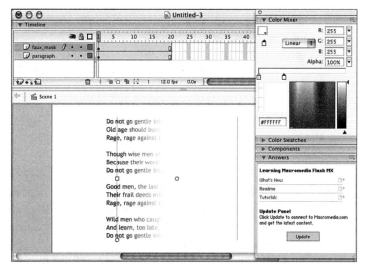

FIGURE 7.15

The Transform Fill tool.

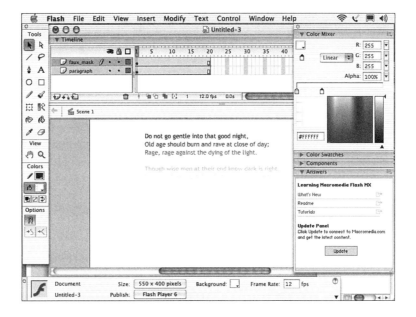
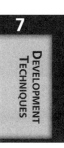

FIGURE 7.16

The gradient filled box is placed toward the bottom of the stage of frame 20.

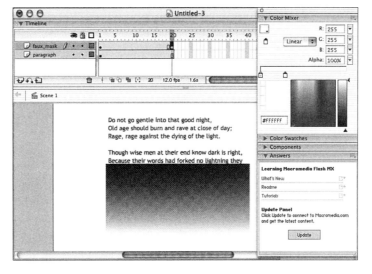

> **Note**
>
> This technique will not work with backgrounds that have patterns or inconsistent colors. The background must be a solid color.

So, you think you're done with masking? Well, you are for now. However, once we move into ActionScripting, you'll see that there are ways to create masks dynamically, without using the layer properties! Furthermore, you can drag masks when and where you want. It's pretty cool stuff.

Loading a Movie

Here comes the good part. If you've been following along since Chapter 1, "What's New in Flash MX?," this is where everything you've learned ties together. We haven't done much in terms of Web site functionality. We've been looking at the features of the program and how different components work. Now we can apply those concepts, along with some new ones, to bring it all home in terms of Web site creation. From this point on, it just gets more advanced. You can really take everything you've learned from this and previous chapters and build on it.

Controlling the main timeline or a movie clip's timeline is easy enough to do. If you have no idea what I'm talking about, refer back to Chapter 5, "Symbols and the Library." Having this ability is fundamental to Web design in Flash. We can, of course, take a few steps beyond this, and you can learn how to use the `loadMovie` action. By using the `loadMovie` action, you can break down and manage separate portions of a Web site, much like separate HTML documents. Aside from site management, this also creates a better experience for the end user. Remember, everything on the Web is about speed. If you can break your Flash site up into several different chunks, instead of one big long movie, you're doing the end users a favor. This way, they are only waiting to download content that matters to them. When they click to go somewhere else, that chunk will get downloaded into the existing Flash movie. If the site is one long movie, the end users have to wait until everything in your Flash movie downloads, even items they might never look at.

> **Note**
>
> When using the `loadMovie` action, you can only load in SWF files. You cannot load in a FLA file at all; it must be in its compressed form. With the addition of Flash MX, you can also load in MP3 files as well as JPGs and GIFs.

From a usability and site-management perspective, the `loadMovie` action is a good thing. You have two different methods for loading movies. The first way involves loading movies or SWF files into different levels. A *level* is much like the Z-Index in dynamic HTML. The level's value will determine how close or how "on top" the movie will appear. For example, if one movie has a level of 1 and another movie has a level of 5, the movie in level 5 will appear on top of the movie in level 1.

It's also important to note that only one SWF file is allowed per level. If you have an existing movie in level 1 and then decide to load a different movie into level 1, the movie being loaded into level 1 will replace the movie currently in that level.

You also need to understand how Flash works in terms of how it positions these external files once they are loaded into a movie. Flash will always load the movie into the top-left corner of the stage. Think of the top-left corner of the movie that is going to be loaded being placed right on top of the top-left corner of the movie that it's being loaded into.

Here's another important item to point: The stage color of the movie will be masked out once it's loaded into an existing SWF file. Therefore, if you need the background color to show up, you must draw a solid box covering the entire stage on the bottom layer of that movie.

Lastly, note that the main timeline is level 0. Rarely will you load a movie into level 0, for that reason. Typically, the main timeline houses a lot of the site's functionality. Of course, if there are scripts and variables between these levels, they can potentially communicate with one another, but again we'll save that stuff for Chapter 10, "Approaching ActionScript," once we get into targeting.

Loading Movies into Levels Using the `loadMovie` Action

In this exercise, you'll load external SWF files into an existing movie. The existing movie looks like an index page of a Web site. You can download the needed files from the Unleashed companion Web site. You'll be loading this content into separate levels. Here are the steps to follow:

1. Open the file `foto_front.fla` that you downloaded from the companion Web site. Notice that it already has several buttons in place.

2. Resave this file in its own folder by choosing File, Save As, and in the Save As dialog box creating a new folder on your desktop. Name the folder `Loader` and save the `foto_front.fla` file inside this new folder.

   You need to create some new movies to load into the `foto_front.fla` file you just saved into the `Loader` folder. Saving all these files in the same directory will simplify the process of writing the paths to these files in your `loadMovie` ActionScript.

3. Create a new document. Choose File, Save As. This will launch the Save As dialog box. Save this document as `loadee1.fla` in the `Loader` folder.

4. Also open the Unleashed common library. If you did not install the Unleashed common library, refer to Chapter 2. If you downloaded it but did not install it, you may choose File, Open as Library and search for `Unleashed.fla` on your computer. Otherwise, choose Window, Common Library, Unleashed.fla.

5. Choose Modify, Document or press Cmd+J (Mac) or Ctrl+J (Windows) to open the Document Properties dialog box. Set the dimensions of the stage to 500×300. You want this movie to be the same dimensions as the movie it's going to be loaded into.

6. In the Unleashed library, in the `Graphics` folder, drag out an instance of foto_page1. When placing this graphic on the stage, it is important that you match up the top-left corner of the graphic with the top-left corner of the stage. To make absolutely sure the graphic is in the top-left corner, with the graphic selected, choose Window, Info to open the Info panel. In the Info panel, type in **0** for the x coordinate and **0** for the y coordinate, as shown in Figure 7.17. This will ensure that the graphic is positioned perfectly in the top-left corner of the stage.

   Notice that the graphic doesn't quite fill the entire stage. The bottom portion seems to be left blank. This was done on purpose. Remember, the background color of the stage will always get masked out. Therefore, by having the bottom portion left blank, it will be invisible when loaded into your main movie, thus revealing the main movie's navigation system. Let's go ahead and put this into practice.

7. Save this document and take note of its name: `loadee1.fla`. Choose Control, Test Movie to test this Flash movie. You might not know it, but you've just created a SWF file! This is the file format used on the Web. When you test a movie, the SWF file is automatically created; in fact, that's what your're viewing in the Test Movie environment. If you go to your desktop and open the `Loader` folder, you'll see two `loadee1` files: the FLA file and the SWF file. This is important because when you use the `loadMovie` action, you can load the SWF file and not the FLA file. Close this document.

8. Open the `foto_front.fla` file again. Highlight the first button, labeled About Us. With this button selected, choose Window, Actions to open the Actions panel. Notice that the Actions panel reads "Actions – Buttons," indicating that any script that you write here will be applied to the selected button.

9. Open the Actions book and then open the Browser/Network book. Locate the `loadMovie` action and double-click it. Notice that some scripts get written for you. Also, there are empty areas you need to fill in when you have the second line of code highlighted. Refer to Figure 7.18.

10. In the URL text field in the top portion of the window, type in the file-name of the movie you made and tested in step 7. It is important that you refer to the SWF version of this file. Therefore, in the URL text field, type **loadee1.swf**. If you didn't save these files in the same directory, you would have to type the entire path to where the SWF file resides.

11. For the Level setting, choose 1. If you were to choose 0, when the movie is loaded, it would knock out the existing interface of the `foto_front` file. By choosing 1, the movie will load on top of the interface, and it will not cover the buttons because of the empty whitespace in the `loadee1` file.

12. Leave the Variables option at its default, don't Send.

13. Save the movie and test it by choosing Control, Test Movie or using the keyboard shortcuts Cmd+Return (Mac) or Ctrl+Enter (Windows). This will launch the movie in the testing environment.

14. After the movie launches in the testing environment, click the first button—the one you applied the action to. Boom! The movie loads into place and feels much like a Web site in terms of functionality. Refer to Figure 7.19.

15. Once you've tested the movie, we're going to load another movie into the `foto_front` file. Therefore, close out of the testing environment to get back into the authoring environment of Flash. Then create a new document.

16. With the new document open, choose Modify, Document. Change the width and height dimensions to 500×300, respectively. Click OK and notice that the document changes to reflect the size you specified.

17. In the Unleashed library, open the `Graphics` folder. In the `Graphics` folder, drag out an instance of foto_page2. Position the graphic at 0,0 for the x and y coordinates. Remember, you can do this by using the Info panel, just as you did in step 4 of this exercise.

18. Save this file as `loadee2` in the `Loader` folder on the desktop. Once you've saved this document, choose Control, Test Movie to export out a SWF of this file. You may want to open the `Loader` folder on your desktop, just to double-check.

19. Open the `foto_front.fla` file again. This time, select the second button. With this button selected, choose Window, Actions. This opens the Actions panel. Note that the title bar reads "Actions – Buttons," which means that whatever action you create will be applied to the selected button.

20. Open the Actions book and then open the Browser/Network book. Locate the `loadMovie` action and double-click it. After double-clicking the action, notice the code that's typed for you, just like in step 7. Highlight the second line of code so that the options above it in the panel become active.

21. In the URL text field in the top portion of the window, type in the filename of the movie you made and tested in step 16. It is important that you refer to the SWF version of this file. Therefore, in the URL text field, type `iloadee2.swf`.

22. In the Location text field, choose Levels in the drop-down menu and type 1 for the level value, as shown in Figure 7.20.

    You're choosing level 1 here because that's what you've chosen for the other movie. Because these two movies have the same level value, only one SWF file can occupy the level at a time. Therefore, if a movie is currently loaded into level 1, and the end user clicks another button to load a different movie into level 1, the movie currently occupying level 1 will be replaced by the new movie.

23. Save the file. Test it by choosing Control, Test Movie. In the testing environment, click the first button to load in `loadee1`, just like you did before. Now, to mix things up, click the second button. Notice that the second movie automatically loads, replacing the existing movie.

24. Close out of the testing environment to get back into the Flash authoring environment. Now you're going to unload a movie manually. Notice the Home button already in the document. Select it and open the Actions panel. In the Actions panel, open the Actions book. Inside the Actions book, open the Browser/Network book. Locate the `unloadMovie` action and double-click it. By default, the second line of code should be selected. Above it are the statements options. Be sure to type 1 for the Level value, as shown in Figure 7.21.

    If you want to unload more than one level on a button, you would have to apply the `unloadMovie` action for every level. You couldn't simply type in each level, separated by commas, in the same line. Here's an example of what the code should look like:

    ```
    on (release) {
    unloadMovieNum(1);
    unloadMovieNum(2);
    UnloadMovieNum(3);
    }
    ```

25. Save and test the movie. Load in a movie. After the movie loads, click the Home button to unload it.

FIGURE 7.17

Positioning the graphic using the Info panel's x and y coordinates.

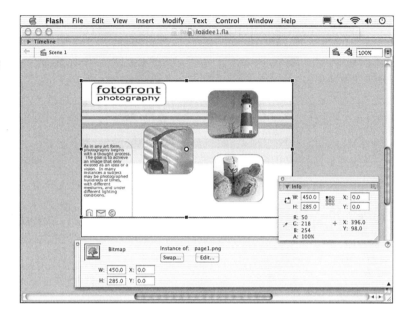

FIGURE 7.18

Notice the empty spaces that need to be filled out in the loadMovie *action.*

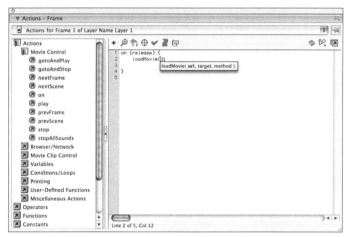

FIGURE 7.19

The foto_front *file with the movie* loadee1 *file loaded inside of it.*

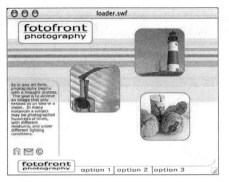

FIGURE 7.20

The URL *is the name of the file we are loading into the movie, and it's loading into level 1.*

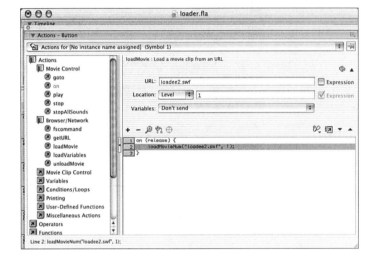

FIGURE 7.21

The unloadMovie *action.*

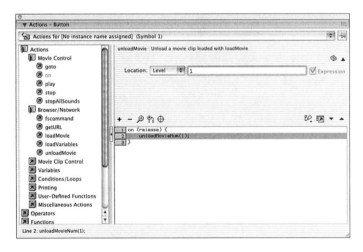

Tip

Visit the companion Web site and look under Chapter 7 to watch the QuickTime movie on loading movies into levels.

This exercise helps get you familiar with loading movies into levels. However, there is another way to load movies into Flash that yields more flexibility: You can load movies into movie clips. The advantage of loading a movie into a movie clip is that the movie clip can be placed anywhere on the stage, so you are not restricted by having the movie always loaded into the top-left corner. Not only that, anything you can do to a movie clip—such as animate it, apply effects, and apply actions—will automatically be applied to any movie loaded into the clip.

Loading a Movie into a Movie Clip

In this exercise you're going to create a button in the `loadee2.fla` file. Also, you have to create a new movie clip that houses nothing. It will be an empty movie clip—a container, of sorts—waiting for a movie to be loaded inside of it. It's important to name the instance of the movie clip so that you can call it in your actions. Here are the steps to follow:

1. Open `loadee2.fla`. Create a new layer and name it **button**. In the new button layer, either create a new button or take one out of the Button common library or the Unleashed library.

2. Create another new layer and call it **mc_placeholder**. Choose Insert, New Symbol. This will launch the New Symbol dialog box. Name the symbol **placeholder**. Make sure it has the movie clip behavior.

3. Click OK. This will place you inside the movie clip symbol editing mode. You want this move clip to be empty, ready to hold a movie that will be loaded into it. Therefore, just click the Scene 1 tab under the timeline. This will bring you back to scene 1.

4. Open the Library by choosing Window, Library. You should see the mc_placeholder movie clip. Drag out an instance and line up the crosshairs with the black box area in the movie, as shown in Figure 7.22.

   When a SWF file is loaded into the movie clip, the loaded movie's top-left corner will line up with the bottom-right corner of the center point of the movie clip.

5. With the movie clip selected, give it the instance name **holder** in the Properties Inspector, as shown in Figure 7.23. Press Return (Mac) or Enter (Windows) to make sure the instance name sticks to the movie clip.

6. Save `loadee2.fla`.

7. Create a new document. Choose Modify, Document to launch the Document Properties dialog box. Change the dimensions of the movie to 200 pixels by 200 pixels. Click OK to close the dialog box.

8. Open the Unleashed common library or choose File, Open as Library and search for the `unleashed.fla` file on your computer.

9. Open the `movie_clip` folder and drag out an instance of slide_show, as shown in Figure 7.24.

10. Save this movie as `picture_slide.fla` in the `Loader` folder on the desktop. Choose Control, Test Movie to export out a SWF file. Close out of the testing environment and close this document.

11. Reopen the `loadee2.fla` file.

12. Select the button on the button layer. Choose Window, Actions to open the Actions panel. Open the Actions book and then the Browser/Network book. Locate the `loadMovie` action and double-click it. As before, this action types the script for you on the right, with the second line of code highlighted.

13. In the options, type **picture_slide.swf** for the URL. For Location, choose Target in the drop-down menu, as shown in Figure 7.25.

14. Place a blinking cursor in the Location text field and click the Insert Target Path icon, as displayed in Figure 7.26. This will launch the Insert Target Path dialog box.

15. In the Insert Target Path dialog box, make sure you have Notation set to Dots and Mode set to Relative. Click the icon of the "holder" instance, as shown in Figure 7.27. Click OK to exit this dialog box.

    It is very important that you have Mode set to Relative. If you set it to Absolute, the movie clip you are calling, when loaded in a movie, will be pointing to a movie clip on the main timeline, which is not good, because the movie clip you are targeting is not on the main timeline but rather in this movie. To learn more about targeting, check out Chapter 10.

16. After clicking OK, you'll notice that the target path has been inserted into the Location text field. Close the Actions panel.

17. Hide or minimize Flash. Locate the `Loader` folder on the desktop. Double-click the `foto_front.swf` file. The file will launch in the Flash 6 player. Once inside the player, click the second button to load in `loadee2`. Once `loadee2` has loaded, click the Slide Show button to see the `picture_slide.swf` file load, as shown in Figure 7.28.

FIGURE 7.22

The movie clip's center point is positioned at the top-left corner of the blank square in the movie.

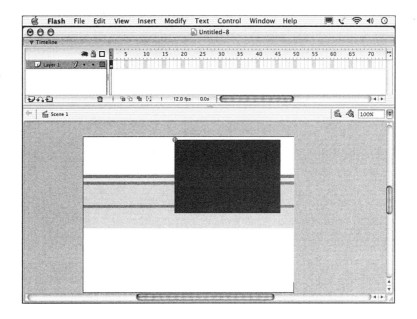

FIGURE 7.23

Name the instance of the movie clip in the Properties Inspector.

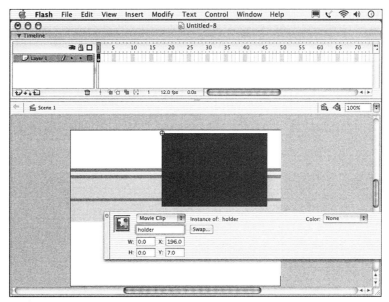

FIGURE 7.24

Place the slide_show movie clip on the stage.

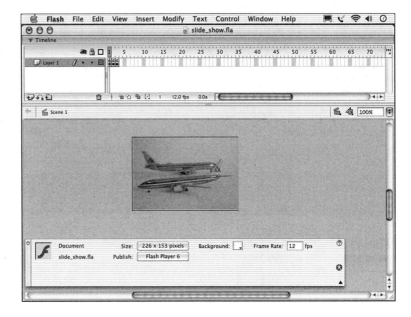

FIGURE 7.25

Choose Target in the Location drop-down menu.

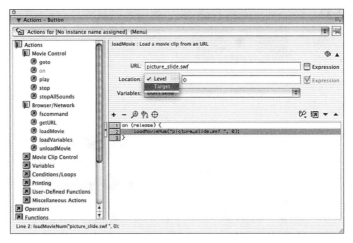

FIGURE 7.26

The Insert Target Path icon.

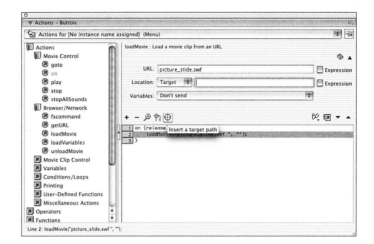

FIGURE 7.27

Notation is set to Dots and Mode is set to Relative in the Insert Target Path dialog box.

FIGURE 7.28

An example of loading a movie into a level and into a movie clip.

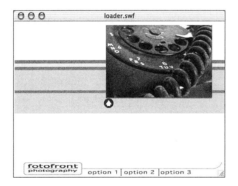

Preloaders

Your `foto_front` file is almost complete; it isn't quite ready for the Web just yet. One of Flash's claim to fame is its streaming format, according to Macromedia. This is really a *progressive* format, as opposed to a streaming format, but here's what it does: Flash automatically plays, and as it's playing frame 1, for example, it's in the process of downloading frame 2, and so on. This is great because you don't have to wait until the entire file is downloaded before you can enjoy it.

Of course, the Web is never a perfect place, and speed often becomes an issue. If Flash is playing frame 1, ideally frame 2 would be completely downloaded before it finishes playing frame 1, but what if frame 2 has a large bitmap graphic and Flash needed more time to download it? The movie playback would suffer because Flash can't play what's not there. Therefore, the movie stops playing. This would continue to happen throughout the entire animation, which doesn't make for the best experience for the end user.

To avoid this type of situation, you can analyze where Flash might have a problem progressively playing frames. When you find such frames, you can preload them, which means you create a small script telling Flash not to play the animation until all the chunky media/ frames have been loaded first.

You've certainly seen preloaders on the Web before. When you go to a Flash site, sometimes it bluntly says "Loading...." Others have neat little animations. These are indicators for the end user that content is being loaded to their machines. In the last exercise of this chapter, we'll create a simple preloader.

Creating a Simple Preloader

In this exercise, you are going to preload the slides in the slide show. Note that in a real-world situation, these slides would have a great deal of difficulty playing progressively. Here are the steps to follow for this exercise:

1. Open the `picture_slide.fla` file. Choose Window, Scene to open the Scene panel. You are going to create a separate scene for your preloading script and animation.

2. Click the plus sign at the bottom of the Scene panel to add a new scene, as shown in Figure 7.29. Double-click the new scene and name it **preload**. Make sure the preload scene appears above scene 1, because they play according to the stacking order in this panel.

3. Test the movie by choosing Control, Test Movie. In the testing environment, choose View, Bandwidth Profiler. This will open the Bandwidth Profiler window, as shown in Figure 7.30.

   You'll notice in Figure 7.30 the many spikes in the graph. If any of these bars rise above the red line, they can't play progressively and need to be preloaded. The red line can be changed to represent different modem speeds. You can access the different modem speeds under the Debug menu. You'll notice the standard predefined modem speeds, as shown in Figure 7.31. However, you also have the option Customize to create your own speed to accommodate faster DSL, cable, and T-1 lines.

4. You can actually get a preview of how the movie will behave under the modem speed conditions set in the Debug menu. Choose View, Show Streaming. Notice on the left side of the window that you can see a streaming percentage of the progress. Above the spikes, you'll notice a green progress bar. Therefore, it's obvious that these frames need to be preloaded.

   It is important to note that if you feel in this situation that frame 40 needs to be preloaded, all frames before frame 40 must be loaded before frame 40 can be loaded.

5. Close out of the testing environment to return to Flash.

6. In the Scene panel, click the preload scene to make it active. In the Unleashed library, open the `movie_clip` folder and find the widget movie clip. Drag out an instance on the stage.

7. It's now time to write your script. Select frame 1 and open the Actions panel. Notice that the title bar reads "Actions – Frame." Therefore, whatever action you write here will be applied to the selected frame (in this case, frame 1).

8. Open the Deprecated book and then the Actions book. Double-click `ifFrameLoaded`. Notice the script that's written for you.

Deprecated simply indicates that there is a more efficient action to use when creating a preloader. Potentially this action will not work in future versions of the Flash player. However, this script will work with the Flash 4, 5, and 6 players just fine. Although more efficient scripts are available, they require a deeper understanding of ActionScript.

9. With the script highlighted, choose Scene 1 from the drop-down menu for the scene. Choose Frame Number for the type and then type **40** for the frame number. This is pretty straightforward. In plain English this simply means, "if frame 40 in scene 1 is loaded." Now you simply have to tell the playhead to do something.

10. Open the Actions book and then open the Movie Control book. Double-click the goto action, which will write additional code, as shown in Figure 7.32.

11. As shown in Figure 7.33, be sure to have the Go To and Play button selected. Also, choose Scene 1 for the scene, Frame Number for the type, and 1 for the frame value. In plain English the script now reads, "If frame 40 in scene 1 is loaded, then go to and play the animation from frame 1 in scene 1."

    Here is what the final script should look like:

    ```
    ifFrameLoaded ("Scene 1", 1) {
        gotoAndPlay("Scene 1", 40);
    }
    ```

    Now, what if frame 40 is not loaded? Then what? If frame 40 is not loaded, the statement is not true, which means Flash will simply ignore it, and the playhead will continue to play. Therefore, you need to stop the playhead from playing before scene 1 and you also need to reanalyze your script. You're now going to set up what's called a *loop*.

12. In the preload scene, insert a keyframe on frame 2. With frame 2 selected, choose Window, Actions to open the Actions panel.

13. Open the Actions book and then the Movie Control book. Then double-click goto. There is nothing to modify after double-clicking. This script is simply telling the playhead to move back to frame 1.

    To recap, the script on frame 1 is looking to see whether frame 40 is loaded. If it's not, the action will be ignored and the playhead will continue to play. As it plays, it hits frame 2 with an action sending it back to frame 1, where it checks again to see whether frame 40 has been loaded. If it has not been loaded, this process continues to repeat. Until the statement for frame 1 is true and frame 40 is, in fact, loaded, the playhead will skip over frame 2 and move right to frame 1 of scene 1 and play from there.

14. Let's test it. Choose Control, Test Movie. Once you're inside the testing view, it may look like nothing has happened. In order to see your pre-loader working, choose View, Show Streaming. You'll see the small widget animation play, as shown in Figure 7.33. Notice on the left the streaming percentage and the green progress bar above the spikes. Once the preloading is complete, the playhead moves to play the animation.

As mentioned earlier, you can create preloaders with more advanced scripting techniques. One such technique includes returning a percentage so that the end user gets an actual readout and a better idea of how long the preloading will take, instead of a small, meaningless animation. We'll discuss percentage preloaders in Chapter 21, "Advanced Interactivity."

7

DEVELOPMENT TECHNIQUES

FIGURE 7.29

Click the Add button to add a new scene in the Scene panel.

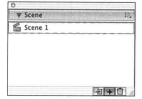

FIGURE 7.30

The Bandwidth Profiler will clue you in on trouble spots for downloading.

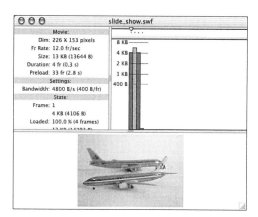

Figure 7.31

Use the different modem speeds under the Debug menu to test and optimize your movie.

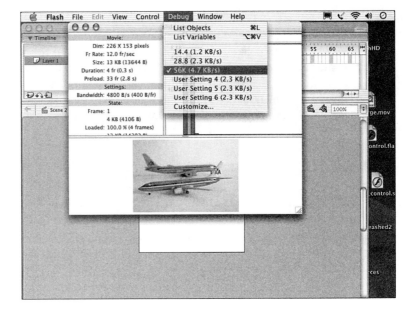

Figure 7.32

The goto *action is placed in the* ifFrameloaded *statement.*

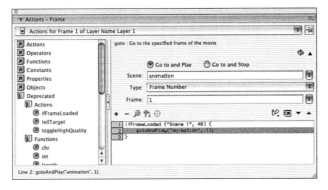

FIGURE 7.33

The animation is preloading.

Publishing

By Todd Coulson

Once all your work is finished, you still aren't quite done. The Flash authoring environment is created within a file with an extension of `.fla`. When you save your work, your entire project is included in that FLA file. The problem is that the only way someone can view your work without you publishing it is if they also own Flash. This is also impractical because then anyone with Flash will be able to open your project and use your graphics, library items, or any other authored event. What's more, anyone without Flash would never be able to see your work. Luckily, the developers at Macromedia have stepped in to save the day with *publishing*. In Flash, publishing is easier and more versatile than in most any other authoring environment. Publishing in Flash also allows you to show your project to millions of online users while giving you the security of knowing your work is protected.

Publishing protects your work, while simultaneously letting the masses view your project. Let's take a look at how to access the Publishing Settings and give your end users the ability to see your work.

Where to Find Publishing

On your menu bar, choose File and then one of the following three items (see Figure 8.1):

- **Publish Settings (Alt+Shift+F12)**. Choosing this option allows you to customize publish settings for the FLA file currently open. This will give you the ability to choose the file format and file-specific options desired for your final output. Be aware that some settings will override the settings created in your project.

- **Publish Preview**. This option allows you to preview the published FLA file in the format of your choice. Only those items selected in Publish Settings can be chosen here for preview.

- **Publish (Alt+F12)**. This option publishes your results of your FLA file without letting you preview your output. This can also be done by going into Publish Settings and clicking the Publish button on the right side of the dialog box.

FIGURE 8.1

*Under the File
drop-down menu,
you'll find the
Publish Settings,
Publish Preview,
and Publish.*

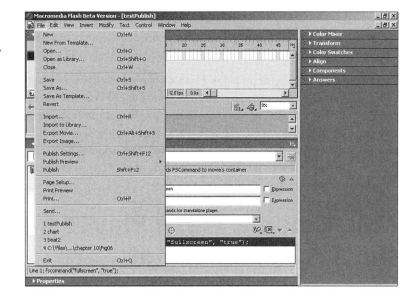

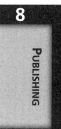

Versatile Formats

Once you're publishing in Flash, you have the option to create multiple formats. The
default publishing settings include a SWF and HTM document. The SWF document,
which is short for *Shockwave Flash* (the Shockwave part of the extension is more associated these days with Director, but the extension has stayed with Flash for continuity), is
viewable in the Macromedia Flash Player. The HTM document that accompanies the
SWF document is set up with OBJECT and EMBED tags that embed the SWF document into
the HTM document. We'll talk more about this later in the chapter.

Flash is highly versatile. It not only publishes to its own format (SWF) but will also publish to the following "alternative" formats: GIF, JPEG, PNG, and QuickTime. The first
three formats are graphic formats. These output images or a series of images to an animation. Therefore, if you have created artwork in Flash on a frame or group of frames,
you can export it to be viewable as an image online or for use in other applications.

The QuickTime format is viewable with Apple's QuickTime Player and is a format for
viewing video. With this format you can import a QuickTime movie into Flash. You simply overlay your own Flash graphics and animations and then publish the whole thing to
be viewable in the QuickTime Player.

Flash also has the ability to publish to either a Mac or PC standalone projector. This
gives you the ability to place your project in a single, self-contained executable file. The

project does not rely on the Flash Player to be viewed, nor do you need any application at all to view it. Simply opening a standalone projector allows end users to view your work on their computers.

One of the truly wonderful points in Flash's favor over many other authoring tools is its ability to publish to a multitude of formats. You can use Flash as an authoring tool for an entire project or Web site, or simply to create portions of projects for usage in other authoring environments or for the Web. As you get further into the publishing aspects of Flash, you will begin to realize the impact Flash has as a tool for your overall creativity. Flash is not simply a Web site creator, a graphics tool, or an animation tool. Instead, it is all three of these wrapped up into one tool.

Macromedia Flash Player 6 and the SWF File Format

As mentioned earlier, the Macromedia Flash file format (SWF) is used for deploying Flash content. It can be read in each of the following ways:

- In Internet browsers that are equipped with the Flash Player. The SWF document must be embedded into an HTM or HTML file in order for the browser to read it.
- Inside Macromedia Director or Authorware, as long as the Flash Xtra is included with the final Director or Authorware project.
- With the Flash ActiveX control in Microsoft Office and other ActiveX hosts.
- Inside the QuickTime Player. Note that depending on which version of QuickTime is being used, some Flash MX functionality may be lost.
- As a standalone movie called a *projector*.

Let's take a look at the first bulleted point for a moment. Internet browsers require the end users to place a plug-in on their browser that allows them to view SWF content online. Look at Figure 8.2 to get an idea of some end users and the versions of the Flash Player they use. Let's suppose Sally has a plug-in for version 4. She will not be able to view the new features created in either version 5 or MX. Barry is surfing the Internet with a Flash Player plug-in for version 3 (Barry's machine is pretty antiquated). Barry will be unable to view any new features of Flash versions 4, 5, or MX. One advantage that Sally does have over Barry is that she is capable of viewing information from versions 1, 2, 3, and 4. Barry is only capable of viewing versions 1, 2, and 3. Mitch is surfing the Internet with the new Flash Player 6. He has the ability to view any of the latest Flash content created in Flash MX or any previous version due to backward compatibility.

FIGURE 8.2

*Every program-
mer must consider
the Flash Player
version their
intended audience
is viewing projects
with. In this exam-
ple, Mitch is the
only end user who
has the ability to
view Flash MX
content online.*

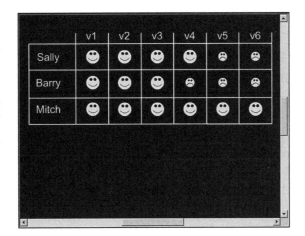

Why are Sally, Barry, and Mitch important to us? They represent the end user who is looking at our projects. Let's say you are creating a Web site on the card game Bridge. Now, not many 20 year olds play Bridge. Some may, but predominantly your audience for this Web site is going to be an older crowd. This target audience might not have the latest plug-in. Therefore, it is important to realize this and publish your project using either the version 3 or version 4 format. This also means creating your ActionScript tailored to the appropriate version. If you are having trouble figuring out which version goes with which piece of ActionScript, just look it up. Click the piece of ActionScript you want to use and then click the book icon on the right side of the ActionScript window. This launches the ActionScript Reference Guide, an example of the guide is displayed in Figure 8.3. This window will tell you which version can handle this piece of code.

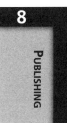

FIGURE 8.3

*An example of
what the
ActionScript
Reference Guide
looks like. This
can be an excel-
lent guide to
determine what
code is specific to
a particular ver-
sion of Flash
Player.*

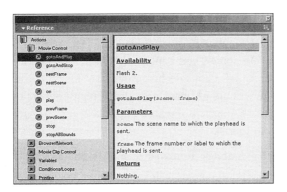

Version Field

Flash has provided a way to go back in time, giving you the ability to choose the version of your Flash document. The resulting SWF document will be tailored to use only the functions of that version and previous versions of the Flash authoring environment. Therefore, choosing Flash MX will be inclusive of all MX functions and ActionScript.

However, publishing in the targeted version is important because it allows you to use code targeted to work with that particular version of Flash and those that precede it. You can select the version you would like to use at the top of the Flash tab within the Publish Settings dialog box, the Version drop-down menu should look similar to Figure 8.4. You can choose any version, from 1 to 6.

FIGURE 8.4

The Flash Version field, located at the top of the Flash tab of your Publish Settings dialog box. This enables you to choose past versions to publish your final SWF file.

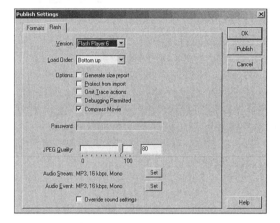

Sound Settings

As you learned in Chapter 6, "Working with Sound in Flash," several compression options are available for the sounds you import into Flash. As mentioned in Chapter 6, it is best to compress your sounds on a case-by-case basis. This will ensure the best quality for your sounds, and you will not just have a single setting throughout your movie. However, if you still choose to have a single setting, Flash does provide this option for you. Here are the steps to follow:

1. Choose File, Publish Settings from your menu bar and click the Flash tab.
2. At the bottom of the Flash tab you will see settings for streaming and settings for event sounds (the difference between these is also mentioned in Chapter 6). Click the Set button next to either of these options. Figure 8.5 shows the sound options appearing within the Publish Settings dialog box.

FIGURE **8.5**

The default values for the sound settings in the Publish Settings dialog box.

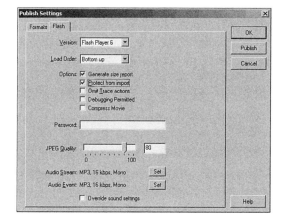

3. Your first option will be the type of compression (refer to Chapter 6 for a listing of types of compressions to use). Select Disable if you want to use your sounds as it is has been set in your project. Select another option if you want to change the compression of your sounds globally.

4. Also based on the type of sound you are using, you may choose a particular sampling rate, level of quality, or bit rate for your sound. Then click OK in the dialog box.

5. Finally, underneath your streaming and event options you have the choice to override the sound settings. Clicking this will throw out the settings you have created in the library and will use the compression you chose earlier this dialog box.

Other Flash Tab Settings

So far you have learned about the Version menu, and we've gone over the sound settings, but what other controls are present in our Flash SWF creation? Figure 8.6 shows the entire Flash tab and the options found there. Here's a list that describes each of them:

- **Load Order**. Use this option to decide how your timeline will load onto the end user's computer. Your choices are limited to top-down and bottom-up (which is the default). However, the main thing to keep in mind is your initialization of variables in ActionScript. If you have items loading before your initialization that rely on some of those variables, your frame might not load correctly. Your use of variables is where you will run into the most problems with the load order. Therefore, it is important to keep your initialization of variables as close to the first thing loaded as possible.

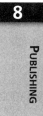

FIGURE 8.6

The options under the Flash tab of the Publish Settings dialog box.

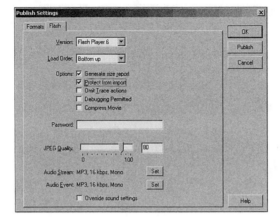

- **Options and Password**. These options allow you to maintain your project. For example, you may want to restrict some users from being able to debug your project or find out some statistics about the file after publishing. Here are the options:
  - **Generate a Size Report**. This is useful in trying to determine which frames are causing problems in your SWF document, which frames are largest, and which frames load quickest. It's also useful for determining the overall size of your project. If your client requests a specific size for a project, you can use this report to target frames and reduce the overall size of a project. It is useful in identifying areas of your project that may be too large to load for your users.
  - **Protect File from Import**. This is highly useful to keep envious designers from stealing your creativity. You can also choose to have a password to allow certain users to view your work (the Password field will become active as you select this option).
  - **Omit Trace Actions**. Trace actions are ActionScript code useful in testing parts of your movie. Trace actions will appear in the output window. Omitting them is only a good idea on your final publish to your end users. It is not a good idea before this, because you may want to use trace actions in the debugging and development of your project.
  - **Debugging Permitted**. This option provides end users with the ability to debug your project from a remote server. This option can be useful if you need outside assistance with your project in the debugging stage. This is also password enabled (so the Password field will become enabled).

- **Compress Movie**. This option is only available with Flash Player 6. It attempts to compress your movie to the smallest size possible. It is set to On by default.

- **JPEG Quality**. This option refers specifically to the JPEG quality within your Flash movie. You have an option range of 0 to 100 for the quality of bitmapped images in your Flash SWF document. Remember, you will have the tradeoff of a larger file size the higher the setting you select. Generally, I like to keep my images up around 90 percent.

Alternative File (JPEG, GIF, and PNG) Settings

Alternative file options are intended to allow you the choice of using a frame (or frames) in your Flash piece outside the project in another a graphical format. Oftentimes you may create artwork in your Flash piece that you want to use in other print pieces or in HTML online. You can publish selected frames from your Flash piece and convert them into workable artwork in either JPEG, GIF, or PNG format. This can also be useful if you want to blur objects in Flash. Simply export a frame from Flash, bring it into Photoshop to apply a blur appearance to it, and import it as a PNG file back into Flash. You can then use the blurred image on in-between frames of your animation to create a blurred look for animation styles. In this section we'll take a look at how to publish a frame or group of frames to alternative formats.

JPEG Settings

It is important to note that JPEG files will export only the frame your playback head is currently in. Therefore, if your playback head resides on frame 20, then frames 1– to 19 will not render out. Figure 8.7 shows a Flash document that is currently resting on frame 110. No other frames will be able to export to JPEG; only 110 will export.

To get to the JPEG settings choose File, Publish Settings, and in the Formats tab, check the box next to the JPEG Image (.jpg) option. If you want the JPEG to possess the same name as the FLA file, make sure the box next to Use Default Names is checked, as displayed in Figure 8.8. This check box is located at the bottom of the Formats tab.

8

PUBLISHING

FIGURE 8.7

Frame 110 is the frame where the playback head of this FLA rests. When this file is published to the JPEG format, only 110 will export. All other frames will be ignored.

FIGURE 8.8

Notice the Use Default Names box is unchecked, so we can choose any name for our JPEG image.

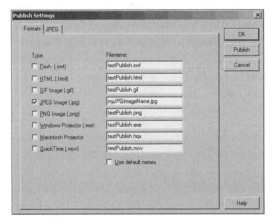

If you want to change the name of the JPEG file, you can uncheck Use Default Names, and automatically all the names under "Filename:" will be editable. Click in the box for the name next to JPEG Image and change the name to something unique. You can also enter a path if you do not want your JPEG to be located in the same file folder as your FLA. You must use a backslash (\) to separate folders and filenames on the PC. On the MAC, use a colon (:) to separate the folders and files in your path.

Immediately after selecting JPEG Image in the Formats tab, you will notice that a tab for JPEG appears along side Formats at the top of the Publish Settings dialog box. Clicking this tab will allow you to choose the settings you want for your JPEG image. Figure 8.9 displays the options available under this tab. These settings are also described in the following list:

FIGURE 8.9

The options of the JPEG tab in the Publish Settings dialog box include the ability to choose the dimensions and the quality of the image to be output.

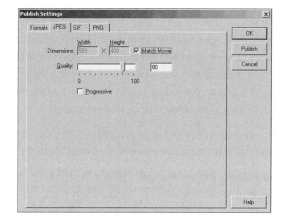

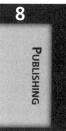

- **Dimensions**. You can choose to have your dimensions match the Flash movie settings (located in Modify, Document in your menu bar), or you can pick your own settings for this file. As always with JPEGs (or any image for that matter), the larger the dimensions the bigger the file size will be. Checking the Match Movie box will gray out the dimensions. Because you already chose the dimensions in the movie settings, there's no need to specify dimensions. If you leave this box unchecked, the Width and Height categories are now editable.

- **Quality**. Based on a value of 0 to 100, this option determines the quality of your image. You need to decide what your objective with the JPEG is. If you are using this image on the Web, you will most likely want to choose a setting in the 50–90 percent range. This way, the image will not look as clean but will load over the Internet faster. If you are creating a JPEG that will eventually be used in a print format, nothing short of 100 percent will be acceptable.

- **Progressive**. This allows your JPEG to load incrementally in a Web browser with a slow connection, which makes your JPEG image to appear to load faster over a slow connection. Again, depending on your audience this option may be useful.

GIF and PNG Settings

The GIF file format is ideal for images that are simple and contain few colors. Examples of these images are cartoons, logos, and signs. The use of fewer colors creates better GIFs in terms of download time and visibility. A GIF generally gives less photo-realistic quality than that of JPEG images. GIFs, when properly optimized, create very small files that load very quickly over slower connections.

When you're publishing images in Flash to the GIF format, Flash will automatically publish the first frame in the file. If you want a different frame marked for export, you must put a frame label in the frame you want exported. That label must be named #static. If you are exporting a series of frames for a GIF animation, Flash will export all the frames of your movie. To select a range of frames to be exported to GIF format, create two frame labels. #First specifies the first frame you want published, and #Last represents the name of the last frame you want published to the GIF. All frames between these two frames will be published, ignoring all other frames in your movie.

Flash can also export an image map for use in specifying URL links in your HTML documents. #map specifies in which frame the map information is located for your GIF file.

Keeping this in mind, let's take a look at the GIF options by clicking the check box next to the GIF Image (.gif) option in the Formats tab again. Then click the GIF tab at the top of the Publish Settings dialog box to open the GIF options. These options are described in the following list and displayed in Figure 8.10:

FIGURE 8.10

The options under the GIF tab in the Publish Settings dialog box offer the ability to choose an animated or static GIF and a choice of palettes for the resulting GIF.

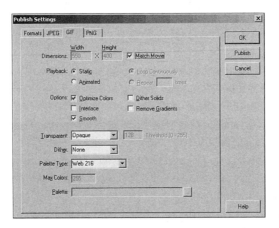

- **Dimensions**. Similar to the JPEG settings, you can also choose the size of your GIF image. Again, you have the choice of Match Movie or your own dimensions. Leaving this check box blank will allow you to enter a width and height for your GIF file.

- **Playback**. Unlike other image formats, GIFs allow you to choose an animation (series of images) or a single image to be included in your file. Choosing Static will gray out the options on the right, because the image will only contain one frame. Choosing Animated will allow you to determine whether you want your animation to loop continuously or to repeat a specified number of loops. Animated GIFs are generally used for ad banners. Just be judicial in your usage of animation on a static HTML page, because your users can be easily annoyed by multiple items moving at the same time on your page.

- **Optimize Colors**. This option removes any unused colors from the GIF file's color table, which means it will only use those colors essential for the image. This is similar to locking in the colors that are needed for your image to look a certain way (locking is used in programs such as Photoshop and Fireworks).

- **Interlace**. Allows the image to display incrementally in a browser as it downloads. This may appear on slower browsers to download the GIF faster. Do not interlace animated GIFs. This is similar to the Progressive option under the JPEG settings.

- **Smooth**. Applies antialiasing to allow your bitmaps to appear smoother. Although bitmaps are not usually used with GIFs, you can use this option to boost the quality of a bitmap being converted to a GIF. Beware though, because images placed on a colored background may gain a gray halo around them. If this occurs, republish the image with Smooth unchecked.

- **Dither Solids**. Applies dithering to solid colors as well as to gradients. Dithering is the way in which colors not in the GIF color palette are read.

- **Remove Gradients**. Turns all gradients to a solid color, using the first color in the gradient as the default. Gradients are often the cause of large file sizes in GIFs because they require many colors to make a smooth transition between two colors.

- **Transparent**. Gives you the ability to make your GIF image transparent, opaque, or possess an alpha value.

    - **Opaque**. Leaves the image's background intact.

    - **Alpha**. Allows you to choose to have a background semitransparent by choosing a value between 0 and 255. A lower value, such as 10, will result in a more transparent background as opposed to a higher value, such as 200.

    - **Transparent**. Removes the background completely from the image.

- **Dither**. Dithering tries to simulate how colors not present in a palette will be displayed in the image. This increases your file size but can improve color quality.

    - **None**. This option will approximate the analyzed color to the closest color in the palette.

    - **Ordered**. Dithers your file with good balance between quality and file size.

    - **Diffusion**. Dithers your file with the best quality but gives up some ability to limit the file size.

8

PUBLISHING

- **Palette Type**. The kind of palette is determined by how many colors you want or how you will display your image over the Web. Your choices of palettes include the following:

    - **Web 216**. Uses the standard 216 colors that are safe to use across the most popular browsers.

    - **Adaptive**. Analyzes colors and comes up with a unique set of colors used to produce the best possible image.

    - **Web Snap Adaptive**. A mix between Web 216 and Adaptive. This option tries to maximize the image quality while using Web 216 colors whenever it deems necessary.

    - **Custom.** Palettes can be imported into Flash and used from programs such as Fireworks. They must be imported using the ACT format. The advantage here is that you get to determine the exact colors you want. Although time consuming, this can be the best alternative, especially for small colored pictures.

PNG files follow almost the same format as GIF, with a few minor differences. You can find a graphical display of the options for PNG files in Figure 8.11.

FIGURE 8.11

The options under the PNG tab in the Publish Settings dialog box offer the ability to choose a bit of depth and a palette for the resulting PNG file.

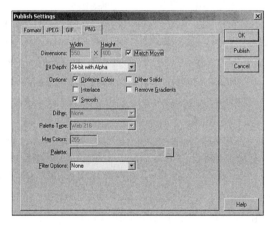

PNG files work primarily off of a bit-depth system that allows you to have transparency within a bitmap format for the image. To enable the transparency, you must select 24 bit with Alpha for your Bit Depth setting. If your image does not call for a transparent effect, choose either 16 or 24 bit to reduce the size of your PNG file.

The other option that PNG provides that GIF does not is the ability to choose a filter. This option attempts to make the bitmap more compressible. It's a system that looks at neighboring pixels to get a sense of what the overall pixel value should be through a line-by-line filtering system. Here are the options available to you for filtering:

- **None.** Turns the filtering option off.
- **Sub.** Evaluates the difference between the pixel prior to the current pixel and the current pixel to gain a value.
- **Up.** Examines the current pixel and the adjacent pixel above it to evaluate the current pixel value.
- **Average.** Takes the adjacent pixels above and to the left of the current pixel to predict a value for the current pixel.
- **Path.** Creates a function out of the top, left-top, and left pixels to arrive at a value for the current pixel.
- **Adaptive.** Analyzes the colors needed to produce the best-quality picture. The file size of an adaptive filtering system can be reduced by reducing the number of colors in your image. However, this option is usually intended for use on machines with millions of colors.

HTML

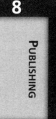

Early in the lifespan of Macromedia Flash, back when it was known as *Future Splash*, the product had little use because ActionScript was not yet a component. However, it was a great graphics tool, and many early developers talked of how Flash worked well as a tool for creating animated GIFs and images for the Web. When Macromedia introduced Flash 3, the game started to change a little bit. Not only were graphic designers finding a use for the tool, but programmers had some leeway by being able to design some interactivity into their projects. That interactivity exploded with Flash 4, when ActionScript was brought into the mix. Flash was now a tool developers could use to create entire Web sites.

Well, not exactly an *entire* Web site, because the Web site still has to get from a SWF file format to your Web page in order for end users to view it. This is where the HTML tab in the Publish Settings dialog box comes into the picture. Flash, upon publishing HTML, will create a document that embeds the Flash SWF into the HTML code to allow the SWF document to be seen by the browser. The code it creates is made up of `OBJECT` and `EMBED` tags, which allow you to specify a Flash SWF to be viewed. Here's an example:

```
<OBJECT classid="clsid:D27CDB6E-AE6D-11cf-96B8-444553540000"

codebase="http://download.macromedia.com/pub/shockwave/cabs/flash/swflash.cab#version=6,0,0,0"
```

```
WIDTH="550" HEIGHT="400" id="testPublish" ALIGN="">
 <PARAM NAME=movie VALUE="testPublish.swf"> <PARAM NAME=quality VALUE=high>
<PARAM NAME=bgcolor VALUE=#FFFFFF> <EMBED src="testPublish.swf" quality=high
bgcolor=#FFFFFF  WIDTH="550" HEIGHT="400" NAME="testPublish" ALIGN=""
 TYPE="application/x-shockwave-flash"
PLUGINSPAGE="http://www.macromedia.com/go/getflashplayer"></EMBED>
</OBJECT>
```

> **Note**
>
> The OBJECT tag would appear between the body tags in an HTML document.
> Upon publishing this HTML file, an HTML file with the preceding code will be
> created.

Let's try publishing this HTML file. First, make sure the HTML box is checked under the Formats tab of the Publish Settings dialog box. If it is checked, you will notice that immediately the Flash box becomes checked as well (if it wasn't already checked before). This is because Flash needs to know what Flash SWF will be used in the code of the HTML. Therefore, it will use the FLA file you have opened as the template for the creation of its code. Your window should look similar to Figure 8.12. Now click the HTML tab at the top of the Publish Settings dialog box. Here are the options you'll find there:

FIGURE 8.12

The options under the HTML tab in the Publish Settings dialog box. Choosing these options will custom-tailor an HTML or HTM file to your specifications. The resulting file must be published in addition to a SWF file.

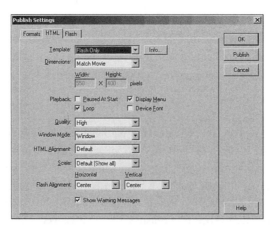

- **Template**. This is the format Flash will use to create the HTML code for you. This is also helpful for creating code on higher-ended Flash/HTML scripting. However, if you are just starting out in Flash, use the default Flash-only template. The default template is set up simply to enter OBJECT and EMBED tags into your HTML to embed the document into the code. Other templates include the following:

- **Detect for Flash**. Detects past Flash Players (for version 3, 4, 5, and 6).
- **Flash Only**. Only places a Flash SWF document in an HTML file.
- **Flash w/ AICC Tracking**. Embeds a Flash file with support for AICC tracking when using Macromedia's Learning component.
- **Flash w/ SCORM Tracking**. Embeds a Flash file with support for SCORM tracking when using Macromedia's Learning component.
- **Flash w/ FS Command**. Embeds Flash in HTML but also lends support for JavaScript in coordination with FS commands.
- **Flash w/ Named Anchors**. Embeds Flash in HTML but allows you to set up labels as anchor points to be used with the Back button of the end user's browser and for book-marking capabilities.
- **Image Map**. Sets up image maps (to be used with the PNG or GIF files you create).
- **Flash with FSCommand**. Provides the ability to work with FS commands (FS commands are discussed later in this chapter).
- **QuickTime**. Displays the SWF in a QuickTime movie from the browser (you must use this template in coordination with the QuickTime tab).
- **Pocket PC 2002**. Assists you in the creation of Flash for handheld devices.

For the purposes of this example, we will work with the default template, but feel free to use a different template to see what code is created with that particular template.

- **Dimensions**. This dialog box will ask you to input the size of your project. A very interesting effect of Flash is that you can choose to have your Flash movie match the movie size, fix it to a different size, or let the browser size determine the size of your piece for you. If you choose Percentage, the size of your browser will be the size of your final project. This is a useful feature when you want every user to see all of your project because it tailors your project to the size of the browser. The drawback to this feature is that your presentation can get stretched. Therefore, if your movie is 640×480 and your user has a browser height greater than the browser width, your presentation will get squeezed to fit the browser size. To prevent this from happening, read about the Scale property, further along in this section.

- **Paused at Start**. Do you want your movie to be paused at the start or run automatically? This sort of a silly option. I'm not sure what reason you would have to pause at the start, but you may let your users choose when they want to start the movie by either clicking a button in the presentation or right-clicking and then clicking Play within the Flash Player. This feature is not used in professional presentations, where navigation will stop and start the presentation and control is in the end user's hand.

- **Loop**. Turning this feature off will stop the SWF at the end of the movie. This is also an irrelevant feature if your navigation is well thought out. Usually Flash programmers like to choose when the movie stops and starts using Flash ActionScript, but if you have a continuously looping cartoon, you may want to activate this feature. If it is activated, Flash will replay from frame 1 when it reaches the end of the movie.

- **Display Menu**. This option allows your end users to have the full menu of items available to them by right-clicking your SWF in the Flash Player. This is a key feature because many developers like the idea of keeping the control in their hands, not the hands of the Flash Player. Deselecting this option will result in just the choice About Flash Player appearing by right-clicking in the Flash Player environment.

- **Device Font**. For Windows machines, you may also want to use Device Font to substitute antialiased system fonts for fonts not installed on the user's computer. This ensures the best quality of legibility for your end users for those text pieces that are set to display with device fonts.

- **Quality**. Lets you determine how well Flash will play back the items in the SWF. If you choose Low Quality, you are favoring the playback speed and performance on slower machines (but giving up appearance quality for items on the screen). Choosing High quality favors better-looking graphics, but your movie could take a performance hit on some slower machines. Check your target audience to see what kind of machines will be used. If their machines tend to be processor intensive, you may select the High quality setting here. If you are not sure, you can choose either Auto High or Auto Low. This will favor either quality of images (High) or speed (Low) and will attempt to improve the opposite feature whenever it deems necessary for better playback. Medium will attempt to give good quality and good speed, but it will not choose on a case-by-case basis. The Best option will give you the best quality available, which sacrifices the speed of the project.

- **Window Mode**. Allows you to change the transparency, positioning, and layering of the Flash movie in question. It does this through changing the WMODE tag in the OBJECT tag of your HTML document. I would highly recommend leaving this option set to Window. This mode attempts to place the Flash piece in its own rectangular window on the Web page and attempts to play back the movie faster than the other options. However, if you plan to deliver your presentation in Internet Explorer 4.0 with ActiveX control, you may want to use the other options. The Opaque Windowless option allows you to place items behind the Flash piece without letting them show through. The Transparent Windowless option allows you to display objects on your HTML page behind the Flash SWF.

- **HTML Alignment**. Positions the Flash piece within the HTML window. The Flash alignment looks at how the Flash movie is placed within the movie window. These tags are highly important when you are attempting to bump your Flash piece up against the edge of your HTML window (for example, if you are opening a pop-up window for your SWF to appear in). If you are attempting to do this, you must choose the Left or Top options so that your movie will move as close to the edge of the browser window as possible.

- **Scale**. Determines how your Flash piece will scale if you did not choose Match Movie in the Dimensions property earlier.

    - **Default**. Tries to display the entire movie without distorting the original image while maintaining the original aspect ratio of your movie.

    - **No Border**. Scales your movie to fill the specified area but may crop your movie in order to keep the aspect ratio of your movie.

    - **Exact Fit.** Displays the entire movie in the area specified, without taking into consideration the aspect ratio. This option may cause distortion of your project on some machines.

    - **No Scale.** Prevents the movie from scaling when the Flash Player is resized.

- **Flash Alignment**. This will attempt to position or crop (if necessary) the Flash piece within the window specified by other alignments.

- **Show Warning Messages**. Checking this option causes Flash to warn you if your options conflict in any way. Flash will let you know whether your settings will generate errors in code.

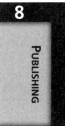

Standalone Projectors

Keep in mind that Flash is versatile—a point that has resonated throughout this chapter. This means you don't have to use the Web at all to display your creation. You can choose to deliver your project on CD-ROM or over a kiosk. This is where the use of standalone projectors is highly useful. You will find the option to publish them by choosing either Mac Projector or Windows Projector (.exe) from the check boxes on the Formats tab, shown in Figure 8.13. Publishing with one of these options checked will create either a file with the extension .exe for the PC or .hqx for the Mac.

FIGURE 8.13

Under the Formats tab of the Publish Settings dialog box, you can choose to publish either Mac or PC stand-alone projector files. You can also give each file its own unique name.

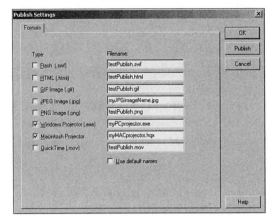

The Mac file cannot be opened on your PC but can be transferred to the Mac to be opened on that platform. However, double-clicking one of these files will execute or play the Flash file you created in its own self-contained format, meaning there's no need for the Flash Player (any version) on the end user's computer in order to play back the project.

FS Commands

If you just double-clicked your executable file, you may have noticed that the project still appears within a window, looking similar to the Flash Player. This is because the project has not been set to Full Screen. In order to give your newly created, self-contained project special features such as Full Screen, you must issue FS commands to Flash to tell it to perform such actions.

FS commands are a series of commands that can, in some cases, pass arguments to the host program of the Flash Player. In this instance, we will be looking at the self-contained executable host. However, you could be using an FS command to send messages to JavaScript within a browser. You may want to use FS commands to talk to Director through strings or events. You can even use FS commands to pass information through Visual Basic or C++.

To access the FS commands, click the first frame of your movie and then go to your Actions palette, also displayed in Figure 8.14. Under the Actions, Browser/Network category you will find a piece of ActionScript for FSCommand. In Normal mode, click this item. Notice that you have a field that's titled Commands for Standalone Player. These are the items you may choose from for the standalone projector.

FIGURE 8.14

In the Actions panel, you can choose FS commands to control the appearance of your projector file. Here, the Fullscreen option is set to True.

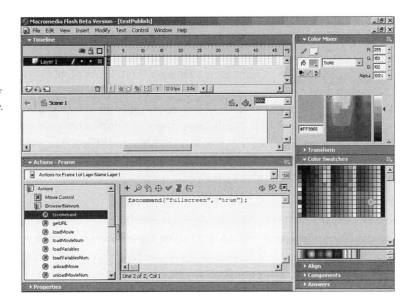

The FS commands available in the ActionScript window include the following:

- Quit. Closes the program and accepts no arguments.

- Fullscreen. Setting this to True will show your projector full screen on the end user's computer. This means it will fill the screen at any cost. The default option, False, will open your project in a window.

- Allowscale. This command, when set to True, will scale your project to reach the corners of your user's screen. A False setting will always reset the project to the size of your movie, leaving the outer spaces of the screen the same color as your document's background color.

- Showmenu. This command is similar to the option Display Menu in the HTML dialog box. Setting this equal to True will provide the whole set of menu items when right-clicking the Flash presentation. Setting it to False will only display the About Flash Player option.

- Trapallkeys. Sends *all* key events to the onClipEvent handler.

QuickTime Settings

Oftentimes, QuickTime can be used to create a solution to problems with sound synchronization. As a example, my company was working on an interactive kiosk in Director.

Each module contained information about wetlands and an activity to teach about the information presented at the front of the module. One activity included cartoons, and we chose to create them in Flash because of its superior animation capabilities. When I imported the Flash SWF cartoons into Director, I ran into a problem. Both Flash and Director are frame-based applications, and I found keeping the synchronization difficult. The more computers we tested on, the more the problem intensified, because one computer's processor could interpret the frame rates of Flash in Director totally different from another computer. Our solution was to publish our Flash document as a QuickTime file and import the time-based product into Director. This way, a time-based movie could drop frames to keep up with the frame rate on slower computers. Presto! Problem solved.

This story demonstrates the flexibility of Flash projects. It also demonstrates one way you can use QuickTime in your projects. Another important use for QuickTime is to add more animation to your movies. Suppose you have a movie to which you would like to add a Flash animation you already have completed in your MOV (the file extension for QuickTime movies). You can import the MOV into Flash and then perform your animation in Flash. When it is published, Flash will place the MOV onto the movie track and the Flash animation on a separate, new track. Now your animation is incorporated into your MOV.

Figure 8.15 shows the default options for the QuickTime tab. Here are the options you need to publish your MOV:

FIGURE 8.15

The options under the QuickTime tab in the Publish Settings dialog box offer the ability to choose various layering and playback options for your resulting MOV file.

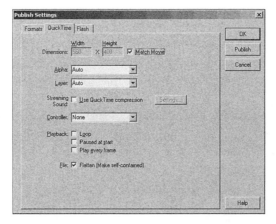

- **Dimensions**. Like the other Dimensions options, here you have the option to match the movie or choose your own dimensions.
- **Alpha**. Choosing Auto (the default) will make sure that when you have no other tracks in your movie (outside of the Flash track), the movie will be opaque. If other

tracks are behind the Flash track, the Flash track will be made transparent to show the other tracks. Choosing Alpha-Transparent, obviously, makes the Flash track transparent throughout the MOV. The Copy option will make the Flash track opaque.

- **Layer**. This option determines where your Flash track is located. Top places it in front of all other objects, whereas Bottom places it behind all other tracks in your movie. The Auto option determines whether any movie items are in front of your movie in the movie's timeline. If there are, your Flash track will play in front. Otherwise, it will play behind the movie track.

- **Streaming Sound**. Do you have sound in your Flash movie? If you do, that sound can be compressed in the QuickTime Player and placed on its own track. Just check this box and fill in the options you need for your sound.

- **Controller.** Specifies the type of controller that will be associated with this MOV file. Here are the options:

    - **None.** Creates a MOV that is a simple file with no control bar attached. This is a useful choice when you're incorporating the QuickTime movie into a Director presentation, where you may use Lingo to control the interface of the MOV.

    - **Standard.** Includes the standard toolbar that allows the user to interact with the MOV file.

    - **QuickTimeVR.** If your Flash file is going to be used in a QuickTimeVR format, choose this option to export your MOV with the QuickTime interaction tools available to the end user.

- **Playback**. Much like the GIF settings, you can choose to have your MOV paused at start, loop at the end of the movie, or play every frame. The last of these three settings could put a strain on your computer's processor because it forces the MOV to play every frame of your SWF, not marrying it to the timeline.

- **File**. Choosing Self-Contained will make sure you have one single document at the end of the publish process. The resulting file will be a single MOV document that "contains" the Flash information within it. Deselecting this option forces you to keep all imported items (such as your original QuickTime movie) in the same locations so that the resulting MOV can reference these items.

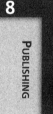

Flash is a highly versatile program. It can create files ready for the Web (SWF and HTML files), self-contained projector files (EXE and Mac projector), images (GIF, JPEG, and PNG), and QuickTime movies with interactivity (MOV). The power of publishing is recognizing the correct medium for your target audience. Picking the proper mix of elements is how your project is going to become successful. Although publishing is one of the last steps in the process of creating a Flash project, you should have an overall sense of which formats you will be using before ever opening the Publish window for your final test. Now that you know the power that Flash possesses, you can utilize its power to the advantage of your clients.

Animation Techniques and Digital Video

By Matt Pizzi

IN THIS CHAPTER

- Controlling Speed
- The Bouncing Ball
- Integrating Digital Video in Flash MX
- Creating QuickTime Movie Controls and a Custom QuickTime Skin

This is a fun chapter. We're going to discuss topics such as traditional animation techniques. You'll see how you can apply techniques used by artists in traditional animation studios to Flash movies. These techniques can add life to your animations, making them more fluid, less rigid, and ultimately more realistic.

You'll also learn how you can incorporate digital video into your Flash movies. Flash MX offers a host of new video support. Flash also integrates with QuickTime 5; in fact, you can build your own navigation and control in Flash to control the QuickTime Player. However, we'll start this chapter by talking about animation techniques.

Controlling Speed

Controlling speed in a Flash movie can be a tricky concept to grasp as you're first learning Flash. It is important to remember that the frame rate (how many frames per second an animation is playing) is not the way to adjust the speed of an animation.

The frame rate is a global setting for the entire Flash movie. The higher the frame rate, the more realistic and fluid your animation will look. The downside to this is that the higher the frame rate, the more powerful the end user's machine must be and the faster the end user's Internet connection must be. As a frame of reference, consider that film plays at 24 frames per second (fps) and digital video plays at 29.97 fps. Ideally, if you're dealing with character animation, the frame rate should be bumped up to 20–25 fps. If you're strictly dealing with interface design, keep it a bit lower (somewhere between 12 and 18 fps). Of course, no standard exists, so you'll have to make a decision concerning what you want the frame rate to be based on your specific circumstances. You must take into account your audience and the content in the site.

Therefore, the question is, how do you control the speed of any given animation in your movie? Keep in mind that the fewer frames used, the faster the animation will look. Go to the Unleashed companion Web site and download the `speed_example.fla` file. Open the document in Flash and notice the three different circles. Also, take note of the timeline, as displayed in Figure 9.1.

One way to view how fast something is moving is to turn on the Onion Skin feature. This is how a traditional animator would look at an animation within a light box. Notice in Figure 9.2 that you see a cascade of all the different frames together.

In Figure 9.2, you'll notice the top animation has large gaps between each circle. This is probably moving a bit too fast for animation in the sense that the end user's eye won't see this circle moving across the screen fluidly. In fact, in traditional animation, this is called *strobing*. Therefore, if you play the animation, the faster circle will almost look like its blinking across the stage.

FIGURE 9.1

The speed example demonstrates how fewer frames create faster animation.

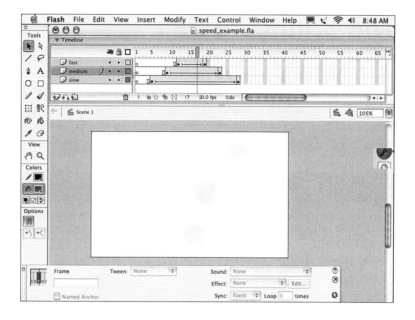

FIGURE 9.2

The speed example with the Onion Skin feature turned on.

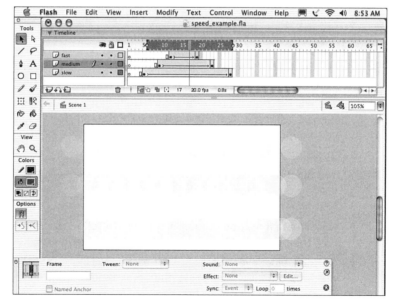

9

ANIMATION TECHNIQUES AND DIGITAL VIDEO

The Bouncing Ball

In this section, we'll work on an exercise to build a bouncing ball. While building this bouncing ball, you'll be learning the fundamentals of animation. You can apply these techniques to many of your Flash animations to create more lively effects. One company that uses these types of techniques throughout its development is Look and Feel New Media (www.lookandfeel.com). Poke around the Web site and some of the portfolio pieces to get an idea as to how you can incorporate these techniques in Flash design.

Bouncing Ball

In this exercise, we'll be using different animation concepts, such as easing, stretching, and squashing, to achieve a realistic effect. Here are the steps to follow:

1. Create a new document. Choose File, Save As and name it bouncing_ball.fla.

2. Create a symbol of a circle by choosing the Oval tool in the Tools panel and then choosing a fill color. Leave the stroke color blank.

3. Draw a circle at the top-right corner of the stage. Click the circle to highlight it and the press F8 on your keyboard to convert it to a symbol. Notice that the Convert to Symbol dialog box appears. Inside this dialog box, in the Name text field, name this symbol circle. Make sure you have the Movie Clip radio button selected for the behavior. Then choose OK.

4. You will be brought into the movie clip symbol editing mode. Click the Scene 1 tab underneath the timeline on the left side to exit out of the editing mode.

5. Double-click layer 1 and name it circle.

   You need to create a motion tween and have this circle follow a path, so let's set this up. Note that this will take a bit more keyframing than some of the animations we created earlier.

6. Now create a motion guide for this ball to follow. In the Layers panel, click the blue Add Motion Guide button, as shown in Figure 9.3.

7. On the Guide layer, using the Pen tool, draw a guide with three arcs. Make the first arc the largest; then make them progressively smaller, as shown in Figure 9.4.

8. On the Guide layer select frame 60, press F5 on your keyboard to insert a frame. Notice that the Guide layer is now extended out 60 frames.

9. Highlight frame 10 of the circle layer and press F6 on your keyboard to inset a keyframe on frame 10. Notice that the timeline is now extended out to frame 10.

10. On frame 10, move the circle from its original position down to the bottom of the stage, at the beginning of the guide, as shown in Figure 9.5.

11. Select frame 1 in the circle layer and in the Properties Inspector choose Motion Tweening from the Tween drop-down menu.

12. Insert a keyframe on frame 18 of the circle layer by selecting frame 18 and pressing F6 on your keyboard. This will extend out the timeline. On frame 18, move the circle from the bottom to the top of the arc, as shown in Figure 9.6.

13. Highlight frame 10 and in the Properties Inspector choose Motion from the Tween drop-down menu. Also, be sure to check the Snap box to ensure that the item stays on the path.

14. Scrub the playhead to make sure the animation is in fact attached to the path. If it isn't, move the circle around the path until the circle snaps to the guide.

15. Insert a keyframe on frame 26 of the circle layer by highlighting frame 26 and pressing F6 on the keyboard. Notice the timeline is extended. With the playhead on frame 26, move the circle from the top of the arc down toward the bottom between the large and medium-size arcs.

16. Highlight frame 18 in the circle layer. In the Properties Inspector, choose Motion from the Tween drop-down menu. Make sure to check the Snap box to ensure the circle will stick to the guide. If your Properties Inspector is not visible, choose Window, Properties.

17. Insert a keyframe on frame 34 of the circle layer by selecting frame 24 and pressing F6 on your keyboard. Notice the timeline is extended. On frame 34, move the circle from the bottom up to the top of the second arc, as shown in Figure 9.7.

18. Highlight frame 26 and in the Properties Inspector choose Motion from the Tween drop-down menu. Make sure to check the Snap box. Scrub the playhead to double-check whether the circle is staying on the guide. If it's falling off the guide, make the necessary adjustments so it will stay on the guide (refer to step 14).

19. Insert a keyframe on frame 41 of the circle layer by selecting frame 41 and pressing F6 on your keyboard. Again, this will extend out the timeline on this layer.

20. With the playhead on frame 41, move the circle from the top of the second arc to the bottom between the second and third arc.

21. Select frame 34 and in the Properties Inspector and choose Motion from the Tween drop-down menu. Make sure to click the Snap check box. Scrub the playhead to check the animation.

22. In frame 45, insert another keyframe by selecting frame 45 and pressing F6 on the keyboard. Notice that the timeline is extended.

23. With the playhead on frame 45, move the circle up to the top of the third arc.

24. Select frame 41 and choose Motion from the Tween drop-down menu in the Properties Inspector. Again, check the Snap box, just to make sure the circle does stick to that motion guide. Scrub the playhead to check the animation.

25. Insert a keyframe on frame 49 of the circle layer by selecting frame 49 and pressing F6 on the keyboard. This will extend the timeline. With the playhead on frame 49, move the circle from the top of the third arc to the bottom at the end of the guide.

26. Highlight frame 45 and choose Motion Tween from the Tween drop-down menu. Check the Snap box and scrub the playhead to see the animation.

27. Now we want the ball to have one final bounce—to bounce right off the stage. Therefore, insert a keyframe in frame 55 by selecting frame 55 and pressing F6 on the keyboard. With the playhead on frame 55, move the circle off the stage, but to make it look like it is bouncing, move the circle up as if there were another arc, as shown in Figure 9.8.

28. Highlight frame 49 and choose Motion Tween from the Tween drop-down in the Properties Inspector.

29. Test the movie!

30. Save the document by choosing File, Save.

FIGURE 9.3

The Add Motion Guide button.

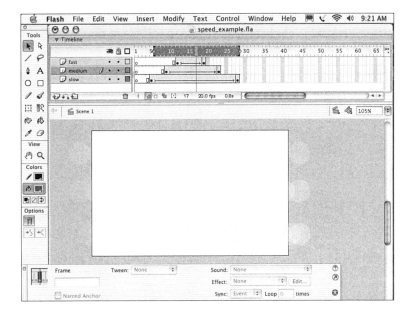

FIGURE 9.4

The Guide layer's three arcs, which help create the bouncing ball effect.

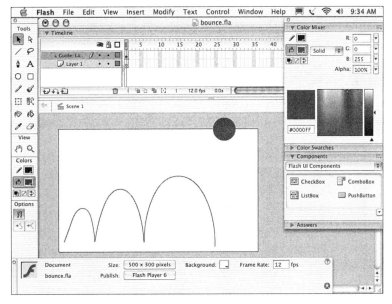

9

ANIMATION TECHNIQUES AND DIGITAL VIDEO

FIGURE 9.5
Move the circle to the beginning of the motion guide on frame 10.

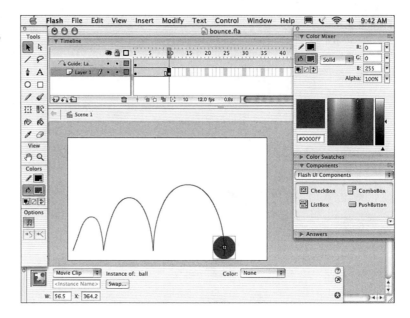

FIGURE 9.6
Notice the circle is placed on top of the first arc.

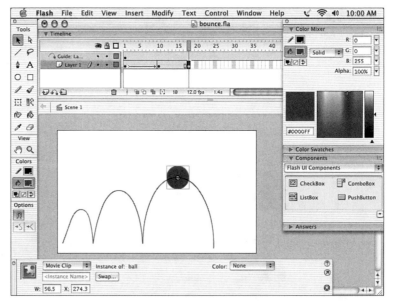

FIGURE 9.7

The circle has been moved from the bottom up to the top of the second arc.

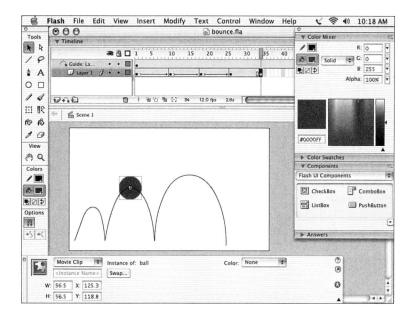

FIGURE 9.8

Move the circle off the stage, but be sure to make the circle look like it's making an upward movement.

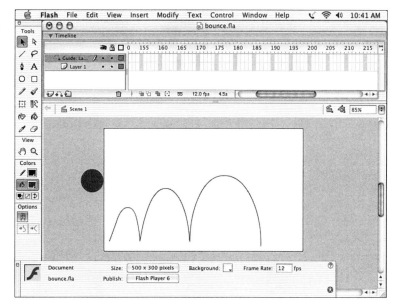

At this point, the animation looks like a bouncing ball, kind of. However, we can improve the appearance of this animation. If you turn on the Onion Skin feature, you'll see that this animation looks very linear, as shown in Figure 9.9. There is no variation in the animation, which means the circle stays the same speed through the sequence. But, we'll fix this. In Figure 9.10, you can view the same animation with Onion Skin as well as outlines, making it a bit easier to see.

FIGURE 9.9

The Onion Skin shows the speed of the animation (in this case, it's linear and rigid).

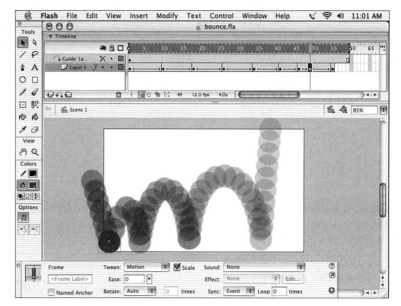

FIGURE **9.10**

The Outline view makes it a bit easier to see the animation.

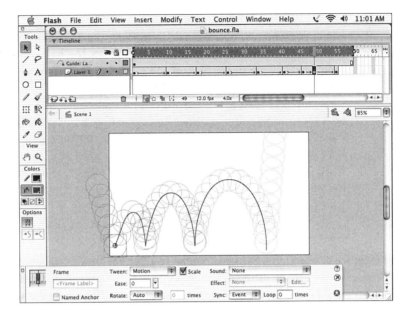

Easing, Squashing, and Stretching

A real bouncing ball has several characteristics when moving you should be aware of when animating. For example, if a ball were to bounce in real life, it would not be one consistent speed. The ball would speed up on its way down due to gravity. On its way up, after it hits the ground, it would spring back. However, before long gravity will take over again and start pulling the ball down. Therefore, the ball as it's bouncing up will gradually slow down before it actually starts moving down again, and it will pick up speed as it starts to move down. Let's begin the next exercise, which will take into account the effect gravity has on a bouncing ball.

Using Easing to Create a Gravity Effect

Follow these steps to use easing to create a gravity effect on the bouncing ball example:

1. Open the `bouncing_ball.fla` file you built in the last exercise.

2. Highlight frame 1 of the circle layer. We want to have the circle ease into the animation, which basically means we need the circle to start off slow and speed up gradually throughout the animation. Therefore, in the Properties Inspector, set the easing of the frame to [nd]80.

3. Highlight frame 10 of the circle layer. Here, we are going to set the easing to "ease out." By easing out of the animation, the ball will slow down as it approaches the top of the arc, much like a real ball would. In the Properties Inspector, set the easing to 65.

4. Scrub the playhead to see the difference in the animation. Repeat steps 2 and 3 for each keyframe. When the circle is at the top of the animation, make sure to ease in; if it is positioned at the bottom, ease out. Do this for the entire animation.

5. Once the easing is finished, test the movie. Already the ball is looking a bit more realistic!

6. Save the movie by choosing File, Save.

In Figure 9.11, the Onion Skin and outline features are turned on. You can see the speed differences between the different easing portions of the animation. Compare Figure 9.10 with Figure 9.11, and you'll see there is a substantial difference in the way the outlines are drawn.

FIGURE 9.11

The momentum of the ball is indicated by the way the outlines in Onion Skin view are drawn.

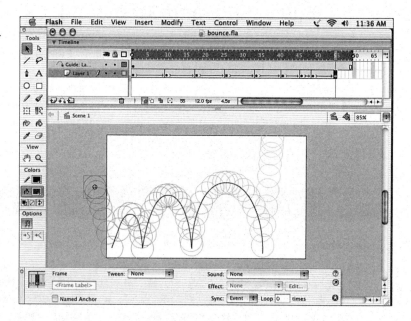

Still, this animation is not as realistic as it should be. To add to the realism, in the next exercise we'll be using an old animation trick—squash.

Using the Squash Animation Technique

When the ball hits the ground, it can't stay in a perfect circle. The air inside the ball will displace, thus changing the shape of the object. In animation, this is called *squash*. In Flash it's very easy to achieve this effect. Follow these steps:

1. Open the movie from the last exercise.

2. Select frame 9 and insert a keyframe by pressing F6 on the keyboard. Also, insert a keyframe on frame 11. The circle layer should now have three keyframes, for frames 9, 10, and 11, as shown in Figure 9.12.

3. In frame 10, highlight the circle. In the Tools panel, click the Free Transform tool to get the bounding box around the circle. Drag the top-middle handle down to squash the circle, as shown in Figure 9.13. After squashing, you may have to tweak the position of the circle. By only having one frame squashed, a snapping effect will result, just like a real ball. Therefore, this would *not* be a good place to try to tween over a few frames so that the effect happens over time. You want the squash effect only to last for a brief moment; it's a subtle technique that has a profound effect of the feel and look of the animation.

4. Now you need to do the same thing for frames 26, 40, and 49. Insert a keyframe before and after each of these frames. On frames 26, 40, and 49, squash the ball using the Scale tool.

5. Test the movie, and you'll see a big difference. Also, refer to Figure 9.14 to see the Onion Skin outlines of this animation; notice the difference between this one and the others you worked on.

6. Save the move by choosing File, Save.

9

ANIMATION
TECHNIQUES AND
DIGITAL VIDEO

FIGURE 9.12

Notice the three keyframes on frames 9, 10, and 11.

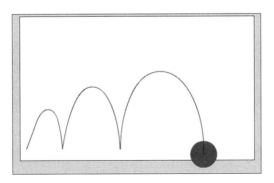

FIGURE 9.13
Squashing the circle using the Scale tool.

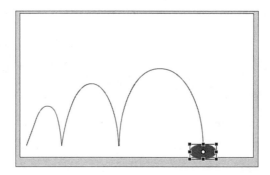

FIGURE 9.14
Notice the squashing in the Onion Skin outlines.

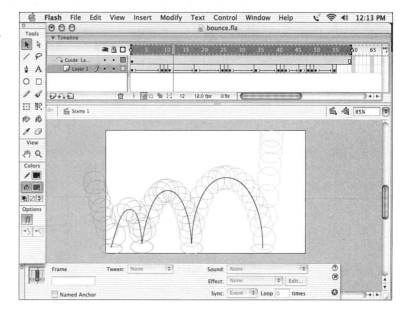

We're getting closer; this animation is almost done. There's still one more technique we can apply to this ball—the stretch effect.

Applying a Stretch Effect to the Bouncing Ball

If the ball squashes once it hits the ground, it's not automatically going to spring back into the shape of a perfect circle. The ball's air will shift it into an oblong shape. In animation, this is called *stretch*. For the bouncing ball example, this effect is pretty easy to achieve, although there are a few tricky spots. Here are the steps to follow:

1. Open up the file from the last few exercises, `bouncing_ball.fla`.

2. Move the playhead to frame 9. Select the circle by clicking it. In the Tools panel, choose the Scale tool. With the bounding box around the circle, drag the top-middle handle up to stretch the circle out. Also, move the cursor outside the bounding box in the top-left corner and slightly rotate it back a few degrees, as shown in Figure 9.15.

3. Scrub the playhead between frames 1 and 10 to see the effect. Now you have to change the next stage of the animation—when the ball bounces back up from hitting the ground. Move the playhead to frame 11 and select the circle. Again, in the Tools panel, choose the Scale tool to get the bounding box around the circle. Pull the middle-top handle up to stretch the circle and rotate it slightly toward the left (the direction in which its moving) a few degrees, as shown in Figure 9.16.

4. Repeat steps 2 and 3 on each set of keyframes where the ball is at the point of hitting the ground.

5. Test the movie! Compare this movie to the one you made in the first bouncing ball exercise. You'll notice a dramatic difference. Look at Figure 9.17 and compare it to Figure 9.10; you'll definitely see the difference in the animation path.

6. Save the movie by choosing File, Save.

FIGURE 9.15

The ball is stretched and tilted slightly.

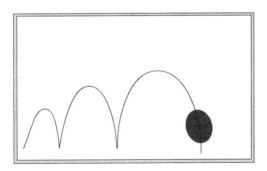

FIGURE 9.16

Stretching and tilting the circle in the opposite direction.

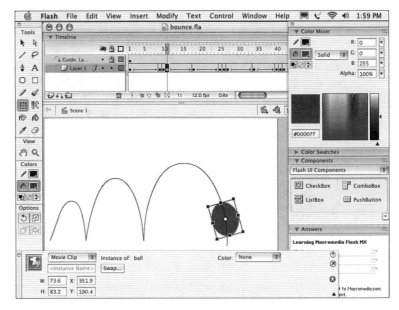

FIGURE 9.17

The Onion Skin outlines of our final animation. There is far more life to this piece than our previous animations.

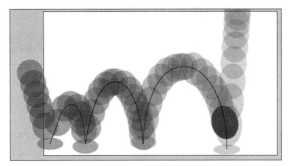

These animation concepts—ease, squash, and stretch—can really prove the difference between an amateur and professional Flash design. Just in the bouncing ball animation, look at the dramatic difference between the starting and ending products. When you're developing Flash content, keep these techniques in mind.

Anticipation and Follow-Through

In this section, we'll look at two additional animation techniques: anticipation and follow-though. If you watch a lot of cartoons, you may already have an idea of what I'm talking about. These techniques are used often in cartoons to give the viewer a hint as to what is coming next. They require just a few frames to get the appropriate appearance. Anticipation will generally have an object shift for a second in the opposite direction of the actual animation. This creates the "anticipated" movement. Follow-through will skew the animated shape in the direction in which it is moving.

Using Anticipation and Follow-Through

In this exercise, we use the techniques anticipation and follow-through to get a better, more fluid looking animation. Here are the steps to follow:

1. Create a new document. Choose Modify, Document. This will open the Document Properties dialog box. Set the Frame Rate text field to 30.

2. Open the Unleashed library by choosing Window, Common Libraries, Unleashed. In the Unleashed library is a folder titled `graphics`. Open the `graphics` folder and find the soccer_ball graphic symbol. Drag an instance out onto the stage.

3. Create a simple motion tween by highlighting frame 20 and inserting a keyframe by pressing F6. Notice that the timeline is extended. With the playhead in frame 20, move the soccer ball to the other side of the stage.

4. Highlight frame 1 and in the Properties Inspector choose Motion from the Tween drop-down menu. This will create the motion tween. Press Return (Mac) or Enter (Windows) to see the animation.

5. Choose File, Save As and name the document `motion_tween`.

   At this point, the animation is pretty basic; it shows an object simply moving from one side of the stage to the other. We'll now use anticipation to make this example more animated.

6. Highlight frame 3 and insert a keyframe by pressing F6. With the playhead on frame 3, select the circle and choose the Transform tool. Skew the soccer ball back, as shown in Figure 9.18. Oftentimes, when an item is going to move in a one direction, you can anticipate that movement with a small jerk in the opposite direction.

7. Highlight frame 6 and insert a keyframe by pressing F6. With the playhead on frame 5, select the circle. Choose the Transform tool again, but this time skew the ball forward slightly, as shown in Figure 9.19.

8. Press F6 in frame 16 to insert a keyframe. Make sure the playhead is on frame 16 and select the soccer ball. In the Tools panel, choose the Scale tool again. Skew the soccer ball even more, as shown in Figure 9.20. This way, as the soccer ball animates, it will skew more over time.

9. If you press Return (Mac) or Enter (Windows), you can see how the beginning portion of the animation looks more lifelike than the previous animation. The only problem is that the ending doesn't look right; therefore, we need to use the follow-through technique to complete this animation. Insert a keyframe on frame 18 by highlighting frame 18 and pressing F6. You may want to turn on Onion Skin and move the soccer ball just a few pixels past the last keyframe. Choose the Transform tool again and skew the ball just slightly in the opposite direction. This will create the appearance that the soccer ball has missed its ending point and will bounce slightly back into position. This produces a realistic effect, making you believe that the soccer ball has some mass to it.

10. Select the last frame in the movie and choose Window, Actions to bring up the Actions panel. Make sure that the title bar of the Actions panel reads "Actions [nd] Frame," which indicates that you'll be applying this action to the selected frame. If the title bar shows something else, be sure to have the frame selected.

11. Open the Actions book and then the Movie Control book. Then double-click the `stop` action. This will apply the `stop` action to the last frame; therefore, the animation will not loop.

12. Test the movie. Choose Control, Test Movie. Notice how much better this animation looks compared to the first one!

13. Save the file as `soccer_ball.fla`.

Figure 9.21 shows the Onion Skin of the animation, which gives you a good indication as to how this animation was built and how it will appear when playing.

FIGURE 9.18

The soccer ball is skewed in the opposite direction.

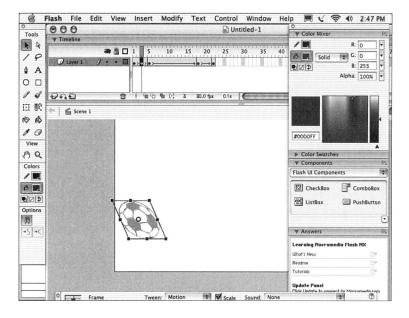

FIGURE 9.19

The soccer ball is now skewed slightly forward.

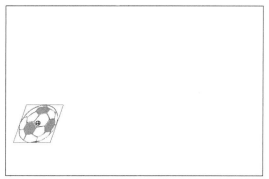

9

ANIMATION
TECHNIQUES AND
DIGITAL VIDEO

FIGURE 9.20
The soccer ball is even more skewed on frame 16.

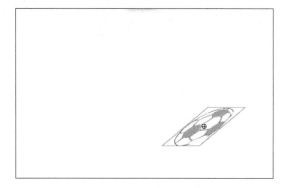

FIGURE 9.21
The Onion Skin of the animation using the anticipation and follow-through techniques.

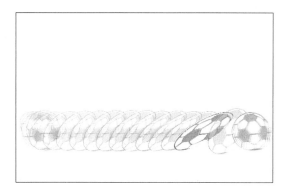

Integrating Digital Video in Flash MX

Flash MX has new, powerful support for video. Video can play natively inside the Flash 6 player. Flash MX supports DV, MPEG, and QuickTime movies as well as the AVI file format. Once the video is inside the authoring environment, you can scale, skew, distort, mask, rotate, and make it interactive using scripting. The Flash 6 player can support video with the addition of the Sorensen Spark codec. It is important to note that the new support for video in Flash is ideal only for short video pieces, no longer than a few minutes or a few megabytes in file size. By no means is the Flash player going to act as a substitute for any of the media players, such as QuickTime or Windows Media Player.

Creating Controls to Play and Stop Video

In this exercise we're going to import some video into Flash. Then we'll create some controls to stop and play a small video clip in Flash. Here are the steps to follow:

1. On the Unleashed companion Web site is a file you can download for this exercise. Depending on your Internet connection, you can download the standard file or the high-quality file. Download the `cali.mov` file from the Chapter 9 section of the Web site. The file is approximately 1.2MB and shouldn't take too long to download. If you have a broadband connection, a larger version, which is just under 12MB, is also available.

2. Once you've downloaded the file, create a new document. In the new document, double-click the first layer and name it **video**.

3. Create a movie clip by choosing Insert, New Symbol. This will launch the New Symbol dialog box. Be sure to give this symbol the movie clip behavior and then name it **video_source**. Click OK, which will bring you inside the movie clip symbol.

4. In movie clip symbol editing mode, choose File, Import. Search for the file `cali.mov` you downloaded earlier. Highlight it and click Open. This will launch the Import Video dialog box, which asks you to either link or embed the video (see Figure 9.22). If you were to link, you'd have to export the Flash movie as a QuickTime movie in order to see the video. By embedding it, the video will play inside the Flash 6 player. Choose Embed and click OK.

5. This will launch the Import Video Settings dialog box, as shown in Figure 9.23. You'll notice that this dialog box has a few options. For now, set Quality to 100, make sure the Import Audio check box is selected, and leave everything else at their defaults. Click OK. Depending on the speed of your computer, this process can vary in time.

   At the top of this dialog box you'll find some vital stats on the movie your bringing in, such as the size, frame rate, and the duration of the movie. Here are the particulars:

   - **Quality**. This option judges the overall quality of the video. It is the biggest contributor to compression artifacting and file size.

   - **Keyframe Interval**. This slider is to set the spacing between keyframes within the movie.

   - **Scale**. This options determines the size at which you import the video. Here, 100% brings the video in at the native size of the file. For this example, the scale is 240 pixels by 180 pixels.

- **Synchronize Video to Macromedia Flash Document Rate.** This is an attempt to synch the video if its frame rate is different from the frame rate for the Flash movie. (I would not rely on this option because it does not work very well.)

- **Number of Video Frames to Encode per Number of Flash Frames.** This option syncs the imported video with the frames per second of the Flash movie. For example, if the Flash movie is playing at 12 fps and the QuickTime movie is saved to play at 24 fps, Flash would have to encode at a ratio of 1:2. Experimenting with this option can produce various results.

- **Import Audio.** This option imports any audio associated with the video file. Note that it depends on how the audio was compressed. The Spark codec, for example, isn't too friendly with the IMA compression standard for audio.

Playing around with these settings is the only way you'll get the desired effect. No standard setting is available that will look good for all video. However, I recommend importing uncompressed or lower-compressed video. This feature only works well with small or short video files. If you are doing a lot of professional work with video in Flash MX, buying Sorenson Squeeze would be a wise investment. Squeeze yields a higher-quality output. Far less artifacting, smaller file sizes, offline compression, and batch processing are just a few of its advantages.

6. After choosing OK, a dialog box may warn you that there are more frames in the video than in your Flash movie. It asks you whether you want it to automatically extend the timeline, as shown in Figure 9.24. This is a huge timesaver—in Flash 5, you would have to calculate how many frames a video file has by multiplying the frame rate by the duration of the clip. Now Flash MX does this automatically. Choose OK. Notice the movie clip's timeline is now full of video.

7. Click the Scene 1 tab to get back to the main timeline. Open up this movie's Library by choosing Window, Library. Drag out an instance of the video_source symbol to the stage. Create a new layer and name it **mask**. Make sure the mask layer is above the video layer.

8. Draw a rounded-corner square around the video. Choose the Rectangle tool in the Tools panel and then click the button in the bottom portion of the Tools panel. This will open the Rectangle Settings dialog box. Set the radius to 12.

9. Draw a rectangle in the mask layer right on top of the video movie clip, as shown in Figure 9.25.

10. Double-click the Layer Properties icon to the left of the layer's name on the mask layer. Choose Mask for the layer type and click OK. Notice that the Layer icon changes to a blue icon, indicating it's ready to mask layers underneath it.

11. Double-click the Layer Properties icon to the left of the layer's name on the video layer. Choose Masked for the layer type and click OK. Notice that the Layer icon changes to a blue icon and that it's indented, indicating it's a slave to the mask layer above it.

12. Lock both layers to get a preview.

13. Now you're going to set up the controls to stop and play the movie. Create a new layer and name it **buttons**. Make sure the buttons layer is on the button. In the Unleashed common library, open up the `buttons` folder. Drag out an instance of Play and an instance of Stop and then position them under the video, as shown in Figure 9.26.

14. Unlock the video layer. Double-click the video clip to go inside the movie clip symbol editing mode. Once inside the movie clip, highlight the first frame and open up the Actions panel by choosing Window, Actions. Open the Actions book and then open the Movie Controls book. Double-click the `stop` action. This will prevent the movie from playing by default.

15. Click the Scene 1 tab under the timeline to return to the main timeline. Highlight the video movie clip and give it an instance name in the Properties Inspector. With the movie clip selected, a text field becomes active in the Properties Inspector. Type the name **videoclip** in this field. Press Return (Mac) or Enter (Windows) to apply the name.

16. Highlight the Play button and open up the Actions panel by pressing F9. In the Actions panel, open the Objects book and then the Movie book. Next, open the Methods book. Then find and double-click the `play` action. Notice that code is written for you; all you have to do is set the target for the instance, as shown in Figure 9.27.

17. Click the Insert Target Path button. This will open the Insert Target Path dialog box, as shown in Figure 9.28. Make sure you have Dots chosen for the syntax and Absolute for the path. Highlight the instance name of the movie clip inside the window and click OK. Your action is now complete, so you can close the Actions panel.

18. Repeat steps 16 and 17, except highlight the Stop button and give it a `stop` action.

19. Test your movie! Notice that it takes a second to export. In a real-world situation, you would create a preloader for this. You can see that you've masked the video and that the Play and Stop buttons work.

FIGURE 9.22

The Import Video dialog box.

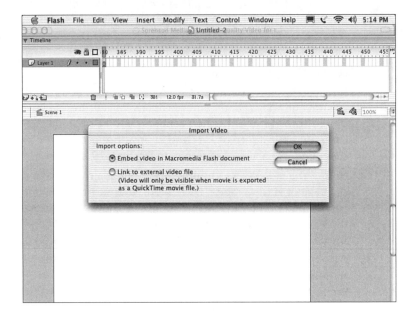

FIGURE 9.23

The Import Video Settings dialog box.

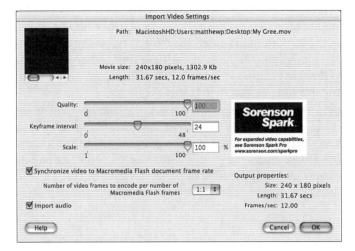

FIGURE 9.24

A warning dialog box concerning the number of frames in the video.

FIGURE 9.25

The mask is directly on top of the video movie clip, and the rectangle has rounded corners.

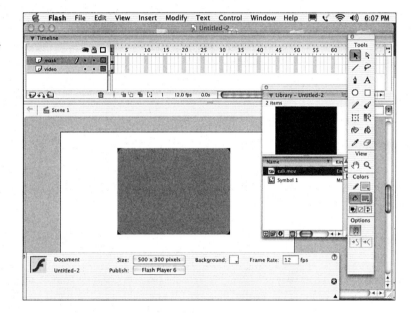

FIGURE 9.26

The Play and Stop buttons under the video clip.

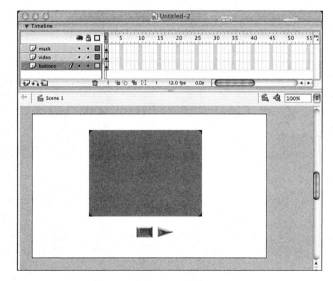

9

ANIMATION
TECHNIQUES AND
DIGITAL VIDEO

FIGURE 9.27

The script that is written for you when you click the play action.

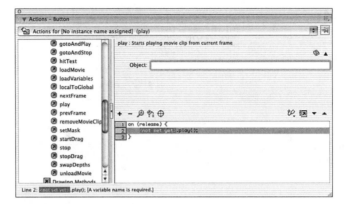

FIGURE 9.28

The Insert Target Path dialog box.

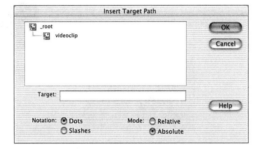

Of course, you can also add fast-forward and rewind buttons using the goto action. This should give you a good understanding of how video is handled in Flash. Remember, you always have the options of animating, scaling, and rotating the video, just to name a few. As long as the video is in a movie clip, everything you can do to a movie clip, you can now do to the video. In fact, if you're not satisfied with the quality of the video, you might consider taking down the alpha of the video, which seems to take away some of the compression artifacts.

Creating QuickTime Movie Controls and a Custom QuickTime Skin

This exercise does require you to have QuickTime Pro. QuickTime Pro is an upgrade (for $29.95) from the standard player edition, but it offers a lot of bang for the buck. It's available from Apple's Web site (http://www.apple.com/quicktime). You will also need an image-creation program, such as Fireworks or Photoshop, and a text editor such as Notepad, simple text, or text edit. This exercise demonstrates a cool way to create a QuickTime movie that looks like your own application. You can change the exterior of the QuickTime player to look the way you want it to. This area of the player you're about to modify is called a *skin*.

Creating a Custom QuickTime Movie

Here are the steps to follow for this exercise:

1. Create a new document. Then choose Modify, Document to bring up the Document Properties dialog box. Make the dimensions of this movie 300[ts]250. Set the frame rate to 15 fps.

2. On the Unleashed companion Web site, download the custom QuickTime files. Choose File, Import and search for the `interface.png` file you downloaded as part of the custom QuickTime files. You'll get a dialog box for PNG import settings. Check the Flatten Image option and then choose OK. Notice that the file is placed on the stage.

3. Create a new layer and name it **video**. With the new video layer selected, choose File, Import and search for the `cali.mov` movie on your computer. Once you find it, choose Open. This will open the Import Video dialog box. Choose Link to External File this time and then click OK. This will launch another dialog box telling how many frames this movie requires. Choose Yes to have Flash extend the timeline for you. Notice that the movie appears on the stage. Position the movie so that the top of the clip is flush with the top of the gray box in the interface, as shown in Figure 9.29.

4. Create a new layer and name it **buttons**. In the Unleashed common library, drag out an instance of the Play and Stop buttons. Place the Play and Stop buttons underneath the video clip.

5. Highlight frame 1 and press F9 on your keyboard. This will open the Actions panel. Open the Actions book, then the Movie Control book, and double-click `stop`. This will stop the movie from playing automatically. Close the Actions panel.

6. Highlight the Play button and press F9 to open the Actions panel. Open the Actions book, then the Movie Control book, and double-click `play`. This will give this button an action of `play` when it is released.

7. Do the same for the Stop button. Highlight the Stop button and press F9 to open the Actions panel. Open the Actions book, then the Movie Control book, and double-click `stop`. This will give the Stop button an action of `stop` when it is released, thus stopping the movie. Notice that you didn't have to target anything; that's because all this is happening on the main timeline.

8. Choose File, Publish Settings. This will open the Publish Settings dialog box. Click the Flash tab. In this section, choose to export using the Flash 4 player, because QuickTime can only understand and is only compatible with Flash 4. Click back to the Formats tab and then check the QuickTime Movie option. Notice that the QuickTime tab appears. For now, the default settings on this tab are fine. To learn more about the QuickTime settings, refer to Chapter 8, "Publishing." Click the Publish button to export the QuickTime movie.

9. In the custom QuickTime files you downloaded earlier, you'll find files named `area_mask.png` and `drag_mask.png`. Make sure these two files, along with the `custom_quick.mov` file, are stored on the desktop.

10. Open a simple text editor such as Notepad, simple text, or text edit. Type the following code:

```
<?xml version="1.0"?>

<?quicktime type="application/x-qtskin"?>

<skin>

<movie src="custom_quick.mov"/>

<contentregion src="area_mask.png"/>

<dragregion src="drag_mask.png"/>

</skin>
```

11. Save the movie as `finished.mov`. This will create a QuickTime movie with the custom interface, as shown in Figure 9.30.

    If you are using Text Edit on the Mac OS X platform, you must choose Edit, Preferences and then make sure the new document format is set to Plain Text and not Rich Text.

12. In QuickTime, choose File, Save As. Name the movie anything you'd like, but it's important to make this movie self-contained. Otherwise, when you move the file off your computer, nothing will appear because it is sourcing everything right now, including the movie and masks.

FIGURE 9.29

The movie clip is flush to the top of the interface box.

FIGURE 9.30

A custom media skin on the QuickTime player.

Approaching ActionScript

By Todd Coulson

IN THIS CHAPTER

In Chapter 9, "Animation Techniques and Digital Video," you learned some techniques for animating using keyframes (that is, placing an object on one frame and then animating across a series of frames). This can often be a timesaver and can give a more realistic look to your animations in a short time. However, you can animate in Flash without using keyframes at all. In fact, this style of animation will allow you to incorporate more interactivity in your projects than using keyframes alone allow. ActionScript is the language that Flash developers use to tell Flash what to do. Actions dictate a set of instructions to Flash to enable your project with more operations. ActionScript can be very simple in nature or highly complex. It all depends on your project's objective. We will start simple in this chapter. However, by the chapter's end, not only will you be able to animate in Flash using ActionScript, but you'll also have a total understanding of the terminology and the rules surrounding the language Flash programmers use.

Object-Oriented Scripting

If you think about people's office skills for a moment, you'll notice many similarities. For instance, many workers can read, write, photocopy, and answer phones. Some of us may be stronger in one area than another, but for the purposes of this example, let's consider everyone as either having a skill or not having a skill. Now, not everyone in an office setting has an equal number of skills. That is why people are placed in departments. Some people might be strong in math skills and are placed in the accounting department. Other workers might be strong in people skills, so they are placed in the sales department. Now imagine that you are the boss of this entire office. Wouldn't it be great if you could just call on a department for a task to be completed correctly for a client? Maybe in some instances you need two or three different departments to accomplish a task for a client. In such a case, you might tell the accounting department to add up some figures for your client's proposal, ask your writing department to draft a report, and then call on your sales team to seal the deal with your client. Tasks would be divided among your company in a fashion similar to Figure 10.1. Notice how some departments are not needed to complete the tasks for the project.

Now think about your office structure in the world of object-oriented programming. You are the boss, so you get to determine what happens and which objects you are going to call upon to complete your project.

Each department would be similar to a *class* in Flash. Classes are groups of data types that control and define the objects of the classes. Just like in the departments in your office, you, the designer, can call on the classes you need to complete a project or action. Figure 10.2 illustrates how a programmer might use objects within a fictitious project. In this example, the programmer has chosen to use movie clip, button, and sound objects in his ActionScript to manipulate the properties in these objects.

FIGURE 10.1

The tasks needed to be performed for this project's completion. Not every department is needed for the project.

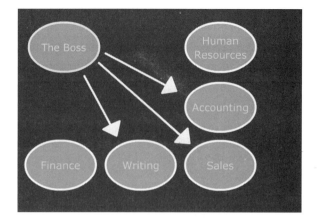

FIGURE 10.2

The Flash programmer has the ability to use different classes of objects to his advantage when developing a project.

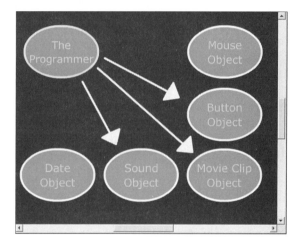

Well then, what is an *object*? Flash has both built-in objects (which basically have their classes created for you and are predefined) and custom objects. Custom objects give you the ability to create your own classes, with their own objects and their own set of properties and methods. To relate this to the example earlier, if you were a boss of a project who needed outside help (none of your departments could handle this set of tasks), you could hire or assemble a team specifically to work on this set of tasks for this particular project. In Figure 10.3 you can see that as a programmer you have the ability to call on classes and objects to perform the tasks you are trying to accomplish.

Figure 10.3

As a programmer, you have the ability to create your own objects and assign properties and methods that work for these objects.

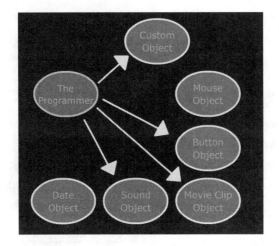

All objects are a collection of properties and methods. Defining these properties and calling these methods will allow you to alter each instance of a particular object that is present in the Flash environment. Objects can be either pure containers of data or graphically represented on the stage of your movie. An example of a data object would be the Date object, which controls the time taken from your system. Calling this object reveals its own Date class properties that can be manipulated. However, nothing will graphically appear on the stage unless you take the data extrapolated from the Date object and place it elsewhere on the stage. All buttons appearing on your stage are graphical instances of the Button class. They have properties that are specific to buttons, but unlike the Date object, they already reside graphically on the stage of your presentation.

Let's inspect your "departments" closer. You may have Earl as an employee. Earl can process all the stacks of paper on his desk in about an hour. He will usually make about 20 mistakes in processing, though. Now Bill takes three hours to process the events but usually makes about four mistakes in his processing. Bill accomplishes his tasks by sorting his papers alphabetically. Earl sorts his stack of papers numerically. If we were relating Earl and Bill to object-oriented programming, their tasks might look like Figure 10.4.

Think of Bill and Earl as different instances of the same object. Bill's properties are different from those of Earl. Also, they have different methods of doing their work, but they still achieve the same tasks. Every object can have different properties. For example, one button instance may be smaller than another button instance. However, they are still from the same class and possess many of the same properties. Notice in Figure 10.5 how one button looks completely different from the other. They are the same object from the same Library member, but they are different instances with different properties.

FIGURE 10.4

The tasks Bill performs are different from those of Earl. These are properties of Bill's work. Also, Bill has a different method of working through his work, much like every class in Flash has different properties and methods that are particular to that class.

	Properties	Methods
Bill	3 hours, 4 mistakes	Alphabetically Ordered
Earl	1 hour, 20 mistakes	Numerically Ordered

FIGURE 10.5

These red buttons are different in size and shape. They are different instances with different height, width, and location properties. However, they are both members of the same object class and also originate from the same Library member.

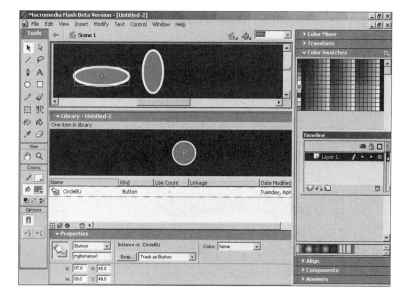

Properties are attributes that create and define an object. For movie clips, this could mean the size of the movie clip and the location of the movie clip. *Methods* are functions assigned to an object that enable the object to carry out specific tasks. These functions could be a single task or multiple tasks, but they will be tasks that are going to be repetitive. Therefore, Flash needs a function to activate that set of commands any time it needs to perform those duties.

Defining classes, objects, methods, and properties are important in being able to define object-oriented programming. Basically, object-oriented programming is the manipulation of object instances through the use of properties and methods available to a particular class.

ActionScript Object Model

Now that we have defined object-oriented programming, let's delve into the rules associated with objects in detail:

- As mentioned previously, objects can either be data objects or graphic items currently located on your stage.

- Top-level objects, such as the `Math` object and the `Date` object, do not require you to create an instance of them in order to use them. Instead, you just use the name of the object and the method following it. This example shows how you would round the number 2.4 to 2:

```
Math.round(2.4);
```

- Built-in objects, such as the `Sound` object, require a new instance of these objects to use them. You would initialize these objects in the following manner:

```
mySound = new Sound();
```

This example shows a variable named `mySound` being equated to the new `Sound` object that is initialized in the statement. It tells Flash that a new `Sound` object is being constructed. This is called a *constructor function*.

- Graphical objects, such as the `MovieClip` object and the `Button` object, can be given an instance name in the Properties panel by clicking them on the stage (any items located on the stage are instances of the items located in your Library). If a `MovieClip` object is created during runtime using either the `attachMovieClip` or `duplicateMovieClip` method, you must give the movie clip an instance name in the method.

- Finally, the graphic objects you create on your stage fall within three categories: movie clips, buttons, and text fields can all be assigned instance names (in the case of text fields, they can also be assigned a variable value) to allow you to control their properties. If you notice a property of these items in the Properties panel, chances are there's a way in ActionScript to control that property at runtime.

The object model in ActionScript allows you to control the objects in Flash. Keep in mind that these objects are not simply visible to you in design mode. These objects are anything that can help you create your project. The objects in your project (the custom and built-in objects) allow you to be more efficient and include more interactivity in your presentations.

Flash's Objects—Movie Clips

The MovieClip object is mentioned constantly when talking about Flash's ActionScript model. That's because of the tremendous power movie clips possess. Think back to Chapter 4, "Flash Animation," which talked about symbols and the Library. You know that movie clips are basically self-contained main timelines. In fact, they actually are their own timelines. With that timeline capability, you can use methods to control a movie clip's play ();, stop();, and gotoAndPlay ("frameName") actions. Furthermore, you have total control of the movie clip's properties, such as position relative to the movie clip's registration point (_x and _y), height (_height) and width (_width), alpha transparency of the clip (_alpha), frames loaded (_framesloaded), and visibility (_visible). What's more, you are not limited to only those properties.

Best of all, movie clips have the ability to talk to each other. Because every movie clip has an instance name, you can call one by name. Therefore, if you are calling an action in clip1, you can tell clip2 to play a different frame and change its visibility to 50 percent. Keep in mind that with objects, ActionScript is intended to heighten your interactivity, so most classes and objects are going to have the ability to interact with each other. Movie clips are no different. You can call on a movie clip from any location in your Flash SWF. You can place actions on buttons, on the root timeline, or even on nested movie clips to tell a particular movie clip to change its properties. This interaction of MovieClip objects is called *addressing*. We'll go deeper into that topic as well as nesting of movie clips later in this chapter. For now, just keep in mind that any movie clip can change properties from any location. Let's try an example using the main timeline.

Exercise 10.1

The starting FLA file for this exercise is a new file. The finished FLA file is 10-01fin.FLA. Here are the steps to follow:

1. Create some artwork on your stage using the graphics tools and select the item you create. I chose to make a circle.

2. With the artwork selected, press the F8 key or choose Insert, Convert to Symbol from the menu options at the top of your screen.

3. This will bring up the Convert to Symbol dialog box. Choose Movie Clip from the three options to choose the type of symbol for your artwork.

4. Choose a name for your movie clip. This will identify your movie clip object in the Library panel. Make sure the name does not conflict with any other Library members in your project.

5. Open your movie clip by double-clicking either the instance on your stage or the library member you just created.

6. Create some animation by clicking on frame 10 of your movie clip timeline, inserting a blank keyframe, and drawing a square. Go to the Properties panel and click the first frame of your timeline. In the Properties panel, choose Shape from the tween options.

7. Create a new layer in your movie clip symbol and name it **actions**. It is a good practice to create a separate layer for your actions. This will make it easy to locate all the actions for a particular frame. Also, when you have several layers in your project, you won't have to scroll through your Timeline panel to find all the actions in a particular problem frame.

8. Create a blank keyframe in the first frame of your new layer. Now go to expert mode in your Actions panel and type the following code:

```
Stop();
```

If you chose to stay in normal mode, choose Actions, MovieControl, Stop to accomplish the same action. This is now your first bit of ActionScript written. Feels good, huh? This is a method used to control the timeline of your movies. No parameters are associated with this action, so there is no need to type anything in the parentheses. You will see later the parentheses can be filled with parameters to further define your actions and methods. I suggest using the expert mode for most of your scripts; however, because you might not feel comfortable typing in the actions yet, I will give you instructions to work in normal mode as well. If you have questions about the normal and expert mode options, see the section titled "Normal Mode and Expert Mode" at the end of this chapter.

My movie clip timeline is shown in Figure 10.6.

9. Go back to the main timeline of your movie by clicking the Scene 1 button located below the timeline. Now, from the main timeline, you're going to make the movie clip play its timeline (remember, movie clips have timelines independent from the main timeline or root-level timeline).

10. In the main timeline, click your movie clip. Then go to the Properties panel for the object you selected. Give your movie clip a unique instance name, such as **myClip**.

11. On the main timeline, make sure there are more frames in your movie than exist in the movie clip. For this example, add 20 frames to the main timeline. On the last frame of your main timeline, type the following script, in a new layer named "actions":

```
myClip.play();
```

12. Press Ctrl+Enter (Cmd+Return on the Mac) to test the movie. You can also access it by going to Control, Test Movie on your menu bar.

FIGURE 10.6

A movie clip timeline with 10 frames and a simple shape tween applied. This is completely independent of the main timeline.

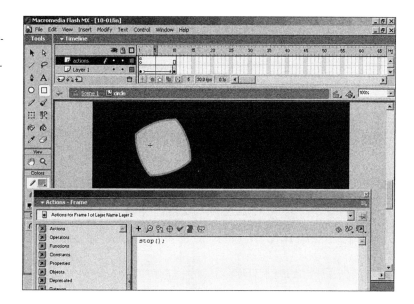

You will notice that the movie plays 20 frames and then plays your movie clip. You are controlling the timeline of the movie clip from the timeline of your movie. You addressed the movie clip you had on your stage by calling the object instance myClip, and then you passed it an action to play its timeline. Mission accomplished! Your first movie clip action has been passed. Save your movie as movieClip.fla so that you can use it in the next example.

Properties

Properties, as mentioned earlier in the chapter, are the attributes that define the instances of objects. Properties are what make instances unique. From within Flash's ActionScript, you access the properties of an object by using the dot operator. This is achieved by typing the object you are trying to access, followed by a dot (.) and then the property you are trying to access. For example, if you were accessing the height of a movie clip that has an instance name of myClip, you would write the following:

```
myClip._height=50;
```

The clip is given a value of 50 pixels. In this case, you use the equals operator (=) and a value that is now associated with the height property of the movie clip instance named myClip.

Properties come in many flavors, and they are specific to an object in your movie. We discussed earlier how a movie clip instance has properties such as height, width, position, and alpha. If, however, you look at the Sound object's properties, you wouldn't find a height or position. A Sound object cannot have a height. This is not a property of the Sound object. However, Macromedia has provided a set of properties specific to the Sound object, such as volume and pan. Therefore, depending on the object, you will have a new set of options to manipulate that object's properties. Let's manipulate the movie you just created to show how the movie clip can change its properties (open the 10.02start.fla file if you are starting from scratch).

Exercise 10.2

The starting FLA file for this exercise is 10-02start.fla. The finished FLA file is 10-02fin.fla. Here are the steps to follow:

1. In the action on the main timeline that plays the movie, delete the code that forces the movie clip to play.
2. Now type the following code in expert mode:

   ```
   myClip._x = myClip._x + 10;
   ```

   If you are creating this in normal mode, choose Actions, Set Variable. Now Flash gives you the option to create an evaluation of two operands. Therefore, in the first blank area, go to Properties, _x. Then, in front of this property, you need to select an object instance to affect. Click the target path button, shown in Figure 10.7, and choose the myClip instance of the movie clip object. Do the same thing for the second blank area, except add "+10" to the end of it.
3. Test your movie by pressing Ctrl+Enter (or Cmd+Return on the Mac).

Target Path Button

FIGURE 10.7

This button, when clicked, will activate the target path you desire.

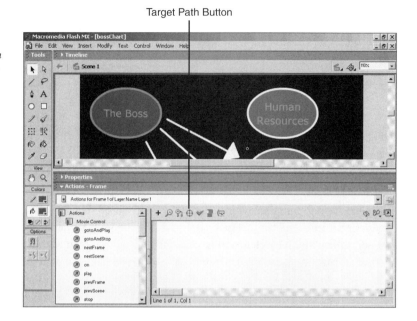

FIGURE 10.7

This button, when clicked, will activate the target path you desire.

Notice how your movie clip moves 10 pixels every time it reaches the action frame on the main timeline. That's because you have altered the x location property for the instance named myClip. Congratulations, you have completed your first animation using ActionScript.

You can also create properties for your object. Suppose you have an object that doesn't have a particular property that you would like to access. You can use the addProperty method to add that property to the object, and you can use a function to assign the property a value. Afterward, your newly added property would be another attribute of the object. The addProperty method is written using the following structure:

```
myClip.addProperty("zProp", this.getZ, this.setZ);
```

Here, myClip represents the path to the object we are adding the property to. zProp is the name of the new property. this.getZ represents the path to a function that retrieves the value of the property, and this.setZ is the path to a function that is invoked to set the value of the property. This style is referred to as the *getter/setter properties*. These are properties created using get and set methods. The second property gets a function to be used, and the third argument of the method retrieves a function to set the property. This is a complex capability of ActionScript and is beyond the scope of this chapter; however, you need to know that it exists. If you would like to learn more about addProperty, check the reference index at the end of this book or other property examples in other chapters.

Variables

Variables are the containers that store your data. They can be set, changed, and updated. Variables can store any data type, which means that you may have a variable that is storing a string one moment and then decide later in your movie that you want it to store a number. The values associated with variables are located on the right side of the equal sign when the variable is initialized or later changed in your project.

It is good form to initialize your variables in the front of your project. Usually on frame 1 of your project, you can just give an initial value to your variable so that Flash has it available when you later change this value. It is also a good organizational technique to do this, because then you have a running list of the variables you are using in your project.

Here are some rules of variable use:

- A variable cannot be a keyword or ActionScript literal. For example, do not name your variable "break". ActionScript will reject it.

- A variable must be unique within its scope, meaning that if you have a variable defined in a block of code, you cannot create another variable with the same name. The variable has to be unique unto itself.

- A variable must be declared a value before you can use it to extract information.

- Variables are always changeable.

- Local variables are available within their own block of code and are created using the var statement within a function. After the block of code is finished, local variables are destroyed by Flash.

- Timeline variables are available to any timeline using a target path. When declaring variables in the timeline, both Set Variable and the assignment operator (=) accomplish the same thing. Using the target path requires the same rules of addressing that pertain to movie clip addressing.

- Global variables are available to any timeline, regardless of their target path. Global variables must be declared with the _global identifier.

- You do not have to specify which data type (for example, a string, number, or boolean) is associated with the variable in question. Many programming languages require you to assign a data type to a particular variable and not interchange data types. In Flash, you may switch data types at a whim. Although it may not always behoove you to do so, because your project can get very confusing if you continuously mix data types.

- Variables can be changed by Flash when it deems necessary. Therefore, if you are assigning a string to be combined with a number, Flash will recognize that the two values are not of the same data type and will attempt to combine them.

With all these rules, it is easy to get confused, so let's try a few `trace` actions and see why they work as variables and why they might not. `Trace` actions allow you to view statements you choose inside the Output window during runtime at the moment the `trace` action is called.

Exercise 10.3

The starting FLA file for this exercise is `10-03start.fla`. The finished FLA file is `10-03fin.fla`. Here are the steps to follow:

1. Open `10.03start.fla` and delete the code previously created on the main timeline.

2. On frame 30 in the main timeline, type the following code:

```
x=3;
trace("x has a value of " + x);
stop();
```

3. Make sure to keep the second x outside the quotation marks preceded by the + operator. Also, if you want to accomplish this using normal mode, choose Actions, Variables, Set Variable from your Actions panel and then simply enter **x** in the first location and **3** in the second location. Then choose Actions, Miscellaneous Actions, Trace to set a message to be placed in the `trace` action.

Your `10-03start.fla` file should look similar to Figure 10.8.

After testing the movie, you'll notice that the Output window appears once the main timeline hits the frame you placed the action on. The message that appears is "x has a value of 3." This is because the second "x" is outside the quotation marks. Flash recognizes this and considers the first part of the message to be a string literal. The second part of the message is a variable that Flash inserts a value for to complete the message. Because of the plus sign, Flash concatenates the two messages.

10

APPROACHING ACTIONSCRIPT

FIGURE 10.8

The timeline with a frame action attached to the end. The Actions panel includes the actions you just wrote.

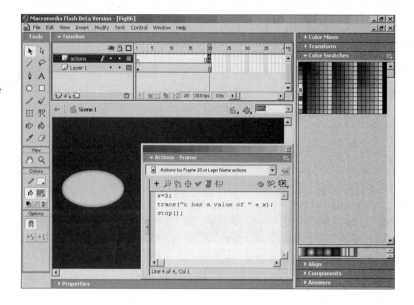

Let's try another direction with this example that should be simple to create. This time, write your actions in reverse, delete the stop action, and see what happens. Your actions should look like this:

```
trace("x has a value of " + x);
x=3;
```

Notice how upon testing the movie the message in the Output window does not include the number 3 at the end of it on the first pass through the action block. That is because we broke one of the rules discussed earlier. You cannot call a variable for a value before it has been assigned a value. The second time the movie loops through, the variable has been assigned a value, so you get the full and complete message (that is, if you remembered to delete the `stop()` action from the last example).

Now let's use a variable in a conditional statement to affect the movie clip. This next example shows you a simple real-world application for using variables.

Exercise 10.4

The starting FLA file for this exercise is `10-04start.fla`. The finished FLA file is `10-04fin.fla`. Here are the steps to follow:

1. In the movie `10-04start.fla`, delete the actions in the main timeline and type the following actions in its place, in expert mode:

```
if (x==3){
    MyClip.play();
}
```

To access the `if` statement using the normal mode, go to Actions, Conditions/Loops, If. After choosing this option, you should see a condition entry box, enter `x==3` in this box. Make sure you include two equal signs. This is how Flash determines the difference between an assignment and a conditional comparison of items. One equal sign equates a value to the variable. Two equal signs compare the two values.

2. Now create a circle using your drawing tools, press F8 to assign it as a new symbol, choose button as the type of symbol, and then give it a unique name for your library reference.

3. Click the button and create another piece of code to toggle the value of the variable:

```
on (release) {
    if (x==3){
        x=0;
    }else{
        x=3;
    }
}
```

The `else` statement can be accessed in normal mode using the same Actions, Conditions/Loops options. The catchall phrase of `else` states that if the value of x is not equal to 3, it will make the variable equal to 3. Your Flash interface should look similar to Figure 10.9.

4. Give your button an instance name. This is not required, but you should get in the habit of naming all the instances brought to your screen for later reference.

5. Test your movie using Ctrl+Enter (Cmd+Return on the Mac).

10

APPROACHING ACTIONSCRIPT

FIGURE **10.9**

The timeline with a conditional statement attached to the button. This code toggles between the two values for the variable. Notice that the button is selected to enable you to see and type actions in this button instance.

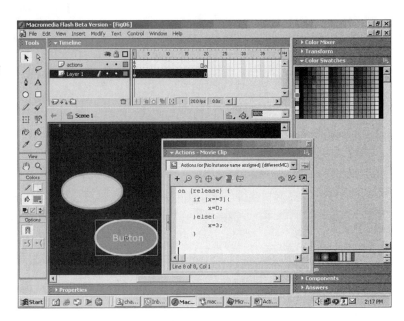

Notice that every time your movie hits the code, it will not animate your movie clip initially because your variable is not associated with the value of 3. If you click the toggle button, the variable's value is changed to the number 3, thus allowing the conditional to work, which in turn allows the animation to occur within the movie clip every time the frame script is tripped. To cease the animation, you simply have to click the toggle button again. This forces the variable's value back to 0, and the if statement in the timeline evaluates to False again.

Methods

As mentioned earlier, methods are functions that carry out specific tasks for an object. Methods can either be created or used from methods built in to the ActionScript model. The following is a method built in to Flash's ActionScript:

```
gotoAndPlay(20);
```

Flash knows that when gotoAndPlay is encountered, a task is going to be carried out. In this case, 20 is a parameter of the goto method. Furthermore, Flash knows that the parameters passed can be in two forms. The first is a number; Flash will take that number and interpret it as a frame number of the timeline specified. The other parameter accepted for the goto method is a string. Flash recognizes a string in the goto method as a frame label.

Methods are also specifically engineered for the object class they are a part of. For example, `getDate` and `getMinutes` are both methods of the `Date` object. Date, time, minutes, and seconds are not at all properties or methods of the `MovieClip` object. Instead, the `MovieClip` object uses methods to carry out its tasks such as `attachMovie` and `loadMovie`.

To find the methods for a particular built-in class, go into your ActionScript panel, click the Objects drop-down list, then choose a category: Core, Movie, Client/Server, or Authoring. Under each of these categories of objects you will find the built-in object classes. Further delving into the object category divulges the methods available for a particular object. Therefore choosing Objects, Core, Date, Methods will divulge all the built-in methods of the `Date` object.

You will also see a set of methods available by choosing Objects, Movie, Movie Clip, Methods. You'll notice further down on the list the `play` method of the `MovieClip` object, which we have used in previous examples.

Functions

Functions are blocks of code that are reusable. Functions can be passed parameters, which are bits of information used within the function's set of actions. Functions are useful because they allow you to write miles of code and call on that block of code anywhere in your project. They are similar to variables in use, because they still require the use of a target path to call them. Functions can also return values back to the programmer, and the programmer can use a function simply to perform a set of tasks on a project.

Functions, like methods and classes, come in both the built-in and custom flavors. The built-in functions can be found in the Actions panel. They include but are not limited to `Boolean`, `escape`, `eval`, `getVersion`, and `String`. Each of these built-in functions can assist you when you want a specific task accomplished.

Custom functions can be created in the following format:

```
function myFunctionName (myArg1, myArg2){
    trace("this is where any actions can go");
    trace("Flash is not limited");
    trace("by the number of actions");
    trace("in a function block");
    x=5;
    trace(x);
    trace(myArg1);
    trace(myArg2);
}
```

Notice first that the word `function` starts you off in the creation of your code. It is followed by the unique name you give to your function. This is followed by a set of parentheses. The items within the parentheses are the parameters the function requires to perform all its tasks. The parameters will be given to the function from the action that calls upon the function (we'll discuss that in a moment). Notice also that you can have as many statements in your function as needed to accomplish your tasks. At the end of your tasks, you create a variable, trace the variable, and then trace both of the parameters of the function. All these variables are limited to the use of the function. They are locally created and cannot be used in other code blocks in other places in your project. These locally created variables are destroyed after the function has ended its tasks. If x were a timeline or global variable, it would have to be called using the target path or the `_global` identifier.

To call on a function, you call it by name from another location in your project. This does not mean you cannot call a function from the same frame as the function, but you would not want to call the function, obviously, from within the same block of code as your function. This could cause damaging errors and isn't logical programming anyway. Therefore, to call the `myFunctionName` function, you would address it much the same way you address variables and movie clips:

```
thePath.myFunctionName(15, "myName");
```

Notice that two parameters are passed to the function. The first, `15`, will now be assigned to the `myArg1` parameter, and the `myName` string will be assigned to the `myArg2` parameter. Let's try an example.

Exercise 10.5

The starting FLA file for this exercise is `10-05start.fla`. The finished FLA file is `10-05fin.fla`. Here are the steps to follow:

1. You guessed it—delete all the code from the main timeline and from the button in the previous example or in `10-05start.fla`.

2. Click a blank keyframe and in the actions frame in the first frame of the movie, type the following code to create the function:

```
function myFunctionName (myArg1, myArg2){
    x=2;
    trace("my name is " + myArg1);
    trace("I own " + myArg2 + " cases of beer");
    trace("I own " + x + " cases of soda");
}
```

> To access `function` in normal mode, choose Actions, User-Defined Functions, Function. Also type **cases of root beer if you are under 21**.
>
> 3. Now on your button place another `onRelease` action (which can be done in normal mode through Objects, Movie, Button, Events, onRelease) and type the following code:
>
> ```
> on (release) {
>     myFunctionName("Todd", 1);
> }
> ```
>
> This statement passes the parameters that will be used in the function. It passes two: `Todd` and `1` (by the way, type your own name if you prefer not to have my name appear in the Output window).
>
> 4. Test your movie using Ctrl+Enter (Cmd+Return on the Mac).

Hey, check it out! You now have a function that places code into the Output window every time you click the button. The code on your button passes the parameters to the function that is located on frame 1 (so you do not need to be on the frame to access the function). The function takes the parameters and executes each line of code.

Let's do one more thing with functions. Here's the next exercise.

Exercise 10.6

The starting FLA file for this exercise is `10-06start.fla`. The finished FLA file is `10-06fin.fla`. Here are the steps to follow:

1. Click your button and press F8.
2. Make the contents of the button nested inside a movie clip and give the new movie clip a unique name for the Library.
3. Give the new movie clip instance an instance name for consistency.
4. Test your movie and click the button.

Oops! You can no longer access the function. That's because you are no longer calling the function from the same timeline. This could be remedied by addressing the function from your button to the main timeline. You could do this by calling the function like this:

```
on (release) {
_root.MyFunctionName("Todd", 1);
}
```

888

8

88

Because you placed _root at the front of the statement calling the function, you have addressed the function properly. We'll talk more about addressing later in the chapter. Now when you test your movie, the button works again.

String Literals Versus Expressions

An expression is any two values that can be evaluated into a single value. An expression is made up of *operands*, or data types that are compared or altered with operators. Operators are the symbols that carry out the comparisons, such as the equal sign (=) or the addition sign (+). Operands could be numbers, strings, or other data types. For example, 1+1=2 is an expression. The 1, 1, and 2 are operands, whereas the + and = signs are the operators. Similarly, z=x+y is also an expression. Flash would analyze all three operands (z, x, and y) and would determine whether a value can be extracted from the operands. Then, using the operators (+ and =), Flash would evaluate the expression.

A string literal is any sequence of characters, numbers, and punctuation marks enclosed in quotation marks. Flash sees these characters as a literal value, meaning that it takes exactly what is encased in the quotation marks as the data. You can use the + operator to concatenate two strings. For example, "My name" + "is Steve" = will evaluate to "My name is Steve". This shouldn't be entirely new; we have used strings in all the trace actions performed thus far in this chapter.

The problem that can be a speed bump for many programmers occurs when the data types become intermixed. If you were to create two variables—one a string and the other a number—Flash will attempt to combine the two data types into one evaluation. If your first variable is myString with a value of "My name is ", and your second variable is myNumber with a value of 32, Flash will combine these two data types:

```
myX= myString+32;
trace(myX);
```

The resulting value of myX would be "My name is 32". This might not yield the you were looking for as a Flash programmer. This is because different data types combined in one statement might just add the number 32 onto the end of the string item. Usually "My name is " would be associated with a name of a person, not a number data type. This is not to say this string isn't correct. Just know that Flash will interpret different data types in different ways. Refer to the "Operators and Operands" section for more information on how Flash refers to its statements.

Addressing and Dot Syntax

Addressing is probably the single most important topic of this chapter. Many problems for novice Flash programmers surround the issue of addressing. Now that most of the terms of Flash ActionScript are floating around in your head, we are going to attempt to have objects, variables, functions, and methods all interact one another through the use of addressing.

Dot syntax is the way in which you use ActionScript to reference items in a project. Items in Flash are separated through the use of the dot (.) operator. Objects, variables, and functions are all slaves to the main timeline. The main timeline is the source for all your communications with items. It is through the use of the dot operator that you can separate items and retrieve certain pieces of data from other parts of your project. Objects, variables, and functions can all be mixed when using dot syntax. However, usually the dot syntax leads off with the object you are aiming to affect. What's more, you can create a nesting of objects and items in your project. For example, you might need to have a movie clip located inside another movie clip. One clip might dictate occurrences for the other clip. Furthermore, you may decide to create timeline variables for each movie clip. Therefore, to reference each of those variables, you might write code similar to

```
_root.myClip1.myClip2.myVar2
```

or

```
myClip1.myClip2.myVar2
```

We'll get into the differences between these two statements later, but both achieve the same thing. They search for myClip1 (movie clip object); then within that clip Flash searches for myClip2 (movie clip object). Finally, inside the myClip2 timeline Flash retrieves the value for myVar2 (a variable). Notice how each object and variable is separated by the dot operator. This makes it easy for Flash to check the hierarchy of objects to find bits of information.

It is also worth mentioning the aliases used in dot syntax. Anytime _root is used in an expression, the statement is referring to the root-level timeline or the main timeline.

The _parent alias refers to a movie clip that is nested inside another movie clip. In the previous example, myClip2 is the child movie clip to myClip1. Therefore, if you were issuing actions from within myClip2 and wanted to affect the properties of myClip1, you could refer to it using the _parent alias.

10

APPROACHING ACTIONSCRIPT

Finally, note the use of `this` in Flash. The `this` keyword is used to refer to the movie clip you are currently calling an action from. Therefore, if you wanted to change the x position of `myClip1` and you were calling the action on a frame from within `myClip1`, you could simply write the expression in the following way:

`this._x`

This refers to the movie clip the action is currently being called from and the `_x` property of that clip. Figure 10.10 displays the use of the `_parent`, `_root`, and `this` aliases for referring to movie clip objects placed on the main timeline. Make note of where the action is placed. The references are for if you are targeting that clip in relation to where the action is being called.

FIGURE 10.10

Using the `_parent`, `_root`, *and* `this` *aliases for referring to movie clip objects placed on the main timeline.*

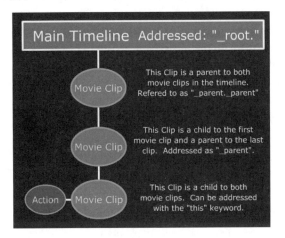

A discussion of dot syntax would not be complete without mentioning how Flash came to include the dot operator as the separator of items. Back in Flash 4, when ActionScript was first being used as a programming language, there was no dot operator. Instead, the slash character (`/`) was used to separate items. Therefore, instead of writing `myClip1.myClip2.myVar2`, you would write `myClip1/myClip2/myVar2` instead. This was once the standard of coding for Flash. It has become a depreciated method of addressing objects in Flash, because Flash has adopted the JavaScript method of separating items with the dot operator. This is important in case you ever need to program for a Flash 4 project or you open a Flash 4 project and need to decipher the code.

Absolute Addressing

Let's think about how we dialed our phones to communicate with each other back in the 80s before cell phones required us to dial area codes for local calls. Would you ever pick up a phone and just talk into it? Well, it would be a really quick call with the dial tone if you did. You would probably not talk to anyone either, except for the recording that says "If you would like to place a call, please hang up." Therefore, you would dial a number to get a hold of your friend. Depending where your friend lived during the 80s, you might dial either a 7- or 11-digit number. If your friend lived next door, you would probably dial seven numbers to contact him. If he lived across the country, you would be forced to dial 11 digits to get connected to his number. Furthermore, you would dial specific numbers to get a hold of a specific individual household. The wrong numbers might lead you to the wrong household. Notice in Figure 10.11 how there are two different ways of communicating by telephone: inserting 7-digit numbers and inserting 11-digit numbers. Flash also has two different types of addressing individual pieces of data or objects: relative addressing and absolute addressing.

FIGURE 10.11

The two different ways of communicating by telephone correspond to the two different ways of addressing individual pieces of data or objects in Flash.

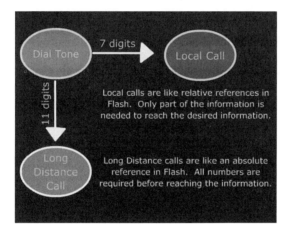

Flash isn't much different. If you do not use addressing, Flash will not connect you to the piece of information you want. Without addressing, you can only work with data on the timeline where your action is called. To address an object in any timeline, you have to call upon the instance name of the object targeted. Furthermore, you can use either relative addressing or absolute addressing to gain access to the information you want to control.

First, an absolute address is based off the main timeline. All communications between objects, variables, and methods must first reference the main timeline, _level0, or the _root-level timeline of the SWF. Absolute addressing, unlike relative addressing, does not concern itself with the location of where the action takes place or with the controlling timeline. It simply tracks down your targeted timeline relative to its position in comparison to the root timeline (in this case, *position* refers to the hierarchy, not the actual x and y positions on the stage). Therefore, if your controlling timeline is located inside a

10

APPROACHING ACTIONSCRIPT

movie clip, you are going to reference the main timeline and then the objects connected to the main timeline to find the targeted item. These concepts are illustrated in Figure 10.12.

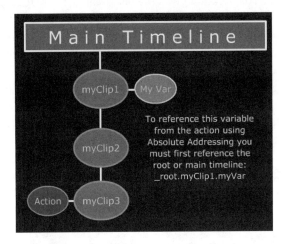

In this figure, notice the relation between the variable, the targeted variable, and the action location, which is inside a movie clip named myClip3. We have no need to refer-ence myClip3 or myClip2 because they are not a part of the hierarchy needed to find the variable. The variable is located in myClip1, a movie clip located on the root-level time-line. Therefore, we only need to reference the root timeline and myClip1 to find the vari-able information contained in the variable named myVar.

The hierarchy is the sequence in which items are relationally spaced on your root level timeline.

In Figure 10.13, the variable is located in myClip2, the second movie clip in the hierar-chy of objects. Therefore, now we have to reference the root-level timeline first, then the first movie clip (myClip1), then the second movie clip (myClip2), and finally the vari-able myVar to retrieve the targeted value.

Figure 10.14 shows a change in the location of the action. Changes in action location, relative to the variable or object targeted, are not integral to the path of an absolute tar-get. Absolute targets are only relative to the main timeline. Therefore, this sample path does not change from the first absolute address example in Figure 10.12. The target to the variable would remain _root.myClip1.myVar or _level0.myClip1.myVar. The sec-ond reference is an alternative that is usually used when you have multiple timelines loaded into your movie. Each time you load a movie onto your SWF timeline, another level is built.

FIGURE 10.13

The variable's location is within myClip2, so the absolute path starting with the root-level timeline would be `_root.myClip1.my Clip2.myVar`*.*

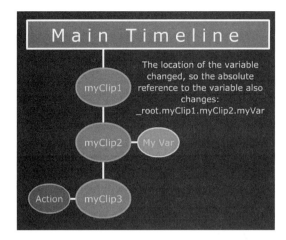

FIGURE 10.14

This figure represents the way actions call on movie clips through an absolute reference. Notice the location of the action and the resulting variable being targeted.

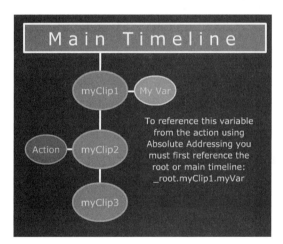

Here, the location of the variable is the same as the first example of absolute addressing. Therefore, the path to find the targeted variable does not change. Absolute addressing always follows the path via the root-level timeline. The only thing that changes in this example is the location of the action, which does not have a bearing on the path to the targeted item.

Let's say the variable is located within the root-level timeline. How would you reference that target path to the variable? It's actually quite easy. Based on the previous figures, you should assume that you would only have to reference the root-level timeline and then the variable. This would read as `_root.myVar`.

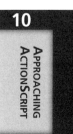

Relative Addressing

Relative addressing as a concept is a lot harder to understand than absolute addressing. This is because relative addressing attempts to target the object using a relative path. The relative path is based first off the location of the action issued or the controlling timeline. From the controlling timeline, you must provide the path to the object you are targeting.

Look at Figure 10.15. You will notice that the action is within myClip1 and the variable myVar is within myClip2. Therefore, there's no need to reference the _root timeline or myClip3 in the target path. The target path consists of three items in this instance: MyClip1.myClip2.myVar. This is because relative addressing communicates with those objects relative to where the action was called.

FIGURE 10.15

The first example of relative addressing. Notice the position of the variable in relation to the action's location. The quickest path to the action is the path that must be provided to Flash.

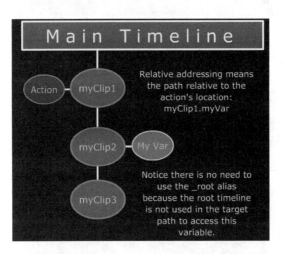

In Figure 10.16 you see a reference to the _parent alias. This is highly useful because, regardless of where the action is called, it will always reference the movie clip that's a parent to the present clip. Therefore, if you move the action, it will always affect the movie clip one level above the action.

Compare Figure 10.16 to Figure 10.17 and notice how the target path does not change. However, the targeted movie clip and the targeted variable within the movie clip will change. The _parent and this keywords allow you to write scripts that can be dropped into any movie clip to affect either the current clip (using this) or the clip one level above (using _parent).

FIGURE 10.16

References to _parent will target one level above the action.

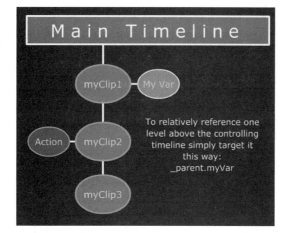

FIGURE 10.17

The _parent keyword is still used, but the clip it affects has changed: the variable is found in myClip1 instead of myClip2.

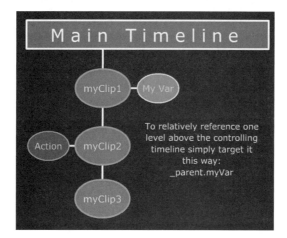

The `this` keyword, as illustrated in Figure 10.18, always targets the current movie clip, but it's more versatile than referencing directly to the clip, as in the first relative addressing example. That's because you do not directly have to call the current clip by an instance name. By saying `this`, you can reuse code on other clips that you want to have similar actions.

Also, note that in all the relative examples we did not directly reference the main timeline. In the second example, we did indirectly reference the main timeline with the use of `_parent._parent` alias references. This seeks the timeline two levels above the action occurrence. Two levels above in the second example turns out to be the main timeline. However, the fact that the main timeline was never directly referenced is in direct conflict to the way in which we referenced items using absolute addressing. Using absolute

10

APPROACHING ACTIONSCRIPT

addressing, you are not allowed to use the this or _parent keywords. Furthermore, absolute addressing is basically set in stone. Moving clips in the target path would break the communication to the clip you're targeting. However, moving the action or the controlling timeline does not alter the target path. In relative addressing, moving the controlling timeline will alter the path unless either the _parent or this keywords are used.

FIGURE 10.18

The this keyword enables you to reference the current movie clip and then refer to other movie clips connected to the current clip in the hierarchy.

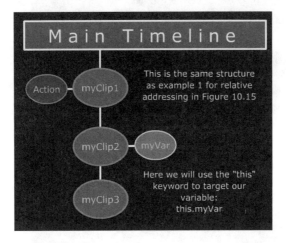

Addressing from Within Nested Movie Clips

Usually the objects that you will target in your path are going to be movie clip objects. It is possible to nest several movie clips inside one another. *Nesting* is a term used to describe the relationship between one movie clip located on the timeline of another movie clip that resides on the main timeline. Whenever two or more movie clips are nested, the movie clips closest to the timeline becomes the parent to the movie clips located farther away from the main timeline. Refer back to Figure 10.10 to see a parent/child relationship.

Now that you have a graphical idea of how nested movie clips, relative addressing, and absolute addressing work, let's attempt to put together some of these relationships in an actual example.

I have provided some artwork on the Web site that will get you started. Open the EastCoast.fla file. Immediately upon opening it, you should notice there are three movie clips on the main timeline, as shown in Figure 10.19. I have placed them in different layers to allow you to see them better. Each movie clip owns an instance name that describes the region of the East Coast by location. The instance names include northEast, middleStates, and southEast. All three of these movie clips are the first movie clip objects in the hierarchy. Now click inside one of these timelines to see how I edited each of the timelines on the first level of the hierarchy. Double-click the northEast movie clip to reveal its timeline.

FIGURE 10.19

Three movie clips located on the root-level timeline.

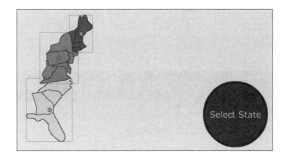

Immediately you will notice that each state is also its own movie clip and owns its own timeline. Therefore, each of the states is nested inside the northEast movie clip timeline. However, each of the states also has its own timeline that can perform animations—just like the northEast timeline can perform animations of its own.

Double-clicking one of the states will show you that the state is nested in the northEast clip. You can see this hierarchy of movie clips along the bottom left of your timeline (see Figure 10.20 for a location of that hierarchy).

FIGURE 10.20

The hierarchy of the root-level timeline Scene 1, movie clip northEast and the movie clip ME. This illustrates a nested movie clip structure.

Currently none of the animations will play in the SWF file, but you should notice the animations have been created for each region and state. The animation will make the state larger and then reduce it back to its original position. I have also included a single button. Currently, it is located on the main timeline. However, you are going to move it around the FLA and place scripts on that button to affect the different movie clips in the scene. You will notice if you click on the button that some scripts have already been started for you. I have separated out in a comment the types of scripts that will be used for absolute references and relative references. Therefore, you can use those comments as a cheat sheet. Just copy and paste the script you want into the body of the script (meaning outside the /* and */ comment symbols) to activate the code.

Absolute Addressing Examples

In the next example, we will examine the EastCoast.fla file in an attempt to see how absolute addressing works.

Exercise 10.7

The starting FLA file for this exercise is EastCoast.fla. The finished FLA file is 10-07fin.fla. Here are the steps to follow:

1. On the button, take the absolute reference for a region and copy and paste it into your button script.

2. Now change regionName to northEast. This is the absolute path to the northEast clip to play its timeline. If you are writing the code on your own, the path for this example should read as follows:

   ```
   _root.northEast.play();
   ```

3. Test the movie.

Notice how the North East region animates, remains there for a moment, and then animates back into position. That's because you sent a play method to the movie clip named northEast, which instructs the clip to play its timeline.

Now pick your favorite northeastern state, because you are going to attempt to make it animate next.

Exercise 10.8

The starting FLA file for this exercise is EastCoast.fla. The finished FLA file is 10-08fin.fla. Here are the steps to follow:

1. On the button, take the absolute reference for a state and copy and paste it into your button script.

2. Now change `regionName` to `northEast` and change `stateName` to `MA` or the state initials of your choice (that is, the instance name of the state movie clip). In this instance, we are going to target two movie clips, and the second one we are going to tell to play its timeline. The path for this example should read as follows:

```
_root.northEast.MA.play();
```

3. Test the movie.

Now you will notice that after testing your movie, the state of Massachusetts will animate. That's because you made an absolute reference to make the nested movie clip MA play its timeline.

Remember, absolute addressing works from the main timeline to the targeted movie clip. Now we're going to prove how moving the location of the action will not affect the script you have written.

Exercise 10.9

The starting FLA file for this exercise is `EastCoast.fla`. The finished FLA file is `10-09fin.fla`. Here are the steps to follow:

1. Click the button and press Ctrl+X (Cmd+X on the Mac) to cut this button from the root-level timeline.

2. Double-click the middleStates movie clip and paste (Ctrl+V on PC or Cmd+V on the Mac) the button into the movie clip scene for middleStates. You might want to paste it onto its own layer. The button must reside on all the frames of the movie clip so that it is always present on the stage.

3. Go back to scene 1 and test the movie.

The great state of Massachusetts still animates. You were still able to affect the northEast timeline from within the middleStates timeline with the same code you used from the main timeline. This is because you used an absolute reference to the targeted movie clip.

Relative Addressing Examples

Now delete the code you have written on the button (if you pasted it from the cheat sheet, just paste it back to its previous location within the comments). Look at the choices for relative addressing. You will notice there are no references to the _root timeline. The first example we'll cover references directly to a movie clip.

Exercise 10.10

The starting FLA file for this exercise is `EastCoast.fla`. The finished FLA files are `10-10Afin.fla` and `10-10Bfin.fla`. Here are the steps to follow:

1. Place the first relative sample script for the button inside the code block and outside the comment.

2. Copy and paste the button back on the main timeline of your movie, like it was originally.

3. Replace `regionName` with `southEast`. Now the path is complete. Remember, relative addressing is relative to where the action is being called, so you do not need to reference the `_root` timeline because the region is one level away from the action in the hierarchy of objects. Your path to the movie clip should read like this:

   ```
   southEast.play();
   ```

4. Test your movie.

5. Now just to prove that relative addressing is relative to where the action is, move your button without changing the script. Cut the button from the main timeline and paste it into the northEast movie clip.

6. Test your movie.

Notice that the button does not work in the second part of this example, but it did work in the first part. That's because in the first part there's a movie clip named southEast one level away from the controlling movie clip (or the clip containing the target path action). Once you moved the clip into the northEast movie clip, however, Flash began searching one level away from where the action is in the northEast movie clip. The only movie clips located one level away from the northEast clip are ME, NH, VT, MA, CT, and RI. Because it does not find the movie clip reference, the button does not work. Try changing the reference to one of the states to see the state animate from where the button is located. Your path should look something like this:

```
CT.play();
```

Now let's run through some quick examples to show how the `this` keyword and the `_parent` alias work.

Exercise 10.11

The starting FLA file for this exercise is `EastCoast.fla`. The finished FLA file is `10-11fin.fla`. Here are the steps to follow:

1. Place your button inside a state of your choice.
2. Copy the button script for _parent into the body of your code. If you are writing the code by hand, just type the following:

   ```
   _parent.play();
   ```
3. Test your movie.
4. Now to prove that the parent will work one level above in the hierarchy, move your button into another state in a different region. Do not change the code on your button.
5. Test your movie.

What just happened? You have written a relative reference that can work in any movie clip you desire. It will always cause the timeline one level above to play its timeline. If you want the main timeline to play from within one of the states, you would use the *_parent._*parent reference. Because we do not have an animation on this timeline, this will not be demonstrated here.

For the last example, delete the code for _parent and paste the code for this into the body of the code on your button.

Exercise 10.12

The starting FLA file for this exercise is EastCoast.fla. The finished FLA file is 10-12fin.fla. Here are the steps to follow:

1. Add some code after this to affect the location of the movie clip. For this example, add 100 pixels to the x location of the movie clip. Your code should look like this:

   ```
   this._x=this._x +100;
   ```
2. Place the button on any movie clip you wish.
3. Test your movie.

Look at that! The clip is moved 100 pixels every time the button is clicked. That's because you told the current movie clip to change its x position (that is, its location of the horizontal plane). Notice also that because the button is part of the movie clip, it will move 100 pixels as well.

10

APPROACHING
ACTIONSCRIPT

ActionScript Structure

Now that you're starting to get an idea of how you can affect different clips, functions, buttons, properties, and variables in a scene, you need to understand better the structure of writing ActionScript in Flash.

Operators and Operands

As mentioned earlier, operators are the symbols in Flash that combine items. The items that operators combine are called *operands*. Operators are located in the Actions panel under Operators. The operands can be variables, target paths, strings, numbers, booleans, and so on. Flash uses the operators to determine how to evaluate the operands that surround a particular operator. For example, the + operator combines two items. The items could be stings, as in this example:

```
"My name is " + "Todd"
```

This evaluates to My name is Todd.

Numbers can also be used, as in the following example:

```
5+x=z;
```

This example uses two variables, which are also operands, and it uses two operators: + and =. The + operator combines the 5 and x operands, where x would represent a variable value that's determined earlier in the code of your Flash movie. Then, the = operator equates the combined value and puts it in the variable z, the third operand.

A set of rules is associated to each operator. Flash must determine how multiple operators will work in conjunction with each other. It's kind of like when you're little and are visiting the amusement park. You push and shove your sister to get on the rides before her. Well, operators are pushing and shoving each other to be the first or last used. This is called *operator precedence*, which is the order in which operators are read. When two or more of the same operators are used, there will be a different order to how those operators are used. This is called *operator associativity*. Certain operators are read left to right; other operators are read right to left. Table 10.1 provides a list of operators and their respective precedence and associativity. The operators at the top have the most precedence.

TABLE 10.1   Key Operators and Related Associativity

Operator	Description	Associativity
+	Unary plus.	Right to left
-	Unary minus.	Right to left
~	Bitwise one's complement.	Right to left
!	Logical NOT.	Right to left
not	Logical NOT (Flash 4).	Right to left
++	Postincrement. Adds 1 to a value.	Left to right
- -	Postdecrement. Subtracts 1 from a value.	Left to right
( )	Function call. Parameters are usually passed here.	Left to right
[ ]	Array element. Items in arrays are placed here.	Left to right
.	Structure member or dot operator.	Left to right
++	Preincrement. Adds 1 to a value.	Right to left
- -	Predecrement. Subtracts 1 from a value.	Right to left
new	Allocates an object.	Right to left
delete	Deallocates an object.	Right to left
typeof	Type of object.	Right to left
void	Returns an undefined value.	Right to left
*	Multiplication of values.	Left to right
/	Division of values.	Left to right
%	Modulo.	Left to right
+	Addition.	Left to right
add	String concatenation (formerly &).	Left to right
-	Subtraction.	Left to right
<<	Bitwise shift left.	Left to right
>>	Bitwise shift right.	Left to right
>>>	Bitwise shift right (unsigned).	Left to right
<	Less than.	Left to right
<=	Less than or equal to.	Left to right
>	Greater than.	Left to right
>=	Greater than or equal to.	Left to right
lt	Less than (string version).	Left to right
le	Less than or equal to (string version).	Left to right
gt	Greater than (string version).	Left to right

TABLE 10.1 continued

Operator	Description	Associativity
ge	Greater than or equal to (string version).	Left to right
==	Equal comparison.	Left to right
!=	Not equal.	Left to right
eq	Equal (string version).	Left to right
ne	Not equal (string version).	Left to right
&	Bitwise AND.	Left to right
^	Bitwise XOR.	Left to right
|	Bitwise OR.	Left to right
&&	Logical AND.	Left to right
and	Logical AND (Flash 4).	Left to right
||	Logical OR.	Left to right
or	Logical OR (Flash 4).	Left to right
?:	Conditional statement.	Right to left
=	Assignment.	Right to left
*=, /=, %=, +=, -=, &=, |=, ^=, <<=, >>=, >>>=	Compound assignment.	Right to left
,	Multiple evaluation.	Left to right

Obviously you don't need to memorize all the precedence and associativity rules surrounding operators, but it is important to keep them in the back of your mind when you are creating code. The way in which you order your operands around with operators makes a difference.

Types of Operators

Operators also fall into categories. For example, some operators are numeric and may perform arithmetic actions; other operators compare operands. Here are some of the different types of operators you may encounter.

Numeric Operators

Numeric operators perform all the arithmetic operations needed for your project. The operators belonging to this category include + (addition), * (multiplication), / (division), % (modulo, which is a remainder of a division), - (subtraction), ++ (increment), and -- (decrement).

Commonly you will see increment and decrement used by programmers as a shortcut to writing out more code. For example,

```
x=5;
x++;
```

is the same as writing this:

```
x=5;
x=x+1;
```

The two addition signs tell Flash to add one to the number. Therefore, both of these instances evaluate to 6.

Furthermore, you have pre and postincrement. Look at the following example, still assuming x=5:

```
if (x++=6);
```

Because the increment comes after x, the comparison is determined before x is incremented. This statement would evaluate to `False`. However, if the increment comes before the x, then a different value could be determined:

```
if (++x=6);
```

Because the increment comes before the variable, the addition will occur before the comparison. Therefore, this statement evaluates to `True`.

Assignment Operators

A single equal sign (=) can be used to assign values in Flash. Therefore, if you want a variable to take on a value of another variable, you would use the = operator to assign them equal to each other. Here's an example:

```
myVar=5;
x=myVar;
```

Both variables are assigned values: x is assigned a value equal to `myVar`, and `myVar` is assigned a value of 5. Alternatively, you could write the following:

```
x=myVar=z;
```

This assigns all variables an equal value. Assignment operators can also be a combination of operators. These include +=, -=, *=, %=, /=, <<=, >>=, >>>=, ^=, |=, and &=. These combination assignment operators can be used to perform a combination of tasks in one operator. Here's an example:

```
x+=20;
```

This statement adds 20 to the value of x. Because we know x equals 5, the expression evaluates to 25. Check this one out:

```
x*=12;
```

In this case, we are using multiplication in the assignment expression. It is the same as saying 5*12=60, but more succinctly.

Equality Operators

Equality operators determine whether items are equal to each other. They yield a true or false output, otherwise known as a *boolean value*. The equality operators include == (tests equality), === (tests for strict equality), != (tests for inequality), and !== (tests for strict inequality).

The == equality operator tests to see whether two values are the same. The key difference between equality and strict equality is that strict equality will not convert data types. Therefore, if two values have different data types, the === operator will yield False always. Here's an example:

```
if (x==5){
    trace("the action has been done")
    }
```

Because of the test for equality, this statement will only occur if the value yielded by the equality operator is True.

Logical Operators

Logical operators compare two boolean values and return a third boolean value. Therefore, if both booleans are equal to True, the logical && operator will return True. If either value is False, the entire logical && expression evaluates to False. Here's an example:

```
if (x<10 || _framesloaded>50){
    trace("the action has been done")
    }
```

This example uses the logical OR statement. Therefore, if either of the statements is true, the logical will return True. Here, we know the value to be 5, which is less than 10, so the entire statement is true, regardless of how many frames have been loaded.

The three logical operators are logical AND (&&), logical NOT (!, which was also used in the equality operator from the previous example), and logical OR (||).

Comparison Operators

Comparison operators are going to blow your mind. They compare two operands and return a boolean value. I bet you didn't see that one coming. Comparison operators include less than (<), greater than (>), less than or equal to (<=), and greater than or equal to (>=). Here's an example:

```
if (x<10){
    trace("the action has been done")
    }
```

Unlike the logical statement, this example has only one comparison. Because x is less than 10, it returns a True value.

String Operators

When the + operator is used with strings, Flash will recognize the data types and concatenate the strings instead of adding them together. Basically, concatenation is the addition of strings, but this isn't the same as the addition of numbers. Instead, it involves attaching two strings together so that they form a complete statement.

The comparison operators also have special values when dealing with strings. Instead of comparing two values for a boolean, comparison operators determine which value comes first in alphabetical order when dealing with two strings.

Loops

A loop is a programming technique in which a task is repeated constantly until a condition is met that ends the loop. Loops come in a variety of flavors. A loop can be a statement that "loops" over a set of frames, with other actions being repeated throughout those frames, or it can be contained within a block statement. The scripting loops that can be placed within a block statement include for, for in, do, and do while. We will go into detail about each of these individually, but for now let's try working with some frame loops.

Exercise 10.13

The starting FLA file for this exercise is 10-13start.fla. The finished FLA file is 10-13fin.fla. Here are the steps to follow:

1. Open the 10-13start.fla movie. It is a continuation of the movie we used in the "Functions" section.

2. Click the movie clip on your stage and press F8. This will create another movie clip (give the new movie clip a name for the Library and an instance name of **blank**). This will now make the first movie clip nested inside a blank movie clip on the second tier of your hierarchy.

3. Inside the timeline for the blank movie clip, add about four frames to the timeline. Also, add some code to affect the next level down, which is the circle movie clip. Type the following code into the Actions panel for the first frame of the blank movie clip:

```
if (circle._x<300){
    circle._x+=10
}
```

4. Test the movie.

   Because the movie only has four frames in the blank movie clip, the timeline will continuously check the code to see whether the circle clip's location is greater than 400. If it is not, the clip is assigned a location of 10 pixels closer to the 400 destination.

5. Add the following code to your clip:

```
if (circle._y>-200){
    circle._y-=10
}
```

Upon testing the movie now, you'll notice that because you added another property and condition for Flash to check, you can animate in a diagonal motion. The clip will continuously loop for as long as the program runs. In fact, even after the clip stops its motion, Flash still checks to see whether the conditions are met.

Note that –300 is used as the number—this is the relation to the coordinates for the circle movie clip, not the coordinates for the circle movie clip in relation to the main timeline.

The `while` Loop

The `while` loops allow you to repeat a statement block as long as a condition remains true. Usually with this type of loop you need some variable in your statement block that will increment each time the statement is executed. While loops are written in the following format:

```
while(condition){
statements();
}
```

The condition part of this code is the driving force that allows the statement to be executed. If the condition returns `False`, the loop ends and goes to the next line of code in the block. Let's try an example.

Exercise 10.14

The starting FLA file for this exercise is `10-14start.fla`. The finished FLA file is `10-14fin.fla`. Here are the steps to follow:

1. On the first frame in the movie, type the following code:

```
stop();
myNum=1
while(myNum<30){
trace("myNum is equal to " +myNum)
myNum++
}
```

2. Test your movie.

If you watched your movie fast enough, which may be physically impossible, you would notice that each line is placed in the Output window, one line at a time, as each loop was executed. Because this loop occurs over the course of one frame, Flash executes it before you enter the next frame. Also, pay special attention to the numbers returned in the Output window. The number 30 is not represented because the number 30 in the `trace` action falls outside the conditional statement. If `myNum` equals 30, it is no longer less than 30. Finally, notice the `myNum++` statement in the code block. This statement allows you to increment the variable, eventually enabling the loop to reach 30.

Without this increment, your loop could fall into the trap of an *infinite loop*, which is a loop that always has a true statement in the condition. This will be a detriment to your computer's system, and most likely your project will be crippled and will not be able to run any further. Therefore, make sure every loop you create has some sort of end to it.

The `do while` Loop

The `do while` loop has been de-emphasized in Flash MX. It was used primarily in Flash 4 to accomplish the same actions as the `while` loop in Flash 5 and now in Flash MX. `Do while` loops have the following format, in case you need to check code from projects completed for Flash 4:

```
do{
    statements();
}while(condition)
```

The `for` Loop

The `for` loop is much more succinct than the `while` loop and much more widely used by programmers. That's because the `for` loop includes the initialization, the increment, and the condition all within the first line of the statement block. For loops are written in the following format:

```
for (initialization; condition; increment){
    statements();
}
```

The initialization gives a value to the variable that will control the statements. You can have more than one variable; just separate the variables by commas. The condition is the same as before: Once the condition returns `False`, the loop ends. The increment is where any variables will change (or *increment*). Let's try an example.

Exercise 10.15

The finished FLA file for this exercise is `10-15fin.fla`. Here are the steps to follow:

1. On any frame in your movie, type the following code:

   ```
   for(myNum=0, x=99; myNum<99; myNum++){
   trace("There are " + x + " bottles of beer on the wall.
   ➥We drank " + myNum + " of them");
   }
   stop();
   ```

2. Test your movie.

Hey, all the beer is gone. One thing you will notice in this example is how you can dictate two variables in one statement. You can also tell the statement to have an end in the first line, thus saving you space compared to using a `while` loop. The `for` loop is certainly very powerful.

The `for in` Loop

This action loops through the properties in an object or elements in an array and executes statements for each property or element. Huh? We haven't talked about arrays yet, so you may be a little confused by this loop. However, don't be distressed—this loop provides a clever way of affecting all the properties associated with an object in your scene. In addition, you can affect the objects that are children of an object in your scene. You would write the `for in` loop in this manner:

```
for (var currentProperty in objectTarget){
    statements(); //Use currentProperty here
}
```

Notice first that `currentProperty` represents the property that the loop is checking at this particular moment. Usually this variable is used in some way in the body of the `for in` loop.

Here's an example of a `for` loop that allow you to play all of the state animations at one time, without animating the middle states' animation timeline.

Exercise 10.16

The starting FLA file for this exercise is `EastCoast.fla`. The finished FLA file is `10-16fin.fla`. Here are the steps to follow:

1. Upon opening the timeline, click the button.
2. Place the following code on the button:
   ```
   for (var name in _root.middleStates){
   _root.middleStates[name].gotoAndPlay(2);
   }
   ```
3. Test your movie.

You just created a loop that allows you to play seven movie clip timelines from one statement block. You can certainly see the power of loops and especially `for` loops.

The Actions Panel

The Actions panel provides the user with all the tools necessary to create ActionScript in his or her project. Let's examine the various tools to better understand how to work within this panel.

Panel Features

When you open the Actions panel, you will immediately notice the Actions toolbox, which runs along the left side of the panel (see Figure 10.21).

It possesses a series of drop-down menus that contain the actions you need to run your projects. Double-clicking one of these will place the action in the script pane. The first level of choices include Actions, Operators, Functions, Constants, Properties, Objects, Depreciated (items that are only used in older versions of Flash), and Flash UI Components. Finally, at the end of this list is an index. If you know the name of the action you want to select, you can do so in the index. Each of the aforementioned categories has the actions listed that pertain to that particular topic.

FIGURE **10.21**

The location of the various objects in the Actions panel.

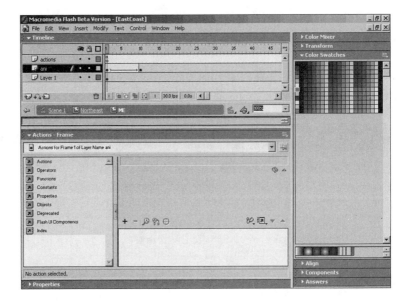

Objects is the most confusing category (see Figure 10.22). Therefore, let's explore its choices first.

FIGURE **10.22**

The book icon represents a set of actions. Here, the Objects category is represented.

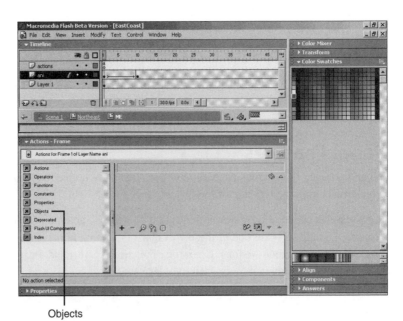

Objects

The first tier of items to select includes Core, Movie, Client/Server, and Authoring. The Core and Movie objects will be the most used, but this tier of object choices is simply a categorization of the types of objects available to you. The second tier of object choices lists the various object classes available to you, which are built in to Flash. Finally, the third tier of choices allows you to access the methods and properties for a particular object class.

Notice the icons that represent the choices with more options and the actual actions that you can select (see Figure 10.23). The selectable actions have the pointer encased in a circle, and the choices are represented by an arrow encased by a book icon. When a book icon is open, it turns into an opened book icon.

FIGURE 10.23

An example of an opened action set followed by an unopened action set and an escape action. The conversion functions set would reveal more choices for actions to be used.

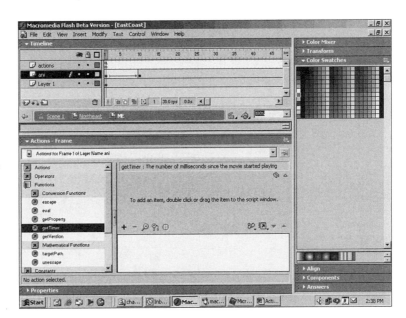

The Actions toolbox can also obtain information about any particular object in it. Click an action of your choice and then click the Dictionary Reference Guide, shown in Figure 10.24, to obtain the information. The Dictionary Reference Guide is located in the upper-left corner of the Actions panel.

The Script drop-down list tells you the location of the current script (see Figure 10.25). This can also be useful to change the location of a script on the fly. In addition, next to this drop-down list is a "pin" button that always keeps the current script in the window, even when you click another part of the Actions panel.

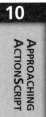

10

APPROACHING
ACTIONSCRIPT

FIGURE 10.24

This book icon represents the dictionary guide. Click it to get detailed descriptions of particular actions.

Dictionary Guide

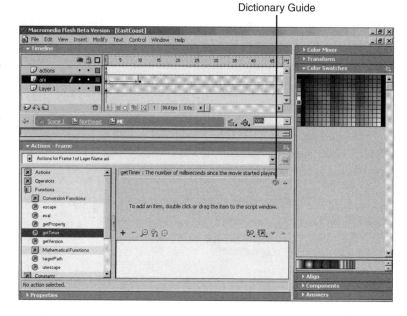

FIGURE 10.25

The script location bar will assist you in knowing the exact position in your project where you are placing the script.

Script Location Bar

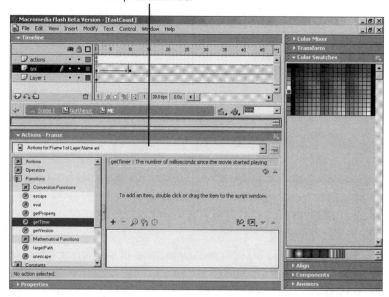

In the upper-right corner of the Actions panel, you'll find the Action panel pop-up menu, which gives you the ability to customize preferences for the panel. You can choose Panel Preferences, Minimize and Maximize the Panel, and Change Modes with this pop-up menu. Other options are available, but we'll cover them in more detail later (see Figure 10.26).

FIGURE 10.26

The pop-up menu for the Actions panel.

Normal Mode	Ctrl+Shift+N
✓ Expert Mode	Ctrl+Shift+E
Go to Line...	Ctrl+G
Find...	Ctrl+F
Find Again	F3
Replace...	Ctrl+H
Check Syntax	Ctrl+T
Show Code Hint	Ctrl+Spacebar
Auto Format	Ctrl+Shift+F
Auto Format Options...	
Import From File...	Ctrl+Shift+I
Export As File...	Ctrl+Shift+X
Print...	
View Line Numbers	Ctrl+Shift+L
View Esc Shortcut Keys	
Preferences...	
Help	
Maximize Panel	
Close Panel	

Looking directly below the Dictionary Reference Guide you'll see the normal mode options area. This is where items in normal mode allow you to alter code. Normal mode attempts to write the code for you based on the input you give Flash. The input items appear in this space.

Below that you'll find the script pane. This is where your scripts show up. It's available in every mode in Flash's Action panel. It displays the script exactly as Flash sees it (see Figure 10.27).

Directly above the script pane are buttons that assist you in your code writing and debugging. In order of appearance, here's a short list of these buttons' purposes:

- **Add New Item to Script**. This option allows you to have a quick drop-down list of all the actions in your panel. This button serves the same purpose as the Actions toolbox. It appears in the old versions of Flash, and Macromedia has decided to keep it in MX.

- **Delete the Selected Actions (normal mode only)**. This button allows you to select a line of code and cut it from your script pane.

- **Find and Replace**. Oftentimes your code will become lengthy, especially on larger projects. These buttons assist you in finding variables, words, or phrases in your code and replacing values for the found text.

10

APPROACHING ACTIONSCRIPT

FIGURE 10.27

The pane in which you can enter code.

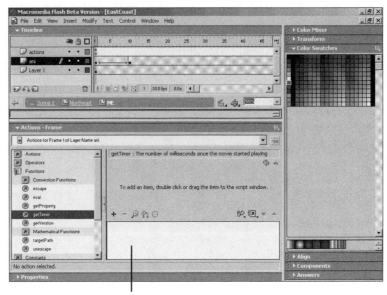

Instruction Pane

- **Insert Target Path**. You may use this button when in need of assistance when assigning your target paths. Sometimes you may become confused by the hierarchy of the movie clips in your scene. This button will display the hierarchy for you.

- **Check Syntax (expert mode only)**. This button checks to see whether any code has been written incorrectly. It places corrections in the output window to clue you in on what code to change.

- **Auto Format (expert mode only)**. This button attempts to format code in an orderly manner, in case you have not been inserting the proper tabs to make your code readable.

- **Show Code Hint (expert mode only)**. This is actually a feature that you can turn on permanently in the preferences of the panel. This button will clue you into what code should be inserted in a particular area where your cursor is located.

Now for the items located on the right side above the ActionScript pane:

- **Action Script Dictionary**. As alluded to before, this opens a quick reference for actions in Flash. This proves much quicker than opening the Help menu every time you have an ActionScript problem.

- **Debug options**. These options allow you to set breakpoints in your code. This becomes useful when you have a piece of code you know has problems. You can put a breakpoint in your code, test your movie, and Flash will halt the presentation to let you view variable values to help you decipher what is problematic in your code blocks.

• **View options**. These options provide another way to change modes in your script pane. Plus, you have the option to add code lines to your script. This is useful when you have several lines of code and you want to quickly find a line. Commonly, the errors that appear in the Output window have a code line attached. If you have code lines turned on, you can find the line specified in the Output window.

• **Up and down arrows (normal mode only)**. These allow you to move code up and down in line order.

Normal Mode and Expert Mode

You've already learned about several of the options available to you in both normal and expert mode. Let's discuss these two options for a moment. First, normal mode should only be used if you are new to Flash. The more you use Flash, the more you will find expert mode faster and easier to work with. The more you work in Flash, the more you will remember some of the codes. This makes your work more efficient, because you will not have to go searching for code. In addition, the normal mode sometimes proves less of a help than expert mode.

For example, in normal mode, in your Actions toolbox go to Actions, Miscellaneous Actions, Evaluate. By double-clicking this you will find that Flash only provides you with a semicolon for code. Writing this code out by hand would certainly be faster than searching for the `evaluate` action in the Actions panel.

Double-clicking any member in the Actions toolbox or clicking an item from the + button allows you to select pieces of text for your script pane. In expert mode, there is less of a need to do this, but the toolbox is still available if you want to click it for a script starter.

Switching from expert mode to normal mode will also serve the same purpose as the Check Syntax button, which makes sure the code you have written is correct. If your code is incorrect, Flash will tell you that it cannot move to normal mode until the script is correct.

Importing and Exporting Scripts

You can create scripts inside Flash and export them to a text file. Also, Flash lets you accomplish the reverse. You can create code in a text file and import it into a Flash file.

To export one of your scripts, click the Actions pop-up menu and choose Export As File. Choose a location for the file and click Save.

To import an outside script, click the Actions pop-up menu, choose Import From File and select the file to be opened from the dialog box.

Finally, you may want a script to be read within Flash but not imported. Basically, this loads a file during the runtime of your movie. You can do this by choosing Actions, Miscellaneous Actions, #include as your action from the Actions toolbox. This allows you to include a path to the file you want opened at that point in your movie. Your script will then become available to your Flash movie.

Actions Panel Pop-up Menu

Here's a laundry list of the items in the Actions panel pop-up menu, located at the upper-left corner of the Actions panel. This list includes the functions of these options:

- **Normal Mode and Expert Mode**. Clicking either of these options changes the mode of the panel. You cannot choose both options.
- **Go to Line**. Allows you to go directly to a line you choose.
- **Find**. Assists you in finding text within your code block.
- **Find Again**. Finds text you attempted to find on your previous attempt or the next occurrence of that text in your code block.
- **Replace**. Replaces text in your code block.
- **Check Syntax**. Checks for errors in your code.
- **Show Code Hint**. Clues you in to the type for a particular area of your code.
- **Auto Format and Auto Format Options**. These buttons allow you to choose options for your formatting. Clicking Auto Format executes the chosen options throughout your code. These options include separating operators with spaces, not having `else` statements bracketed by curly braces, having a space after function statements, and other options.
- **Import and Export Scripts**. These options are discussed in the preceding section.
- **Print**. Prints out thecurrent script.

- **View Line Numbers**. Places numbers next to every line of code in your script for easy location.

- **View Esc Shortcut Keys**. Places shortcut key combinations that write certain scripts for you on the fly. You can view the shortcuts by checking this option and viewing the action in the Actions toolbox.

- **Preferences**. These preferences are also available through Edit, Preferences and clicking the ActionScript Editor tab. This option will give you a number of further options to choose from when viewing your panel, including the following:

  •**Automatic Indentation**. Indents lines in the code you write where Flash deems necessary. You can also dictate a number of spaces to indent.

  •**Code Hints**. Automatically gives you code hints (even in expert mode) after writing partial parts of code. Flash attempts to clue you in as to what to write next. You can place a delay for the code hints to appear, if you think many of the code hints are unnecessary, but you still want the option to see them.

  •**Text Options**. You can change the font and size of text to be viewed in your Actions panel.

  •**Syntax Coloring**. Gives you the option to change colors of items that you want to be alerted to. Therefore, if you want to customize the appearance of items in your Actions panel, such as the background, text colors, colors of keywords, and so on, you can have those options changed.

- **Help**. Brings up Flash's help pages.

- **Maximize Panel**. Extends the size of the Actions panel to maximize your viewable area.

- **Close Panel**. Closes your panel for the time being.

As you can see from the length of this chapter, Macromedia has spent a lot of time building up its ActionScript language. ActionScript packs a lot of power and arms you with the ability to animate without frames, control the objects included in a movie, alter properties of an object, and instruct different areas of your movie from frame, button, or movie clip actions.

Understanding that object-oriented programming is the manipulation of objects in a scene in order to create interactivity for the end user is the key concept of this chapter. Objects are instances of classes that make up your project's content. Every object can be manipulated through changing its properties or calling a method to tell the object to perform a particular task.

10

APPROACHING ACTIONSCRIPT

Furthermore, `MovieClip` objects are special objects available to you. Not only are they graphically represented, but they also have a timeline independent of the main timeline. Therefore, targeting a timeline and telling it to perform actions from a controlling timeline will enable you to communicate between different movie clips and across several timelines. This is called *addressing*. All the timelines in a Flash FLA work in coordination with each other to complete the project in the way you've chosen. Therefore, you must target specific actions to work in conjunction with specific actions from Flash.

Also, several types of actions can assist you as a programmer. Loops enable you to repeat a block of code several times until a conditional statement proves false. For example, loops enable you to accomplish tasks for as long as the user has his mouse pressed down or for as long as a variable is equal to a certain number.

Functions, like loops, enable you to repeat a block of code. However, unlike loops, functions are called upon. Therefore, if you call on a function only once, it will execute the function block one time. If you have a function called every time the user clicks a button, the functions block could be executed several times.

ActionScript controls the movies you create. It guides your projects, but you are the conductor of these projects. Much like an orchestra conductor has the ability to tell the strings section to play a certain note, you have the ability to tell a sound to play or tell a movie clip to move across the screen. Furthermore, when you add variables to your project that will be defined by a user's interaction, the project's interactivity and usability skyrocket.

Data Types and Variables—In Depth

By David Vogeleer

In this chapter we discuss different types of data and variables that store data.

Data, simply put, is anything and everything you want it to be, including text, numbers, and logical representations (known as Boolean data). In its most raw form (binary code), data is represented as a bunch of zeros and ones, which comprises the basic data computers use as their primitive language.

Types of Data Types

Before we get into any major details about any of the data types, let's briefly look at the different data types in Flash:

- **String**. Any piece of data to be listed as basic text (for example, "This is a string data type"). Notice the quotation marks, which signify that this is a string.

- **Number**. Any piece of data to be listed as an integer with a numeric value (for example, 1, 44, -10, 21.7, and -0.8 are all legal number data types).

- **Boolean**. This is a logical representation used for conditions and results of certain formulas (`true` and `false` are the only two Boolean data types).

- **Null and undefined**. These are used when there is no presence of data.

- **Array**. This is used for lists of data (it is its own data type).

- **MovieClip**. This is used for movie clip instances (it is its own data type).

- **Object**. This is used with user-defined or built-in classes of data.

The two most commonly used data types are strings and numbers. We will go into greater detail on these two and discuss the different parts of them.

First, let's take a look at these data types and see how easily they can be misinterpreted:

```
"My name is David."     // this is a string datatype
1234                    // this is a number datatype
"1234"                  // this is a string datatype
1+2+3                   // this is a number datatype
"My name "+"is David"   // this is a string datatype
'Single quote marks'    // this is a string datatype with single quote marks
```

These are the basic forms of the string and number data types. The text to the right with the double forward slashes (//) just represents comments in the code (the interpreter skips this text completely).

We will go over conversion in the "Changing the Types of Values in Variables" section later in this chapter.

The String Data Type

The string data type can be categorized as any amount of text between quotes. This includes characters, numbers, and certain properties of movie clip instances.

Creating a String

To create a string, place some text between quotation marks, as shown here:

```
"this is a string literal"
//that was simple enough
```

Another way of creating a string using the string data type is to declare a new string with the new constructor:

```
new String("this is a string literal")
```

Also, you can set this equal to a variable (which we will discuss later in this chapter):

```
var myString = new String("this is a string literal")
```

Empty Strings

You do not have to put anything between the quotes for it to be a string literal. You can just place an opening and closing set of quotes to create an empty string, as shown here:

```
""        // an empty string with double quotes
''        // an empty string with single quotes
```

Although this is an empty string, it is not equal to the null or undefined data types. In the following example, we first start a new file by going to File in the toolbar and choosing New (Ctrl+N). Then we use an `if` statement in the actions of the first keyframe in the main timeline and test it by going to Control in the toolbar and selecting Test Movie (`if` statements are discussed in Chapter 12, "Statements and Expressions—In Depth"):

```
if ("" != null) {
trace ("An empty string is not equal to null");
}
// output: An empty string is not equal to null
```

Notice that we use a `trace` function that, when the movie is tested, displays our output in the Output window. You'll see how to use this empty string at the end of this chapter.

Quotes

As you have seen, all string literals must be surrounded by quotes. These quotes can be single quotation marks (') or double quotation marks ("), but you must close with the same type of quotation mark you started with. Here are some examples:

```
"double quotes"       //legal string
'single quotes'       //legal string
"double to single'    //illegal string
'single to double"    //illegal string
```

If you do not close with the same quotation mark you opened with, you will receive this error:

```
String literal was not properly terminated
```

However, you can put quotation marks inside quotation marks, as shown here:

```
'Then David said: "These are quotes inside a string"'
//this is a legal string containing a quote within it
```

You do need to be careful, though, because a single quotation mark can also be used as an apostrophe. This can cause errors if you are not paying attention. Here's an example:

```
'He wasn't going to go'
//the interpreter reads this as 'He wasn' and throws up an error message
```

If we had used opening and closing double quotation marks instead of single quotation marks here, the interpreter would not have thrown the error. However, let's say we want to use single quotation marks anyway. In this case, there is a workaround: the escape sequence.

Escape Sequences

Escape sequences are string literals used with a backslash (\). This tells the interpreter to use the following character or character representation.

Here are some basic escape sequences:

```
\"      double quote escape sequence
\'      single quote escape sequence
\\      backslash escape sequence using the backslash not as an escape sequence
```

Let's take a look at our example again, but this time using the escape sequence:

```
'He wasn't going to go'
//as before, this will cause errors and not display the proper text
'He wasn\'t going to go'
//now using an escape sequence, the problem is solved, and the
//interpreter reads it correctly
```

Now the interpreter reads the string correctly. Remember, you only have to use the quote escape sequences when you have one quotation mark (double or single) in between the opening and closing quotation marks of a string; if you have two, they cancel each other out .

Manipulating Strings

String manipulation includes creating new strings, joining strings, and much more. In this section, we'll start with the easy tasks and work our way up.

Joining Strings

Joining strings is as simple as putting a plus operator (+) between two string literals. Here's an example:

```
"This is " + "a string literal"
// the interpreter translates this as "This is a string literal"
```

Notice the space after "is" in this example. This space is necessary in strings; otherwise, the string would appear like this: `"This isa string literal"`. Alternatively, we could use a space string to make the code appear clearer, as shown here:

```
"This is" + " " + "a string literal"
// the interpreter translates this as "This is a string literal"
```

Note that the space string is not equal to the empty string we discussed earlier:

```
if (" " != '') {
trace ("A space string is not equal to an empty string")
}
// output: A space string is not equal to an empty string
```

Also, even though it has been depreciated in Flash MX, you can use the operator add to join strings together:

```
"This is " add "a string literal"
// the add operator works just like the + operator
```

You can also add strings by setting them to variables:

```
var fName = "David";
var lName = "Vogeleer";
var space = " ";
trace (fName + space + lName);
// output: David Vogeleer
```

Here, all we did was set each string to a variable and then add the variables.

Another way to add strings with variables is to set the same variable to an additional string with an assignment operator. Here's an example:

```
var name = "David ";
name+="Vogeleer";
trace (name);
// output: David Vogeleer
```

And, of course, we can create a new string by adding a string to a variable that contains a string, as shown here:

```
var fName = "David ";
var fullName = fName + "Vogeleer";
trace (fullName);
// output: David Vogeleer
```

The concat Function

Using dot syntax, the concat function acts similarly to the assignment variable (+=) we looked at earlier. Simply attach it to a string with another string in the brackets:

```
var name = "David ".concat("Vogeleer");
trace (name);
// output: David Vogeleer
```

And, of course, you can attach the concat function to a variable:

```
var fName = "David ";
var fullName = fName.concat("Vogeleer");
trace (fullName);
// output: David Vogeleer
```

Now let's put a variable in the parentheses instead of a string literal:

```
var fName = "David ";
var lName = "Vogeleer";
var fullName = fName.concat(lName);
trace (fullName);
// output: David Vogeleer
```

This technique can even handle multiple expressions:

```
var name = "This is ".concat("a"+" ".concat("string " + "literal"));
trace (name) ;
// output: This is a string literal
```

Not only can you use multiple joining expressions, but you can also embed concat functions within concat functions.

Indexing Characters in Strings

Characters inside of strings can be indexed, stored, and displayed. Each character in a string has a specific index, starting with the first character at the index zero (0). The indexing of strings always starts with 0 instead of 1 in Flash; therefore, the second character has an index of 1 and the third character has an index of 2, and so on.

The `charAt` Function

You can use the `charAt` function with strings to see characters at a defined index. Just attach the function to a string and place a number in the parentheses that represents the index you wish to grab. Here's an example:

```
trace("David".charAt(2));
// output: v
```

This function can also be attached to a variable holding a string:

```
var name = "David";
trace (name.charAt(2));
// output: v
```

What's more, you can use a variable in place of the number in the parentheses:

```
var place = 2;
var name = "David";
trace (name.charAt(place));
// output: v
```

The `length` Property

The `length` property provides a way to determine the number of characters in a given string. Simply attach it to a string, and it will return a numeric value. Here's an example:

```
trace ("Unleashed".length);
// output: 9
```

> **Tip**
>
> The last character in a string will always be *string*.length minus one.

Of course, this property can also be attached to a variable holding a string, as shown here:

```
var title = "Unleashed";
trace (title.length);
// output: 9
```

Even though you might not consider a space to be a character, ActionScript does:

```
var title = "Flash Unleashed";
trace (title.length);
// output: 15
```

In this example, the output is 15 instead of 14 because the space is counted as a character.

Using the `length` property combined with the `charAt` function, we can identify every character in a word based on a defined function (more on functions in later chapters). Here's an example:

```
//first create the function
function list (myString) {
//use a loop statement to cycle through
//all the characters in the string
for(i=0;i<myString.length;i++){
     trace (myString.charAt(i));
}
}
//create our string
var title = "Unleashed";
//run the function on our string
list(title);
// output: U
//         n
//         l
//         e
//         a
//         s
//         h
//         e
//         d
```

The `indexOf` Function

The `indexOf` function takes a given character, looks for it in a string, and returns the character's index. As before, you can attach it directly to a string or a variable holding a string. Place the character you are looking for in the parentheses as a string literal, like so:

```
//attach the function directly to a string
trace ("Flash".indexOf("a"));
// now create a variable and attach the function to the variable
var title = "Unleashed";
trace (title.indexOf("e"));
// output: 2
//         3
```

In the second part of this example, the `indexOf` function found the first index of *e*, but let's say we now want to find the next one. To do this, we just place a starting index in the function after the character we are looking for and separate them with a comma:

```
var title = "Unleashed";
trace (title.indexOf("e",4));
// output: 7
```

In this case, we put in the index of the character following the first *e* and the `indexOf` function found the next one with no problem.

You can also look for certain strings of characters with the indexOf function. Just place the string in quotes, just like you would a single character. The indexOf function will return the first index of the first character in the string you are looking for:

```
var title = "Unleashed";
trace (title.indexOf("she"));
// output: 5
```

The Output window displays the index of the first character in the string you're looking for (in this case, *s*).

Here's another nice feature of the indexOf function: If it does not find the character or characters in the string, it will display -1 in the Output window when you trace it:

```
var title = "Unleashed";
trace (title.indexOf("o"));
// output: -1
```

Let's take a look at what happens when we look for the letter *u* in the same string:

```
var title = "Unleashed";
trace (title.indexOf("u"));
// output: -1
```

The indexOf function could not find *u* in this case because Flash reads upper- and lower-case letters as completely different characters.

This can be useful when you're using forms in Flash. For example, let's say your company is willing to pay for in-state shipping to its customers, but if the recipient is outside the state, he or she must pay the shipping. Therefore, when users enter another state in the shipping form, they are greeted with a message reminding them to include shipping costs (otherwise, a thank-you message appears):

```
//first create our variables
var homeState = "VA";
var thankYou = "Thank you for your order";
var reminder = "Please remember to include shipping";
//now create the if statement
if (enteredState.indexOf(homeState) == -1) {
    message = reminder;
} else {
    message = thankYou;
}
```

This code determines whether the variable homeState is in enteredState and sends the appropriate message.

The `lastIndexOf` Function

Like the indexOf function, the lastIndexOf function searches a string for a character or group of characters. However, unlike the indexOf function, which starts at the beginning of the string and moves toward the end, the `lastIndexOf` function starts at the end and works toward the beginning.

Also, this function works the same as the `indexOf` function in that you simply attach it to a string or variable holding a string and place the desired character or characters in parentheses, followed by a comma with a starting index. If no starting index is defined, the starting index automatically becomes the last character in the string. Here's an example:

```
var title = "Unleashed";
trace (title.lastIndexOf("e"));
// output: 7
```

Although this function may not seem like much, consider that the following code is what it would take to do the same thing without the built-in `lastIndexOf` function:

```
function theLastIndexOf (myString,searchFor){
     for (i=0;i<myString.length;i++){
          if (myString.charAt(i)==searchFor) {
               found = i;
          }
}
     trace (found);
}
var title = "Unleashed";
theLastIndexOf(title,"e");
// output: 7
```

The `substring` Function

Many times, it is necessary to pull more than one character from a string. Flash has a few built-in functions for this task. One of them is the `substring` function.

The `substring` function attaches to strings and variables like other functions. However, in the parentheses, you put the starting and ending index, separated by a comma. Here's an example:

```
trace("Unleashed".substring(2,7))
// output: leash
```

Now let's attach it to a variable and leave out the ending index:

```
var title = "Unleashed";
trace (title.substring(2));
// output: leashed
```

As you can see, without an ending index, the `substring` function grabs all the characters from the starting index onward.

So far we have put in numbers representing the starting and ending indexes. Now let's use a variable instead of a number. This will make the function more dynamic. For example, let's say you would like to pull the ZIP Code out of the last line of an address:

```
var line3 = "Richmond, VA 23866";
finalSpace = line3.lastIndexOf(" ");
zip = line3.substring(finalSpace+1);
trace (zip);
// output: 23866
```

This takes the last space in the third line and makes it the starting point. It then grabs everything after that, which in this case is the ZIP Code.

If, by mistake, you place the ending index first and the starting index second, the interpreter will switch them for you:

```
var title = "Unleashed";
trace (title.substring(7,2));
// output: leash
```

Even though the numbers were reversed, the interpreter still retrieves the correct information.

The `substr` Function

The `substr` function acts similarly to the `substring` function. However, in place of an ending index, you put the desired number of characters to be returned. The `substr` function still uses a starting index like the `substring` function. Here's an example:

```
var title = "Unleashed";
trace (title.substr(2,5));
// output: leash
```

If you have a starting index but not a designated number of characters to pull, the `substr` function will begin at the starting point and pull all the following characters:

```
var title = "Unleashed";
trace (title.substr(2));
// output: leashed
```

You can also place a negative number in the starting index, and the `substr` function will start counting from the end toward the beginning using the specified number of spaces:

```
var title = "Unleashed";
trace (title.substr(-4,2));
// output: sh
```

The `slice` Function

The `slice` function acts similarly to the `substring` function, except you can use negative numbers in the starting and ending indexes, as shown here:

```
var title = "Unleashed";
trace (title.slice(2,-2));
// output: leash
```

The split Function

The `split` function is a unique function when it comes to manipulating strings. It divides a string into separate strings that can be stored in an array (more on arrays in Chapter 15, "Arrays").

Attach the `split` function to a string or variable and in the parentheses place the delimiting character. Here's an example:

```
var title = "Unleashed";
trace (title.split("e"));
// output: Unl,ash,d
```

This example separates the original string based on the letter *e*. This is very powerful because you can take apart a sentence and store each individual word as its own variable or within an array as elements. Let's take a look:

```
//first, create a variable holding the string
var title = "Flash MX Unleashed";
// then set an array equal to the string with the function attached
myArray = title.split(" ");
//display the entire array
trace (myArray);
//display just the first element in the array
trace (myArray[0]);
// output: Flash, MX, Unleashed
//          Flash
```

Now you can see some of the capabilities this function has. You can sort, store, and send all this data in a nice, clean format thanks to the `split` function.

The toLowerCase Function

Earlier, we ran into a problem when trying to find a lowercase *u* in the word *Unleashed* because Flash does not treat lowercase characters the same as uppercase characters. This problem can be overcome with either the `toLowerCase` function or the `toUpperCase` function. Both work the same, except one coverts characters to lowercase and the other to uppercase.

Let's go over `toLowerCase` first. When you want to find a lowercase letter in a string with uppercase letters, you must first convert all the uppercase letters to lowercase. This can be done on an individual basis with a lot of tedious coding, or you can simply attach the `toLowerCase` function directly to the string. Here's an example:

```
var title = "Unleashed";
title = title.toLowerCase();
trace (title);
// output: unleashed
```

In this case, we converted the uppercase *U* to a lowercase *u*. Now we can run the `indexOf` function like before and view the results:

```
var title = "Unleashed";
title = title.toLowerCase();
trace (title.indexOf("u"));
// output: 0
```

The `toUpperCase` Function

The `toUpperCase` function is identical to the `toLowerCase` function, except instead of lowercasing a value in a string, it uppercases it. Attach this function like you would any other function with nothing in the parentheses:

```
var title = "Unleashed";
title = title.toUpperCase();
trace (title);
// output: UNLEASHED
```

Like the `toLowerCase` function, the `toUpperCase` function affects the entire string.

The `charCodeAt` Function

We've talked about how Flash reads upper- and lowercase letters as different letters. This is because Flash doesn't see them as letters at all but rather as code points. Flash has two built-in functions for dealing with code points: the `charCodeAt` function and the `fromCharCode` function.

The first, the `charCodeAt` function, takes characters at defined indexes of strings and returns the code point value in a numeric form. Attach this function like you would any other function, and in the parentheses put the index of the character you're interested in. Here's an example:

```
var title = "Unleashed";
trace (title.charCodeAt(2));
// output: 108 (the code point for the letter "l")
```

The following code goes through any string and displays each character's code point in the Output window:

```
//create the function
function listCodePoints (myString){
//set the loop statement to run through each character
for(i=0;i<myString.length;i++){
//trace each characters code point
```

```
        trace (myString.charCodeAt(i));
    }
}
//create the variable to hold the string
var title = "Unleashed";
//run the function
listCodePoints(title);
// output: 85
//        110
//        108
//        101
//        97
//        115
//        104
//        101
//        100
```

Putting a negative value in the index place will always return the value NaN (Not a Number, covered later in this chapter in the "NaN" section):

```
var title = "Unleashed";
trace (title.charCodeAt(-2));
// output: NaN
```

The `fromCharCode` Function

Unlike the `charCodeAt` function, the `fromCharCode` function allows you to put code points in parentheses, and it translates them back to their string characters. Attach this function to a string data type and put the code points you would like to see in parentheses, separated by commas:

```
//create the variable to hold our string
var title ;
title = String.fromCharCode(85,110,108,101,97,115,104,101,100);
trace (title);
// output: Unleashed
```

> **Tip**
>
> The `fromCharCode` function must be attached to a string data type when it is run; otherwise, it will return Undefined.

Unicode-Style Strings

Another way to create a string is by using Unicode-style escape sequences. The basic form of a Unicode escape sequence starts with a backslash character, then a lowercase u, followed by a four-digit number:

```
var title = "\u0055\u006e\u006c\u0065\u0061\u0073\u0068\u0065\u0064"
trace (title);
// output: Unleashed
```

Now you can type in Unicode format in strings. The only real reason you would want to do this is to get those characters you can't simply type from the keyboard, such as the copyright symbol ([cr]), which in Unicode is \u00A9.

You can also type Unicode in shorthand format by replacing the \u00 with \x, as shown here:

```
trace ("\u0068");
trace ("\x68");
// output: h
//         h
```

The Number Data Type

The next data type we'll discuss is the number data type. Numbers come in all sorts of forms and are used for lots of different reasons, ranging from counting, to mathematical properties of movie clips, to expressions. Let's look at a few of examples:

```
1                   //legal number
4.998               //legal number
3+4                 //legal number
_x                  //legal number representing a horizontal position
string.length       //legal number representing the length of a string
0123                //legal number representing an octal number
10e2                //legal number using exponents
0x000000            //legal hexadecimal number
"1234"              //not a legal number, but a string literal
```

The two basic types of numbers supported by Flash are integers and floating-point numbers. Integers are whole numbers (positive or negative). Floating-point numbers are also positive or negative, but they include decimal points as well as fractional values (which are converted to decimal values).

Integers have two basic rules:

- They cannot contain decimals or fractional values.
- They cannot go below Number.MIN_VALUE or above Number.MAX_VALUE.

Some of the basic integers are raw numbers, such as 428 and 1200. These numbers are plain and simple. However, another example of an integer is a hexadecimal number, which is often used in color-coding (0x999999, for instance). Yet another form of integer is an octal number, such as 0123, which translates to the following:

(1×64) + (2×8) + (3×1)

Floating point numbers include decimal values, fractional values, and exponents. Exponents are defined by using the letter *e* followed by a number. This number represents the number of zeros. Here's an example:

```
trace (10e2);
// output: 1000
```

Creating a Number

One way to create a number is to simply type it:

```
4
```

You can also use the number data type in conjunction with the `new` constructor to create a number:

```
new Number(4);
```

Now you can set it equal to a variable:

```
var myNumber = new Number(4);
trace (myNumber);
// output: 4
```

Solving the Problem of Repeating Decimal Points

Because computers have difficulties with defining repeating decimal places and can sometimes misrepresent a number with multiple decimal places, it's a good idea to round or drop the decimal places with built-in methods `Math.round` and `Math.floor`.

When using the `Math.round` method, simply place the number or variable holding the number in parentheses, and the method will round it to its nearest whole value, thus creating an integer:

```
trace (Math.round(1.23333));
trace (Math.round(1.566666));
// output: 1
//          2
```

The `Math.floor` method, on the other hand, completely drops the decimal places from the number and creates an integer. Its use is the same as the `Math.round` method:

```
trace (Math.floor(1.23333));
trace (Math.floor(1.566666));
// output: 1
//          1
```

These methods will be discussed in greater detail in later chapters.

Predefined Values for Numbers

Even though you can create almost any number manually, Flash has a few values for numbers built in to it. Ironically, the first predefined value for a number is Not a Number (NaN).

NaN

Rarely would you set a number equal to NaN, but occasionally you might see this value in the Output window when the number you are trying to use is not a number. A NaN value can be the result of placing text inside a number data type or trying to divide zero by zero. Here's an example:

```
var seatsAvailable = new Number("lots");
trace (seatsAvailable);
// output: NaN
```

Because NaN is not a number, variables with this value cannot be equal to each other:

```
//create our variables
var seatsAvailable = new Number("lots");
var seatsTaken = new Number ("a few");
//create the if statement to see if it is not equal
if (seatsAvailable != seatsTaken) {
trace("These two are not equal");
}
```

MAX_VALUE and MIN_VALUE

Flash has limitations as to what a number can be. Two of these limitations are `MAX_VALUE` and `MIN_VALUE`. Currently, the maximum allowable value for a number is 1.79769313486231e+308, and the minimum allowable value is 4.94065645841247e-324.

This doesn't mean a number has to be between these two values. For example, a number can be lower than `MIN_VALUE`, as shown here:

```
//create our variable
var myNumber = -1;
//create an if statement to see if myNumber
//is lower than the MIN_VALUE
if (myNumber < Number.MIN_VALUE) {
     trace ("myNumber is lower than MIN_VALUE");
```

```
}
// output: myNumber is lower than MIN_VALUE
```

This is because `MIN_VALUE` is the minimum value a number has to be, not the largest negative number. To see the largest negative number, set `MAX_VALUE` to negative and run the same code:

```
//create our variable
var myNumber = -1;
//create an if statement to see if myNumber
//is lower than the -MAX_VALUE
if (myNumber < -Number.MAX_VALUE) {
trace ("myNumber is lower than -MAX_VALUE");
}
// output: (nothing because -1 is not smaller than -MAX_VALUE)
```

POSITIVE_INFINITY and NEGATIVE_INFINITY

If, by some chance, you create a number greater than `Number.MAX_VALUE`, the value will be `Infinity`. Likewise, if you create a negative number larger than `-Number.MAX_VALUE`, the value will be `-Infinity`.

Predefined values are built in to Flash that represent `Infinity` and `-Infinity`. They are `Number.POSITIVE_INFINITY` and `Number.NEGATIVE_INFINITY`.

Using these predefined values, we can test whether a number is infinite in the code:

```
//create our variable
var myNumber = Number.MAX_VALUE * Number.MAX_VALUE;
//create the if statement
if (MyNumber == Number.POSITIVE_INFINITY){
trace ("Both numbers are infinite");
}
// output: Both numbers are infinite
```

Bonus Numbers

Here's a list of more predefined `Math` constants:

- `Math.E`. The natural base for a logarithm. The approximate value is 2.71828.

- `Math.LN2`. The natural logarithm of 2. The approximate value is 0.69314718055994528623.

- `Math.LN10`. The natural logarithm of 10. The approximate value is 2.3025850929940459011.

- `Math.LOG2E`. The base-2 logarithm of `MATH.E`. The approximate value is 1.442695040888963387.

- `Math.LOG10E`. The base-10 logarithm of `MATH.E`. The approximate value is 0.43429448190325181667.

- `Math.PI`. The ratio of the circumference of a circle to its diameter, expressed as pi. The approximate value is 3.14159265358979.

- `Math.SQRT1_2`. The reciprocal of the square root of one half. The approximate value is 0.707106781186.

- `Math.SQRT2`. The square root of 2. The approximate value is 1.414213562373.

Numbers are the basis of almost all object-oriented programming. In the next chapter, "Statements and Expressions," you'll see a lot of ActionScript that involves using numbers.

Boolean Data Type

The next data type we'll discuss is boolean. Boolean data types are logical answers in the form of true or false. Also notice that these words cannot be used as variables or identifiers in ActionScript because they are strictly boolean data types. Let's take a look at a use of boolean:

```
var alarm = true;
if (alarm == true) {
    trace ("Wake me up!");
}else{
    trace ("Let me sleep in.");
}
// output: Wake me up!
```

Because `alarm` is set to `true`, the `if` statement is true and traces the appropriate message. If the alarm had been set to false, the `else` statement would have taken effect.

Boolean can be used in many ways, and we'll examine this data type in more detail in Chapter 12.

Null Data Type

The null data type is a representation that a variable has no data or definable data (string, number, boolean, and so on). Null will not show up in the Output window unless assigned in the code.

> **Tip**
>
> Null must be assigned manually; the interpreter will not assign it.

Because null is a representation of no data, it is only equal to itself and the undefined data type. Here's an example:

```
if (null == undefined) {
     trace ("no data equals no data");
}
// output: no data equals no data
```

Undefined Data Type

Much like null, undefined represents the absence of data. However, unlike null, there are a few ways for undefined to be assigned:

- It can be manually assigned in the Actions panel.
- The interpreter will assign it if a variable does not exist.
- The interpreter will assign it if a variable has no value.

Let's take a look at the undefined data type in action.

```
var title;
trace (typeof(title));
// output: undefined
```

Like null, because undefined represents the absence of data, it is only equal to itself and null.

Array Data Type

Arrays are used to hold lists of data and sometimes even lists of lists. Here's an example of an array:

```
myArray = new Array("David","Mike","Bart");
```

For more on arrays, see Chapter 15.

Movieclip Data Type

Although this is not a conventional data type, you cannot convert to this data type from another. It is important in that you can manipulate instances of movie clips by using this data type.

Movieclip acts more like a class of an object than a data type. You can set its properties, and the property changes will be shown in the movie clip on the main stage. For exam-

ple, if you wanted to make the instance "circle" on the main stage have a 50 percent Alpha setting, you would use the following:

```
Circle._alpha = 50;
```

For more on the movieclip data type, see Chapter 13, "Movie Clip Objects."

Object Data Type

The object data type is used to set up ActionScripted objects in Flash. Here is an example of a dog object and a property of the dog object:

```
//Create the object
dog = new Object();
//Assign a property
dog.type="Beagle";
//Display the property in the output window
trace(dog.type);
```

Variables

Now that we have covered data, let's take a look at what holds this data—variables.

Data without variables only lives for a second; once the interpreter has passed it, its lifespan is over. Variables are like Tupperware: They can hold data for long periods of time, and whenever you want that data, you just go to the variable and it's still there. A variable can hold any type of data, including: strings, numbers, Boolean values, and even other variables.

A downside to variables is that they can only hold one piece of data. Arrays, on the other hand, can hold multiple pieces of data (see Chapter 15 for more information).

Making a Variable

A variable can be created in several different ways. Let's start with the easiest method, which is the one we will be using most often. You simply use the keyword var to start the process and then name the variable. You close the line with a semicolon so that the interpreter knows the line has finished. Here's an example:

```
var myVariable;
```

That's easy enough. Now let's assign it some data:

```
var myVariable = "Unleashed";
//we set myVariable to the string literal "Unleashed"
```

Unlike many other programming languages, ActionScript does not require you to declare what type of data you are holding in a certain variable, nor does the data have to stay the same, but more on that later on.

You do not actually need the keyword var to declare a variable (although the code is easier to follow when you're looking through it); the interpreter will recognize that a variable has been declared when data is assigned. Here's an example:

```
myVariable = "Unleashed";
//we still declared a variable, but without the keyword var
```

Another way to declare a variable is by using the set identifier. In the parentheses, you declare the variable's name as a string literal and then set its value after a comma:

```
set ( "myVariable", 6 );
trace (myVariable);
// output: 6
```

We have looked at assigning variables with single pieces of data; now let's look at one assigned with an expression:

```
var myVariable = 2+4;
trace (myVariable);
// output: 6
```

This time, we are going to assign a variable to another variable:

```
var myVariable = "Unleashed";
var variable2 = myVariable;
trace (variable2);
// output: Unleashed
```

You can create multiple variables with the same data using equality marks to separate them, as shown here:

```
var myVariable = variable2 = variable3 = "Unleashed";
trace (myVariable);
trace (variable2);
trace (variable3);
// output: Unleashed
//         Unleashed
//         Unleashed
```

You can even assign a variable to an expression using other variables:

```
var myVariable = 4;
var myVariable2 = 2;
var addedVariables = myVariable + myVariable2;
trace (addedVariables);
// output: 6
```

Changing Data in Variables

Now that you have seen how to create variables and add data to them, let's see how to change the data in them.

The process is as simple as reassigning data to the variables:

```
var myVariable = "Unleashed";
trace (myVariable);
myVariable = "Flash";
trace (myVariable);
// output: Unleashed
//         Flash
```

What's more, the new data doesn't have to be of the same type:

```
var myVariable = "Unleashed";
trace (myVariable);
myVariable = 6;
trace (myVariable);
myVariable = false;
trace (myVariable);
// output: Unleashed
//         6
//         False
```

This time, we changed `myVariable` from a string literal to a number and then to a boolean data type.

Another way to change a variable is to add to it. Here's an example:

```
var myVariable = "Flash";
trace (myVariable);
myVariable = myVariable + " Unleashed";
trace (myVariable);
// output: Flash
//         Flash Unleashed
```

Here, all we did was set the variable equal to itself plus another string. There is an easier way of doing this—by using an assignment operator, called the *addition assignment* (+=).

We'll use the same code as before but replace the long, written method of adding additional text with this new way:

```
var myVariable = "Flash";
trace (myVariable);
myVariable +=  " Unleashed";
trace (myVariable);
// output: Flash
//         Flash Unleashed
```

Now let's look at another variable that uses an incremental operator to increase its value.

Incrementing and Decrementing Variables

As you have just seen, you can add to already created variables. Now let's look at how to do it with numbers.

First, create a movie clip with a small circle centered in it and place it on the main stage. Then, go into the object actions of that movie clip instance and place the following code in it:

```
//lets create our variable when the instance loads
onClipEvent (load) {
i = 0;
}
onClipEvent (enterFrame) {
//lets increase our variable one at a time
i = i + 1;
trace (i);
}
// output: (it will start with 1, and increase by 1 constantly)
```

That was the old way of adding to variables; now let's do it the new way:

```
//lets create our variable when the instance loads
onClipEvent (load) {
i = 0;
}
onClipEvent (enterFrame) {
//lets increase our variable one at a time
i += 1;
trace (i);
}
// output: (it will start with 1, and increase by 1 constantly)
```

That looks better, but there's still an easier way to increase a variable by one each time, and that's by using the increment operator (++):

```
//lets create our variable when the instance loads
onClipEvent (load) {
i = 0;
}
onClipEvent (enterFrame) {
//lets increase our variable one at a time
i ++;
trace (i);
}
// output: (it will start with 1, and increase by 1 constantly)
```

That was great! However, if we want to increase our variable by more than one at a time, we'll have to go back to the addition assignment because the increment operator only increases at a rate of one at a time.

Data Types and Variables—In Depth

CHAPTER 11

315

11

DATA TYPES AND
VARIABLES—
IN DEPTH

Now that we have these numbers, let's make them move the movie clip to the right. While still in the object actions of the movie clip, use the following code:

```
//lets create our variable when the instance loads
//lets create our variable when the instance loads
onClipEvent (load) {
i = this._x;
}
onClipEvent (enterFrame) {
//lets increase our variable one at a time
i ++;
this._x = i;
}
```

Now when you test the movie, the little circle will move to the right one pixel at a time.

Technically, you could have written the preceding code like this:

```
onClipEvent (enterFrame) {
_x++;
}
```

We've covered increment variables, so now let's review decrement variables. These variables are the exact opposite of increment variables because they take away one at a time.

Let's look at our previous code with the circle move clip. Using the same code, replace instances of **++** with **- -**, which will cause the variable to decrease:

```
//lets create our variable when the instance loads
//lets create our variable when the instance loads
onClipEvent (load) {
i = this._x;
}
onClipEvent (enterFrame) {
//lets increase our variable one at a time
i --
this._x = i;
}
```

Now the circle moves to the left one pixel at a time.

Empty Variables

As you know from previous sections, an empty variable has a value of undefined. We can use this to test whether a variable is being used. We use an `if` statement to test whether a variable is equal to undefined; if it is, the variable needs to be filled. Let's take a look at an example:

```
var title;
if (title == undefined) {
```

```
trace ("This variable is empty");
}else{
trace ("This variable has information in it");
}
// output: This variable is empty
```

Because the variable we created has yet to be assigned any data, it is automatically valued as undefined and the `if` statement value is `true`.

Comparing Variables

Oftentimes when using variables, you'll want to compare one against another (for password verification, memory games, and high score validation, for example).

When you're comparing variables, it's important that they are the same data type. Keep that in mind until we get to the next section.

Let's start with a password-verification example. We'll use a predefined password and a user input password and compare them. If they are equal, we'll run some specific code; if they are not equal, we'll run different code. Here are the steps to follow:

1. Start a new file by going to File, New in the toolbar.

2. Create two more layers on the main timeline and label the layers Actions, Input, and Validate, respectively.

3. Now create a movie called "validate" that has a rectangle in it with the text "Validate" over top of it. Place this movie on the Validate layer of the main timeline and label its instance name "validate."

4. In the Input layer, choose the Text tool and draw a text box. Change the type to Input and choose Show Border Around Text so you can easily see the text box when we test the movie. Then choose Password for the line type instead of Single Line (this will place asterisks instead of characters in the text box). Then label the Var label input. The settings should look like Figure 11.1.

5. Now for the actions. In the first keyframe of the Actions layer, place this code:

```
//We first create the password
password="flash";
//Now we set the button actions for the validate movie
validate.onPress = function (){
//this will check to see if the password and the input match
    if(input==password){
        trace("You may enter");
    }else{
        trace("You do not have clearance");
```

```
//This clears the input field
        input="";
    }
}
```

FIGURE 11.1

Creating the
Validate button.

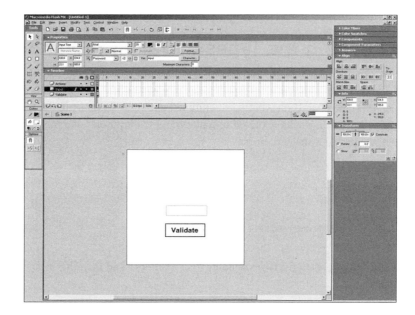

When you test the movie, note that if you enter the correct password, it issues a welcome message in the Output window; otherwise, the output window displays a different message and clears the user input field.

As another example of using variables, let's try to determine whether a new score is the high score.

Create a new file as before in previous examples (Ctrl+N) and put the following code in the first frame of the main timeline:

```
//first create the current high score
highScore = 1200;
//then create a new score to rival the high score
newScore = 1300;
//now create the if statement that will determine and adjust the high score
if (newScore > highScore){
highScore = newScore;
trace ("congratulations, the new highscore is " + highScore);
}else if (newScore == highScore) {
trace ("You are now tied for 1st at " + highScore);
```

```
}else{
trace ("Your score of " + newScore + " was not good enough");
}
// output: congratulations, the new highscore is 1300
```

Test the movie. Then go back and change the variables to see different results.

Changing the Types of Values in Variables

You may have noticed in the preceding high-score example that we were adding two different types of values into one statement. So, what does that make the value of the statement? That depends on what was combined and how. Because in the previous example we added a string with text in it to a number, the interpreter automatically converted the entire thing to a string.

Now let's take a look at using the `typeof` function to check the value of a given variable:

```
var name = "Kevin ";
var age = 35;
var combined = name + age;
trace (typeof(combined));
// output: string
```

Let's suppose we have two variables (one a number and the other a string containing numbers):

```
var year = "1967"
var age = 35;
var combined = year + age;
trace (typeof(combined));
// output: string
```

This still comes back as string. However, if we subtract them, the result changes, as shown here:

```
var year = "1967"
var age = 35;
var combined = year - age;
trace (typeof(combined));
// output: number
```

When the variables are subtracted, the interpreter converts the combination to a number.

Although the conversion has taken place in the `combined` variable, it has not affected the original values. Automatic conversion only works when evaluating an expression.

When using a boolean in an expression involving a number, the conversion will always be to a number, as shown here:

```
var answer = true;
var age = 35;
```

```
var combined = year + age;
trace (typeof(combined));
// output: number
```

Same goes for a boolean and a string. Both data types will always convert to a string:

```
var answer = true;
var age = "35";
var combined = year + age;
trace (typeof(combined));
// output: string
```

As far as conversion goes, what does the interpreter convert each element to? To find out, let's take a look at the next few lists.

To string conversions:

- A number converts to a string literal equal to that number (for example, 123 to "123").
- A boolean converts to "true" if true and "false" if false.
- Undefined converts to "undefined".
- Null converts to "undefined".
- NaN converts to "NaN".
- An array converts to a list of elements separated by commas.

To number conversions:

- A string containing numbers converts to a numeric value represented in those numbers.
- A string not containing numbers converts to NaN.
- Undefined converts to 0.
- Null converts to 0.
- A boolean converts to 1 if true and 0 if false.
- NaN converts to NaN.
- An array converts to NaN.

To boolean conversions:

- A string with a nonzero number converts to true.
- A string containing zero converts to false.
- An empty string converts to false.
- A number converts to true if it's a nonzero number and false if it's zero.

- Undefined converts to false.
- Null converts to false.
- NaN converts to false.
- An array converts to true.

Converting Variables Using Functions and Methods

Now that you know what values convert to, let's see how to convert them. We will start the conversions by using the toString method.

The toString Method

This method acts like any of the previous methods we've discussed. Simply attach it directly to a data type you would like to convert to a string or attach it to a variable you would like to convert. There are no arguments in the parentheses. Here's an example:

```
var age = 35;
age.toString();      //Converts the variable age to a string
false.toString();    //Converts the boolean datatype false to a string
(50).toString();     //Converts the number 50 to a string
                     // the parentheses are there as to not
                     // confuse the interpreter into
                     //thinking it was a decimal point
```

The String Function

To use the String function, simply place the variable or data type you would like to convert in the parentheses, and the function will convert it to a string:

```
String(myVariable);
String(123);
String(null);
// the String function converts all of these datatypes to a string datatype
```

Using Operators

You have already seen that using a plus sign (+) will convert numbers and variables to a string, as shown here:

```
500 + "string";      //Converted to a string
myVariable + "";     //Using an empty string to convert variables to a string
```

You can also convert a data type to a number by subtracting zero from it:

```
"123" - 0            //Converts the string to a number
"Flash" - 0          //Becomes NaN due to lack of numbers to convert
myVariable - 0       //Converts value of myVariable to a number
```

The `Number` Function

This function acts nearly identically to the `String` function. Place the variable or data you wish to convert in between the parentheses, and the function will convert it to a number:

```
Number(myVariable);        //Converts value of myVariable to a number
Number("Unleashed");       //Becomes NaN
Number("1234");            //Becomes the number 1234
```

This function is great for converting input fields that are string literals.

The `parseInt` and `parseFloat` Functions

These functions convert strings to numbers much like the `Number` function. However, unlike the `Number` function, these two functions can pull numbers out of text, as long as the first non-space character is a number.

Let's take a look at the `parseInt` function, which is for pulling whole integers (remember from earlier, integers have no decimals or fractional values). Just attach this function like you would any other function and place the variable or string you want to convert in the parentheses:

```
var idNumber = "123abc";
trace (parseInt(idNumber));
// output: 123
```

The `parseFloat` function works in much the same manner, but it pulls floating numbers instead of integers:

```
var idNumber = "123.487abc";
trace (parseFloat(idNumber));
// output: 123.487
```

If the first non-space character is anything but a numeric value, the function returns NaN:

```
var idNumber = "abd123.487";
trace (parseInt(idNumber));
// output: NaN
```

In case you're wondering what happens when you use `parseInt` on a floating number, the following example shows that the function will return everything up to the decimal point:

```
var idNumber = "123.487abc";
trace (parseInt(idNumber));
// output: 123
```

However, if you use the `parseFloat` function on an integer, it will return the same value as the `parseInt` function:

```
var idNumber = "123abc";
trace (parseFloat(idNumber));
// output: 123
```

The `Boolean` Function

Converting to a boolean is as easy as using the `String` or `Number` function. Place the variable or data type in the parentheses, and the `Boolean` function converts it to a boolean:

```
Boolean(myVariable);    //Converts the value of myVariable to Boolean
Boolean(123);           //Converts to true
Boolean(0)              //Converts to false
```

Longevity of Conversions

We have been converting data types from left and right over these last couple of pages, but how long do these conversions last? If you are just converting a raw data type or the value of a variable, the conversion only lasts as long as the interpreter reads it (which is less than a second). However, if you set a variable equal to the conversion, it lasts as long as the variable lasts, or until it is changed again. Here's an example:

```
var myVariable = 10;
trace (Boolean(myVariable));
trace (myVariable);
// output: true
//         10
```

As you can see, the conversion just lasted long enough for the result to be traced; then it went back to normal. Now let's set the converted value to a variable:

```
var myVariable = 10;
myVariable = Boolean(myVariable);
trace (myVariable);
// output: true
```

Now the variable `myVariable` is a boolean data type.

The Scope of a Variable

So far, we have placed variables on the main timeline and in a movie on the main timeline. It's now time you learned about the scope of variables and how to overcome the shortcomings of the local scope of variables.

Timeline Variables

Whenever a variable is created or defined on a timeline, it is available to every frame on that timeline as well as any buttons that have been placed on the stage associated with that timeline.

Any code placed in the object actions of a movie clip instance can access variables on the timeline of that movie, but not the timeline the movie is in. Here's an exercise to make this clear:

1. Start a new file like before.

2. Create a movie called myMovie. On this movie clip's timeline, in the first frame, place the following code:

```
var myVariable = "Success";
```

In the second frame of the movie, place this code:

```
//this will stop the movie from looping
stop();
trace (myVariable);
```

3. Now create a new layer and place a rectangle on that layer. Highlight the rectangle and press F8 on your keyboard to convert it to symbol (or select Insert, Convert to Symbol on the toolbar). Then choose Button. Now you have a button on the time-line. Go into the actions of this button and place the following code:

```
on (press) {
        trace (myVariable);
}
```

You're done with this movie. Go to the main timeline, place your new movie on the main stage, and test it.

You should see the word *Success* pop up in the output window, and when you click the rectangle button, the variable should appear again (see Figure 11.2).

FIGURE 11.2

*A successful
implementation of
a timeline
variable.*

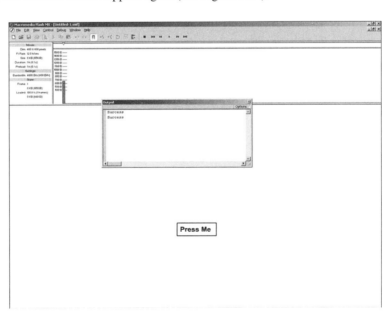

Dot Syntax

Dot syntax enables code to see from one timeline to the next, either by direct route with the use of instance names or with special predefined tags such as _root and _parent. Just remember that each level must be separated by a dot, hence *dot syntax*.

The _root and _parent tags are constants: _root is always the main timeline and will never change, but _parent is relative to where you are using it, and it always goes up one level.

Another part of dot syntax involves using the instance names of symbols. For example, if you want to know the horizontal position of myMovie on the main timeline, you would type the following:

```
_root.myMovie._x
```

If you need to know myVariable in the movie myMovie, which is embedded in theMovie, which in turn is on the main timeline, you would use this:

```
_root.theMovie.myMovie.myVariable
```

The _root Tag

The _root tag represents the main timeline; everything on it can be accessed like so:

```
_root.whatever
```

Let's look at an example of this:

1. In the movie you created earlier, go into the object actions and place the following code:

```
onClipEvent (load) {
        trace (theVariable);
        trace (_root.theVariable);
}
```

2. On the main timeline in the first frame, place this code:

```
var theVariable = "theRoot";
```

Now test the movie again. Here's the output:

```
// output: undefined
//          theRoot
//          Success
```

The movie came back with undefined because the variable could not be found in its local scope, but in the root it found the variable with ease.

The _parent Tag

The _parent tag is used in dot syntax to refer to one step up. Parents can be overlapped like this:

```
_parent._parent
```

However, no more than two parents are allowed to connect together.

Now go back into the object actions of the movie you created earlier and replace its code with the following:

```
onClipEvent (load) {
    trace (_parent.theVariable);
}
```

Now test again:

```
// output: theRoot
//         Success
```

This time, the _parent part of the dot syntax looks up one level and finds the variable.

Now let's get the _root timeline to find the vertical position of the movie.

1. Name the instance of the movie "myMovie."

2. In the first frame of the main timeline, add this line of code:

   ```
   trace(_root.myMovie._y);
   ```

Now test the movie. The first line you see in the output window should be a number representing the vertical position of myMovie.

Although this may seem tedious and difficult to understand, thanks to a new identifier in Flash MX called _global, a lot of these problems can be solved.

The _global Identifier

Introduced in Flash MX, the _global identifier creates data types that can be seen from all parts of the Flash movie without the use of dot syntax and target pathing.

Just attach the _global identifier to what you would like to make global; then you can access it from anywhere in the Flash movie.

1. Start a new Flash movie. Then on the main timeline, in the first frame, place this code:

   ```
   _global.myVariable = "Omnipotent";
   ```

2. On the stage, draw a rectangle and convert it to a symbol (F8). Call it draw1.

3. Convert it again and, this time, call it draw2.

4. Convert it for a third time and call it draw3.

5. Open up your library (Ctrl+L) and go into draw1. In the first frame of the timeline, place the following code:

```
trace (myVariable);
```

Now test the movie:

```
// output: Omnipotent
```

Is that powerful or what? You have just traced a variable on the main timeline from another timeline that is imbedded into three separate movies.

If you happen to create a local variable with the same name, only ActionScript attempting to access it locally will be affected; it will not affect the global variable.

An Applied Example

You have learned a lot of fun stuff in this chapter (and some not-so-fun stuff). Let's end with an easily applied example of how to use variables. Follow these steps:

1. Start a new Flash movie and make its dimensions 400×400 (Ctrl+M) in the stage properties.

2. Now draw a circle on the main stage, but not too big—about 50×50 should do. Convert this circle to symbol and make it a movie clip.

3. Open up the Actions panel and go into the object actions of the movie and place the following code:

```
onClipEvent (load) {
//create all our variables
friction = .5;
pointX = Math.round(Math.random()*400)
pointY = Math.round(Math.random()*400);
}
onClipEvent (enterFrame) {
//set our if statements to move at different speeds
//based on distance, and to pick a new spot once the
//designated spot has been reached
if (Math.round(_x) != pointX){
    _x+=(pointX-_x)*friction;
}else if (Math.round(_x) == pointX){
    pointX = Math.round(Math.random()*400);
}
if (Math.round(_y) != pointY) {
    _y+=(pointY-_y)*friction;
}else if (Math.round(_y) == pointY){
```

```
        pointY = Math.round(Math.random()*400);
    }
}
```

In this example, the `if` statements are saying that if the object is not at its designated spot yet, adjust its position based on the distance it is from the designated spot. Then, once it has reached the spot, pick a new spot and keep moving the circle.

Note that you can adjust the friction to achieve some interesting effects.

Statements and Expressions—In Depth

By David Vogeleer

IN THIS CHAPTER

- Statement Syntax
- Object Statements
- Flow Modifiers

This chapter covers statements and expressions. Even though we have not formally gone over statements, you have already used them. A *statement* is simply a small piece of code made up of keywords, operators, and identifiers. Statements can be in one of six different categories:

- **Declaration statements**. These statements involve declaring variables, creating functions, setting properties, declaring arrays, and so on. Here's an example:

```
var myVariable;              // declares a variable
    myObject._x = 235;       //setting the horizontal position
    myArray = new Array ();  //creating an array
function myFunction (){      //creates a function
```

- **Expressions**. These include any type of legal expression. Here's an example:

```
i++;                    //increase a variable
lName + space + fName;  //combining variables
```

- **Flow modifiers**. These include any statement that disrupts the natural flow of the interpreter reading the ActionScript. There are two subtypes of flow modifiers: conditional statements and loop statements.

  Conditional statements use Boolean answers to determine what to do next or what *not* to do next. Here's an example:

```
if (inputName == userName){
    if (inputPassword == password){
    gotoAndPlay("startPage");
}else {
    displayMessage = "Double check you password";
}
}else if (inputName != userName){
if (inputPassword == password){
    displayMessage = "Double check your user name";
}
}else{
    displayMessage = "Double check all your information";
}
```

  Loop statements run until a defined condition has been met. Here's an example:

```
for (i=0; i<30; i++) {
    trace (i);
}
```

- **Predefined functions**. Functions that are predefined in ActionScript. Here's an example:

```
trace ("function");        //a simple trace function
gotoAndStop (2);           //a playback function
getProperty( myMovie, _x );  //gets the horizontal position
```

- **Object statements**. Statements that deal with and manipulate objects. Here's an example:

```
myGrades = { tests: 85, quizzes: 88, homework: 72 };
for (name in myGrades) {
    trace ("myGrades." + name + " = " + myGrades[name]);
}
//output: myGrades.tests = 85
//        myGrades.quizzes = 88
//        myGrades.homework = 72
```

- **Comments**. This last category is one of a kind. It includes comments used in code merely as information for the user while in the actions panel; the interpreter will skip over these comments. Here's an example:

```
//this is a comment used in ActionScript;
```

Breaking up statements into these simple categories is only to help you understand the different types and uses of statements. We will go over a few of these categories in more detail later in this chapter.

Now, let's look at some of the basics of building these statements.

Statement Syntax

As you've seen, statements are keywords, operators, and identifiers joined together to accomplish certain tasks. For instance, in the following code, `var` and `new` are the keywords, `Array ()` is the identifier, and the equal sign is the operator:

```
var myArray = new Array ();
```

As you'll notice, a semicolon has been placed at the end of this statement. This semicolon tells the interpreter that the statement is complete and to move on to the next one. The semicolon is not required, and the interpreter will move on without it. However, it is good coding etiquette to place one there.

Also, it is good etiquette to place each new statement on its own line. Again, this is not necessary, but it is a good practice to follow. You can see this for yourself by examining the following two segments of code. Which code section is easier to read?

```
myVariable = "Flash";
myVariable += " Unleashed";
trace (myVariable);
//output: Flash Unleashed

myVariable = "Flash"; myVariable += " Unleashed"; trace (myVariable);
//output: Flash Unleashed
```

Although the output is the same, the first section of code is much easier to read than the second. Note the spacing between each part of the statement. Oftentimes this is a necessity for the interpreter to correctly identify each part. However, even if this spacing is not always required, it is *always* a good rule to follow.

Statement Block

Some statements have multiple statements associated with them, particularly *flow modifiers*. These statements have statements within them that appear between brackets. Let's take a look at an example:

```
if (book == "Flash Unleashed") {
    trace ("Your on the right track");
}
```

The first statement is an `if` statement (`if` statements are discussed in greater detail later in this chapter) that contains a function statement. Notice that not only is the `trace` function held between brackets, but it is indented as well. This indentation is not a requirement but is used for improved readability. In Flash MX, you can turn on the option to have statements indent automatically: Choose Auto Format under the ActionScript preferences or press Ctrl+Shift+F. You can even adjust the settings of the automatic formatting under Auto Format preferences.

Also, note that the lines with brackets do not have semicolons, but the lines between the brackets do. What's more, the closing bracket is aligned with the beginning of the line that the opening bracket is on. Again, this is not a requirement; it's just placed this way for ease of readability.

The closing bracket is required if an opening bracket is used; otherwise, the interpreter will send an error message like this one:

```
Statement block must be terminated by '}'
```

Even though the earlier code is in brackets, because only one statement is held within the `if` statement, the use of brackets is not required. Instead, the code can be written like this:

```
if (book == "Flash Unleashed") trace ("Your on the right track");
```

As a personal preference, I use brackets in conditional statements, even if they are not required, just for consistency.

Another type of statement that uses brackets is a user-defined function. Here's an example:

```
function myFunction (myVariable){
     trace (myVariable);
}
var name = "David";
myFunction (name);
//output: David
```

Again, the statement held within the function appears between brackets and is also indented for easy reading and consistency.

Now that we have gone over some of the basic syntax of statements, let's cover some of the statement categories in more detail.

Object Statements

This section covers a couple of the statements associated directly with objects (which will be discussed in later chapters). These include the `with` statement and the `for in` statement.

The `with` Statement

The `with` statement is for controlling multiple properties of an object without the hassle of retyping the object over and over again. Just place the object's name in the parentheses, and the properties listed between the brackets are the ones affected for that object. Here's an example:

```
//first create an object
myObject = new Object();
with (myObject){
     _x = 50;
     _y = 100;
     _alpha = 75;
}
```

Another use of the `with` statement involves associating it with a movie clip and using some of the new drawing features available in Flash MX.

First, create an empty movie clip and place it on the main stage. You accomplish this by going to the title bar and choosing Insert, New Symbol (or by pressing Ctrl+F8 on your keyboard). Then you can name it whatever you like, but make sure it is a movie clip type. For this example, name it myMovie. After that, go back to scene 1 and open the Library by choosing Window, Library (Ctrl+L), choosing your movie, and dragging it onto the stage. Now, place the following actions in the object actions of your movie:

```
onClipEvent (enterFrame) {
     with (this){
```

```
        lineStyle (1, 0x397DCE, 150);
        lineTo (_root._xmouse,_root._ymouse);
    }
}
```

Using `with` allows you to associate the drawing actions with a single movie at once, instead of having to associate each action individually, like this:

```
onClipEvent (enterFrame) {
    this.lineStyle (1, 0x397DCE, 150);
    this.lineTo (_root._xmouse,_root._ymouse);
}
```

As you have seen, the `with` statement can be very powerful, especially if it's assigned to a function, as in this example:

```
function myFunction (myMovie){
    with (myMovie){
        _x=50;
        _y=20;
        trace (myMovie._name);
    }
}
```

Now, all you have to do is call the function on any movie clip and all the properties and functions associated with the `with` statement will be applied to that clip.

The `for in` Statement

The `for in` statement is an advanced loop statement that's associated directly with objects. Unlike other loop statements, which run based on a defined condition, the `for in` statement runs until all properties of the assigned object are evaluated.

The syntax for this statement can be difficult, so its important that you read this section carefully. Start with the `for` keyword; then add an opening parenthesis and the keyword `var`. Following that, name the variable that will hold each property for the object; then add the keyword `in`. Next, place the name of the object you are using followed by a closing parenthesis and an opening bracket. Between the brackets is where you'll place the code that will use the properties of the object. Let's take a look at a generic template:

```
for (var myProp in myObject){
    //the code to use the properties;
}
```

This seems simple enough, so now let's go over how to use the properties. There are two types of property calls: one calls the property's name, and the other calls the property's value.

The first type of property call simply uses the variable you created to hold the properties. An example will help make this clearer.

First, let's create an object we can use for the rest of the exercise; then we'll use the `for in` statement to call each properties' name in this object:

```
var contact = new Object();
contact.name = "David";
contact.age = 22;
contact.state = "VA";
for (var myProp in contact){
        trace (myProp);
}
//output: state
//        age
//        name
```

In the preceding example, we traced the variable we created to hold each property in our object. As you'll notice, it does not start at the beginning but rather at the end, and it moves toward the beginning.

Now that you know how to pull the names of the properties, let's go over how to pull the values of each property. To get the value of each property, use the object's name (in this case, `contact`) and connect it to the variable we created inside of brackets. Here is the example:

```
var contact = new Object();
contact.name = "David";
contact.age = 22;
contact.state = "VA";
for (var myProp in contact){
        trace (contact[myProp]);
}
//output: VA
//        22
//        David
```

You know how to get the names of the properties, and you just saw how to get the values. Now let's combine the two:

```
var space = " "
var contact = new Object();
contact.name = "David";
contact.age = 22;
contact.state = "VA";
for (var myProp in contact){
        trace (myProp + ":" + space + contact[myProp]);
}
//output: state: VA
//        age: 22
//        name: David
```

Let's not stop there; let's take a big step forward and set the `for in` statement to a function. Then we'll place all the properties of the object in an array with named elements (see Chapter 15 "Arrays," for more on arrays):

```
var contact = new Object();
     contact.name = "David";
     contact.age = 22;
     contact.state = "VA";
     var myArray = new Array();
function makeArray (myObject){
     for (var myProp in myObject){
          myArray[myProp] = myObject[myProp];
     }
}
makeArray(contact);
trace (myArray.name);
//output: David
```

While we are on the subject of arrays, note that you can also pull each element out of an array using the `for in` statement, as if it were a property of an object. Here's an example:

```
var myArray = new Array ("David",22,"VA");
var space = " ";
for (var element in myArray){
     trace (element + ":" + space + myArray[element]);
}
//output: 2: VA
//        1: 22
//        0: David
```

The `for in` statement also works on named array elements, as you can see here:

```
var myArray = new Array ("David",22,"VA");
myArray.city = "Richmond";
var space = " ";
for (var element in myArray){
     trace (element + ":" + space + myArray[element]);
}
//output: city: Richmond
//        2: VA
//        1: 22
//        0: David
```

Now that we have discussed object statements, let's move on to flow modifiers.

Flow Modifiers

So far, we have gone over ActionScript as a language that executes code, one line after the other, without stopping. Now we are going to go over some statements that redefine how ActionScript functions.

Flow modifiers are statements that adjust the natural order the interpreter takes when reading ActionScript. When the interpreter hits a flow modifier, it doesn't just run the statement and move on. Instead, it runs the statement to see whether a condition has been met. If the condition hasn't been met, sometimes the interpreter will move on, but other times it will stay at that spot until the condition has been met. In most cases, this condition is user defined.

The first of the flow modifiers we'll cover is the conditional statement.

Conditional Statements

Conditional statements are statements that are executed only when their conditions have been met. These conditions are based on Boolean values (either `true` or `false`). Here's an example of how a conditional statement acts:

```
if (true){
     //do something;
}
```

You'll often use conditional statements in situations where you want to test whether to run certain code. Without these condition statements, every piece of ActionScript you place in the Actions panel would run without being checked for whether it is necessary or even correct.

An example would be a game where, after the user has finished, the ActionScript checks whether this user's score is higher than the present high score. If it is, the user's score becomes the new high score. However, if the user's score is not higher than the present high score, the new score will not replace the present one.

The code for this might look something like the following:

```
if (userScore > highScore) {
     highScore = userScore;
}
```

Everything between the parentheses is the *condition*, and the symbol between the two variables is the *comparison operator*. Before going on with more examples of conditional statements, we should go over each of the comparison operators and their uses.

Comparison Operators

If everything between the parentheses in a conditional statement is the condition, then the comparison operator is the type of condition. This operator tells the conditional statement how to evaluate the data in the condition. Here's a list of the comparison operators:

- Equality (==)
- Inequality (!=)
- Less than (<)
- Less than or equal to (<=)
- Greater than (>)
- Greater than or equal to (>=)
- Strict equality (===)
- Strict inequality (!==)

Equality Operator (==)

This operator determines whether two pieces of data are equal to one another. Here's are some examples:

```
var title = "Unleashed";          //creates our variable

if (title == "Unleashed"){        //evaluates to true

if (title == "Not Unleashed"){    //evaluates to false
```

Inequality Operator (!=)

This operator determines whether two pieces of data are *not* equal (note the exclamation point before the equal sign). Here are three examples:

```
var title = "Unleashed";          //creates our variable

if (title != "Unleashed"){        //evaluates to false

if (title != "Not Unleashed"){    //evaluates to true
```

Less than Operator (<)

This operator determines whether the variable on the left has a lower value than the variable on the right. Here are three examples:

```
var myAge = 22;
var yourAge = 20;
var myName = "David";
var yourName = "Caroline";    //create all the variables we need

if (myAge < yourAge){         //evaluates to false

if (yourName < myName){       //evaluates to true
```

Less than or Equal to Operator (<=)

This operator evaluates whether the data on the left is less than the data on the right. If this is true, or if they are equal, the condition will evaluate to true. Here are a few more examples:

```
var myAge = 22;
var yourAge = 22;
var myName = "David";      //create all the variables we need

if (myAge <= yourAge){      //evaluates to true

if ("David" <= myName){     //evaluates to true
```

Greater than Operator (>)

This operator determines whether the data on the left is greater than the data on the right. Here are three examples:

```
var myAge = 22;
var yourAge = 20;
var myName = "David";
var yourName = "Caroline";   //create all the variables we need

if (myAge > yourAge){        //evaluates to true

if (yourName > myName){      //evaluates to false
```

Greater than or Equal to Operator (>=)

This operator determines whether the data on the left is greater than the data on the right, and if they are equal, the condition will evaluate to true. Here are three examples:

```
var myAge = 22;
var yourAge = 24;
var myName = "David";      //create all the variables we need

if (myAge >= yourAge){      //evaluates to false

if ("David" >= myName){     //evaluates to true
```

Strict Equality (===)

This operator not only determines whether the values are equal but also whether they are the same type of value. Notice the triple equal sign, as opposed to the double equal sign for the regular equality operator. Here are four examples:

```
if (5 == 5){      //evaluates to true

if (5 == "5"){     //evaluates to true
```

```
if (5 ===5){        //evaluates to true

if (5 === "5"){    //evaluates to false
```

Notice how that with an equality sign, the string value "5" is evaluated as being equal to the number 5, but with strict equality, they are not equal.

Strict Inequality (!==)

This operator not only determines whether the values are not equal but also determines whether the values are not the same type (note the exclamation point in front of the double equal signs). Here are four examples:

```
if (5 != 5){        //evaluates to false

if (5 != "5"){      //evaluates to false

if (5 !==5){        //evaluates to false

if (5 !== "5"){     //evaluates to true
```

Strict equality and strict inequality are new additions to the comparison operators in Flash MX. They are very useful, not only for determining whether two values are the same but also whether they are being used the same.

Now that we have gone over the comparison operators, let's get back into the conditional statements, starting with the `if` statement.

The `if` Statement

You have been using the `if` statement for sometime without a formal introduction, so let's start with the basics of how this statement works.

The `if` statement works like a simple "yes or no" questionnaire: If `true`, then run the code in the curly brackets; if `false`, skip the code in the curly brackets and move on.

The `if` statement starts out with the keyword `if` and is followed by a condition, which is any comparison expression held within parentheses. This is followed by an opening curly bracket, which is followed by all the ActionScript that is to run if the condition evaluates to `true`. Finally, a closing curly bracket finishes the statement.

The simplest of `if` statements involves actually placing a Boolean value right into the condition, as shown here:

```
if (true){
      trace ("True");
}
if(false){
```

```
        trace ("False");
}
//output: True
```

In this case, only "True" will be traced, because that is the only condition that comes back true. The condition that was set to false is skipped once it is evaluated.

You can also use the numeric equivalent to the Boolean representation to accomplish the same effect:

```
if (1){
        trace ("True");
}
if(0){
        trace ("False");
}
//output: True
```

Again, only "True" is traced because 0 is equal to the Boolean value false. This is a good tool for evaluating numbers, because any number greater than zero will be considered true. Here's an example:

```
var myScore = 88;
var previousScore = 86;
if (myScore-previousScore){
        trace ("I've improved");
}
//output: I've improved
```

You can also use variables in if statements that hold values that translate to Boolean values or are Boolean values themselves:

```
var myVariable = 1;
if (myVariable){
        trace ("True");
}
//output: True
```

Another great feature of the if statement is that it can check whether a movie clip instance exists. Simply place the name of the instance in the condition, and if this instance exists, the if statement will evaluate to true; otherwise, it will evaluate to false.

Let's look at an example of this. First, create a shape on the main stage and then convert it to a symbol by going to the toolbar and selecting Insert, Convert to Symbol (F8). Then, name the instance myMovie.

Next, create a new layer and call the layer actions.

Then place the following code in the first frame on the main timeline in the actions layer:

```
if (myMovie){
        trace ("myMovie exists");
}
//output: myMovie exists
```

See Figure 12.1 to see what it is supposed to look like.

FIGURE 12.1

Place the movie clip on the main stage in its own layer and label the instance myMovie.

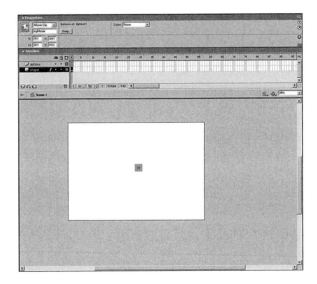

This is great, but if we want to check for a certain movie on the go, we set it to a function, as shown here:

```
function findMovie (myMovie){
        if (myMovie){
                trace ("myMovie exists");
        }
}
findMovie(myMovie)
```

Now whenever the movie exists on the same timeline as the function, when the function is invoked with the proper name, the phrase will be displayed in the output window.

You can also test a single variable to see whether it is "not true" in a conditional statement using the logical NOT operator.

The Logical NOT Operator (!)

The logical NOT operator is used to show inequality or to test whether something is false. Place an exclamation point in front of the variable you wish to test as "not true," as shown here:

```
var myVariable = false;
if (!myVariable) {
      trace ("myVariable is false");
}
//output: myVariable is false
```

This, when used in conjunction with the function we just created, can determine whether there is no instance of a specific movie on the stage:

```
function findMovie (myMovie){
      if (!myMovie){
            trace ("myMovie does not exist");
      }
}
findMovie(myMovie)
```

The function we created determines whether the movie does not exist, and if it doesn't, the trace function is run.

Now that you've seen the basic workings of the if statement, we'll cover nested if statements.

Nested if Statements

Nested if statements are if statements held by other statements to check more than one condition. You simply put the nested statement in as if it were a regular statement held within the original if statement. Here's an example:

```
var title = "Unleashed";
var name = "David";
if (title == "Unleashed"){
      if (name == "David"){
            trace ("They both match");
      }
}
//output: They both match
```

If the nested if statement evaluates to false, even with the original if statement evaluating to true, the trace function will not be run. Here's an example:

```
var title = "Unleashed";
var name = "David";
if (title == "Unleashed"){
      if (name == "Kevin"){
```

```
            trace ("They both match");
    }
}
//output: (nothing)
```

If the original `if` statement evaluates to `false`, the nested `if` statement will not even be evaluated. Again, the `trace` function will not be run. Here's an example:

```
var title = "Unleashed";
var name = "David";
if (title == "Flash"){
    if (name == "David"){
            trace ("They both match");
    }
}
//output: (nothing)
```

Now that you have seen how to evaluate multiple conditional statements using nested `if` statements, let's do the same thing using a logical operator.

The Short-circuit AND Operator (&&)

In the condition part of an `if` statement, you can place multiple conditions using the short-circuit AND operator. After the first condition, place a space, followed by two ampersands (&&) and then the second condition. Let's look at our previous example:

```
var title = "Unleashed";
var name = "David";
if (title == "Unleashed" && name == "David"){
    trace ("They both match");
}
//output: They both match
```

As with nested `if` statements, both conditions must evaluate to `true` in order for the entire condition to evaluate to `true`. Here's an example:

```
var title = "Unleashed";
var name = "David";
if (title == "Unleashed" && name == "Kevin"){
    trace ("They both match");
}
//output: (nothing)
```

You can place many of these operators in a single conditional statement for checking multiple conditions, as shown here:

```
var title = "Unleashed";
var name = "David";
if (title == "Unleashed" && name == "David"  && true){
    trace ("Everything is working");
}
//output: Everything is working
```

Now that you know how to check multiple conditions to see whether each is true, let's see whether any of the conditions are true using another logical operator.

The Logical OR Operator (| |)

Oftentimes you'll want to see whether any one of a set of conditions is correct. To do this without the logical OR operator requires multiple if statements with the same response over and over again, if any of the conditional statements are met. Let's take a look at what this would look like:

```
var name = "David";
var age = 22;
if (name == "David"){
     trace ("One of them are correct");
}
if (age == 33) {
     trace ("One of them are correct");
}
//output: One of them are correct
```

Because the first conditional statement evaluates to true, the trace function is run. But what if both the if statements evaluate to true?

```
var name = "David";
var age = 22;
if (name == "David"){
     trace ("One of them are correct");
}
if (age == 22) {
     trace ("One of them are correct");
}
//output: One of them are correct
//        One of them are correct
```

The problem we encounter using multiple if statements to determine whether one of them evaluates to true is that if they are both correct, both sections of code are executed, thus creating duplication. We could overcome this by using a test variable to hold a value if the first conditional statement is met. Instead, however, we are going to use the logical OR operator. The syntax of this operator is | | (Shift+\). Place this operator between conditions in the condition statement, separating them with a space on both sides. Let's take a look at this using our previous example:

```
var name = "David";
var age = 22;
if (name == "David" || age == 22){
     trace ("One of them are correct");
}
//output: One of them are correct
```

Now the interpreter reads the statement and checks to see whether the first condition is met. If so, it skips the second condition because of the OR operator and runs the trace function. If the first condition is not met, the interpreter evaluates the second condition, and if this condition is met, the trace function is run. If neither condition is met, the interpreter simply moves on.

With the OR operator, you can check to see whether any one of multiple conditions will be met. Here's an example:

```
var name = "David";
var age = 22;
if (name == "Kevin" || age == 33 || true){
      trace ("One of them are correct");
}
//output: One of them are correct
```

Because neither of the first two conditions evaluates to true, the third condition is evaluated to true and the trace function is run.

Another type of conditional statement is known as the *conditional*. We'll cover this type of conditional statement before moving on because it acts very similar to an if statement.

The Conditional (?:)

The conditional is more of an expression than a conditional statement, although it does have a conditional statement in it.

The syntax is a condition followed by a question mark, a value (which we'll call *value 1*), a colon, and then another value (which we'll call *value 2*).

If the condition evaluates to true, the expression's value is equal to value 1. If the condition does not evaluate to true, the expression's value is equal to value 2.

This is nice if you want to run a simple conditional statement without typing a lot. Here's an example:

```
var myVariable = 1;
var myVariable2 = 2;
var myVariable3 = (myVariable < myVariable2) ? myVariable : myvariable2
trace (myVariable3);
//output: 1
```

Let's look at another applied example:

```
var password = "flash";
var userPassword = "flash";
trace ((password == userPassword) ? "Correct": "Incorrect");
//output: Correct
```

As you'll notice, the previous conditional statement not only does something if the condition evaluates to `true` but also if it does not evaluate to `true`. We can also create a statement that will run if the conditional is not met. These statements are called `else` statements.

The `else` Statement

An `else` statement is used with an `if` statement. If the `if` statement does not evaluate to `true`, the `else` statement runs its code.

The syntax for `else` statements is like the syntax for other conditional statements, except it has no conditions. It runs when the evaluator reaches it. Here's an example:

```
var name = "David";
if (name == "Kevin"){
    trace ("The name is Kevin");
}else{
    trace ("The name is not Kevin");
}
//output: The name is not Kevin
```

Because the `if` statement does not evaluate to `true`, the `else` statement is run. If the `if` statement does evaluate to `true`, the `else` statement is not read by the interpreter. Here's another example:

```
var name = "David";
if (name == "David"){
    trace ("The name is David");
}else{
    trace ("The name is not David");
}
//output: The name is David
```

Now let's take a look at a more practical example of using the `else` statement, this time as an age-verification check:

```
//create a date object
var date = new Date();
//get the year
var year = date.getFullYear();
var inputYear = 1980;
//see the difference in inputYear and year
var age = year-inputYear
//evaluate if they are old enough
if (age >= 21) {
gotoAndPlay ("welcome");
}else{
gotoAndPlay ("tooYoung");
}
```

Now that you have seen what the `else` statement can do when joined with an `if` statement, let's look at the `else` `if` statement to see how it works.

The `else` `if` Statement

The `else` `if` statement allows you to run through several conditional statements in your code, and each is only read if the preceding conditional statement does not evaluate to `true`.

The syntax for the `else` `if` statement is nearly identical to the `if` statement, except that it has a preceding keyword of `else`, as demonstrated here:

```
var title = "Unleashed";
if (title == "Flash") {
      trace ("The title is Flash");
}else if (title == "Unleashed") {
      trace ("The title is Unleashed");
}else {
      trace ("We don't know what the title is");
}
//output: The title is Unleashed
```

Now that you understand the significance of the `else` `if` statement, let's take a look at the same code but *without* the `else` `if` statement:

```
var title = "Unleashed";
if (title == "Flash"){
      trace ("The title is Flash");
}else{
      if (title == "Unleashed") {
            trace ("The title is Unleashed");
      }else{
            trace ("We don't know what the title is");
      }
}
//output: The title is Unleashed
```

Besides fewer lines being required, the code is much easier to read in the first example than it is in the second one.

So far we have covered the `if` statement, the `else` statement, and the `else` `if` statement. Now let's go over another type of conditional statement: `switch`. We'll also discuss some of its methods.

`switch, case, default, and break`

A `switch` statement is used much like an `if` statement: It evaluates a condition and runs the code associated with that condition if the condition evaluates to `true`.

Statements and Expressions—In Depth
CHAPTER 12

349

12

STATEMENTS AND
EXPRESSIONS—
IN DEPTH

The syntax is difficult to understand, so don't feel bad if you don't get it the first time around.

The statement starts with the keyword switch, followed by a value in a set of parentheses and then an opening curly bracket. The value in the parentheses is usually a variable that you are looking for in strict equality (===) in your set of cases.

After the opening curly bracket, you begin to use the keyword case, followed by a space and another value and a colon. After the colon, you can put in any code you want to execute if the case evaluates to true. The value before the colon is what the switch is searching on, and it can be any data type. After the code you want to execute, place the keyword break to stop the code from going on to the next case without evaluating it.

Then, after all your cases, place the keyword default and a colon and then the code to be executed if none of the cases evaluates to true.

That's a lot to do, so before we look at an applied example, let's see what all this looks like:

```
switch (mainValue) {
    case value1:
        //code to be executed;
        break;
    case value2:
        //code to be executed
        break;
    case value3:
        //code to be executed
        break;
    default:
        //default code to be executed
}
```

The preceding is fairly generic. Now let's see it using real information:

```
var name = "David";
switch (name) {
case "Kevin":
    trace ("Kevin is the name");
    break;
case "Caroline":
    trace ("Caroline is the name");
    break;
case "David":
    trace ("David is the name");
    break;
case "Kim":
    trace ("Kim is the name");
    break;
```

```
default:
      trace ("There isn't a name");
}
//output: David is the name
```

As previously stated, the break keyword plays a big part in executing this code smoothly. To prove this point, let's see what happens without it:

```
var name = "David";
switch (name) {
case "Kevin":
      trace ("Kevin is the name");
case "Caroline":
      trace ("Caroline is the name");
case "David":
      trace ("David is the name");
case "Kim":
      trace ("Kim is the name");
default:
      trace ("There isn't a name");
}
//output: David is the name
//        Kim is the name
//        There isn't a name
```

And of course, if the variable is not found, the default keyword will execute its code:

```
var name = "Mike";
switch (name) {
case "Kevin":
      trace ("Kevin is the name");
      break;
case "Caroline":
      trace ("Caroline is the name");
      break;
case "David":
      trace ("David is the name");
      break;
case "Kim":
      trace ("Kim is the name");
      break;
default:
      trace ("There isn't a name");
}
//output: There isn't a name
```

We have covered the basics of conditional statements. Now it's time to move to the next group of flow modifiers: loop statements.

Loop Statements

Much like conditional statements, loop statements use conditions to modify the flow of ActionScript. Unlike conditional statements, loop statements run continuously until the condition has been met.

We have already seen one loop statement—the `for in` loop statement used with objects. This statement is specific to objects; the other loop statements we'll cover have a different syntax than the `for in` loop statement.

Let's jump right in with our first loop statement: the `while` loop.

The `while` Loop

The `while` loop runs similarly to an `if` statement: If the condition is true, the statement runs its code. Unlike an `if` statement, however, a `while` loop will start over and run again until the condition is no longer true.

The `while` loop's syntax is very similar to that of the `if` statement as well, except it uses the keyword `while`, followed by the condition and an opening curly bracket that encloses the ActionScript to be run while the condition is true, along with a closing curly bracket that ends the statement.

Because the statement will run until the condition is not true, you must make sure the loop will eventually end. Otherwise, processor power can be affected and errors can occur. Let's take a look at an example:

```
var i = 0;
while (i < 4) {
     trace (i);
     i++;
}
//output: 0
//        1
//        2
//        3
```

Notice that we put an incremental variable in the code to be run while the condition is true. This incremental variable is what shuts down the loop. Let's see what would happen if we didn't have that incremental variable:

```
var i = 0;
while (i < 4) {
     trace (i);
}
//output: (an error message that says that a script in the movie is causing
//the flash player to run slowly, and then it asks do you want to abort)
```

This is why ending a loop statement at some point is very important. Another way to cause the loop statement to end is to use a break script. We covered the keyword `break` in the earlier section on `switch` statements. Now we're going to use it to end loops.

The `break` Keyword

The `break` keyword is often used to end long-running loop statements. The syntax is simple: Place the keyword `break` at the end of the code you would like run while the condition is true and follow it with a semicolon to end the line.

Let's take another look at our previous unstopping loop statement, but this time with the `break` keyword added:

```
var i = 0;
while (i < 4) {
      trace (i);
      break;
}
//output: 0
```

Because the condition is true, the loop statement is run until the point where the interpreter hits the `break` keyword. After reaching `break`, the interpreter moves as if the condition is no longer true.

The `while` loop can also be used to duplicate movie clips much easier than manually duplicating them.

To do this, place a movie clip of a square on the main stage with the instance name myMovie (see Figure 12.2).

FIGURE 12.2

Again, place the movie clip on the main stage in its own layer and label the instance myMovie, but this time, put it near the top-left corner of the stage.

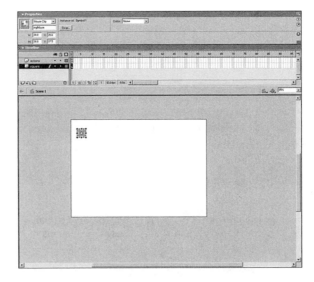

Then, create a layer called actions and place the following code in the first frame of this layer:

```
var i = 0;
var amount = 7;
while (i<=amount) {
    duplicateMovieClip("myMovie", "myMovie"+i, i)
    myMovie._y =i * myMovie._width;
    myMovie._x =i * myMovie._width;
    i++;
}
//this simply cleans the first duplicated movie
myMovie0._visible = false;
```

Now test the movie by going to the toolbar and selecting Control, Test Movie (Ctrl+Enter).

Now you have steps (see Figure 12.3). Even if you want to duplicate each instance of the movie clip manually, you would have a line for each single time you create a new instance.

FIGURE 12.3

Once the movie is tested, it should look similar to a staircase effect.

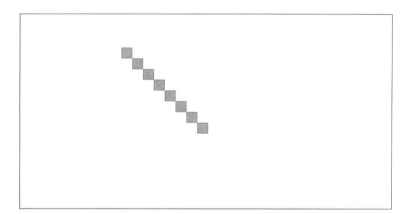

You can also set the condition to something a little more dynamic, such as the `length` property of a string or array. Let's take a look:

```
var date = new Date();
var fullDate = new Array();
fullDate.push(date.getDate());
```

```
fullDate.push(date.getMonth()+1);
fullDate.push(date.getFullYear());
var i = 0;
while (i < fullDate.length){
        myDate +=fullDate[i];
        if (i < fullDate.length-1){
                myDate += "-";
        }
        i++;
}
trace (myDate);
```

Now you have a nice-looking full date that's dynamic! These are just a few of the hundreds of ways the `while` loop can be used. Other examples might included running a game "while" the character has enough energy or having a date- and time-sensitive security lock on a site that "while" the date is before a set date, no one can enter the site.

Next, we'll take a look at another type of loop statement: the `do while` loop.

The `do while` Loop

The `do while` loop works identically to the `while` loop in that it runs its code while the set condition evaluates to `true`. The syntax, however, is completely different.

The syntax for the `do while` loop starts with the keyword do, followed by an opening curly bracket. Then comes the code to be executed while the condition evaluates to `true`. On the next line, following the last line of code to be executed, is a closing curly bracket followed by the keyword `while`, which is then followed by the condition inside a set of parentheses. Finally, a semicolon is used to end the line. Let's take a look at a generic template:

```
do {
        //code to be executed while true
}while (condition);
```

That's the basic format of the `do while` loop. Now let's revisit a couple of previous examples to see how they can be used with `do while`. Here's the first example:

```
var i = 0;
do{
        trace (i);
        i++;
}while (i<4);
//output: 0
//        1
//        2
//        3
```

This is just a basic loop with an incremental variable. Now let's revisit the duplicate movie example and see how it would work with a do while loop:

```
var i = 0;
var amount = 7;
do{
     duplicateMovieClip("myMovie", "myMovie"+i, i)
     myMovie._y =i * myMovie._width;
     myMovie._x =i * myMovie._width;
     i++;
} while (i<=amount);
//this simply cleans the first duplicated movie
myMovie0._visible = false;
```

Just like before, the staircase appears (see Figure 12.4).

FIGURE 12.4

Here again is the staircase effect after you test the movie.

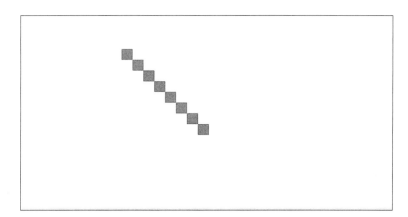

As you can see, the do while loop works identically to the while loop, just with different syntax.

Let's move on to our next loop statement: the for loop.

The for Loop

The for loop works like the other loop statements. It has a condition as well as code to be executed while the condition evaluates to true. The difference is that the condition as well as the incremental variable are held in the same area.

The syntax of the for loop begins with the keyword for, followed by an opening paren-thesis. However, instead of placing the condition first, you create an incremental variable and set a value to it. This variable is followed by a semicolon. After the first semicolon, you create your condition, which again is followed by a semicolon. After the second semicolon, you adjust your incremental variable according to how you want it to work so that the loop will have an end. Then use a closing parenthesis and an opening curly bracket to end the line. The code to be executed begins on the following line, and the statement ends with a closing curly bracket. Here's the generic template of the for loop:

```
for (incremental variable; condition; adjustment of our variable){
//code to be executed
}
```

You may find this difficult to understand without real information, so let's put some in:

```
for (var i = 0; i<4; i++){
      trace (i);
}
//output: 0
//         1
//         2
//         3
```

In this case, we created our incremental variable, i, and put a condition in i<4. Then we increased our variable so that the loop will end eventually.

This is all pretty basic, but we can put it to a function and make it more dynamic by attaching the function to whatever we want.

Next, we'll create a basic function using our for loop, and we'll separate each character in a string, place each character in an array that we create (more on arrays in Chapter 15), and then reverse the array and place it back into a variable as a string. Here's the code:

```
//create a function with just one variable
String.prototype.reverseString = function (){
//create a blank array
myArray = new Array();
//get each character and put it in the array
      for (i=0;i<this.length;i++){
            myArray[i] = this.charAt(i);
      }
//reverse the array
      myArray.reverse();
//use an empty string to join each character
//then set it equal to the original string
      this = myArray.join("");
      trace (this);
```

```
}
//create a variable holding a string literal
var name = "David";
//call function
name.reverseString()
//output:divaD
```

In this function, we use the `for` loop to make sure we retrieve each character in our string.

You can also use nested `for` loops to pull even more information out of data types. This next example takes strings in an array and counts each one. Then it returns the string that appears most often (notice the use of nested `for` loops). Here's the code:

```
//create the function
Array.prototype.stringCount = function (){
//create the sort function so the elements are put in alphabetical order
     function alphabet (element1,element2) {
          return (element1.toUpperCase() < element2.toUpperCase());
     }
     this.sort (alphabet);

//create the variables we need
     preCount = 1;
     count = 0;
     for(var i=0; i<=this.length-1; i++){
          for(var j=(i+1); j<=this.length-1; j++){
//change the element with the .toUpperCase () method when counting
//because flash distinguishes between upper case and lower case letters
               if(this[i].toUpperCase()==this[j].toUpperCase()){
                    preCount+=1;
//check to see if the new element has a higher frequency than the previous
                    if (preCount > count) {
                         count = precount;
                         preCount = 1;
                         name = this[i];
                    }
               }

          }

     }
//then the answer is changed  to upper case and displayed in the output window
     trace (name.toUpperCase());
}
//example array
var myArray = new Array
("David","fred","George","John","Mike","fred","mike","Fred")
//run the function
myArray.stringCount ();
//output: Fred
```

You can also place multiple variables and conditions in loop statements, but this tends to produces surprising results.

Multiple Conditions in Loop Statements

Using multiple conditions in loop statements can serve a variety of purposes when you are dealing with multiple objects. For instance, we'll create two variables, i and j, and set them to 0 and 3, respectively. Then we'll increase each by 1 and test them both with a "less than 5" condition. First, we'll use the logical OR operator and test it; then we will use the short-circuit AND operator and test it. Finally, we'll discuss the results.

When placing multiple variables in for loops, separate them with commas, as shown here:

```
for (var i = 0, j = 3; i<5 || j<5;i++,j++){
    trace ("j="+j);
    trace ("i="+i);
}

//output j=4
//       i=1
//       j=5
//       i=2
//       j=6
//       i=3
//       j=7
//       i=4
```

Now we will use the short-circuit AND operator:

```
for (var i = 0, j = 3; i<5 && j<5;i++,j++){
    trace ("j="+j);
    trace ("i="+i);
}
//output j=3
//       i=0
//       j=4
//       i=1
```

This time, j counts up to 4 and i counts to 1.

This seems almost backwards to what you learned about these two operators as they relate to conditional statements, because in loop statements, as long as a condition is true, the code will run. Therefore, in the case of the OR operator, as long as either of the conditions evaluates to true, the statement will run. When we used the AND operator, on the other hand, they both had to evaluate to true for the statement to continue to run.

That just about covers loop statements. However, you should know that using loop statements is not the only way to create loops in Flash. There are also event handler loops as well as timeline loops. Let's discuss them next.

Event Handler Loops

In Chapter 17, "Event Handlers," we will cover event handlers in more detail. For now, though, we're just going to cover one: the onClipEvent (enterFrame) handler. This clip event is placed inside a movie clip instance and runs constantly. You can use conditional statements to create a mock loop, if you want.

For example, let's say you want to wait a little bit before moving on to the next frame of a movie. You could use this code in conjunction with another clip event handler called load. Let's take a look:

You could place the following in the object actions of any movie clip for the event handlers to work properly:

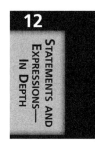

```
onClipEvent (load){
     i=0;
}
onClipEvent (enterFrame){
     if (i>=50){
          trace ("go to next frame");
     }else{
          trace ("not yet");
     }
     i++;
}
```

Now, because of onClipEvent (enterFrame), the movie will not move on until i is equal to 50.

Another type of loop is the timeline loop, which is covered next.

The Timeline Loop

A timeline loop uses a timeline and a set number of frames in that timeline to continuously play through a movie. Let's see one in action.

First, go to the second frame of the main timeline and insert a blank frame by going to the toolbar and choosing Insert, Blank Key Frame (F7).

Now, in the first frame of the main timeline (on the same layer, because there should only be one layer), place the following code:

```
trace ("This is a loop");
```

Now when you test this code, you will see "This is a loop" a bunch of times, until you stop the movie from running.

You can also use `goto` functions to create a conditioned timeline loop. As an example, place three keyframes on the main timeline and use the following lines of code on the indicated frames. Here's the code for frame 1:

```
i = 0;
```

Here's the code for frame 2:

```
i++;
```

Finally, here's the code for frame 3:

```
if (i<5){
      trace (i);
      gotoAndPlay (2);
}else {
      stop();
}
```

The output is the numbers 1–4.

Note

In Chapter 21, "Advanced Interactivity," you can see a conditional statement used with a dynamic text field to create a preloader that returns the percentage loaded.

Working with the Movie Clip Object

By Matt Pizzi

The movie clip is by far the most important object in Flash. It's unique in many ways, but probably the most obvious characteristic is that it's the object represented graphically on the stage, unlike other objects, such as the sound or math object. Because the movie clip is a physical object, in the sense that you can actually see it, it provides a good starting point for any type of Flash development or interactivity.

Objects have properties associated with them. You can modify or change these properties to achieve interactivity and special effects. In this chapter, we're going to go through some general exercises that can be easily applied to many different situations. The first series of exercises is based on changing the movie clip's x position to animate the object without tweening.

Creating Animation Using ActionScript

In this exercise, we are going to assign properties to a movie clip to move it across the stage. We are going to change the objects x position in a step-by-step, methodical way. First, we will create the animation and then actually have the object move across the stage using just scripting, without any tweening. After you understand how this works, we'll mix it up a bit and change some things randomly, such as the speed of the animation. After that, we'll duplicate the movie clip so that there are more than one of them moving across the stage, and they'll be moving at different speeds using randomly assigned values. Finally, we'll control the movie clip to wrap around the stage. Once we've animated it, it will continue to animate all the way off the stage to the point where you can't see it anymore. When the movie clip gets close to the point of animating off the stage, we'll set it to go back around to the opposite side of the stage for a wrapping effect. Ready? Here are the steps to follow:

1. Navigate to the companion Web site, `http://www.flashmxunleashed.com`, and in the Chapter 13 section, find the `walking_man.fla` file and download it.

2. Once you've downloaded the file, open it in Flash. You'll notice it contains a movie clip of a stick figure. Test the movie to see the animation. You'll notice that the stick figure is walking in place; we'll animate the stick figure so that it moves across the stage as well.

3. Highlight the movie clip and open the Actions panel by choosing Window, Actions. This will launch the Actions panel. Press Shift+Cmd+E (Mac) or Shit+Ctrl+E (Windows) to switch the Actions panel into expert mode. Don't worry, we'll take this one step at a time, and besides you will be an expert soon enough. Keep in mind that it's simply faster to script in expert mode.

4. Turn on line numbering. This will make reading the various exercises a bit easier, especially when I call refer to a specific line number. To do this, select the Action panel's submenu in the top-right corner and choose View Line Numbers.

5. Click the plus sign to open the drop-down menu in the Actions panel, as shown in Figure 13.1.

6. Choose Actions, Movie Clip Control, OnClipEvent. You'll notice that the on action is typed, and Flash provides a hint scroll box for you to choose a condition, as shown in Figure 13.2.

7. You need this action to be evaluated again and again. When you're using the clip event handler, the enterFrame condition can be used to have a single-frame loop command. Therefore, scroll in the hint scroll box and double-click enterFrame, or just type it in the parentheses. Now, whatever action you write after this will loop, meaning it will run again and again.

8. After the last curly bracket in line 1, press Return or Enter. You'll notice that Flash MX provides automatic formatting and that the text is indented on the second line. Here, you need to set or change the x position of the movie clip. To change this, type **this._x**. By typing this, you're talking to the movie clip you have selected, and _x, of course, refers to this movie clip's x position on the stage.

9. Now you want this movie clip's x position to equal something, because at this point the script doesn't affecting anything. Therefore, you need to add to the script a value that this._x can equal. Go ahead and add the following to the script:

```
this._x = this._
```

This means that the value of the x position in its current position is equal to whatever value that is. Therefore, if the x position of the movie clip is 250, the value equals 250. Again, the movie clip is not moving. To make it move, you need to add a mathematical expression.

10. Because the script has the x position equaling itself at this point, the only thing you need to add is some math. For example, you can have the x position equal its current position plus 5. This way, every time the script runs, the x position of the movie clip equals its current position plus 5, which will make the movie clip animate. The final script should look like this:

13

```
onClipEvent (enterFrame){
this._x = this._x + 5;
}
```

11. Test the move and see the man walk across the stage. Pretty cool, huh?

12. Save this file as walking_across.

FIGURE 13.1

This drop-down menu can access all the actions in Flash.

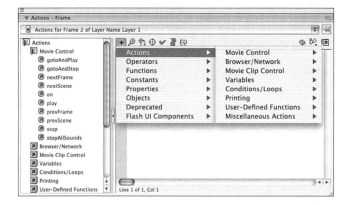

FIGURE 13.2

Flash MX's new hinting feature in the ActionScript editor.

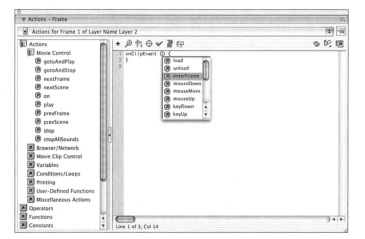

Generating Random Values

With Flash, you have the ability to create animations with certain elements being dynamic. In the case of our walking man, every time you visit the site, the animation is exactly the same. With Flash, however, that doesn't necessarily have to be the case. Because you assign the values of the movie clip's x position through ActionScript, instead of assigning a value that is constant, you can assign a random value. This way, every time the movie loads, a different value is assigned to the script, making the movie clip move at different speeds.

Creating a Random Speed for an Animated Object

Here are the steps to follow for this exercise:

1. Open the `walking_across.fla` file you used in the last exercise. Highlight the walking man and open the Actions panel.

2. Notice that the script from the last exercise is still in place. In line 2, you added 5 to the current location of the x position of the movie clip. In this case, 5 is a constant, meaning it never changes—at least until now. Delete the 5 and leave a blinking insertion point. Click the plus sign in the Actions drop-down menu and choose Object, Core, Math, Methods, random. The `random` method picks a value from 0 to 1. The problem with this is that we need a larger number than 1. Moreover, we would prefer whole numbers. As is, the `random` method could return a value such as .001 or even .00007, and these values are not great enough to show a visible difference within the animation. Test the movie just see what happens. Not much. So again, more math needs to be done.

3. Now you want multiple whatever random value is returned by a greater number—let's say 20. Beyond that, you also need this number to be a whole number (.00007 doesn't do you any good, but the number 7 would). Therefore, you must multiple by 20 and make whatever the value is a whole number by using the `int` function to change it to an integer. Here's what the script will look like:

```
onClipEvent (enterFrame) {
    _x = _x + int(Math.random() *20)
}
```

4. Test the movie. Notice that you're getting a jerky movement. This is because you are generating a different number every time the script is run. This action is in the looping `enterFrame` event handler. In the next step, you're going to write an initialization script to create one random number and use that value in the looping statement.

5. Put a blinking cursor in front of the `on` action in line 1. Click the plus sign to activate the Action drop-down menu. Choose Actions, Movie Clip Control and choose On Clip Event. This time choose `load` for the event handler.

13

WORKING WITH THE MOVIE CLIP OBJECT

6. Place a blinking cursor after the last curly bracket in line 1. Press Return (Mac) or Enter (Windows) to move it down to the next line. Notice that the cursor automatically indents thanks to Flash's new auto-format feature. Now you're going to set a variable. Name the variable `xvalue`. Make the variable equal to `int(random ()*20)`.In the second action underneath, change the script so that it reads `_x + xvalue`. Here is what the script should look like:

```
onClipEvent (load) {
    xvalue = int(Math.random()*20)
}
onClipEvent (enterFrame) {
    this._x = this._x + xvalue
}
```

7. Test the movie a few times, and each time the speed of the walking man should be a bit different. If you were looking for more dramatic results, you could simply multiply the `Math.random` object by something larger than the number 20. This is not foolproof, though. Sometimes the value returned will be 0. If you needed value that equals at least 1 every single time, you can either add 1 to the end of the statement or use an `if` statement to check for that condition and an `else` statement to do something about it. For the purposes of this exercise, we'll be okay. If the movie doesn't animate every now and then, this may make the final piece a bit more interesting.

8. Choose File, Save As and name the movie `walking_across2.fla`.

Using If/Else Logic to Control the Movie Clip's Movement

In the last exercise, you were able to control the x position of the movie clip by adding to its existing value. The only problem is that when the man gets to the end of the stage, he keeps walking (in fact, if you didn't close the SWF file, he'd still be walking in the middle of nowhere). Therefore, let's have the man wrap around the stage so that when he walks off the right side of the stage, he immediately shows up on the left side of the stage. Here are the steps to follow:

1. Open the `walking_across2.fla` file, which you either saved from the last exercise or downloaded from the Unleashed companion Web site.

2. Select the clip and open up the Actions panel. You need an `if` statement to evaluate the location of the movie clip. This document is 550 pixels wide, so you need to

check whether the x position of the movie clip is equal to or greater than 550. If it is, then you need to set it back to 0, which is the left side of the stage. Place a blinking cursor after the last curly bracket on line 4. Press Return (Mac) or Enter (Windows) to move down to the next line. Type **if (this._x >= 550) {**. Hit Return or Enter again to move down to the next line and type **this._x = 0**. This script will check to see whether the x position of the move clip is greater 550. If it is (or if that statement is true), the script will then set the x position of the movie clip to 0. The final script should look like this:

```
onClipEvent (load) {
    xvalue = int(Math.random()*20)
}
onClipEvent (enterFrame) {
    if (this._x >= 550) {
        this._x = 0
    }

    this._x = this._x + xvalue
}
```

3. Test the movie. As the animation plays, you'll notice that if the man walks off on the right side of the stage, he immediately shows up on the left side of the stage, creating a wrap effect.

4. Save this as smart_man.fla; we'll refer to this file again later.

Controlling Movie Clip Properties and Working with ActionClips

One of the most powerful aspects of ActionScript is the ability to control the properties of objects. With a movie clip object, for example, you can control its position on the stage. You can also control its scale, its rotation, its alpha (transparency), and much more. In this section, we are going to work on a file that incorporates most of these settings. We're also going to look at movie clip symbols that contain nothing but actions. They're just containers you can call to trigger certain events or actions. These types of movie clips are often referred to as *ActionClips* or *ScriptClips*.

Changing Scale Properties with Continuous Feedback Buttons

In this exercise you're going to change an object's properties. You're going to create some controls that will give you, or an end user, precise and total control over the object's appearance. To get more familiar with the different properties of objects, open up the Properties book located inside the Objects book in the

Actions panel. We'll look at the most common properties in this exercise. Here are the steps to follow:

1. Create a new document. Choose Modify, Document Properties to open the Document Properties dialog box. Make sure the movie is running at 25 frames per second and that the dimensions of the stage are 550 pixels by 400 pixels. Choose any background color you like and then click OK.

2. In the Unleashed Common Library, open up the graphics folder. Find any graphic you like and drag an instance of it onto the stage. Once the graphic is on the stage, highlight it and press F8 to convert it to a movie clip symbol. Give it any name you like and make sure it does, in fact, have a movie clip behavior. Click OK. If you're brought into the movie clip symbol editing mode, click back to scene 1. With the movie clip symbol selected, give it an instance name of **controlme** in the Properties Inspector's Instance Name text field.

3. Name the current layer **movieclip**. Create a new layer and name it **buttons**. Open the Unleashed Common Library found under the Window menu. Inside the Library, open the buttons folder. Drag out two instances of a button of your choice.

4. Next you need to create a movie clip, and this movie will house nearly all the actions. There won't be any artwork for this movie clip; it is strictly for containing the scripts to make this piece functional. These types of movie clips are often referred to as *ActionClips* or *ScriptClips*. Choose Insert, New Symbol. This will open the New Symbol dialog box. Name the symbol **ActionClip** and be sure to give it a movie clip behavior by clicking the Movie Clip radio button. Click OK. This will bring you into the movie clip symbol editing mode. Click the Scene 1 tab to get back to the main timeline.

5. Back in scene 1, create a new layer and name it **actions/labels**. Open the movie's library by choosing Window, Library. You'll see the movie clip symbol ActionClip; drag out an instance on the stage. You'll notice that it looks like a tiny circle with a crosshair, as shown in Figure 13.3. This is because it doesn't have any physical content. With it still selected, give the symbol an instance name in the Properties Inspector. Type in **StoredActions** in the Instance Name text field. Press Return (Mac) or Enter (Windows) to make sure the instance name sticks.

Now on the stage you have a movie clip with an instance name of controlme, an empty movie clip with an instance name of StoredActions, and a set of buttons on the stage, all of which are shown in Figure 13.4.

6. You're now ready to control the movie clip. The first thing you'll change is its scale. The button on the left will be used to increase the scale, and the button on the right will be used to decrease its scale. You may want to type a plus sign on top of the button on the left and a minus sign on the button on the right, as shown in Figure 13.5.

7. Double-click the StoredActions movie clip. Place a `stop` action in frame 1. Press F6 on your keyboard to insert another keyframe. Highlight the new keyframe and open the Actions panel. In the Actions panel, you're going to create a variable. Name the variable `_root.controlme._xscale` and have it equal `_root.controlme._xscale + 10`. Do the same for `yscale`. These variables are going to equal the current x and y scale of the object plus 10. You also need to set up a multiple frame loop so that this script runs every time a button is pressed and continues to run until the button is released. The code should look like this:

```
_root.controlme._xscale = _root.controlme._xscale + 10;
_root.controlme._yscale = _root.controlme._yscale + 10;
```

Oftentimes programmers want to use the `setProperty` action at this point. After all, now that you have this variable, don't you need to take the value that it contains and apply it to the `_xscale` and `_yscale` properties? No. The way you named your variables cuts out this line of code. The variable name targets the properties `_xscale` and `_yscale`. Therefore, when you make the variable equal a value, that value is automatically applied to the property targeted in the variable naming convention. This is a more efficient way to code.

8. Highlight frame 2 and in the Properties Inspector label it **increase**. Press Return or Enter to make sure the label sticks.

9. Highlight frame 3 and insert a keyframe. With frame 3 selected, press F9 to open the Actions panel. Click the plus sign and choose Actions, Movie Control, gotoAndPlay. Type in 2 for the frame. This is what the script should look like:

```
gotoAndPlay(2);
```

It would also be acceptable to type in the label of the frame instead of the frame number. This would be beneficial if there's any reason to add or move frames around on the timeline. However, this is unlikely because there is no animation, so we'll stick with using frame numbers.

10. Click back to scene 1 to get to the main timeline. Highlight the positive scale button and then press F9 on your keyboard to bring up the Actions panel. Click the plus sign to activate the Actions drop-down. Choose

Actions, Movie Control, On. Choose `Press` as the event handler. Then choose Objects, Movie, Movie Clip, Methods, gotoAndPlay. Place a blinking cursor in front of the `gotoAndPlay` method and type in **`_root.StoredActions`**; the argument will be `increase`. After this script, you have set up another event handler so that when the mouse is released, the script tells the StoredActions playhead to move to frame 1 where there is a `stop` action. The final code on the button looks like this:

```
on (press) {
    _root.StoredActions.gotoAndPlay("increase");
}
on (release, releaseOutside) {
    _root.StoredActions.gotoAndStop(1);
}
```

The event handler `on (press)`, which is a mouse press, will trigger the next line of actions. The second line targets the StoredActions instance and tells it to play the increase frame. The forth line's event handler, `on (release, releaseOutside)`, will trigger the action on the fifth line. We included `on releaseOutside` because if the end user moves the mouse away from the button and then releases the mouse, the button will not play the fifth line, which essentially stops the action, so the movie clip will still increase in size even though the intention of the end user was to stop it from growing. The fifth line's action targets the StoredActions instance and tells it to go to and stop on frame 1 so that it stops running the action on the release frame. All the buttons you'll create for the next few exercises will function the same way.

11. With this completed, you can now test the movie! Choose Control, Test Movie. Click the plus sign and watch the movie clip increase in size, as shown in Figure 13.6.

12. You now have to set up the opposite effect—decreasing the movie's size. Double-click the StoredActions movie on the stage. Insert a keyframe on frame 4. You may want to copy and paste the code from frame 2 (it's going to be almost the same). After pasting the code into frame 4, change all instances of plus signs (+) to minus signs (-). The final code should look like this:

```
_root.controlme._xscale = _root.controlme._xscale - 10;
_root.controlme._yscale = _root.controlme._yscale - 10;
```

13. Label frame 4 **decrease**. Insert a keyframe on frame 5 and give frame 5 an action of `gotoAndPlay (4);`. It's important to note that you could also call the frame label here instead of the frame number.

14. Click the Scene 1 tab to come back to the main timeline. Highlight the positive button and press F9 to open up the Actions panel. Highlight all the actions and choose Copy. Highlight the "minus sign" button and paste the actions. Simply change the name of the frame label to **decrease** instead of increase. The final code should read as follows:

```
on (press) {
    _root.StoredActions.gotoAndPlay("decrease");
}
on (release, releaseOutside) {
    _root.StoredActions.gotoAndStop(1);
}
```

15. Test the movie! You'll notice that the man on the tractor decreases in size. You'll also notice a small problem. When the movie gets smaller than zero, it starts increasing in size. That's because it's reading negative numbers after zero. Because it can't tell the difference between negative values and positive values, our movie looks broken. So let's fix it.

16. Double-click the StoredActions movie clip. Select frame 4 and open the Actions panel. You need to add an `if` statement: If the x and y scales are equal to or less than zero, then set and keep the value at zero. Here's the proper syntax:

```
_root.controlme._xscale = _root.controlme._xscale-10;
_root.controlme._yscale = _root.controlme._yscale-10;
if (_root.controlme._yscale<2) {
    setProperty("_root.controlme", _yscale, 2);
    setProperty("_root.controlme", _xscale, 2);
}
```

The `if` statement simply evaluates whether the movie clip's x and y scales are less than 2, and if they are less than 2, the statement sets the x and y scales equal to 2. Therefore, each scale can never be smaller than 2. You'll notice that we only check to see whether the y scale is less than 2. This is because we have written the script so that x and y are scaled up and down equally, so if the y scale is less than 2, then so is the x scale. Notice in Figure 13.7 that the movie clip never disappears, nor does it flip around and scale back up.

17. Test your movie to make sure its working.

18. Save the document as `property_change.fla`.

13

WORKING WITH THE MOVIE CLIP OBJECT

FIGURE 13.3

The empty movie clip on the stage.

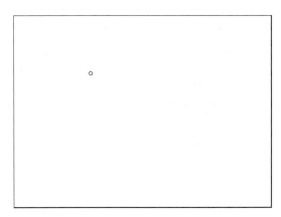

FIGURE 13.4

All the objects currently on the stage.

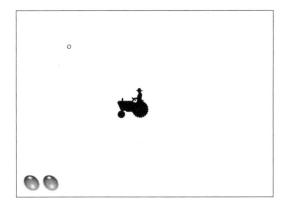

FIGURE 13.5

Type a plus sign and a minus sign on the buttons to make them more user friendly.

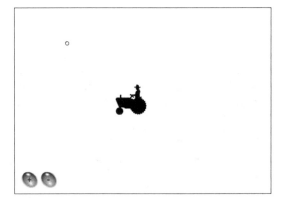

FIGURE 13.6

The symbol increases in size.

FIGURE 13.7

The symbol doesn't get any smaller than a 2×2 pixel.

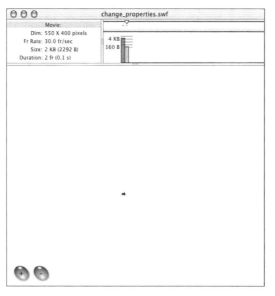

Now that you can increase and decrease the scale of the symbol, let's move its position up and down as well as from left to right.

Changing the X and Y Position of the Movie Clip

First things first. For this exercise, you'll need to drag out four more instances of the buttons. You may want to draw arrows on them (that is, up, down, left, and right arrows) as displayed in Figure 13.8. Now follow these steps:

1. Open the `property_change.fla` file from the last exercise.

2. Double-click the StoredActions symbol to enter the movie clip symbol editing mode. Insert a keyframe in frame 6 and label it **up** in the Properties Inspector.

3. Press F9 to open the Actions panel. You need to write a script to change this movie clip's y position in negative numbers to move it up, because the top of the stage is on the zero y axis. This script will be very similar to the earlier script, with a few differences in the properties you're going to change. The script should look like this:

```
_root.controlme._y = _root.controlme._y - 10;
if (_root.controlme._y <=0) {
    setProperty("_root.controlme", _y, 400);
}
```

The first line sets the variable to equal the current y position plus 10. In the second line, the `if` statement looks to see whether the object has moved off the visible part of the stage. If so, the script resets the object's y position to be 400, which in this case is the bottom of the stage.

4. Insert a keyframe on frame 7 and add the following script to the frame:

```
gotoAndPlay(6);
```

This will set up the multiple frame loop.

5. Click back on the Scene 1 tab to get to the main timeline. Highlight the button with the up arrow. Press F9 to open the Actions panel and write a script to target the StoredActions "up" frame. The script should read as follows:

```
on (press) {
    _root.StoredActions.gotoAndPlay("up");
}
on (release, releaseOutside) {
    _root.StoredActions.gotoAndStop(1);
}
```

6. Test the movie. Notice that the movie clip moves up, and when it moves off the top of the screen, it wraps and appears again at the bottom of the stage, as shown in the split view in Figure 13.9.

This works great except for one thing: In the testing environment, scale the movie clip way up so that it appears about 500-percent larger than its current size. Now click the up-arrow button, and you'll notice that the object wraps down to the bottom before it ever really leaves the top. There's a reason for this. In step 3 of the script, the `if` statement checks to see whether the movie clip symbol's y property is ever less than zero and, if so, sets it to 400. Well, that's exactly what's happening here. The script is using the crosshairs or center point of the movie clip for its y property.

So how do you fix this? You could get the dimensions of the movie clip and use those values in the expression. For example, if the movie clip is 100 by 100 pixels, then a sure fix would be to take half of that value, because it changes the movie clip's position based on the center point, and add or subtract it from the expression. Therefore, when the center point moves off the top of the stage, the top half of the symbol is already gone; it's the second half you have to worry about, so you could just add 50 to the coordinates in the script so that it reads as follows:

```
_root.controlme._y = _root.controlme._y - 10;
if (_root.controlme._y <=-50) {
    setProperty("_root.controlme", _y, 450);
}
```

Of course, your values may differ from these, depending on your symbol. To find the dimensions of your symbol, select it and open the Info panel by choosing Window, Info. Here you'll find the symbol's width and height in pixels. Take half of those numbers and plug them into your script; then test your movie. You'll see it works wonderfully. Well, it works fine until you scale the object up, which is when it gets messed up like the last time. This is because the number you hard coded into the script is only good if the movie clip symbol stays at the same size. If it gets scaled up or down, the number used in the script needs to change. In the example, the movie clip is 100 by 100. If you scale it up to, say, 325 by 325, then half of 325 is not 50, which means the script is wrong again.

How do you fix this? Luckily there are some additional properties you can use to make the values you're setting in this statement dynamic. You'll be using the width and height properties in the next step.

7. Instead of setting the movie clip to a constant value such as 0 or 400, you can set the value to half the size of the current state of the movie clip. All you have to do is get the current height and current width of the movie clip and divide it by 2 and then use that as the value to set the position of the object. Here is what the script will look like:

```
_root.controlme._y = _root.controlme._y - 10;
if (_root.controlme._y <=-_(root.controlme._height/2)) {
    setProperty("_root.controlme", _y, 400+(_root.controlme._height/2)
);
}
```

The first line sets the variable, which in turn sets the property of the y position of the movie clip on the stage. The second line of code evaluates whether or not the movie clip's y position is less than or equal to half the height of the movie clip instance. If it is less than or equal to that value, the movie clip's y position is set on the third line of code to half the height of the movie clip plus 400, which will move the movie clip to the bottom of the stage.

8. You now have to do the same for the down button, left button, and right button. Fortunately, you can copy a lot of the scripts. Double-click the StoredActions movie clip on the stage. Insert a keyframe on frame 8. Label this frame **down**. You now have to write the logic to move the movie clip down. All you really have to do is copy the script on the "up" frame and just change the negatives to positives and swap a few numbers around. The final script should look like this:

```
_root.controlme._y = _root.controlme._y + 10;
if (_root.controlme._y >=400+(_root.controlme._height/2)) {
    setProperty("_root.controlme", _y, -(_root.controlme._height/2) );
}
```

On the first line you are now adding 10, instead of subtracting it. For the second line, you are looking for a number greater than or equal to 400 plus the height of the movie clip instances. Remember, 400 is the height of the stage. On the third line, if you find that the number on the second line is in fact greater than or equal to that value, the y position property of the movie clip is set to equal negative half the height of the movie clip.

9. Insert a keyframe on frame 9 and press F9 to open the Actions panel. You need to create the multiple frame loop, so place the action `gotoAndPlay(8);` on frame 9. Click the Scene 1 tab to return to the main timeline.

10. Highlight the down button and apply this action:

```
on (press) {
    _root.StoredActions.gotoAndPlay("up");
}
on (release, releaseOutside) {
    _root.StoredActions.gotoAndStop(1);
}
```

11. Test the movie! Perfect, now let's just get the right and left buttons to work.

12. Double-click StoredActions and insert a keyframe on frame 10. Label this frame **left**. The script to move the object to the left is very similar to the previous two buttons (really, the biggest difference is changing the y position to the x position and taking into account the width of the stage instead of the height). Here's the final script:

```
_root.controlme._x = _root.controlme._x - 10;
if (_root.controlme._x <= -(_root.controlme._height/2)) {
    setProperty("_root.controlme", _x, 550+(_root.controlme._height/2)
);
}
```

After working with the other buttons, you'll probably find this bit of code to be a bit more self-explanatory. The first line sets a variable, and the variable's value is the current x position of the object (10). Again, this will ultimately set the property as well. The second line just checks to see whether the object has moved off the stage by factoring in the width of the object. If it is moving off the stage, you send it back to the opposite side of the stage by adding 550 (the stage's width) plus half the width of the movie clip symbol.

13. Insert a keyframe on frame 11. Give it a simple gotoAndPlay (10); action. Click the Scene 1 tab to move back to the main timeline.

14. Highlight the left-arrow button. You need to apply a script that will target the StoredActions movie clip and tell it to play frame 10. The final script looks like this:

```
on (press) {
    _root.StoredActions.gotoAndPlay("left");
}
on (release, releaseOutside) {
    _root.StoredActions.gotoAndStop(1);
}
```

15. For the right-arrow button, double-click StoredActions to enter the symbol editing mode. Insert a keyframe on frame 12 and label it **right**. Here you will add the same script that's on frame 10, but you'll flip the numbers. The final script should look like this:

```
_root.controlme._x = _root.controlme._x + 10;
if (_root.controlme._x >= 550 +(_root.controlme._height/2)) {
    setProperty("_root.controlme", _x, -(_root.controlme._height/2) );
}
```

The first line, again, sets the x position of the movie clip through a variable. You'll notice that it equals the current x position plus 10. The second line evaluates whether or not the clip is off the stage by adding the stage size to half the width of the movie clip. If the movie clip is off the stage, the x position's value is set to half the width of the movie clip, moving it to the opposite side of the stage.

16. Insert a keyframe in frame 13 and give it a `gotoAndPlay (12);` action.

17. Click the Scene 1 tab, highlight the right-arrow button, and apply this action:

```
on (press) {
    _root.StoredActions.gotoAndPlay("right");
}
on (release, releaseOutside) {
    _root.StoredActions.gotoAndStop(1);
}
```

18. Test the movie. Pretty cool, huh?

19. Save the movie by choosing File, Save As. Name it `property_change2.fla`.

FIGURE 13.8

The buttons have arrows indicating which direction each one will move the movie clip.

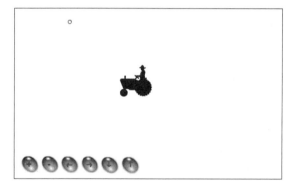

FIGURE **13.9**

*The movie clip on
the left is about to
move off the stage.
The movie clip on
the right appears
at the bottom after
it has completely
moved off the top
of the stage.*

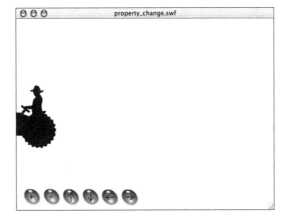

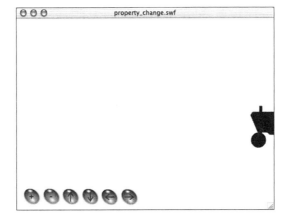

13

WORKING WITH
THE MOVIE CLIP
OBJECT

Changing a Movie Clip Object's Rotation

At this point in the file, you can move the object all around on the stage and
even change the movie clip's scale. Let's now take a look at how you can
change its rotation as well. Follow these steps:

1. Drag out another instance of the button on the stage. You're going to
   make this a rotate button. Try to draw a circular arrow, as shown on
   Figure 13.10.

2. Go ahead and double-click the StoredActions movie clip on the stage to
   enter the movie clip symbol editing mode.

3. Select frame 14 and insert a keyframe by pressing F6. With frame 14 still selected, label it **rotate** in the Properties Inspector. After that, press F9 to open the Actions panel. You now need to set a variable and make the variable equal the current rotation of the movie clip plus 10. Here's what the script should look like:

```
_root.controlme._rotation = _root.controlme._rotation + 10;
```

The first line does, in fact, set a variable, which in turn sets the property. The variable is the current rotation of the movie clip plus 10. By adding to the current rotation, you'll be rotating the object clockwise; if a negative number were used, you'd be rotating the object counterclockwise.

4. Insert a keyframe on frame 15 and in the Actions panel give it an action of `gotoandPlay (14);`.

5. Click the Scene 1 tab to get back to the main timeline. Highlight the last instance of the button and open the Actions panel by pressing F9. You need to give this button an action that targets the StoredActions movie clip and tell it to play the "rotate" frame. Here's what the script will look like:

```
on (press) {
    _root.ActionClip.gotoAndPlay("rotate");
}
on (release) {
    _root.ActionClip.gotoAndStop(1);
}
```

6. Test the movie to view and check your rotation button. As shown in Figure 13.11, the movie clip symbol is rotating clockwise!

7. For additional practice on your own, try creating a button that rotates the object counterclockwise. If you get stuck, check the Unleashed companion Web site for help or download the finished file from `http://www.flash-mxunleashed.com` and deconstruct what I did.

8. Save the document by choosing File, Save As and name it `rotate.fla`.

FIGURE 13.10

Notice the circular arrow on the last button.

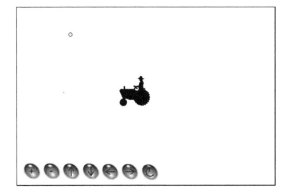

FIGURE 13.11

The movie clip symbol is rotated.

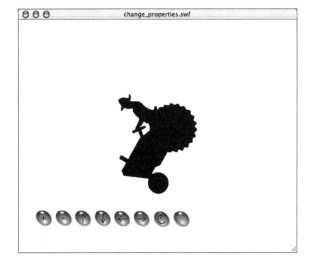

Changing the Alpha of a Move Clip

The last exercise for this movie involves controlling the movie clip's alpha. By changing the alpha of the movie clip, you can make it disappear. To do this, follow these steps:

1. Be sure to have the `rotate.fla` file open. On the main timeline, drag out another instance of your button. Then double-click the StoredActions movie clip to edit the symbol.

2. Once you're inside the symbol, highlight frame 16 and press F6 to insert a keyframe. In the Properties Inspector, label this frame **alpha**. With the frame still selected, bring up the Actions panel by pressing F9, if it isn't already open.

3. Now you need to set a variable to change the movie clip's current alpha. Remember, this button is going to make the symbol disappear, so you want to subtract from its current value. Then you need to set the movie clip's alpha property to equal the variable you're going to set in the first line of the script.

However, you're going to need an `if` statement, because if the end user keeps clicking the button after the alpha of the movie clip equals zero, the value will equal a negative number. What's more, if you create another button that *increases* the alpha value after it has been decreased, the user will need to click the button a few times to get past zero and into the positive range, making it appear that it takes longer than it should to get the expected results. For example, if the end user clicks the negative alpha button 10 times after the alpha equals zero, it now has a value of –100. If you create a positive alpha button, the user would have to click it 10 times just get the value back to zero, which means for the first 10 clicks, nothing would seem to happen, and the end user would think something is broken. Therefore, you need an `if` statement to check whether the alpha value is equal to zero, and if it is, set it to zero so that it stays at zero.

```
        Here's what the code should look like:
_root.controlme._alpha = _root.controlme._alpha - 10;
if (_root.controlme._alpha <=0) {
    setProperty("_root.controlme", _alpha, 0);
}
```

The first line sets a variable to equal the movie clip's current alpha minus 10. The second line sets the movie clip's alpha property to equal the variable. The third line evaluates whether or not the alpha property is less than or equal to zero. The forth line is a condition. If the evaluation is true, meaning that the alpha property is less than or equal to zero, then the fourth line sets the alpha property to equal zero; therefore, the alpha can never have a value less than zero.

4. Highlight frame 17 and insert a keyframe. Give this frame an action of `gotoAndPlay(16)`.

5. Click the Scene 1 tab to get back to the main timeline. In scene 1, highlight the alpha button. Press F9 to open the Actions panel. You need to target the StoredActions instance and tell it to move the playhead to the "alpha" frame. Here's the code:

```
on (press) {
    _root.StoredActions.gotoAndPlay("alpha");
```

```
    }
on (release, releaseOutside) {
    _root.StoredActions.gotoAndStop(1);
    }
```

6. Test the movie. Notice that the alpha button works, as shown in Figure 13.12.

7. Now create a button that increases the alpha property's value. You can repeat steps 1 through 6. The only thing that changes is in the script on the frame of the StoredActions instance. That script should add 10 instead of subtract 10, and of course all instances of 0 become 100. Here's the code:

```
_root.controlme._alpha = _root.controlme._alpha + 10;
if (_root.controlme._alpha >=100) {
    setProperty("_root.controlme", _alpha, 100);
    }
```

FIGURE 13.12

The movie clip's alpha property decreases when the button is pressed.

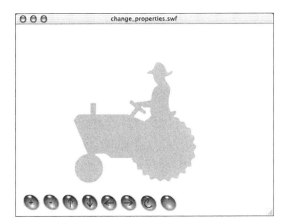

Controlling movie clip properties is at the heart of ActionScript. These basic exercises are designed to get you familiar with how properties work. The scripts in these exercises have been streamlined and yield the best performance. Everyone scripts differently, however, so if you feel you would have written your script in a different way, that's fine. Having the master ActionClip allows you to have continuous feedback buttons, which sure beats clicking the button every time you want to change its property by a value of 10. This way is far more user friendly. Also, because the script is contained in an ActionClip, it's more portable, and you can use this clip in many different movies.

Duplicating Movie Clips

The `smart_man.fla` file has an animation of a stick figure walking. He walks at a random speed that's assigned when the movie first loads. Because all the actions are in the instance of the movie clip, you can make duplicates of this movie clip and have many stick men walking around on the stage. To make copies, hold down the Option key (Mac) or Alt key (Windows) and then click and drag a duplicate. Drag as many instances as you want onto the stage. You'll notice that six instances appear in Figure 13.13.

FIGURE 13.13

Six instances of the stick figure walking around on the stage.

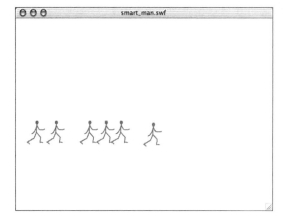

This works fine with such a low number, but what if you want 50 of these guys on the stage? You can use the "duplicate movie clip" action (`duplicateMovieClip`) to achieve this result dynamically.

When a movie clip is duplicated, the new instance is loaded into a depth level. A *level* is much like a layer, as discussed in Chapter 7, "Development Techniques." Movie clips on lower depth levels appear below movies on higher depth levels. The first movie clip instance is automatically assigned a depth level of 0. Any movie that has been duplicated must be assigned a different depth level. If it is assigned a depth level that is already occupied by an instance, the resident instance will be removed from that level and replaced with the new duplicated instance.

You can only apply a `duplicateMovieClip` action to an existing instance, and the action will make an exact copy of the instance it is duplicating, writing over all the properties of the current instance. Movies that are duplicated will always start on frame 1, regardless of what frame the parent instance is on during the time of duplication. If, for some reason, the main or parent movie clip that is being duplicated is deleted, all duplicated instances will be deleted as well. Variables in the parent movie clip are not copied into the duplicated movie clips.

You can apply the `duplicateMovieClip` action to a movie clip object as a method. Let's go ahead and take a look at some ActionScript and see how to apply this action to the `smart_man.fla` file.

Duplicating Movie Clips

Here are the steps to follow for this exercise:

1. Open the `smart_man.fla` file. If you saved this file with the duplicated instances we experimented with at the beginning of this section, delete them so that there is only one.

2. Highlight the stick figure on the stage and give it an instance name of **man** in the Properties Inspector.

3. Select frame 1 and press F9 to open the Actions panel. The first thing you need to do is target the movie clip instance. Then you can attach the `duplicateMovieClip` action and fill in the parameters. Here is the code:

   ```
   _root.man.duplicateMovieClip ("man1", 1);
   ```

   First, the instance "man" is targeted. Then the `duplicateMovieClip` action is attached as a method and given two parameters. The first parameter is the instance name of the new duplicated movie, and the second is the level it should load into. The instance name has to be something other than the instance name of the parent movie clip. Also notice that we're putting this action on the frame and not in the movie clip. If you put it in the movie clip, each duplicated movie clip would have this action as well, and the duplication would never stop.

4. Choose Files, Save As and name this movie `two_men.fla`. Test the movie. As shown in Figure 13.14, you'll have two walking men on the stage.

   Note that this is a duplicate of the parent instance. If you were to scale the man so that he is much larger, the duplicated movie clip would carry over those same characteristics, as demonstrated in Figure 13.15. This would apply in any situation that involves changing the properties of the parent instance, including color, alpha, scale, rotation, and so on.

   Now, if you want 50 different instances, you just have to write this line of code 50 times, right? Well, no. That's not any better than copying the instance 50 times. Therefore, let's write something that will be a little more dynamic.

5. Highlight frame 1 and press F9 to open the Actions panel.

6. You now need to create a single frame loop. You want this loop to run the same action, in a slightly different way, until it has met a certain condition. To create this loop, you are going to use the `For` action. Place a

blinking. Click the plus sign for the Actions menu and then choose Actions, Conditions/Loops, For. In the script window, you'll see the hint box shown in Figure 13.16.

7. The hint box is looking for the following three conditions:

   - `init`. This initializes a variable and is a starting point for the actions.

   - `condition`. This compares the variable against a condition to see whether it is true or false. If the variable has met the condition and is true, the loop will stop running.

   - `next`. This increments the variable so at some point the condition will be true. Here's what the top part of the script should look like to duplicate six walking men:

   ```
   For (a=1; a<5; a=a+1) {
   }
   ```

   The first thing you do is set the variable a to equal 1, which is a good starting point. Next, you want six walking men on the stage, so you want this loop to keep running until you have five duplicates (the five duplicated instances plus the parent totals six). That's why the condition is a<5;, because as long as it is less than 5, you want the script to continue running. Finally, you increment it using a=a+1 so that every time the loop passes, the number will increase, eventually getting to 5, which when it reaches that point the condition will be true and the action will stop running. If you don't increment this loop action, the duplication will become so complex that the Flash player will either stop or crash (or, even worse, your computer will crash).

8. The action you need to run in the loop statement is the `duplicateMovieClip` action. Cut and paste that action inside the `for` action's curly brackets.

   If you leave the `duplicateMovieClip` action alone, you really won't see a difference. Right now it will keep duplicating the movie and naming the new instance **man1** and putting it in level 1, replacing anything in that level. That's why you need to make this action a bit more dynamic.

9. You need to give each instance that is duplicated a different name. You do this by concatenating (or joining together) a literal part of the name, in this case "man," with a variable, in this case a. Because a will have a different value each time the action is run, the instance name will also have a different value. Therefore, you'll end up with man1, man2, man3, and so on. You're also going to do the same for the levels, because you

want all these instances to have different levels so that they don't replace one another. The final script should look like this:

```
for (a+1; a<5; a=a+1) {
    _root.man.duplicateMovieClip ("man" + a, a);
}
```

10. Test the movie. As shown in Figure 13.17, six men appear on the stage.

11. Save the movie as duplicated_man.fla.

FIGURE 13.14

The duplicated movie clip on the stage.

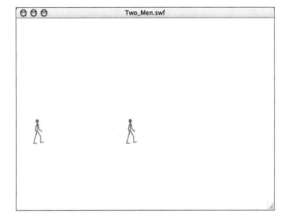

FIGURE 13.15

The duplicated movie clip will duplicate all the properties of the parent movie clip instance.

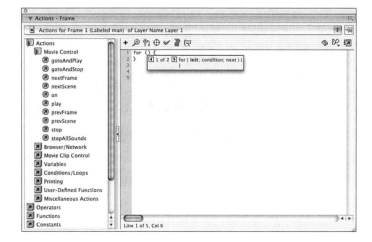

CHAPTER 14

Functions

By David Vogeleer

So far we have covered some of the basics of ActionScript, including variables, statements, and movie clip objects. Now we'll get into functions.

A *function* is basically a reusable piece of code. Once a function is created, it can be used over and over again, without you rewriting the code. This is very powerful, not only because it can save on file size but also because it will make your code much easier to read and manage.

This chapter covers the topics of creating functions, using the built-in functions, and using functions as methods and objects. Instead of just talking about functions, let's jump right in and create one.

Creating a Function

Creating a function is as easy as using the keyword `function`, providing a name for the function, followed by a pair of parentheses for parameters (we discuss the topic of parameters in more depth later), and placing whatever code you want between two curly brackets. It looks something like this:

```
function myFunction(){
    //script to run in function
}
```

Now that you know what a function looks like, you can create one of your own. To begin, open a new Flash movie, click the first frame in the timeline, open the ActionScript panel (F9), and place the following code:

```
function myFunction (){
    trace ("My first function");
}
```

Now you have your own function, with a simple `trace` statement placed within the curly brackets. However, if you tested your movie at this point, nothing would happen. This is because all you have done so far is create a function; now you need to run it.

Running the Function

Now that you have your function, let's make it work for you. To run this function (also called *invoking* the function), you start with your function name, followed by a set of parentheses to hold our parameters, and you finish with a semicolon to end the line, as shown here:

```
function myFunction (){
    trace ("My first function");
}
```

```
myFunction();
//output: My first function
```

That was easy. You simply created a function and then invoked it to see the statements run and the message displayed in the output window.

Let's now look at another way of creating functions. This way starts with the function name. Then you set it equal to the keyword `function`, followed by a set of parentheses and the curly brackets for holding your code. Here's an example using a generic template:

```
myFunction = function(){
    //script to run in function
}
```

Now let's put this into practice with the previous example:

```
myFunction = function(){
    trace("My second function");
}
myFunction();
//output: My second function
```

Now you have seen two basic ways of creating functions and running them. So far, all you have done is run a simple `trace` statement. Now let's put some script in it that you can really use. We'll start with a function that fades out a movie:

```
function fadeOut(){
    myMovie._alpha -= 5;
}
//now invoke the function
fadeOut();
```

Every time this function is invoked, the movie clip myMovie will decrease its `_alpha` value by 5.

That was simple, but what if you only wanted to fade to a certain point? You can place conditional as well as loop statements within functions to perform a condition test.

Here's the same example, but this time we're using an `if` statement to only allow myMovie to fade to a certain point:

```
function fadeOut(){
    if(myMovie._alpha >50){
        myMovie._alpha-=5;
    }
}
//now invoke the function
fadeOut();
```

14

FUNCTIONS

Now the function will check whether the movie clip has faded to the designated point yet. If it has reached the designated point, the function still runs, but the statements in the `if` statement will not.

Now, suppose you want to set the point where the alpha will fade differently for two different functions that are invoked. This is where parameters come in.

Using Parameters in Functions

So far you have seen how to create functions and place scripts inside them. This is not very dynamic, though, in that once the information is in the function, it cannot be adjusted for different situations. Now we'll use parameters to change this limitation.

Parameters in a function act similarly to variables in ActionScript. They can be changed on the fly whenever the need arises. You place the parameters in parentheses following the name of the function, which looks something like this:

```
function myFunction(parameter){
    //script involving parameter;
}
```

This is simply the generic template, so let's look at some examples next. The first example runs a simple `trace` statement:

```
function myTrace(name){
    trace(name);
}
//now we will run the function twice with two different parameters
myTrace("David");
myTrace("George");
//output: David
//        George
```

This is a basic example, so let's return to the previous fading example and see how to use parameters with conditional statements.

Like before, you want to set a point that your movie clip will fade to, but this time you'll use three parameters—the instance name of the movie clip, the point to fade the movie to, and the amount to fade the movie by. In this example, you'll use a loop statement instead of a conditional statement:

```
function fade(movie, fadePoint, amount){
    while(movie._alpha > fadePoint){
        movie._alpha -= amount;
    }
}
//now the function is made, let's run it on a couple movies
```

```
fade(myMovie,50,5);
fade(myMovie2,20,2);
```

The preceding code would be placed in the timeline where both movies reside.

So far we have used functions to perform basic repetitive tasks using code that we want to consolidate and use whenever we want without having to rewrite the entire script. Now let's make the functions give us back information.

Functions That Return Values

Currently we are using functions to run repetitive code using parameters, but all the functions are doing is running code. Now let's make them give back some information. To do this, we'll use the `return` statement.

The `return` statement does two things. First, when the interpreter reaches the `return` statement, it causes the function to end. Second, it returns the value of an expression assigned to it, but the expression is optional. Here is a generic template:

```
function functionName (parameters){
    //script to run when function is invoked
    return expression;
}
```

Now let's look at an example of using the `return` statement to end a function. This example contains a conditional statement, and if the condition is met, the function will end and will not run the remaining code:

```
function myFunction (num){
    if(num>5){
        return;
    }
    trace("Num is smaller than 5");
}
//Now we invoke the function twice
myFunction(6);
myFunction(3);
//output: Num is smaller than 5
```

Even though the function is run twice, because the conditional statement in the first function is met, the `return` statement is run and the function is ended. In the second function, the conditional statement is not met, and the `trace` statement is run.

This time, let's use the `return` statement to return a value back to us based on an expression we apply to the `return` statement:

```
function fullName (fName,lName){
    return fName+" "+lName;
```

```
}
//now we set the a variable to the function
myName = fullName("David", "Vogeleer");
trace(myName);
//output: David Vogeleer
```

All we did was set the function to a variable, and the `return` statement returned the value of the expression we assigned to it to the variable.

Using `return` statements, you can nest functions within functions and even use them as parameters.

Nested Functions

Nested functions can be a great tool if you want to run a repetitive set of scripts within a function but use the result differently in each function. Let's take a look at a couple functions—the first will square a user-defined number, and the second will combine two squared numbers by using the return value from the first function:

```
function square(num){
    return num*num;
}
//Now create the second function
function combineSquares(){
    square1 = square(2);
    square2 = square(3);
    return square1 + square2;
}
//Set the variable to the second function
myNum = combineSquares();
trace(myNum);
//output: 13
```

The preceding code uses the first function (`square`) and nests it within a second function (`combineSquares`) to return a value that uses the returned value of the `square` function.

Now let's create a function that uses another function as a parameter. We'll use the same example as before, but this time we'll set the `square` function as a parameter:

```
function square(num){
    return num*num;
}
//Now create the second function
function combineSquares(square1, square2){
    return square1 + square2;
}
//Set the variable to the second function
myNum = combineSquares(square(2),square(3));
```

```
trace(myNum);
//output: 13
```

As stated, you can nest functions within themselves for repetitive use if you want to use the result differently in each function.

We have talked about creating and using functions in many different ways; now let's see the scope of a function.

Function Scope

The scope of a function is like the scope of a variable; it is only directly available (called by name, instead of dot syntax mapping to the function) in the following ways:

- If the function is called on the same timeline it was created in.
- If the function is called from a button when the function resides on the same timeline as the button that called it.
- If the function is called within a movie clip where the function was created on the timeline of that movie.

In Flash 5, if none of these criteria were met, you had to use dot syntax to map to the function you created. In Flash MX, you can use the global object to create a function that is available throughout the entire Flash movie and all its timelines. (We will discuss the global object later in this chapter.)

First, let's discuss how to map to functions using dot syntax.

Mapping to a Function

There are two basic ways of mapping to a function:

- **Using movie objects**. In this case, *root* refers to the root timeline of the current level the script is run on, and *parent* refers to the movie clip or object that contains the movie clip or object with the script. If a script using the _parent object is placed within a movie, the script looks to the movie containing itself. Also, _level*N* refers to the *n*th level in the standalone Flash player or the Flash movie.

14

FUNCTIONS

> **Note**
>
> parent can be used twice in a row, but no more than twice in a row.

- **Using movie names**. An example is `myMovie.myFunction();`. Notice that every movie object or movie name used in dot syntax is separated by a period.

Now that you have seen some generic tags for using dot syntax to map to functions, let's look at a few examples of using them:

```
_root.myFunction ()                //invokes the function in the root timeline
_parent.myFunction()               //invokes the function in the parent timeline
_parent._parent.myFunction()       //invokes the function in the parent of the
                                   //parent timeline
_root.myMovie.myFunction()         //invokes the function in myMovie which is
                                   //located on the root timeline
```

As mentioned before, thanks to Flash MX, using dot syntax is no longer a necessity when trying to reach a function from a timeline that's different from the one it was created on.

The `global` Object

The `global` object is introduced in Flash MX. This new object has the power to allow functions and other data types to be reached from the entire movie. It can transform any variable, array, function, or object into a globally available data type. This way, you can create all the variables, functions, and whatever else you need to call upon in the main timeline and reuse them over and over again.

The generic template looks like this:

`_global.datatype`

We could go on for several pages talking about this new object, but for this chapter, we'll use it in the context of functions. Therefore, let's look at the generic template:

```
_global.functionName = function(parameters){
    //script to be run
}
```

Now that you have seen the general form of a global function, let's jump right in and create one.

We'll start with a simple `trace` function, with no parameters this time, and place this script in the main timeline:

```
_global.myFunction = function(){
    trace("My first global function");
}
```

You can now call this function from anywhere within the entire Flash movie and on any timeline, provided there is not a local function with the same name, which will cause the interpreter to use the local function instead.

The preceding example was straightforward, and so is the next one. This time, we are going to use parameters with the function but still use a trace statement as the script:

```
_global.myFunction = function(name){
    trace(name);
}
```

Now whenever this function is invoked from anywhere, whatever is placed as its parameter will be displayed in the output window when the movie is tested.

These two examples are great, but they do not show the true power of what the global object can do. The next example requires a little more effort and understanding to see how the object works.

First, start a new movie (Ctrl+N). On the main stage, draw a circle and then convert it to a movie clip symbol (F8).

Now in the timeline that your circle resides in, create another layer and place the following actions in the first frame of the new layer:

> **Note**
>
> This layer should be blank. Technically, you can place code in layers where symbols reside, but this is not a good habit.

```
_global.frictionSlide = function(friction,movie,distance,startX){
    newX = startX + distance;
    if(movie._x <= newX){
        movie._x+=(newX-movie._x)*friction;
    }
}
```

Now that this code is on the main timeline, you can put the function and a variable in your symbol. Therefore, open up the object actions for the circle movie clip you created and place this code in it:

```
//create a variable that the value will stay permanent
onClipEvent(load){
currentX = this._x;
}
//now invoke our function
onClipEvent(enterFrame){
    frictionSlide(.2,this,200,currentX);
//notice how the function can be invoked without a direct path to the function
}
```

14

FUNCTIONS

When you test the movie, the circle will slide slightly to the right and then slow down. You can adjust the parameters for when you call the function to have it do different things. We placed the variable in the `load` event because, if it were within the `enterFrame` event handler, the variable would change and the movement would never stop.

Of course, because this function is global, it can be called from anywhere, and the parameters can be changed for each movie clip.

Also note that, as shown in the preceding code, the global function calls a local variable. The next section covers some rules involved with calling variables regarding functions.

Variables and Functions

When using variables in conjunction with functions, you need to follow several rules to avoid errors and increase consistency.

First, you should be cautious when using a variable name that's the same as the name of a parameter in the function when they both reside in the same script. This should be common sense (if for no other reason than for the sake of organized code), but let's say it happens anyway.

Create a variable and call it `myVariable`; then create a function and have it trace `myVariable`:

```
var myVariable = "Flash";
//now create the function with no parameters
function myFunction (){
    trace(myVariable);
}
//now run the function
myFunction();
//output: Flash
```

In this instance, the interpreter does not find `myVariable` anywhere in the function, so it begins to look outside the function, and it runs into the variable you created, which is named `myVariable`, and grabs the value of that variable.

Now let's see what happens when you use a parameter with the same name. Using the same code as before, simply add a parameter with the same name as the variable you created:

```
var myVariable = "Flash";
//now create the function
function myFunction (myVariable){
    trace(myVariable);
```

```
}
//now run the function
myFunction("MX");
//output: MX
```

This time, the interpreter found `myVariable` within the function itself, as a parameter name, and ignored the variable that was created before the function was created.

Finally, let's add a variable inside the function with the same name as the parameter and the variable you created before the function (again, using the same code as before):

```
var myVariable = "Flash";
//Now create the function
function myFunction (myVariable){
    myVariable = "Unleashed";
    trace(myVariable);
}
//Now run the function
myFunction("MX");
//output: Unleashed
```

This time the interpreter found the variable `myVariable` inside the function and didn't bother with the parameter or the variable you created before you created the function.

So now you know how the interpreter looks for variables: First, it looks in the function itself; then it looks at the parameters, and finally it looks outside the function.

The variables available within the function are not available outside the function. Let's take a look at an example:

```
//First create the function
function myFunction (myVariable){
    myVariable = "Unleashed";
    trace(myVariable);
}
trace(myVariable);
//output: undefined
```

Because we attempted to trace the variable itself instead of running the function, the interpreter could not find the variable. Fortunately, this problem can be overcome. A variable can be pulled from a function under its own set of rules, as follows:

- The function must be invoked before a variable can be pulled from it.
- The variable pulled cannot have the same name as a parameter in the function.
- The variable created in the function cannot be a locally created variable.

Now let's go over some examples of these rules. As you saw earlier, you cannot pull a variable out of a function that has not been invoked yet. Therefore, let's invoke the function `myFunction` but first remove the parameters:

14

FUNCTIONS

```
//First create the function with no parameters
function myFunction (){
    myVariable = "Unleashed";
}
//Now run the function
myFunction();
trace(myVariable);
//output: Unleashed
//This time, place the parameter myVariable back in and let's see what happens.
function myFunction (myVariable){
    myVariable = "Unleashed";
}
//Now run the function
myFunction();
trace(myVariable);
//output: undefined
```

As you can see, because the variable we are trying to pull out has the same name as the parameter in the function, the trace statement traces undefined. This is not because the function has a parameter; it is because the names are the same. As shown next, if we change the name of the parameter, the trace statement returns the value we are looking for:

```
//First create the function and change the parameter
function myFunction (anyVariable){
    myVariable = "Unleashed";
}
//Now run the function
myFunction();
trace(myVariable);
//output: Unleashed
```

Now let's discuss the difference between a locally created variable and a variable that can be pulled from a function. In this next example, we'll create two different variables in two different ways, but both from inside the function. Then we'll run the function and attempt to pull both variables. We'll go over the results after the script. Here's the code for this example:

```
//First create the function with no parameters
function myFunction (){
    var A = "Flash"
    B = "Unleashed";
}
//Now run the function
myFunction();
trace(A);
trace(B);
//output: undefined
//       Unleashed
```

This time, variable A was not traced because using the keyword var inside a function creates a local variable that cannot be used outside the function. Variable B was traced correctly because it was not created locally like variable A was.

The next section will take functions a step further. As far as parameters are concerned, all we have covered involves using them to pass information to the script of a function. Now you'll see how to use them as objects.

Arguments

Arguments are the parameters you define when you invoke any function, and you can use the predefined arguments object of all functions to your benefit.

The arguments object of any function is more like an array (refer to Chapter 15, "Arrays," for more on arrays). And like an array, you can call specific parameters as well as the number of total parameters.

Let's start with the number of arguments in a given function. Gathering this information is as easy as using the length property.

The length Property

The length property of the arguments object found in all functions returns a value that represents the number of parameters a user has defined when a function is invoked. The generic template looks like this:

```
function functionName(parameters){
    //code to be run in the function
    arguments.length;
}
```

As you'll notice, you must use the length property as well as the arguments object inside the function. (The length property is also a property of arrays as well as a property of strings and can be used outside a function only in that context.)

Now let's see this property in a real example. Create a function with two basic parameters and trace the length of the arguments, like so:

```
function myFunction (x,y){
    trace (arguments.length);
}
//now run the function
myFunction(5,6);
//output: 2
```

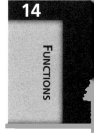

14

FUNCTIONS

The function runs, and the number of parameters are displayed in the output window. However, as mentioned before, the `length` property returns the number of arguments when the function is invoked, not created. To see what I mean, here is an example:

```
//create a function with two parameters
function myFunction(x,y){
    trace(arguments.length);
}
//now invoke the function, but add a parameter
myFunction (5,6,7);
//output: 3
```

Now that you have seen how to find the number of arguments, the next step is to pull individual arguments out of the entire set.

To call individual arguments, you use the `arguments` object and a numerical value held in brackets. The generic template looks like this:

```
function functionName(parameters){
    //code to be run in the function
    argument[N]
}
```

With this generic template, place a number (*N*) in the brackets that represents the argument in that position. However, note that arguments begin counting at 0 instead of at 1, so the first element looks like this:

```
argument[0]
```

Here is an example using this method of pulling individual arguments:

```
//create a function with three parameters
function myFunction(x,y,z){
    trace(arguments[1]);
}
//now invoke the function
myFunction(2,4,6);
//output: 4
```

Because arguments begin counting at 0 instead of at 1, the second argument is labeled `[1]` instead of `[2]`.

Now, using this method combined with the `length` property, you can create some amazing code. Let's take a look at an example that creates a global function that adds all numbers placed as parameters:

```
//first create a function with no parameters
function addArgs(){
//now use a loop statement to total the argument values
    for(var i = 0; i<arguments.length; i++){
```

```
            numTotal +=arguments[i];
    }
//display the total in the output window
    trace (numTotal);
}
//now invoke the function
addArgs(1,2,3);
//This can also work with combining strings.
//first create a function with no parameters
function combineStrings(){
//create a variable that will hold a string literal space
    space = " ";
//now use a loop statement to combine the strings
    for(var i = 0; i<arguments.length; i++){
//now convert each argument to a string for consistency
        total +=arguments[i].toString()+space;
    }
    trace (total);
}
//now invoke the function
combineStrings("Flash","MX","Unleashed");
```

Another great use of this technique involves creating an array that can hold the arguments outside of the function, because, as previously stated, the arguments object cannot be used outside the function. Here's an example:

```
//first create a function with no parameters
function createArray(){
//create an array to hold the arguments
    myArray = new Array();
    for(var i = 0; i < arguments.length; i++){
        myArray.push(arguments[i]);
    }
    return myArray;
}
//set a variable equal to the array
var argsArray = createArray(1,2,3,"One","Two");
//display new array in output window
trace(argsArray);
//output: 1,2,3,One,Two
```

These are just a few examples of using the length property combined with pulling individual arguments.

So far, you have seen functions used as easily repeatable code that can be changed, as needed, by using parameters. However, you can also use them for more than just actions because they are also considered objects.

14

FUNCTIONS

Functions as Objects

Using a function as an object may seem a bit unorthodox, but this actually greatly increases the usability of a function. To create a function object, you assign it without the parentheses and use it like an expression. Also, because the function is an object, you can move it around like any other type of data.

Here is an example using the built-in function trace() (built-in functions are discussed in the "Functions Built In to Flash" section):

```
//First, we set a variable to the trace function, but without parentheses
myFunction = trace;
myFunction("This function is now an object");
//output: This function is now an object
```

As you can see, the trace function is sent to the variable myFunction as an object, and because the variable is equal to the function, we invoked the function using the variables name.

Now let's look at another way of using the trace function as an object—this time we'll create our own function and set what we want displayed as a property of it:

```
//First, create the function
function myInfo (){
    trace(myInfo.name);
}
//Assign a property called name to the function
myInfo.name = "David";
//Run the function
myInfo();
//output: David
```

Assigning properties to functions is easy because of the built-in function object. You can even assign multiple properties to your functions. Now, suppose you would like to see a list of all the properties in a function. You can use the for in loop statement to pull properties of objects. (For more on loop statements, see Chapter 12, "Statements and Expressions—in Depth.")

To use the for in loop statement, place the keyword for ahead of an opening parenthesis. Then place the keyword var followed by your variable's name (in this case, functionProp). Then place the keyword in followed by the name of the object (the function's name, in this case). Finally, place a closing parenthesis, then opening and closing curly brackets inclosing the script you want to run while the loop looks through the properties. Here's what it looks like:

```
//First, create the function
function myInfo (){
```

```
}
//Now assign properties to it
myInfo.fName = "David";
myInfo.lName = "Vogeleer";
myInfo.age = "22";
myInfo.location = "Virginia";
//now use the for in statement to look through our properties
for(var functionProp in myInfo){
    trace("The property "+functionProp+" equals "+myInfo[functionProp]);
}
//output: The property location equals Virginia
//         The property age equals 22
//         The property lName equals Vogeleer
//         The property fName equals David
```

Notice that, in this example, we not only called the name of the property but also the value by using the function's name and the property we wanted to call in brackets. Because we used a dynamic variable, we did not have to put it in quotes. However, to call a single property of a function using brackets, you must place the name of the property in quotes, as shown in the following code:

```
//First, create the function
function myInfo (){
}
//Now assign the property to it
myInfo.age = "22";
trace(myInfo["age"]);
//output: 22
```

Let's take it another step forward by creating multiple functions with multiple properties. Then we'll store each function in an array. (As mentioned earlier, arrays are covered in greater detail in Chapter 15.) After that, we'll call all the properties of all the functions to be displayed in the output window, and because we stored the functions in the array as objects, we can invoke the functions by using the array.

First, we'll create the functions we need and, in the first one, store the `trace` statement we'll use at the end of the code. After that, we'll assign the properties to the functions. Then we'll create the array and store the functions in the array as objects. Finally, we'll run a script that looks through each element of the array as well as displays each property in each element.

After that, we'll invoke our first function using the array as a shortcut. Here's the code:

```
//First, create the functions
function myInfo (){
//This script is for later use
    trace("Traced from myInfo");
}
```

14

FUNCTIONS

```
function flashInfo (){
}
//Create the properties for each function
myInfo.fName = "David";
myInfo.age = "22";
flashInfo.version = "MX";
flashInfo.player = 6;
//Now create the array to hold the functions as objects
var functionArray = new Array();
//Place the functions in the array
functionArray[0] = myInfo;
functionArray[1] = flashInfo;
/*
Finally we create the script to search through the array
and trace all of our properties with their values
*/
for (var myElement in functionArray){
    for (var functionProp in functionArray[myElement]){
        trace("Property "+functionProp);
    }
}
//and because the function is stored as an object in the array
//we can call it using the array
functionArray[0]();
//output: Property player
//        Property version
//        Property age
//        Property fName
//        Traced from myInfo
```

In the preceding code, we used only two functions and two properties for each function. You can, however, increase both, and the script will still function properly.

Now that you have seen functions used as repeatable sets of code and as objects, let's move on to using them as methods to be used in conjunction with objects.

Functions as Methods

Before we get into using functions as methods, you need to know what a method is. A method is a function used in conjunction with an object. A method can perform a desired task on an object or can be used to gather information from that object.

We call methods just like we call functions, using parentheses; however, methods are attached to objects using dot syntax. Here is a generic template for calling a method:

```
object.method();
```

The preceding template is just for calling a method; to assign a method, you drop the parentheses, like this:

```
object.method;
```

Now that you have the generic templates to go by, let's start creating a few methods. First, we'll place a simple `trace` function within a function we create. Then we'll create a generic object, called `gObject`, and assign a property of `gObject` to our function. Then we'll invoke it by using the entire name, including the property. Here's the code:

```
//First, the function
function myFunction(){
    trace("Flash MX Unleashed");
}
//Then the generic object
gObject = new Object();
//Now the property of the object
gObject.title = myFunction;
//Now invoke the method
gObject.title();
//output: Flash MX Unleashed
```

Using a method is stronger than using a function when dealing with an object in that the method can manipulate the object itself. Take a look at the following code to see the function created and then reworked to change the object:

```
//First, the function
function myFunction(){
    trace("Flash MX Unleashed");
}
//Then the generic object
gObject = new Object();
//Now the property of the object
gObject.title = myFunction;
//Now create a new property
gObject.name = "David";
//Rewrite the function
function myFunction(){
    trace(this.name);
}
//Invoke the method
gObject.title();
//output: David
```

In this code, you can see how changing the function completely changes the property title of the `gObject` object.

Functions can also get information from objects when used as methods. Let's start by looking for a single property in an object and then have the function return its value instead of tracing it directly. Then we'll trace the method. Here's the code:

```
//First, create the object
gObject = new Object();
//Now add two properties to our object
gObject.age = 22;
```

14

FUNCTIONS

```
gObject.ageVerify = getAge;
//Here, create the function, and have it look for the property
function getAge (){
    return(this.age);
}
trace(gObject.ageVerify());
//output:22
```

That was a lot of work for not a big payoff. We could have simply traced the property itself. Therefore, let's build on the previous example and combine multiple properties in an expression that we may want to use again and again.

In this example, we'll create an object called `myCircle`. Then we'll create a function that gets the circumference and the area of the object. The idea is that no matter how often the properties we use change, the function will perform the same calculation on our object. Here's the code:

```
//First, create the object
myCircle = new Object();
//Now add two properties to our object
myCircle.radius = 5;
myCircle.circumference = getCircumference;
myCircle.area = getArea;
//Here, create the functions
function getArea (){
    return Math.round(Math.PI*Math.pow(this.radius,2));
}
function getCircumference (){
    return Math.round(Math.PI * 2 * this.radius);
}
//Finally, invoke the methods
trace(myCircle.area());
trace(myCircle.circumfrence());
//output: 79
//         31
```

Note that we use `Math.round()` in these functions to keep the answers smaller. The preceding code shows that methods can be quite powerful when used in an expression. You can change the value of `radius` to verify that the formula will still calculate correctly, or you can even apply the functions as methods to other objects for the same results.

Methods do exist in Flash without us creating them. As a matter of fact, it is difficult to write ActionScript without using methods. They are too numerous to list here, because nearly each object has its own set of methods.

Let's look at just a few examples of code using some of the built-in methods. This first example takes each word out of a `String` object and places them in an array using the `split` method:

```
//First, create our string
myString = "Flash MX Unleashed by Sams Publishing";
//Now create an array to hold our words
var myArray = new Array();
//Now use the split method and a "space" as a delimiter
myArray = myString.split(" ");
//And trace the array to see what happened
trace(myArray);
//output: Flash,MX,Unleashed,by,Sams,Publishing
```

The next example uses built-in methods to do the exact opposite of what the previous example does. In this example, we will convert the array back to a string using the `join` method for the `Array` object:

```
//First, create our array
myArray = new Array("Flash","MX","Unleashed","by","Sams","Publishing");
//Now, using the join method, we are going to set the array to a variable
myString = myArray.join(" ");
//Finally trace the string to see our results
trace(myString);
//output: Flash MX Unleashed by Sams Publishing
```

The final example of using built-in methods tells us what day of the week it is. We first have to create a basic array holding all the days of the week, and the rest is up to the method. Here's the code:

```
//First, create our array holding the days of the week
day = new Array
("Sunday","Monday","Tuesday","Wednesday","Thursday","Friday","Saturday");
//Next we create a date object to use our method with
myDate = new Date();
myDay = myDate.getDay();
//Finally we combine the information from our method with the
//array to get the days name
trace(day[myDay]);
//output: (the day of the week depending on what day it is)
```

As mentioned earlier, these are just a few examples of using some of the built-in methods found in Flash.

Speaking of being built in to Flash, the final section of this chapter covers some of the built-in functions found in Flash.

Functions Built in to Flash

We have covered ways of creating and manipulating user-defined functions thus far. Now we'll focus on some of the built-in functions Flash has to offer. We'll briefly go over some basic built-in functions. Then we'll go over what Macromedia considers to be an ActionScript-defined function. Finally, we'll discuss some of the depreciated functions.

Because you know what functions look like, I'll only briefly label the parts:

```
stop()              //stops a movie clip from playing, and has no parameters
play()              //plays a movie clip, and has no parameters
gotoAndStop(5)      //goes to a specified frame (the parameter) and stops
trace("Flash")      //displays parameter in output window
```

This list just goes on and on.

Flash, however, does recognize a few functions to be in a "functions" category. But before we go into them in any great detail, however, we need to go over a special function that deals with functions on the same timeline as itself: the `call` function.

The `call` Function

The `call` function is an interesting function that's brought all the way from Flash 4. This function can run code from any given frame without moving to that frame. It is a depreciated function, and Macromedia recommends using the keyword `function` to make code available throughout the timeline, as we discussed earlier. However, it's still good to know how to use the `call` function in case you ever have the need to.

The generic template is straightforward. Use the keyword `call`, followed by a string representing the frame label or a number representing a frame number, enclosed in parentheses. Here is the generic template:

```
call(frame);
```

Now that you know what it looks like, let's use the `call` function in an example. Start a new movie by going to File, New (Ctrl+N). Then create a new layer. Name the top layer **labels** and the bottom layer **actions**. Then place two more keyframes in each layer (F7).

Open the Actions panel for the first frame on the actions layer and place this code there:

```
stop();
```

This will stop the play head from moving past this frame. Next, in frame 2 of the same layer, place this `trace` statement:

```
trace("This is code from frame two");
```

Then in the final frame of the actions layer (frame 3), place this `trace` statement:

```
trace("This is code from the labeled frame");
```

Now we turn our attention to the labels layer. In the third frame of this layer place the label "labeled." When you're done, your screen should look similar to Figure 14.1.

FIGURE **14.1**

The project thus far.

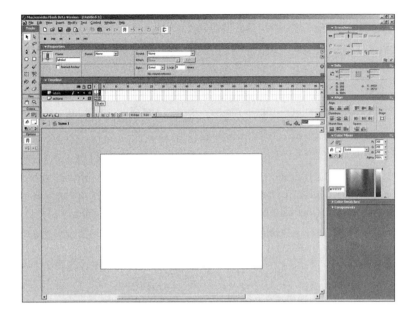

If you were to test this movie right now, nothing would happen. This is because of the stop function in frame 1. If stop were removed, both trace statements would run repeatedly, over and over again, while the movie loops through. However, when you place these next actions after stop, both statements will be run, but only once, and the frames still will never be reached by the play head. Therefore, place the following code in the first frame of the actions layer, and at the end, it will look like this:

```
stop();
call(2);
call("labeled");
//output: This is code from frame two
//        This is code from the labeled frame
```

Test the movie. There you have it—the code that was placed in the frame 2 as well as the third frame which was labeled "labeled" runs without the play head ever reaching these frames.

Now that we have covered this unique function, let's move on to some more built-in functions. Flash has predefined a couple of categories for functions in the Actions panel. The first is *conversion functions*.

14

FUNCTIONS

Conversion Functions

Conversion functions perform a specific task on objects: they convert objects. Each of the five main data types has its own conversion script that will change it to another data type.

The generic template utilizes the keyword of the object you are trying to convert to, and the expression you are trying to convert follows, enclosed in parentheses, as shown here:

```
converter(expression);
```

We will use the following example to change some data from one type to another. After each step, we will use the trace statement and the typeof operator to display the data type of each object following the conversion. Here's the code:

```
//Start off with a simple string
myString = "string";
trace (typeof myString);
//Now we begin converting the same object
//again and again while checking after each time
myString = Number(myString);
trace (typeof myString);
myString = Array(myString);
trace(typeof myString);
myString = Boolean(myString);
trace(typeof myString);
myString = Object(myString);
trace(typeof myString);
//Finally back to a string
myString = String(myString);
trace(typeof myString);
//output: string
//          number
//          object
//          boolean
//          object
//          string
```

> **Note**
>
> When converting to an array with the Array conversion function, whatever is being converted will be placed in the first element of the array, and not separated into individual elements.

Converting data types is an important part of using ActionScript. You can convert numbers from input text fields (all types of information from input text fields are strings; see

Chapter 19, "Working with Text," for more information) into true number data types. You can convert boolean data types into strings to use in sentences.

Let's now move on to the next category of functions: mathematical functions.

Mathematical Functions

Mathematical functions execute mathematical operations on expressions you assign to them. You may be thinking addition, subtraction, and so on, but these operations are much more advanced. Only four mathematical functions are listed in ActionScript:

- isFinite
- isNaN
- parseFloat
- parseInt

The first two of the mathematical functions, isFinite and isNaN, act more like conditionals. Let's see how they work individually.

The first, isFinite, checks to see whether the expression entered is a finite number. If the number is finite, the function returns True. If the expression is not finite (or *infinite*), the function returns False. Here is an example in which we test two numbers and trace the results:

```
trace(isFinite(15));
//evaluates to true
trace(isFinite(Number.NEGATIVE_INFINITY));
//evaluates to false
```

The second of these two functions, isNaN, works in the same manner. It checks to see whether the expression entered is not a real number. If the expression is not a real number, the function returns True. If the expression is a real number, the function returns False. Let's take a look:

```
trace(isNaN(15));
//evaluates to false
trace(isNaN("fifteen"));
//evaluates to true
trace(isNaN("15"));
//evaluates to false
```

Even though the last example is in fact a string, the interpreter converted it to a number when it was evaluated. Keep this in mind when evaluating numbers as strings.

The next mathematical function is parseFloat. This function takes numbers out of a string literal until it reaches a string character. Then it converts what it has removed into a true number data type. Here are a few examples:

```
trace(parseFloat("15"));
//output: 15
trace(parseFloat("fifteen"));
//output: NaN
trace(parseFloat("20dollars"));
//output: 20
```

As you can see in the last example, the function only takes the number and drops the rest of the string.

The last mathematical function is `parseInt`. This function can perform the same task as the `parseFloat` function, but it can also use a radix, which is useful when working with octal numbers. Here is an example:

```
trace(parseInt("15", 8));
//output: 13 (a representation of the octal number 15
//that has been parsed)
```

A few more functions are defined directly in ActionScript, including `getProperty()`, `getTimer()`, `targetPath`, and `getVersion()`, all of which return information. There is also `eval`, `escape`, and `unescape`, which perform their desired tasks on expressions.

We have covered a great deal of information about functions; now let's look at some depreciated functions and alternatives to their use.

Depreciated Functions

If you have worked in Flash 4 or even Flash 5, you may notice some of the functions are not where they used to be. No, they are not completely gone, but they are *depreciated*, which means that ActionScript provides new ways of performing the same tasks, and although these functions are still available for use, they might not be in the next release. Therefore, it is a good idea to get out of the habit of using them.

We'll go over each depreciated function briefly and discuss alternatives to their use.

chr

The `chr` function converts a numeric value to a character based on ASCII standards. It has been replaced by `String.fromCharCode`. Here are examples of both:

```
//The old way
trace(chr(64));

//The new way
trace(String.fromCharCode(64));

//output @
//        @
```

int

The `int` function takes a number with a decimal point and drops the decimal point. It has been replaced by `Math.floor`. Here are examples of both:

```
//the old way
trace(int(5.5));
```

```
//the new way
trace(Math.floor(5.5));
```

```
//output: 5
//        5
```

length

The `length` function returns the number of characters in a string or variable holding a string. It has been replaced by `String.length`. Here are examples of both:

```
//First create a variable holding a string
myString = "Flash";
```

```
//the old way
trace(length(myString));
```

```
//the new way
trace(myString.length);
```

```
//output: 5
//        5
```

mbchr

The `mbchr` function, like the `chr` function, converts a numeric value to a character based on ASCII standards. It has been replaced by `String.fromCharCode`. Here are examples of both:

```
//the old way
trace(mbchr(64));
```

```
//The new way
trace(String.fromCharCode(64));
```

```
//output @
//        @
```

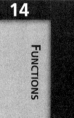

mblength

The `mblength` function, like the `length` function, returns the number of characters in a string or variable holding a string. It has been replaced by `String.length`. Here are examples of both:

```
//First create a variable holding a string
myString = "Flash";
```

```
//the old way
trace(mblength(myString));

//the new way
trace(myString.length);

//output: 5
//        5
```

mbord

The `mbord` function converts a character to a number by using the ASCII standard. There is no replacement, but this function is still depreciated. Here is an example:

```
trace(mbord("@"));
//output: 64
```

mbsubstring

The `mbsubstring` function removes a set number of characters from a string. It has been replaced by `String.substr`. Here are examples of both:

```
//First, create a variable to hold a string
myVar = "Unleashed";

//the old way
trace(mbsubstring(myVar, 0, 2));

//the new way
trace(myVar.substr(0, 2));

//output: Un
//        Un
```

ord

The `ord` function, like the `mbord` function, converts a character to a number by using the ASCII standard. There is no replacement, but this function is still depreciated. Here is an example:

```
trace(ord("@"));
//output: 64
```

random

The `random` function returns a random number from a expression given. It has been replaced by `Math.random`. Here are examples of both:

```
//the old way
trace (random(5));

//the new way
trace (Math.floor(Math.random()*5));
//output: (2 random numbers between 0-4)
```

substring

The substring function, like the mbsubstring function, removes a set number of characters from a string. It has been replaced by String.substr. Here are examples of both:

```
//First, create a variable to hold a string
myVar = "Unleashed";

//the old way
trace(substring(myVar, 0, 2));

//the new way
trace(myVar.substr(0, 2));

//output: Un
//        Un
```

This is the last of the depreciated functions.

That's it for all the functions. We have gone over everything, from creating functions to using depreciated functions. We have even covered using functions as objects and methods.

Just remember that functions are mainly used as blocks of repetitive code, parameters are used to slightly modify functions for different uses, and methods are functions attached to objects.

14

FUNCTIONS

Arrays

By David Vogeleer

IN THIS CHAPTER

What Is an Array and How Does It Work?

Back in Chapter 11, "Data Types and Variables—In Depth," we discussed different data types, including variables. Variables can hold one piece of data or another data type, including another variable. Like variables, arrays can hold any type of data, including strings, integers, and Booleans. They can also hold other data types, including variables and other arrays (called *nested arrays*), which we will discuss later in this chapter.

In this chapter, we will go over what an array is, how to create one, and how to retrieve, manipulate, and delete data from arrays with an applied example at the end.

So let's jump right in and see what an array is made of.

Deconstructing an Array

As stated earlier, an array is a data type that can hold multiple pieces of information. Here's an easy way to imagine this: A variable is like a chair, and it can hold one person (one piece of data). On the other hand, an array is more like a bench, and it can hold multiple people (multiple pieces of data).

Each piece of data in an array is called an *element*. Each element is automatically assigned the name of the array and a unique number called its *index*, which is enclosed in brackets. However, the first element in an array is not assigned the number 1; it is instead assigned the number 0 because arrays start counting at zero instead of one.

Therefore, the first element in the array myArray is labeled myArray[0]. Likewise, for the seventh element in the same array, you would use myArray[6].

This indexing is great for holding and retrieving sequential information.

The number of elements in an array is known as its *length*, and we will cover this topic in greater detail later in the chapter when the properties of an array are discussed.

Creating an Array

Now that you know what an array is and what it does, let's discuss how to create one. There are several different ways to create an array; however, we will be dealing mainly with the new operator and the Array constructor to build our sample array.

Open a new movie, click the first frame of the main timeline, and open the Actions panel. When creating arrays using the new operator and the Array constructor, start by setting a variable. Then make the variable equal to the new operator combined with the Array constructor, followed by a set of parentheses and then a semicolon (to end the line of code). Here's an example:

```
var myArray = new Array();
```

You're done! You just created your first array, so let's take a look at it. Start by adding the following to your code:

```
var myArray = new Array();
trace(myArray);
```

Now test your movie by going to the toolbar and choosing Control, Test Movie. When you test your movie, an output window will open because of the trace function in the code. However, nothing appears in the window, as shown in Figure 15.1. That's because there is nothing in our array. Let's go back and add some data to the array.

FIGURE 15.1

An empty output window for your movie.

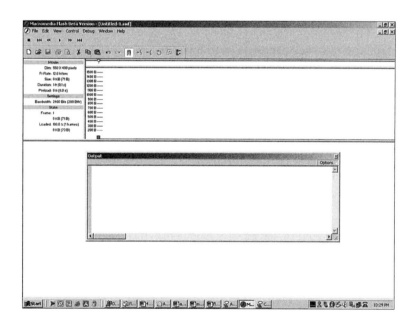

Each element in an array is labeled with the array's name and an integer that represents its position inside of the array. The first element in an array will always have an index of 0, followed by 1, and so on. Because you have already created the array, you will label the new elements manually. Under where you created the array, type the array name and then 0 in brackets, like this:

```
var myArray = new Array();
myArray[0] = "fName";
```

```
myArray[1] = "lName";
trace(myArray);
//output: fName, lName
```

Now that you have data in the array, you can continue to add elements, However, it's much easier to create the elements right in the beginning. So, let's do that next. Also, notice this time that the output of the code is preceded by comment marks (//). Such comments do not affect the code at all and are merely for explaining some of the actions in it. The output will appear in the code like this from now on.

You will still be using the original code, but when you create the array this time, you will create it with data inside. Elements in an array can be of any data type, as discussed earlier. Let's use a couple strings to start with. When putting elements in an array when it is created, place them in the parentheses and separate them with commas, like this:

```
var myArray = new Array("fName","lName");
trace(myArray);
//output: fName, lName
```

Another way of creating an array with information doesn't involve the new operator or the array constructor. You can simply set a variable equal to the elements you want in the array, but instead of putting them inside parentheses, place them between brackets, as shown here:

```
var myArray = ["fName","lName"];
trace(myArray);
//output: fName, lName
```

This traces the same as the other examples. However, just remember that when you do not use the new operator and the array constructor, you must place the elements in brackets.

You can even put just one piece of data in the array when you create it, but make sure it is not an integer. Otherwise, some surprising results will happen. Let's take a look.

Use the same code as before but replace what is in the parentheses with the number 5 (note that the output of the code is shown within the code using comment marks):

```
var myArray = new Array(5);
trace(myArray);
//output:  ,,,,
```

When you test the movie, notice that it doesn't display the number 5 but instead displays four commas. This is because when you place only an integer in an array, it creates that many blank elements.

You can also store variables in arrays just like any other type of data, and the data stored in the variables will display in the array:

```
var myName = "David";
var myAge = 22;
var myArray = new Array(myName, myAge);
trace(myArray);
//output: David, 22
```

Besides variables, arrays can also hold other arrays (called *nested arrays*). Nested arrays are useful for holding multiple lists in one place. Just place the name of the array as an element, as you would a variable:

```
var myNames = new Array("fName","lName");
var myArray = new Array("age",myNames);
trace(myArray);
//output: age, fName, lName
```

The second array simply encompasses the first array. However, if you trace the last element in myArray, you will see that it doesn't separate the elements from myNames. Let's take a look at this:

```
var myNames = new Array("fName","lName");
var myArray = new Array("age",myNames);
trace(myArray[1]);
//output: fName, lName
```

As you can see, even though it appears that when we added myNames to myArray, the elements came over as individual elements, in fact the entire array came over as one element. Just keep this in mind when you add arrays to arrays.

Retrieving Information from an Array

When retrieving information from an array, use the index of the array element to pull that specific piece of data, as shown here:

```
var myArray = new Array("fName","lName","age");
trace(myArray[1]);
//output: lName
```

In this example, we simply call the second element in myArray, which has the index of 1 because arrays start counting at 0.

There is a way to count the number of elements within an array—using the length property. It is the only property that an array has. Just attach the length property to any array with a period, and it will return the length. Here's an example:

```
var myArray = new Array("fName","lName","age","location");
trace(myArray.length);
//output: 4
```

> **Tip**
>
> Remember, the last element in any array will always have the index of
> `array.length` minus 1.

When combined with loop statements, the `length` property can be used to retrieve
sequential information.

This example lists each element vertically in the output window, as opposed to all in one
line. Create a movie and then place this code in the object actions of the movie:

```
onClipEvent(load){
        var myArray = new Array("fName","lName","age","location");
        i = 0;
}
onClipEvent(enterFrame){
if (i<myArray.length){
        trace(myArray[i]);
        i++;
        }
}
//output: fName
//         lName
//         age
//         location
```

This is just a simple example of how to use a loop statement and the `length` property.

Adding Elements to Arrays

So far we have created an array and placed elements in the array; now lets add elements
to an array. There are a couple ways of accomplishing this. Let's start with the simple
method and move into the more dynamic method.

You can start by setting the `length` property of an array. Setting the `length` property of
an array will add as many blank elements to that array as you specify—but again, the last
blank element will have the index of the length minus 1. Here's an example:

```
var myArray = new Array();
myArray.length = 10;
trace(myArray);
//output: ,,,,,,,,, (9 commas)
```

Using the `length` property to add elements will only add blank elements to the beginning.

Now we will add elements that actually have data in them. Start by creating an array and adding elements using the index of the elements, as shown here:

```
var myArray = new Array("fName","lName");
trace(myArray);
myArray[2] = "age";
myArray[3] = "location";
trace(myArray);
//output: fName, lName
//        fName, lName, age, location
```

That was pretty easy. All we did was add elements manually by looking at the next index of the array and assigning an element to it.

Now we will make it more dynamic. Create a button and place it on the main stage. Then add these actions to the first frame of the main movie:

```
var myArray = new Array();
i = 0;
```

Now add these actions to the object actions of the button you just placed on the main stage:

```
on(press) {
        thisLength = myArray.length;
        myArray[thisLength] = i;
        i++;
        trace(myArray);
}
//output: (depending on how many times you click the button, increasing
//output continued: numbers starting at 0)
```

Let's take a look at what we did. First, we created an array and a variable that equals zero. Then, we added actions to a button that, when pressed, will set the element with the index of the array's length to the variable *i*. The variable *i* will be increased by 1 each time the button is clicked. Finally, we traced the array.

Well, that was pretty dynamic, but we had to write some code that lets us know what the next index of the array should be. Now we're going to talk about an array method that will do the checking for us: the push method.

The push Method

The push method is great when you want to add elements to the end of an array without checking the length. Just assign the method to the array using a period and put what you want to add in parentheses following the push. Take a look at the following example:

First, create a movie and put it on the main stage. Then add these actions to the object actions of the movie:

```
onClipEvent(load) {
    var myArray = new Array();
}
onClipEvent(keyDown){
    theKey = String.fromCharCode(Key.getAscii());
    myArray.push(theKey);
    trace(myArray);
}
//output: (every key you press depending on how many
// and which key(s) you press)
```

This example is a simple keystroke recorder to show how easily the push method works. It simply "pushes" the keystroke to the end of the array.

If, at first, when pressing keys in the test screen, you do not see anything, click the mouse on the stage. Even though a keyDown event is taking place, the mouse must be clicked inside at least once for the event to take place.

You can also push more than one element at a time into an array. In this example, we will add two pieces of data at the end of the array using the push method:

```
var myArray = new Array("fName","lName");
trace(myArray);
myArray.push("age","location")
trace(myArray);
//output: fName, lName
//        fName, lName, age, location
```

Here, we just added two elements to myArray simultaneously using the push method.

You can add any kind of data type using the push method, as shown in the following example:

```
var myArray = new Array("fName","lName");
trace(myArray);
var x = 10;
var anotherArray = new Array("age","location");
var y = 5 + x;
myArray.push(x,y,anotherArray);
trace(myArray);
//output: fName, lName
//        fName, lName, 10, 15, age, location
```

Here, we've added a variable, an expression, and even another array to our original array using the push method.

As an interesting aside to what the push method for arrays can do, you can check the new length of an array while using the push method to add elements, as shown here:

```
var myArray = new Array("fName","lName");
trace(myArray.push("age","location"));
```

```
trace(myArray);
//output: 4
//        fName, lName, age, location
```

You can even substitute this method of returning the length for the `length` property in some cases. Here's an example:

```
var myArray = new Array("fName","lName");
trace(myArray.push(myArray.push()));
trace(myArray);
//output: 3
//        fName, lName, 2
```

Because this method adds the number before it checks the length using the `push` method, it adds the number 2, representing the length of the array, instead of 3.

The `push` method is great for gathering repetitive information for retrieval. Some examples might be providing back and forward control inside the Flash movie and recording users' information for the next time they visit.

Another example is a search function that searches inside an array and returns the frequency and positions of the element you are looking for:

```
//First, create the function and label your variables
function searchArray(theArray,lookFor) {
//Then create an array to hold the positions
            var position = new Array();
        //Use a for loop statement to check through each element
            for (var i = 0; i <=theArray.length-1; i++) {
        //Use an if statement to compare each element to what you're looking for
                if (theArray[i] == lookFor) {
        //If the element matches, add to the position array
                        position.push([i]);
                }
            }
        //Lastly, trace the results
            trace("The frequency is " + position.length);
            trace("In position(s) " + position);
}
var myArray = new Array("fName","lName","age","location","age");
searchArray(myArray,"age");
        //output: The frequency is 2
        //        In position(s) 2, 4
```

This is just another example of how to use the `push` method and the `length` property to retrieve elements from an array.

Another method you can use to add elements to an array is the `unshift` method.

The unshift Method

The unshift method works identically to the push method, except, instead of adding elements to the end, it adds them to the beginning. Here's an example:

```
var myArray = new Array("fName","lName");
trace(myArray);
myArray.unshift("age");
trace(myArray);
//output: fname, lName
//        age, fName, lName
```

Again, the unshift method adds elements to the beginning of an array. Therefore, each of the original elements' indexes are increased. For instance, fName will go from myArray[0] to myArray[1], and age will become myArray[0].

Also, like the push method, the *unshift* method can be used to show the length of an array:

```
var myArray = new Array("fName","lName");
trace(myArray.unshift("age","location"));
trace(myArray);
//output: 4
//        age, location, fName, lName
```

Like the push method, unshift traces the new length and adds elements to the array, but unlike push, it adds them to the front of the array.

The splice Method

The splice method is one of the more powerful methods of arrays. Not only can it add elements to an array, but it can also delete elements and place elements in the middle of arrays. Its syntax is very similar to the other methods we have talked about, except it has multiple parts:

```
myArray.splice(startingIndex,deleteNumber,itemsToAdd);
```

Let's take a look at the first part, the part that will delete items from the starting point forward. Attach the method like you would any other, and in the parentheses, place the index of where you want to start deleting items from the array:

```
var myArray = new Array("fName","lName","age","location","phone");
myArray.splice(2);
trace(myArray);
//output: fName, lName
```

The method started with the second index, which was age, and deleted all remaining elements. The elements were permanently removed. As a matter of fact, if you check the length of myArray after the splice, the value will be 2.

Now that you know how to delete from one index to the end, let's see how to remove a certain number of elements from a starting point. Use the same code, only this time, in the parentheses place a comma after the starting point and put in however many elements to remove. Here's an example:

```
var myArray = new Array("fName","lName","age","location","phone");
myArray.splice(2,2);
trace(myArray);
//output: fName, lName, phone
```

This time the method removed elements from the starting index we assigned and permanently removed the number of elements we assigned. If you check the length, it will return the value 3.

The last step of the `splice` method is to add elements in the middle of the array, beginning with the starting point. Again, we will be using the same code as before. This time after the number representing the number of elements to remove, we'll place another comma and then add the elements in while separating them with commas:

```
var myArray = new Array("fName","lName","age","location","phone");
myArray.splice(2,2,"fax","email");
trace(myArray);
//output: fName, lName, fax, email, phone
```

This time, the `splice` method removed the number of assigned elements at the assigned starting point and added elements at the starting point. Again, when adding elements, you can add any type of data, including variables and other arrays.

Now let's add elements to the middle of an array without deleting any elements. This time, we'll use the same syntax but set the number of items we want to delete to zero:

```
var myArray = new Array("fName","lName","age","location","phone");
myArray.splice(2,0,"fax","email");
trace(myArray);
//output: fName,lName,fax,email,age,location,phone
```

Because we set the number of items to delete to zero, the method simply adds the elements in at the index we listed and slides the other elements over.

The `splice` method has yet another great use. It can return the values of the items removed. Here's an example:

```
var myArray = new Array("fName","lName","age","location","phone");
trace(myArray.splice(2,2));
//output: age,location
```

In this case, instead of showing what the array looks like after the splice, the method shows what elements were removed. At this point, if you trace the array, it will show the new array with these elements removed. This is really useful if you want to remove certain information from one array and place that information in another array. Here's an example:

```
var myArray = new Array("fName","lName","age","location","phone");
anotherArray = myArray.splice(2,2);
trace(anotherArray);
trace(myArray);
//output: age, location
//         fName, lName, phone
```

This time, we removed items from an array and placed them in a new array called `anotherArray`.

You can even add elements to the original array while removing elements from it and placing them into a new array. Using the same code as before, this time we'll add an element to the original array:

```
var myArray = new Array("fName","lName","age","location","phone");
anotherArray = myArray.splice(2,2,"fax");
trace(anotherArray);
trace(myArray);
//output: age, location
          fName,lName,fax,phone
```

That was simple enough. We removed two elements and placed them in a new array while adding an element to the original array.

To summarize, the `splice` method can almost do it all. You can use it to add, remove, and change the elements inside an array. It can even be used to create new arrays.

Another method used for adding elements to arrays is the `concat` method.

The concat Method

The `concat` method works similarly to the `push` method in that it adds elements to the end of an array. However, it does not affect the original array. Instead, it creates a new array with the new elements.

To demonstrate the `concat` method, let's use our sample array. Now we can create another array by adding elements to the original with the `concat` method:

```
var myArray = new Array("fName","lName","age");
var anotherArray = myArray.concat("phone","fax");
trace(anotherArray);
//output: fName, lName, age, phone, fax
```

The new array, `anotherArray`, has both the elements from the original array, `myArray`, and the new elements we add to the end. If you trace `myArray`, nothing changes because the `concat` method only affects the new array it creates.

One nice thing about the concat method is that when adding an array to another array, it separates the elements and adds them as singular elements. Let's take a look at two examples: one using the push method and the other using the concat method.

Here's the example that uses the push() method:

```
var myArray = new Array("fName","lName");
var anotherArray = new Array("age","location");
myArray.push(anotherArray);
trace(myArray[2]);
//output: age, location
```

And here's the example that uses the concat() method:

```
var myArray = new Array("fName","lName");
var anotherArray = new Array("age","location");
myArray = myArray.concat(anotherArray);
trace(myArray[2]);
//output: age
```

In the first example, we used the push method to add the second array to myArray. Notice that it doesn't separate the elements into their own individual elements. Instead, it places the entire array in myArray[2]. In the second example, we used the concat method to add the second array to myArray. When the concat method is used, array elements are separated into individual elements.

> **Note**
>
> Unless you set the array equal to itself, the concat method will not permanently affect the original array.

Even though concat will separate the elements in an array into individual elements, it will not separate nested arrays. Here's an example:

```
var myArray = new Array(["fName","lName"],["age","location"]);
var anotherArray = myArray.concat(myArray);
trace(anotherArray[0]);
//output: fName, lName
```

Naming Array Elements

Most array elements are numbered, but they can also be named. Naming array elements is an easy way to keep information organized within an array. None of these named elements can be manipulated by array methods, nor can they be seen when the array is traced.

15

ARRAYS

There are two ways to create named array elements. The first uses dot syntax, and the second uses brackets and string literals. Here's an example of both methods:

```
var myArray = new Array();
myArray.fName = "David";
myArray["age"] = 22;
trace(myArray);
//output: (nothing)
```

We first created an array to hold the named elements and then we attached the first element using dot syntax and set it equal to a string. Then we attached the next named element using brackets and a string to name it, and we set its value to a number. Finally, we traced the array, but there were no results. This is because, as previously stated, when you trace an array, named elements will not appear. You have to call the named elements individually. Therefore, using the same code as before, we will trace both named elements individually when tracing the array:

```
var myArray = new Array();
myArray.fName = "David";
myArray["age"] = 22;
trace(myArray["fName"]);
trace(myArray.age);
//output: David
          22
```

This time, when we traced the elements individually, the trace was successful.

Named array elements will also not show up in the array's length. Here's an example:

```
var myArray = new Array();
   myArray.fName = "David";
   trace(myArray.length);
//output: 0
```

Now that you know how to add elements to an array, let's cover how to remove them.

Removing Array Elements

Just like adding elements, removing them has several different options. We will start with the simple options and then move into using the array methods.

The first option for removing elements from an array is using the `delete` operator.

The `delete` Operator

This `delete` operator is misleading. It does not actually delete the element in the array; it merely sets the element to `undefined`. To use this operator, type **delete** then use a space to separate the array element you want to "delete" by using its index. Here's an example:

```
var myArray = new Array("fName","lName");
trace(myArray[0]);
delete myArray[0];
trace(myArray[0]);
//output: fName
         undefined
```

As you can see, when we traced the first element in `myArray` before we used the `delete` operator, it displayed `fName`. Then after we used the `delete` operator, the output of the first element became `undefined`. Also note that the length of an array after the use of the `delete` operator will stay the same—even though the operator removes the data in the element, it does not remove the element itself.

The `delete` operator can also be used on named array elements, as shown here:

```
var myArray = new Array();
myArray.fName = "David";
trace(myArray.fName);
delete myArray.fName;
trace(myArray.fName);
//output: David
         undefined
```

Just like indexing array elements, the `delete` operator simply removes the value of the element, but the element is still in the array.

To remove the element itself, we have a few choices. The first involves using the `length` property. Then there are the `pop`, `shift` and `splice` methods.

Removing Elements Using the `length` Property

Using the `length` property to remove elements in an array is very similar to using it to add elements. Just create an array and set its length, like so:

```
var myArray = new Array("fName","lName","age","location");
trace(myArray);
myArray.length = 2;
trace(myArray);
//output: fName, lName, age, location
//        fName, lName
```

Using the `length` property to remove elements is a very simple way to get rid of everything that comes after the desired length of the array.

The `splice` Method Revisited

The `splice` method was already covered earlier in this chapter. This time, however, we'll use it for the removal of elements in an array.

You can use the `splice` method in two different ways when removing elements. The first way removes all elements beginning with the starting index you define. The second way sets the number of elements to remove at the starting index. Here's an example:

```
var myArray = new Array
("fName","lName","age","location","phone","fax","email");
trace(myArray);
myArray.splice(5);
trace(myArray);
myArray.splice(2,2);
trace(myArray);
//output: fName, lName, age, location, phone, fax, email
//fName,lName, age, location, phone
//fName, lName, phone
```

The first `splice` sets the starting index and removes all elements at and beyond that point. The second `splice` sets the starting index and the number of elements to remove and then actually removes those elements. Another method used for removing array elements is the `pop` method.

The pop Method

The `pop` method can be thought of as being the "archenemy" of the `push` method. Whereas the `push` method adds elements to the array, the `pop` method removes singular elements from the end of the array. Its syntax is the same as the other methods—just attach the method to the array you want to remove elements from, as shown here:

```
var myArray = new Array("fName","lName","age","location");
myArray.pop();
trace(myArray);
//output: fName, lName, age
```

In this example, the `pop` method simply dropped the last element in the array completely and changed the length of the array.

The `pop` method can also return the value of the element it removes. Here's an example:

```
var myArray = new Array("fName","lName","age","location");
trace(myArray.pop());
//output: location
```

The next method for removing array elements is the `shift` method.

The shift Method

If the `pop` method is the archenemy of the `push` method, then the `shift` method is the archenemy of the `unshift` method. The `shift` method removes one element from the beginning of an array and decreases its length by one:

```
var myArray = new Array("fName","lName","age","location");
myArray.shift();
trace(myArray);
//output: lName, age, location
```

Also like the pop method, the `shift` method returns the value of the element it removes:

```
var myArray = new Array("fName","lName","age","location");
trace(myArray.shift());
//output: fName
```

But what if we don't want to get rid of the elements in an array and instead just want to change them?

Changing Elements in Arrays

Now that you know how to add and remove elements, let's discuss how to change them. We will create an array, trace it to see the original, change the first element to something else by using the index, and then trace it again to see the difference as shown in the following code:

```
var myArray = new Array("fName","lName");
trace(myArray);
myArray [0] = "age";
trace(myArray);
//output: fName, lName
//        age, lName
```

That was pretty simple. We just renamed the first element, just like renaming a variable. What's more, changing named array elements is just as easy, as shown here:

```
var myArray = new Array();
myArray.age = 21;
trace(myArray.age);
myArray.age = 22;
trace(myArray.age);
//output: 21
//        22
```

The next section covers in greater detail nested arrays and how they can be used and manipulated.

Advanced Nested Arrays

Earlier in this chapter, we briefly discussed nested arrays (arrays held within other arrays). Now we are going to discuss some advantages to using these nested arrays. First, let's go over again how to create one. The example we'll use here involves the starting five of a basketball team by position. This example shows the following information:

- Points scored

- Shots taken

- Total rebounds

We will start with just the first two positions and combine them, as shown here:

```
var PG = new Array(12,15,4);
var SG = new Array(20,22,5);
var team = new Array(PG,SG);
trace(team);
//output: 12,15,4,20,22,5
```

Now that we have the data entered in, we could get the point guard's rebounds from the team array, without showing the other elements. To do this, we assign an index to the indexed element. This may sound complicated, but it's not. We want to know how many rebounds the point guard has (the third element in the first element of the team array). Here's the code we'll use:

```
var PG = new Array(12,15,4);
var SG = new Array(20,22,5);
var team = new Array(PG,SG);
trace(team[0][2]);
//output: 4
```

Success! We retrieved an individual element from a nested array. This is a very powerful tool when you have massive arrays with many nested arrays. Now let's take this a step further. We'll add the rest of the team and this time get the total for each category and place this information in an array called totals. We'll also divide the totals, as they are being calculated, by the main array's length property to get the averages for the players and then place that information into another array called averages. Here's the code:

```
//First, get all the players ready with their stats in their own array
var PG = new Array(12,15,4);
var SG = new Array(20,22,5);
var SF = new Array(11,13,8);
var PF = new Array(18,14,16);
var C = new Array(20,17,21);
//Now combine all the players arrays into one array called "team"
var team = new Array(PG,SG,SF,PF,C);
var totals = new Array();
var averages = new Array();
//Now lets create the loop statement that will perform all the necessary
//tasks we want
for(var i = 0; i<team[0].length; i++){
        for(var j = 0; j<team.length; j++){
```

```
//Place the total of each sub-element into the totals array
     totals[i]+=team[j][i];
//Divide the total of each sub-element by
//the main array's length to get the //average
     averages[i]+=(team[j][i])/team.length;
     }
}
trace(totals);
trace(averages);
//output: 81, 81, 54
//       16.2,16.2,10.8
```

In this example, we drew information in sequence from the nested arrays, totaled each column, and placed the totals in another array. We also successfully got the averages for all the players and placed them in another array. This is just one of the many possibilities for using this method.

Additional Array Methods

So far we have gone over methods for adding and removing elements. Now we will go over some other array methods for manipulating elements within an array.

The `toString` Method

Oftentimes, you might want to set an array equal to a variable, but when you set a variable equal directly to an array, the script simply copies the array over to that variable and stores each element as its own element. We'll use the `toString` method, which you saw before in Chapter 11, to convert an entire array to one string, with each element separated by commas:

```
var myArray = new Array("fName","lName");
var anotherArray = myArray;
var myVariable = myArray.toString();
trace(anotherArray[0]);
trace(myVariable[0]);
//output: fName
//        undefined
```

This example shows that when we copied `myArray` into `anotherArray`, an exact copy of the original array was created. Then we copied the same array to `myVariable`, but attached the `toString` method to it. When we tried to trace a singular element out of `myVariable`, *undefined* was returned. So now let's drop the index of `myVariable` and see what happens:

```
var myArray = new Array("fName","lName");
var anotherArray = myArray;
```

```
var myVariable = myArray.toString();
trace(anotherArray[0]);
trace(myVariable);
//output: fName
//         fName, lName
```

Notice that the elements are separated with commas and spaces when the array becomes a string. But what if you want to separate each element with some other character? The join method can accomplish this.

The `join` Method

Similar to the toString method, the join method converts all elements in an array to one string to place in a variable. Unlike the toString method, however, the join method separates each element the way you want it to. Again, just set this method to an array like you would any other method and then place whatever data type you want to separate the elements with between the parentheses. It can be a string, a number, a variable, or any other type of data. Here's an example:

```
var myArray = new Array("fName","lName","age","location");
var myVariable = myArray.join("--");
trace(myVariable);
//output: fName--lName--age--location
```

Alternatively, you can leave the parentheses blank, which causes join to act just like the toString method:

```
var myArray = new Array("fName","lName","age","location");
var myVariable = myArray.join();
trace(myVariable);
//output: fName,lName,age,location
```

You can even put in an expression, as shown here:

```
var myArray = new Array("fName","lName","age","location");
var myVariable = myArray.join(2+2);
trace(myVariable);
//output: fName4lName4age4location
```

Now let's look at another method for arrays—the slice method.

The `slice` Method

Like the splice method, the slice method can grab elements from an array and place them into a new array. Unlike the splice method, however, the slice method does not affect the original array. Here's an easy way to think of these methods: The splice method is like cutting, and the slice method is like copying.

The syntax for the `slice` method is the same as the `splice` method—you can set the starting point and how many elements you want to copy. Here's an example:

```
var myArray = new Array("fName","lName","age","location");
var anotherArray = myArray.slice(2);
trace(anotherArray);
trace(myArray);
//output: age, location
//         fName, lName, age, location
```

The `slice` method copies the elements, starting with the declared index, to the last element of the original array and places them in a new array without affecting the original array.

You can also set the ending index of the elements you wish to copy:

```
var myArray = new Array("fName","lName","age","location");
var anotherArray = myArray.slice(2,3);
trace(anotherArray);
//output: age
```

So far, these methods have removed, added, and shifted elements. Now let's change the order of them with the `reverse` method.

The reverse Method

The `reverse` method is exactly what it sounds like—it's a method for reversing the order of all the elements in an array. Once an array is created, you can attach the `reverse` method to it, like so:

```
var myArray = new Array("fName","lName","age","location");
myArray.reverse();
trace(myArray);
//output: location, age, lName, fName
```

The `reverse` method is used mainly for reversing already sorted arrays. The next section shows you how this method is used.

Sorting Arrays

Sorting plays an important role in using arrays. With sorting, you can put names in alphabetical order, put prices from greatest to least, and even see who has the highest score so far in a video game.

There are two types of sorting: One involves a general sort of the elements in an array, and the other involves the sorting of nested arrays.

Let's go over the general `sort` method. Just attach this method like you would any other method, and it sorts somewhat alphabetically. Here's an example:

```
var fName = new Array("David","Mike","George","Matt","Kim");
fName.sort();
trace(fName);
//output: David,George,Kim,Matt,Mike
```

The sort worked fine. So why did I mention it will sort "somewhat" alphabetically? As you'll notice, all the strings in the `fName` array start with a capital letter. However, change the first letter in "David" to a lowercase *d* and see the results:

```
var fName = new Array("david","Mike","George","Matt","Kim");
fName.sort();
trace(fName);
//output: George,Kim,Matt,Mike,david
```

This time, "david" is moved to the back, even though it's the same name. The `sort` method does not recognize "david" as being the same as "David" because it doesn't look at the letters themselves; instead, it looks at their keycodes (discussed in Chapter 11), in which capital letters come before lowercase letters. There are solutions to this, however, and that is where the arguments to the `sort` method come in. You can assign arguments to control how the `sort` method will sort.

Assigning an argument to the `sort` method can be difficult, depending on how advanced you want to get. Let's start small. We'll create a function that controls the sort and then we'll set the function as the argument to the sort. The following example uses an array of ages and sorts them from greatest to least:

```
function bigToSmall(element0,element1){
        if (element0 < element1){
                return 1;
        }else if (element0 > element1){
                return -1;
        }else {
                return 0;
        }
}
var age = new Array(12,21,13,24,48);
age.sort(bigToSmall);
trace(age);
//output: 48, 24, 21, 13, 12
```

In this example we created a function. This function must contain two elements that represent elements in the array. Then we created an `if` statement that determines how to sort the elements. The result of the `if` statement should be negative if you want the first element to appear before the second element and positive for the other way around. After creating the function, we created the array. Then we sorted the array according to our function.

Now that's a pretty large function for just a simple sort. We can shorten it, though, by setting the `return` statement to an expression:

```
function bigToSmall(element0,element1){
        return element1-element0;
}
var age = new Array(12,21,13,24,48);
age.sort(bigToSmall);
trace(age);
//output: 48, 24, 21, 13, 12
```

Now that you know how to create a function to use in the `sort` method, let's revisit the `fName` array from earlier and sort it alphabetically, regardless of case:

```
function alphabet(element0,element1) {
    return (element0.toUpperCase() > element1.toUpperCase());
}
var fName = new Array("David","andy","mike","George","john");
fName.sort(alphabet);
trace(fName);
//output: andy, David, George, john, mike
```

By using the `toUpperCase` method for strings, we convert each element in the array to the same style (you can also use the `toLowerCase` method). This way, when the sort is run, it will compare the elements equally because the same case is used for all elements.

The sortOn Method

The *sortOn* method, a new addition to the array methods in Flash MX, is an extremely tricky method to use. This method sorts nested arrays by the value of a specific named element in each array. The syntax is similar to other methods covered so far, but in the parentheses, you put the named field you want to sort all the nested arrays by. Each of the nested arrays you want to sort must have that named field in it. Let's take a look at an example:

```
var one = new Array();
one.a = "a";
one.b = "b";
one.c = "c";
var two = new Array();
two.a = "b";
two.b = "c";
two.c = "a";
var three = new Array();
three.a = "c";
```

```
three.b = "a";
three.c = "b";
var myArray = new Array(one,two,three)
trace(myArray[0].a);
myArray.sortOn("b");
trace(myArray[0].a);
//output: a
//        c
```

In this example, we first created the three arrays we are going to put in our main array. In each of the nested arrays, we created three named array elements: one, two, and three. Then we set each of the three named elements to three different string literal letters: a, b, and c. Next we shuffled each of the values so that the arrays will not be equal to each other. Then, we placed each of these three arrays in myArray. After that, we traced the named element a in the first nested array of myArray. Then we ran the sort based on the named element b in all the nested arrays. After the sort, we traced myArray again based on the named element a in the first array element, and this time it was c. Therefore, the sort was successful.

Applied Example

We have gone over lots of code and different examples of how to use some of the methods of arrays. Now let's look at an applied example of arrays at work. We are going to create a mouse recorder that, after a certain length of recording, will replay the recorded positions of the mouse.

First, we must create the necessary symbols for the movie:

1. Create a movie symbol with an arrow graphic that's centered at the point of the arrow. Name this symbol **arrow** (see Figure 15.2).

FIGURE 15.2
The "arrow" symbol.

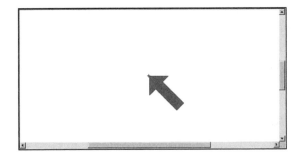

2. Create a movie symbol with a dynamic text field labeled "count". Name this symbol **count** (see Figure 15.3).

FIGURE **15.3**

The "count" symbol.

3. Create a button symbol to move from frame to frame. Name this symbol **button** (see Figure 15.4).

FIGURE **15.4**

The "button" symbol.

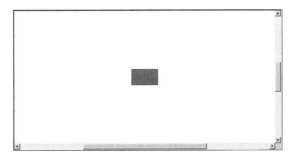

Next, on the main stage, create five layers with the following labels:

- Actions
- Labels
- Count
- Arrow
- Button

The movie will consist of three keyframes. In the Labels layer, label the frames like this:

- start
- record
- playRecord

Now we will move to the Actions layer. In the first frame, place this code:

```
stop();
//Create our arrays to hold our data
var mouseX = new Array();
var mouseY = new Array();
```

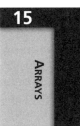

Also, in the first keyframe of the Buttons layer, place a button instance. Then place the following code in the object actions of the button:

```
on(press) {
        gotoAndStop("record");
}
```

Next, on the Count layer, place a count instance on the stage in the second keyframe and then place the following code in the object actions:

```
onClipEvent(load) {
//Create a variable to adjust the length of the recording
//as well as an incremental variable
        time = 200;
        i = 0;
}
onClipEvent(enterFrame){
//Then use a loop statement to check if time is up
        if(i < time){
//Record the positions of the mouse and place them
//in the arrays on the main stage
                _root.mouseX.push(_root._xmouse);
                _root.mouseY.push(_root._ymouse);
        this.count = i;
        }else {
//When count is over, go to the next frame
                _root.gotoAndStop("playRecord");
        }
        i++;
}
```

Then, on the Arrow layer, place an arrow instance on the main stage in the third keyframe and place these actions in it:

```
onClipEvent(load){
//Create incremental variable again
        i=0;
}
onClipEvent(enterFrame){
//as long as the you are not at the end of the array
//keep playing
        if(i<_root.mouseX.length){
//Set the positions of this arrow equal to positions
//held in arrays on the main timeline
                _x = _root.mouseX[i];
                _y = _root.mouseY[i];
                i++;
        }else {
//When it's over, go to the beginning
                root.gotoAndStop("start");
        }
}
```

That's it! Now test the movie and have some fun coming up with your own experiments using arrays. Also note that the higher the frame rate, the smoother the animation will play.

Summary

We have gone over all the basics of arrays. We have touched on each of the predefined methods as well as some of the theories and ideas behind them.

Components

By David Vogeleer

This chapter covers the brief history of Smart Clips and why they were created. Then it moves into a new feature of Flash MX—components, which are the new Smart Clips. Components provide a way of creating reusable customizable interface pieces. We will go over this new feature and how to use each built-in component. Then we will continue with how to create your own with custom icons.

Let's start in the beginning with Smart Clips.

The History of Smart Clips

Back in Flash 5, Smart Clips were created so that developers and programmers could design interface pieces to be reused over and over again without the user having to go into the Actions panel to adjust the variables. Instead, the user could use a graphical interface to adjust individual settings of the movie clip.

This concept gave people with little or no programming background the ability to design and implement interfaces made entirely from Flash.

This power did not come without a price, however; the file size of the Smart Clips became an issue. Smart Clips are noticeably larger in size than the original movies converted to Smart Clips. If the developer can code the interface and make it a smaller file size, then the novelty of having a nonprogrammer adjust the settings loses its value.

In Flash MX, however, Smart Clips have given way to components.

Introduction to Components

Flash user interface components (*UI components* for short) are movie clips that have been created with special methods and other ActionScript so that through an interface, major variables can be adjusted to create interface pieces that can be customized for individual needs.

You can create your own components, which you'll do later in this chapter, but Flash also includes its own set of UI components, and they can be found in the Components panel, as shown in Figure 16.1. To open this panel, go to the menu bar and choose Window, Components (Ctrl+F7).

FIGURE **16.1**

The Components panel.

Here's a list of each component with a description of how it is used:

- **CheckBox**. Single choice: yes or no.
- **ComboBox**. A display showing a list of choices from which only one can be chosen.
- **ListBox**. A display showing a list of choices from which one or several can be chosen at once.
- **PushButton**. Invokes a defined function when clicked or when Enter/Return is pressed.
- **RadioButton**. This is a single choice within a group of choices; only one in a group can be chosen.
- **ScrollBar**. Attached to a dynamic text field. This component can be used to scroll the text up and down, as well as left to right.
- **ScrollPane**. Attached to a movie. This component can be used to scroll the movie's viewable area vertically as well as horizontally.

Before we go over in detail how to use and customize each of these components, you need to know how to add them to a movie and adjust their parameters.

Adding Components to a Movie

Adding components to a document can be accomplished in two different ways. The simplest way is to drag an instance of the component onto the stage. The more difficult way is to add them to the Library and then use ActionScript to attach them to a movie clip or the main stage itself. We'll start with the simpler method and then use the more difficult one.

Note that we'll be working in Live Preview mode. Live Preview allows you to see the changes you make to the component's parameters immediately after you change them, instead of having to test the movie to see them. To turn on Live Preview, go to the menu bar and choose Control, Enable Live Preview. If you see a check mark beside that option, it is already on.

Manually Adding Components

The first thing you need to do is start a new file. Go to the menu bar and choose File, New. Make sure to dock the Components panel if it is not already docked so that you can see the full stage. Figure 16.2 shows the Components panel docked.

Now, press and drag the icon for CheckBox onto the stage. You will use all the default settings for this example.

When you test the movie, you now have a working check box.

FIGURE 16.2

The station is docked so you can see the whole stage.

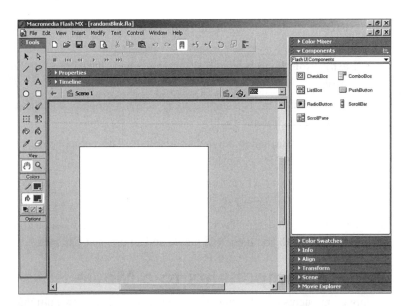

In the next section, you'll place a component on the stage using ActionScript.

Adding Components with ActionScript

This example is more advanced than the previous one and requires more steps. You'll use the `attachMovie` statement to place a component on the stage. Here is the generic template:

```
movie.attachMovie(identifier, newInstanceName, depth);
```

Because you have already included the CheckBox component on the stage, you can skip the first of the following steps:

1. Drag out an instance of Check Box component you would like to use on the stage.

2. Remove the instance of the component from the stage, because you are going to attach it with ActionScript later. (Hightlight the component and hit delete.)

   All UI components already have the correct linkage properties and an identifier. The identifier in the linkage properties is used when ActionScript attaches a movie to another movie. The identifier for UI components is the letter F, followed by the component's name and then by the word Symbol. For example, the CheckBox component has the identifier FCheckBoxSymbol.

   When you bring any UI component onto the stage, the library receives a folder called Flash UI Components. In this folder are several other folders, plus the component itself with its own icon. To view the linkage properties of the component, open the Library (Ctrl+L), double-click the Flash UI Components folder, right-click the component, and then choose Linkage.

3. Open up the Actions panel for the first keyframe in the timeline and place this code:

```
//This will place the Component on the main stage
_root.attachMovie("FCheckBoxSymbol", "myCheckBox", 0);
//This will give the CheckBox a label
_root.myCheckBox.setLabel("Check Me");
```

Now you can test the movie. The result should look similar to what's shown in Figure 16.3.

Note

Remember, if you are going to place a component using ActionScript, you must first drag an instance of it from the components panel onto the stage so that the component will be available in the Library.

Notice that you set the label of the CheckBox component. This is one of the many parameters associated with components. We'll discuss setting parameters next.

FIGURE 16.3

The check box component in action.

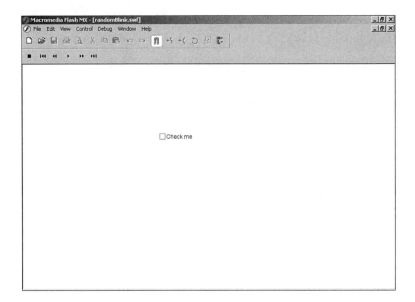

Setting Parameters

The parameters of a component are what make it customizable. They allow users to set different aspects of each component individually, without having to open the Actions panel. Each component has its own parameters, which will be discussed later in this chapter.

Parameters can also be set in two different ways. The first method involves manually setting them through the Component Parameters panel or through the Properties panel when the component is highlighted. Both can be seen in Figure 16.4. Notice in the Properties panel that the Parameters tab is selected. This must be selected; otherwise you will see the properties of the component as a movie clip instead of the parameters of the component. The second way of setting parameters is, of course, through ActionScript.

You'll first learn how to set parameters manually. Then we'll cover how to set them with ActionScript.

Manually Setting Parameters

You will continue to use the CheckBox component, so start a new file and drag an instance of the CheckBox component onto the stage (refer back to Figure 16.2). Now look at the parameters of this component either in the Properties panel or in the Component Parameters panel. Here's a list of the parameters you should see with a description of each:

- **Label**. This is a string that will be displayed with the component.

- **Initial Value**. This is a Boolean value telling the component to start as checked (True) or unchecked (False).

- **Label Placement**. This sets the position at which the label will be placed: Left or Right. Note that the label also acts as a hit area (clickable area) for selecting the component.

- **Change Handler**. This a string that calls a function that must be defined on the same timeline as the component. The function will only be called when a user checks or unchecks the check box (for more on Change Handler, see the section on passing information to and from ActionScript).

FIGURE 16.4

You can set the properties of components in both the Properties panel and the Component Parameters panel.

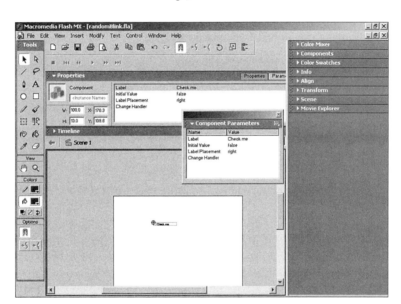

Now that you have seen what the parameters are, let's change them for the current component. Change the Label parameter from Check Box to True/False. Leave the Initial Value parameter at False. Change the Label Placement parameter to Left and leave the Change Handler parameter alone for now.

Test the movie to view the check box you've just created. Now we're going to adjust the settings from ActionScript.

Setting Parameters Through ActionScript

Each component has a set of methods that can be found under "Flash UI Components" in the Actions panel. These methods not only can retrieve parameters from components but can also set and reset the parameters of components.

We'll continue with the CheckBox component you've placed on the main stage. You do not have to adjust the parameters back manually; in this case, you'll do it with ActionScript.

However, before you can adjust the parameters, you have to name the instance. In the Properties panel, name the instance of the CheckBox component `myCheckBox`.

Once the instance name has been set, create a new layer and call the layer **actions**. In the first frame of the actions layer, place this code:

```
//First, label the CheckBox
myCheckBox.setLabel("Check me please");
//Then position the label
myCheckBox.setLabelPlacement("left");
//Set the initial value
myCheckBox.setValue(true);
//Finally set the width of the label, which is also
//the hit area of the CheckBox
myCheckBox.setSize(120);
```

Notice that you've set the width of the component by using the `setSize` method. You can set the width and height of a component using the `_width` and `_height` properties, but this will not affect the layout, only the dimensions. This means that if the text is too large for the text box and you use `_width` to adjust it, only the actual dimensions will change, not the width of the text box.

You can also adjust the width of a component using the Free Transform tool by highlighting the component and going to the menu bar and choosing Modify, Transform, Free Transform or pressing the Q key on the keyboard.

Each component differs as to whether the width and the height can be adjusted. We'll go over the details of each component in the next section, when we cover built-in UI components.

Built-in UI Components

Flash MX comes bundled with several built-in UI components, which were briefly discussed earlier. In this section we'll go over each one individually, including a list of parameters and uses, specifics of the components, and an example of each one.

We'll start with the component you've been working with so far—the CheckBox component.

The CheckBox Component

Because we've discussed the basic fundamentals of the CheckBox component already, this subsection will be brief.

The CheckBox is an interface piece that can be set to True or False and usually represents a "yes" or "no" answer. Here is the list of parameters with descriptions for the CheckBox component:

- **Label**. This is a string that will be displayed with the component.
- **Initial Value**. This is a Boolean value telling the component to start as checked (True) or unchecked (False).
- **Label Placement**. This sets the position at which the label will be placed: Left or Right. Note that the label also acts as a hit area for selecting the component.
- **Change Handler**. This a string that calls a function that must be defined on the same timeline as the component. The function will only be called when a user checks or unchecks the check box.

The CheckBox component can have its width changed with `setSize`, but not its height. Here is a generic template for the `setSize` method for this component:

```
MyCheckBox.setSize(width);
```

Do not forget that the width of the text field is not just for the text but also for the hit area of the check box.

You have seen several examples of check boxes throughout this chapter, but here is another:

1. Create a new file (Ctrl+N).
2. Drag an instance of the CheckBox component onto the stage.
3. Change its parameters as follows:
    •For Label, enter **Over 21**.
    •Set Initial Value to False.
    •Set Label Placement to Right.
4. Test movie by going to the menu bar and choosing Control, Test Movie (Ctrl+Enter).

This was a brief review of the CheckBox Component. Next we'll cover the ComboBox component.

The ComboBox Component

The ComboBox component is a drop-down, scrollable list of single-selection choices, meaning that only one choice can be selected at one time.

The list of choices is considered a zero-based list, which means that the first choice is in position 0, the second choice is in position 1, and so on. This is because when you're creating a list using the component's parameters, you are creating an array to hold the list. (Arrays were covered in Chapter 15, "Arrays.")

The scrollable list can also be moved with keystrokes. Here is the list of them:

- **Down arrow**. Moves down one line
- **Up arrow**. Moves up one line
- **Page Down**. Moves down one page of choices
- **Page Up**. Moves up one page of choices
- **End**. Moves to the last choice
- **Home**. Moves to the first choice

Also, the list can be set to Editable. The Editable function indicates that an input text field will appear at the top of the combo box that acts like a search window for the list of choices. Here are the parameters associated with the ComboBox component:

- **Editable**. Sets whether a search box is available.
- **Labels**. This is an array of strings representing the choices in the list.
- **Data**. This is another array of strings that represents the values of each choice in the list.
- **Row Count**. This is a number representing how many choices to display at once; the default value is 8.
- **Change Handler**. This is a string representing a function that resides on the same line as the component. This function is run anytime a user makes a selection from the list or, if the ComboBox component is set to Editable, when the user types something and presses Enter in the combo box.

You can set the width of the ComboBox component, but not the height. This can be done with the Free Transform tool (Q) or by using the `setSize` method, as shown in this generic template:

```
MyComboBox.setSize(width);
```

As an example, let's create a list of colors to choose from. You'll set the window to display fewer than the total number of choices so that the scrollbar will appear. Follow these steps:

1. Create a new file (Ctrl+N).

2. Drag an instance of the ComboBox component onto the stage.

3. Change the parameters as follows:

   - Set Editable to False.

   - For Labels, enter **Green**, **Yellow**, **Red**, **Blue**. To do this, double-click the brackets in the List parameter or click the magnifying glass at the end of the parameter when the parameter is selected. When this is done, the Values dialog box appears, as shown in Figure 16.5. The plus sign is used to add elements, and the minus sign is used to remove them. The arrows move the selection bar up and down in the list. Therefore, click the plus sign four times to add four elements. To change the value of the elements, double-click them and type in the list of colors.

   - In the Rows parameter, change the number from 8 to 3. This will display only three of the four elements at a time, thus causing the scrollbar to appear.

4. Finally, test the movie by going to the menu bar and choosing Control, Test Movie (Ctrl+Enter).

FIGURE 16.5

The Values panel, used for setting elements in arrays for components.

Let's move on to another type of list—the ListBox component.

The ListBox Component

The ListBox component is a drop-down, scrollable list similar to the ComboBox component, However, unlike the ComboBox component, which only allows one selection at a time, the ListBox component can have several choices chosen by the user at once.

Also like the ComboBox component, the ListBox component is a zero-based list, which means the first element in the Labels parameter is at the 0 index, the second element is at the 1 index, and so on.

Of course, keystrokes can be used to control the ListBox component. Here's the list of keystrokes:

- **Down arrow**. Moves down one line
- **Up arrow**. Moves up one line
- **Page Down**. Moves down one page of choices
- **Page Up**. Moves up one page of choices
- **End**. Moves to the last choice
- **Home**. Moves to the first choice

The ListBox component, however, is not editable like the ComboBox component is. The ListBox component has four main parameters:

- **Labels**. This is an array of strings that represents the choices in the list.
- **Data**. This is another array of strings that represents the values of each choice in the list.
- **Select Multiple**. Enables the user to make more than one selection from the list at one time. This is useful for allowing the user to choose all the choices that apply.
- **Change Handler**. This is a string representing a function that resides on the same line as the component. This function is run anytime a user makes a selection from the list.

You may have noticed that Row Count is not a parameter in the ListBox component. This particular component uses a window that only displays a certain number of choices, which is determined by the height. Yes, you can adjust the height and the width of the ListBox component with the Free Transform tool (Q) or via the setSize method. Here's the generic template for setting the size of a ListBox component:

```
myListBox.setSize(width, height);
```

Alternatively, you can set the width by itself using the setWidth method, like this:

```
myListBox.setWidth(width);
```

> **Tip**
>
> If you set the width using the setSize method but do not set the height, the component will only be tall enough to display two items at once.

In the following example of a ListBox component, you are going to create a list of sports that the user can choose from to indicate which ones he or she plays. Follow these steps:

1. Create a new file (Ctrl+N).
2. Drag an instance of the ListBox component onto the stage.
3. Change the parameters as follows:
   - For Labels, enter **Basketball**, **Baseball**, **Hockey**, **Football**, **Golf**, **Bowling** by using the Values dialog box (refer back to Figure 16.5).
   - Set Select Multiple to True.
4. Test the movie by going to the menu bar and choosing Control, Test Movie (Ctrl+Enter).

   You now have a working list of choices from which a user can choose multiple selections. Notice that the scrollbar is present but is not necessary. You can change this with just a little more work using the `setAutoHideScrollBar` method. If this method is set to `True`, it will detect whether the entire list is visible at once. If the entire list is indeed visible, then the scrollbar will not be shown.
5. Name the instance of the ListBox component **myListBox**.
6. Create a new layer and name it **actions**.
7. In the first keyframe of the actions layer, place this code:

   ```
   MyListBox.setAutoHideScrollBar(true);
   ```
8. Test the movie again.

Now the list box looks much nicer. If you were to go back and add more elements or adjust the size so that not all the elements are visible at once, the scrollbar will reappear. Therefore, it is a good policy to always set the `setAutoHideScrolBar` method to `True`.

The next component we'll discuss is the simplest of them all, but it still deserves your attention. It's the PushButton component.

The PushButton Component

The PushButton component is a simple component to understand. Its only use is as a clickable button. The PushButton component has only two parameters:

- **Label**. This is a string that will appear on the button and is centered.
- **Click Handler**. This is similar to the Change Handler parameter found in other components. It is a string that represents a function that resides on the same time-line as the component. This function is called when a user presses and releases the push button.

The width and height of a push button can be adjusted using the Free Transform tool (Q) or the `setSize` method. The `setSize` method for this component has the following generic template:

```
myPushButton.setSize(width,height);
```

The PushButton component does not have a `setWidth` method, so you must set the size using the `setSize` method. If you do not include a height for the method, the height will be the same height as the text field, so it isn't a huge deal if you decide to leave the height out.

In the following example, you will create a simple button with a label. Here are the steps to follow:

1. Create a new file (Ctrl+N).
2. Drag an instance of the PushButton component onto the stage.
3. For the Labels parameter, enter **Press Me**.
4. Now test the movie by going to the menu bar and choosing Control, Test Movie (Ctrl+Enter).

When you test the movie, turn on the Bandwidth Profiler by going to the menu bar and choosing View, Bandwidth Profiler (Ctrl+B). Notice that the size of this single button is over 30KB. We'll discuss this further in the section "Downsides of Components."

The next component we'll discuss is the RadioButton component. It has some unique attributes, and you can create groups of RadioButton components.

The RadioButton Component

The RadioButton component is unique among the other components in that it can be grouped with several other RadioButton components to form multiple choices that are mutually exclusive, meaning that only one radio button in a group can be selected at a time.

The parameters for the RadioButton component are as follows:

- **Label**. This is the text that will appear with the component; it also acts as the hit area for the component.
- **Initial State**. This is a Boolean value telling the component to start as checked (True) or unchecked (False). Only one radio button in a group can be set to True. If other radio buttons are set to True, the last one set will remain True and the others will change to False.

- **Group Name**. This is the name of the group of radio buttons that will be associated with each other; only one in the group can be selected at one time.
- **Data**. This is the information associated with the RadioButton component.
- **Label Placement**. Set the position at which the label will be placed: Left or Right.
- **Change Handler**. This is a string representing a function that has been defined on the same timeline as the component. This function is invoked when a user selects a radio button from a group.

You can set the width of a RadioButton component, but not the height. To set the width of this component, you can use the Free Transform tool (Q) or the setSize method, like this:

```
myRadioButton.setSize(width);
```

What's more, you can set the width of multiple radio buttons in a group using the same method, like this:

```
myRadioGroup.setSize(width);
```

In the following example, you'll create two groups of RadioButton components. One will have two choices, and the other will have three choices. Here are the steps to follow:

1. Create a new file (Ctrl+N).
2. Drag an instance of the RadioButton component onto the stage.
3. Open the Library (Ctrl+L) and then open the Flash UI Components folder and drag another RadioButton component onto the stage.

Tip

You should not pull multiple components from the Flash UI Components panel; this will increase file size unnecessarily. Instead, once an instance is on the stage, drag copies of the component from the Library in the Flash UI Components folder in the Library (Ctrl+L).

4. Using the Align panel (Ctrl+K), align both radio buttons vertically and put them near the left edge of the stage.
5. Change the parameters of these buttons as follows:
    - For the Label parameter, enter **Yes** for the top radio button and **No** for the bottom radio button.
    - Set the Initial State parameter of both to False.

- For the Group Name parameter of both components, enter **choices**.
- Set the Label Placement parameter of both components to Right.

6. From the library, drag three more instances of the RadioButton component onto the stage and align them vertically near the left edge, but slightly away from the first group.

7. Change the parameters of these three RadioButton components as follows:

- For the Label parameter, enter **Top**, **Middle**, and **Bottom** for the top, middle, and bottom radio buttons, respectively.
- Set the Initial State parameter of all three components to False.
- For the Group Name parameter, enter **position** for all three components.
- Set the Label Placement parameter of all three components to Right.

8. Test the movie by going to the menu bar and choosing Control, Test Movie (Ctrl+Enter). The result is shown in Figure 16.6.

You now have two groups of RadioButton components in which only one item in each group can be selected at one time.

FIGURE 16.6

The radio button in action.

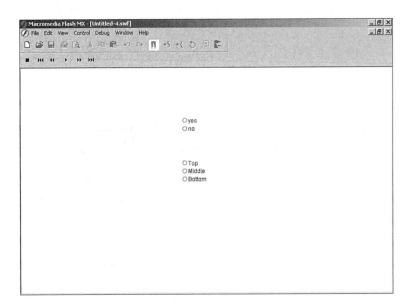

The last two components in the Flash UI components family are different from the others. One scrolls text, and the other scrolls movie clips. The first of the two is the ScrollBar component.

The ScrollBar Component

The ScrollBar component is used for adding a vertical and even horizontal scrollbars directly to dynamic or input text fields (an input text field is another type of dynamic text field). You'll find more information on text fields in Chapter 19, "Working with Text."

Without scrollbars, the text field would have to be large enough to display all the text at once. With the ScrollBar component, you can set the text field's size to whatever you wish and use the scrollbars to move the text up and down, or even left to right, in the text field.

You associate a ScrollBar component with a text field by dragging the component onto the text field near the side on which you would like it to appear. Alternatively, you can type the text field's instance name into the Target TextField parameter.

The ScrollBar component might look familiar to you. This is because other components use the ScrollBar component, which means that if you have one of these components that use the ScrollBar component, you already have the ScrollBar component in your Library and should pull it from there.

Here's a list of the other components that use the ScrollBar component:

- ComboBox
- ListBox
- ScrollPane

Here are the two parameters for the ScrollBar component:

- **Target TextField**. This is the instance name of the text field you would like the ScrollBar component to control. This parameter will be filled automatically when you drop the ScrollBar component on the text field.
- **Horizontal**. This states whether the ScrollBar component is meant to control the text field vertically (False) or horizontally (True).

The ScrollBar component will size itself to fit when you drop it on a text field. If you need to resize the text field after the ScrollBar component has been placed on it, simply drag the ScrollBar component off, resize the text field, and drop the ScrollBar component back on it.

You can also adjust its length by using the Free Transform tool (Q) or the setSize method for ScrollBar components, which has the following generic template:

```
myScrollBar.setSize(length);
```

In the following example, you will create a dynamic text box and place a ScrollBar component on this text field to control it. Here are the steps to follow:

1. Create a new file (Ctrl+N).

2. Create another layer. Name the top layer **actions** and the bottom layer **text**.

3. In the text layer, choose the Text tool (T) and then choose Dynamic for the type. Draw a rectangle that's about 70 by 70; you can adjust this in the Properties panel.

4. Label the instance of the text field **myText**.

5. Now, in the actions layer, go to the first keyframe, open the Actions panel, and place this code:

```
//This will make the text field multiline and wrap
myText.multiline=true;
myText.wordWrap=true;
//This will put text in the text field
myText.text="This is my first time using a ScrollBar
Component and I like it already";
//This will put a box around the field
myText.border=true;
```

6. Back on the text layer, drag an instance of the ScrollBar component onto the stage, dropping it onto the text field you created near the field's right or left side, depending on where you want the scrollbar. The ScrollBar component should attach itself when you release it.

7. Once the ScrollBar component has been attached, check its parameters to ensure that myText is in the Target TextField parameter and that Horizontal is set to False.

8. Finally, test the movie by going to the menu bar and choosing Control, Test Movie (Ctrl+Enter). It should look similar to Figure 16.7.

Now onto the last Flash UI component—the ScrollPane component.

The ScrollPane Component

The ScrollPane component does for movie clips what the ScrollBar component does for text fields. The ScrollPane gives you the ability to display a section of a large movie clip.

However, unlike the ScrollBar component, the ScrollPane component cannot be attached directly to a movie clip. It must draw in the movie clip from the Library through the linkage identifier.

Also, all fonts displayed in the ScrollPane component must be embedded fonts. You cannot use device fonts. But remember, if all that needs to be scrolled is text, you should use the ScrollBar component instead. Here's a list of parameters for the ScrollPane component:

- **Scroll Content**. This is a string representing the symbol linkage identifier for the movie clip that is to be displayed.

- **Horizontal Scroll**. This parameter sets whether a horizontal scrollbar is to be present (True) or not (False). You can use Auto to allow the ScrollPane component to decide for itself whether the scrollbar is needed.

- **Vertical Scroll**. This parameter sets whether a vertical scrollbar is to be present (True) or not (False). You can use Auto to allow the ScrollPane component to decide for itself whether the scrollbar is needed.

- **Drag Content**. This is a Boolean value stating whether or not the user can move the content of the ScrollPane component just by dragging the content itself.

FIGURE **16.7**

Just associate a scrollbar with a text field, and you can scroll the content of that text field.

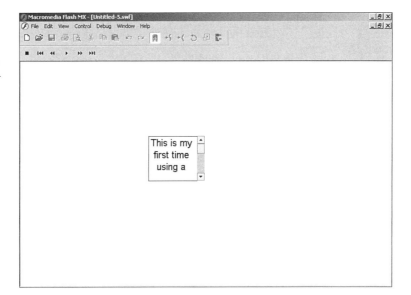

> **Note**
>
> Because the ScrollPane component can decide whether the vertical or horizontal scrollbar is needed (or both), it is recommended that you use the default value, Auto.

Both the height and the width of the ScrollPane component can be adjusted either with the Free Transform tool (Q) or by using the setSize method, like this:

```
myScrollPanel.setSize(width,height);
```

In this example, you'll create a movie clip that holds a graphic you either design or import. Then you'll make some adjustments in the linkage properties of this movie clip. Finally, you'll set the ScrollPane component to draw in your movie clip. Here are the steps to follow:

1. Create a new file (Ctrl+N).

2. Create a new movie clip by going to the menu bar and choosing Insert, New Symbol (Ctrl+F8).

3. Choose Movie Clip and name it **picture**.

4. In this new movie clip, either create a graphic or import one by going to the menu bar and choosing File, Import (Ctrl+R).

5. Go back to the main stage and open the Library (Ctrl+L).

6. Right-click the picture movie clip and then click Linkage.

7. Check the Export for ActionScript option (which is required for the ScrollPane component to get the movie). The string "picture" should then pop up in the identifier. Also, the option Export in First Frame should become checked. If the identifier does not appear, simply type it in and then click OK.

8. Now drag an instance of the ScrollPane component onto the stage.

9. Change the parameters of the ScrollPane component as follows:

   • For the Scroll Content parameter, enter **picture**.

   • Leave Horizontal Scroll set to Auto.

   • Leave Vertical Scroll set to Auto.

   • Set the Drag Content parameter to True.

10. Test the movie by going to the menu bar and choosing Control, Test Movie (Ctrl+Enter). It should look similar to Figure 16.8.

That's the last of the Flash UI components. So far, you have seen how to use each of them, but you haven't learned how to use the information passed to and from them. Therefore, the next section covers how these components interact with ActionScript.

FIGURE 16.8

Your ScrollPane component will look different depending on what graphic you either created or imported into the picture movie clip.

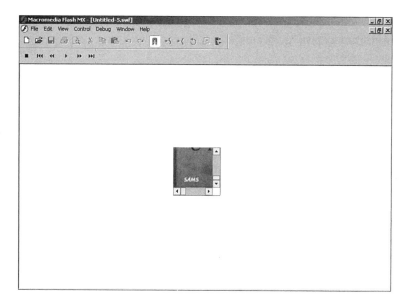

Passing Information to and from ActionScript with Components

You have seen how easy it is to implement and use the components we have covered so far; however, they are useless (except for the ScrollBar and ScrollPane components) unless you can pass information from them to ActionScript.

The first step involves using a parameter that calls a function that is defined on the same timeline as the component. There are two types of this parameter:

- Change Handler
- Click Handler

The Click Handler parameter is the PushButton component's equivalent to the Change Handler parameter that the other components have. You create the function on the timeline with this template:

```
function handlerName (instanceName){
    //script to be run
}
```

Notice the parameter `instanceName` in this generic template. This is for identifying which component has had the event. Here's a quick example of using the Click Handler parameter:

1. Create a new file (Ctrl+N).

2. Create another layer. Call the top layer **actions** and the bottom layer **button**.

3. Drag an instance of the PushButton component onto the main stage in the button layer.

4. Set the PushButton component's parameters as follows:

    - For Label, enter **Click**.

    - Set Click Handler to `onPress`.

5. Now in the first keyframe of the actions layer, place these actions:

```
function onPress (){
    trace("A button has been pressed");
}
```

6. Test the movie (Ctrl+Enter).

That was simple. Notice that because you do not have more than one button, you don't need a parameter. In the next example, however, you will use parameters.

This next example involves retrieving information from the component. You do this by using `get` methods. Each component has its own set of `get` methods, but each component that holds information or contains a choice has a `getValue` method. Follow these steps to use the `getValue` method in a ComboBox component:

1. Create a new file (Ctrl+N).

2. Create another layer. Call the top layer **actions** and the bottom layer **combo**.

3. Drag an instance of the ComboBox component onto the main stage in the combo layer.

4. Set the ComboBox component's parameters as follows:

    - For the Labels parameter, use the Values dialog box to enter **Comedy**, **Drama**, **Mystery**, **Romance**.

    - Set the Change Handler parameter to `onSelect`.

5. In the first keyframe of the actions layer, place these actions:

```
//Create the function and use a parameter to make it dynamic
function onSelect (choice){
    trace(choice.getValue());
}
```

6. Test the movie (Ctrl+Enter).

When you test the movie, every time you select a choice from the drop-down list, the value will be displayed in the output window.

Also notice that because you used a parameter in the function, the function can call the value of any component with `onSelect` as a change handler.

Now you'll combine these last two examples to create a very small form that can be reset and display a choice. First, you'll create a small form with two RadioButton components and two PushButton components. The PushButton components will have the same Click Handler parameter, but one pushbutton will reset the radio buttons, and the other pushbutton will trace the results of the RadioButton group. Here are the steps to follow:

1. Create a new file (Ctrl+N).
2. Create another layer. Call the bottom layer **components** and the top layer **actions**.
3. In the components layer, drag an instance of the PushButton component onto the stage.
4. Highlight the PushButton component, copy it (Ctrl+C), and then paste the copy onto the main stage (Ctrl+V).
5. Set both of components side by side.
6. Label the instance names of these buttons as follows:
    - Label the left component's instance **reset**.
    - Label the right component's instance **result**.
7. Change the reset PushButton component's parameters as follows:
    - For Label, enter **Reset**.
    - Set Click Handler to `clicked`.
8. Change the result PushButton component's parameters as follows:
    - For Label, enter **Result**.
    - Set Click Handler to `clicked`.
9. Now in the same layer, drag a RadioButton instance onto the main stage and create a copy of it like you did to the PushButton component.
10. Place both RadioButton components side by side, above the PushButton components.
11. Label the instances of the RadioButton components as follows:
    - Label the left component's instance **female**.
    - Label the right component's instance **male**.

12. Now change the Label parameter of both RadioButton components to the same as their instance names, set the Group parameter of each to **gender,** and use the defaults for the other settings. At this point, your stage should look like Figure 16.9.

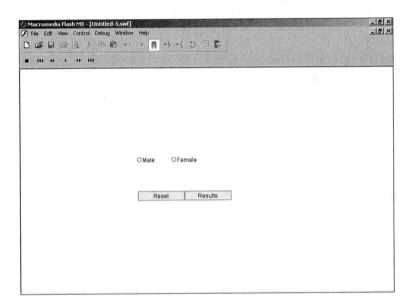

13. Now in the first keyframe of the actions layer, place this code:

```
//Create the function
function clicked (button){
//Check to see which button is being pressed
    if(button == reset){
//Reset the RadioButtons
        male.setState(false);
        female.setState(false);
    }else if(button == result){
//Display the results in the output window
        trace (gender.getValue());
    }
}
```

14. Test the movie by going to the menu bar and choosing Control, Test Movie (Ctrl+Enter).

When you test the movie, you will be able to choose an option from the group of radio buttons, and you can use the pushbuttons to reset the choices or trace what has been selected.

You used the `getValue` method that is associated with the group of radio buttons. Now, go back to the components and add these to the radio button parameters:

1. For the male radio button, place **1** in the data parameter.
2. For the female radio button, place **2** in the data parameter.

Now when you press the results button, it will not display the label of the radio button in the Output window but instead will display either 1 or 2, depending on the choice you have made.

For a larger example, go to the companion site for this book and look under the Chapter 16 section.

So far you have learned how to implement the family of Flash UI components and how to pass information to and from these components, but you have not learned how to make them look different from one another. The next section explains how to change the look of your components.

The Appearance of Components

Every component you have seen so far has been gray, white, and black. There is no real flair to the generic forms of the components, so in this section, you will learn how to change that. As usual, you have more than one way of accomplishing this task. You can do it manually, which is not only difficult but oftentimes even more difficult to reverse if you change your mind. You also have different ways of changing the look of components using ActionScript, and we will mainly to focus on these methods, but first I'll explain how you can change components manually.

Making Manual Changes to the Look of Components

For most movie clips, which are what components really are, you can double-click them and move down the hierarchy of how they are put together to edit certain parts. Unfortunately, you cannot double-click components to edit them. You can, however, right-click them and choose either Edit, Edit In Place, or Edit In New Window. You can also open up the Library (Ctrl+L), open up the `Flash UI Components` folder, and then open up the `Component Skins` folder to see all the graphics used.

As you go through some of the clips, you may notice ActionScript that controls the components. It is strongly recommended that these actions go untouched, unless you are a highly experienced ActionScripter.

Yes, you can adjust the color and look of all the graphics of the components this way, but it is very tedious to search all the way down to the individual graphics. What's more, if you have to make a change again, it is ever more difficult to go back.

You can, however, control major component pieces, such as the arrow and the font color, of all components using ActionScript. Therefore, let's move in that direction and focus on the ActionScript side of changing how components look.

Changing the Appearance of Components with ActionScript

You have more than one way of changing the appearance of components with ActionScript, so we'll start with the basics. To change a single aspect of a single component, you can use the `setStyleProperty` method of that component, like this:

```
myComponent.setStyleProperty("componentProperty", value);
```

A list of all the properties associated with the component can be found in the Actions panel under FStyleFormat, Properties.

Here's a small example that changes the scroll track color of a ScrollBar component:

1. Create a new file (Ctrl+N).
2. Add a layer. Call the bottom layer **scroll** and the top layer **actions**.
3. Drag an instance of the ScrollBar component onto the stage in the scroll layer and name the instance **myScroll**.
4. In the first keyframe of the actions layer, place this code:
   ```
   //this will change the track of the ScrollBar to blue
   myScroll.setStyleProperty("scrollTrack",0x397DC7);
   ```
5. Test the movie (Ctrl+Enter) to see the blue track.

That was easy enough, but if you have multiple components using similar pieces, you'll want to change more than just one component's property at a time. Therefore, you'll want to create a color scheme.

Because components share certain aspects with one another, such as the scrollbar arrow or how the text is formatted in the text fields, it is easy to change entire schemes of components using the `globalStyleFormat` method. Here's a template:

```
globalStyleFormat.componentProperty = value;
```

In this example, you'll place a CheckBox component and a RadioButton component on the stage, and with one script, change the look of the font for the both of them. Follow these steps:

1. Create a new file (Ctrl+N).

2. Add a layer. Call the bottom layer **components** and the top layer **actions**.

3. In the components layer, drag an instance of the CheckBox component and an instance of the RadioButton component onto the stage.

4. Use the default settings for both.

5. In the actions layer, place this code in the first keyframe:

```
//First we create the format we want to use
globalStyleFormat.textItalic=true;
globalStyleFormat.textColor=0xFF0000;
globalStyleFormat.textUnderline=true;
//Then we apply it, otherwise nothing happens
globalStyleFormat.applyChanges();
```

6. Test the movie (Ctrl+Enter) and see the new text format you created.

Do not forget to apply the changes to the components using the applyChanges method. Note that you could have just changed a single property by calling the property in the applyChanges method in the last line, like this:

```
globalStyleFormat.applyChanges("textColor");
```

You can also create several different formats and apply each one to different components using the newFStyleFormat object. You use this object like you would the globalStyleFormat method. Let's take a look at this object in an example. Here are the steps to follow:

1. Continue from the previous example with the RadioButton and CheckBox components.

2. Name the instance of the RadioButton component **myRadioButton**.

3. Name the instance of the CheckBox component **myCheckBox**.

4. Replace the actions in the actions layer with these:

```
//Create our different formats
checkFormat = new FStyleFormat();
radioFormat = new FStyleFormat();
//Now adjust the properties of each format
checkFormat.check=0xFF0000;
checkFormat.textUnderline=true;
radioFormat.textColor=0x397000;
radioFormat.textBold=true;
//Now assign the formats to the Components
radioFormat.addListener(myRadioButton);
checkFormat.addListener(myCheckBox);
```

This time, instead of using the applyChanges method, you use the addListener method. This method is much easier to control because if you want to take the format away, you can use the `removeListener` method. However, using the `removeListener` method will produce surprising results and not remove the entire format. Therefore, it is recommended that if you want to change back to the original format of a component during playback, you should create a default format and set the component to that.

You can now change colors and formats of individual components as well as all components at once. Now let's move onto something bigger—let's actually change the graphic using the `registerSkinElement` method.

> **Note**
>
> Changes made to the look of a component will not show up until playback.

The `registerSkinElement` Method

Registering skin elements is not as easy as it sounds. You do not just create a movie and change the name. Each graphical skin element in the `Component Skins` folder has a "readme" layer as the top layer. This is where you must register your skin. You can find instructions in the actions of this readme layer.

In the following example, you're going to change the check mark for a CheckBox component to a red X. Here are the steps:

1. Start by creating a new file (Ctrl+N).
2. Drag an instance of the CheckBox component onto the stage.
3. Open the Library (Ctrl+L).
4. Open the `Flash UI Components` folder.
5. Open the `Component Skins` folder.
6. Open the `FCheckBox Skins` folder.
7. Open the `fcb_check` movie clip.
8. In the first layer of the `fcb_check` movie clip (the readme layer), in the first frame, open the Actions panel.
9. At the bottom of the script, you can see the registration code.
10. Now that you're in the `fcb_check` movie clip, on the stage is a small check mark graphic that has an instance name of `check_mc`. You can delete this movie altogether and create your own with the same name, or you can edit the movie.

11. In this example, you'll edit the movie. Therefore, double-click the check mark to enter the movie and edit it. Once in the movie, notice the thin green lines; these are used to guide you and show you how big to make the graphic.

12. Highlight and delete the check mark graphic.

13. Using the Text tool, create a static text field, choose red for the font color, and type the letter **X**.

14. Once this is done, break it apart by going to the menu bar and choosing Modify, Break Apart (Ctrl+B).

15. Now use the Free Transform tool to make the X fit in between the thin green lines, as shown in Figure 16.10. You'll probably need to zoom in to see this better.

16. Test the movie and click the check box. Now instead of a little black check appearing, a red X appears instead.

Although this was a simple example, look at the number of steps it took. To change the skins on more advanced elements such as the scroll buttons, it may be easier to break them apart and register different parts all at once instead of just one single graphic.

FIGURE **16.10**

You replace the check mark with a red X.

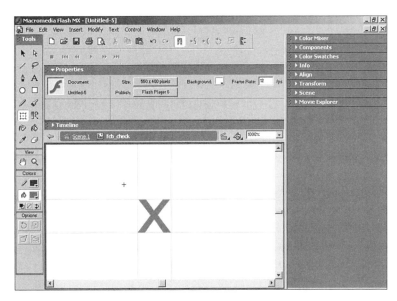

If, by chance, something bad happens and you can't go back, simply drag a new instance of the same clip onto the stage and choose Replace Existing Component (Not Undoable) and click OK. This will take you back to square one.

We've covered a lot of information and yet we've only talked about the components built in to Flash. Now let's move onto creating your own components.

Creating Components

Creating components can be rewarding. Once your component is complete, anyone can use it, even if the user is not a programmer. This section covers how to create a custom component as well as how to create its own icon for use later.

In this next example, you'll create a rectangle whose color can be changed. Follow these steps:

1. Create a new file (Ctrl+N).
2. Create a new movie clip and call it **myRectangle** (Ctrl+F8).
3. Draw a rectangle in the center of the screen (R).
4. Now create another layer and call it **actions**. In that layer, place the following code (which we'll discuss next):

```
//This starts the Component
#initclip
//Create the rectangle class
function recClass (){
    this.recColor = new Color(this);
    this.changeColor();
}
//This will control the inherit properties of recClass
recClass.prototype = new MovieClip();
//This will change the color at playback
recClass.prototype.changeColor = function () {
        this.recColor.setRGB(this.myColor);
}
//This is the most important step, registering the class
Object.registerClass("FRectangle", recClass);
//This ends the clip
#endinitclip
```

Note that `#initclip` and `#endinitclip` are what holds the block of code for components. They serve no other purpose than that.

The first thing this code does is create a class for your object. Then it creates a movie clip to use in the inheritance of the properties. Next, a method is created to change the color of `recClass`. Then this class is declared, which is very important when using components. This links `recClass` to the movie with the identifier of `FRectangle`. Now that you understand the code you've placed in the actions layer, let's move on to the second set of steps for this exercise:

1. Go to the main stage and open the Library (Ctrl+L).

2. There should be only one movie (the myRectangle movie) because that is all you created. Right-click this movie and choose Component Definition.

3. The Component Definition dialog box will appear, as shown in Figure 16.11. Add parameters with the plus sign and set the values of these parameters as follows:

   - For Name, enter **Color**.

   - For Variable, enter **myColor**.

   - For Value, enter **0**.

   - For Type, enter **Color**.

FIGURE 16.11

The Component Definition dialog box.

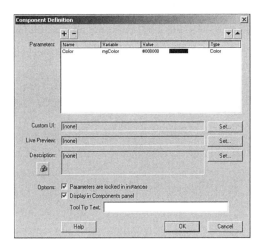

4. Click OK. Now the icon in the Library changes. You'll next create a custom icon to import.

   Use any imaging software to create a GIF, PNG, or JPG with the dimensions of 24 by 20 pixels.

5. Once you have created your icon and have saved it, go to the menu bar and choose File, Import To Library and map to the icon.

6. Now the icon will appear in your Library.

7. Create a folder in your library called `FcustomIcons`.

8. Place the icon you imported in the `FcustomIcons` folder and name it the same name as the component, myRectangle.

9. Close the library and then reopen it. Now you have your own icon representing your first component.

10. Right-click the component again and choose Linkage.

11. Check Export for ActionScript and name the identifier **FRectangle**.

12. Now drag an instance of your new component onto the stage and adjust the parameters to see it change color when you test the movie. Remember, changes will not take place until playback.

That was terrific. You created your own component and a custom icon to go with it.

You can have the component appear in the Components panel by dropping a copy of the Flash file into the `Components` folder found in Flash MX. Depending on the operating system, it appears in different places in the Flash MX folder. Also, once this file is in the folder, you must close out of Flash MX and restart it.

You have seen all the benefits of using Flash UI components as well as how straightforward it is to create your own components. However, components are not all good, as we'll discuss in the next section.

The Downside to Components

Components provide a great way to reach more people with Flash and enable them to create their own custom interfaces, but like their predecessor, Smart Clips, components have their problems.

In Flash 5, Smart Clips were used, but the file size created by Smart Clips made them nearly not worth building for the Web. Components have improved on this, but not to a dramatic degree. For example, the PushButton component you created earlier in this chapter is over 25KB in size. Now that in and of itself is not large, but we're only talking about a single button.

Also, dragging multiple components of the same type onto the stage from the Components panels instead of just dragging one and then dragging the rest from the Library increases file size even more. Just keep this in mind when you are using components and always copy instances out of the Library.

Finally, the last section of this chapter briefly covers a few resources on the web for components.

Flash UI Component Resources

From the beginning, the Flash community on the Web has been a great resource for gathering information on the particulars of Flash and its uses. Since the launch of Flash MX,

more and more sites have popped up with resources for Flash MX, you can find a list of them in Appendix A. Here are a few that focus on components:

- `http://www.macromedia.com/support/flash/applications/creating_comps/`
- `http://www.flashcomponents.net`
- `http://www.were-here.com/forums/forumdisplay.php?forumid=45`
- `http://www.waxpraxis.org`
- `http://radio.weblogs.com/0106797/`

Also, don't forget to download additional sets of components from Macromedia at the following site:

`http://www.macromedia.com/desdev/mx/flash/articles/components.html`

You will need the Macromedia Extension Manager to download them.

Event Handlers

By Todd Coulson

What Is an Event Handler?

Let's consider your daily morning routine. You wake up in the morning. You walk down the stairs and sit down for breakfast. You pour the milk and lift the spoon to your mouth to eat a bite of your cereal. Therefore, the handlers in your daily routine would consist of `on wake`, `on walk`, `on pour`, and `on eat`. Now let's think about the actions you perform in your daily routine; they consist of waking up, traveling down the stairs, and eating a nutritious breakfast. (I prefer Cheerios myself.) Looking at your actions, we could surmise that you probably prefer to wake up only once, although with your snooze alarm, this may become five or six times if you're like me. You probably will travel to the breakfast table only once. You will probably only pour the milk and the cereal only once as well. However, the action of eating will happen numerous times. Each time you bring the spoon to your mouth would count for another action. Think about this in code format. Would you want to write a different action every time you performed an action in the morning? The code would certainly get messy. In fact, it might look something like this:

```
Wake up.
Hit alarm.
Wake up.
Hit alarm.
Wake up.
Hit alarm.
Wake up.
Hit alarm.
Wake up.
Hit alarm.
Travel to breakfast table.
Pour cereal.
Pour milk.
Lift spoon to mouth.
Eat.
Lift spoon to mouth.
Eat.
Lift spoon to mouth.
Eat.
```

The preceding example, without the use of handlers, only gets you to eat three bites of your cereal. I usually eat a lot more than that. Therefore, we could simplify your breakfast behavior with the use of *handlers*, which are little bits of code that *handle* when your actions are used. This makes your breakfast routine much simpler. It might now look more like this:

```
On wake{
    Hit alarm and wake up;
}
on walk{
```

```
    Travel to breakfast table;
}
on pour{
    pour cereal into bowl;
    Pour milk into bowl;
}
on eat{
    Lift spoon to mouth;
    Eat;
}
```

There you have it! Your whole morning routine specified in Flash ActionScript. Well, not exactly the ActionScript language the way Macromedia has specified, but rather our own human interpretation. What can you learn from this? Handlers will tidy up your work. Instead of having to write down each time you wake up (which, remember, for me is like six times), our handler will execute the hitting the alarm and the waking up actions every time the on wake handler is called. Furthermore, notice the on eat handler. Before you only got three bites of your breakfast. However, with the new handler method of scripting, you can have your whole breakfast in one tidy little handler. It will execute code every time your event occurs.

ActionScript Handlers

The preceding script is a real-world example of how your day would go if written in code. Think of your daily morning ritual as a simile for Flash's ActionScript model. However, on eat, on travel, and so on are not the handlers of Flash's ActionScript. ActionScript uses handlers to take care of the tasks it needs to determine when events will occur. These include events such as onLoad, which would create code when a movie clip is loaded into your SWF. You can also use events to determine what your end user's actions are. These might include mouse events, such as on (press), on (rollover), and onMouseDown. These are all examples of how Flash writes its actions within the ActionScript model. Other events occur in a certain order or at a certain time, such as onLoad, onEnterFrame, and onUnload. These events happen whenever a particular order occurs within your project. For example, an end user will never have control over the playback head entering a frame. Furthermore, an end user will not be able to, say, load this movie clip. It's the job of Flash and the programmer to determine when a movie clip may load or when to enter a new frame.

Where to Write Handlers

Event handlers are written to buttons and movie clips or through the use of methods in any other part of your movie.

You must keep a few rules in mind when writing your event handlers. Here's a list of rules for your button and movie clip handlers:

- Buttons use on (*event*) handler actions. Movie clips require onClipEvent handlers. A clip event cannot be added to a button, and an on handler cannot be used in the movie clip format.

- Both movie clip and button actions can use methods to affect either movie clip or button instances without the script being attached to that particular instance. This is helpful when you need a handler for a movie clip that was created using the attachMovie or duplicateMovieClip action.

- You can attach onClipEvent and on actions only to instances that have been placed on the stage in authoring mode.

- Event handler actions only work when the instance is on the screen. The action will not work if your instance is unloaded from your SWF.

- You may attach as many handlers as you like to a script. You may not attach more than one of the same handler to a script. Therefore, if you already have an instance of on (press), you will not have to write it again in the same script.

- If you want a handler to pertain to every instance of a library member, you must create a class and assign a prototype to that class. The prototype will allow you to define a method that will be used throughout the class. Individual instance handlers will override any prototype method defined in your script.

Creating a Button

Table 17.1 provides an introduction to the various types of handlers that can be used within a button's ActionScript or outside the button's ActionScript using methods of the instance.

TABLE 17.1 Event Handlers Commonly Associated with Button Events Performed by the End User

Event Handler Actions	*Event Handler Methods*	*Action Description*
on (press)	onPress	When the user presses a button
on (release)	onRelease	When the user releases a button
on (releaseOutside)	onReleaseOutside	When the user presses a button but releases the mouse outside the button area
on (rollOver)	onRollOver	When the user's mouse enters the button area

TABLE 17.1   Event Handlers Commonly Associated with Button Events Performed by the End User

Event Handler Actions	*Event Handler Methods*	*Action Description*
on (rollOut)	onRollOut	When the user's mouse leaves the button area
on (dragOver)	onDragOver	When the user drags his mouse over a button
on (dragOut)	onDragOut	When the user drags his mouse out of a button
on (keyPress"...")	onKeyDown, OnKeyUp	When the user presses in or lifts up on a key on the keyboard

Now let's practice using these handlers to see them in action. The actions we'll write inside the handlers are trace actions to follow how these handlers are activated. A trace action displays a message of your choice in the output window when a particular handler has been executed. Here are the steps to follow for this exercise:

1. Create a button. The graphics aren't important for this exercise, so just create a circle on your screen using the Circle tool.

2. Select the button and press F8 on your keyboard. This allows you to make that circle a button instance. Give it a unique library name and then click OK.

3. Double-click your button instance and edit your button's graphics so that there is a different graphic for the Over and Down states. This means selecting your graphic in frame 1 and copying it into the other frames. Then change the properties on frames 2 and 3 to change the look and feel of the Up and Over states. For example, you could change the color of your button.

4. Now go back to scene 1 of your newly created movie. Click your button and open up the Properties panel.

5. In your Properties panel, give your button a unique instance name. This will be unique to only this instance of the button and will differentiate it from other instances of the same library member dragged onto your stage.

6. Now go to your Actions panel and open Actions, Movie Control, On. This will open up your handler choices. If you are in Normal mode, you will see all the choices of button handlers available to you. Select Press and deselect rollover.

7. Click the on action again. This time select release. Continue the process until every action has a different handler. Do not do this for keyPress (this handler is only for buttons that have input focus).

8. Switch to Expert mode.

9. Inside each of these handlers type a message to go with what the handler does. For example, under the on Press handler type the following:

Trace("The user pressed the button.");

When you are finished, your code should look something like Figure 17.1.

FIGURE 17.1

The Flash authoring environment and Actions panel for use with the button event handlers. The trace *actions will help you monitor your movie in the Flash Player.*

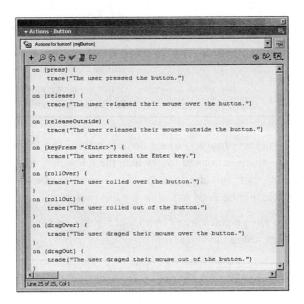

```
on (press) {
    trace("The user pressed the button.")
}
on (release) {
    trace("The user released their mouse over the button.")
}
on (releaseOutside) {
    trace("The user released their mouse outside the button.")
}
on (keyPress "<Enter>") {
    trace("The user pressed the Enter key.")
}
on (rollOver) {
    trace("The user rolled over the button.")
}
on (rollOut) {
    trace("The user rolled out of the button.")
}
on (dragOver) {
    trace("The user draged their mouse over the button.")
}
on (dragOut) {
    trace("The user draged their mouse out of the button.")
}
```

10. Now press Ctrl+Enter (Cmd+Return on the Macintosh) and test your movie in the Flash Player. You will notice that as you roll your mouse into the button, the output window appears. Executing actions that trip the other handlers will continue to place messages in the output window. Look at Figure 17.2 for an example of what your output window would look like once your code is executed. Remember that trace actions place the messages you send to the output window. This is helpful in troubleshooting the code you have written.

11. Save your work to use later in this chapter.

The key point to keep in mind here is that any actions you place within these handlers will execute when the user completes one of the actions. For example, the one little handler for on (rollover) will execute actions every time the user rolls his mouse over the button. Every handler will execute its actions when that handler is tripped.

FIGURE **17.2**

The Flash Player MX environment displaying trace *actions, inside different handlers, in the output window.*

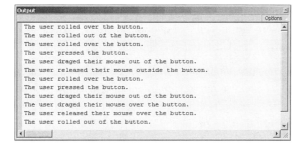

Movie Clip Handlers

Table 17.2 provides an introduction to the various types of clip event handlers that can be used directly on a movie clip using ActionScript or outside the movie clip's ActionScript using methods of the instance.

TABLE 17.2   Clip Event Handlers That Can Manipulate the User's Actions in Coordination with Movie Clip Instances

Event Handler Actions	Event Handler Methods	Action Description
onClipEvent (load)	onLoad	Executes actions when a movie clip loads
onClipEvent (unload)	onUnload	Executes actions upon unloading the movie clip from a SWF
onClipEvent (enterFrame)	onEnterFrame	Executes actions every time a new frame is entered and the movie clip is present on the stage
onClipEvent (mouseDown)	onMouseDown	Executes when the user's mouse is down
onClipEvent (mouseUp)	onMouseUp	Executes when the user's mouse is up
onClipEvent (mouseMove)	onMouseMove	Executes code when the user's mouse is moving
onClipEvent (KeyDown)	onKeyDown	Executes code when the user presses a key
onClipEvent (keyUp)	onKeyUp	Executes code when the user lifts his finger off a key on the keyboard
onClipEvent (data)	onData	Executes code when data is received from an outside source

Welcome to `ClipEvent` handlers. These handlers have a lot of scripting potential. `ClipEvent` handlers were introduced to ActionScripters in Flash 5 and really gave programmers a better way to track the end user's motions.

Let's think about the `mouseMove` handler. Because we know every instance while the mouse is in motion, we can also put an action within the handler to track the coordinates of the mouse. Therefore, not only do we know the mouse is moving, but we also know where the mouse is located in the project.

Let's try the same exercise we executed on a button, but this time using `onClipEvent`. Here are the steps to follow:

1. Create some artwork on your screen. Select it and press F8 to convert the artwork to a movie clip.

2. Go into your Properties panel and give your movie clip a unique instance name. This will differentiate it from the other instances of this library member that you use in your score.

3. Click the movie clip instance on the stage. In the Actions panel, choose Actions, Movie Clip Control, onClipEvent. If you are in Normal mode, you will see a series of radio buttons representing the handlers you can choose for your `onClipEvent`. If you are in Expert mode, don't fret—a drop-down menu will appear if you have Code Hints turned on in your action preferences.

4. Choose `load` for one handler. Then choose another clip event handler and choose `unload` for the second clip event.

5. Inside each handler, place a `trace` action that will be unique to what the `load` and `unload` handlers actually do.

6. Now go to the timeline and move the keyframe for your movie clip to frame 30 of your movie. Then add frames to frame 50. Your Flash interface should look similar to Figure 17.3.

7. Press Ctrl+Enter (Cmd+Return on the Macintosh). Export your movie and notice that the `load` `trace` action will occur in about three seconds (if your movie is set to 12 fps). Your movie clip will remain on the screen for about two seconds and then your unload message will appear. After this message, you will not see your movie clip again, because the SWF loops to frame 1. This cycle will continue for as long as you keep the movie open.

8. Save your work to use in future work.

The previous examples use handlers that have already been set; the end user has no control over when the movie clips are loaded or unloaded. The only way we could give the user such control is if we had a button that sends the end user to a frame that includes the movie clips.

FIGURE 17.3

The Flash author-ing environment and Actions panel for use with the onLoad *and* onUnload *han-dlers.*

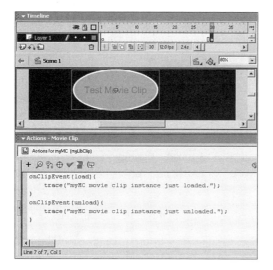

17

EVENT HANDLERS

Let's extend our examples to look at some more movie clip handlers, where the control is in the authoring environment:

1. Select another onClipEvent handler and choose enterFrame for the event.

2. Place a trace action that will be unique to this action. Your ActionScript should resemble Figure 17.4 when finished.

FIGURE 17.4

The Flash author-ing environment and Actions panel for use with the onEnterFrame *han-dler.*

3. Place a `stop` action on the first frame where the movie clip is present on your timeline.

4. Press Ctrl+Enter (Cmd+Return on the Macintosh) to test your movie.

5. Save your work to use this project later.

You'll notice that lots of messages appear in the output window now. That's because
every time you enter a new frame, and the movie clip is present on your stage, a new
message will appear. Because the movie clip is not on the stage in the first 30 frames, no
messages appear. That means that as long as the movie clip is on the stage, the
`enterFrame` handler will work. No movie clip means no handler, which means no `trace`
action.

Now let's start to look at the user-controlled handlers. Follow these steps:

1. Delete the word `enterFrame` from your `onClipEvent` handler and type in
   mouseMove in its place.

2. Retype a different message to represent the `mouseMove` handler's purpose.

3. Go to the timeline and delete the first 30 frames and place a `stop` action on the
   first frame of your movie. Your timeline and ActionScript should be similar to
   Figure 17.5 upon completion.

FIGURE 17.5

*The Flash
authoring environ-
ment and Actions
panel for use with
the onMouseMove
handler.*

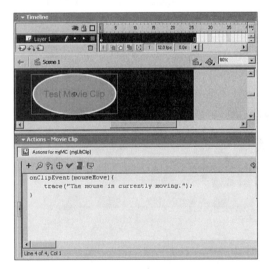

4. Press Ctrl+Enter (Cmd+Return on the Macintosh) to test your movie in the Flash
   Player.

Now keep in mind the scope of the movie clip handlers. They will only happen as long as the movie clip is on the stage. Because you placed a `stop` action, the movie clip is always on the stage. Therefore, `onClipEvent` will always be searching to see whether the mouse is moving. As long as you move your mouse, the `trace` action occurs. If you stop your mouse, the `trace` actions cease to accumulate in the output window. This is really useful when trying to follow the user's mouse location in relation to the project.

We can also track the user's mouse events and keystrokes as well. To do so, follow these steps:

1. Delete the last `mouseMove` handler and click `onClipEvent`, choosing `mouseDown` for the event. Create separate `ClipEvent` handlers for `mouseUp`, `keyDown`, and `keyUp`. Your code should look similar to Figure 17.6 when finished.

2. Save your work so you can use this file later.

FIGURE 17.6

The Flash authoring environment and Actions panel for creating mouse button and keyboard events. These events are end user controlled, meaning the user determines when these events occur.

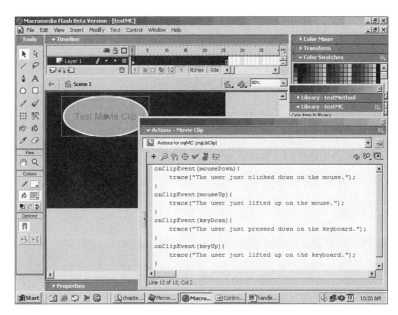

3. Press Ctrl+Enter (Cmd+Return on the Macintosh) to test the movie.

Notice that if you do not click the movie clip, you will still get a message in the output window. Also notice that any key you press will elicit a message in the output window. You must use other actions to trap a particular key or trap a particular location on the screen to further control the user's response. In the meantime, you will notice that the handlers only look for the user's mouse clicks or keystroke hits. These actions will not execute at any other time in the project.

The data event occurs when data has been brought in from another source. If you wanted to bring in XML data or variables from a text file, Flash has included a handler that tells you when that data is available to you.

Methods

You will also notice in both of the tables provided earlier in this chapter that event handler actions and event handler methods are listed. You may be wondering, "What is a method of a handler?" Methods allow you to issue a script located away from the instance you are targeting. Still, you have control over the same handlers if the script is attached to a movie clip or button instance. Think about movie clips for a moment. You may be creating movie clips using the `attachMovie` action. This will attach the newly created instance of a library member during the runtime of the project. You are unable to attach scripts to that instance. However, through the use of methods, you can still control the instance. You'll learn how to manipulate your movie clips and buttons with the use of methods in the next example.

To write these methods, you can choose any frame in your movie to place in your script. The format for writing a method is as follows:

- If you're in Expert mode, start with Actions, User Defined Functions, Method. This will show you the format for how to write your method. In the first red area, place the target path to the instance of the button or movie clip you wish to use with the method. In the second area, place the method you would like to use to interact with the instance of your object.
- If you are in Expert mode, you are going to want to type your method similar to this:

```
myMC.onMouseMove = function() {
    trace("The mouseMove handler is invoked.");
};
```

Here, `myMC` represents the path to the targeted movie clip. Keep in mind that we're referencing this using relative addressing, and our movie clip is located on the root level of the timeline. If we were addressing it using absolute addressing, the first line would read `_root.myMC.onMouseMove=function(){`. Either way is fine.

Now that you have a better handle on how to write methods, let's go through a quick example using the `trace` actions again. Follow these steps:

1. Open up your movie clip file and your button file (if you saved them previously; if not, just create two library items—one button and one movie clip). Carry the button from your library in your button movie to the library of your movie clip movie.

2. Now bring two copies of your button onto the stage. You should now have one movie clip and two buttons present on your stage.

3. Strip all items of any ActionScript because we are going to write new scripts.

4. Make sure every item has a unique instance name. That means if you have two buttons, name each one something different. Remember that everything on the stage can be unique, even if they are the same library item. For this example, you can name your movie clip `myMC` and your buttons `myButton1` and `myButton2`.

5. Now click the first frame in your movie and type the following code in the Expert mode of your Actions panel:

```
Stop;
myButton1.onPress = function() {
    trace("Button 1 has been pressed. Works just like the
[ic:ccc]handler attached to a button");
};
myButton2.onPress = function() {
    trace("Button 2 has been pressed. Works just like the
[ic:ccc]handler attached to a button");
};
myMC.onMouseMove = function() {
    trace("The mouseMove handler is invoked. See works just like the
[ic:ccc]mouseMove Clip Event");
};
```

Notice that you have a separate method for each of the objects in the stage. Remember, you can assign more than one method to a particular instance. For the purposes of this exercise, we are only using one method per movie clip. If you have followed the steps in this exercise, your Flash authoring environment should look similar to Figure 17.7.

Also notice that you have a `mouseMove` handler. Therefore, when you go to test your movie, any mouse movement should be picked up by the `myMC` movie clip instance. Also, the handlers on each of the buttons should react when either button is clicked. However, a different message should appear with each individual button instance clicked.

6. Press Ctrl+Enter (Cmd+Return on the Macintosh) to test your movie in the Flash Player environment.

FIGURE 17.7

*The Flash author-
ing environment
and Actions panel
for creating meth-
ods to control but-
tons and movie
clips from loca-
tions other than
on the instances.*

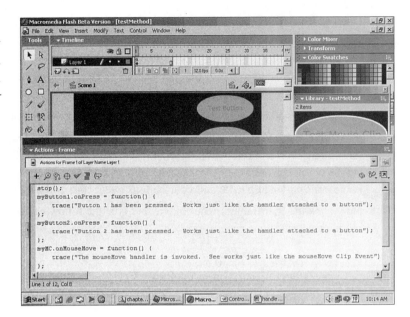

Attach Movie and Methods

Using methods instead of event handlers has two advantages. The first advantage is that
any movie created during runtime cannot have a script attached to it. Remember that if
the movie clip is being dynamically created, you have no way of placing a script to affect
that clip unless it is nested inside another blank movie clip. Methods allow you to use the
same handlers on your dynamically created movie clips. We'll get to that in a moment.

The second advantage is the ability to have one location for all the major scripts for your
buttons and movie clips. Keep in mind that this is a housekeeping preference. If you need
your scripts to be organized, then using methods could provide some organization. If you
like to place your script right on the clip or button you are working with, that works, too.

Now let's try creating a movie with an `attachMovie` action. Therefore, delete the movie
clip on your stage presently, and let's get to writing some code:

1. Go to the library member of your movie clip. Right-click the movie clip and click
   Linkage from the drop-down menu. In this dialog box, choose Export for
   ActionScript and give your movie clip a unique identifier. This provides Flash the
   opportunity to know which movie clip from the library will be used when the
   `attach` action is called. For this example, choose `myMCid` for the identifier name.
   To see what the Linkage Properties dialog box looks like and where to input your
   identifier, refer to Figure 17.8.

FIGURE 17.8

The Linkage Properties dialog box. Pay special attention to the location of myMCid, *which is the unique identification for the* TestMov *library item.*

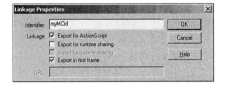

2. Now go back to your script on the first frame of the movie. Right after the stop action, insert an attach action. You can find this from the Actions panel by going to Objects, Movie, Movie Clip, Methods, attachMovie. The script for this method will not work if you place the attachMovie action after your handler, because the handler would be called before the movie clip; it won't be able to find the instance. Methods have to be available on the timeline at the time an action is being invoked.

3. Now you need to input into your attachMovie code the location where the clip will be attached. Therefore, in front of your attachMovie action, type **_root** so that you can place the movie clip on the root level of the timeline.

4. Next you need to identify the movie clip you want attached to your movie. Therefore, inside the arguments of the attachMovie action (inside the parentheses of the script), type in the name of the identifier you gave to your movie clip's library member (in this example, myMCid).

5. Now place a comma next to your identifier and give your newly created movie clip a unique movie clip instance name. You keep the same name used in the last example, myMC, but you'll need to make sure your old movie clip from the last example is no longer on the stage if you are using the same movie for this example.

6. Next you need another comma and then a level to place the movie clip on. This is important when you're attaching multiple movie clips to provide some dimension order as to where on the stage those clips are placed in relation to other items on the stage. In this example, just type **number 1** because you can place it first on your stage. If you have written your code correctly, your stage should look similar to Figure 17.9.

7. Press Ctrl+Enter (Cmd+Return on the Macintosh) to test your movie's outcome in this example.

8. Save your movie to use in the next example.

FIGURE 17.9

The Actions panel with an `attachMovie` *action added to create an instance of a newly created movie clip at run-time of this movie. Notice there is no movie clip on the stage during authoring mode.*

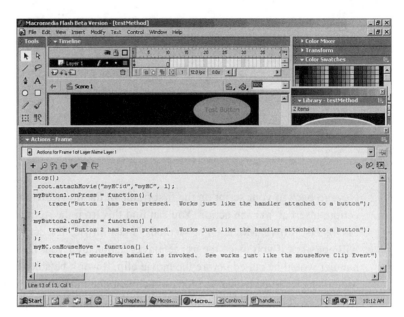

Notice how this movie reacts the same exact way the last movie did, with one exception: The movie clip isn't present in the authoring environment. Instead, it's created using the `attachMovie` code. Yet, you're still capable of tracking the `mouseMove` action with a handler that targets the newly created movie clip. This cannot be done on the actual movie clip because it is not present in the authoring environment to select the item for inputting code.

Event Handlers and the Prototype Object

Having handlers is a great tool. But what happens if you want the same action to occur for every instance of a particular symbol. You are out of luck, right? Wrong. As usual, Macromedia has given you a way to have your handlers react no matter what instance is on the stage. Furthermore, your handlers will react to either attached movies or movies placed on the timeline because you will still make use of methods. Finally, you can mix your master code with code that belongs locally to an instance. In that case, the code attached to the instance will override the overall class code.

In the next example, we will define methods in the prototype object. The prototype is a property of a constructed class, meaning that you need to first create a class, which will be assigned to a symbol in your Library via the linkage identifier. The class can then inherit properties or methods from other classes you designate. The prototype properties and methods defined will be inherited for each instance of the symbol created either in authoring mode or during runtime.

Open the movie you used in the last example. You are going to use the same graphics but discard the actions from the previous example. Here are the steps to follow:

1. Create a duplicate of the movie clip and create different artwork for the newly created movie clip in your Library.

2. Go to the Linkage Properties dialog box for each movie clip and give each library member a different identifier.

3. Now on the first frame of your movie, you'll create the code for the first class. Go to Expert mode in the Actions panel. The first line of code will appear as follows:

```
function mySymbolClass(){}
```

This piece of code makes `mySymbolClass` the name of the newly defined class.

4. Next you want to inherit the methods from the `MovieClip` class. You can do this with the following code:

```
MySymbolClass.prototype=new MovieClip();
```

5. Now that you have your prototype created, you can use those methods to create actions that will occur anytime an instance is onscreen. This can be done in the following fashion:

```
MySymbolClass.prototype.onLoad=function()
[ic:ccc]{trace ("Pink Movie Clip loaded");}\
```

6. Next you have to create some code that will register your class. This is done with the following code:

```
Object.registerClass("myMCid", mySymbolClass);
```

Notice, here, that `myMCid` is the same as the linkage name assigned the movie clip symbol in the Linkage Properties dialog box in the previous example. The registration associates `myMCid` with the class you just created.

7. Notice especially in the code where the linkage name is used in both the Library and the ActionScript code.

   In my piece, I changed the colors of one of my movie clips to yellow, so I now have one movie clip that is pink and one that is yellow. This allows me to notice a difference in export mode, when we move to another frame containing a different movie clip. I gave my pink movie clip an ID of `myMCid` and my yellow movie clip an ID of `myMCid2`. In my code I have repeated step 4 to create a `mouseDown` method that sends the playback head to another frame. I also duplicated steps 5 and 6 to create another class for my other movie clip in my library, keeping in mind to give the duplicated movie in the Library a different linkage name. If you have followed the steps correctly, your code will look similar to Figure 17.10.

FIGURE **17.10**

Flash will associate the linkage name with the class constructed. MyMCid is used for the first class, mySymbolClass. MyMCid2 is used for association with the second class, mySymbolClass2.

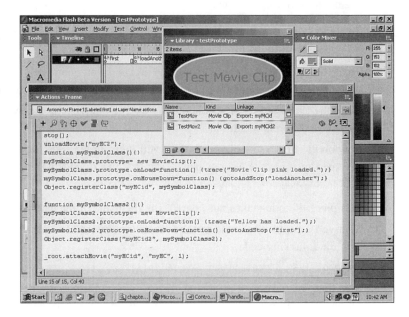

8. Now you still haven't created any items on the stage. Use `attachMovie` to create one instance of each of your movie clips in your library. First, make two blank keyframes on our root timeline (separated by a few empty frames). Give frame labels to each of the blank keyframes you create.

   Make sure the label names coordinate with the names you placed on your `goTo` action in the `mouseDown` method of your prototype, if you followed the code typed into Figure 17.10.

9. In each of the keyframes, create code to attach a movie clip instance to the root level of the timeline and another piece of code that will unload the movie clip in the opposite keyframe. Your code for these frames should look like this:

```
first keyframe
unloadMovie("myMC2");
_root.attachMovie("myMCid", "myMC", 1);
second keyframe
unloadMovie("myMC");
_root.attachMovie("myMCid2", "myMC2", 2);
```

   Make sure that if you are writing either of these pieces of code on the same frame as your class construction that you place the `attachMovie` action after the construction code. You run the risk of the code not running because it has no members on the stage to associate the method with.

10. Press Ctrl+Enter (Cmd+Return on the Macintosh) to test your movie. Every time a movie clip loads, you should see a trace action in the output window, as shown in Figure 17.11. Furthermore, when you click on the stage, your main timeline should switch to the alternate keyframe label.

FIGURE 17.11

This Flash Player 6 environment shows that the frame has switched to the yellow movie clip frame, and the output window reflects which movie has been loaded most recently.

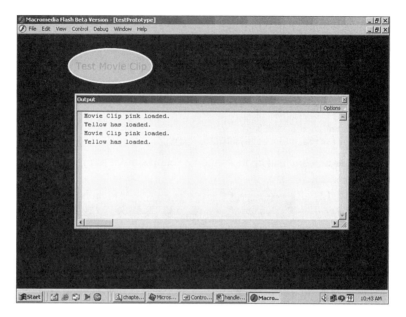

You may be thinking, "That's great, but we basically accomplished the same thing with the method being placed on a frame." Actually, the prototype allows you to have control over every instance created of your library. Therefore, let's create a couple of instances to prove that the same `onload` method is activated for two different instances of the same movie clip. Follow these steps:

1. Place two more blank keyframes with unique frame labels attached to them.

2. Place a button on each of the frames in your movie and place a basic `gotoAndPlay` action on it. Set up each button with its own unique instance name and tell each action to play the next frame in the sequence of frame labels.

3. You will also have to delete the `mouseDown` methods placed on the movie in the previous example. We are only going to use the `onLoad` statements for this demonstration.

   In the first keyframe, create code to unload the last movie in your fourth labeled frame. Also, create code to attach a movie to your frame. In the second labeled frame, unload the movie from your first label and attach a new instance of the pink movie clip. Repeat the process for each of the last two keyframes using the yellow movie clip item instead. Now, your code on each keyframe should resemble the following:

```
first keyframe
unloadMovie("myMC4");
_root.attachMovie("myMCid", "myMC", 1);
second keyframe
unloadMovie("myMC");
_root.attachMovie("myMCid", "myMC2", 1);
third keyframe
unloadMovie("myMC2");
_root.attachMovie("myMCid2", "myMC3", 1);
fourth keyframe
unloadMovie("myMC3");
_root.attachMovie("myMCid2", "myMC4", 1);
```

Your timeline and code should be set up similar to Figure 17.12.

FIGURE 17.12

Code for the prototype method example on multiple items. The first two keyframes should be separate instances of the first movie clip. The last two keyframes should create separate instances of the second movie clip. Also, the class information from the last example should be present on the first frame of your movie.

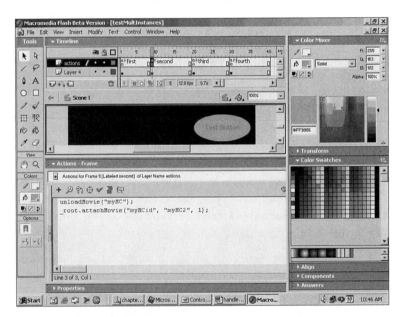

4. Now you want to test your movie. Notice that the `load` command is the same for the first two button clicks. The second two clicks load the message for the yellow movie clip. However, all four movies have individual instance names. Therefore, the same code is being executed for each of the movie clips in your scene that originated from the same library member.

The unique item to be learned from the second example of the prototype object is that the same output statement is being executed for two completely individual instances of the same movie clip. That is the beauty of the prototype of a constructor class.

Handlers control the daily laundry list of tasks performed during an end user's experience. They can be handlers to control the timeline in the Flash authoring environment, to control when items such as movie clips or outside variable information is loaded, or to control or monitor user interaction with your stage. Therefore, handlers are important tools in creating your code. They save you time by repeating a set of actions every time a handler is called.

Furthermore, onClipEvent, introduced in Flash 5, is an incredible tool for monitoring where the user's mouse is located, when the user moves his mouse, or to cause actions to occur at a constant rate with the enterFrame event. Clip events are always attached to movie clips, but you do not need anything in a particular movie clip to be able to use the clip event handlers.

Methods give you the ability to monitor your SWF files. You can monitor when attached movies load, you can still have access to all the events present with the event handler actions, and you can place your scripts conveniently in individual places on your timeline.

Finally, you learned that you can create a class that will use the prototype object to attach your methods to every instance of a particular library member. This is useful if, for instance, you want to know the moment when a particular movie clip is loaded. Every instance of the movie clip could tell you this information, with the prototype object inheriting the methods of the movie clip class.

17

EVENT HANDLERS

CHAPTER 18

ActionScript's Built-in Objects in Action

By Matt Pizzi

IN THIS CHAPTER

At this point, you've worked with many aspects of ActionScript. This chapter's focus is exclusive to dealing with the predefined objects inside of ActionScript. Before we dive into this topic, let's review what an object actually is. You'll find that some of the terms and concepts have been discussed in different areas of this book; it's necessary to bring them back for this light review.

Scripting languages, such as ActionScript, categorize information in different groups called *classes*. Instances of these classes are called *objects*. If you were to create a class, first you would define all its properties. For example, if you were to create a "car" class, it would have properties (or characteristics) such as color, engine size, and wheels. It would also have behaviors, or *methods*. These methods might be accelerate, turn, and stop.

In Flash, all instances of a movie clip are instances of the `MovieClip` class. All buttons are instances of the `Button` class. Flash MX has several different prebuilt classes you can work with. Of course, you can always build your own classes and objects, but we'll save that topic for the end of the chapter. Flash MX categorizes the prebuilt objects as follows:

- **Core objects**. These objects are all built on the ECMA specification and can be found in other scripting languages such as JavaScript. These objects include `Arguments`, `Array`, `Boolean`, `Date`, `Function`, `Math`, `Number`, `Object`, and `String`.

- **Movie clip objects**. These objects are specific to ActionScript and include `Accessibility`, `Button`, `Capabilities`, `Color`, `Key`, `Mouse`, `MovieClip`, `Selection`, `Sound`, `Stage`, `System`, `TextField`, and `TextFormat`.

- **Client/server objects**. These objects are designed to carry communication between a client or an end user's computer to a Web server and database. These objects include `LoadVars`, `XML`, and `XMLSocket`.

- **Authoring objects**. These objects are used for customizing the Flash MX authoring environment.

Throughout this chapter we'll be looking at many of the predefined objects. Of course, some will be left out because they are covered in other chapters. For example, there will be no mention of server-side scripts or middleware integration. This book has several chapters devoted to those topics.

We've already looked at the `MovieClip` object, but ActionScript offers a series of predefined objects as well. Each of these objects has different properties you can change. For example, you could change the x and y scale of a movie clip. These are properties of the `MovieClip` object. We're going to look at properties for other objects as well. For example, the `Sound` object has a `volume` property, but obviously the `MovieClip` object does not.

The Mouse Object

Being able to create your own environments in which you, as a developer, have more control than in traditional Web-development architectures is what makes using Flash so attractive to Web designers. So, if you have total control over what music the listener hears or how a user interacts with your design, why not change the cursor's appearance? At first this may not sound all that practical, but think of the possibilities. Suppose you were to create an outer-space game, for example. You could instantly change the end user's cursor into a space ship. In other words, you can control the total experience right down to the cursor. Let's perform a quick exercise so that you can get familiar with the Mouse object.

Using the Mouse Object to Create a Custom Cursor

To create a custom cursor, you need to drag a movie clip out of the Library. When dragging the movie clip, you're going to use the predefined Mouse object to hide the visibility of the mouse cursor, thus showing only the movie clip you're dragging. Here are the steps to follow:

1. Open a new document. Open the Unleashed Common Library by choosing, Window, Common Libraries, Unleashed. Open the graphics folder and drag out an instance of any graphic symbol onto the stage.

2. With your symbol highlighted, choose Insert, Convert to Symbol to launch the Convert to Symbol dialog box. Name the symbol **new_mouse** in the Name text field. Highlight the Movie Clip radio button to give this symbol a movie clip behavior. Then click OK.

3. Highlight the move clip and open the Actions panel by pressing F9. You need some things to happen based on this script. For example, you need to start dragging the mouse. You also need to hide the standard cursor. To accomplish these tasks, use the following code:

```
onClipEvent (load) {
    startDrag(this, true);
    Mouse.hide();
}
```

Here's what the code means: To begin, the event handler is loaded, which means this action will run when the movie is loaded. The startDrag action starts the dragging operation, but it has two conditions. The first is the *target*, or what you want to start dragging. In this case, this is targeted, which simply means "this instance of the movie clip." The second condition is true, which will lock the tip of the cursor to the center of the movie clip. If you leave this condition out, you will get unpredictable results, and when the end user moves the mouse around, the movie clip will not look like it is responding appropriately.

4. Test the movie by pressing Cmd+Return (Mac) or Ctrl+Enter (Windows). Notice that you don't see the standard cursor but rather the movie clip you designated as the draggable object. See Figure 18.1 for an example.

FIGURE 18.1

Creating a custom cursor in Flash is easy.

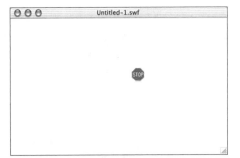

Note

Refer to the Unleashed companion Web site, located at http://www.flashmxun-leashed.com, to see a QuickTime movie tutorial on making custom cursors.

Hiding standard cursors is only one use for the Mouse object. You can also show the mouse. Maybe you've created a game, and in this game the player is a worm trying to dodge hungry fish. You could create a custom cursor of a worm MovieClip. If a fish gets to close, it could swallow the worm. At that point, you could use the showMouse() action to reveal the standard cursor again, proving that, in fact, the worm was swallowed by the big bad fish.

The Mouse object is one of the more basic objects. Let's now dive into something a bit more complicated—the Date object.

The Date Object

The Date object allows you to do many things. Most commonly, though, developers use it to display the current time or date in a Flash movie. The most complicated aspect of the Date object (and its not really too complicated) is formatting the information to display.

It's important to know that the Date object will capture the time and date information from the system calendar and clock of the end user's machine. If a user in Boston is looking at your site at the same time as someone in Los Angeles, ideally the Boston user should see Boston time (if the system preferences are set up properly), and the user in Los Angeles should see West Coast time. This is pretty handy, and it's not too complicated to pull off. The next exercise will show you how.

Using the Date Object to Display the Time

The first thing you must do to begin this exercise is create a new Date object. You'll also put an action on a movie clip; this way, you can use the onClipEvent (enterFrame) event handler so that the action will loop, thus giving the user constant and accurate feedback concerning the current time. Here are the steps to follow:

1. Create a new document. In this new document, choose the Text tool and then click the stage to place an insertion point. In the Properties Inspector, choose Dynamic Text in the drop-down menu. In the Var: text box in the Properties Inspector, provide a variable name of time, as shown in Figure 18.2.

2. Covert the text field to a movie clip symbol by pressing F8 or choosing Insert, Convert to Symbol. This will launch the Convert to Symbol dialog box. Here, be sure to give the symbol a movie clip behavior and type **date_mc** in the Name text field. Then click OK.

3. With the movie clip selected on the stage, press F9 to open the Actions panel. In the script, you have to define a new Date object. In order to this, you need to create a new variable that has a value of a new Date object. Here's the code:

```
onClipEvent (enterFrame) {
    time = new Date();
}
```

The clip event, enterFrame, loops to keep the time current, and the second line sets the value of the variable to the new Date object.

4. Test your movie. In Figure 18.3 the date and time is shown in Greenwich Mean Time. This is nice and all, but maybe it's too much information.

   In the next steps, you are going to take measures to reformat this text so that you get the time with an appending AM. or PM.

5. For this part of the exercise, you need to change some of the code. First, you need to create a new variable for the new date. Second, you need to create a function to format the time the way you want it to appear. When formatting the time, you must be aware that it's possible the value returned might be 9:9, for example, which stands for 9:09. Therefore, you'll need to create an `if` statement to check whether the minute value is less than 10. If it is, you'll concatenate a literal 0 to place in front of the single-spaced digit. Then you need to create a variable to get the actual hour. This will allow you to create another variable to check whether the hour is less than 12. If it is, you need to display AM. Otherwise, you'll display PM. You then have to set your time variable to equal all the variables you've set up. Phew! It's not that bad, I promise. Here's the code:

```
onClipEvent (enterFrame) {
    dateObject = new Date();
    function format(number) {
        if (number<10) {
            return "0"+number;
        } else {
            return number;
        }
    }
    if (dateObject.getHours()>12) {
        myhour = dateObject.getHours()-12;
        amPm = "pm";
    } else {
        myhour = dateObject.getHours();
        amPM = "am";
    }
    time = myhour+":"+ format(dateObject.getMinutes())+" "+amPM;
}
```

Notice that you still have the `enterFrame` event handler to continually update the time. This way, if the user is at your site for 10 minutes, the time will update to reflect this. If you set it on `Load` instead, the event handler would only return the time for when the page actually loads.

You've also defined a new `Date` object, appropriately named `dateObject`. Next, you established a new function called `format` with a parameter called number. (You'll use this later to format the minutes.) Then you created an `if` statement to evaluate whether the `number` parameter is less than 10 and to perform the following action in the code (and if not, to perform the `else` condition). The second `if` statement checks for the AM and PM values mentioned in step 5. You also set the `time` variable to equal the `myhour` variable to return the hour of the day. Finally, you concatenate a literal colon (:). The colon creates time separators for `dateObject`'s `getMinutes` method, which is formatted using the `format` function. Then, of course, you concatenate this to the `amPM` variable to display either AM or PM, depending on the time of day. Notice the space (" ") literal, which provides some space between the minutes and the `amPM` value.

6. Test the movie! Notice that in Figure 18.4 the time is formatted with the hour and minutes separated by a colon, followed by either AM or PM.

   Now for one final touch: Let's add the month, day, and year. This is the easy part.

7. In scene 1, double-click the movie clip housing the `time` variable. Inside the movie clip, add another dynamic text field and provide a variable name of `month`.

8. Click the Scene 1 tab to return to the main timeline. You want the date to be formatted as 7/19/02, for example.

9. Open the Actions panel with the movie clip selected. After the `time` variable, create a new one named `month`. For its value, you just need to use `dateObject.getMonth`, `dateObject.getDate()`, and of course `dateObject.getminutes()`. You'll want to separate these with forward slashes as well. Here's the line of code:

   ```
   month = (dateObject.getMonth() + 1)
   +"/"+dateObject.getDate()
   +"/"+dateObject.getFullYear();
   ```

   Notice with the `dateObject.getMonth` action that you are adding 1. This is because the `getMonth` method returns a value from 0 to 11 (0 representing January and 11 representing December). By adding 1 to that value, you'll get the appropriate numeric value in your date format.

10. Test the movie. Figure 18.5 shows the successfully formatted time, along with the month, day, and year.

FIGURE 18.2

In the Properties Inspector, Dynamic Text is chosen from the drop-down menu, and it has a variable name of time.

FIGURE 18.3

Unformatted time.

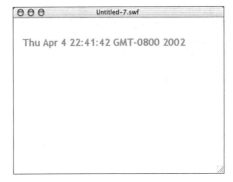

FIGURE 18.4

The time is formatted to our specifications.

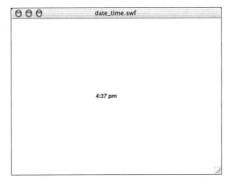

FIGURE 18.5

The time and date are formatted properly.

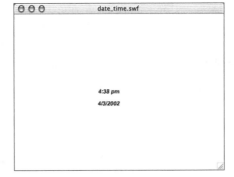

Of course, the Date object can be used for purposes other than displaying the time and date. A sample use would be to have a changing graphic in your site to represent the time of day. You could take four of the same outdoor pictures at different times of the day. Ideally, the pictures would be during sunrise, midday, sunset, and evening. You could create a movie clip with four frames and place one of these pictures on each different frame, in sequential order. Using the Date object, you could determine the time of day, which in turn would the determine which frame of the movie clip the playhead should be on. You can download an FLA file called date_time.fla that uses this example on the Unleashed companion Web site at http://www.flashmxunleashed.com.

The Color Object

The Color object can quite powerful. It allows end users to choose specific colors for various items, or it can even be used to select random colors. This way, every time a visitor comes to the site, the background color could be different, for example. We're now going to work on an example that changes a car's color. There are a couple different ways you can do this: You can set the color to a new solid color, or you can apply an effect that behaves more like a highlight.

Changing a Symbol's Color Through ActionScript

For this example, you're going to set up four buttons—a red, green, yellow, and blue button. The yellow button will change the entire item of the car symbol to a solid yellow color. The last three will preserve the detail of the artwork and just change the tint to a new color.

1. Create a new document. In this document, create four buttons—a red, green, blue, and yellow button. Once you are done with the buttons, align them along the bottom of the stage. If you forget how to make buttons, refer to Chapter 5, "Symbols and the Library."

2. Open the Unleashed Common Library by choosing Window, Common Libraries, Unleashed. If you haven't installed the Unleashed Common Library, but you've downloaded the file, simply choose File, Open As Library and search for unleashed.fla on your computer.

3. In the graphics folder, drag out an instance of "car" and place it above the buttons on the stage, as shown in Figure 18.6.

4. With the car graphic selected, convert it to a movie clip symbol by pressing F8 on your keyboard. This will open the Convert to Symbol dialog box. In the Name text field, type **color_change** to give it a new name. Make sure you select the Movie Clip radio button for the symbol's behavior. Click OK.

5. Highlight the car on the stage. In the Properties Inspector, give this movie clip an instance name of **colorTarget** (remember to avoid spaces in the naming conventions of your instances).

6. Highlight the yellow button on the stage and press F9 to open the Actions panel. Here, you need to apply an action to set the color of the movie clip to solid yellow. You'll be using the `Color` object for this. In the `color` object, you'll use `setTransform` to change the color using a certain hexadecimal value. Here's the code:

```
on (press) {
    c = new Color(_root.colorTarget);
    c.setRGB(0xFFFF00);
}
```

When the button is depressed, the variable `c` is set equal to a new `Color` object. You're setting the RGB value of `c` to equal `0xFFFF00`, which is yellow.

7. Choose File, Save As and name the movie `car_color1.fla`. Test the movie. Although it doesn't actually show the color yellow, you can tell that a solid color is shown in Figure 18.7. It looks pretty good; however, all the detail of the car has been replaced with the solid yellow color as well. You'll notice some areas are left white; that's because those areas have no color value, so what you're really seeing is the stage.

8. Highlight the red button and press F9 to open the Actions panel. This time you're going to apply a new color using a slightly different technique. First, you're going to set up a new `Color` object called `carColor`. Then you'll set up a new object called `colorRed`. This is a generic object, and you'll be able to assign the following color properties to it:

   - ra. Represents the red channel percentage (-100 to 100)
   - rb. Represents the red channel offset (-255 to 255)
   - ga. Represents the green channel percentage (-100 to 100)
   - gb. Represents the green channel offset (-255 to 255)
   - ba. Represents the blue channel percentage (-100 to 100)
   - bb. Represents the blue channel offset (-255 to 255)
   - aa. Represents the alpha channel percentage (-100 to 100)
   - ab. Represents the alpha channel offset (-255 to 255)

   Of course, with all these properties (especially considering their value ranges), it may be difficult to gauge what your color will look like. Luckily, all these settings are identical to the Advanced option in the Color drop-down menu in the Properties Inspector. Therefore, you may want to experiment with colors there before you start your scripting.

After experimenting with the colors, , you'll set the `carColor` object to use the `setTransform` method to assign a value of `colorRed` to your generic object. Here's the code:

```
on (release) {
    carColor = new Color (_root.colorTarget);
    colorRed = new Object ();
    colorRed.ra = 80;
    colorRed.rb = 255;
    carColor.setTransform(colorRed);
}
```

These numbers are simply made up; feel free to use your own values.

9. Test the movie and click the red button. Notice that the car turns reddish. You can still see the majority if the detail in the car.

   In this case, you're just changing the tint. Now click the yellow button. The car is yellow again. Now click the red button again. Hmmm. It seems as though something's not working. Remember, you are applying a red channel percentage and offset values, which means the result will look different if the starting color is different. Therefore, you need to set the movie clip's color back to its original style before applying the new color tints.

10. Highlight the red button and open the Actions panel. You have to create an `on (press)` event handler so that as the button is pressed, the actions will reset the movie clip back to its original appearance for a brief moment, until the `on (release)` event handler is triggered, and those actions run, changing the car's appearance again. Here's what the code will look like:

```
on (press) {
    carColor = new Color (_root.colorTarget);
    original = new Object ();
    original = {
        ra: '100',
        rb: '0',
        ga: '100',
        gb: '0',
        ba:    '100',
        bb:    '0',
        aa: '100',
        ab:    '0'
    }
    carColor.setTransform (original);
}
on (release) {
    carColor = new Color (_root.colorTarget);
    colorRed = new Object ();
    colorRed.ra = 80;
```

```
        colorRed.rb = 255;
        carColor.setTransform(colorRed);
    }
```

11. Test the movie. Click the yellow button to change the cars appearance. Now click the red button. For a brief moment, you'll notice that the car's original style is restored.

12. Repeat step 10 for the blue and green buttons. Remember, inside these new Color objects, you'll want use ga and gb or ba and bb, depending on which button you're working on.

FIGURE 18.6

Four buttons on the stage with the car.

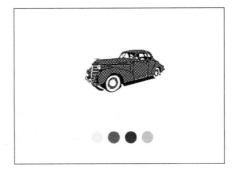

FIGURE 18.7

The entire car is a solid color.

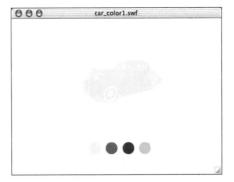

The Color object can be powerful. It is useful in many applications, especially for e-commerce. For example, suppose you live in Los Angeles and your car got keyed; you would need a new paint job (really, you would). You might get on the Web and shop around for a body shop to paint your car. A savvy body shop would have pictures of all the popular models of cars, and you could select your car's make, model, and so on.

Once you have chosen your car from the database, you could choose different colors to paint your car. Using a script like the one you just created, you could see a picture of your car in the various colors you've chosen.

Creating Random Color Values

In Chapter 13, "Movie Clip Objects," you animated a stick figure walking across the screen. We're now going to open that file and create a random color for each instance of the walking figure.

Applying Random Colors

1. Open the `smart_man.fla` file you worked on in Chapter 13. If you no longer have that file, you can always download it from the Unleashed companion Web site.

2. Test the movie just to refresh your memory about what you created. You have six stick figures walking across the stage at random speeds. Now you're going to a random color value them.

3. Highlight the stick figure on the stage and press F9 to open the Actions panel. In the current actions you will notice there are already two event handlers: one for `on load` and the other for `enterFrame`. If you put the random color action within the `enterFrame` event handler, each stick figure will change its color every time this action runs because it is a looping statement. However, if you put the action in the `on load` event handler, the random color will be calculated only once.

4. Within the `onClipEvent (load);` event handler, you need to define a new `Color` object. You also have to define what you're going to apply this new color object to. Finally, you have to assign random color values to red, green, and blue's color channels and alpha settings. Here's the final code:

```
onClipEvent (load) {
    xvalue = int(Math.random()*20)
    manColor = new Color (this);
    colorDefine = new Object ();
    colorDefine.ra = random (100);
    colorDefine.rb = random (255);
    colorDefine.ba = random (100);
    colorDefine.bb = random (255);
    colorDefine.ga = random (100);
    colorDefine.gb = random (255);
    manColor.setTransform(colorDefine);
}
onClipEvent (enterFrame) {
```

```
        if (this._x >= 550) {
            this._x = 0
    }

        this._x = this._x + xvalue
    }
```

This is much like the code for the previous example in this chapter. The exception this time is that the color is being applied dynamically instead via a color button. Also, the `random` function is generating a random number, up to the value in parentheses.

5. Test the movie. Figure 18.8 shows that all the stick figures have different colors that are set randomly. Test the movie a few more times just to see the random colors being generated.

6. Save the document as `random_man.fla`.

FIGURE 18.8

The stick figures have different color values.

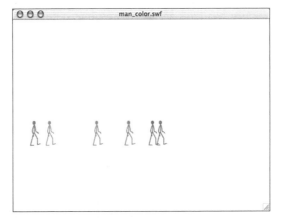

The Sound Object

When using the `Sound` object, you can control a sound's volume and balance. In order to control the sound, you must export it from the Library. Once the sound is exported, you can then can attach it to the `Sound` object. This is commonly known as *instantiating*.

Creating a Volume Slider

For this exercise, you will need some looping music. You can download some from the Unleashed companion Web site, or you can always visit Flash Kit (www.flashkit.com), which offers hundreds of free sound loops. Here are the steps to follow for this exercise:

1. Create a new document. Choose File, Import. Import the sound file you just downloaded by searching for it on your computer and choosing Open.

2. Open the movie's Library by choosing Window, Library. Select the sound in the Library; then in the Library's option menu (in the top-right corner) choose Linkage. This will open the Linkage Properties dialog box, as shown in Figure 18.9.

3. In this dialog box, check the Export for ActionScript box. Type the name **Music1** in the Identifier text field. Then click OK.

4. Highlight frame 1 by clicking it; then open the Actions – Frame panel by pressing F9. You now need to attach the sound. The first thing you have to do is to set a variable. Then you'll make that variable equal the new Sound object. Next, you'll create a statement by choosing evaluate in the Miscellaneous Actions book. In that statement, you'll attach the sound Music1 to your new sound object, s. Finally, you'll choose evaluate again and this time attach the start method to s. Here's what the code will look like:

```
s = new Sound;
s.attachSound("Music1");
s.start();
```

5. Test the movie. You should hear the music playing. Close out of testing mode to get back to Flash.

6. Now we're ready to create a slider to control the volume. Create a small circle using the Oval tool. Choose any fill and stroke color you like. After drawing the circle, select it and press F8 to launch the Convert to Symbol dialog box. Here, choose the Button behavior and name the symbol **circle_button**. Click OK.

7. Now that the circle is a button, you must convert it to a move clip. Remember, to create a draggable movie clip, it's best to have a nested button symbol. With the button selected, press F8 to open the Convert to Symbol dialog box again. Choose Movie Clip for the behavior and name the symbol **circle_mc**. Click OK.

8. Double-click the circle to enter the movie clip symbol editing mode. Select the button and press F9 to open the Actions panel. Here, you have to make the movie clip draggable. Choose the plus sign to open the Actions drop-down menu. Choose Actions, Movie Clip Control, startDrag. Be sure to set the event handler to press. For the conditions, leave the target blank and do not choose the Lock Mouse to Center option. Also, type in **left, top, right,** and **bottom** in their respective fields. You'll give these variables a value in the movie clip. After that, set a variable called dragging to equal true. Here's the code:

```
on (press) {
    startDrag("", false, left, top, right, bottom);
    dragging = true;
}
```

9. After the last curly bracket, add a stopDrag action to the existing code. Make sure the event handler is release, releaseOutside. After choosing the stopDrag action, set the variable dragging to equal false. Here's the final code for the button:

```
on (press) {
    startDrag("", false, left, top, right, bottom);
    dragging = true;
}
on (release, releaseOutside) {
    stopDrag();
    dragging = false;
}
```

10. Save the movie as sounds.fla. Test the movie. Notice that the volume slider works!

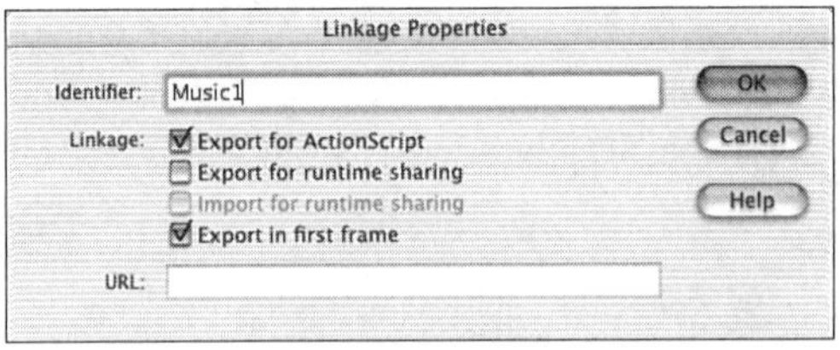

FIGURE 18.9

The Linkage Properties dialog box.

As you can see, the Sound object can add value to your Web site. It allows you to interact with your end users. This way, if they feel a sound is too loud, they have the option of turning down the volume within your Flash movie. In the next exercise, we'll create a slider to control the balance of the sound. Note, however, that you will only hear a difference if you have stereo speakers installed on your computer.

Creating a Balance Slider

Creating a slider to control the balance of a sound is very similar to creating a volume slider, which you did in the previous exercise. Here are the steps to follow:

1. Open the sounds.fla file. Select the circle movie clip on the stage. Holding down the Option (Mac) or Alt (Windows) key, click and drag the circle somewhere else on the stage. This will make a copy of the button, as shown in Figure 18.10.

2. The actions on the button inside the movie clip will stay the same. However, you need to make adjustments to the actions on the movie clip. Select the movie clip and press F9 to open the Actions panel. Here, you need to change some of the actions. First, delete the math so that bottom equals only _y. Set left to equal _x -50 and set right to equal _x +50. Also, set a new variable called center to equal _x. Now, the top part of your code should look like this:

```
onClipEvent (load) {
    top = _y;
    left = _x -50;
    right = _x + 50;
    bottom = _y ;
    center = _x;
}
```

Setting the variables top and bottom to _y will set the y axis to equal the circle's current position. Setting center to _x sets the x axis of the circle to its current position. By subtracting 50 from left, you can use that value to set the pan to the left speaker. The same is true for the right.

3. You now have to adjust the second portion of the ActionScript. Right now it sets the volume, but you need to set the pan. Therefore, type **_root.s.setPan** over the "set volume" script. The condition will be _x - center * 2. Therefore, it will get its initial value from the x position when the movie is loaded. Then, as the circle is dragged to either the left or the right, the x position value will change. The changed number will be multiplied by 2. The maximum number to the left or right is 50 or –50, respectively, but by multiplying the number by 2, it can equal 100 or –100,

thus fully shifting the balance to the left speaker or the right speaker, respectively. Here's the final code for the movie clip:

```
onClipEvent (load) {
    top = _y;
    left = _x -50;
    right = _x + 50;
    bottom = _y ;
    center = _x;
}
onClipEvent (enterFrame) {
    if (dragging ==true) {
        _root.s.setPan((_x-center)*2);
    }
}
```

4. Test the movie. You should now be able to change not only the volume but also the balance.

FIGURE 18.10

A duplicated circle movie clip.

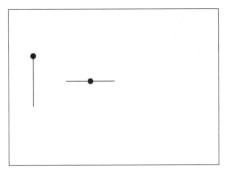

The Math Object

Flash comes with a lot of built-in Math objects. In order to use them, however, you will have to remember concepts taught to you in trigonometry. We're going to create an example using the walking stick figure. You can download the file for this exercise at the Unleashed companion Web site located at http://www.flashmxunleashed.com.

The Math Object in Action

In this exercise, you're going to create a very low-level, interactive game of sorts. Basically, you're going to convert your cursor into a bottle of water, and the walking stick-figure man is going to follow this cursor's every move.

Apparently he's thirsty, but once he reaches the cursor (the bottle of water), the bottle will disappear and he'll stop walking. As soon as you move the cursor away from the walking man, the bottle will appear and the man will start chasing it again.

What does this have to do with the Math object? The movement of the man following the cursor is all calculated based on the angle between the movie clip (the walking man) and the cursor (the bottle of water). Here are the steps to follow for this exercise:

1. Open the math_man.fla file you downloaded from the companion Web site.

2. You first need to get the walking man movie clip to follow the mouse. Select the movie clip and press F9 to open the Actions panel. In the Actions panel, you need to set the property of the movie clip based on the location of the mouse. You need to first add the onClipEvent handler with enterFrame as the condition. Again, this will create a loop that constantly evaluates where the mouse is. You need to set a setProperty action and within this action you want to set the action's target to this and choose _x for the property. The value will be the current position minus the value of the current position minus the current x position of the mouse divided by 10. Here's the code:

```
onClipEvent (enterFrame) {
    setProperty (this, _x, this._x - (this._x - _root._xmouse)/10);
    setProperty (this, _y, this._y - (this._y - _root._ymouse)/10);

}
```

3. Test the movie. It's not going to work properly just yet, but you do want to see whether the script is working. The man should be walking backwards when the mouse is moved to the left side of the stage, as shown in Figure 18.11.

4. Because people don't typically walk backwards, you'll want to fix this. You want the man to always point in the direction of the mouse. Therefore, you have to find the relationship between the movie clip and the mouse and subtract their x and y positions; this value you can use when finding the radians of the arc by using the Math object arctangent2. Of course, you don't need radians—you need *degrees*. You can take the value in radians and divide using 180/pi. The Math object contains an object for pi. Finally, after you get this value, you can set the rotation property of the movie clip to equal that value. Here's the code:

```
onClipEvent (enterFrame) {
    setProperty (this, _x, this._x - (this._x - _root._xmouse)/10);
    setProperty (this, _y, this._y - (this._y - _root._ymouse)/10);
```

```
    x = _root._xmouse-this._x;
    y = _root._ymouse-this._y;
    Radians = Math.atan2(y, x);
    Degrees = Radians*(180/Math.PI);
    setProperty(this, _rotation, Degrees);
}
```

5. Test the movie. Now the man is always pointing in the direction of the mouse. The only bad part, as shown in Figure 18.12, is that the man walks upside down (which is even worse than him walking backwards). You'll need to fix this glitch.

6. Now you need to check whether the variable `Degrees` is either greater that 90 degrees or less than –90 degrees. If it is, you'll need to scale the man to -100, thus inverting him. Here's the final code:

```
onClipEvent (enterFrame) {
    setProperty(this, _x, this._x-(this._x-_root._xmouse)/10);
    setProperty(this, _y, this._y-(this._y-_root._ymouse)/20);
    x = _root._xmouse-this._x;
    y = _root._ymouse-this._y;
    Radians = Math.atan2(y, x);
    Degrees = Radians*(180/Math.PI);
    setProperty(this, _rotation, Degrees);
    if (Degrees>90 || Degrees<-90) {
        setProperty(this, _yscale, -100);
    } else {
        setProperty(this, _yscale, 100);
    }
}
```

7. Test the move. All is well. The man now does not walk backwards or upside down. Next, you have to change the mouse to a water bottle. Then you have to detect collisions between the cursor and the movie clip to have the man stop walking.

8. Save this document as `arctangent.fla`.

FIGURE 18.11

The movie clip is yielding undesired results.

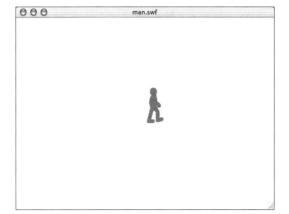

FIGURE 18.12

The man is now walking upside down.

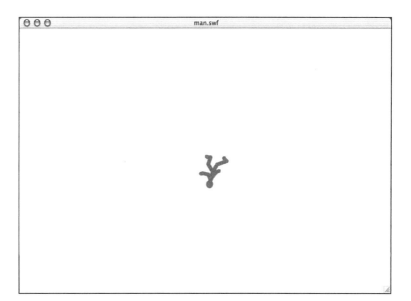

Basic Collision Detection

This exercise finishes up the previous one. Begin by opening up the `arctan-gent.fla` file; then follow these steps:

1. Open the Library and drag out an instance of the bottle movie clip. With it selected, press F9 to open the Actions panel and apply the same action you used in step 3 of the first exercise of this chapter. Here is the code:

```
onClipEvent (load) {
    startDrag(this, true);
    Mouse.hide();
}
```

2. Test the movie. Notice that the man is now following the bottle.

   You now want to check to see when the man walks into the bottle. When he does, you want him to stop walking and you want the bottle to disappear. However, once you move the mouse again, you want the man to follow it and you want the bottle to be visible again.

3. Select the walking man movie clip and press F9 to open the Actions panel. Here, you need to create another `if` statement. The statement is going to check whether the center point of the bottle movie clip intersects with the shape of the walking man. You can check by the shape of the `MovieClip` object. Flash will do an okay, but not perfect, job of evaluating the shape. If a collision does occur, you want to hide the bottle and you want to stop the walking man movie clip. If a collision does *not* occur, you want to show the bottle as well as the man walking. Here's the code:

```
onClipEvent (load) {
    startDrag(this, true);
    Mouse.hide();
}
onClipEvent (enterFrame) {
    if (this.hitTest(_root.man._x, _root.man._y, true)) {
        setProperty(this, _visible, 0);
        _root.man.stop();
    } else {
        setProperty(this, _visible, 1);
        _root.man.play();
    }
}
```

4. Test the movie. Notice that when the walking man gets close to the bottle, it will disappear and he will stop walking. However, once you move the mouse the bottle reappears, and the man starts walking again.

The `Math` object is very powerful, although it may require you to brush up on some old math skills. Once you have a good handle on the `Math` object, the scripting is the easy part.

CHAPTER 19

Working with Text

By David Vogeleer

IN THIS CHAPTER

- The Text Field Basics
- ActionScripting Text Fields
- Interfacing Text Fields with Outside Data

Using text is one of the most important forms of communication, and Flash has taken this into account. As a matter of fact, Flash MX provides greatly increased capabilities for dealing with and manipulating text fields.

This chapter has three major sections dealing with the following topics:

- The basics of text fields
- Using ActionScript with text fields
- Interfacing text fields with outside data

With this in mind, let's get right into the basics, starting with the interface itself.

The Text Field Basics

This section covers the basics of creating text fields manually and provides some uses of these text fields. However, to get started, let's first discuss the interface of the text field.

Text Field Interface

When you select the Text tool by clicking the letter *A* button in the Tools panel or by pressing the T key on the keyboard and then click the stage, the Properties panel changes, similar to what's shown in Figure 19.1. The letter *A* in the upper-left corner signifies that the Text tool is selected.

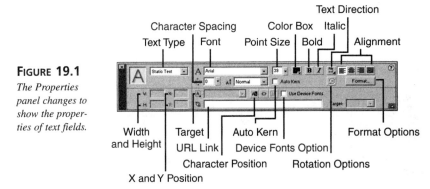

FIGURE 19.1
The Properties panel changes to show the properties of text fields.

If you are used to Flash 5, you'll immediately notice that all the options are placed in one panel instead of several panels. Next to the letter *A* is the Text Type drop-down menu, which has three options. The default setting is Static Text. Here is a list of all the options and what they mean:

- **Static Text**. Text that is placed during production. It does not change throughout the playback of the movie and can only be adjusted at the production level.

- **Dynamic Text**. This text field may also hold text during production, but at runtime the text can be manipulated by ActionScript to display whatever is required.

- **Input Text**. This is a text field that can have text placed in it during production, but at runtime it can be used to send information to the player or ActionScript via the text the user types in.

All these options are covered in greater detail as the chapter progresses. Following the Text Type drop-down menu, moving from left to right, you will find the basic formatting features for text, including font, size, color, bold, italics, direction, and alignment, as well as the Format submenu, where you can set margins and spacing. A new feature of MX allows you to change the direction of text via the Text Direction button. This feature enables text in the text box to be displayed horizontally, as we're used to seeing it, or vertically, as shown in Figure 19.2.

FIGURE 19.2

See how the text goes vertical just by choosing the option.

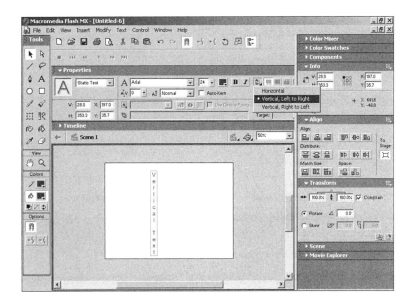

19

WORKING WITH
TEXT

Right below the font type, you'll find the spacing and position options available, including the Auto Kern option. Then, at the bottom of the Properties panel is an input box for placing a URL if a hyperlink is desired in the text field. This is followed by another drop-down menu for choosing the target type of the URL.

Finally, under the Text Type menu are four info boxes showing the position and size of the text box. This is a new feature for specifying text options and will become more useful as we go through the details of using text fields.

When you select Dynamic Text instead of Static Text in the Text Type menu, the menu changes to look like Figure 19.3. Some features available to Static Text are not available to Dynamic Text. However, other features become available, so let's focus on them.

FIGURE 19.3

The Properties panel is focused on the text field and set to Dynamic Text.

The first new feature that appears is a box right below the Text Type drop-down menu. This box is used for naming the instance of the text box, another new feature of Flash MX. For the first time, text fields can now be seen as objects inside of ActionScript (more on that in the section "ActionScripting Text Fields").

The next available feature is the Line Type drop-down menu. The options are Single Line (default), Multiline, and Multiline No Wrap.

After the Line Type drop-down menu, three buttons are shown. Each of these buttons controls a certain feature of dynamic text fields:

- **Selectable**. This feature allows the text in the field to be highlighted and copied to the Clipboard of a user's computer.

- **Render Text as HTML**. This feature allows native HTML tags to be used in conjunction with dynamic text to give some format to the text. (This feature is covered in greater detail in the last section, "Interfacing Text Fields with Outside Data.")

- **Show Border Around Text**. This feature gives the text box a white background and a black hairline border.

The next box is the Var: (variable) declaration box. This is used for labeling the text field with a variable name to use in conjunction with ActionScript when in text is drawn from either a local data type or an outside source. Do not confuse the variable name with the instance name. If both the variable name and the instance name are the same, undesirable results can be produced. A newly available feature for dynamic text is the Edit Character Options menu, which allows you to imbed the font you are using in the dynamic text field by selecting all characters or certain characters. This feature can be useful if you are using a font that is not readily available on most computers. Even though this feature does increase the overall file size, it is often worth the price to show your particular font. If this feature is not used, and the user does not have the desired font, the text box will be converted over to the system font.

The option for text fields is Input Text. Again, an input text field is used primarily for users to enter information that can be stored and used by the player. Input Text has the same options as Dynamic Text, plus a Set Maximum Characters option. This option can be used to set the maximum number of characters a user can place in an input text field. This can be useful if you are looking for a certain type of information, such as the year, in which case the category will have no more than four characters. Lastly, for input text fields as well as dynamic text fields, a small blue circle with a white figure in it appears on the left of the Text Properties panel. This is another new feature of Flash MX that's worth mentioning. It's called the Edit Accessibility feature, and it assists in making content found on the Web more accessible to individuals with disabilities. It is only supported in the Flash 6 player, and users must be running the Windows operating system. This is a big step in making the Web a more accessible environment for all who come to it. More information can be found on Macromedia's site regarding this new feature at `http://www.macromedia.com/macromedia/accessibility/features/flash/`.

So now that you know all about the interface, you can finally use it. Let's start with static text.

Static Text

Static text is produced during the production of a Flash movie, and once the movie is run, the text cannot be adjusted. During production, however, you can adjust the text. You can adjust individual words and even characters by changing their color, size, font, and so on.

We've already covered all the options in the Properties panel for static text; however, there is a new addition for static text found in Flash MX that we haven't discussed: Distribute to Layers.

In Flash 5, when you would break apart a text box, all the letters that were contained in that text box became shapes. Now when we break apart a text box, each letter becomes a text box. If they are broken apart again, then they become shapes, but if they are not broken apart, they can be easily sent to individual layers that will be automatically labeled with each letter. Let's take a look.

Create a static text box and type in **Text**. Highlight the text box and go to the menu bar and choose Modify, Break Apart (or press Ctrl+B on your keyboard). Figure 19.4 shows what this should look like. Notice that the text is still on one layer.

FIGURE 19.4

Notice that each letter in the text field is now its own text field.

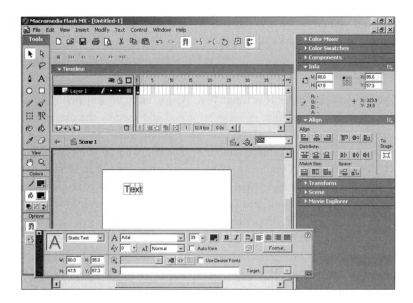

Now, go back to the menu bar and chose Modify, Distribute to Layers (Ctrl+Shift+D). Now each letter is on its own layer, and each layer has been named with the appropriate letter. Also, notice that the layer in which the entire text field previously resided is now empty (see Figure 19.4).

FIGURE 19.5

Now each letter has its own layer with the name of the layer being set to the letter itself.

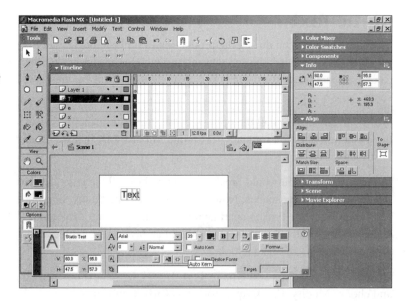

This capability is great if you want to modify individual letters with tweening.

Now let's move on to the next important part of text in Flash—the dynamic text field.

Dynamic Text Fields

Dynamic text fields provide a great way of displaying information in text format without you having to type in the text field manually. Setting text to a dynamic text field is just like setting text to a variable. As a matter of fact, when you create a dynamic text field, you assign it a variable name in the Var input box. Then, in ActionScript, you assign the variable name you have given to the text field and set it equal to whatever you want the text to say.

Let's go ahead and create a dynamic text field. Follow these steps to create a movie (we'll use this movie for the remainder of the section):

1. Start a new movie and add a layer.
2. Name the top layer `actions` and the bottom layer `text`.
3. In the text layer, create a dynamic text field by selecting the Text tool, choosing Dynamic Text in the Text Type drop-down menu from the Properties panel, and drawing a rectangle with the Text tool on the main stage.
4. Label this text box `myText` in the Var: field.

Now that you have the main stage set up, open the Actions panel in the first keyframe of the actions layer and insert this action:

```
myText = "My first dynamic text"
```

Test the movie, and you will see your text displayed on the screen. That was great! You just created your first dynamic text field, but it doesn't seem all that dynamic at this point. It simply takes text out of the ActionScript and displays it. You could have just as easily written this text in a static text field. Therefore, let's now make this text truly dynamic.

Add another layer under the text layer and call it `button`. Then create a button on this layer and place these actions in the object actions of the button:

```
on(press){
        i++;
    myText = i;
}
```

Next, replace the actions in the actions layer with these:

```
//create a variable to be increased
i = 1;
myText = i;
```

Now test the movie again. This time, when you click the button, the number (i) is increased and displayed. You can now begin to see how dynamic text fields can be used.

This next example requires a bit more coding. You are going to create a digital clock that will continually run.

First, start a new file (Ctrl+N). Name the layer **text**. In the text layer, create a dynamic text field, label the variable `myText`, and choose Show Border Around Text so that you can see it easily.

Then, make sure the text field is highlighted and convert it to a symbol (press F8). Select the movie clip and name it **clock**.

In the object actions of the clock movie that holds your text field, place these actions:

```
onClipEvent (enterFrame){
//Create a date object to get and hold the time
    myDate = new Date();
    hours = myDate.getHours();
    minutes = myDate.getMinutes();
    seconds = myDate.getSeconds();
//hours are in military form, so we change it to regular form
    if(hours > 12){
        hours = hours - 12;
    }
//Create a variable to hold our time
    myTime = hours+":"+minutes+":"+seconds;
//Set myTime to the dynamic text field
    myText = myTime;
}
```

Now you have a dynamic digital clock. If you like, you can add more date objects to it, including the date and year. You can also download this example from the Web site.

We'll come back to the topic of dynamic text fields later in this chapter when we work through ActionScripting text fields. Right now, let's move on to the other type of dynamic text field—the input text field.

Input Text Fields

Input text fields, like dynamic text fields, can display data from ActionScript. However, unlike dynamic text fields, input text fields can pass data from the user to ActionScript to be used and stored.

Let's look at an example so that you can see what an input text field looks like and how it works. Create a new file (Ctrl+N). Name the first layer **text**. Then create another layer and call it **Input**. Create a third layer labeled **actions**.

In the text layer, create a dynamic text field, label the variable `myText`, and choose Show Border Around Text both in the Properties panel.

Highlight the text field and convert it to a symbol (press F8). Select the movie clip and name it **display**.

Next, in the Input layer, select the Text tool, choose Input Text Field as the option in the Text Type drop-down menu of the Properties panel, and draw a rectangle with the Text tool. Label the variable of this text field **input**. Also, select Show Border Around Text as a property of the input text field. Again, this will make it much easier to see when you test the movie.

Now, in the text layer, open up the object actions of the movie containing the dynamic text (display). Place this code in it:

```
//This will set the dynamic text to input immediately
onClipEvent(load){
    myText = _parent.input;
}
//This will reset the dynamic text whenever the user
//mouse clicks on the stage
onClipEvent(mouseDown){
    myText = _parent.input;
}
```

Finally, in the first keyframe of the actions layer, place this code:

```
//This will initially set the input box
input = "Type in here";
```

Now when you test the movie, you will see two strings of text both reading "Type in here." Enter some text in the input text field and then click anywhere on the stage to reset the dynamic text field.

Input text fields are great for making a Flash movie more interactive for the user. You can use them to get personal information, get answers to questions on a quiz, or even to control movie clips with directional input.

We've covered the basic creation and use of each type of text field, but so far we've created all the text fields and made changes to their format manually. Now let's discuss how to make text fields and manipulate them in ActionScript.

ActionScripting Text Fields

One of the most upgraded areas in Flash MX is the ability to create, remove, and control text fields dynamically from inside ActionScript.

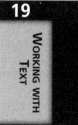

The first step involves learning how to create text fields with ActionScript. After that, all your text boxes will be created from ActionScript.

Creating Text Fields with the `createTextField` Method

You create a text field with ActionScript by attaching it to a movie clip instance. The generic template looks like this and is explained in the following list:

```
myMovie.createTextField(name, depth, x, y, width, height);
```

- `myMovie`. The name of the movie in which the text field is being created
- `name`. The instance name of the text field
- `depth`. An integer representing the stacking order of the text field
- `x, y`. The horizontal and vertical coordinates relative to the movie in which the field is being placed
- `width, height`. The horizontal and vertical size relative to the movie in which the field is being placed

Before you jump right in and start creating text fields, you should know some default values associated with the `createTextField` method:

Property	Default Value
type	"dynamic"
border	false
background	false
password	false
multiline	false
html	false
embedFonts	false
variable	null
maxChars	null

We'll go over how to change some of these values as well as what to change them to when we cover the properties of a text field. For right now, the default values are what we want to use. Also, so that we can work from the main timeline easily, we're going to create the text field in the _root movie.

Start by creating a new file (Ctrl+N). Then open up the actions layer (the only layer in the new file) and in the first frame place these actions:

```
//This will create a text field in the root level, and
//set it at the top left corner
_root.createTextField("myText",1,0,0,100,100);
```

There you have it—your first ActionScripted text field! However, at this point it doesn't contain any text. Earlier, when you created text fields manually, you applied a variable name to them in order to place text inside. When creating text fields with ActionScript, you are doing more than just creating a text field—you are creating a `TextField` object. This object has many properties, two of which are `text` and `htmlText` (we will go over `htmlText` in detail in the last section). These properties enable you to set text to a text field, and you attach these properties like you would any other property.

Let's add some more code to what we have already. Your entire code should now look like this:

```
//This will create a text field in the root level, and
//set it at the top left corner
_root.createTextField("myText",1,0,0,200,100);
//Now set a string equal to the text property of myText
myText.text = "My first coded text field";
```

Test the movie, and you will see the string appearing on the screen using the default settings.

Now that you know how set text to your text field, let's modify the text field itself to see changes in the text box.

You can change anything from ActionScript that can be changed manually, including text size, color, border, background, and so on. Again, you set these properties like any other property of an object. Let's go over a few of them with some basic examples. You can use the same text, or you can change it.

Let's start by adding a border and a background and then changing the text color. Place the following code in the first frame of the main timeline:

```
//This will create a text field in the root level, and
//set it at the top left corner
_root.createTextField("myText",1,0,0,100,100);
//Now adjust some of the settings of the text field itself
myText.border=true
myText.borderColor=0xFF0000;
myText.background=true;
myText.backgroundColor=0x0000FF;
myText.textColor=0xFFFFFF;
//Now set a string equal to the text property of myText
myText.text = "Some Patriotic Text";
```

Notice that in order to change the color of the border and the background, you have to turn them on first. If you don't, neither the border nor the background will be visible.

Also notice that we changed the properties of the text field a little, so when you test this movie, a blue box with a red border and some white text will appear.

These are not the only properties we can change. We can also change the type of text field.

This time, let's create a password that a user will have to give in order to "gain access". But instead of gaining access, a welcome message or wrong answer will be displayed in the Output window depending on what is placed in the input text field.

To begin, create a new layer and call it **button**. On this layer, place an instance of a button on the main stage. Then, in the object actions of the button, place this code:

```
on(press){
//This will check whether the password is correct
    if(input.text == password){
        trace("Welcome");
    }else{
        trace("Incorrect Password, please try again");
    }
}
```

Now, in the first keyframe in the other layer, place the following actions, which will create an input text field that uses password characters to hide the user's input. This code also places a border around the text field and creates another text field displaying a label for the input field:

```
//First, create the password
password = "radius";
//Now create two text fields
_root.createTextField("input",1,0,0,100,15);
_root.createTextField("passwordText",2,0,15,100,15);
//Here we change some properties for the input text field
input.type="input";
input.password=true;
input.border=true;
input.maxChars = 10;
//Now set the properties of the label
passwordText.selectable = false;
passwordText.autoSize = "center";
//Put text to the label
passwordText.text = "Password";
```

You have an input text field with a border that, when typed in, only displays asterisks. You also have a dynamic text field that labels the input box; this text field cannot be highlighted. Also note that you can place more than one text field at a time at the same depth within the same movie; the last field created will simply overwrite the previous one.

So far you have been able to control your text boxes and add text to them, but you haven't changed the text itself to a large degree. In addition to `TextField`, Flash MX has added `TextFormat` as a new object. Let's discuss how to use this new object.

The `TextFormat` Object

The `TextFormat` object acts similarly to a style sheet. You first create the `TextFormat` object and then apply the format to the text field by using the `setTextFormat` method. First, however, you must learn how to create a `TextFormat` object. Start with this generic template:

```
formatName = new TextFormat ();
```

Once you've created this, set the attributes to the format object. Here's an example:

```
formatName.bold = true;
```

Once you have made all the formatting changes you want to make, you apply the `TextFormat` object to a text field, like this:

```
myText.setTextFormat(formatName);
```

or

```
myText.setNewTextFormat(formatName);
```

The difference in these two lines of code is that `setNewTextFormat` is applied to newly inserted text by a user or by using the `replaceCel` method.

Also note that you do not have to apply the text format to the entire text; you can declare an index point as well as an ending index point. You'll learn more about this as the section progresses. Now let's look at some of the default values associated with the text itself:

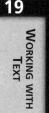

Property	Default Value
font	"Times New Roman"
size	12
textColor	0x000000
bold	false

Property	Default Value
italic	false
underline	false
url	" "
target	" "
align	"left"
leftMargin	0
rightMargin	0
indent	0
leading	0
bullet	false
tabStops	[ ] (empty array)

Now that you know what the format of the text is by default, you can change these properties for any given situation.

Let's create a format and then create a text field to handle that format. Then we'll apply the format to the text field. Start with a new, clean file. Then place these actions in the first keyframe:

```
//First we create our format
myFormat = new TextFormat();
//Create formatting rules for this format
myFormat.bold=true;
myFormat.italic=true;
myFormat.align="center";
myFormat.size = 15;
//Now create the text field
_root.createTextField("myText",0,0,0,150,100)
//Apply properties to the text field
myText.multiline=true;
myText.wordWrap=true;
myText.text="Creating text fields in ActionScript is a very powerful tool"
//Apply the format to our text
myText.setTextFormat(myFormat);
```

When you test the movie, you will have a nice-looking piece of text like Figure 19.6 because you formatted it the way you wanted to.

Let's take this a step further and highlight the word *red* in the color red and underline it in another piece of text. We'll also apply a format to increase the size of the entire text. We do this by using a starting index and an ending index when we assign the format to the text. If the starting and ending index is not entered, TextFormat will change the format of the entire text field. The generic template for this is as follows:

```
myText.setTextFormat(startIndex, endIndex, formatName);
```

FIGURE 19.6

The text is formatted to the Format *object you created with all of its options.*

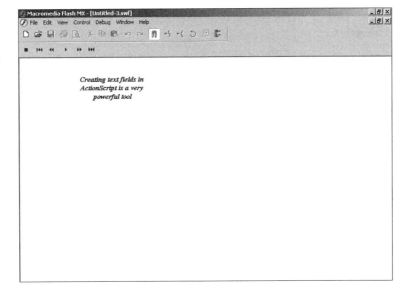

Now that you have seen the generic template, let's continue with the example. First, clear out all the code in the first keyframe and replace it with this:

```
//First we create our formats
redFormat = new TextFormat();
increaseSize = new TextFormat();
//Declare the rules for this format
redFormat.color=0xFF0000;
redFormat.bold=true;
redFormat.underline=true;
increaseSize.size=24;
//Now create the text field
_root.createTextField("myText",0,0,0,150,150);
//Apply some properties to the text field
myText.multiline=true;
myText.wordWrap=true;
myText.text = "The color of that apple is red";
//Now apply the increaseSize format to the whole thing
//Then apply the redFormat to the word red using index points
myText.setTextFormat(increaseSize);
myText.setTextFormat(27,30,redFormat);
```

Now when you test the movie, all the text will be increased to point size 24, and the word *red* will appear in bold and in the color red, as shown in Figure 19.7.

FIGURE 19.7

The word red *is now the color red, bold, and underlined because we used starting and ending indexes.*

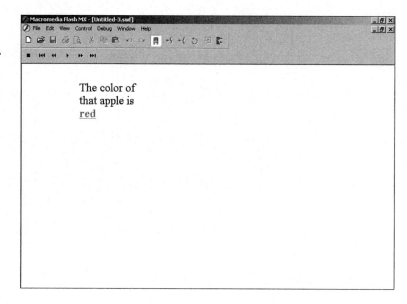

We changed the single word *red*, as shown in Figure 19.7, by setting starting and ending indexes, but this technique is not very dynamic. Instead, you can use variables that change in place of generic numbers.

In this next example, each letter of the text will change color in a loop, one at a time, and then go back to normal.

First, open a new file (Ctrl+N). Then create a movie clip by going to the menu bar and choosing Insert, New Symbol (Ctrl+F8). Name the movie clip **text**. Then go back to the main stage. Open the Library and drag the "text" movie clip onto the stage.

Now, in the object actions of this empty movie clip, place the following code:

```
onClipEvent(load){
    this.createTextField("myText",0,-75,-75,150,150);
    myText.text="This text continually blinks";
    myText.multiline=true;
    myText.wordWrap=true;
//Create our generic text format
    generic = new TextFormat();
    generic.size = 20;
    generic.align="center";
//Here create the blink format
    blink = new TextFormat();
    blink.color = (0xFF0000);
    blink.bold=true;
    blink.size=18;
```

```
//Set another text format to make each letter go back to normal
   clear = new TextFormat();
   clear.color = (0x000000);
   clear.bold=false;
   clear.size=20;
//set the initial format
myText.setTextFormat(generic);
//set the incremental variable
i=0;
}
onClipEvent(enterFrame){
//this conditional statement sets the change of the format
//while the incremental variable rises
   if(i<=myText.text.length){
       myText.setTextFormat(i,i+1, blink);
       i++;
   }else{
//this resets the variable i
       i=0;
   }
//this cleans each letter after the format has gone through
   myText.setTextFormat(i-3, i-1, clear);
}
```

Now test the movie.

This is a neat little effect in which each letter changes to the color red, increases to 18-point size, and then goes back to normal when the next letter changes. This effect involves no manual drawing or formatting—everything you see is created and formatted from inside the ActionScript. Even though this example shows a very dynamic way of changing individual letters in a text field, we can still improve upon it.

An issue that has turned some people away from using Flash to build an entire Web site is the difficulty involved in searching text for strings and returning something to the user. Now, using some of the techniques we have discussed thus far and some ingenuity, we can search a text field and highlight what we are searching for.

Again, starting with a new movie, follow these steps:

1. Create a new layer so that there's a total of two layers.

2. Name the top layer `actions` and the bottom layer `button`.

3. In the button layer, place an instance of a button (which we will come back to in step 5).

4. In the first frame of the actions layer, place this code:
   ```
   //First, create the formats for the text
   search = new TextFormat();
   clean = new TextFormat();
   ```

```
//Now create the rules of these formats
search.size=17;
search.color=0xFF0000;
clean.size=14;
clean.color=0x000000;
clean.font="Arial";
//Create the text fields
_root.createTextField("input",0,0,0,100,20);
_root.createTextField("myText",1,0,25,150,200);
//Now the properties of the text fields
input.type="input";
input.border=true;
input.text="type here";
myText.multiline=true;
myText.wordWrap=true;
myText.text="This is how to use what we have covered
and search through a text field.";
//Create a simple variable we will use when we search
var space = " ";
//Finally, apply the clean format to both fields
myText.setTextFormat(clean);
input.setTextFormat(clean);
```

If you test the movie at this point, both text boxes appear with text in them and are formatted using the "clean" format.

5. After the code has been placed in the first frame of the actions layer, return to the button, and in the object actions of the button, place this:

```
on(press){
//this will reset the entire format first to clean the text field
    myText.setTextFormat(clean);
//this uses a space to make sure it doesn't not look at part
//of a word as the whole word
    searchFor = space+input.text;
//this makes sure it is not case sensitive
    searchText = myText.text.toUpperCase();
//Finally, this sets the index points of where to set the format
    myText.setTextFormat(searchText.indexOf(searchFor.toUpperCase()),
searchText.indexOf(searchFor.toUpperCase())+searchFor.length, search);
    }
```

And there you have it. Test the movie and try out the search engine (see Figure 19.8). It can search for single words or groups of words, depending on what you type into the input field. Also, this file is available for download on the Web site.

FIGURE **19.8**

A basic search function for finding the first appearance of a group of letters in a text field.

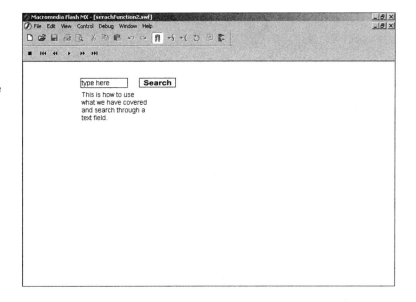

So far you have seen some nice methods for dealing with text fields. However, all we have done is to use information typed in the ActionScript as text. Oftentimes, though, you will want to be able to update text without opening Flash. This can be done by using external data, and that's what the next section covers.

Interfacing Text Fields with Outside Data

Interfacing with external data to draw into a text field can be a very powerful technique. You can update news or personal information quickly and easily.

To bring in text from outside the Flash file, you'll use the loadVariables and loadVariablesNum methods. The difference in the two is that loadVariablesNum loads information into a level number, whereas loadVariables loads information into a movie. Here are generic templates of both methods:

```
loadVariables(targetPath, myMovie);

loadvariablesNum(targetPath, levelNumber);
```

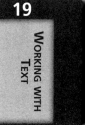

Note

If you are in normal mode and mistakenly place a level number in the `loadVariables` method, the interpreter will switch `loadVariables` automatically, but if you are in expert mode and do the same thing, the code will not function properly.

In this section, we'll mainly be using the `loadVariablesNum` method to load text right into the root of a movie by using level zero. But before we start loading and manipulating this text, let's take a look at what kind of format we should be putting this text in.

External Text Format

When creating documents to load into Flash movies, you should save them as `.txt` files or `.as` files. These are the easiest formats to use.

Here are a few rules to know about external files that load in as text:

- Set the information to a variable like you would in Flash.
- Separate your variables with the ampersand (&), without spaces.
- Do not put quotations around your strings unless you would like them to be seen in the text field.
- All information drawn in from external files comes over as a String data type.

Here's an example of a text file that can be loaded easily into a Flash movie:

```
question1=What kind of room has no walls?&answer1=A mushroom
```

Although this is not much of a text file, you can see how the ampersand separates the variables, that there are no quotation marks, and that there's no extra space between the variables.

Now that you have the generic template to use to load text as well as the format for the text file, let's try a small example. Here are the steps to follow:

1. Start by creating a new file.
2. Save this file to your project directory and call it `loadingText`.
3. Create a text file with Notepad that has the following text:
   ```
   loadedText=This is loaded text from outside the Flash movie.
   ```
4. Save this file in the same project directory as `loadableText.txt`.

5. Go back to Flash. In the first frame of the main timeline, put this script:

```
//First, load the variables
loadVariablesNum("loadableText.txt", 0);
//Now create the text field
_root.createTextField("myText",1,0,0,200,100);
//Set the properties of the text field
myText.multiline=true;
myText.wordWrap=true;
//Create a function that waits for the data to be loaded
//then places it in the text of our text field
_root.onData = function(){
    myText.text=loadedText;
}
```

Provided that both the text file and the Flash file are saved in the same directory, when you test this movie, the text will appear in the text field you created.

You've now learned how to get text from outside the Flash file to load into a text field, and you have yet to manually create anything.

Even though you are using an external source for text, you are still not using a lot of text. If, by chance, you were to have more information in the text file than could be displayed at once in the text field, you would need to provide the ability to move the text up and down, and in some cases from side to side, to be able to view it all. This is where the built-in properties associated with scrolling text fields come in.

Scrolling

Scrolling is not a new feature to Flash, but in Flash MX you can use the new hscroll and maxhscroll properties with text fields, which we will discuss after we discuss the vertical scrolling property, scroll. When scroll is increased, the text moves up. When scroll is decreased, the text moves down.

Vertical Scrolling

You can create an example that uses vertical scrolling by following these steps:

1. Create a new file and save it to your project directory as scrolling.

2. Create a new text file in Notepad that holds enough text to scroll. Here's an example:

```
scrollableText=It is always darkest before the dawn,
 so if you are going to steal your neighbors paper,
that is the time to do it.
```

3. Save this file to the desktop as scrollText.txt.

4. Back in Flash, on the main stage, create another layer and call it **button**; then call the top layer **actions** like before.

5. On the buttons layer, place two instances of a button on the far-left side of the stage and line them up, one on top of the other. Name one of these instances **myButton** for spacing purposes of the text field.

6. In the top button, place the following actions:

```
//This button will scroll the text back down
on(press){
    myText.scroll−;
}
```

7. In the bottom button's actions, place these lines of code:

```
//This button will scroll the text up
on(press){
    myText.scroll++;
}
```

8. In the first frame of the actions layer, place this script:

```
//First, load the variables
loadVariablesNum("scrollText.txt", 0);
//Now create the text field
_root.createTextField("myText",1,myButton._width,0,100,40);
//Set the properties of the text field
myText.multiline=true;
myText.wordWrap=true;
myText.border=true;

//Create a function that waits for the data to be loaded
//then places it in the text of our text field
_root.onData = function(){
    myText.text=scrollableText;
}
```

When you're all done, test it. Your results should look similar to what's shown in Figure 19.9.

Horizontal Scrolling

In Flash MX, you can do more than just scroll text up and down; you can also scroll text left and right. This can be great for displaying messages that you want to flow from left to right.

Let's create an example in which, while the user holds the mouse button down, text scrolls back and forth until the mouse button is released.

For this example, you first need to start a new file (Ctrl+N) and name the layer **actions**, as you have been doing.

FIGURE **19.9**

The buttons will scroll the text up and down when they are pressed.

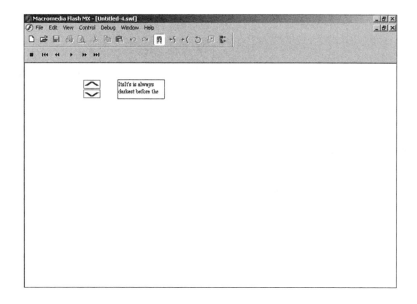

Then, in the first frame of the actions layer, place these actions:

```
//First, create the text field in the upper left corner
_root.createTextField("myText",0,0,0,50,20);
//Now assign the properties and text
myText.border=true;
myText.text="This is horizontal scrolling at its finest";

//Set the scroll speed, the higher the number, the faster it scrolls
scrollSpeed=3;

//Create functions to control when it is scrolling and when it stops
_root.onMouseDown = function (){
    scroll=true;
}
_root.onMouseUp = function (){
    scroll=false;
}

//This function will do the scrolling
_root.onEnterFrame = function(){
    if(scroll){
        myText.hscroll+=scrollSpeed;
    }
    //These next two conditionals control the direction
    if(myText.hscroll==myText.maxhscroll){
        scrollSpeed=-3;
    }else if(myText.hscroll==0){
```

```
        scrollSpeed=3;
    }
}
```

Now when you test the movie, you will see a text field with some text in it. If you click and hold down the mouse button on the stage, the text will scroll back and forth until the mouse button is released. This example is available for download from the Web site.

Earlier in this chapter, we briefly talked about a certain type of text that can be used in text fields, and now we'll cover it in greater detail. The type of text I'm referring to is HTML, which stands for Hypertext Markup Language. If you have ever worked on a Web site, you know what HTML is. Text fields in Flash support the HTML format, and the next section provides the details.

HTML in Text Fields

Before we start using the HTML format in our text fields, you need to know how to prepare the text fields for it. When creating the text field, you'll use a property called `html` whose default value is `false`. You must first change this property to `true`. You have become accustomed to setting text equal to `TextField.text`, but in order to accept HTML text, you set it to `TextField.htmlText`. Let's take a look at the generic template for preparing text fields for HTML-formatted text:

```
//First, create the text field
_root.createTextField("myText",0,0,0,150,50);
//Now set the properties
myText.html=true;
myText.htmlText = "<B>This is bold text</B>";
```

It is that simple. However, notice the instances of <B> and </B> on either side of the text. These are HTML tags you will use to tell the interpreter what to do with the sections of text. Here's a list of some of the main tags and their uses:

- <B></B>. Creates bold text
- <I></I>. Creates italic text
- <U></U>. Creates underlined text
- <FONT COLOR="#397DCE"></FONT>. Changes the font color
- <FONT SIZE="18"></FONT>. Changes the font size
- <FONT FACE="Arial"></FONT>. Changes the font type
- <A HREF="http://www.macromedia.com"></A HREF>. Creates a hyperlink
-
. Creates a line break

Now, let's create a text file with HTML formatting and then draw it into a text file. For this example, you're going to create a grocery list that will use bulleted points. Here are the steps to follow:

1. Create a new file in Flash, call it `groceryList`, and save it to the project folder.

2. Create a text file in Notepad with the following code in it:

```
theTitle=<B>The <I>Grocery</I> List</B>&gList=Bacon<BR>Eggs
        <BR>Hashbrowns<BR>Orange Juice<BR>Milk
```

3. Save this file in the same directory as the Flash file and call it `theList.txt`.

4. Back in the Flash movie, place this code in the first frame:

```
//First, load the variables
loadVariablesNum("theList.txt", 0);
//Create the text formats
titleFormat = new TextFormat();
listFormat = new TextFormat();
//Create the rules for these formats
titleFormat.align="center";
titleFormat.size=15;
listFormat.bullet=true;
listFormat.size=13;
//Create the text fields
_root.createTextField("title",0,0,0,150,25);
_root.createTextField("list",1,0,25,150,100);
//Create the properties for these text fields
title.border=true;
title.html=true;
list.html=true;
list.border=true;
list.multiline=true;
list.wordWrap=true;
//Finally, use a function that waits for the data
//to load the text and format it
_root.onData = function(){
    title.htmlText=theTitle;
    list.htmlText=gList;
    title.setTextFormat(titleFormat);
    list.setTextFormat(listFormat);
}
```

Test the movie. As long as the files are located in the same place, the end result will look similar to what's shown in Figure 19.10.

Note that when you set the text fields to the HTML format in the ActionScript, you have to wait for the text to be loaded into the player first; otherwise, if you try to format the text before it is completely loaded, the interpreter will format the text field. Then, when the text is loaded, it will be overwritten by the default format.

19
WORKING WITH TEXT

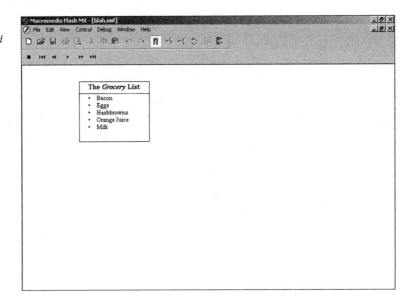

We have gone over how to use basic HTML tags to format text even before it reaches the text field. Also, you've seen how to reformat already HTML-formatted documents to better control the appearance of the text. Now we're going to go over how to use JavaScript in text fields based on some fundamental HTML tags.

JavaScript in Text Fields

JavaScript is another object-oriented programming language developed for browsers. It can perform tasks ranging from giving a simple alert to opening completely custom windows based on your specifications.

You can get to JavaScript by using the <A HREF> tag in HTML. Let's jump right into an example.

To begin, create a new movie and place the following code in the first frame of the main timeline:

```
//First we create the text field
_root.createTextField("alert",0,0,0,50,40);

//Change some of the properties so it can except html
alert.html=true;
alert.htmlText="<A HREF='javascript:alert(&quot;Warning,
you are not ready&quot;);'>"+"Warning</A HREF>";
alert.border=true;
```

When you test the movie and click the warning, a browser window will open up because JavaScript must run in a browser.

You can, however, publish the movie by selecting File, Publish (Shift+F12). This will create an HTML document that holds your Flash movie. If you then open this HTML document, the script will run considerably faster because the browser is already open.

The JavaScript you just included is very basic; this example involves the creation of a JavaScript function, and the HTML tag will call the function based on a few constraints that you define.

First, start a new movie (Ctrl+N). Then create the text box and all its attributes in the first frame of the main timeline. Use the following code:

```
//First, create the format
myFormat = new TextFormat();
myFormat.bold=true;
myFormat.size=18;
//Create the text field
_root.createTextfield("openWindow",0,0,0,75,25);
//Now set some of the properties
openWindow.border=true;
openWindow.borderColor=0xFF0000;
openWindow.html=true;
openwindow.htmlText="<A HREF='javascript:cornerWindow
(\"http://www.macromedia.com\",600,600);'>Open Window</A HREF>"
```

In this case, you have to publish the file to place the JavaScript function in the HTML of the document. After the movie has been published, open the HTML file that was created with it using Notepad or another program so that you can see the HTML. Then place the following JavaScript between the header tags of this HTML document:

```
<script language="JAVASCRIPT" type="TEXT/JAVASCRIPT">
<!—
if(screen){
topPos=0
leftPos=0
}
function cornerWindow(thePage,wt,ht){
leftPos= 0
topPos = 0
newWin1 = window.open(thePage,'aWin','toolbars=no,
 resizeable=no,scrollbars=yes,left='+leftPos+',
top='+topPos+',width='+wt+',height='+ht)
}
// —>
</script>
```

19

WORKING WITH TEXT

Once you've done this, save the page and close it. Then open the HTML document again in a browser environment and watch the code create a custom window like the one shown in Figure 19.11.

FIGURE 19.11

*The Flash docu-
ment in the HTML
file opens a cus-
tom window using
JavaScript that's
embedded in the
HTML.*

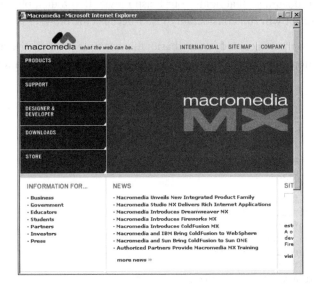

This code is great for displaying the titles of news articles, for example. Then, for more information, users can click a title to read a particular article, which comes up just how you want it to.

That just about ends our discussion of text fields in Flash. Remember that text is a crucial part of getting your ideas or your clients' ideas out to the right people. Also keep in mind that everything you have done with text fields in this chapter can be completely coded from ActionScript, which gives you greater power when creating custom interfaces.

Let's end this chapter with a fun experiment that displays text one character at a time, just like a typewriter. To do this, first create a new movie and in the first frame of the main timeline, place the following actions:

```
//First create the text formats
start = new TextFormat();
type = new TextFormat();
//Assign rules to these formats
start.color=0xFFFFFF;
type.color=0x000000;
//create an incremental variable
j=0;
```

```
//Now create the text field
_root.createTextField("myText",0,0,0,100,100);
//Modify some a property of the text box
myText.selectable=false;
myText.multiline=true;
myText.wordWrap=true;
//Add the text
myText.text="This experiment is just for fun";
//Apply the start format to the text
myText.setTextFormat(start);
//Now create a function to adjust the format of our text
_root.onEnterFrame = function(){
    if (j<=myText.text.length){
        myText.setTextFormat(j,j+1,type);
        j++;
    }
}
```

Now when you test the movie, it will appear that the text is being typed in one letter at a time. What's more, by modifying different parts of the script, you can adjust the effect to do whatever you like.

Debugging

By Todd Coulson

CHAPTER 20

Writing Proactive ActionScript

The first and best way to debug is to write code that does not create errors. This means planning your project from start to finish. The first day you sit down to create your project, start thinking about mapping out the way in which interaction will be created. That means thinking about the placement of variables, thinking about a hierarchy structure for your movie clip objects, and also thinking about how your graphics will work in coordination with the code you write. The trick is to have as much of this thought process mapped out before you even open Macromedia Flash MX. Flash is a tool that assists in creating interactive programs. It is not the tool that dictates creativity. That comes from the human brain—your human brain. Therefore, your project should have a starting map that will be referred to constantly throughout the project's lifespan. This is not to say the map is unchangeable; however, following a road map will help you steer clear of pitfalls and the dreaded "bug."

Another common programming technique is to comment code. This not only helps in writing ActionScript but also assists any other designers or programmers viewing the project to contribute their work. Comments are delineated in Flash with the // sign. For multiline comments, place /* at the beginning of the text and */ at the end of the text to be commented. You place comments to divulge the purpose of a variable, to show how a block of code works, and to show why a function is called in a particular place, among other things. There is almost no limit to the amount of comments you can place in a project. Don't write paragraphs of comments, but little single line notes which will greatly explain your code. Even the most experienced coders will run into mental blocks as to what they were trying to accomplish on projects they worked on in previous years. Comments can clear up these mental speed bumps.

Comments can also come in a variety of colors. Flash MX allows you to change the color codes on the various types of code you write. Go to Edit, Preferences and click the ActionScript Editor tab. Under the option for syntax coloring you can change the color of your ActionScript text, background, comments, keywords, strings, and identifiers. I highly recommend sticking with the default colors, which would make your comments gray, but if you do decide to change the color of your ActionScript, make sure you remain consistent from Flash document to document, and make sure the text colors make sense. For example, if you are going to change the comment color, don't make it a color that closely resembles the color of keywords. Furthermore, I would recommend making the color of your commented text red so that any person viewing your code would know that red text is a warning that a comment is being used. Using green or purple text for comments might not get the point across like red would. Regardless of the color of your comments, your ActionScript should be littered with commented, colored text throughout.

The trace action is an invaluable tool. In many cases, using trace actions is even better than using the debugger for following the values of variables and checking code with notes in your project—especially if you already know an area of code has proved problematic. A trace action can be called in the following manner:

```
Trace ("any text here to display a message");
Trace (myVariableName);
```

The former code uses a trace action that will place the exact message in the output window. The latter trace action will place the variable's value in the output window. The latter example is more useful when you're trying to track what a value is in a particular point in your code. The former example can be used when you're just trying to figure out how an action in Flash works. Then you could just sub out the trace action for the code you want placed in a particular code block. If you don't want end users to view trace actions in your project, choose File, Publish Settings, click the Flash tab of items to publish, and check the box labeled Omit Trace Actions. You can find the Omit Trace Actions check box in Figure 20.1.

FIGURE 20.1

*Omit Trace
Actions will hide
all trace actions
from your end
users.*

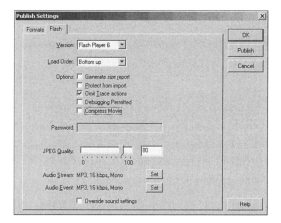

Naming Conventions

If you run into problems in Flash concerning your addressing of movie clips, make sure you have named every clip in the target path correctly. This means ensuring there are no extra spaces at the end of the instance names. Also, make sure your movie clips are in the correct order. Be meticulous about the hierarchy and make sure to follow it exactly when writing code in the target path. Any mistyping of letters or additional spaces will throw the path off and will not allow the code to run properly.

20

DEBUGGING

While writing your code, make sure your ActionScript does not conflict with itself. One way to do this is to place actions on the top layer of every timeline. Also, it's usually helpful to not include any graphics on the top layer. Otherwise, you could mistakenly put two conflicting actions on the same frame. Make sure your variables are set up in a particular way to ensure the success of your project. A variable is set to make sure your project navigates in a certain way. If you have two variables that cancel each other out, parts of your project may become defunct.

Make sure your items in Flash are all unique. You will run into fewer errors if every object has its own identifier. Don't provide a movie clip with a name and then provide a variable with the same name. It will be harder to track down items when you are scanning the Movie Explorer for an object or piece of code. Furthermore, follow a convention of writing your code. Commonly, ActionScript programmers like to name variables and objects with lowercase letters for the first word in a name and use a capital letter to start the second word in the object's name, with no space in between the words. For example, a variable would be written as

```
myVarName
```

but not

```
myvarname
```

or

```
My Var Name
```

Remember, this is just a style of preference. Using underscore characters (_) for your spaces is a matter of choice. Just stay consistent in coding ActionScript. Do not mix and match styles; this causes harder searches of code and makes the process more difficult on other programmers who may be looking at your work.

Also, save your work constantly. It is good to have several versions of your project. Constantly save your work that you know to be functioning properly to a "current" or "final" file. That way, old versions of your project can be used as a guide or a fallback. If you only work in one file, you are highly likely to save some code you didn't necessarily want. Going back one or two versions can save many headaches.

Finally, remember that bugs happen! They are as inevitable as death and taxes. Oftentimes bugs are due to an oversight in coding. At other times bugs are caused by a game plan gone wrong. The key to catching bugs is paying attention to the flow of your project. Understand how your project is expected to work and how your project currently flows in relation to the code. This will often accentuate what bugs may be present in the project. The next section identifies ways of finding and fixing the bugs in your projects.

It will help you to be more efficient in solving problems related to bugs and allow your project to be error free when you go to publish it.

Identifying Bugs

As mentioned earlier, there are several ways to restrict the number of bugs that occur in your project. However, we all know that bugs are going to happen anyway. For example, you may have a button that isn't responding to an action, a handler might be missing some syntax, or your variables might not be changed based on a mislabeled target path. Whatever the problem, tools are available to rescue you. Tools such as the Output window, the Watcher, the Bandwidth Profiler, and the Debugger can assist you in identifying bugs in your project.

One problem with discovering bugs is that code blocks are read by Flash in a very short period of time. Within milliseconds, Flash tries to accomplish the tasks set out in a code block. Just watching a movie in the Flash Player will not always allow the human eye to pick up what problems are currently in the project. Furthermore, variables are used in basically all the projects in which you write ActionScript, and you cannot see these variable values simply by watching the movie in the Flash Player. Let's open the ECdebug.fla file and work through some of the debugging techniques to find values for the variables and decipher what bugs may be present in the project. The ECdebug.fla file is a tampered file, in which the programmer has taken a lackadaisical approach to writing code. The use of debugging techniques and the Flash interface will help clean up the code and place objects to perfect the project. Currently none of the buttons work. However, when we finish cleaning up the FLA file, there should be a working preloader, buttons labeled "Choose Region" and "Choose State" that reveal more buttons underneath them, and buttons corresponding to each state and region, which animate their particular part of the East Coast. Currently, none of that functionality is working, but code has been written in an attempt to make it work. In the next few sections, we will pinpoint the problems with this file.

Output Window

The Output window allows Flash to talk to the programmer. When errors are created in code, the Flash Output window alerts you to the facts associated with the error. When you need to know the variables or objects in your code, the Flash Output window will list those items for you. Finally, when you want to know whether a particular piece of code is working, trace actions can appear in the Output window to let you know that the code is being executed. For Exercise 20.1, we'll open up the ECdebug.fla file and use the Output window to find problems with this code.

Exercise 20.1

Here are the steps to follow for this exercise:

1. Immediately upon opening `ECdebug.fla`, save the movie and call it `ECdebugCorrect.fla` so that you do not confuse it with the original file.

2. Test the movie using the Control, Test Movie menu command.

3. The Output window should immediately appear, alerting you to an error in the code. The window should produce the error shown in Figure 20.2.

4. Close the Flash Player and leave the Output window open so that you can refer to it while changing your code in the Actions panel during authoring mode.

5. The Output window has instructed you to go to the symbol named RegionMenu. Therefore, double-click the symbol in the movie with that name. This symbol happens to correspond to the movie clip symbol that houses the buttons for the region names and is located on the upper-right area of the stage.

6. Upon entering this movie clip symbol, check the layer names for the layer "choose." In this layer you will find one button. It has an instance name of myChoiceReg. Click once on this button and open the Actions panel to investigate the code attached to the button.

7. The output window shows you that line 1 needs to have a symbol to terminate the code block.

8. In your Actions panel, turn on the line-numbering feature. You can do this by pressing Ctrl+Shift+L (or Cmd+Shift+L on the Mac) or by clicking the Actions panel menu options and choosing View Line Numbers. This step really isn't necessary for this code, but it shows you how you can now easily locate line number 1 in the code block to identify where the problem is occurring.

9. Look at this statement. Notice that there is a curly brace ({) to open the `on release` statement, a curly brace to start the conditional statement, and a curly brace to start the `else` statement. However, if you look at the closing braces (}), you'll see that indeed we are missing one to compliment the `on release` statement. Therefore, in the final line of code, add a closing curly brace to end the statement.

10. Test the movie. This should remove the error from the Output window. In fact, because this was the lone syntax error in this project, the Output window will not appear again. Leave the Flash Player open for our next exercise.

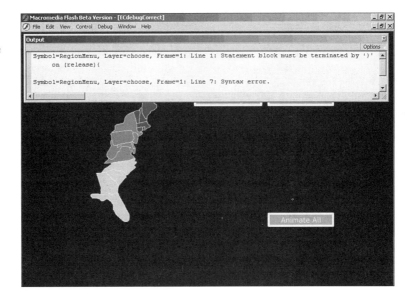

FIGURE 20.2
The Output window assists you in finding the line and object where incorrect ActionScript syntax occurs.

Bandwidth Profiler

The Bandwidth Profiler allows you to view streaming as if you were looking at a file using a particular modem speed. It also gives you vital statistics about the size of frames and the overall size of a project. The value of the Bandwidth Profiler is that you can target parts of your project to optimize and rework certain sections of it.

Now simply looking at this movie, it might appear to be perfectly normal. However, our programmer has missed some key components, which you'll fix in Exercise 20.2.

Exercise 20.2

Here are the steps to follow for this exercise:

1. Without clicking any of the buttons (which aren't working anyway) go to the Flash Player menu bar and click View, Bandwidth Profiler. This will bring up a bar graph view of what the project looks like. Now you have the ability to view how many bytes are located in the movie on any given frame. Your Bandwidth Profiler should look similar to the one shown in Figure 20.3.

   This lets you know what frames have a lot of information and may need further optimization. It also tells you which frames will trip up the pace of the presentation if the project is not preloaded.

20

DEBUGGING

2. Now, from your menu bar, choose Debug‡ 56K (4.7 KB/s). This will allow you to test the project as though you were an end user looking at the project streaming over a 56K modem. If you want to target other stream rates, you can choose Debug‡ Customize... to specify another rate. For now, we will test using 56K.

3. Go to the menu bar and choose View, Show Streaming. Now your project will run as if it were streaming over a 56K modem. Notice how the project stutters on all the frames with a lot of content. This means Flash cannot load the project faster than the animation of the objects on the screen. This is suspect to not having a preloader built into the project. Therefore, let's leave the Flash Player for a moment.

4. Save your FLA as `ECdebugCorrect.fla`.

5. Go to the second frame of the root-level movie timeline and let's look at the code under the layer named "actions."

6. Notice a function initialization and some initialization of variables. After that, you'll find a block of code that is surrounded by comment marks. Apparently the programmer of this piece of code neglected to take out the comment marks, which is necessary to run the preloader. Therefore, delete the instances of `/*` and `*/` from the code block. Now we have a preloader. This is important for halting the movie while it loads the necessary pieces to run smoothly over a 56K modem. Also, you will notice that the percentage of the bytes loaded is calculated in the variable named `percentLoaded`, which is also associated with the dynamic text box object named `percentPre`.

7. Test the movie using Ctrl+Enter (Cmd+Return on the Mac).

8. Go to your Flash Player menu bar and click View, Show Streaming again. Notice how the percentage of the movie will show once the first frame is loaded and your user has a graphical representation of how long until the program is started. Also notice how the playhead remains on frame 1 while the rest of the movie loads; this is also represented graphically in Figure 20.4. Once it gets to 100 percent, the movie plays the rest of the animation on the main timeline.

You can see how valuable a tool the Bandwidth Profiler can be for viewing a project's flow. It allows you to test your movies under ideal end-user modem specifications without having to physically hook up any connections or alternate machines.

Now, the next step is to optimize the graphics in frames where the kilobytes seem to be high.

9. Open up the Bandwidth Profiler in the Flash Player environment for `ECdebugCorrect.swf`. Notice that frame 31 is right around 8KB.

10. Go to frame 31 in the root-level timeline of the FLA. Click the frame that holds the content for the outlines of the states.

11. With the Arrow tool selected, click on the lines of the states, then click the Straighten button until you feel all the lines are straightened out sufficiently. Disregard the look of this piece for the moment. You should have several straight lines surrounding the states, causing the states not look like correct. However, for the purpose of this demonstration, you'll want to see the states with optimized lines.

12. Test the movie and look at the Bandwidth Profiler for frame 31. Notice how the kilobytes for this frame now hover around 4KB. Other frames may also be affected by the line straightening, but for now we're just looking at frame 31.

13. Go back to your FLA and press Ctrl+Z (Cmd+Z on the Mac) a number of times to undo the straightening you did in step 11.

14. Save your work.

FIGURE 20.4

The newly created ECdebugCorrect.swf file with a preloader added to the code. Notice the location of the playhead.

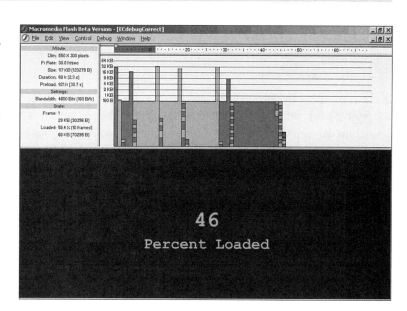

FIGURE 20.3

The Bandwidth Profiler allows you to see the graphical representation of a project in bytes per frame.

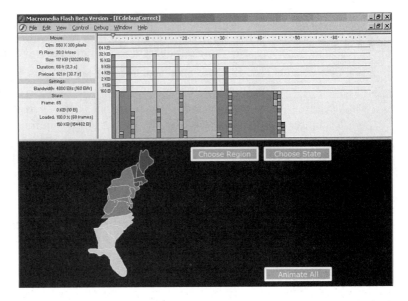

If you get this graphical representation below the red line in the Bandwidth Profiler, no preloader will be necessary for the frame. This is less important for this movie because our programmer decided to leave preloading code for us. However, if a file needs to be a specific size for a client (say, under 100KB), the Bandwidth Profiler could decipher which frames are too high in size and target those frames for optimization, as it did for frame 31.

The project is not finished yet. We still haven't checked to see whether all the parts of the project work yet. Go to the end of the project's timeline in the Flash Player and click around on the various buttons. Notice how none of them work. Clicking the Animate All button, for instance, animates nothing. Also, we want to get the Choose State button to react much the same way the Choose Region button reacts (you already fixed the Choose Region button when you completed Exercise 20.1).

Identifying Values Attached to Variables

Oftentimes the bugs in a project remain because variables are not being tracked correctly. You may have wanted a variable changed at a point in your project but forgot to change it. Sometimes you may be changing variables in places where it is unnecessary. Luckily, Flash allows you to track the values of variables during the runtime of your projects.

For the purposes of Exercise 20.3, we are going to target the Choose State button to determine why it does not toggle between showing and hiding other buttons' options. Here are the steps to follow:

Exercise 20.3

Here are the steps to follow for this exercise:

1. Open the `EcdebugCorrect` file, if it isn't already opened.

2. Double-click the StateMenu movie clip. Look around at how the piece is set up. Click the actions. Notice that the variable named `open`. It is set `open=0` in two places. This should be a red light already, but we are going to investigate this variable using the Flash Player. Also notice that there are two labels. One named open, and one named close. Click the various buttons in this movie clip to familiarize yourself with the clip's structure. Do not change any code attached to the buttons; just observe them and how the project is set up.

3. Go back to the root-level timeline and test the movie. When your movie has loaded all the objects, select Debug, List Variables from the menu bar in the Flash Player. Notice that all the timeline variables present in the project are listed and show the value associated with each variable. All the global variables would also be listed in here, if the project had global variables associated with it. The local variables in functions would not be listed here. However, toward the end of the list, you'll notice that `open` is listed twice and has the value of 0 in both cases. We now know that the variables are being read correctly in both movie clips.

4. Press Ctrl+Enter (Cmd+Return on the Mac) to test the movie in the Flash player. Click the Choose Region and Choose State buttons in your SWF.

5. Choose Debug, List Variables again from the menu bar. Your Flash Player should look similar to Figure 20.5.

   Notice that the value for the Choose Region button has changed to 1, whereas the value for Choose State has remained at 0. This is the second time we have been clued in to a mislabeled variable causing the code to be faulty.

   Before we fix the variable value, let's look at one more maneuver for finding values of variables during testing in the Flash Player. Go back to authoring mode.

6. Open the StateMenu movie clip you investigated earlier. On the button for Choose State, place the following code:

   ```
   trace(open);
   ```

7. This will show you what the value is any time the Choose State button is clicked.

8. Test the movie. Notice that the Output window appears with the value 0 for the `open` variable.

9. Click the Choose State button and notice that the value for the variable open remains at 0.

10. Go back to authoring mode and into the movie clip StateMenu. You have now seen three times that the open variable is not changing values properly. Therefore, go to the frame labeled "open" and look at the code in the Actions panel. Change the value of open to 1. If you are confused as to why we are changing it here, check the way in which the variables are set up in the RegionMenu movie clip. That clip toggles back and forth properly.

11. Test the movie. What happened? The variable still didn't work. Something else must be wrong. We will fix this second problem next.

12. Save your work to ECdebugCorrect.fla.

FIGURE 20.5

The Output window containing the values of variables and movie clips located currently on the timeline. Notice the value of open.

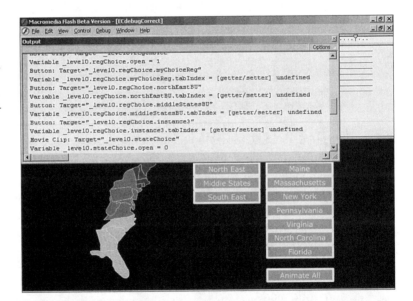

Note

When you selected Debug, List Variables, you may have noticed an option called List Objects. As you might expect, this option allows you to view all the objects included in the SWF file in the Output window.

The Debugger

The Debugger is a tool that allows you to track values of variables, follow hierarchies of objects, and "watch" values throughout your project. It provides yet another way in which you can follow values to analyze bugs in your projects. In Exercise 20.4 you will use the Debugger to track problems remaining in the project.

Exercise 20.4

Here are the steps to follow for this exercise:

1. Open the movie `ECdebugCorrect.fla`.

2. In the Flash authoring environment, choose Control, Debug Movie. Notice that the SWF opens with the Debugger available for viewing. It also pauses the movie at the start of the project.

3. Using the Script pull-down menu on the right side of the panel, choose the script for the button named chooseStateBU.

4. Next, place a breakpoint on the second line of this code. You can accomplish this by choosing a code from the Navigate to Other Scripts button on the right side of the Debugger. Then right-click a line of code and choose Set Breakpoint. This will pause the project when this point in the code is reached. Your debugger should look like the one shown in Figure 20.6. However, the gold arrow in the figure will not show up until this piece of code has been "broken," meaning that you executed the statement in the project and Flash is now executing this line of code.

5. Now click the play button on the debugger to run the movie.

6. Test the problematic Choose State button and watch the Debugger pause the movie at the breakpoint you set.

7. In the Debugger, an indicator is located over top of your breakpoint. This shows the location where Flash is reading the code. Flash is slowing down the processing of the script and allowing you to see its thought process.

8. If you click the button in the display window, you can also see the variable under the Variables tab to follow the progress again of how it is being set.

9. Note that the variable is evaluating `open1` to be not equal to `1`. Therefore, Flash will skip the first conditional of the statement. Instead, upon you clicking the Step In Script button, the Flash script will go to the `else` option of the conditional. This is expected for the first time running through the script. For a list of the types of buttons available in the Debugger, refer to Figure 20.7.

20

DEBUGGING

FIGURE 20.6

The Debugger stopping at a breakpoint on the second line of the problematic button script.

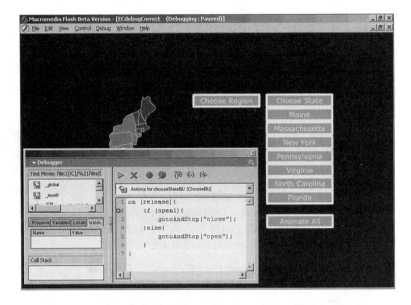

> **Note**
>
> The Step Over button is only useful for stepping over the script of a user-defined function. In all other instances, it reacts the same exact way the Step In Script button does.

FIGURE 20.7

The Step buttons and script indicator in the Debugger. Click the Step In Script button to view the next logical step in the Flash programming.

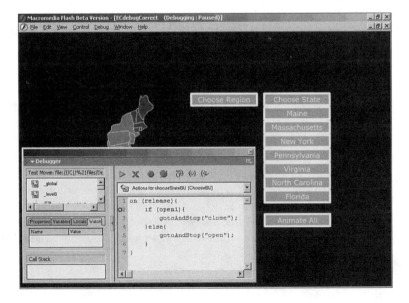

10. Click the Choose State button again to determine the thought process of Flash for the second run through the script. The second time, notice that open1 is still being interpreted by Flash as not equal to 1. This means Flash will skip over moving the playback head at this point in the code.

11. With this new information, you can return back to authoring mode, now that you know open1 is not the correct variable. In fact, the programmer shouldn't have named the variable open1. Perhaps his hand slipped while typing and he accidentally typed 1 at the end of line 2 of the button's code. Therefore, go to the StateMenu button and change the conditional to search for the value open, not open1.

12. Test the movie. You will find that both the buttons now toggle. Save the ECdebugCorrect.fla file.

Finding the bug in this code may have been a little easy to pick out. However, sometimes it takes a couple passes for your eyes to locate a bug in your project. Sometimes you will see the variable values in the Output window but not pick up on why the code doesn't work until you look in the Debugger. Sometimes it will take "watching" a variable in the Watcher to pick up on a problematic piece of code. The important thing to remember is not to give up. The errors you make in coding can be solved with a combination of logic and patience.

The Watcher

Now that we know both of the buttons work, let's watch the two open variables using the Watcher. This will ensure that the variables are working correctly. Exercise 20.5 shows you one final way to track the variables in a movie. Much like the trace action, the method used in this exercise will target a single variable of your choice; however, unlike the trace action, the Watcher will follow the progress of the variable as its value changes for the duration of the movie playback.

Exercise 20.5

Here are the steps to follow for this exercise:

1. Open the ECdebugCorrect.fla file and choose Control, Debug Movie to open ECdebugCorrect in the Flash Player 6 environment. You will notice a series of tabs on the Debugger as well as a window that displays a list of all the objects in a scene. Figure 20.8 shows the display list and the Variables tab.

   Click the _level0.regChoice movie clip object in the display list.

2. Click the Variables tab and right-click the variable open.

20

DEBUGGING

3. Right-click the variable open and choose Watch to set this variable to be watched by the Debugger.

4. Click the _level0.stateChoice movie clip object and in the Variables tab, right-click the variable open and choose Watch to watch this variable as well.

5. Click the Watch tab in the debugger. Notice how both the variables just selected appear in the Watcher. Your Watch tab should look similar to Figure 20.9. Now click both buttons in the SWF and notice how the values change.

FIGURE 20.8

The display list and Variables tab in the Debugger.

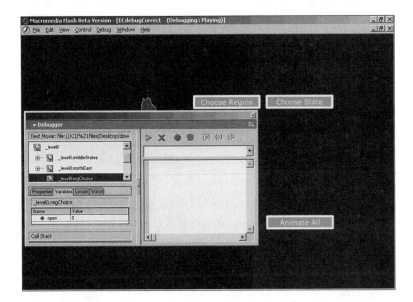

The Watcher can be a valuable tool when you know a variable is not acting right. It allows you to click around your SWF and test to see changing values of variables, without you needing to place several trace actions throughout your code.

FIGURE 20.9

The Watch tab, looking for the value of each open variable.

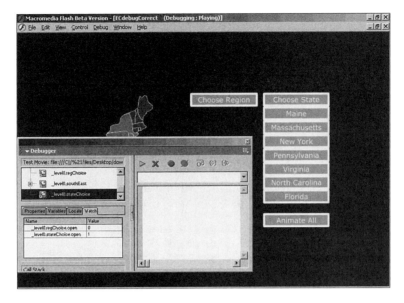

Mislabeled Target Paths

One common mistake novice programmers make involves not being able to keep names straight. You have the name of the movie clip symbol, the name of any instances of that symbol, and the names of any variables on the timeline inside the movie clip—and that's just movie clips. Add button instances, nested clips, and other objects in the scene, such as sound, and things can get cluttered quickly. That's why the naming convention for your items is of paramount importance in your programming.

Naming conventions help you keep track of items and enable you to avoid problems in the future. However, you'll most likely encounter a slip in your foolproof plan for naming movie clips (especially because every clip needs an instance name for addressing, and you are likely going to have several dozen movie clips in your projects). Exercise 20.6 will assist you in finding problems with misnamed target paths. In testing the sample movie, you may have noticed that some of the region names and all the states did not target the correct paths.

Exercise 20.6

Here are the steps to follow for this exercise:

1. Open the movie `ECdebugCorrect.fla`.
2. Open up the movie and click the movie clips in the scene. Look at the instance names assigned to each clip.

20

DEBUGGING

3. Double-click each of the region movie clips and look at the names of the states.

4. Write all the instance names down on a piece of paper so you can remember exactly how they are typed.

5. Double-click the RegionMenu movie clip to see what code is written for the buttons of the three different regions.

6. Notice the path for the Northeast region:

   ```
   _root.northEast.Maine.play();
   ```

   This is in conflict with attempting to play the northEast timeline. In fact, it won't play any timeline because there is no movie clip named Maine in the FLA.

7. Delete `Maine` from the target path.

8. In testing the SWF, we noticed that the middleStates movie clip plays as expected when the button is clicked. Therefore, check the target path of the final button, southEastBU, in the RegionMenu movie clip. Figure 20.10 displays the Actions panel and shows how going back to the panel and checking codes can often reveal misspellings of paths or misrepresented paths in your addressing of movie clips.

9. You will find that this target path is also suspect:

   ```
   _root.southEast.play;
   ```

10. Instead of the movie clip being referenced incorrectly (the clip being targeted is southEast), this time the method needs to be finished. Therefore, insert two parentheses after the word *play*, like so:

    ```
    play();
    ```

    This will complete the method for this button.

11. Now that we have fixed some errors in the RegionMenu movie clip, let's investigate the target paths for the StateMenu movie clip. Double-click the movie clip and investigate the path on the button for Maine.

12. Earlier we noticed that the path has an error in the way in which the instance of Maine is referenced. If you open the Library, you'll notice that our programmer forgot to reference the movie clip instance and instead referenced the movie clip library name. Therefore, make sure to change this to the instance name, which happens to match the initials for the state. In other words, change the path

    ```
    _root.northEast.Maine.play();
    ```

to now read as follows:

```
_root.northEast.ME.play();
```

13. Now do the same for the rest of the state buttons (our programmer has absentmindedly made the same mistake on all the state buttons).

14. The one other problematic target path in this movie is on the Animate All button. Therefore, check the code included on that button:

```
animateAll();
```

Even though this is a function being called, it still needs to follow a target path. Because no functions are written to the StateMenu movie clip's timeline, let's assume that this button is misplaced. Click Ctrl+X (Cmd+X) to cut this button.

15. Go to the root level of the timeline and search for this function. You will notice `animateAll` is in the second frame of the movie; it was initialized before the preloader. Paste (Ctrl+V or Cmd+V) the button onto the main timeline of the movie.

16. Test the movie. Now all the buttons are working in this project. I have left one final problem in the project for a later example. Save your `ECdebugCorrect.fla` file and ponder that tidbit while we discuss changing values.

FIGURE **20.10**

Testing the paths of all the movie clips will smooth many of beginning programming problems. Just make sure your target path matches the target path of your instance names for movie clips and objects.

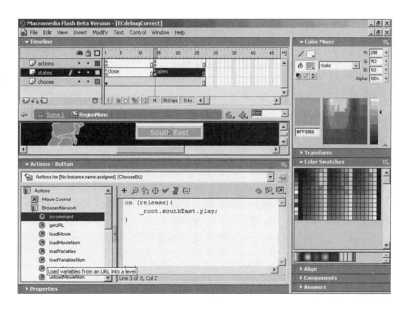

Changing Variable and Property Values

Most of the techniques discussed in this chapter have focused on discovering bugs in your project. Keep in mind, though, that debugging shouldn't always be about the eradication of "bugs." It should be about making your project perfect—finding the best appearance for your project, with the interactivity that keeps users coming back to use it. This can also be achieved through the use of the Debugger. The Debugger allows you to change values of properties (size, position, height, width, and so on) and values of variables to see how your project would look with those changed values. To learn more about this, proceed to Exercise 20.7.

Exercise 20.7

Here are the steps to follow for this exercise:

1. Open and test your `ECdebugCorrect.fla` file to view the `ECdebugCorrect.swf` file in the Flash Player. Right-click the screen and open the Debugger.

2. Within the Debugger window, you have already been to the Variables tab. Note that a tab labeled Properties is available to you as well. Click a movie clip object in the display list. In this case, choose `_level0.northeast`.

3. Click the Properties tab. All the properties of the `_level0.northeast` movie clip object are available for you to edit, except for the ones shown in gray. These cannot be changed.

4. Select the `alpha` property and change its value to `40`.

5. Select the `_x` value and change it to `150`. Your Debugger should look something like Figure 20.11.

   Notice how the properties of your clip have changed for the purposes of the SWF.

6. Close the SWF in the Flash Player and look at your FLA.

All the properties are still like they were previously. Changing property values in the Debugger will not change values in the FLA. This gives you the ability to look at how a project could look using different colors, placements, and sizes, without damaging the original content.

To access the variables, you can click the Variables tab of any timeline that possesses a variable, or you can click the _global button in the display list to get a list of all the global variables in the project. All the variables you see in the Variables tab can be edited. Just like with the properties, this will not change the value of the variables in the

FLA. It will only temporarily change the values for testing purposes. In the previous example, where the toggle's variable open needed to be changed to 1, we could have changed the variable's value during runtime to see how the toggle would react to the value being 1 at a particular moment. This would have given us another clue as to why the value was not working properly.

FIGURE 20.11

The properties of the northEast movie clip in your SWF. These values can change the appearance of your SWF for testing purposes but will not change the values within your FLA.

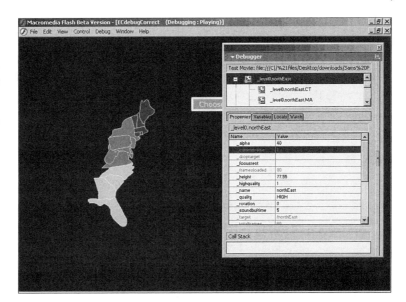

Debugging from Remote Locations

Troubleshooting should come from many different sources. Your learning should never end. One day you might solve a problem by reading a newsgroup online. Reading Macromedia tech notes can help you solve many of the general troubleshooting problems you'll encounter. Sometimes you may have an effect you want to get exactly right, which may be found in an online reference. Other times you may find the answer you're looking for in the reference materials in this and other books. The point is, you have an endless source of knowledge to tap into while debugging your projects. One such source can come in the form of help from other programmers. Are you out of luck with getting them your file to test and debug? Of course not. Macromedia allows you to share your project with users who you want to look at your project through the use of a remote server location.

20

DEBUGGING

Enabling Flash with the Ability to Debug Remotely

Exercise 20.8 shows you how to debug movies that are located on a server away from your computer. However, before you can place files on a server for the world to see, you must follow some steps to enable the file to be debugged remotely. This exercise goes over the items that need to be included in your project to allow for debugging remotely.

Exercise 20.8

Here are the steps to follow for this exercise:

1. Select File, Publish Settings in your `ECdebugCorrect.fla` file.

2. On the Flash tab of the Publish Settings dialog box, select Debugging Permitted. If you want your project to be protected from theft, provide a password in the Password box. This box is displayed in Figure 20.12.

3. Open the Debugger using any of the following menu commands:
   - Control, Debug Movie
   - File, Export Movie
   - File, Publish Settings, Publish

4. Flash creates two files: a SWF file, which is the file needed for viewing the project, and an SWD file, which is needed for viewing breakpoints in the Debugger of the SWF.

5. Both the SWF and SWD files must remain alongside each other on the server location you choose. Place both files on the server.

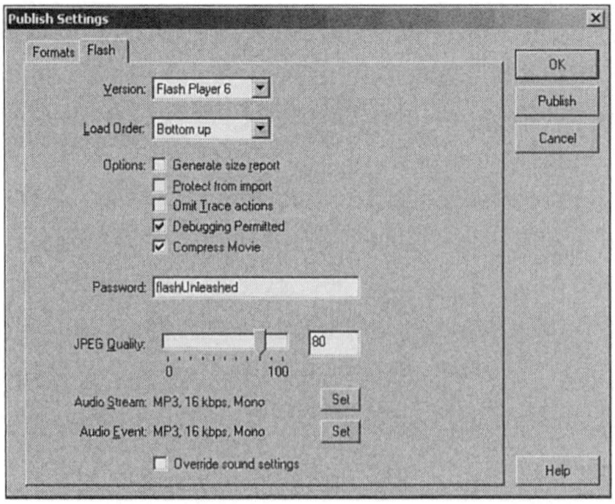

FIGURE 20.12

The publish settings needed to enable debugging in your SWF file.

Activating the Debugger from the Server

The previous exercise looked at enabling Flash to use a server. Exercise 20.9 shows you how to use a server to debug a file that is not located on your computer. You will need access to a server to debug the movie in this exercise, so if you do not have access to a server, you can skip this exercise.

Exercise 20.9

Here are the steps to follow for this exercise:

1. In Flash, choose Window, Debugger.

2. From the Options pull-down menu in the upper-right corner of the panel, choose the Enable Remote Debugging option.

3. Open either a browser window or the Flash Player standalone application.

4. Open the remote file using its location path.

5. This should open the Remote Debug dialog box. Choose either the Localhost or Other Machine option. Here are explanations of these options:

   - **Localhost.** If the Debug Player and the Flash authoring environment are on the same computer as the one on which you are viewing the file, then choose Localhost.

   - **Other Machine.** Allows you to debug from a computer that lacks the proper authoring and debugging tools or lacks Flash MX. Refer to Figure 20.13 to view the dialog box that appears with these options.

6. Enter the password for the Debugger, as shown in Figure 20.14.

   Remember the problem we had at the end of Exercise 20.6? Let's try to find that bug. Start by looking at the function script we wrote in the second frame of the movie.

7. Place a breakpoint in the first line of the function.

8. Play the Debugger and click the Animate All button.

9. The Debugger will show each of the actions in the statement block as you click the Step In script button. You'll notice that the middleStates movie clip did not play. Check the target path of the middleStates line in the custom function. Here's how it currently reads:

```
_root.middle.play();
```

10. Change the value so that the path includes the entire middleStates instance name. It should now read as follows:

    ```
    _root.middleStates.play();
    ```

11. Publish the movie and place it back on the server for any further testing you would like to perform.

FIGURE 20.13

The Remote Debug dialog box prompts you to enter the location of the Flash authoring environment.

FIGURE 20.14

Enter the same password initialized in the Publish Settings dialog box for the file.

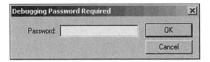

You've now finished debugging a file using many of the debugging techniques included in the Flash Player and the Flash authoring environment. Of course, in the real world your debugging wouldn't finish until you and many of your coworkers approve the project. Testing is important, and it must be done thoroughly. Make sure you let as many people use the project as possible before calling your project complete.

Proper debugging involves many steps. Furthermore, these steps begin when your project begins, not simply at the end of your project. Using tools in Flash, you can decipher which problems are occurring. What's more, you can slow the speed at which Flash reads each line of code to determine which objects are holding variable and property values at runtime. This will allow you to determine whether your interactivity map at the beginning of your project is matching the logic that Flash interprets in your ActionScript.

Advanced Interactivity

By Matt Pizzi

IN THIS CHAPTER

- Creating Draggable Objects
- Creating Interactivity with the Mouse
- Creating Preloaders That Return Accurate Information
- Creating Custom Scrollable Objects
- Creating Dynamic and Draggable Masks

This chapter is devoted to creating interactivity with the end user. Flash design, often-times, is all about how the developer can interact with the end user. This is what pushes Web development forward. Having the ability to interact with users makes the Web more usable and ultimately more enjoyable.

We are going to be looking at ActionScripts that can produce such interactivity. Again, I want to show you general concepts that can be applied to any given project. ActionScript is about learning concepts and then taking those concepts and making them fit to cater to your specific project.

Creating Draggable Objects

Creating an object that the end user can drag is a little tricky because in order for the user to drag an object, it must be a movie clip. You can use clip events that cater to drag-ging movie clip objects; however, the easiest way to create a precise, draggable object is to also make it a button. Therefore, what you need is a button nested inside of a movie clip symbol.

Dragging Objects

In this exercise you are going to create a movie clip that you can drag around the stage. Although this exercise isn't all that advanced, it provides the building blocks for more complex tasks. You can download a completed version of this project called `Gato_Puzzle_Finished.fla`, located at `http://www.flashmxun-leashed.com`. Here are the steps to follow:

1. Create a new document. Choose Modify, Document to change this movie's dimensions to 400 by 400 pixels. Choose any background color you like and change the frame to be 22 frames per second. These settings aren't so important in terms of the functionality of the draggable movie clip. Click OK.

2. Draw a circle on the stage. Choose any fill and stroke color.

3. Highlight the circle by double-clicking it to select both the fill and stroke. Then convert it to a symbol by choosing Insert, Convert to Symbol. Give this symbol a button behavior by choosing the Button radio button. Name this simply **button_drag**. Click OK.

4. Highlight the button on the main timeline and, with it selected, press F8 to convert it to a symbol. This time, give it a movie clip behavior and name it **drag_mc**. Click OK.

At this point, you have a movie clip symbol with a button nested inside of it. Now you need to give the button an action to start dragging the movie clip if it has been pressed and to stop dragging the movie clip when the mouse is released.

5. Double-click the movie clip instance on the stage. This will bring you inside the movie clip symbol editing mode. Once inside this mode, select the button and press F9 to open the Actions panel.

6. Click the plus sign to activate the Actions drop-down menu. Choose Actions, Movie Control, On. For the event handler, choose press from the hint list or just type **press**.

   We're using press here because it's more natural and familiar to computer users. When you click something onscreen, you expect to be able to move it, and when you release the mouse, you expect to stop dragging the selected item.

7. Press Return (Mac) or Enter (Windows) after the last curly bracket in line 1. Notice the auto-format feature automatically indents your text on the next line. In the Action drop-down list, choose Actions, Movie Clip Control, startDrag. You need to add some conditions to this action. First, you need to target a movie clip. Because you want to drag the movie clip you're inside of, the target can simply be this. As for the next condition, type **true** to lock the mouse to the center of the movie clip. By doing this, the center of the movie clip will attach to the tip of the mouse. This means when you're dragging the object, it always looks like you're dragging it from the center.

8. Test the movie. Notice, as shown in Figure 21.1, when you click the object, you begin to drag it.

   To be able to stop dragging the object entails the use of the stopDrag() action.

9. Highlight the last curly bracket in your script. Click the plus in the Actions drop-down menu and choose Actions, Movie Control, On. This will type the on action. Choose release from the hint list menu or just type it.

10. Press Return or Enter after the curly bracket in line 1. Notice the cursor automatically indents. Here, you need the stopDrag action. Click the plus sign in the drop-down menu and choose Actions, Movie Clip Control, stopDrag, or you can just type **stopDrag()**. The final code should look like this:

```
on (press) {
    startDrag(this,1);
}
on (release) {
    stopDrag();
}
```

You'll notice that you don't have to provide a target to stop dragging the object. The stopDrag action specifies to stop the current "drag" action; therefore, you don't need to target the movie clip.

11. Test the movie. Pretty good, huh? Note that you're going to create many different interactions with ActionScript in this chapter that will require you to understand how this exercise works. All exercises from this point on assume you know how to create a draggable object.

FIGURE 21.1

Dragging a movie clip object. Notice the cursor is a finger, representing the drag.

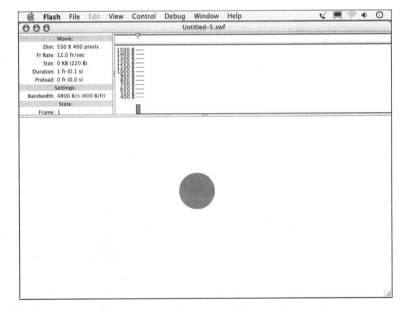

We're now going to take a look at what you can do with draggable objects. One common feature you might want to create is a shopping cart in which you literally drag an object you want to buy into a bin. Also, think about the types of games you could create, such as puzzles, for example. Keep reading, because you're going to create one in the next exercise.

Creating Complex Drag-and-Drop Interactions

In this exercise you're going to learn how to create a jigsaw puzzle using a picture of my cat, Gato. Here's how the puzzle will work: The puzzle pieces will randomly scatter every time the movie is loaded. If the end user places a puzzle piece in the right location (or close to the right location), it will snap in place. Otherwise, the piece will return to its original location. So, here it goes:

1. Navigate to the Unleashed companion Web site located at `http://www.flashmxunleashed.com` and go to the Chapter 21 section. Find the `gato_puzzle.fla` file and download it.

2. Open the `gato_puzzle.fla` file. Figure 21.2 shows a photograph of Gato and a graphic representing the outline for the puzzle.

3. The first thing you're going to do is cut up the picture of Gato to make the separate puzzle pieces. You'll use the puzzle pattern as your guide; think of it as a cookie cutter of sorts.

4. Select the picture of Gato and choose Modify, Break Apart. This will make the photograph of Gato a primitive shape. Drag over the puzzle pattern item and place it right on top of Gato, as shown in Figure 21.3.

5. With the puzzle pattern still selected, choose Modify, Break Apart to make it a primitive item. Click away from the puzzle pattern to deselect it. Perfect! You've just cut Gato up into a bunch of shapes. If you select any piece, you'll notice that it is separate from the rest of the photograph, as shown in Figure 21.4.

6. Now you have to convert each of these puzzle pieces into movie clip symbols by choosing Insert, Convert to Symbol or by pressing F8. Highlight the first puzzle piece in the top-left corner and work your way right. Convert each piece using the name Gato1, Gato2, and so on. Do this until all the puzzle pieces are movie clip symbols. When you're finished, you should end up with 11 puzzle pieces that are all movie clip symbols, as shown in Figure 21.5.

7. Highlight each piece and give it an instance name. Name the first one **gato1**, the second **gato2**, and so on, until each has an instance name. You can name the instance of the movie clip through the Properties Inspector.

8. Once each piece has an instance name, highlight all of them. Note that you can't choose Select All; you have to hold down the Shift key and click each puzzle piece. If you choose Select All, you also select the puzzle outline, which you do not want to do in this case. Once all pieces are selected, hold down the Option (Mac) or Alt (Windows) key and click and drag copies of them to the right, as shown in Figure 21.6. These will act as the drop targets.

9. You now need to move the original puzzle pieces to a separate layer. Select the puzzle pieces as you did in the last step, by holding down the Shift key and selecting each one. Once they're all selected again, cut them by choosing Edit, Cut or by pressing Cmd+X (Mac) or Ctrl+X (Windows).

10. Create a new layer and name it **Puzzle Pieces**. Name the original layer **drop targets**.

11. Turn off the visibility of the Puzzle Pieces layer by clicking the bullet under the eye column in the Layers panel. Notice that the puzzle outline becomes visible. Highlight the outline and group it by pressing Cmd+G (Mac) or Ctrl+G (Windows). Move the outline over the drop targets on the right, as shown in Figure 21.7. Save your file as Gato_Puzzle.fla.

12. Highlight each of the drop target movie clips by clicking them and adding the word *target* to the end of their instance names in the Properties Inspector. For example, the instance name for the first drop target movie clip should now be gato1target. It's important only to add the word *target* with no space, leaving the rest of the name the same. You'll see why as you start working with interactions a bit more; for now, just trust me. Do this for each instance. When naming them, you may also want to choose alpha in the Effect drop-down menu and bring the alpha slider down to 10%. When you're done, all the instances should have a new name and a lower alpha percentage, as shown in Figure 21.8.

13. Double-click each puzzle piece movie clip to enter into movie clip symbol editing mode. You'll notice that once you're inside the symbol, the picture is a primitive object, as shown in Figure 21.9. Select the primitive artwork and press F8 to convert it to a symbol. Make sure you give it a button behavior; this way, you can give the button an action to drag the parent movie clip. Name it **Gato1_button**. Do this for each of the puzzle pieces.

    As we begin to look at some ActionScript for this exercise, you're first going to get one puzzle piece to work properly. Once that happens, you'll apply the script to all the other pieces.

14. Now you're ready to do some scripting. Start off by adding dragging functionality to one of the puzzle pieces. Double-click the first puzzle piece to enter the symbol editing mode. Select the button and give it the following startDrag and stopDrag actions (just like you did in the first exercise):

```
on (press) {
    this.startDrag();
}
```

```
on (release, releaseOutside) {
    stopDrag();
}
```

15. Test the movie. You'll notice that you can drag the puzzle piece, but it appears behind the other pieces. To fix this, you need to change its depth level. Whatever puzzle piece is selected needs to have the highest depth level of all the movie clips. Create a new layer and name it **actions**. On the first frame of the actions layer, create a variable named depthValue and set it equal to 1. Now, every time a puzzle piece is selected, you can add to the variable and then assign a depth level of the selected movie clip to equal that variable.

16. Now you're going to swap the depth level of the selected movie with the current value of the variable depthValue plus 1. Make sure you're inside the movie clip symbol and that you're applying this action to the button. Here's what the code will look like:

```
on (press) {
    _root.depthVaule = _root.depthValue +1;
    this.swapDepths(_root.depthValue);
    this.startDrag();
}
on (release, releaseOutside) {
    stopDrag();
}
```

17. Test the movie. Nice! Each movie clip you select always appears in front.

    Now, how about making the movie clip actually snap to or land in the appropriate location? If the movie clip being dragged comes close to its destination, you want it to snap there, so the end user knows he did something right. The first thing we need to discuss is the drop target property. The drop target property will return an absolute path as to where the instance being dragged has been dropped. You then have to compare that path with the location of the target movie clip instance. You'll compare them using the eval function. If, in fact, the comparison indicates the dropped location is equal to the location of the dragged object, you want to set the dragged movie clip's x and y coordinates to the same as those of the target clip. If the drop target isn't close to being equal to the location of the dragged object, you want the dragged movie clip to return to the original position it was in when the movie first loaded. Phew! Okay. Let's try it. Before we do, make sure you save your file. Choose File, Save As and save the file as Gato_Puzzle2.fla.

It's important to note that in order for the drop target to be considered equal to the dragged object, the cursor must be within the dimensions of the target. In fact, 99 percent of the movie clip can look like it's in the right place, but if the cursor doesn't break the dimensions of the target, it will not be considered equal to the dragged object.

18. After the stopDrag action, you need to create an if statement that checks whether the movie clip that has stopped being dragged is equal to the drop target. Here's the code:

```
on (press) {
    _root.depthVaule = _root.depthValue +1;
    this.swapDepths(_root.depthValue);
    this.startDrag();
}
on (release, releaseOutside) {
    stopDrag();
    if (eval(this._droptarget) == eval("_root."+this._name+"tar-
get")) {
        this._x = eval(this._droptarget)._x;
        this._y = eval(this._droptarget)._y;
    }
}
```

Line 8 contains the if statement. You'll notice that it's checking to see whether the movie clip being dragged is equal to the target movie clip in the left side of the stage (== is the comparison operator to test equality). You'll see that the target is _root, which targets the main timeline. The _name property refers to the instance name of the movie clip, and because you named all the target movie clips the same name as the draggable puzzle pieces, with just the word *target* added, all we have to do is concatenate the instance name with the word *target*. On the next line, if the statement is True, you are setting the x and y coordinates of the dragged instance to equal the x and y coordinates of the target movie clip. This will produce a snapping effect when the user is a few pixels off.

19. Test the movie. It's looking good, but you're still not done.

You'll notice two things: First, if you drag a puzzle piece into the right location, it snaps into place there, but you can start dragging the piece again if you want to. However, we want the piece to get locked down after it's in the right location, so once a piece is in the right place, you can't move it away anymore. Second, what happens if the puzzle piece isn't dropped in the right location? In this case, we'll want the piece to move back into its original location.

20. To lock down the movie clip after it has reached the proper location, all you have to do is set a variable. After setting the x and y coordinates of the dragged movie clip to equal the x and y coordinates of the target movie clip, you'll create a symbol called finish, and you'll have it equal True. Right after the on (press) action you need to create an if statement to see whether the variable finish is equal to True. If it isn't equal to True, you'll carry on with the actions that follow the if statement. If it is equal to True, you don't continue on. The operator to check for inequality is !=. Here's the code:

```
on (press) {
    if (finish != true) {
        _root.depthVaule = _root.depthValue+1;
        this.swapDepths(_root.depthValue);
        startDrag(this);
    }
}
on (release, releaseOutside) {
    stopDrag();
    if (eval(this._droptarget) == eval("_root."+this._name+"tar-
get")) {
        this._x = eval(this._droptarget)._x;
        this._y = eval(this._droptarget)._y;
        finish = true;
    }
}
```

21. Next you need to set a variable of the movie clip's current x and y location when the object is clicked by the end user. Then, in the `release` portion of the script, if the drop target isn't equal to the target movie clip, you want to send it back to the original x and y coordinates set so just the puzzle piece is dragged. Here's the final code:

```
on (press) {
    xpos = this._x;
    ypos = this._y;
    if (finish != true) {
        _root.depthVaule = _root.depthValue+1;
        this.swapDepths(_root.depthValue);
        startDrag(this);
    }
}
on (release, releaseOutside) {
    stopDrag();
    if (eval(this._droptarget) == eval("_root."+this._name+"tar-
get")) {
        this._x = eval(this._droptarget)._x;
        this._y = eval(this._droptarget)._y;
        finish = true;
    } else {
        setProperty(this, _x, xpos);
        setProperty(this, _y, ypos);

    }
}
```

22. Now the logical thing would be to apply this script to each puzzle piece. However, because you never targeted a specific movie clip instance, this clip is very portable. Therefore, you're going to export this script out and save it as an ActionScript file. Then, in each instance of the puzzle piece, you'll use an `include` action to include this `.as` file. First of all, save this file as `Gato_complete.fla` in a folder on your desktop named `puzzle`. If you don't have this folder on your desktop, create it. Once the file has

been saved, open the Actions panel where all the actions are stored. In the panel's submenu, choose Export As File, as shown in Figure 21.10. When you export the file, save it as `puzzleScript.as` in your `puzzle` folder. If you do not save the files in the same directory, you have to type the appropriate path. You can always download this `.as` file from the companion WEB site located at `http://www.flashmxunleashed.com`.

23. Once the file has been exported, type in the following action for each of the nested buttons of the puzzle piece movie clip:

```
#include "puzzleScript.as"
```

24. Test your movie! Of course, the puzzle is pretty easy to complete, because all the puzzle pieces are put together initially. Therefore, you need to create one last script to randomly scatter the pieces on the stage.

25. Highlight one of the movie clips and press F9 to open the Actions panel. You're going to put a script on the movie clip this time. Basically, all you have to do is set some variables that will randomly select a number within the confines of the dimensions where you want to scatter these objects. Then you have to set the x and y properties to equal that variable. The stage is 600 by 355 pixels, and of course you want to scatter the puzzle pieces on the left side of the targets, so that brings the width dimension down to roughly 300 pixels. Therefore, you need to select random numbers from 1 to 300 for each the x and y coordinates. Here's the code:

```
onClipEvent (load) {
    randomxpos = random(300);
    randomypos = random(330);
    setProperty(this, _x, randomxpos);
    setProperty(this, _y, randomypos);
}
```

26. Again, instead of copying this code to all the instances, export the script as `randomScript.as` and save it in your `puzzle` folder. Then on each instance type `#include"randomScript.as"`.

27. Test the movie. Notice that all the puzzle pieces get scattered randomly, as shown in Figure 21.11. Pretty fun, huh? Be sure to visit the Unleashed companion Web site to see other ways you can customize the puzzle to make it more challenging. You can also download a complete working file of this puzzle called `Gato_Puzzle_Finished.fla`.

FIGURE 21.2
A picture of Gato and the puzzle pattern.

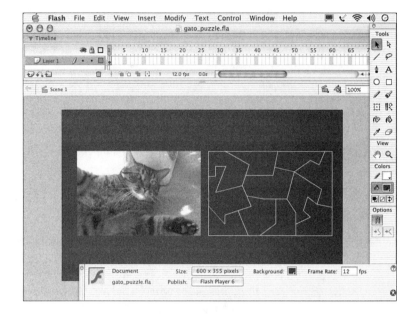

FIGURE 21.3
The puzzle pattern is placed directly over the photograph of Gato.

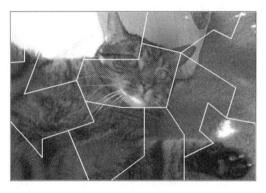

FIGURE 21.4

The puzzle piece selected is separate from the rest of the image.

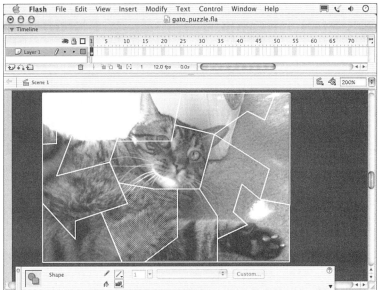

FIGURE 21.5

Eleven movie clip symbols make up the puzzle. Notice that all the movie clip symbols are selected.

FIGURE 21.6

The puzzle pieces have been duplicated.

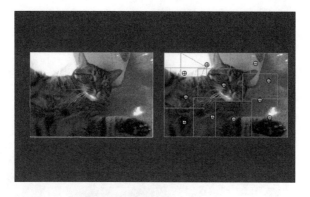

FIGURE 21.7

The puzzle outline has been placed over the drop targets.

FIGURE 21.8

All the puzzle pieces have a lower alpha setting.

FIGURE 21.9

Inside the movie clip symbol is a primitive piece of artwork.

FIGURE 21.10

Choose Export As File from the Actions panel's submenu.

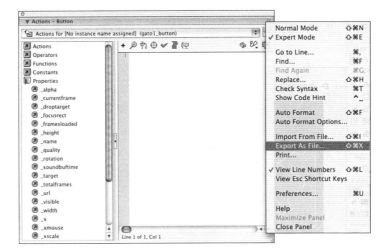

FIGURE 21.11

All the puzzle pieces are randomly placed on the stage.

Creating Interactivity with the Mouse

One of the most popular tricks in Flash development is creating a sliding menu based on the location of the mouse. Usually the menu will move in the opposite direction of the mouse. We're going to look at how to create such a navigation system. This script really doesn't have anything we haven't looked at already; we're going to be using some of the things you learned earlier in the book and apply them to this next exercise. You can download a finished version of this file called `menu_slide.fla` by going to the Unleashed companion Web site and navigating to the Chapter 21 section. Here are the steps to follow:

1. Create a new document. Choose Modify, Document to open the Document Properties dialog box. Set the dimensions of the stage to 400 by 325 pixels. Choose a background color and set the frame rate to 15 frames per second. Click OK.

2. Open the Buttons Common Library by choosing Window, Common Libraries, Buttons.fla. Find any button you like and drag out multiple instances of it until you have enough in a row to equal the width of the stage, as shown in Figure 21.12.

FIGURE 21.12

Several instances of the same button in a line across the stage.

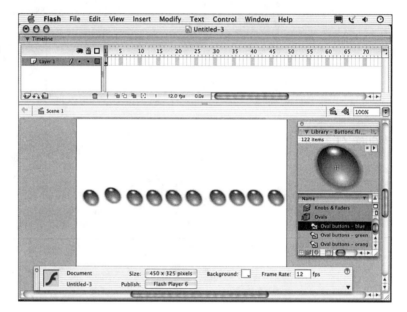

3. With all the instances selected, open the Align panel by choosing Window, Align. If you are not familiar with the Align panel, experiment with different buttons to get acquainted with their behaviors. Align the buttons so that they're spaced evenly, as shown in Figure 21.13.

4. With all the instances highlighted, convert them to a movie clip symbol by pressing F8. This will launch the Convert to Symbol dialog box. Name this symbol **Slide_Nav** and give it a movie clip behavior. Click OK.

5. You're now ready to start applying some actions to the movie clip. You want change the x position of the button movie clip based on the position of the mouse. Basically, what you need to do is find the x position of the mouse and subtract that number from the x position of the movie clip. As you might have guessed, that number is probably going to be too large, so you'll have to divide it as well. Select the movie clip and press F9 on your keyboard to open the Actions panel. Type the

following code (if it seems too complicated, review Chapter 10, "Approaching ActionScript"):

```
onClipEvent (enterFrame) {
    movement = __root.xmouse/18;
    this._x = this._x + movement;
}
```

FIGURE 21.13

The button instances are evenly spaced and aligned with the Align panel.

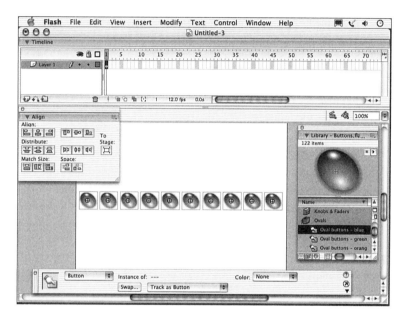

The first line, of course, is the event handler `enterFrame`, which allows these actions to run over and over again. The second line sets a variable to equal the x position of the mouse divided by 18 because the number returned by just the x position of the mouse would might be far too large, so you just cut it down a bit. Finally, the third line sets the x position of the movie clip to equal its current location plus the value of movement.

6. Test the movie. You can see some things work okay, but not quite the way we envisioned. First of all, the navigation bar moves in the same direction as the mouse, so what we can do is make the total value negative. However, then the mouse would only move in one direction, because it will only be getting negative values. Therefore, what you have to do is zero out the location by subtracting using a number that's half the size of the stage. By doing that, you get values on the positive and negative sides of the spectrum, making the navigation bar move in the opposite direction of the mouse, both to the left and right. Here's the code:

```
onClipEvent (enterFrame) {
    movement = ((200 - _root._xmouse)/18)
    this._x = this._x + movement;
}
```

The first line hasn't changed since the last time; in fact, all the changes are on the second line. Notice that you're subtracting the x position of the mouse from 200, which is half the width of the stage, and then dividing that value by 18 to slow the movement down.

7. Test the movie. Looking good. Still one kink we have to work out, though.

   If you move the mouse all the way over to the right and pause for a moment, the navigation bar moves off the stage, and that's bad. We want the navigation bar to move as far right as possible and stop when only one button is left visible. Same goes for the left side.

8. You need to write a script that checks whether the navigation movie clip is moving too far to the left or the right. The first thing you need to do is move the movie clip off the stage so that only one button is showing and then open the Info panel by choosing Window, Info. Here, you can get the x coordinate for the location of the movie clip, as displayed in Figure 21.14. It's important to have the center squared selected when getting the coordinate.

FIGURE 21.14

Get the x coordinate of the navigation movie clip from the info panel.

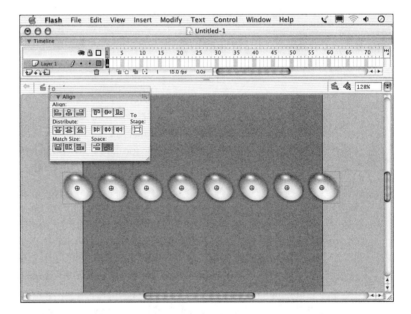

9. You now need to write an `if` statement that checks whether the x position is either less than –171 or greater than 576. Note that your numbers may vary slightly depending on which button you used and what its size is. Here's the code:

```
onClipEvent (enterFrame) {
    movement = ((200-_root._xmouse)/18);
    if (this._x <-171 || this._x >576) {
        movement = 0;
    }
    this._x = this._x+movement;
}
```

The third line is the one that's different here. You'll notice an `if` statement checking to see whether the x position of the movie clip is less than –171, which is the value needed to display only one button on the left side, or greater than 576, which is the value needed to display only one button on the right side (note that `||` stands for logical `OR`). If either one of these conditions is true, the variable movement will be set to 0.

10. Test the movie. It's almost perfect. The only problem with this script is that once the navigation bar reaches the right or left side limit, it stops and doesn't move again after it stops. The is because you are setting the variable movement to 0, and if movement equals 0, the navigation bar is not moving. Therefore, you need to add a condition to check whether the x position is greater than or less than certain values, but at the same time check to make sure that these times the `movement` value is also greater than or less than 0. Here's the final script (note that `&&` is a logical AND):

```
onClipEvent (enterFrame) {
    movement = ((200-_root._xmouse)/18);
    if (((this._x < -171) && (movement < 0))
|| ((this._x > 574) && (movement > 0))) {
        movement = 0;
    }
    this._x = this._x+movement;
}
```

11. Test the movie. Perfect! Figure 21.15 shows that when the navbar moves too far to the left, it will automatically stop.

Moving objects based on the location of the mouse can create some great interactions with your end users. Make sure, if you are using this as a slide navigation tool, that you use it wisely. It's important that the end user understands what it is and how it works. If a tool is not usable, no matter how cool it is, you've failed as a Web designer.

FIGURE 21.15
The navigation bar stops when it moves too far to the left.

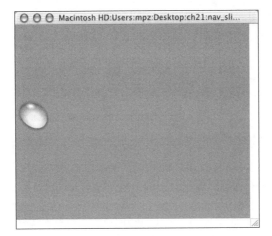

Creating Preloaders That Return Accurate Information

Oftentimes, preloaders are nothing more than eye candy for the end user as a movie is preloading. That's okay, but with ActionScript, we can give the end user the precise amount of the movie that has been downloaded. In the next exercise, you're going to create a preloader that returns a percentage of the amount of a movie that has been downloaded. This will be a streaming percentage, so you can see it increase constantly. To complete and follow along with the next exercise, you will have to download a file from the companion Web site. The file you need to look for under the Chapter 21 section of the site is slide_show.fla.

Creating a Preloader That Streams a Percentage

Now that you have the file downloaded to your computer, go ahead and open it in Flash. You'll notice that the file has six frames. The first frame contains nothing, while the other five have photographs on them, with a set of buttons to navigate through each. The first frame will act as our preloader, so the following five frames will play appropriately. Notice that this document is not divided into scenes. Scenes are generally problematic when scripting a single frame looping statement for preload.

1. In frame 1, choose the test tool and then click once on the stage to insert a blinking cursor. Extend out the size of the text box by grabbing its top-right corner and dragging it to the right until it's about 300 pixels long.

2. With a blinking cursor still in the text box, in the Properties Inspector, change the type to dynamic text using the drop-down menu.

3. In the Var: text field, enter **loadedFile**.

4. Highlight the dynamic text field on the stage and convert it to a movie clip symbol by pressing F8. In the Convert to Symbol dialog box, name this symbol **preloader_mc**. Be sure to give it a movie clip behavior.

5. Test the movie. In the testing environment, choose Window, Bandwidth Profiler. You'll see the spikes for each frame holding a picture, so you'll want these preloaded.

6. Close out of the testing environment and come back to frame 1. You need to write a script on the movie clip. You'll be using the `enterFrame` event handler so that the script can run again and again. You need to evaluate whether the number of bytes loaded equals the total bytes of the movie. If so, you can move out of the preloading scene and into the slideshow scene. If they're not equal, you need to set the variable `loadedFile`, which divides the bytes loaded by the total bytes and then returns a value in decimal format. You'll round that number and multiply it to get a value that looks more like a percentage. Here's the code:

```
OnClipEvent (enterFrame){

        If(_root.getBytesLoaded() == _root.getBytesTotal()){

        gotoAndStop (2);

{else{

        _root.stop

}

percentLoaded=Math.round((_root.getBytesLoaded)))

/(_rot.getBytesTotal()) * 100);

loadedFile = "File is" + percentLoaded + "% loaded.";
```

The first line uses the `enterFrame` event handler. The second line checks whether the bytes loaded are equal to (==) the total bytes of the movie. If the statement is true, the third frame of the movie will play, which happens to be the first frame of the slideshow. The fifth line sets a variable that divides the bytes loaded by the total bytes, and that value is rounded and multiplied by 100. The sixth line sets the variable, which also happens to be the text field on the stage. This will literally display the value in the movie file and is concatenated with the value of the `percentLoaded` variable, which is also concatenated with a literal of "percentage loaded".

7. Test the movie. Be sure to choose Show Streaming under the View menu. The movie is shown in Figure 21.16.

FIGURE 21.16

The streaming percentage during the preload process.

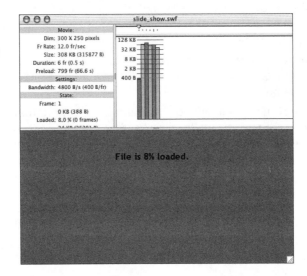

Creating a preloader that returns useful feedback is beneficial to the end user when a download might take a while to complete. You can find a completed copy of this file located on the companion Web site http://www.flashmxunleashed.com.

Creating Custom Scrollable Objects

It's simple to create scrolling dynamic text, but what if the text isn't dynamic? Or what if you have something that you want to scroll that isn't necessarily text? This next exercise will help you create a scroll system for anything.

Creating Custom Scrollbars

For this exercise, you need to set up a scrollbar with two buttons—one that scrolls content up, and one that scrolls content down. You also need to create a draggable box between the two that also scrolls or moves the content up and down, just like an operating system. Basically, you'll be setting the property of the scrollable object to the opposite value of the draggable box. Let's start by building these items. Here are the steps to follow:

1. Create a new document. Choose Insert, New Symbol to launch the New Symbol dialog box. Name the symbol **Scroll** and make sure to give it a movie clip behavior. Click OK, and you'll be placed inside the movie clip symbol editing mode.

2. Still inside the movie clip Scroll, rename layer 1 **Text**. Create a new layer by clicking the Add Layer button at the bottom of the Layers panel. Name this new layer **Scroll bars**. Create one more new layer and name it **Actions**. Make sure the Actions layer is on top, as shown in Figure 21.17.

3. Inside the movie clip symbol Scroll, make sure the Text layer is selected. Open the Unleashed library by choosing Window, Common Libraries, `unleashed.fla`. If you didn't store the Unleashed library in your common libraries but downloaded the file from the companion Web site, choose File, Open As Library and search for the `unleashed.fla` file on your computer. In the Unleashed library, double-click the `movies` folder and drag out an instance of Dylan_Thomas, as shown in Figure 21.18.

FIGURE 21.17

The three layers, with the Actions layer on top.

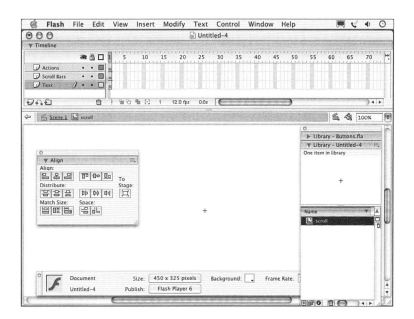

FIGURE 21.18
*Place an instance
of the
Dylan_Thomas
movie clip on the
stage.*

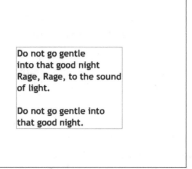

Do not go gentle
into that good night
Rage, Rage, to the sound
of light.

Do not go gentle into
that good night.

Creating Dynamic and Draggable Masks

New in Flash MX is the ability to create a dynamic mask. This means you can use any movie clip instance to mask out any other movie clip instance.

Dynamic Masks

For this exercise, you're going to need a bitmap graphic. If you don't have a bitmap graphic, you can always download a picture of the chicken car on the Unleashed companion Web site. Once you've done this, follow these steps:

1. Create a new document. Import the bitmap graphic by choosing File, Import and locating the file on your computer. Now choose Open. Notice the bitmap is shown on the stage (see Figure 21.19).

2. Select the bitmap and press F8 on your keyboard to convert it to a symbol. In the Convert to Symbol dialog box, name the symbol **Graphic** and make sure you choose the Movie Clip radio button. Click OK.

3. With the new movie clip symbol selected, give it an instance name in the Properties Inspector. Name it **graphic**.

4. Choose the Oval tool in the Tools panel and draw a circle off the stage. If you draw the circle on top of the bitmap, you won't see it because it will disappear behind the bitmap. It's better to draw the shape away from the graphic, as shown in Figure 21.20.

5. After drawing the circle, select it and press F8 to convert it to symbol. In the Convert to Symbol dialog box, name the symbol **circle** and give it a movie clip behavior. Click OK.

6. With the circle selected, press F9 to open the Actions panel. In the Actions panel, open the Actions menu and choose Objects, Movie, Movie Clip, Methods, setMask. Notice the red highlight in the script, as shown in Figure 21.21. Here in the red highlighted area, you have to target which movie clip will be masked. In this case, it will be graphic. In parentheses, type in the name of the movie clip to use as the mask. Here's the code:

```
onClipEvent (enterFrame) {
    _root.graphic.setMask(this);
}
```

7. Test the movie. In Figure 21.22, the circle movie clip is masking out the bitmap movie clip.

8. Close out of the testing mode. You now want to make this movie clip draggable. Double-click the movie clip to enter the movie clip symbol editing mode.

9. Inside the symbol editing mode, notice that the circle is a primitive shape. Select it and press F8 to convert it to a button symbol. In the Convert to Symbol dialog box, name the symbol **button1** and give it a button behavior. Click OK.

10. With the new button symbol selected, press F9 to open the Actions panel. You can now follow steps 6 through 10 of the draggable objects exercise in this chapter or you can type the following code:

```
on (press) {
    startDrag(this, true);
}

on (release) {
    stopDrag();
}
```

11. Test the movie. As shown in Figure 21.23, you can now drag the movie clip anywhere within the Flash movie.

Note

Visit http://www.flashmxunleashed.com to see a QuickTime movie explaining this concept further.

FIGURE 21.19

The bitmap graphic on the stage.

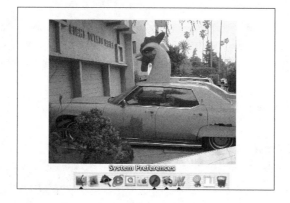

FIGURE 21.20

Draw the circle away from the bitmap.

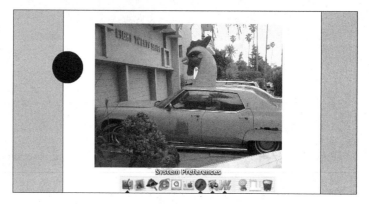

FIGURE 21.21

Notice the high-light in the ActionScript.

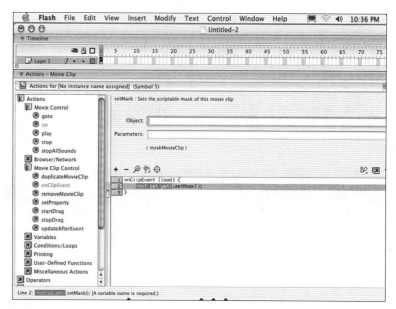

FIGURE **21.22**

The circle movie clip is masking out the bitmap movie clip.

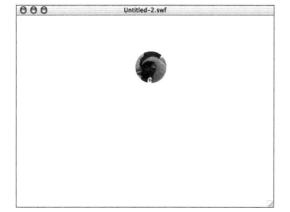

FIGURE **21.23**

The circle movie clip is draggable.

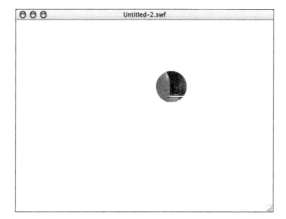

The dynamic mask is a new feature in Flash MX. It offers tremendous flexibility in your development because you do not need to designate certain layers to be mask or masked layers. You can download a finished example of this exercise at the companion Web site. The file is `dynamic_mask.fla`.

CHAPTER 22

Interfacing with JavaScript

By Matt Pizzi

IN THIS CHAPTER

- Creating a Pop-up Window
- Triggering an Alert Dialog Box
- Having Fun with JavaScript

Sometimes in Flash you may find it necessary to have the Flash player call or trigger a JavaScript with the HTML document in which the Flash file resides. This can open up a whole new world of possibilities. Such techniques aren't used all that often; for the most part, if you need Flash to perform a task, you can probably come up with some ActionScript to cater to your needs. However, there is always that situation where you may need to call a JavaScript.

Creating a Pop-up Window

The first topic we're going to look at is probably the most practical application for using ActionScript to communicate with JavaScript—opening a pop-up browser window. This has to be done in JavaScript, because JavaScript can talk directly to the Web browser, whereas ActionScript cannot.

Creating a Pop-up Window Using JavaScript

First, you need to create a document that will contain the content for the pop-up window. If you use an HTML editor such as Dreamweaver or GoLive, you can create an HTML page here. The pop-up can even be a Flash movie. You'll find some files you can download and use from the companion Web site. This will save you some time in preparing for this exercise. Here are the steps to follow:

1. Open the `start.fla` file, as shown in Figure 22.1.

2. Just so you are familiar with the file that will be used in the pop-up window, open the file `video.html` that you downloaded from `http://www.flashmxunleashed.com`. Figure 22.2 shows that this is an HTML document with a QuickTime movie embedded in it.

3. With the `start.fla` file open, choose File, Publish Settings to open the Publish Settings dialog box, as shown in Figure 22.3.

4. Make sure the HTML box is checked and then click the HTML tab. In the HTML tab, you can leave everything set to the defaults.

5. Publish the movie to create the SWF file and the HTML document. In the next step, you'll add some JavaScript to the HTML document Flash generated.

6. You need to write a JavaScript within the HTML document that is going to house your main SWF file to create the pop-up window. I don't want to get into a detailed explanation of the JavaScript here. You'll probably have a good idea of what the script does based on the ActionScript exposure you've had in the last few chapters. This is actually a simple script—it just uses an `open` method. Here's the JavaScript code that needs to be added to the HTML document:

```
<SCRIPT language="JavaScript">
    function popUp (url, name, attributes)
    {
        window.open(url, name, attributes);
    }
</SCRIPT>
```

Just to play it safe, here's the entire HTML document with the JavaScript:

```
<HTML>
<HEAD>
-
<TITLE>:QuickTime Movie:</TITLE>
<SCRIPT language="JavaScript">
    function popUp (url, name, attributes)
    {
        window.open(url, name, attributes);
    }
</SCRIPT>
</HEAD>
<BODY bgcolor="#FFFFFF">
<OBJECT classid="clsid:D27CDB6E-AE6D-11cf-96B8-444553540000"
 codebase="http://download.macromedia.com/pub/
shockwave/cabs/flash/swflash.cab#version=6,0,0,0"
 WIDTH="550" HEIGHT="400" id="start" ALIGN="">
 <PARAM NAME=movie VALUE="start.swf">
<PARAM NAME=quality VALUE=high>
<PARAM NAME=bgcolor VALUE=#FFFFFF>
<EMBED src="start.swf" quality=high
bgcolor=#FFFFFF  WIDTH="550" HEIGHT="400" NAME="start" ALIGN=""
 TYPE="application/x-shockwave-flash"
PLUGINSPAGE="http://www.macromedia.com/go/getflashplayer"></EMBED
>
```

```
</OBJECT>

</BODY>

</HTML>
```

Now that you have this script inside the HTML document that start.swf is nested in, you can call that JavaScript from within the Flash movie using the getUrl action.

7. Open the start.fla file in Flash again. Select the button next to the label Click to Play Movie. You need to give this button an action to call the JavaScript method inside the HTML document.

8. Press F9 to open the Actions panel with the button selected. Using the plus sign button to access the Actions drop-down menu, choose Actions, Movie Control, On. Choose either Press or Release for the event handler.

9. Place a blinking cursor after the curly bracket in line 1 and press Return (Mac) or Enter (Windows) to advance the cursor down to the next line. In the Actions drop-down menu, choose Actions, Browser/Network, getUrl. This will type in the getUrl action. For the conditions, you need to fill in all the parameters for the JavaScript popUp method. Here is the code:

```
on (press) {
    getURL("javascript;popUp ('video.html',"+" 'Video',
'toolbar=no, location=no, "+" directories=no,
status=no, menubar=no, "+" scrollbars=no, resizable=0,
height=300, "+" width=3250, top=50, left=50')");
}
```

The getURL action applies these conditions to the JavaScript popUp method. Video.html is the name of the file, Video is the name of the window, and the rest of the parameters set the window to be either True or False. Oftentimes when using this type of pop-up window, you will not have a status bar, scrollbar, resize handles, and location bar, and you'll set an absolute height and width for the dimensions of the window. This way, it looks more like a window and less like a Web browser. Figure 22.4 displays the anatomy of the Web browser window.

10. Test the movie in a Web browser. Notice that when you click the button, the window pops up just like in Figure 22.5.

11. You can also have this pop-up window move to specific x and y coordinates. Instead of having the window appear and cover important content in the Web site, you can move it off to the side a bit. The code is fairly simple. Open the `video.html` file. Before the closing head tag (`</head>`), type in this code:

```
<script language="JavaScript">
    window.moveTo (500,400);
</script>
```

I decided to position the pop-up window at 500x and 400y. Feel free to set these coordinates to whatever is best for your situation.

12. Test the movie. You'll notice that the document pops up in the same location initially, but after a brief moment you'll see it change to the new coordinates.

22

INTERFACING WITH JAVASCRIPT

FIGURE 22.1

Open start.fla *and work with this file.*

FIGURE 22.2

This document will be the window that the JavaScript will pop up.

FIGURE 22.3
*The Publish
Settings dialog
box.*

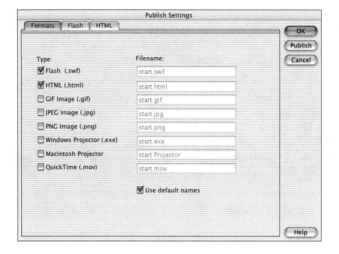

Button Bar   Location Bar   Scroll Bar

FIGURE 22.4
*The anatomy of a
browser window.*

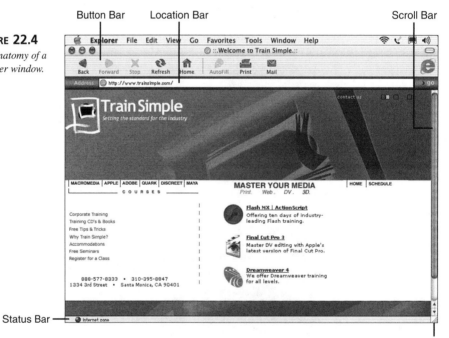

Status Bar

Resize Handles

FIGURE 22.5

The window pops up in front of the main movie. This is Flash talking to the JavaScript within the HTML document.

Triggering an Alert Dialog Box

You might want to trigger an alert dialog box for many different reasons. Say, for example, you're checking passwords, and an end user's password doesn't match up. In this case, you could fire off an alert dialog box. This is especially true when you're dealing with sites that are not entirely built in Flash. Sites that combine Flash animation with traditional HTML design may find this very useful. If the majority of a site is HTML, but the navigation system is built in Flash, then if something needs attention, popping up a Flash dialog box may seem a bit weird. This is where you could call a JavaScript method from within the small Flash piece of the Web page.

Creating an Alert Message

In this exercise, you're just going to create a new document and place a button on the stage. When you click that button, an alert dialog box will pop up. In a real-world situation, you probably wouldn't have this functionality on just a button, but it could be part of a condition in another script. Say, for example, you have an online quiz that keeps the user's score. If, for some reason, the end user's score isn't high enough, you could trigger an alert dialog box telling the user to retake the test to proceed.

This exercise will help you get some of this functionality down. To begin, follow these steps:

1. Create a new document and open the Document Properties dialog box by choosing Modify, Document. In the Document Properties dialog box, change the dimensions of the stage to equal 400 by 300 pixels. In this document, you're going to ask the end user some questions. You're going to store the answers in a variable.

2. With static text, type in the question **Do you prefer Pepsi or Coke?**.

3. Now you need to place three buttons next to the question so the user can answer it by choosing either Pepsi, Coke, or None. Open the Buttons Common Library by choosing Window, Common Libraries, Buttons. Find three buttons of your choice and drag them out onto the stage. Again, with static text, type a small label under each of these buttons, as shown in Figure 22.6.

4. You'll ask one more question. Type the question **Would you prefer to surf or ski?**. Then drag out three instances of the button and label them Surf, Ski, and None, respectively. Now you should have two questions with six buttons, as shown in Figure 22.7.

5. Create a dynamic text box on the stage and give it a variable name of **message**. Make sure the text is white because you don't want the end user to see it. You must have the text box (you can't just have a variable) because the JavaScript is going to use this text box.

6. Highlight the first button, which is the Pepsi button. Press F9 to open the Actions panel. When this button is pressed, you want to set the variable message. Therefore, in the Actions window, type

    ```
    on(press) {
    message = "Pepsi is good."
    }
    ```

    You'll notice the text is in quotes. Therefore, this is what will literally show up—nothing has to be evaluated, and no math needs to be applied to it.

7. Repeat step 6 for the other two top buttons. Make up any sentence you want the variable to equal. (Try to make it funnier than mine.) Watch the length of your text, though, because large amounts of text could end up causing problems.

8. Now you have to apply similar actions to the last set of buttons. However, the only difference is what the variables are going to equal. Because this is the second question, that means there is a good chance the user answered the first one already, and you don't want to delete that answer.

Rather, you want to add to it with whatever answer the user comes up with for this question. Therefore, highlight the Surf button and press F9 to open the Actions panel. The code is almost the same but with one small difference. Here's the code:

```
on(press) {
Message = message + ", and you surf too! Cool dude."
}
```

The only difference here is preserving what the variable may already equal from the first question and just concatenating the two answers. You'll notice, however, the word message on the right side of the equals sign is not in quotes. This is because you want the value of message, not literally the word *message* typed out. Quotes signify literals, remember.

9. Repeat step 8 until the other two buttons have actions applied to them.

10. Drag out one more button and put the label Done next to it, as shown in Figure 22.8.

11. With the Done button selected, press F9 to open the Actions panel. Give this button an action that will trigger a JavaScript, and use the contents of the variable to fill the alert dialog box. Here is what the code should look like:

```
on (release) {
    a = "javascript:showAlert('"+_root.comment +"')";
    getURL(a);
}
```

12. Save the document as alert.

13. Now you need to Publish this document. Choose File, Publish Settings to open the Publish Settings dialog box. Make sure the HTML and Flash formats are selected and then click the Publish button. You're almost done.

14. Now you need to edit the HTML to include the JavaScript method for the alert dialog box. Open the HTML document that Flash created when you published the movie in any HTML editor. The HEAD portion of the HTML should look like this:

```
<HTML>
<HEAD>
<meta http-equiv=Content-Type content="text/html;  charset=ISO-8859-1">
```

```
<TITLE>alert_try</TITLE>
<SCRIPT = "javascript">
     function showAlert (message) {
          alert (message);
     }
</SCRIPT>
</HEAD>
```

15. Test the movie. It's shown in Figure 22.9.

As you can see, it's fairly easy to incorporate JavaScript functions into your ActionScript. Calling them using the `GetUrl` action allows Flash to communicate with the browser. You can download the completed file for this exercise on the companion Web site, located at `http://www.flashmxunleashed.com`.

FIGURE 22.6

The three labeled buttons after the question.

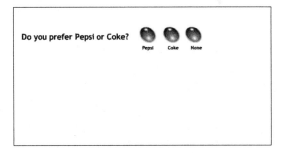

FIGURE 22.7

Now there are two questions with six buttons.

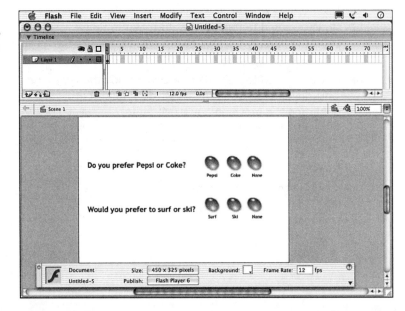

FIGURE 22.8

The Done button.

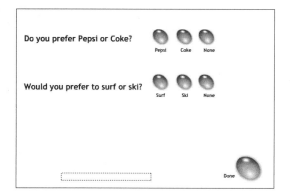

FIGURE 22.9

The ActionScript is interfacing with the JavaScript.

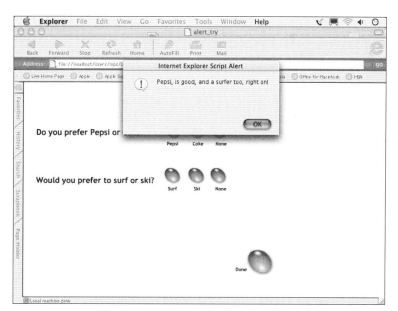

Having Fun with JavaScript

The great thing about ActionScript and JavaScript is that they're both fun to work with. You can do a lot of cool stuff with both scripting languages. However, they are really designed to do two different things. ActionScript is for Flash, and it provides Flash with incredible power in terms of interactivity and usability. JavaScript is pretty similar but is geared for Web browsers and client-side scripting tasks by Web surfers. In the next exercise, you are going to shake your browser window (the JavaScript part) based on two objects colliding (the ActionScript part).

Shaking the Browser Window

In this exercise you're going to place two objects on the stage. When you drag one of the objects on top of the other, the browser window will start shaking. It's a pretty cool effect. Here are the steps:

1. Let's start off by creating the collision detection. You need to create a draggable object, and when that object is dropped on or collides with another object on the stage, the browser will shake.

2. Create a movie clip circle. Apply some hit test actions to it for the collision. Here's the code:

```
on (press) {
    startDrag("");
    orig_x = this._x;
    orig_y = this._y;
}
on (release) {
    stopDrag();
    if (this.hitTest(_root.rightTarget)) {
        this._x = _x;
        this._y = _y;
    } else {
        this._x = orig_x;
        this._y = orig_y;
    }
}
```

Test the movie and notice that the circle is draggable.

3. Create another movie clip symbol, this time making the shape a square. Save the movie as shake.fla by choosing File, Save As.

4. Publish the Flash movie. To publish it, choose File, Publish Settings. This will open a dialog box. In this dialog, be sure to have the HTML box checked. Click Publish.

5. Now we'll write the JavaScript code in an HTML document that Flash created when the document was Published. You can type the code as you read it, which is actually the best way to learn, or you can download the code the Unleashed companion Web site. It's called browser_shake.js.

Here's the browser-shaking code courtesy of `Javascript.internet.com`:

```
<SCRIPT LANGUAGE="JavaScript1.2">
<!-- Free JavaScript - http://javascript.internet.com -->
    function shake_xy(n) {
    if (self.moveBy) {
        for (i = 10; i > 0; i--) {
            for (j = n; j > 0; j--) {
            self.moveBy(0,i);
            self.moveBy(i,0);
            self.moveBy(0,-i);
            self.moveBy(-i,0);
            }
          }
        }
      }
    function shake_x(n) {
    if (self.moveBy) {
        for (i = 10; i > 0; i--) {
            for (j = n; j > 0; j--) {
            self.moveBy(i,0);
            self.moveBy(-i,0);
            }
          }
        }
      }
    function shake_y(n) {
    if (self.moveBy) {
        for (i = 10; i > 0; i--) {
            for (j = n; j > 0; j--) {
            self.moveBy(0,i);
            self.moveBy(0,-i);
```

```
            }
          }
        }
      }
      //-->
      </SCRIPT>
```

4. To have the browser shake, drag the green circle into the green square. The browser will begin to shake.

This type of interaction with JavaScript offers unlimited possibilities in your Flash Web development. In this chapter, we reviewed some basic examples to get your feet wet, but all the concepts we covered can apply to any type of JavaScript interaction. For example, you can have Flash communicate with cookies, which offers many benefits, especially for e-commerce applications.

You can download a finished working file of this last exercise at the companion Web site, `http://www.flashmxunleashed.com`.

CHAPTER 23

Creating a Flash Game

By Randy Osborn

IN THIS CHAPTER

- Create the Basics First
- Add Elements to the Game
- Arrays in Games
- Use External Files for Easily Updating Games
- Save Games and High Scores
- Final Words of Wisdom

Although Flash started out as a way to add animation and life to a Web page, it has slowly become the de facto standard for creating all things interactive on the Web. Even games are much easier to create now that Flash can be programmed using basic principles of object-oriented programming. Flash MX gives you virtually unlimited control for creating games and interactive animations. This chapter covers some of the basics as well as more advanced techniques of game programming in Flash, giving you the power to take your games to the next level.

For the first part of this chapter, we'll create a top-scrolling, arcade-style game that illustrates many of the techniques used in programming for a variety of games—techniques ranging from multiple-object collision detection, to dynamic creation and destruction of objects and enemies, to quick and simple player control. So, let's get right into the game-creation process.

Create the Basics First

Whenever I create a game, I build the engine first and the graphics for the finished product second. This does a few things for me. First, it allows me to focus on creating a good game—pretty graphics won't make a good game, but they can make a good game better. Second, building the basic engine for the game allows me to prove that it can be done. Just about any game can be made in Flash, but sometimes a seemingly simple idea can be very difficult to create. By building the engine first, you don't waste your time making graphics for a game concept that may change along the way. Finally, it forces me to make my code as dynamic as possible. By programming with dynamic code, you allow graphics to be changed and game play to be tweaked without having to go in and modify a bunch of code every time a change is needed.

Movie Setup

You will start by creating a three-frame movie that is 480 by 640 pixels and has a frame rate of 36 fps. I recommend using a higher frame rate than the default frame rate of 12 fps because movement will appear much smoother. This happens because the code being used to move objects is evaluated at a faster rate. Next, create two layers. Name the bottom layer **player ship** and the top layer **actions**. The game we'll create has at least three very basic elements: a player ship, the player ship's ammo, and enemy ships. Therefore, we'll start by creating those elements. You can create these objects throughout the exercise yourself or use the ones in the FLA (`shooter.fla`) for this project, which can be downloaded from <INSERT DOWNLOAD SITE HERE>.

Initialize Variables in the First Frame

Insert a keyframe on the first frame of the actions layer by selecting the first frame and then choosing Insert, Blank Keyframe. Put the following code on the first frame of the actions layer. This will define and initialize some variables we'll be using later:

```
// initialize global variables
playerLives = 3;
playerSpeed = 10;
ammoSpeed = 15;
newAmmo = 50;
enemySpeed = 10;
maxEnemies = 10;
stageWidth = 480;
stageHeight = 640;
```

Now insert a blank keyframe on the second frame of the actions layer. We'll use this frame to define the functions we'll be calling later on. Finally, insert a blank keyframe on the third frame of the actions layer and place a `stop()` action on the third frame.

Player Ship Movement

The only object we will place on the stage to begin with is the player ship. You can now create the player ship movie clip from scratch or use the one provided in the FLA for this exercise. Place it somewhere near the bottom center of the stage on the first frame of the `player ship` layer and give it an instance name of **ship**. Your setup should look something like what's shown in Figure 23.1.

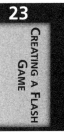

FIGURE 23.1

Player ship setup.

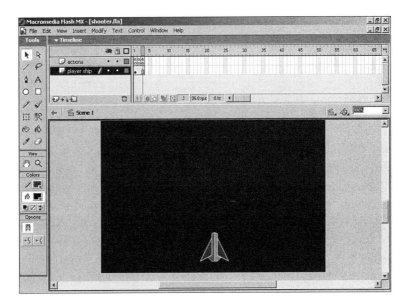

Now you can attach the code that controls player movement directly to the player ship movie clip. To do this, select the player ship movie clip on the stage and type the code into the Actions window. Be sure the movie clip is selected, not the frame on the main movie timeline. Here's the code:

```
onClipEvent (load) {
    this.onEnterFrame = function() {
    if (Key.isDown (Key.RIGHT) && this._x < _root.stageWidth - this._width/2 ) {
        this._x += _root.playerSpeed;
        }
    if (Key.isDown(Key.LEFT) && this._x > this._width/2) {
        this._x -= _root.playerSpeed;
        }
    if (Key.isDown(Key.UP) && this._y > this._height/2) {
        this._y -= _root.playerSpeed;
        }
    if (Key.isDown(Key.DOWN) && this._y < _root.stageHeight - this._height/2) {
        this._y += _root.playerSpeed;
        }
    }
}
```

Let's break this code up a bit and look at it. We'll start with the first line:

```
onClipEvent (load) {
}
```

This tells Flash to evaluate all the code following it, one time, when this movie clip enters the stage.

```
onEnterFrame = function() {
}
```

This tells Flash to evaluate all the code following it continuously at the movie frame rate, while the movie clip is on the stage. This is perfect for player movement, because it is constantly being evaluated and offers a quick response to any key presses.

```
if (Key.isDown (Key.RIGHT) && this._x < _root.stageWidth - this._width/2 ) {
    this._x += _root.playerSpeed;
    }
```

This part of the code does a few things. First, it tells Flash to look for the right-arrow key being pressed; then it tells Flash to check whether the x position of the player's ship is within the boundaries of the stage. It does this by getting the width of the player ship and dividing that by two (`this._width/2`), because the x position of the player's ship is measured from its center point. It then subtracts that value from the width of the stage, which is represented here by the global variable `_root.stageWidth`, which we defined on the first frame of the movie by setting it equal to 480, the width of the movie. If both of these conditions are met, Flash moves the player ship movie clip that these actions are attached to, this, on its x axis by setting its x position equal to its current value, plus the value defined by _root.playerSpeed in the first frame of the movie. By using the previous variables instead of literal numbers, we allow ourselves to change the shape, size, and speed of the player ship and the dimensions of the final game without needing to go in and replace a lot of "hard-coded" numbers with new numbers.

```
if (Key.isDown(Key.LEFT) && this._x > this._width/2) {
    this._x -= _root.playerSpeed;
    }
if (Key.isDown(Key.UP) && this._y > this._height/2) {
    this._y -= _root.playerSpeed;
    }
if (Key.isDown(Key.DOWN) && this._y < _root.stageHeight - this._height/2) {
    this._y += _root.playerSpeed;
    }
```

These three if statements check for the left-, up-, and down-arrow keys being pressed and whether the constraints of the player's ship are within the stage dimensions. UP and DOWN use the property _height to check the height of the player's ship and _root.stageHeight, which is defined in the first frame as 640, the height of the movie.

You can now save your version and test the movie. Use the arrow keys to move the ship around the screen.

Attach Enemies and Make Them Move

The next element to add is the enemy ships. Create two movie clips—name one **enemy ship** and name the other **enemy ship code**. The enemy ship movie clip will contain the enemy ship code movie clip on its first frame. We'll place enemy ship on the stage dynamically using attachMovie. In order to use attachMovie, you must give the movie clip you will be attaching a *linkage* name. This can be found in the "Advanced" section when you create your movie clip, as shown in Figure 23.2.

Alternatively, you can add the linkage name after the movie clip is created by selecting Linkage from the Library menu. In this case, we have a movie clip called enemy ship and the linkage name is enemy. You want to be sure you select Export for ActionScript and Export in First Frame in the Linkage menu. This makes the movie clip accessible at the start of the game and allows Flash to place it on the stage dynamically. A very effective way of using attachMovie is to make an empty "container" movie clip that holds another movie clip that has all the code you need to use attached to it. For this game, we have created the movie clip enemy ship, which contains the movie clip enemy ship code on its first frame. The enemy ship code movie clip contains the actual graphic image of the enemy ship that you want to use. Next, we'll attach all the enemy movement code to it. This way, every time you call the attachMovie clip action to attach the enemy ship code movie clip to the stage, they'll all be using the same movement code.

FIGURE 23.2

*Click "Advanced"
to reveal linkage
options.*

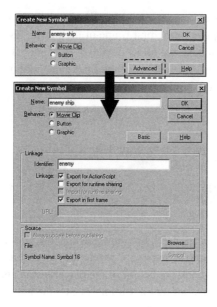

To attach the movement code, you need to edit enemy ship and put the movement code
on the enemy ship code movie clip that is in the first frame. Select the enemy ship code
movie clip and add this code to the Actions window:

```
onClipEvent (load) {
    randomSpeed = random (3);
    this.onEnterFrame = function() {
        _parent._y += _root.enemySpeed + randomSpeed;
        _parent._x += randomSpeed;
        if (_parent._y>_root.stageHeight +_parent._height*2) {
            _parent.removeMovieClip();
        }
    }
}
```

Let's look at the code a little closer. Like with the player movement code, the
`onClipEvent (load)` action evaluates the code that follows it, one time, when the movie
clip appears on the stage. Here's the next line of code:

```
randomSpeed = random (3);
```

This creates a variable we can use to add a little variety to the movement of the enemy
ships. We then use the `onEnterFrame = function()` action to continuously evaluate
the following code while the movie clip is present in the frame:

```
_parent._y += _root.enemySpeed + randomSpeed;
_parent._x += randomSpeed;
```

The first line moves the enemy ship across the y axis of the stage at the rate set by `_root.enemySpeed`, plus the random value we created when this movie clip entered the stage and assigned to the variable `randomSpeed`. The second line adds a little more variety to the movement of the enemy ships by using the same random variable that's used for speed to move an enemy ship just slightly across the x axis as it flies towards the player's ship.

```
if (_parent._y>_root.stageHeight +_parent._height*2) {
    _parent.removeMovieClip();
    }
```

Finally, this `if` statement checks the location of the movie clip on the y axis of the main stage. If the movie clip has moved two times its height in pixels below the bottom of the stage, then this statement removes the movie clip.

Now that we've created the enemy ships and written the code that moves these ships in the right direction, we need a way to place them on the stage. To do this, create an empty movie clip and call it **enemy generator**. This movie clip will not be seen in the final movie, but we will need it on the stage in order for the final movie to work properly. Place this movie clip at the top of the stage and double-click it to edit it. On the first frame, you can create text at the center point that identifies it as "enemy generator." This way, you can always identify it from the main stage as the enemy generator. Keeping track of "blank" movie clips by identifying them with text on the first frame becomes important later when you might have many more "blank" clips placed around the stage (see Figure 23.3).

FIGURE 23.3

Labeling off-screen movie clips with text on the first frame will help keep things organized on the stage.

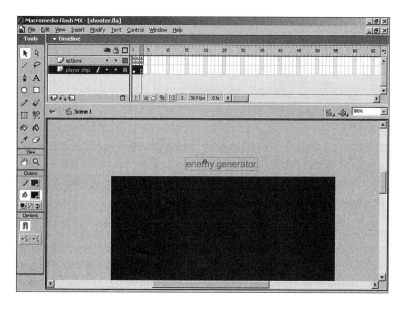

On the 16th frame of the enemy generator movie clip, insert a key frame and add the following action:

```
_root.createEnemy();
```

This will call the function `createEnemy` every time the playhead hits this frame (approximately twice a second in this 36-fps movie). This frame length can later be adjusted to create more or fewer enemies on the stage. We'll now create the function `createEnemy` on the second frame of the main movie timeline. We'll put this function in the second frame, because in order for a function to work properly, it must be on a frame that the Flash movie has loaded and the playhead has passed through.

On the second frame of the main movie timeline, put the following code to define the `createEnemy` function:

```
function createEnemy() {
    newEnemy++;
    if (newEnemy == maxEnemies) {
        newEnemy = 1;
    }
    _root.attachMovie("enemy", "enemy"+newEnemy, newEnemy);
    setProperty(eval("enemy"+newEnemy), _x, _root.stageWidth-random
➥(_root.stageWidth));
    setProperty(eval("enemy"+newEnemy), _y, -eval("enemy"+newEnemy).
➥_height/2));
}
```

Here's how the code breaks down:

```
newEnemy++;
```

This increments the variable `newEnemy`, setting it to its current value (+1). We will use this variable to give the newly attached movie clips unique names. Here's the next bit of code:

```
if (newEnemy == maxEnemies) {
    newEnemy = 1;
    }
```

This checks whether the new enemy being attached is equal to the value of `maxEnemies`, which we have set to 10 on the first frame of the movie. If it does equal 10, then 10 enemies have been created, and we can set the variable `newEnemy` back to 1 and continue attaching movies in this cycle.

```
_root.attachMovie("enemy", "enemy"+newEnemy, newEnemy);
```

This is the `attachMovie` code that I mentioned earlier. `_root.attachMovie` indicates that we are attaching this movie clip to the root level of our movie and not to another movie clip. `"enemy"` is the unique linkage name we gave the enemy ship movie clip earlier so that Flash can find this movie clip in the Library. `"enemy"` + `newEnemy` gives the attached movie clip a unique instance name, and `newEnemy` tells Flash at which depth level to attach this new instance of the movie clip.

Now that we have identified which movie we are attaching and have given it a new name, we need to give it coordinates and place it on the stage. This is what the following code is for:

```
setProperty(eval("enemy"+newEnemy), _x, _root.stageWidth-random
➥(_root.stageWidth));
setProperty(eval("enemy"+newEnemy), _y, -eval("enemy"+newEnemy)._height/2));
```

The first line tells Flash to set the x position of `eval("enemy"+newEnemy)`, the newly created instance of the movie clip, equal to the width of the stage, minus a random number that can be between zero and the value of `_root.stageWidth`. This will place the enemy ships randomly across the top of the stage. The second line sets the y position of the newly created enemy ship just above the top of the stage, based on half the total height of the enemy ship.

Now the movement and placement code for the enemy ships is complete. You can now save and test the movie. The enemy ships are now flying toward the player's ship, and you can use the arrow keys to dodge them.

Make the Player's Ship Shoot

Now that enemy ships are flying toward your player's ship, you've got to have a way to shoot them down. First, we'll create the player's ammo in a way that's similar to how we created the enemy ships. We'll build a "container" movie clip that holds another movie clip with the movement code attached to it.

Create a new movie clip using Insert, New Symbol and call it **ammo**. In the Linkage menu, give it the unique name, **ammo**, and be sure you select Export for ActionScript and Export in First Frame, the same as you did when you created the enemy ship. Then edit the ammo movie clip and put your ammo code movie clip on the first frame. You may create the ammo code movie clip now by using Insert, New Symbol and then drawing your graphic on the first frame of the new movie clip, or you can use the graphic provided in the FLA for this exercise. The ammo code movie clip should have the graphic for the ammo in it. Now that it is on the first frame of the ammo movie clip, select it and add the following code in the actions window:

```
onClipEvent (load) {
    this.onEnterFrame = function() {
        _parent._y -= _root.ammoSpeed;
        for (i=0; i<_root.maxEnemies; i++) {
            if (_parent.hittest("_root.enemy" + i)) {
```

23

CREATING A FLASH GAME

```
        trace ("HIT");
      }
   if (_parent._y <-10) {
      _parent.removeMovieClip();
      }
   }
 }
}
```

The most important part of this code is the `for` loop. We have already used the other code on the enemy ship code movie clip to move the clip across the stage and remove it when it leaves the stage. Let's examine the `for` loop:

```
for (i=0; i<_root.maxEnemies; i++) {
   if (_parent.hittest("_root.enemy" + i)) {
      trace ("HIT");
   }
```

This `for` loop constantly examines whether or not this movie clip is touching an enemy ship movie clip. By using the `for` loop in the `onEnterFrame` action, we continuously run the statement in the loop many times a second, making it a reliable way to check for a hit between the two movie clips. In the `for` loop, we initialize the statement by setting `i=0`. We then check to see whether `i<_root.maxEnemies`, which we have set to 10 in the first frame of the main movie timeline. Finally, we increment i by using `i++`, giving the `for` loop a way to end the statement when `i=9`. Every time the loop runs through, it checks to see whether the ammo movie clip that this code is attached to is touching an enemy ship movie clip by using `hittest("_root.enemy" + i)`. If the ammo movie clip is touching any of the enemy ship movie clips, `hittest` returns true and the message `HIT` is sent to the Output window.

Now that we have the code to move the ammo movie clip across the stage, we need a way to place the clip on the stage and make it look like it's being shot from the player ship movie clip. A very simple way to do this is to create a button using Insert, New Symbol and call it **fire button**. Place some text on the first frame of fire button to identify it and place it just off the bottom of the stage, near the center. The player will never see this button, but it will still be working for us as our fire button. Now select fire button and add the following code to it:

```
on (keyPress "<SPACE>") {
   newAmmo++;
   shipX = _root.ship._x;
   shipY = _root.ship._y-_root.ship._height/2;
   _root.attachMovie("ammo", "ammo"+newAmmo, newAmmo);
   setProperty(eval("ammo"+newAmmo), _x, shipX);
   setProperty(eval("ammo"+newAmmo), _y, shipY);
}
```

Let's break this code up a little and see what it's doing. Here's the first line:

```
on (keyPress "<SPACE>")
```

With this code, Flash checks for the spacebar being pressed and evaluates the code following each time the spacebar is pressed.

```
newAmmo++;
```

This code causes Flash to increment the variable `newAmmo` each time to give each ammo movie clip a unique name and place it on the next level of the main movie when we attach it to the stage. The initial value of `newAmmo` is set to 50 on the first frame of the main movie timeline. Because two dynamically attached or duplicated movie clips cannot exist on the same level of the main movie, we set `newAmmo` to 50 so that we don't use the same level as any of the enemy ships being attached at the same time.

```
shipX = _root.ship._x;
shipY = _root.ship._y-_root.ship._height/2;
```

In this bit of code, `shipX` and `shipY` are temporary variables we will use to define the top and center of the player ship movie clip.

```
_root.attachMovie("ammo", "ammo"+newAmmo, newAmmo);
```

This code causes Flash to attach the new instance of the ammo movie clip using `_root.attachMovie` and the unique linkage identifier ammo.

```
setProperty(eval("ammo"+newAmmo), _x, shipX);
setProperty(eval("ammo"+newAmmo), _y, shipY);
```

Using the temporary `shipX` and `shipY` variables, this code attaches the new instance of ammo to those coordinates. Now it looks like the shot being fired is coming from the front of the player's ship.

You can now save and test the movie. You should be able to move the player's ship around and fire shots at the enemies coming toward you. When one of your shots passes through an enemy ship, you should see the word HIT appear in your Output window, because of the `trace` action we used on the ammo code movie clip.

Now that we know the code for the hit detection is working, we can add an effect to the enemy ship movie clip so that enemy ships appear to explode when hit. We can add this effect by editing the enemy ship movie clip. Insert a blank keyframe on the first frame of the enemy ship movie clip using Insert, Blank Keyframe and put a `stop()` action on it. Next, we need to insert a blank keyframe at frame 2. Here, we can add the explosion effect. Then, at the end of this effect, we insert another blank keyframe and add one action to that frame:

```
this.removeMovieClip()
```

This simply tells this movie clip to remove itself after the explosion effect is over.

Now we need to add a little more code to the hit detection on the ammo code movie clip. Instead of using the `trace` command to send the word HIT to the Output window, we need to tell the enemy movie clip that we just hit it, to play the explosion animation, and then remove itself. Here is how the final code for the hit detection on the ammo code movie clip should look:

```
onClipEvent (load) {
    this.onEnterFrame = function() {
        _parent._y -= _root.ammoSpeed;
        for (i=0; i<_root.maxEnemies; i++) {
            if (_parent.hittest("_root.enemy" + i )) {
            eval("_root.enemy"+i).gotoAndPlay (2);
            _parent.removeMovieClip();
            }
        if (_parent._y <-10) {
            _parent.removeMovieClip();
            }
        }
    }
}
```

We have replaced the initial `trace` action with two lines of new code:

```
eval("_root.enemy"+i).gotoAndPlay (2);
_parent.removeMovieClip();
```

This gets the name of the enemy just hit and tells that movie clip to go to and play frame 2. Frame 2 of the enemy movie clip is the start of the explosion animation. After that plays through, the movie clip goes to the keyframe with the code to remove itself. We now have the effect of the enemy ships exploding when the player's shots hit them. We have also added the action `_parent.removeMovieClip();` to remove the ammo movie clip from the stage.

Check for the Enemy Ship Hitting the Player's Ship

We've got a solid start to the game now, but what if one of the enemy ships crashes into the player's ship? This will cost the player one life and blow up both ships. The simplest way to do this is to add the hit detection to the enemy ships. This way, the enemy ships will constantly be checking for a collision with the player's ship. To do this, we will write another function on frame 2 of the main movie timeline. Select frame 2 of the main movie and below the `createEnemy()` function write a new function called `hitCheck(thisEnemy)`. It should look like this:

```
function hitCheck(thisEnemy) {
    if (thisEnemy.hittest(ship) && _root.playerDead!=1) {
        thisEnemy.gotoAndPlay(2);
        _root.ship.gotoAndPlay(2);
    }
}
```

We'll be passing this function a variable from the enemy ship movie clip that is calling it. That variable, `thisEnemy`, will contain the instance name of the enemy ship movie clip. Then Flash will check the following `if` statement:

```
if (thisEnemy.hittest(ship) && _root.playerDead!=1) {
    thisEnemy.gotoAndPlay(2);
    _root.ship.gotoAndPlay(2);
    }
```

The `if` statement checks whether the enemy ship movie clip has hit the player's ship *and* checks whether the player is not already dead and in the "respawning" time. The `if` statement uses the logical operator `&&` to make sure both statements return `True` before executing the code in the `if` statement. We will set the `_root.playerDead` to `True` or `False` from the player ship movie clip later; for now, we are checking to make sure it is not equal to `True`. If both these statements return `True`, the enemy ship is destroyed in the same manner as a shot hitting it by going to and playing frame 2. The player's ship is also told to blow up by going to and playing frame 2, but those frames do not exist yet. We will need to create the player explosion and respawning animation next. Now that we have the function created and named, we need to call it from the enemy ship code movie clip. Edit the enemy ship movie clip and select the enemy ship code movie clip. Then add the following code to the `onEnterFrame` action:

```
_root.hitCheck (_parent);
```

This will constantly call the `hitCheck(thisEnemy)` function we just wrote. Notice that it is passing the variable `_parent`, which is a property containing the instance name of the enemy ship movie clip. The code on the enemy ship code movie clip should now look like this:

```
onClipEvent (load) {
    randomSpeed = random (3);
    this.onEnterFrame = function() {
        _parent._y += _root.enemySpeed + randomSpeed;
        _parent._x += randomSpeed;
        if (_parent._y>_root.stageHeight+_parent._height*2) {
            _parent.removeMovieClip();
        }
        _root.hitCheck (_parent);
    };
}
```

23

CREATING A FLASH GAME

Now, we just need to add the player's ship explosion and respawning animation, and this section of code will be complete. In the `hitCheck(thisEnemy)` function, we told the player ship movie clip to go to and play frame 2, using `gotoAndPlay(2)`, if an enemy ship collides with it. We can now edit the player ship movie clip and insert a blank keyframe to frame 2 by selecting frame 2 and using Insert, Blank Keyframe. This is where we will put the player ship explosion animation and also where we will set a couple of variables. Add the following three lines to frame 2 of the player ship movie clip:

```
_root.playerLives -= 1;
_root.playerDead = 1;

play();
```

The first line takes one of the player's lives away. The variable `playerLives` is initially set on the first frame of the main movie timeline. The second line is a temporary variable we will set while the player's ship goes through its "respawn" animation. This will allow the player a second or two to recover without immediately dying again. The `play()` action at the end tells Flash to keep playing after this frame. After the player ship explosion animation plays through, add a blank keyframe and put the following action on it:

```
if (_root.playerLives == 0) {
    _level0.gotoAndStop ("gameover");
}
```

This checks to see whether the player is out of lives by comparing the variable `playerLives` to 0. If the player has no more lives left, we use `_level0.gotoAndStop ("gameover");` to tell the main timeline to go to the frame labeled gameover. We will create this frame next, but first we will finish with the player's ship respawn animation. If the player has at least one life left, the movie clip continues playing. Following this frame, we will need a respawn animation to show the player that he is still playing but can't be killed immediately. To do this, we'll make the player ship movie clip blink on and off a couple of times. At the end of the respawn animation, add one more keyframe and put the following action on it:

```
_root.playerDead = 0;
```

This tells the enemy ship movie clip's `hitCheck(thisEnemy)` function that the player is back in the game and can be killed again if hit by an enemy ship.

To finish this section, add a new blank keyframe to the main movie timeline and call it **gameover**. Then write the text **GAME OVER** in the center. This will be the final screen the player sees when he runs out of lives.

You can now save and test the movie and shoot down enemy ships as they hurl toward you. It's almost a complete game, but we can add a few more things to make it better.

Add Elements to the Game

First, we will add a score. To do this, create a dynamic text field on the main movie time-line and give it the variable name **score**. Put the text field in the first frame of a new layer called **HUD**, which stands for Heads Up Display. We will use this frame for sending feedback elements to the player, such as score, lives remaining, and enemies missed. Then put some static text next to it identifying it as the player's score. You can add the action `score = 0;` to the first frame of the main movie timeline on the actions layer to set the initial value of this variable. Then simply add the following action to the ammo code movie clip in the `for` loop to increase the score each time an enemy ship is destroyed:

```
_root.score += 50;
```

This will increase the player's score by 50 points each time an enemy is destroyed. The complete `for` loop on the ammo code movie clip should look like this now:

```
for (i=0; i<_root.maxEnemies; i++) {
    if (_parent.hittest("_root.enemy" + i)==1) {
    eval("_root.enemy"+i).gotoAndPlay (2);
    _root.score += 50;
    }
}
```

You can now save and test the movie and watch as your score goes up when you destroy enemy ships.

We can also indicate the number of lives remaining to the player in a similar fashion. Create a dynamic text field on the main movie timeline in the HUD layer and give it the variable name **playerLives**. Put some static text next to it identifying it as the number of lives the player has remaining. We have already defined the variable `playerLives` on the first frame when we wrote the code to detect whether the game is over. This dynamic text field will now update with the number of lives the player has remaining after each time the player crashes into an enemy. The final bit of feedback we can give the player is how many enemy ships he has missed. Again, create a dynamic text field and give it the variable name **missed**. Place it on the first frame of the main movie timeline on the HUD layer and put some static text next to it indicating it is the number of enemies the player has missed. You can add the action `missed = 0;` to the first frame of the main movie timeline on the actions layer to set the initial value of this variable. Then you can add the following code to the enemy ship code movie clip in the `if` statement to increase the missed amount by one, each time an enemy ship reaches the bottom of the screen:

```
_root.missed += 1;
```

23

CREATING A FLASH GAME

When adding this code to the `if` statement, be sure you add it before the `removeMovieClip()` action; otherwise, it will not be evaluated before the clip is removed and therefore will not work. The `if` statement on the enemy ship code movie clip should now look like this:

```
if (_parent._y>_root.stageHeight+_parent._height*2) {
    _root.missed += 1;
    _parent.removeMovieClip();
    }
```

Now you can save and test the movie and see all three of the new elements working the way they should. Let a few enemies get by and watch the `missed` variable go up. Let an enemy crash into you and watch the `playerLives` variable go down. Your game should now resemble what's shown in Figure 23.4.

FIGURE 23.4

The shooter game in action.

Now when you play the game, it runs pretty much how you would expect it to, except for one thing: When you shoot an enemy with more than one shot, the hit detection on the following shot thinks it is still hitting the enemy. Instead, it is actually hitting the explosion animation, but this animation is part of the enemy ship movie clip. Technically, this is correct, but it is not the right behavior for the game. We need to update the hit detection code on the ammo code movie clip to check for the enemy ship exploding before returning `True`. Here's the new bit of code you need to add to the `if` statement:

```
eval("_root.enemy" + i).exploding != 1
```

This checks for the variable `exploding` within the enemy ship movie clip to see whether it is not set to `True`. If the enemy ship is playing the explosion animation, then `exploding` will be set to `True` and the `if` statement will return `False` and not evaluate the hit detection code again. Here's what the full `if` statement should look like after adding the new code:

```
if (_parent.hittest("_root.enemy" + i) && eval("_root.enemy" + i).
➥exploding != 1)
```

The `if` statement uses the logical operator `&&` to make sure *both* statements return `True` before executing the code in the `if` statement.

All you need to do now is set the variable `exploding` from within the enemy ship movie clip. You can add the following code to the first frame of the explosion animation on the enemy ship movie clip:

```
exploding = 1;
```

This sets `exploding` equal to `True`, which can now be evaluated by the `if` statement in the ammo movie clip. Now when you shoot a few shots into an enemy, the explosion animation plays only once. This is the behavior we would expect in the game.

One last touch we can add to the game is an intro screen so that the game doesn't start before the user is ready. On this same screen, we can tell the users what keys to use for controls and any other information we want to relay to the user before he starts playing the game.

Create a new movie clip on the first frame of the HUD layer by using Insert, New Symbol. Give it the instance name of **info** and then edit it to add your text. After adding the text you want to the first frame of the info movie clip, you need to add a button for the user to click when he is ready to play. Create a new button on the first frame under the information text and put some text on the button that indicates it's the start button. Now add a blank keyframe to the info movie clip on the second frame. The complete info movie clip should have the information text and the start button on the first frame. The second frame should be blank. On the first frame, select the start button and add the following code to the Actions window:

```
on (release) {
    _root.info.gotoAndStop (2);
    _root.enGen.gotoAndPlay (2);
}
```

This code tells the info movie clip to go to frame 2, which is the blank frame we just created. Then it tells the movie clip enGen to go to frame 2 and play. In order for this second line of code to work, we need to give the enemy generator movie clip the instance name of enGen and modify that movie clip just a little. Do that now. First, select the enemy generator movie clip on the main stage and give it the instance name of **enGen**. Now double-click it so we can make a few modifications to it. Add a stop() action to the first frame so that it doesn't immediately start creating enemies when the movie is started. Next, add the following line of code to the last frame on this clip, the same frame that calls the createEnemy() function:

```
gotoAndPlay (2);
```

This will tell the enemy generator clip to keep looping and creating enemies after the user clicks the start button. The last frame of the enemy generator clip should now have these two lines of code:

```
_root.createEnemy();
gotoAndPlay (2);
```

You can now save your version of the game and test it. You may also download the complete version (shooter.fla) to compare with your final version at <ENTER DOWNLOAD SITE HERE>.

We could do many more things to make this game more fun. Here's a list of elements you can try adding yourself to make your own unique version of the game:

- A shield for the player ship
- Accelerate enemy ships after a certain score is reached
- Send enemy ships in waves or make them appear from the bottom of the screen occasionally
- An "enemies killed" indicator
- Limited ammo supply with ammo indicator
- A high-score list (an exercise for which you'll find later in this chapter)

This exercise is just a starting point in understanding the way Flash can attach and remove movie clips dynamically and perform multiple-target hit detection using a simple for loop. Now let's look at using arrays in game programming.

Arrays in Games

Arrays provide a very flexible and powerful way of storing variables for gaming. Arrays can contain all kinds of information that can be referenced from any point within a movie. You could use an array to store names representing the individual cards in a deck of cards, or the names for elements that are found by a player in an adventure game. In this section, we'll use arrays to store essential data for a random terrain generator. You can download the FLA (random_terrain.fla) at <ENTER DOWNLOAD SITE HERE>.

Random Terrain Generator

This example uses a very simple graphic for terrain, but this same concept can be used for any type of terrain. When you make the image for your final terrain, you need to be sure that the "up" and "down" sides of the terrain are the same height. To help with this, you can turn on the grid in Flash and set it to the width of the final pieces. Then use this grid to help you cut up your terrain into equal widths and heights. Your setup should look something similar to what's shown in Figure 23.5.

When you get the terrain cut into the pieces, you will need to make them into movie clips. For this example, you can name them **land1** through **land19**. Note that for each "up" piece and "down" piece, I've added an equal-height "level" piece for the possibility of flat ground. We'll be attaching these pieces dynamically, using `attachMovie`, so these movie clips will need to put into empty "container" movie clips. A very effective way of using `attachMovie` is to make an empty "container" movie clip that holds another movie clip that has all the code you need to use attached to it. You can name these **a1** through **a19** and give them the corresponding linkage names **a1** through **a19**. Now that you have the terrain movie clips created and linked, we can start with the code to attach, move, and remove each piece dynamically. In the first frame of the main movie timeline, create the arrays by adding the following code:

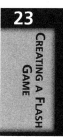

FIGURE 23.5

The basic pieces used for the random terrain generator.

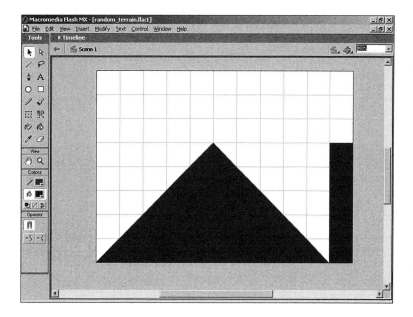

```
choose1 = new Array ("a2","a3","a19");
choose2 = new Array ("a2","a3","a19");
choose3 = new Array ("a4","a5","a17");
choose4 = new Array ("a4","a5","a17");
choose5 = new Array ("a6","a7","a15");
choose6 = new Array ("a6","a7","a15");
choose7 = new Array ("a8","a9","a13");
choose8 = new Array ("a8","a9","a13");
choose9 = new Array ("a10","a10","a11");
choose10 = new Array ("a10","a10","a11");
choose11 = new Array ("a9","a12","a13");
choose12 = new Array ("a9","a12","a13");
choose13 = new Array ("a7","a14","a15");
choose14 = new Array ("a7","a14","a15");
choose15 = new Array ("a5","a16","a17");
choose16 = new Array ("a5","a16","a17");
choose17 = new Array ("a3","a18","a19");
choose18 = new Array ("a3","a18","a19");
choose19 = new Array ("a1","a1","a1");
```

These arrays define the possible choices for each piece to attach to itself as it moves from the right side of the stage to the left. Each piece can either attach an "up" piece, a "down" piece, or a "level" piece, with a few exceptions. You can use Figure 23.6 to help you keep track of the possibilities for each piece.

FIGURE 23.6

Draw a diagram by hand or in Flash to keep track of the different terrain piece combinations.

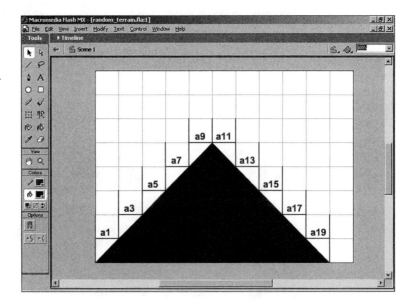

The highest "level" piece cannot go any higher, so we've given it a tendency to call another level piece. We've added the same number twice in the array so that when we write the code for it to pick a random piece, it will have a better chance of staying level. You could give it an equal tendency to go "down" or even force it to go "down" by changing the possibilities to more or all of one number. Now let's write the code to attach each movie clip, move it across the stage from right to left, and remove itself when it reaches the left side of the stage. We can do this by defining a function that will be called from each movie clip. First, we'll attach the code to each movie clip that is in each container clip. Edit a1 and select land1, the movie clip on the first frame. Now write the following code for the land1 movie clip:

```
onClipEvent (load) {
    this.onEnterFrame = function (){
        _root.moveAndUpdate (_parent,_name);
    }
}
```

All this does is call the function moveAndUpdate and pass the function two very important variables. The first is the instance name of the container movie clip, and the second is the name of this movie clip. The container movie clip will be given a name dynamically, but we will name this movie clip ourselves—give the land1 movie clip an instance name of **choose1**. You can now put the previous code on movie clips land2 through land19 by opening and editing their container movie clips a2 through a19. Don't forget to name each movie clip that you are attaching the code to so that _name can pass the instance name to the function. For this example, you can use choose1 through choose19 for the instance names of the movie clips; this is important for later. Now let's look at the function moveAndUpdate that we are calling from these movie clips. You can write this function on the first frame of the movie to be sure it is loaded and can be referenced by each movie clip:

```
function moveAndUpdate (instance,currentPiece) {
    if (instance._x == 550) {
        var upOrDown = random(3);
        nextPiece =(eval(currentPiece)[upOrDown]);
        startX = instance._x;
        _root.i++;
        _root.attachMovie(nextPiece , "land" + _root.i, _root.i);
        setProperty(eval("_root.land" + _root.i),_x, startX+45);
        setProperty(eval("_root.land" + _root.i),_y,_root.base);
    }
    if (instance._x < -100) {
        instance.removeMovieClip();
    }else{
        instance._x -= 5;
    }
}
```

This function receives two important variables from each clip: `instance` is used to check the position of the movie clip and move it across the stage, and `currentPiece` is used to check the possibilities for the next piece to appear. The first part of the code checks the x position of the movie clip to see whether it equals 550. The movie clips will pass over this point only one time, so this case will only be true once to generate the next piece of land placed behind this piece. Now let's look at how we use the arrays to choose the next piece of terrain:

```
nextPiece =(eval(currentPiece)[upOrDown]);
```

This is how we access the arrays and choose a random direction for the terrain. This function is passed the variable `currentPiece` from each movie clip. We defined each instance earlier as choose1 through choose19, so now we know which piece is calling this function. We can use `eval()` and the array accessor `[]` to access the corresponding array and pull a random name from that array:

```
startX = instance._x;
_root.i++;
```

We find the x position of the movie clip that called this function (which should equal 550) and increment `i`, which is a global variable we're using in order to give each instance a unique name and depth level in our movie. Here's the code:

```
_root.attachMovie(nextPiece , "land" + _root.i, _root.i);
setProperty(eval("_root.land" + _root.i),_x, startX+45);
setProperty(eval("_root.land" + _root.i),_y,_root.base);
```

Then we attach the movie clip that has the linkage name that we assigned `nextPiece` from the array, and we give it a new name and depth. We then set the position of that movie clip to appear directly behind the movie clip that called it and at the base y position of the movie, which we can define later. Now we just need to move this movie clip across the stage and remove it when it gets off the stage. Here's one way you can do this:

```
if (instance._x < -100) {
    instance.removeMovieClip();
}else{
    instance._x -= 5;
}
```

This part of the `moveAndUpdate` function will be constantly called by each movie clip. It simply moves each clip across the x axis by 5 pixels each time, and when the x position of the movie clip becomes less than -100, the movie clip removes itself.

Finally, we can add a few pieces of initializing code to the first lines of the first frame and then place the first piece to start the terrain generation. Here's the code:

```
i = 1;
base = 400;
```

This will initialize i and give us a base of 400, since the movie is 550 by 400. Then we can create a blank keyframe on frame 2 of the main movie timeline and add the following code:

```
_root.attachMovie("a1", "land" + _root.i, _root.i);
setProperty(eval("_root.land" + _root.i),_x, 550);
setProperty(eval("_root.land" + _root.i),_y,base);
stop();
```

This will place the first piece of terrain, a1, in the correct position and start the terrain generation as it moves across the screen from right to left.

Now that the terrain generator is working, we could easily add hit detection to it by entering the following code into the updateAndMove function:

```
if (instance.hitTest(object)) {
    trace ("HIT");
}
```

In this case, hitTest will be evaluated for every instance of the terrain during every frame of the movie. Just throw in a player ship and some enemies and you've got a side-scrolling arcade-style game.

Use External Files for Easily Updating Games

Using external files to store variables is a good way to make your games easy to update. Trivia games provide a good example for using external files to store questions and answers that can be changed without needing to open the source file and change the text inside. This section provides a few tips for using external files to load variable data. First, you can format your external text file in an easy-to-read fashion by using the ampersand and comment delimiters, like this:

```
//Question number 1
&Q1=First question&
//
//Answers to question number 1
&Q1A1=First choice&
//
&Q1A2=Second choice&
//
&Q1A3=Third choice&
//
&Q1A4=Fourth choice&
//
//The correct answer for question 1
```

```
&Q1ca=Q1A1&
//
//Finished loading
&loading=done&
```

With this formatting, you can keep your variables organized and easy to read. Be sure
you start *and* end each line defining a variable with an ampersand. You can use the comment delimiter (//) to add comments to the code so that anyone opening the text file
knows how to use and update it. It's important to note that when you load variables from
a remote file, it may take a few seconds to actually load them in from the text file.
Because of this, it's good to set a "finished loading" variable and then check for that
variable within a loop in the Flash file, like this:

```
if (loading == "done") {
    gotoAndStop ("questions");
}else{
    gotoAndPlay ("loading");
}
```

With this simple loop, you will ensure that all variables before the "loading" variable are
loaded into the movie before continuing.

Save Games and High Scores

A great new feature in Flash MX is the `SharedObject`, which allows data to be stored on
the user's hard drive, much like a browser cookie. By defining a `SharedObject` and giving it a unique name, you can write data to and retrieve data from the `SharedObject` in
the form of variables. This is a great way to create a local high-score list or a list of the
user's top scores for any given game. It also allows entire games to be saved, by storing
all the pertinent variables as the user exits and then retrieving those variables and restor-
ing the game upon the user's return.

Let's look at how to create, write to, and read from a `SharedObject`. Create a new file to
try out this next exercise. You can add all the code for this exercise to the first frame
actions. The following statement shows how to create a `SharedObject`, by giving it a
unique name and returning it to a variable. If the `SharedObject` does not exist already on
the user's hard drive, it is created. Otherwise, it is returned, and in both cases we can
now read from and write to the `SharedObject` by using the variable name we returned it
to (in this case, `score`). Here's the statement:

```
score = SharedObject.getLocal ("highScores");
```

Now we can add a property to the `SharedObject`:

```
score.data.highscore = 5000;
```

When we assign the new property, the data is not immediately written to the disk. The data is written upon exiting the Flash Player or when there are no more references to the `SharedObject`. We can, however, force the data to be written by using the following line:

```
score.flush();
```

The `flush` command tells Flash to immediately write to the `SharedObject`, and now we can reference the `SharedObject` and check the high score, as shown here:

```
trace (score.data.highscore);
```

This should display 5000. If we exit the movie and reopen it later, we need to retrieve the `SharedObject` before we can read from it again:

```
score = SharedObject.getLocal ("highScores");
trace (score.data.highscore);
```

This will display 5000 again, because the data is stored in the `SharedObject` until we overwrite it.

To show this whole process in action, I've created a very simple "high-score list" movie (`highscores.fla`) that can be downloaded from <INSERT DOWNLOAD SITE> and viewed in Figure 23.7.

FIGURE 23.7

Complete high-score list.

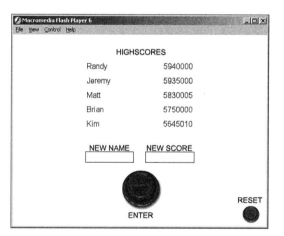

This allows you to enter a name and high score to illustrate how to keep track of personal high scores on a user's machine. Create a new movie and on the first frame of the main movie timeline, you create the `SharedObject` like we did earlier:

```
score = SharedObject.getLocal ("highScores");
```

You can also create some dynamic text fields on the stage in the first frame (in this example, they're called highScore1 through highScore5 and highScoreName1 through highScoreName5). You also need two input text fields for the new name and new score that you want to enter (in this example, newName and newScore). Finally, you need two buttons—one to enter the new name and new score and one to reset the data in the SharedObject and clear the high-score list.

Insert a blank keyframe on the second frame of your main movie by using Insert, Blank Keyframe. Now, in the second frame of the main movie timeline, you can write some actions to set the high score list to its previous state by reading the data from the SharedObject. If this is the first time this movie has been opened, you need to set the initial score values equal to 0 so that the new numbers can be evaluated properly. Here's what the first half of the code for the second frame looks like:

```
highScoreName1 = score.data.highScoreName1;
highScoreName2 = score.data.highScoreName2;
highScoreName3 = score.data.highScoreName3;
highScoreName4 = score.data.highScoreName4;
highScoreName5 = score.data.highScoreName5;
highScore1 = score.data.highScore1;
highScore2 = score.data.highScore2;
highScore3 = score.data.highScore3;
highScore4 = score.data.highScore4;
highScore5 = score.data.highScore5;
```

This assigns the proper values to the text fields by reading the data from the SharedObject and assigning those values to the existing text fields. If this is the first time running this movie, you need to be sure the score variables are numbers and not strings or undefined, as shown here:

```
if (highScore1 == undefined) {
    score.data.highScore1 = 0;
    highScore1 = 0;
}
if (highScore2 == undefined) {
    score.data.highScore2 = 0;
    highScore2 = 0;
}
if (highScore3 == undefined) {
    score.data.highScore3 = 0;
    highScore3 = 0;
}
if (highScore4 == undefined) {
    score.data.highScore4 = 0;
    highScore4 = 0;
}
if (highScore5 == undefined) {
    score.data.highScore5 = 0;
```

```
    highScore5 = 0;
}
score.flush();
```

This will check whether or not the score data in the SharedObject is undefined. If it is the first time running the movie, or not enough values were entered the first time running the movie, this will assign zeros to the undefined scores. The flush() statement at the end forces Flash to update the SharedObject with the new values before continuing to the next frame.

On the third frame of the main movie, insert another blank keyframe and simply place a stop() action in it. This allows the user to input a new name and a new score value. When the Enter button is clicked, the code on it tells the main movie to go to the next frame and play. Insert a blank keyframe on the next frame of the main movie for the next block of code. The statements we'll be adding to this frame take the newScore value and check it with the existing scores. If the new score is higher than the lowest score, it gets added to the list. Here's how you can check the values and update the SharedObject with the new score and new name.:

```
if (newScore > parseInt(highScore1)) {
    score.data.highScore5 = score.data.highScore4;
    score.data.highScore4 = score.data.highScore3;
    score.data.highScore3 = score.data.highScore2;
    score.data.highScore2 = score.data.highScore1;
    score.data.highScore1 = newScore;
    score.data.highScoreName5 = score.data.highScoreName4;
    score.data.highScoreName4 = score.data.highScoreName3;
    score.data.highScoreName3 = score.data.highScoreName2;
    score.data.highScoreName2 = score.data.highScoreName1;
    score.data.highScoreName1 = newName;
    newScore = "";
    newName = "";
}
```

The first thing you check is whether the new score is higher than the current high score:

```
if (newScore > parseInt(highScore1))
```

You need to use the parseInt command for the highScore1 variable so that Flash knows that you are comparing numbers and not strings. If the new score is higher than the current high score, you update all the values in the SharedObject by shifting everything down one row. If the new score is not greater than the highest high score, you check to see whether it is greater than the next highest score *or* equal to the highest high score using else if:

```
else if (newScore == parseInt(highScore1) || newScore > parseInt(highScore2)) {
    score.data.highScore5 = score.data.highScore4;
    score.data.highScore4 = score.data.highScore3;
    score.data.highScore3 = score.data.highScore2;
```

```
    score.data.highScore2 = newScore;
    score.data.highScoreName5 = score.data.highScoreName4;
    score.data.highScoreName4 = score.data.highScoreName3;
    score.data.highScoreName3 = score.data.highScoreName2;
    score.data.highScoreName2 = newName;
    newScore = "";
    newName = "";
}
```

This time, you shift all values down one, except for the highest score. If the new score is not greater than this score, you add another else if statement and check it against the next highest score, and so on.

After checking the score and updating the SharedObject, if necessary, you add a flush() statement to the end so that you can update the dynamic fields on the stage with the correct data. Insert one more blank keyframe in the final frame of the main movie timeline. Here, you put the final statements needed to update the text fields and send the playhead back to frame 3 so that the user can enter a new name and a new score:

```
highScoreName1 = score.data.highScoreName1;
highScoreName2 = score.data.highScoreName2;
highScoreName3 = score.data.highScoreName3;
highScoreName4 = score.data.highScoreName4;
highScoreName5 = score.data.highScoreName5;
highScore1 = score.data.highScore1;
highScore2 = score.data.highScore2;
highScore3 = score.data.highScore3;
highScore4 = score.data.highScore4;
highScore5 = score.data.highScore5;
gotoAndStop (3);
```

The reset button can be used to clear the high-score list by setting all the values in the SharedObject to zero or blank. It then sends the movie to the frame for updating the visible text fields. Here's the code:

```
on (release){
    score.data.highScore5 = 0
    score.data.highScore4 = 0
    score.data.highScore3 = 0
    score.data.highScore2 = 0
    score.data.highScore1 = 0
    score.data.highScoreName5 = ""
    score.data.highScoreName4 = ""
    score.data.highScoreName3 = ""
    score.data.highScoreName2 = ""
    score.data.highScoreName1 = ""
    score.flush();
    gotoAndPlay (5);
}
```

The high-score list I have created is definitely not the most efficient or dynamic way of creating a high-score list. I chose to use this example to better illustrate sending and retrieving data from the SharedObject and how to update it on the fly.

Final Words of Wisdom

With each new release of Flash, the game programmer's life gets easier. New tools, functions, and built-in objects give the game programmer more flexibility and make creating complex games and interactivity easier. Flash gives the game programmer all the tools necessary; it just takes a little experimentation and exploration to use these tools in novel and interesting ways.

Getting and Sending Data

By Matt Pizzi

IN THIS CHAPTER

- Formatting Dynamic Text with HTML Tags
- Creating Scrolling Text
- Sending a Form to an E-mail Account

This chapter is about how you can send data and load external data into a Flash movie. The concepts we're going to review in this chapter are different from some of other dynamic chapters. The other chapters deal specifically with moving data in and out of Flash using a server-side scripting language such as ColdFusion or ASP.

The first topic we're going to look at is how to load in content dynamically through a text file. Say, for example, a news organization has a Flash Web site, and this Web site provides up-to-the-minute traffic information. Chances are it wouldn't be too cost effective to have a Flash developer waiting to update the site with the news traffic information. A better scenario would be to have anyone in the office capable of typing to create the updates through a text file. By dynamically sourcing the contents of the text file, the Flash movie can be updated without someone ever having to edit inside of Flash.

Update a Flash Movie Dynamically Through a Text File

To follow along in this exercise, you can download the `news_traffic.fla` file from the Unleashed companion Web site, located at `http://www.flashmxun-leashed.com`, and navigate to the Chapter 24 section. Here are the steps to follow:

1. Open the `news_traffic.fla` file. Notice the file is just a movie with a bitmap graphic on layer 1, as shown on Figure 24.1.

2. Double-click layer 1 and rename it **bitmap**. Click the Insert Layer button at the bottom of the Timeline panel. Notice a new layer is created above the bitmap layer.

3. Double-click the new layer and name it **text**. Lock the bitmap layer so that you don't edit it by accident.

4. With the text layer selected, choose the Text tool. Click and drag out a box covering the majority of the stage, as shown in Figure 24.2.

5. You're going to use this text box to provide the viewers with detailed traffic information around Los Angeles. After drawing the text field, you need to give it a dynamic type. In the Properties Inspector in the Type drop-down menu, choose Dynamic. Give it a variable name of **traffic**. Make sure to set its line type to Multiline.

6. Create a small text field in the top-left corner of the stage, just above the traffic text field, as shown in Figure 24.3. After dragging out the text field, give it a dynamic type in the Type drop-down menu in the Properties Inspector. Give this text field a variable name of **date**.

7. Create a new folder on your desktop and name it `varloader`. Save this document as `loadvars.fla` in the `varloader` folder. On your computer, open Notepad, Simple Text, Text Edit, or even Word or AppleWorks—any application that can save a TXT document will do.

8. Inside the text editor, type **traffic**=. Then after the equal sign type in a description for the traffic, as shown in Figure 24.4.

9. After typing the description for the traffic, without a space, type the **&date**=. Spaces are not allowed when you're dividing up variable names. The ampersand joins the new variable with the text. After the ampersand type in today's date.

10. Save the document as `report.txt` in the same directory as the `news_traffic.fla` file. You can also download this file from the companion Web site located at `http://www.flashmxunleahsed.com`.

11. Open up the `news_traffic.fla` file. Select frame 1 and open the Actions panel by pressing F9. Click the plus sign in the Actions drop-down menu and choose Actions, Browser/Network, loadVariables. In the URL text field, type the name of your text document, which is `report.txt`. If the file is not saved in the same directory (the `varloaders` folder on the desktop), you must address it properly or move the TXT file into the `varloaders` folder. Leave everything else at the defaults. You need to load into level 0. Here's the final code:

```
loadVariablesNum("report.txt", 0);
```

12. Test the movie. Notice the text is loaded in dynamically, as shown in Figure 24.5.

13. Save the document as `traffic_loader1.fla`.

FIGURE 24.1

The `news_traffic` *file consists of a large bitmap graphic.*

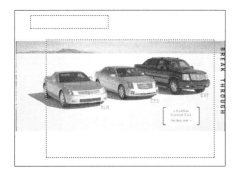

24

**GETTING AND
SENDING DATA**

FIGURE 24.2

The text box is almost the same size as the stage.

FIGURE 24.3

The small text field in the top-left corner of the stage.

FIGURE 24.4

Type in a description for the traffic report.

FIGURE 24.5

The text is dynamically loaded into the movie.

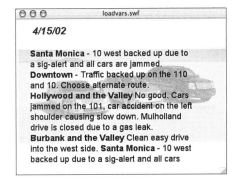

Formatting Dynamic Text with HTML Tags

When loading in text, you can actually use some HTML tags to do formatting. In the `traffic_loader1.fla` file you've been working with, you can change the appearance of the text that loads into the text field. The most important part, of course, is to check the HTML check box in the Properties Inspector, as shown in Figure 24.6.

FIGURE 24.6

Checking the HTML box allows for HTML formatting.

The downside here is that HTML text will actually be generated, and HTML text is not antialiased, thus generating jagged-looking text. However, this can actually be an advantage with smaller text, which tends to look blurry when antialiased. Therefore, a crisper appearance is provided.

You have some limitations when using HTML text. The main one being only a limited number of HTML tags are supported. Here's a list of those tags:

- `<a>`
- `<b>`
- `<i>`
- `<p>`
- `<u>`
- `<br>`

- `<font face>`
- `<font size>`
- `<font color>`

That's it. No other tags will work.

Tip

If you include the font outlines of a typeface and you use a `<b>` or `<i>` tag, the text may disappear. The reason is that generally a bold or an italic typeface is a separate outline that must be included.

With the HTML check box now selected, open the `report.txt` file and add some of the HTML tags just listed. You can also download this file from `http:/www.flashmxunleashed.com`. Save the text document and test the movie. Figure 24.7 shows the difference in the text. Save the Flash file as `traffic_loader2.fla`.

FIGURE 24.7

The newly formatted text using HTML.

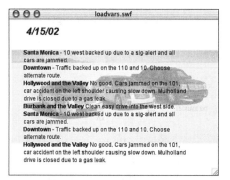

Creating Scrolling Text

In Chapter 1, "What's New in Flash MX?," we looked at how to use components to create a scrollbar for dynamic text. In Chapter 16, "Components," we looked at how to modify the appearance of the standard scrollbar components. These tasks were easy and work great, but what if you want to make your own scroll buttons or you need to scroll something other than text? Never fear. You can always create your own scrollbars, which is a pretty painless task.

Create Scrolling Text

Be sure to have the `traffic_loader2.fla` file open. You're also going to have to edit some parts of your text file, so have it open as well. Here are the steps to follow:

1. Download the `report2.txt` file from the companion Web site. You need to add some additional text in order to scroll. For this example, you'll create different regions to display traffic situations all over Los Angeles, as shown in Figure 24.8.

2. In the `traffic_loader2.fla` file, create a new layer and name it **buttons**. You can use the buttons in the common library, or you can create your own. Whatever the case, place two buttons on the stage and position them so that one looks like a scroll-up arrow and the other looks like a scroll-down arrow, as shown in Figure 24.9. Rotate and transform the buttons, if necessary, to have the arrows pointing in the appropriate direction.

3. With the scroll-up arrow button selected, press F9 on the keyboard to open the Actions panel. Here, create an `on (press)` event handler and set a variable. The variable should be `traffic.scroll` (`traffic` being the name of the dynamic text field and `scroll` being the action to be performed). For the new `traffic.scroll` variable, set its value to be `traffic.scroll + 1`, where 1 stands for the number of lines to scroll up. Here is the final code for the top button:

    ```
    on (press) {
        traffic.scroll = traffic.scroll+1;
    }
    ```

4. Test the movie. Notice the traffic text scrolls up each time the up-arrow button is pressed, as shown in Figure 24.10.

5. You now need to get the down-arrow button to scroll down. Basically, the script is the same, except you'll subtract 1 instead of adding it. Here's the final code for the down-arrow button:

    ```
    on (press) {
        traffic.scroll = traffic.scroll-1;
    }
    ```

6. Test the movie. Notice that the text now scrolls up as well as down.

24

GETTING AND SENDING DATA

FIGURE 24.8

Notice all the different regions in the report.

FIGURE 24.9

Two buttons representing the scroll-up and scroll-down arrows.

FIGURE 24.10

The text can be scrolled up.

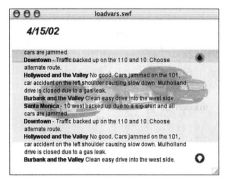

You can download the completed file on the companion Web site located at
`http://www.flashmxunleashed.com`.

Sending a Form to an E-mail Account

The most frequent question I get from my students when I teach class is, how can I send form data to an e-mail account? There are really two different ways. The first way is the easiest way in the sense that all you need to do is make clever use of the getURL action. The second way is a bit more sophisticated and really opens the door up to a great deal of possibilities because it uses Common Gateway Interface (CGI), which is server-side scripting. It's more powerful and lays the groundwork for you to interact with any CGI script, not just the one you're about to create in the next exercise. You can preview the completed exercise by downloading eMailDone.fla from the companion Web site located at http://www.flashmxunleashed.com.

Sending Form Data to an E-mail Account

In this exercise, you're going to send information that an end user fills out in a form to a specified e-mail address. Here are the steps to follow:

1. Create a new document. In this new document, set up four different text fields. Make the first one single line, input text, and give it a variable name of **name**. Create a second input text field, this time make it a multi-line text field and give it a variable name of **address**. Create a third, single-line text field and give it a variable name of **homephone**. Finally, create a fourth, single-line text field and give it variable name of **cellphone**. Next, type these variable names next to the text fields so that the end user knows what information you're looking for, as shown in Figure 24.11.

2. With frame 1 selected on the timeline, press F9 to open the Actions panel. You need to set up some variables that you can use when opening the e-mail program on the client's machine.

3. Set a variable for the e-mail address you want to send the form to. Also, you need to set one for the subject and for the mailto action. Here's the final code for frame 1 (of course, yours may vary depending on which e-mail account you want to send the information to):

```
email = "mpz@flashmxunleashed.com";

contact = "Matthew Pizzi";

mailto = "mailto:" + contact + "<" + email + ">";

subject = "Flash Form Feedback";

stop ();
```

Notice that there's a stop action at the end of the script to avoid the movie playing beyond frame 1.

4. Highlight frame 10 and insert a blank keyframe by pressing F7. In this new keyframe, type on the stage **Thank you for submitting the form.**, as shown in Figure 24.12.

5. Move the playhead back to frame 1. Drag out an instance of a button from a common library or create your own. This will act as the submit button.

6. With the button selected, press F9 on your keyboard to open the Actions panel. You need to use an event handler to apply the getURL action. Here's the final code:

```
on (press) {
    getURL ("mailto:mpz@flashmxunleahsed.com" +
"?subject" + _root.subject + newline + "&body" +
"Name:" + name + newline + "Address:" + address +
"Home Phone:" + homephone + "Cell Phone:" + cellphone);
    _root.gotoAndStop(10);
}
```

7. Test the movie and fill out the form. After filling out the form, notice that the movie does go to frame 10, as shown in Figure 24.13. The e-mail client opens on the end user's machine with all the information appended to the e-mail, as shown in Figure 24.14.

FIGURE 24.11

All the text fields have labels next to them.

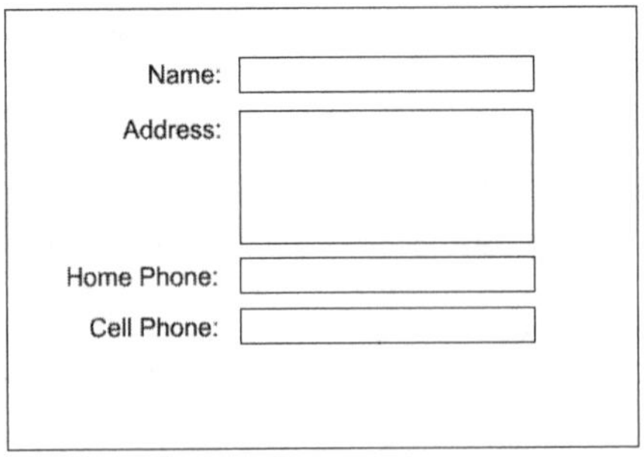

Name:	
Address:	
Home Phone:	
Cell Phone:	

FIGURE 24.12

The stage is empty except for the text you just typed.

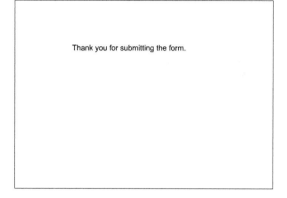

FIGURE 24.13

The movie goes to frame 10.

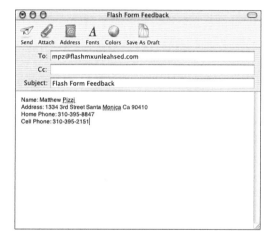

FIGURE 24.14

The e-mail client has all the information already filled out.

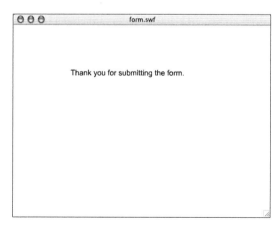

You can download a complete working file from the companion Web site located at `http://www.flashmxunleashed.com`.

It's pretty easy to send or move information out of a Flash movie and into an e-mail program. Next, we're going to take a look at how to get the Flash movie to work with a CGI script.

Download the `Flash_Form.fla` file from the companion Web site. You'll notice it's a completed form with text boxes. All you need to do is add the CGI script. Here are the steps for this exercise:

1. Open the `Flash_Form.fla` file you downloaded from the Unleashed site. Create a new layer and name it **submit**.

2. With the submit layer active and the playhead on frame 1, drag out a button instance from the Common Library. If you forget how to open the Common Library, choose Window, Common Library, Buttons.fla.

3. With the button selected, press F9 to open the Actions panel. You need to use the `getUrl` action to send this form to the CGI bin of your Web server. We'll use the `POST` method for this. You also need to set up some variables to set the e-mail address where the form should be submitted. You also are going to set up a variable to create a subject for the e-mail, and you're going to call an HTML document that the browser can move to once the action is completed. Here's the final code:

```
on (release) {
    _MAILTO = "mpz@trainsimple.com";
    _SUBJECT = "Try";
    _THANKS = "thanks.htm";
    getURL("http://www.flashmxunleashed.com
/cgi-bin/tmail/tmail.cgi", "", "POST");
}
```

You are welcome to use this CGI script for testing, but if you have a high production server, you'll need to acquire your own CGI script. You can download the completed file from the companion Web site.

An Introduction to Flash and ColdFusion Integration

Dennis Baldwin

CHAPTER 25

In this chapter we're going to briefly cover Flash and ColdFusion integration, along with some of the new ActionScript classes built in to Flash MX. This might seem a bit overwhelming at first, but once you've covered the basic principles, you'll be well on your way to developing the next generation of integrated applications. We'll take a brief look at components, some of the previous Flash methods, and Macromedia Flash Remoting service, which consists of new ActionScript classes as well as the Flash Gateway. We'll end up walking through a basic application that goes into detail using some of the new components that ship with Flash and ColdFusion MX. Of course, you could still develop this application using the previous methods, such as loadVariables, getURL, and the XML object. Not that these methods aren't up to the task, but the functionality built in to the new products provides for better performance and reliability. You will also see that the integration is tighter, meaning you don't have to deal with common workarounds to get Flash and ColdFusion to talk to each other. What's more, you'll get a taste of using the Macromedia Flash Remoting service component to communicate with leading Web application servers. Macromedia has worked hard to bring tighter integration among its flagship products, which is a strong selling point for ColdFusion MX. This allows developers and designers to create robust Flash applications that increase usability and introduce a new era of Internet applications.

With Flash MX, Macromedia introduces the next generation of Internet applications and development. Designers and developers have the capability to work together to create robust Flash applications. This goes beyond using Flash as a visual element; instead, it's used to create a unique user experience integrated with a powerful database back end. This allows for the separation of application logic and the Flash user interface. Designers can create the Flash UI while developers concentrate on creating reusable components. Developers can pass these components on to designers, where all they need to do is specify certain parameters and default values for the components to work. This not only separates application logic from the Flash UI but allows designers and developers to work in conjunction—which gives new meaning to Internet development.

Now with the MX versions of Flash and ColdFusion, Macromedia has brought the client and server closer together. The communication is still done over HTTP but with a new format called the *Action Message Format* (AMF). AMF is part of Macromedia Flash Remoting service, which Macromedia has introduced in Flash and ColdFusion MX. You're now able to access the client ActionScript classes that will communicate with the Flash Gateway, the server-side component of Macromedia Flash Remoting service. In previous versions of Flash, most integration with application servers such as ColdFusion was accomplished with getURL, loadVariables, and the XML object. These methods are still available in the Flash 6 player, but AMF is preferred when dealing with integers, recordsets, arrays, and structures.

Many people have frowned upon the nature of Flash because, in the past, it has been used to create useless intros and animations. (I use the term *useless* loosely because there was a point in time when Flash intros were exciting and unique.) Now it seems like just about every site has a Flash intro with a "skip intro" button. This chapter aims to go beyond using Flash as an animation tool by integrating unique user experiences with database back ends. Flash MX provides new meaning to Internet applications via the ability to interact with enterprise application servers and display on devices such as PDAs, game consoles, and smart phones. This will allow designers to create a Flash UI that displays consistently across multiple platforms. Developers can create application logic to interact with the Flash UI and provide dynamic content wherever the Flash movie is being viewed.

Components

Along with increased usability, the development process is improved because designers and developers can work together to create Flash applications. Flash MX has built-in components that are similar to smart clips but offer more functionality. You have the ability to access all sorts of properties, parameters, and methods of these clips. They can be found in the Components panel (Window, Components) and can simply be dragged and dropped onto the stage. Figure 25.1 shows the default components panel that ships with Flash MX.

FIGURE 25.1

Flash MX Components panel.

These are the default components that ship with Flash, and they allow for more control of forms and maintaining data. You can also download Components Panel Set 2 from the Macromedia Exchange (`http://www.macromedia.com/exchange/flash`).

You will need the Macromedia Extension Manager to install the second set, but these components are free and well worth the time they'll save you in the future. Hundreds of components are available on the Macromedia Exchange, and you can even feel free to submit your own. Many components are added daily, making this a great place to start when building your application. Figure 25.2 shows the second component set.

FIGURE 25.2

Flash MX Components Panel Set 2.

These components contain many methods and properties that add interactivity and functionality to your Flash movies. For more information on components, look in the ActionScript dictionary under *F*. You'll see in a later example that these components come in very handy when integrating with ColdFusion. Not only that, they save you hours of development time when creating Flash applications. For example, at some point you'll have the need to use a scrollbar in one of your applications. Coding a scrollbar isn't considered anything complex, but it can definitely be time consuming. The purpose of components is to provide reusable code so you don't end up reinventing the wheel.

Not only do components save time but they offer a way for designers and developers to work together when creating Flash applications. Components provide a way to separate the code from the display. Developers can create custom components and pass them on to junior-level developers or designers to include in their movies. The designer simply needs to know how to set a few properties or parameters for the clip, and everything else is taken care of. This provides for a rapid application development (RAD) environment for Web teams. Libraries of custom components can be developed and reused in future projects, which can save hours of development and debugging time.

Creating custom components is beyond the scope of this chapter but is something worth investigating. If you've ever developed a repetitive task within Flash, it may be time to consider creating custom components and code that can be reused in your applications.

Previous Integration Methods

In previous versions of Flash, Macromedia introduced ways to communicate with application servers over HTTP. These methods included getURL, loadVariables, and the XML object. Each method has its pros and cons and is still available in the Flash 6 player. Although we'll briefly cover these methods, you'll be introduced to new ways of accomplishing these tasks.

getURL

The getURL method was introduced in the Flash 2 player, but the GET and POST options are only available to the Flash 4 player and above. This has always been a good way to send data to the server, but it calls for the Flash movie to redirect the browser to another page. This usually consists of a Flash movie sending variables to a non-Flash page, which in turn processes the data. This is also a one-way path because you can only send data from Flash but not retrieve it.

loadVariables

The loadVariables method was a great addition to the Flash 4 player, providing the ability to send data via GET or POST. The advantage of using loadVariables is that the Flash movie makes an HTTP request to the server without having to redirect the Flash movie. This is all handled behind the scenes. The problem with loadVariables is that the data needs to be URL encoded and sent in name/value pairs. This prevents sending and receiving complex data such as arrays, objects, and recordsets. There are ways to accomplish sending complex structures to and from Flash, but this requires a good bit of ActionScript knowledge, and these workarounds generally require more overhead from the Flash player.

The XML Object

The XML object provides a great way to send and receive complex data structures to and from Flash. This was introduced in Flash 5 and works seamlessly with servers that transfer information using XML packets. Sending data using the XML object provides structure to your data as well as increased speed and reliability. The XML parsing and performance has improved dramatically in the Flash 6 player. In version 5, an XML packet that contained many child nodes ran poorly, and the preferred method was to use XML packets that contained attributes instead of nodes. Now XML packets can contain many child nodes, and the performance gain is substantial. Although performance has increased, you should still take caution as to how much data you're loading. It is still recommended that you break your data up into pieces if you're dealing with lots of information. This can reduce strain on the Flash player and improve the end-user experience.

If you need to interact with different application servers that utilize XML, then using the XML object is the preferred method. Because performance and reliability have increased, it would be advantageous to become familiar with the XML object and use it in your applications.

As you can see, these previous methods all have their pros and cons. If you're dealing with simple integration, then getURL and loadVariables are both up to the task. If you have the need to transfer structured data in an efficient manner, consider using the XML object. Make sure you analyze your application before development. Outline a specification document that will help you determine whether you can use these older methods to accomplish your task.

If you're looking to build a robust Flash application where Flash will serve solely as the front end, you should explore the new Macromedia Flash Remoting service components. We'll discuss Macromedia Flash Remoting service and then get our hands dirty with an account management application that will go into detail of Flash and ColdFusion MX integration.

Macromedia Flash Remoting service

Macromedia Flash Remoting service serves as the layer of communication between Flash and the application server. Developers will now be able to interact with different application servers, such as ColdFusion MX, Java, and .NET servers. All communication will be handled via the new Action Message Format (AMF), which works over HTTP. The server-side component of Macromedia Flash Remoting service, known as the *Flash Gateway*, allows developers to make calls from Flash to the application server. New Macromedia Flash Remoting service classes are now available in ActionScript that allow

Flash to communicate with the server through the Flash Gateway. These classes are known as *NetServices* and offer increased performance and functionality over the older methods.

Figure 25.3 shows the relationship between Flash, Macromedia Flash Remoting service, and the application server.

FIGURE 25.3

The relationship between Flash, Macromedia Flash Remoting service, and the application server.

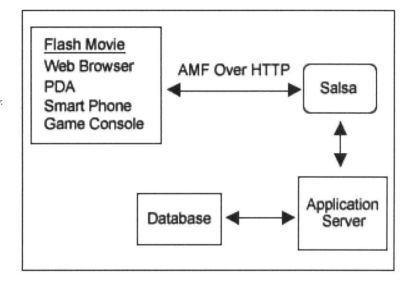

You'll become more familiar with Macromedia Flash Remoting service and how it works when we take a look at the sample application for this chapter. The Macromedia Flash Remoting service component, from a user's standpoint, is completely invisible. It was designed to make the developer's life easier by creating a standardized method of developing and debugging entire Flash applications.

A Basic Account Management System

Now that you have a basic grasp of the server-side functionality, we're going to walk through an entire application that utilizes some of the new features. As mentioned earlier, this application could be developed the old way using `loadVariables` or the `XML` object. Our goal is to walk through the development of an application that shows the power and capabilities of these Macromedia Flash Remoting service components. There are so many new server-side components that it's almost like learning an entirely new program. Because we can't cover everything in this chapter, it will be just enough to intrigue you and get you started developing your own Flash/ColdFusion MX applications.

This example requires that you have ColdFusion MX installed and running. You'll also need the Flash MX add-ons, which contain the ActionScript classes and components necessary to connect to the Flash Gateway and help you debug your application. The application will be tested and run from localhost, and you can change this to whatever your IP address or hostname is. You'll see this specified in the ActionScript code shortly.

Getting Started

Copy the file `ch25.zip` to your Web root `c:\neo\wwwroot`. Now unzip this file and make sure the files reside in `c:\neo\wwwroot\flashexamples\ch25`. This directory structure is key to developing the application. Of course, you can change the structure, but this should be reflected within the Flash ActionScript code. Your directory structure should look similar to Figure 25.4.

FIGURE 25.4

Account management directory structure.

This application will demonstrate a user account management system in which data records can be updated and deleted from the Flash UI. The Flash Gateway, the server-side component of Macromedia Flash Remoting service, will be used to transmit information between itself and the application server. The application server will then query a database and pass information back to the Flash Gateway. Figure 25.5 demonstrates the communication process.

FIGURE 25.5

The communication process via Macromedia Flash Remoting service.

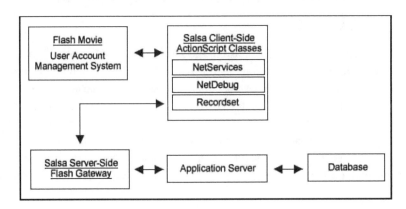

Macromedia Flash Remoting service requires the use of ActionScript classes along with server-side creation of Macromedia Flash Remoting service services in ColdFusion MX. As you can see, Macromedia Flash Remoting service serves as the bridge between Flash and the ColdFusion application server. The following account management application will introduce the code and techniques to build dynamic Web applications. Let's get started.

Files in the Application

First off, we're going to take a look through each of the files and get a basic of understanding of what they do. Following is a list of files included with this application that can be found in /wwwroot/flashexamples/ch25/:

- Accountmanagement.fla
- Accountmanagement.html
- Accountmanagement.swf
- Application.cfm
- deleteUser.cfm
- getUserInfo.cfm
- getUserList.cfm
- updateUser.cfm
- users.mdb

The Database

The key to any Web application is the database along with the structure. If you take a look at users.mdb, you'll see the design of the table, as shown in Figure 25.6.

The data structure is very straightforward, and you'll see that UserID is the primary key for the users table. This is what we'll use to pass between the Flash Gateway and ColdFusion when updating and deleting records. Other information will be passed, but the user ID is unique to each user and lets us know which record to update or delete.

The ColdFusion Templates

Now we're going to take a look at each of the ColdFusion templates. Application.cfm simply serves to store the Data Source Name (DSN), which in this case is accountmanagement. This is set as a global request variable and will be called from other templates when making database queries. The DSN will need to be set up through the ColdFusion Administrator, which is shown in Figure 25.7. You can change the DSN to any name you prefer—just make sure this is consistent in the Application.cfm template and the ColdFusion administrator.

25

FLASH AND
COLD FUSION
INTEGRATION

FIGURE 25.6

*Database struc-
ture for user's
table.*

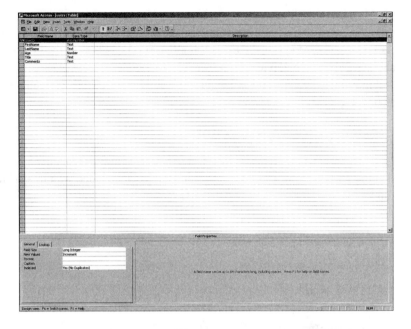

FIGURE 25.7

*Managing ODBC
data sources in
ColdFusion
Administrator.*

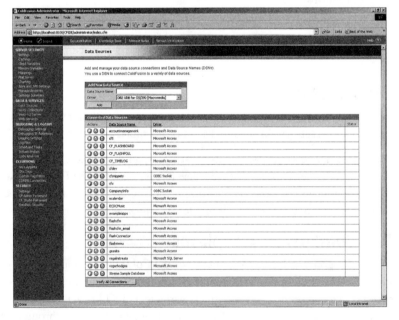

We'll take a brief look at the rest of the templates in the order they'll be accessed throughout the application. The `getUserList.cfm` template is used to populate the List Box component within Flash. Figure 25.8 shows the communication process, which grabs information from ColdFusion and populates the list box. You'll see that this component has tremendous functionality and can even be controlled using the up and down arrows on your keyboard. When a selection is made, a change-handler function will be called (in this case, it calls the `getUserInfo.cfm` template).

FIGURE 25.8

Communication between Flash and the application server to retrieve the user list.

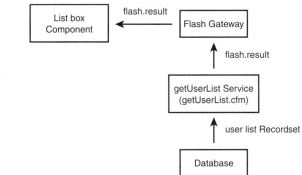

The `getUserInfo.cfm` template is used to query the database and grab the selected user's information, as shown in Figure 25.9. Once a selection is made from the list box, a unique user ID is passed to the template. The user ID is passed through the Flash Gateway, and the template queries the database via the user ID. The recordset is then passed back to Flash and handled accordingly to display the user's information.

FIGURE 25.9

Communication between Flash and the application server to retrieve the user's information.

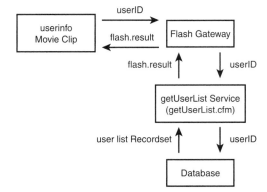

Once the information has been loaded into the Flash UI, the user can then edit the text fields and modify the data. If the Update button is clicked, a change handler is called that will send the user ID along with the other data to the `updateUser.cfm` template through the Flash Gateway. The template will then update the database via the unique user ID. After the database has been updated, another call to the `getUserList.cfm` template is made that will update the list box in case any names have been changed.

Similarly, once the Delete button is clicked, the user ID will be passed to the `deleteUser.cfm` template. The record will be removed from the database via the user ID. Once the record has been removed, we'll call the `getUserList.cfm` template again to display the most current list of names.

The Flash File

The Flash source file, `Accountmanagement.fla`, contains all the ActionScript, components, and graphics that create the front end of the sample application.

The compiled Flash file, `Accountmanagement.swf`, is what will be displayed in the `Accountmanagement.html` file. We'll be accessing this HTML page when we're not testing inside the Flash Integrated Development Environment (IDE).

We're now going to take a detailed look at the source code and how it interacts with the Flash Gateway. We'll also look into the NetConnect Debugger, which will make your life easier when debugging applications.

Movie Structure

Let's open the Flash source file and look at the overall structure of the sample movie. The structure of this movie consists of two main movie clips that handle the display of information. The first clip is actually a List Box component and is assigned an instance name of `userList`. You can view instance names of movie clips in the properties panel. The next movie clip is given an instance name of `userInfo` and will be used to display the user's information along with the Update and Delete buttons. The `userInfo` clip also contains a couple of subclips that display different response messages, depending on the user's selection. There are a few other graphical elements you can see while looking through the movie structure displayed in Figure 25.10.

FIGURE 25.10

The `Account-management.fla` *movie structure.*

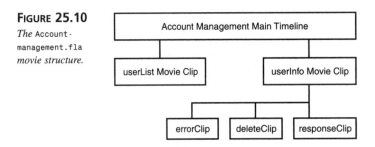

Understanding the Code

In frame 1 of the main timeline, you'll see most of the ActionScript code necessary to run the user-management application. For learning purposes, most of the code resides here, because it's easier to follow than having to search for code within different movie clips. It's always good practice to build modular code (that is, code that's broken into components). The code is centralized, but you'll see that it is broken into different components that handle different functions. The first two lines of code are `#include` statements that load the `NetServices` and `NetDebug` classes into the movie once it has been published from the Flash IDE:

```
// include the Macromedia Flash Remoting service client-side classes
#include "NetServices.as"
#include "NetDebug.as"
```

These classes are part of the client-side component of Macromedia Flash Remoting service. As mentioned earlier, you'll need to install the Flash MX add-ons, which include these classes as well as the NetConnect Debugger component. The `NetServices` class is used to create the two-way connection between Flash and the Flash Gateway. The `NetDebug` class is used in conjunction with the NetConnect Debugger (Window, NetConnect Debugger). If you do not intend on using the debugger, it is not necessary to include it in your code. This will help reduce file size, even though it doesn't add much. I would recommend using the debugger while testing and then commenting it out or removing it once you've finished debugging. After the proper classes are included, we can make the connection to the Flash Gateway:

```
// lets make sure we only run this block of code once
if (initialized == null) {
// set initialized to true so we don't run this again
var initialized = true;
//
NetServices.setDefaultGatewayUrl("http://127.0.0.1:8100/flashservices/
➥ gateway");
var gatewayConnection = NetServices.createGatewayConnection();
var userService = gatewayConnection.getService("flashexamples.ch25", this);
}
```

The connection to the gateway only needs to be established once. Therefore, we check for the existence of the variable `initialized`. If it doesn't exist, the `if` statement will run and set it to `True`, meaning it will only run once. After the initial connection is made, we can make as many calls and data transfers as necessary throughout our application. The default gateway URL specifies the gateway we'll be connecting to on the local machine. You can also specify a secure protocol (HTTPS) to be used with the Flash Gateway. The next line of code actually creates the connection to the Flash Gateway and sets it to the `gatewayConnection` variable. A URL string can also be specified as a parameter for this method, but Macromedia recommends specifying the URL in the `setDefaultGatewayURL` method. Once the connection has been made, we connect to our service directory under `flashexamples.ch25` and set this to the `userService` variable. We will now be able to make calls to our Macromedia Flash Remoting service server-side services via the `userService` variable.

We'll now be accessing service functions, which correspond to the ColdFusion templates mentioned earlier, to handle our data. The first service function we'll look into is the getUserList function:

```
function getUserList() {
    userService.getUserList();
}
getUserList();
```

The order in which this code is specified doesn't matter. We can place the call to getUserList before the function declaration. The user list service is called several times throughout the application and is used to load or reload data into the List Box component. Note that when we make a call to a service function, we'll be waiting for the data to be returned from the Flash Gateway. To capture the results, we need to specify a result function that will capture the data. All data returned to service functions will be sent to the function with _Result appended to the name (for example, getUserList_Result):

```
// initialize the array to store our list elements
var valueList = new Array();
function getUserList_Result(resultRecordset) {
    for (i in resultRecordset.items) {
        // grab the id, first name, and last name to store in tempObj
        var userid = resultRecordset.items[i].userid;
        var firstname = resultRecordset.items[i].firstname;
        var lastname = resultRecordset.items[i].lastname;
        // create a temporary object that will
➥ contain the id, first name, and last name
        // the first name and last name will be
➥ labels and the id will be our data
        // then set it in the array which will be used to populate our userlist
        var tempObj = new Object();
        tempObj.label = firstname + " " + lastname;
        tempObj.data = userid;
        valueList[i] = tempObj;
    }
        // set the user list
        userList.setDataProvider(valueList);
}
```

When the movie initially plays, we call the getUserList service, and the recordset is sent back to getUserList_Result. This function is used to loop through the items of the recordset, and we set them to local variables in Flash. In this case, we're dealing with the userid, firstname, and lastname of each user. While we're looping through the recordset, we create a temporary object to store the object's label and data. The label for the list box is the user's first name and last name, which will display in the list box. We also set the data for each user in the temporary object, which is userid. The data variable is invisible to the user and is what we'll use to grab the user's information, update it, and delete the record. Through each iteration of the loop, we set the temporary object and then append it to the `valueList` array. Once the looping has completed, we take the `valueList` array and place it in the `setDataProvider` method of the `userList` list box. Remember that `userList` corresponds to the instance name of the List Box component on the stage. See Figure 25.11 to view the populated List Box component.

FIGURE 25.11
User list display in the Flash movie.

The `setDataProvider` method of the List Box component is one of many methods we have access to with the new Flash MX components. To learn more about the methods and properties of components, be sure to view the ActionScript dictionary under *F*.

So far, you've seen the code that loops through the user list recordset. Now you need to see what's happening on the server side. If you look at the server-side code in `getUserList.cfm`, here's what you'll see:

```
<cfquery datasource="#request.dsn#" name="getusers" dbtype="odbc">
select userid, firstname, lastname
from users;
</cfquery>
<cfset flash.result=getusers>
```

In this query, we're grabbing a recordset from the database that contains the user's ID, first name, and last name. These results are then set in `flash.result`, which will be passed back to the `getUserList_Result` function in Flash.

If you're familiar with ColdFusion, you'll see that a new variable scope has been introduced. That's right, we now have access to the Flash variable scope, which will pass the result to the Flash Gateway and then to the Flash movie. Here is a list of the variables within the Flash scope:

- `flash.result`. A variable that will be passed to the Flash movie
- `flash.params`. A structure of parameters passed from the Flash movie
- `flash.pagesize`. Specifies the number of records passed to the Flash movie at a time

The `flash.result` variable can pass strings, integers, recordsets, arrays, structures, and Boolean values to the Flash movie. This makes it easier to send structured data, such as recordsets, to Flash movies than in the past.

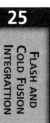

25

FLASH AND
COLD FUSION
INTEGRATION

So we've successfully made our initial request to the server and populated the list box with our results, not too shabby! Now the next step is to handle the event of a user clicking one of the list box entries. What we want to do is display the information for the selected user. With the List Box component, we have access to a change-handler method. This calls a custom function that we specify whenever the selection within the box changes. Select the List Box component on the stage and view the properties. You'll see that we call the `handleSelected` function for the change handler:

```
function handleSelected() {
    var selectedID = userList.getSelectedItem().data;
    getUserInfo(selectedID);
    userInfo.gotoAndStop(2);
}
```

The function initializes the `selectedID` variable and sets the user ID to it. The `data` variable corresponds to the user ID and was set earlier by our `getUserList_Result` function. Once again, UserID serves as the unique key for our users and allows us to retrieve, update, and delete user data.

We now make a call to the `getUserInfo` service, which queries the database and returns the information for the selected user. After the call is made to the server for the user information, we tell the `userInfo` movie clip to go to and stop on frame 2. This all happens instantaneously, and while the `userInfo` clip is sent to frame 2, we wait for the Flash Gateway to return the recordset to `getUserInfo_Result`:

```
function getUserInfo_Result(resultRecordset) {
        // grab the values from the recordset
        var userid = resultRecordset.items[0].userid;
        var firstname = resultRecordset.items[0].firstname;
        var lastname = resultRecordset.items[0].lastname;
        var age = resultRecordset.items[0].age;
        var title = resultRecordset.items[0].title;
        var comments = resultRecordset.items[0].comments;
        // set the values in the userinfo clip for display
        // the userid will be used to update and delete users
        userInfo.userid = userid;
        userInfo.firstname = firstname;
        userInfo.lastname = lastname;
        userInfo.age = age;
        userInfo.title = title;
        userInfo.comments = comments;
}
```

The function waits for the recordset object that is passed back from the `getUserInfo` service. The necessary variables—userid, `firstname`, `lastname`, age, `title`, and comments—are pulled from the recordset and then placed in the `userInfo` clip for display. The output of the `userInfo` clip is shown in Figure 25.12.

FIGURE 25.12

User information display in the Flash movie.

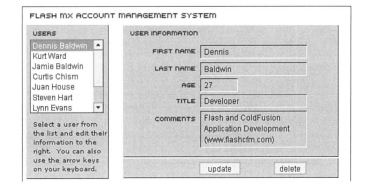

Let's take a look at the server-side ColdFusion `getUserInfo` service and the code that handles this task:

```
<cfset userid = flash.params[1]>
<cfquery datasource="#request.dsn#" name="getuserinfo">
select userid, firstname, lastname, age, title, comments
from users
where userid = #userid#;
</cfquery>
<cfset flash.result=getuserinfo>
```

The first `<cfset>` statement grabs the user ID that is passed from the Flash `getUserInfo(userid)` function and sets it to a local CF variable. Next, we query the database using the user ID and place the results of the recordset in the `flash.result` variable. This is passed through the Flash Gateway and back to Flash and is handled by the `getUserInfo_Result` function.

So far, everything we've covered has been read-only type interaction. Now we're going to look into updating and deleting user information and the code that will handle these tasks.

If you look inside of the `userInfo` clip, frame 1 contains the necessary ActionScript functions to handle the update and delete actions. These functions are declared in frame 1 and await a user event once the movie clip is sent to frame 2. In frame 2, you'll see the dynamic text fields along with the Update and Delete buttons. These buttons are also new components that ship with MX, called *pushbuttons*. The buttons have a click-handler method that is called whenever one is clicked.

The Update button's click handler is the `updateUser` function. When the button is clicked, the function is called and the `updateUser` service is put to work:

```
function updateUser() {
    // make sure that all fields are filled out
```

25

FLASH AND
COLD FUSION
INTEGRATION

```
// simple validation to see if data exists in the text field
if(firstname != '' && lastname != '' && age != ''
&& title != '' && comments !='') {
    // go to frame 3 which will display the response message
    this.gotoAndStop(3);
    // call the update user service to update the database contents
    // the result will be returned to updateUser_Result in _root
    _root.userService.updateUser(userid, firstname, lastname,
age, title, comments);
    // refresh the user list in case a firstname or lastname was changed
    _root.userService.getUserList();
    } else {
    // send error message that one or more fields are missing
    errorClip.gotoAndPlay(2);
    }
}
```

This function performs basic validation, just to see whether the fields actually have any data in them before the service is called. If there is no data in the fields, we target the clip errorClip and tell it to play. This basically prompts the user to fill out these fields. If there is data in the fields, the userInfo clip is sent to frame 3, which displays a sub-clip called responseClip and displays an "Updating Database" message.

The updateUser service is then called (note that we call it from root because that's where updateUser_Result resides). We pass the userid, firstname, lastname, age, title, and comments parameters to the updateUser service. The ColdFusion updateUser.cfm template will take these parameters and update the database with the new information:

```
<cftry>
<cfset userid = flash.params[1]>
<cfset firstname = flash.params[2]>
<cfset lastname = flash.params[3]>
<cfset age = flash.params[4]>
<cfset title = flash.params[5]>
<cfset comments = flash.params[6]>
<cfquery datasource="#request.dsn#" dbtype="odbc">
update users
set firstname='#firstname#', lastname='#lastname#',
age=#age#, title='#title#', comments='#comments#'
where userid = #userid#;
</cfquery>
<cfset flash.result=1>
<cfcatch>
<cfset flash.result=0>
</cfcatch>
</cftry>
```

With this template, we're basically setting the parameters passed from Flash, through the gateway, to local CF variables. The query then updates the user's information based on the user ID. You'll see that we've introduced a `<cftry>…<cfcatch>` statement that will tell us whether the update was successful. If it is successful, we send a value of 1 (`True`) back to Flash. If it is not successful, we send 0 (`False`).

With these values, the `updateUser_Result` function will then determine what response to send to the user through the `userInfo.responseClip` movie clip:

```
function updateUser_Result(success) {
    if(success) {
    // update successful so display the success message
    userInfo.responseClip.gotoAndPlay("success");
    } else {
    // update failed so display the failed message
    userInfo.responseClip.gotoAndPlay("failed");
    }
}
```

If the update is successful, we target `responseClip` and tell it to go to and play the success frame. This will display a message of "success" to the user. After this message is finished displaying, the _parent clip of `responseClip`, which is `userInfo`, is sent back to frame 2. The new information is displayed, and a call is made to the `getUserList` service. The reason for the call to `getUserList` is to refresh the list box with the new `firstname` and `lastname` values if the record was updated.

The last piece of the puzzle involves handling the Delete pushbutton if it's clicked. You'll see that the sequence of events is very similar to the update action. The click handler for the Delete button is the `deleteUser` function, which resides in frame 1 of the `userInfo` clip.

Before we let users delete any information, we first need to prompt them to confirm that this is what they want to do:

```
function deleteUser() {
    // set the current userid in the delete clip
    // the userid will be passed from the delete clip to the deleteUser service
    deleteClip.userid = userid;
    // play the delete clip
    deleteClip.play();
}
```

We set the `userid` inside of `deleteClip`, which resides in frame 2 of the `userInfo` movie clip. After we set the `userid`, we then tell the delete movie clip to play. This will display a prompt and then let the user click a Yes or No button to confirm. The click handlers for both of these buttons reside in frame 1 of `deleteClip`:

```
function deleteUser() {
    // call the deleteUser service which will returned
    // to deleteUser_Result in _root
    _root.userService.deleteUser(userid);
}

function doNotDeleteUser() {
    // return the current clip to frame 1
    this.gotoAndStop(1);
}
```

If the Yes button is clicked, we call the `deleteUser` service, pass the `userid`, and wait for the response in `_root`. The `deleteUser_Result` function will wait for the response and, if successful, display a "success" message. If it fails, a "failed" message is displayed:

```
function deleteUser_Result(success) {
    if(success) {
    // delete successful so display the success message
    userInfo.deleteClip.gotoAndPlay("success");
    // reload the user list since the user has been deleted
    userService.getUserList();
    // reset the userinfo fields until another user has been selected
    userInfo.firstname = "";
    userInfo.lastname = "";
    userInfo.age = "";
    userInfo.title = "";
    userInfo.comments = "";
    } else {
    // delete failed so display the failed message
    userInfo.deleteClip.gotoAndPlay("failed");
    }
}
```

We also need to reset the fields in the `userInfo` clip when deleting the user, which can be seen in the preceding code snippet. The last thing we'll look into is the code for the ColdFusion `deleteUser.cfm` template:

```
<cftry>
<cfset userid = flash.params[1]>
<cfquery datasource="#request.dsn#" name="getuserinfo">
delete from users
where userid = #userid#;
</cfquery>
<cfset flash.result=1>
<cfcatch>
<cfset flash.result=0>
</cfcatch>
</cftry>
```

Once again, we set the `userid` passed from Flash to a local CF variable; then we perform a delete query based on the `userid` variable. If the query is successful, we send a value of 1 to Flash; if the query is not successful, we send a value of 0. The `deleteUser_Result` function will take care of the rest and determine what message to display to the user.

Debugging

An application is never complete without some knowledge of how to debug it and fix anything that might be broken. This application should run perfectly out of the box, but not without troubleshooting and debugging during development. This is where the `NetDebug` class comes in handy. In Flash MX we now have access to this class and a nice tool called the NetConnect Debugger. To enable this during testing go to Window, NetConnect Debugger. Make sure you enable this before you test the movie. Figure 24.13 shows the NetConnect Debugger in action.

FIGURE 24.13

NetConnect Debugger window.

This window displays all calls made to the Flash Gateway and any results sent back to Flash. It lists any parameters that are available, along with all sorts of useful information to improve debugging. If errors are occurring or you're not receiving the expected results, this is a great place to troubleshoot your application. You'll also see error codes and messages if your application doesn't work correctly. Take some time to get familiar with this window because it will definitely save you time and frustration in the future.

There's a lot of information to soak in here, but once you grasp some of the concepts in this application, you'll find that the new Macromedia Flash Remoting service services are very intuitive and provide for almost unlimited possibilities.

Advancing Your Skills

This application would not be complete without the ability to add new users to the database. That's why we challenge you to use what you've learned in this chapter to apply "Add User" functionality. You will then be able to add users to the database, modify their information, and delete them if necessary.

Also consider using shared objects to store data locally on the user's machine. You could let users log in and have their personal information pulled into Flash from the local machine without having to send a request to the server. This would save from having to making any unnecessary calls to the server. Once the information is updated, you could send the information to the server and also save it locally for the next time the information is displayed.

Another area to explore is ColdFusion components that are new to ColdFusion MX. Components provide for a means of reusing code that is stored in a single location. You can invoke methods on components and receive method results. These are similar to Flash components in that they provide for RAD and allow you to separate application logic from the display code. ColdFusion components are stored in files with a `.cfc` extension.

Summary

As mentioned earlier, you have unlimited possibilities with Flash and ColdFusion MX. The Web is constantly changing and so are the tools and applications utilized in today's Web market. It's key to stay at the forefront of Internet application development. We need to be able to build cutting-edge applications in less time, and Macromedia has provided us with the technology to do this.

CHAPTER 26

Integration with ASP

By Dan Waters

Now that you have discovered the endless aesthetic and functional ability of Flash MX, you are equipped with an extraordinarily powerful design tool. It is time to broaden the horizons once again. Not only does Flash MX facilitate the creation of beautiful, professional design; it also provides the developer with different ways of accessing data from a variety of locations.

You have seen how ColdFusion works with Flash MX. Now, we'll explore another solution for linking your database with a Flash movie: Active Server Pages. Using a combination of the techniques discussed in this chapter, you will be able to create a myriad of dynamic, Flash-based data solutions. What's more, you aren't restricted to any particular language. As long as you have the appropriate tools and a suitable algorithm, you can provide your users with precious dynamicity from virtually any source.

Popular applications of this technique include, but are in no way limited to, customized colors, text, guest books, message boards, search engines, user profiles, shopping carts, greeting cards, games, and even full-fledged data browsers (which you will be building at the end of this chapter).

It is helpful to note that most of the communication between Flash and a server-side scripting language is done on the part of the server. Flash should always act as the interface and should handle as little of the processing as possible. This leads to a pleasing conclusion: Flash can be used to display almost anything returned by your language of choice (assuming your language provides some form of output function).

Before we begin, you will learn exactly what you need to harness the power of Flash and ASP. A few software items are required, and you must have a particular server configuration accessible to you if you wish to use ASP.

We will start by covering the basics and theory behind data transmission. Following the basic overview, we will discuss how to send data from Flash to ASP. Then, you will learn how to send data from ASP to Flash. Using information from these sections, we will build a working model, step by step, from the ground up. Following this example, we will discuss databases and the code necessary to open, display, and manage them. This will be followed by a database project. After completing this somewhat long project, we will discuss limitations concerning images and sounds and how to overcome them with Flash MX. At the end of the chapter, you will be presented with a project that can be downloaded from the Web site accompanying this book.

Getting Started

Three major components are involved in the development of a successful Flash-based data solution: Macromedia Flash, a Microsoft-based Web server (or Unix running Chili!ASP) and a preferred text editor. Here are the particulars:

- **Macromedia Flash**. The code presented in this chapter is written for Flash 5 or Flash MX and is designed to run on the Flash 6 player.

- **A Web server**. You need access to a Web server that supports some kind of server-side scripting language, such as CGI, PHP, ASP, ColdFusion, or even Perl. The code in this chapter was built and tested on a Windows XP Professional server. It will also work on Windows NT, Windows 2000, or Windows 95/98.

- **A text editor**. You need a text editor to write your ASP code. Generally, Notepad will suffice for small ASP projects. If you need a flamboyant development environment, Microsoft Visual InterDev handles ASP files, data sources, and project files, complete with syntax highlighting and function hints.

When you have these tools, make sure your server is set up correctly by completing these tasks:

- **Configuring for Windows XP Professional/2000/NT**. Install the latest version of Internet Information Services (IIS). It usually comes with the product CD and can be installed using the Add/Remove Programs menu. If you are running a version of Windows NT older than 4.0 or are experiencing problems accessing a data source, you may need to upgrade Microsoft Data Access Components (MDAC). MDAC and other data access items can be found at `http://www.microsoft.com/data`.

- **Configuring for Windows 95/98**. You can test your Flash and ASP programs on a Windows 95 or Windows 98 machine. To do so, you must install Microsoft Personal Web Server. This comes with the NT 4 Option Pack. The Option Pack can be downloaded from `http://www.microsoft.com/ntserver/nts/downloads/recommended/NT4OptPk/default.asp`.

  Although it is referred to as the *NT 4* Option Pack, the installer will not copy NT files if it detects a Windows 95 or Windows 98 operating system.

- **Configuring for UNIX or Linux**. For ASP programs to run on a UNIX or Linux machine, you must have a component installed that processes ASP. A popular one is Chili!ASP, which can be found at `http://www.chilisoft.com`.

When you have set up the server, you can test the status of your scripting language by writing a small program to output the date, as shown here:

```
<%@Language="VBScript"%>
<%
    Response.Write FormatDateTime(Now(), 1)
%>
```

Save the small script as `test.asp`. Then upload to your server and access it via its absolute path (that is, `http://localhost/test.asp`). If it outputs the date, ASP is most likely working correctly. To further test your system's functional ability, download `SystemTest.zip` from

```
http:www.samspublishing.com
```

and run `SystemTest.asp` from the `http://` protocol.

The last thing you will need is a working knowledge of VBScript and ASP, and experience programming in ActionScript. The ASP examples also assume that you have experience working with Microsoft Access. If ASP is not your strong suit, a great place to learn is `ASP101.com`. Programming experience in any server-side scripting language will be beneficial.

The Concept

Both Flash and ASP have the ability to send data to and receive data from other environments. Naturally, this implies that Flash and ASP can talk to each other using similar methods. The trick to successfully integrating Flash and ASP is rather simple: Gather data from the user in ASP or Flash, format it to the liking of its destination environment, and send that formatted data on its merry way. Program flow and data management are vital to the success of any integration endeavor.

If you have experience with sending variables across the Web, you are probably familiar with a *query string*, which is a sequence of variables and values appended to a Web address that allows another page to receive results from the previous page. Let's examine a simple HTML form:

```
<FORM ACTION="qs.asp" METHOD="GET">
    <INPUT TYPE="hidden" NAME="last_name" VALUE="Smith">
    <INPUT TYPE="submit">
</FORM>
```

A dissection of the code reveals that the form sends data to the file `qs.asp` using the GET method. (The GET method generates a query string, whereas the POST method does not.) It defines a variable called `last_name` and gives it a value of `"Smith"`. When the Submit button is clicked, the user will be taken to the following URL:

```
qs.asp?last_name=Smith
```

The portion of this URL following the question mark is what we are interested in: `last_name=Smith`. As more variables are defined, the query string becomes longer. Each variable and value pair is separated by an ampersand:

```
qs.asp?last_name=Smith&first_name=John&middle_initial=Q
```

The format shown here is called the Variable Definition String (VDS). This is the format in which Flash sends and receives variables. Conveniently, it is also what you will end up with if you URL-encode the correct parts of a properly formatted string in ASP. Specifically, the value following the equal signs (=) must be "URL encoded," whereas the equal signs and variable names themselves should not be URL encoded. This is to ensure that sentences and other groups of letters with special characters (such as white-space) will be translated into Flash properly. When such a string is loaded into Flash, Flash will transform those values into variables within its own memory and initialize them accordingly. Once you import a list of variables, the variables are within the scope of Flash. Let's assume you have written a text file called `variables.txt`, which resides in the same folder as your FLA document. This file should contain only one line, as shown here:

```
size=Medium&color=Navy+Blue&style=Mandarin+Collar
```

This string appears to define the attributes of a particular shirt: a medium navy blue dress shirt with a mandarin collar. You can load these variables into Flash offline using the `loadVariablesNum` function:

```
loadVariablesNum("variables.txt", 0);
```

This call will open `variables.txt`, extract the VDS it finds in the file, and parse that line of text. You will then have access to three variables, already defined by the string:

Variable	Value
_root.size	Medium
_root.color	Navy blue
_root.style	Mandarin collar

As long as the string you load into Flash has URL-encoded values and is in the proper VDS format, Flash will be happy to accept your definitions.

Now, let's try generating a variable definition string using ASP code. The following code below will generate a valid definition string:

```
<%@Language="VBScript"%>
<%
    Option Explicit
    Dim var(3), i, count
    i = 0
    count = 3
    var(0) = "Flash"
    var(1) = "And"
    var(2) = "ASP"
    Do While i < count
        Response.Write "Var" & i & "=" & var(i) & "&"
        i = i + 1
    Loop
    Response.Write "i=" & i
%>
```

This code defines an ASP array of three elements. The loop structure creates a variable/value pair in a VDS and appends additional pairs until the loop condition becomes false. Then it sends the finished VDS to the HTTP response.

When writing your finished VDS to the browser, make sure you have not written anything else to the response. This includes HTML tags or text of any sort. For Flash to read the variables, only the VDS may be transmitted back to the movie. To make sure you are doing this correctly, view the output of your ASP script without using Flash, but with the proper parameters to provide output (just access the script online, with a query string if necessary). Then, view the source. The only thing you should see in the source code is a line of text—your VDS.

Save this code as `test.asp` in a directory on your Web server. In order for it to work, it must be hosted on a server matching the requirements described earlier. Furthermore, you must access it "online," meaning via a URL similar to this:

```
http://localhost/FlashUnleashed/test.asp
```

A URL in this format instructs your Web server to run the script.

The following URL will attempt to "download" the file from another location on your computer and therefore will not work:

```
file://C:\Inetpub\wwwroot\FlashUnleashed\test.asp
```

You should receive output in your Web browser that looks like this:

```
var0=Flash&var1=And&var2=ASP&i=3
```

This VDS initializes four variables in your Flash movie when loaded:

Variable	Value
Var0	Flash
Var1	And
Var2	ASP
i	3

Passing the value of the variable i is good practice, because oftentimes you will need to know exactly how many relevant variables you retrieved in your ASP script and successfully sent to the Flash movie. If you explore the ASP code, you will notice that i is initialized to 0 and incremented each time the loop iterates. It can be used effectively in loops as a *sentinel* value, or as a total value, such as how many results of a search were found.

The VDS format is used to initialize variables in Flash more appropriately than to initialize variables in ASP, although this is possible if necessary. There are two easy ways to initialize Flash variables with such a string: You can either trail the filename of the movie with a query string in the <OBJECT> code, or you can send a VDS-formatted string back to Flash using a loadVariablesNum call.

The length of the VDS is not visibly limited, although I have found it does impact the length of time it takes for Flash to initialize all the variables. A good rule of thumb is to try and keep the number of values you are passing low. For example, if you have 100 test questions with four answers each, do not load 500 variables into Flash. Just run a loop in the Flash movie to load five variables each time. Instead of having a variable scheme such as question_427, 427a, 427b, 427c, & 427d, you could have question, a, b, c, & d and update them using loadVariablesNum each time a new question is to be delivered.

Sending Data from Flash to ASP

The trip from Flash to ASP is much easier on data than the other way around. When you send variables in Flash using the loadVariablesNum or getURL function, you can access them in ASP using the ASP Request collection, like so:

```
<%
    Option Explicit
    Dim MyName    ' As String
    MyName = Request("myname")
%>
```

The line that grabs the variable from Flash—Request("myname")—can be written in three different ways:

Notation	*Refers To*
`Request("myname")`	*myname* from POST or GET
`Request.Form("myname")`	*myname* from POST only
`Request.QueryString("myname")`	*myname* from GET only

You can also specify to load all the variables into (or send variables from) a specific movie clip. This is essential in situations where you want to send variables local to a particular movie clip. To specify a movie clip whose variables you want to send, follow the syntax of the `loadVariablesNum` and `getURL` functions:

```
loadVariables ("myscript.asp", "_root.UserDataClip", "POST");
```

The preceding command would send all the variables in the movie clip with an instance name `UserDataClip` to `myscript.asp` using the POST method. The second parameter specifies the absolute path to the movie clip or the level from which to send your variables. Refer to Chapter 29, "ActionScript Reference," for more information on this function.

If you need to open a new browser window and are able to send all the variables in the current clip, you can use the `getURL` function (note that you cannot specify a source clip or level for variables using `getURL`):

```
getURL ("myscript.asp", "_blank", "POST");
```

Note

Keep in mind that if you decide to use an ASP script in conjunction with `getURL` or `LoadVariables`, you will be unable to see results using Flash's Test Movie feature. You must actually export the SWF file to the server.

Let's apply some of this knowledge and start experimenting.

Example 1: Passing Values From Flash to ASP

We'll begin by creating a new Flash document. Let's call it `ex1.fla` to help us keep track of the examples in this chapter. Here are the steps to follow:

1. In the first keyframe, create a text box. In Text Options, choose Input Text. Give it the variable name `myname`.

2. Create a standard four-state Submit button and drop it onto the stage in the first keyframe.

3. Right-click the Submit button and edit its actions. Then enter these lines into the Actions window:

```
on (release) {
    getURL ("ex1.asp", "_self", "POST");
}
```

This will redirect your page to `ex1.asp`. Remember, if you want to send or receive variables in Flash without physically leaving the movie, the `loadVariablesNum` function is ideal. However, we do not need this functionality for this particular example.

4. Now, close the Actions window and publish the movie. The work on the Flash side is done.

5. Create a new ASP page in your text editor of choice. The aim of this page is to print out exactly what Flash sent you. It's not very impressive, but it is a fundamental stepping stone. Here's the code:

```
<%@Language="VBScript"%>
<%
    Option Explicit
    Dim strMyName
    strMyName = Request.Form("myname")
    Response.Write "Your name: " & strMyName
%>
```

6. Save this code as `ex1.asp`. Then, visit the HTML page via your Web server, submit your name, and test to make sure it works. You should receive one line of output, which tells you your name (or the name you entered). The input screen is shown in Figure 26.1, and the output screen is shown in Figure 26.2.

If you don't get the expected output, make sure your server configuration is as specified in the "Getting Started" section of this chapter. Also, make sure you are accessing your HTML page via the `http://` protocol; otherwise, you will be asked to download your own `ex1.asp` file, and it will not work.

FIGURE 26.1

The Flash input screen submits the text you entered to the ASP script.

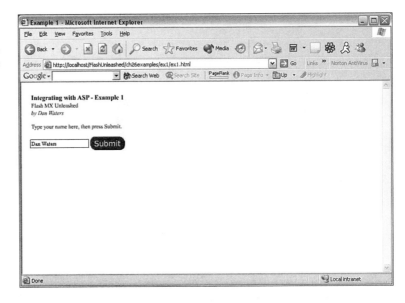

FIGURE 26.2

After you submit your information via Flash, ASP reads in what you inputted and prints it back out.

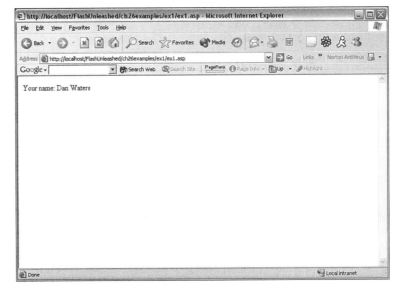

Sending Data from ASP to Flash

Two effective methods of data transferal from ASP to Flash are available: the "one-shot" method, which initializes the movie with some starting values, and the reusable method, which utilizes the `loadVariablesNum` function. We will build an example using `LoadVariablesNum` later in this chapter.

The "one-shot" approach is accomplished by writing a query string into the object code, which embeds the Flash movie in an HTML page. The following code demonstrates a simple HTML or ASP page that plays a Flash movie:

```
<HTML>
<HEAD>
 <TITLE>Embedding A Flash Movie In An ASP Page</TITLE>
</HEAD>
<BODY>
<CENTER>
 <OBJECT
 classid="clsid:D27CDB6E-AE6D-11cf-96B8-444553540000"
codebase="http://download.macromedia.com/pub/shockwave/
cabs/flash/swflash.cab#version=6,0,0,0" WIDTH="550"
HEIGHT="400">
  <PARAM NAME=movie VALUE="movie.swf">
  <PARAM NAME=quality VALUE=high>
  <PARAM NAME=wmode VALUE="transparent">
<EMBED SRC="movie.swf" QUALITY="high" WIDTH="550" HEIGHT="400"
TYPE="application/x-shockwave-flash"
PLUGINSPAGE="http://www.macromedia.com/shockwave/
download/index.cgi?P1_Prod_Version=ShockwaveFlash"
WMODE="transparent">
</EMBED>
 </OBJECT>
</CENTER>
</BODY>
</HTML>
```

Now, let's say you want the movie to know the results of a previous form submission when it begins playing. For example, if the page that brought you to this Flash page sent a variable called `strName`, you could initialize the Flash movie with the value of `strName` without ever calling `loadVariables`. Here's an example:

```
<HTML>
<HEAD>
 <TITLE>Embedding A Flash Movie In An ASP Page</TITLE>
</HEAD>
<BODY>
<CENTER>
 <OBJECT
 classid="clsid:D27CDB6E-AE6D-11cf-96B8-444553540000"
codebase="http://download.macromedia.com/pub/shockwave/
cabs/flash/swflash.cab#version=6,0,0,0" WIDTH="550"
HEIGHT="400">
  <PARAM NAME=movie VALUE="movie.swf?strName=<%=Request("strName")%>">
  <PARAM NAME=quality VALUE=high>
```

```
   <PARAM NAME=wmode VALUE="transparent">
<EMBED SRC="movie.swf?strName=<%=Request("strName")%>"
QUALITY="high" WIDTH="550" HEIGHT="400"
TYPE="application/x-shockwave-flash"
PLUGINSPAGE="http://www.macromedia.com/shockwave/
download/index.cgi?P1_Prod_Version=ShockwaveFlash"
WMODE="transparent">
</EMBED>
 </OBJECT>
</CENTER>
</BODY>
</HTML>
```

The bold portion of this code is the part that initializes our Flash movie with a variable, or string of variables. It's exactly like sending variables from one ASP page to another using the GET method. You specify a filename and trail it with a query string (in this case, a VDS). The <% and %> markers break into ASP code. The equals sign (=) indicates an inline Write command, which tells ASP to print Request("strName"). So, when you run the Name form and enter a value such as "Dan Waters," your Flash movie will receive a VDS containing strName=Dan+Waters and will initialize that variable. However, these variables are only defined in level 0 of the movie, in _root. The inline variable-definition technique is best suited for small amounts of data. It can also be used in conjunction with the loadVariables technique. In fact, the combination of these two methods can be very useful. For instance, if you are browsing through a database recordset in a Flash interface and you need to switch to a different interface, but maintain the same records in the new interface, you can refresh the ASP page in which the Flash is embedded with a different record number. That way, Flash can notify ASP of where to start looking for records.

Let's build a small project to apply this concept.

Example 2: Passing Values From HTML to Flash

In this example, we'll create an HTML form that allows users to specify their name and age. It will also allow them to adjust the size of the movie using a drop-down list. Here are the steps to follow:

1. Start by building a simple HTML page. You want to utilize form components, which takes inputs from the user and submits them to an ASP script residing on your server somewhere. An example of such a form is shown here (this is ex2.html, the input page):

```
<HTML>
 <HEAD>
  <TITLE>ex2</TITLE>
 </HEAD>
```

```
<BODY>
<FORM ACTION="26-ex2-display.asp" METHOD="POST">
 <TABLE BORDER=1 CELLPADDING=5 CELLSPACING=0>
  <TR>
   <TD ALIGN="left" VALIGN="center">
    Name
   </TD>
   <TD ALIGN="left" VALIGN="center">
    <INPUT TYPE="Text" NAME="strName"><BR>
   </TD>
  </TR>
  <TR>
   <TD ALIGN="left" VALIGN="center">
    Age
   </TD>
   <TD ALIGN="left" VALIGN="center">
    <INPUT TYPE="Text" NAME="strAge"><BR>
   </TD>
  </TR>
  <TR>
   <TD ALIGN="left" VALIGN="center">
    Display Size
   </TD>
   <TD ALIGN="left" VALIGN="center">
    <SELECT NAME="Size">
     <OPTION VALUE="Square">300x300 (Square)
     <OPTION VALUE="Fullscreen">Fullscreen
    </SELECT>
   </TD>
  </TR>
  <TR>
   <TD COLSPAN=2 ALIGN="center" VALIGN="center">
    <INPUT TYPE="submit" VALUE="Display Movie">
   </TD>
  </TR>
 </TABLE>
</FORM>
</BODY>
</HTML>
```

This form takes three inputs and submits them to an ASP page. The script itself actually performs a small amount of "data preparation," which is used to decide how to display the movie. The other two values are written directly into the <OBJECT> code, which will display the received information in a Flash movie. Therefore, you'll need a Flash movie.

2. Create a new movie. Call it `ex2.fla`. I have created a very simple, small movie with two dynamic text boxes in it. The variable names of the dynamic text boxes must match the variables you send in the VDS to be displayed properly. So, for this example, I have given one text box the variable name `strName` and the other `strAge`. The Size field is not used in the Flash movie, because it is implemented by dynamically specifying the `WIDTH` and `HEIGHT` parameters in the `OBJECT` and `EMBED` tags.

3. This simple setup is all that needs to be done using this method, so export the movie as `ex2.swf`.

Now, let's write the necessary ASP page to display the Flash movie.

4. We will copy some standard HTML object code to embed the Flash movie and mark some areas where dynamic values need to be implemented. Here's the code (call it `ex2-display.asp`):

```
<%@Language="VBScript"%>
<%
    ' Processing the form values
    Dim strName, strAge, nMovieWidth, nMovieHeight
    Select Case Request("Size")
        Case "Square":
            nMovieWidth=300
            nMovieHeight=300
        Case "Fullscreen":
            nMovieWidth="100%"
            nMovieHeight="100%"
        Case Else
            nMovieWidth=300
            nMovieHeight=300
    End Select
    strName = Server.URLEncode(Request("strName"))
    strAge = Server.URLEncode(Request("strAge"))
    ' End form processing
%>
<HTML>
<HEAD>
  <TITLE>26-ex2</TITLE>
</HEAD>
<BODY>
<CENTER>
  <OBJECT
classid="clsid:D27CDB6E-AE6D-11cf-96B8-444553540000"
codebase="http://download.macromedia.com/pub/shockwave/
cabs/flash/swflash.cab#version=6,0,0,0"
WIDTH="<%=nMovieWidth%>" HEIGHT="<%=nMovieHeight%>">
<PARAM NAME=movie
```

```
VALUE="26-ex2.swf?strName=<%=strName%>&strAge=<%=strAge%>">
 <PARAM NAME=quality VALUE=high>
  <PARAM NAME=wmode VALUE="transparent">
<EMBED SRC="26-ex2.swf?strName=<%=strName%>&strAge=<%=strAge%>"
QUALITY="high" WIDTH="<%=nMovieWidth%>" HEIGHT="<%=nMovieHeight%>"
TYPE="application/x-shockwave-flash"
PLUGINSPAGE="http://www.macromedia.com/shockwave/
download/index.cgi?P1_Prod_Version=ShockwaveFlash"
WMODE="transparent">
</EMBED>
 </OBJECT>
</CENTER>
</BODY>
</HTML>
```

The top part of this code processes the form from the previous HTML page. It determines how to display the size of the movie and displays it full screen, if there is invalid input. Then, it encodes the strName and strAge variables so that they are in a suitable format (VDS) when sent to Flash.

To write the value of an ASP variable quickly and easily, you can use this notation:

```
<%= variableName %>
```

This is an inline ASP Response.Write command. Its only function is to print out the value between the ASP start and ASP end tags. This value can be concatenated with string values added to numbers, or acquired by calling a function, but you should avoid using Sub routines in that small area.

In the OBJECT and EMBED tags in ex2-display.asp, there are inline Write commands that dynamically specify the width and height, which can either be 300 by 300 or 100% by 100% (full screen). Whenever the filename of the movie is specified, the inline Write command is seen again:

```
ex2.swf?strName=<%=strName%>&strAge=<%=strAge%>
```

If you break this line up logically, you will see that this is nothing more than a simple VDS. So, if you feed the ASP script your name and age (for instance, Dan Waters for strName and 19 for strAge), the preceding string would transform into the following string:

```
ex2.swf?strName=Dan+Waters&strAge=19
```

When this is sent to Flash, it initializes _root.strName to Dan Waters and _root.strAge to 19. These variables are ready to use in your ActionScript, if you choose to do so.

Now, try it out. Access `ex2.html` via your server and fill in the form. Upon clicking Display Movie, you should be redirected to `ex2.asp`, which will display the Flash movie as you directed it.

Building a Working Model

It's time to tie the Flash-to-ASP and ASP-to-Flash concepts together. In this next exercise, we will re-create Example 2. However, we'll use a Flash movie for the form instead of an HTML page. On top of that, we'll use absolute Flash object paths and tweening to create a simple dynamic animation. Specifically, we will play a movie clip containing a tween, which contains text received from ASP.

When you first load the page, all the fields will be blank except for Name, which is initialized by Flash to "Unidentified Person" using ActionScript. You will be able to resize and change the contents of the movie using Flash itself.

Example 3: Data Transmission in a Flash/ASP Hybrid Environment

The ASP page we created in Example 2 can also be used for our current example, because the code to display the movie does not change. We just need to create a new Flash movie that sends variables to the page it is displayed in. This example will only consist of three files: the source FLA file, the ASP page that displays and refreshes the movie, and the SWF file. To complete this exercise, follow these steps:

1. Copy your code from Example 2 and replace all occurrences of `ex2.swf` with `ex3.swf`. Save the page as `ex3.asp`. Let's write the display type into the movie also. You need to add two lines below the `End Select` line in the ASP:

   ```
   Dim Size
   Size = Server.URLEncode(Request("Size"))
   ```

2. Update the variable definition strings in the `<PARAM NAME="movie">` and `<EMBED>` tags to load one more variable:

   ```
   ex3.swf?strName=<%=strName%>&strAge=<%=strAge%>&Size=<%=Size%>
   ```

   You can recycle your old Flash movie, too. However, we need to make a few alterations to allow proper functionality.

3. Convert all the previously dynamic text boxes to input text boxes. This will allow you to update the Flash movie. You can specify full screen or square mode simply by typing **Fullscreen** or **Square** in that input box.

4. We need a movie clip that has a dynamic text box in it so we can access the text directly using ActionScript. Create a new movie clip called Greeting Text. Place a dynamic text box in the first keyframe and give it the variable name `Text`.

5. Create a new movie clip called Greeting. Drop an instance of Greeting Text in the first frame and give it the instance name `GreetingAnim`.

6. Create a motion tween that, for the sake of simplicity, lasts 5 to 10 frames. Both the first and last keyframes should contain `GreetingAnim`, the instance of Greeting Text you created. The tween itself can be anything you wish, as long as you place a `Stop` action in the last frame so that the user will be able to read it. In the provided example, a position tween is used.

7. Now we need to take care of that greeting animation. Make sure you have labeled all the relevant movie clips with the instance names specified previously. In the first frame of the main timeline, add these frame actions:

```
if(strName eq "")
{
    strName = "Unidentified Person";
}
_root.Greeting.GreetingAnim.Text = "Hello, " + strName + "!";
```

This code checks to see whether `strName` has been defined. If not, it sets the name to "Unidentified Person" so that the tween will still work. Then, it uses absolute paths to set the text in the tween to a special greeting message.

8. Finally, drop a Submit button onto the stage and give it a `getURL` action to refresh the values and redisplay the movie:

```
on (release) {
    getURL ("ex3.asp", "_self", "POST");
}
```

This will refresh the mounting page with updated values in the Flash VDS. The values will correspond to whatever you have entered in the input text boxes.

Now, export the movie as `ex3.swf` and try it out. The tween should update itself as you enter your name differently. The values in the boxes should also update themselves. If you are having troubles, refer to the standard troubleshooting routine mentioned in the previous examples.

Concept Check

We've come a long way so far. Let's take a rest and review what you have learned:

- The Variable Definition String (VDS) is a query string with URL-encoded variable/value pairs, each separated by an ampersand. The VDS is instrumental to correct functionality when sending data from ASP to Flash.

- You can load variables into Flash from a text file (offline) or a script (online). A text file contains a single VDS, whereas a script can contain any multitude of commands and operations, as long as it generates a single VDS.

- There are two overall methods of receiving variables in Flash: using the `loadVariables` command and using the inline VDS, which is written into the `<OBJECT>` tag's `Movie` parameter and the `<EMBED>` tag.

- There are two overall methods of sending variables in Flash: via the `loadVariables` command and via the `getURL` command. Use the latter if you plan to display a page rather than a movie, or if you wish to refresh a movie with new values.

Getting Started with Databases

You may have noticed that in the previous examples, we haven't really touched on the `loadVariables` command. Then again, we haven't encountered a situation where it is necessary to use this command. One such situation involves invisibly loading data from a database into your Flash movie, without opening up a new window or leaving the interface. To do this, tell Flash to instruct your ASP script to go get some data, put it in the VDS format, and send it back to your Flash movie.

A handy thing about ASP and other scripting languages is that you don't necessarily have to open up a new browser window or redirect the user to the page. An ASP script can run invisibly and still return a value (or a set of values). In this section, we're going to use this property of server-side scripting to retrieve data using ASP, send a VDS to Flash, and create an integrated data system using Microsoft Access.

This also means that providing error handling is absolutely necessary. If you have a "loading" loop that waits for variables to load from ASP, you would never know the ASP script is malfunctioning. Generally, in this situation, the loading loop continues forever without loading something from ASP. This is when you need to debug the script by itself.

Let's start with some review of ASP data concepts. This section is not designed to teach you ASP but rather assumes a working knowledge of the language. ASP references can be found all around the Web; for instance, `ASP101.com` is a vast reference with plenty of examples.

Basic ADO Concepts

A data solution in ASP using Microsoft ActiveX Data Objects (ADO) consists of three main entities: the `Connection` object, the `Recordset` object, and the SQL string.

The `Connection` object is of type `ADODB.Connection`. It is the part of your script that actually connects to a database. You need to create the `Connection` object using

```
Set objConnection = Server.CreateObject("ADODB.Connection")
```

After creating the object, you must define a connection string and then open the connection. Here is a connection string for a Microsoft Access database, which we will be using in later examples:

```
DRIVER={Microsoft Access Driver (*.mdb)};uid=Username;pwd=Password;DBQ=filepath
```

The `UID` and `PWD` parameters are optional unless your Access database is password-protected (which is a good idea). If it is password-protected, `UID` should be Admin.

The file path must be absolute to the server, so you must use `Server.MapPath("file-name")` to reference the file path.

A great list of other connection strings can be found at the following site:

```
http://www.able-consulting.com/ADO_Conn.htm
```

A complete ASP statement to create, define a connection string for, and open a connection would look like this:

```
Set objConn = Server.CreateObject("ADODB.Connection")
objConn.ConnectionString = "DRIVER={Microsoft Access Driver (*.mdb);" & _
"uid=Admin;" & _
"pwd=CapnCrunch;" & _
"DBQ=" & Server.MapPath("test.mdb")
objConn.Open
```

The `Recordset` object is of type `ADODB.Recordset`. It contains—you guessed it—a given set of records. What the recordset contains is determined by the SQL statement you use to sort your data. You must initialize the `Recordset` object using

```
Set objRS = Server.CreateObject("ADODB.Recordset")
```

Then, you must open a recordset in the following manner:

```
objRS.Open strSQL, objConn, adCursorType, adLockType
```

In the preceding Open statement are four parameters. First, strSQL is the SQL string used to specify which fields and records in your database are to be opened. It can be any valid SQL statement. Next, objConn is a valid, open Connection object. Finally, adCursorType and adLockType are constants that specify how the recordset can be accessed and scrolled through. The Recordset object also has several very useful methods that allow us to manipulate its data, such as AddNew, Update, Delete, MoveFirst, and MoveNext. You will learn more about these methods in upcoming examples.

The SQL string requires some background knowledge of the Structured Query Language. We won't be using very many SQL commands in this chapter, just to keep things simple. Some commands we will be using are SELECT, INSERT, UPDATE, DELETE, FROM, WHERE, and ORDER BY. If you are unfamiliar with SQL, it is not too difficult to grasp after working with it for a while, so don't worry.

Note

You must close all Connection and Recordset objects when you are done with them; otherwise, your server will hang and be unable to respond to other queries. You must also set these objects equal to Nothing. At the end of each of your ASP scripts (that use databases), you should have a code block similar to this:

```
<%
    ' Clean up objects and say goodbye.
    objRS.Close
    Set objRS = Nothing
    objConn.Close
    Set objConn = Nothing
%>
```

Also, if you are using a Do…While loop to extract all your records, make sure you are using the MoveNext method of the Recordset object before you give the Loop command. If you fail to do this, the loop will execute forever.

Data Retrieval and Management Techniques in ASP

The process of retrieving data from your database in ASP can be very simple or very complex, depending on the approach you take. The data that lands in your Recordset object is entirely dependent on your SQL string, which can be very short and defined in one statement, or very long and defined across multiple lines. It is obviously best to keep this string simple (to lessen the load on the server), but sometimes it isn't possible, especially if you are designing a solution in which the user specifies what data to display, such as a customized search engine.

Building the SQL string is very important. You must also remember to debug the string if you are not getting the results you expect. To do this, run the ASP script you are designing with the required parameters and use `Response.Write` to reveal exactly what your SQL string consists of, making sure the syntax is correct and that you are selecting the correct fields from the correct tables:

```
Response.Write strSQL
```

You should always loop through all records in the recordset, even if you expect to find only one result matching the query. It never hurts to display more than one option. To do this, construct a loop and continue to build on the VDS. In other words, add data to your running VDS with each reiteration of the loop.

Most retrieval techniques use the SQL `SELECT` statement when opening the recordset. However, it is also appropriate to use the `Connection.Execute(strSQL)` method, which executes a SQL statement on the database connection. You can set a recordset equal to this function. This is useful if you will be making multiple selections in your script.

You really only need three other SQL commands to be able to fully manage a database: `UPDATE`, `INSERT INTO` and `DELETE`. These commands can be performed directly on your database using the `Connection.Execute(strSQL)` method, as you will see in the final project. Under the right conditions, it's not even necessary to use these commands to perform these actions because ADO has some built-in methods for the `Recordset` object. As long as you have an opened recordset, you can use any of the following methods of the `Recordset` object:

Recordset *Object Method*	*What It Does*
`rs.AddNew`	Creates a new record in the table
`rs.Update`	Updates the database
`rs.Delete`	Deletes the current record

Note

These methods will not work if you have obtained your `Recordset` object using the `Connection.Execute` method. You must have a recordset opened using the ADO `Open` command.

After using any of these ADO methods or actually altering the contents of data, you must call rs.Update and then close the recordset using rs.Close.

To simply update one field of a record, you would access it the same way you would access a variable from the Request collection, as shown here:

```
rs("field_name") = newvalue
```

Remember, this section is about ASP and ADO, *not* Flash. The only thing you need to worry about to remain "Flash friendly" is to send back your data in a VDS.

Before we dive into the first example using ASP and databases, let's make sure you know exactly how to approach such a development task. Many factors are involved in successfully integrating these two technologies. Insufficient mastery in even one area can foreshadow many nights spent staring blankly at your monitor. To avoid such frustrating and counterproductive midnight sessions, let's make sure to get started on the right foot.

Developing Your Application

Creating an application that utilizes two intertwined technologies can be very difficult. Now that we are getting involved with complex data solutions, it should help to outline an almost-foolproof method of designing your solution.

Step 1: Analyze Your Project

You've finally been contracted by The Company to build their integrated solution. But where do you start? Just like any other well-developed application, a lot of planning must take place before you even open up Flash or InterDev. Many people tend to skip this phase and dive headlong into writing code. Unless you are a very skilled and experienced programmer and designer, you may be faced with desperate situations later ("Why didn't I think of this problem before?").

The first thing you need to do is sit down, away from the computer, with a pen and pad. Write down the major goals you wish to accomplish in the development of this site. What kind of technology is available to you? What language are you going to be coding in? Answering these questions now will save you much grief in the long run, especially if you develop the whole site in ASP and find that your destination server is Unix without Chili!Soft. Are you developing a conservative business site in which the dynamic nature of the site is the top priority, or is it a promotional site with more animation and a few ASP bells and whistles? Get an idea of how much code you are going to put into this project and estimate how long it will take you to write the basic infrastructure. This will also aid in the process of estimating the total hours you need to spend in front of the monitor.

A lot of people tell me they are attempting to write a shopping cart or e-business gadget of a similar genre involving transactions and so on. That is the good stuff. You don't see many Flash shopping carts out there today, and the primary reason is that, oftentimes, developers simply get sick of making it! And, why do they get sick of developing it? Most likely, it's because they didn't have these few key concepts down about Flash and ASP integration.

So, before you even lay a hand on those peripherals, sit down and get your materials together.

Step 2: Condense the Data

Now that you know exactly how you plan to approach the project, create a list of information tidbits that you will need to consummate the data processing. If you are designing a member profile viewer, you will want to have access to information such as the members' first name, occupation, age, location, and so on. These variables are what will inevitably be sent to Flash, so make sure you have a very complete list. If you are unsure about the inclusion of a variable, include it as long as it doesn't seem totally extraneous. Then, go back to your ASP file and see if you can return all these variables in the variable definition string format. Often, this takes a lot of work, but it's absolutely necessary.

Step 3: Get Your Backend Working

No, this doesn't mean "start dancing." What many developers do not directly realize is that Flash has absolutely nothing to do with their database. They think and think and think about how they can write values to their DB via Flash without even looking to ASP, though they know it must be an integral part of their project somehow.

The fact that Flash has absolutely nothing to do with your database can't be stressed enough. Flash has nothing to do with anything external, other than your Web-based scripts or local programs (if you're using the projector format). So now what?

Get your backend working. That's the bottom line. Write, refine, and test your backend code using structured code methodology. Don't even touch Flash just yet. Get it all figured out, work out the bugs, and when you are absolutely sure that your backend performs its desired function, move on to Step 4.

Step 4: Design Your Flash Interface

Eventually, the time will come when you need to start producing some visible content! Work on your layout. Sometimes it helps to do it on paper first and then put it into the digital world. Whatever helps you get an idea should be how you design your interface. When you need to load dynamic data, load a lot at the same time to avoid a lot of loading screens. Allocate one frame for the Load Variables action. The next few frames should be a loading animation, using loading actions like the ones I provide in the next example. The frame after the loading animation should display the necessary variable data. Set these frames up and don't worry about ActionScript just yet; rather, focus on the layout itself and keeping space for the necessary frames.

Step 5: Apply ActionScript

See the upcoming example for tips on how to use ActionScript to achieve the results you need with ASP and an external source. Apply these techniques wherever needed in your movie. After you've scripted everything, there's only one thing left to do....

Step 6: Test Vigorously

Now, beta-test a lot. Find anything that might be a potential problem and correct it. If you change something in the Flash movie, clear your temporary Internet files to make the changes evident. If it seems that at this point your focus is straying and you feel a little burnt out, take a break from the system and analyze it with your head. Think about new ways the problem could be solved, such as a revision of your algorithm or determine workarounds for whatever problems you may have.

> **Tip**
>
> Sometimes a little time off is all it takes to get back into the swing of things, so do not kill yourself finishing your project. This applies to many other areas of design and occupations even broader than the scope of computing. Many programmers and designers have their best ideas and solutions when their brains are literally in "beta" mode—sending out slower, more relaxed brain waves and thus allowing more natural thought processes to occur.

Integrating with ASP and Microsoft Access

The time has come for us to truly start experimenting with these techniques. The true usefulness of integrating Flash with ASP lies in the ability to integrate with data stores, making your Flash movie a wonderful vehicle for your content!

The next few examples will be collective components of a rather large project that will reinforce and consummate your knowledge and skill. The project itself has four phases, each of which has individual and unique design specifications to encourage modular and successful programming and design habits. By the first couple of examples, you will have a well-formed foundation in Flash and ASP integration.

In the next example (ex4-1), we will create a Flash-based user profile system. Each user will have personal data that can be displayed in Flash. In ex4-2, we will add the buttons to this system. In the third phase, we will add a search feature in another page to find employees by name or position. In phase 4, we will add the ability to log in and update the database through Flash, or even add/remove users. Our database will have a new field, Icon, that is a representative JPEG avatar of sorts for each member of our database.

The scenario: You have been hired to create the staff profile system for SomeCorp Designs, a small imaginary Web-design firm. Ten total employees need to be entered into the database. Three of the employees have the same last name, so you will also learn how to deal with multiple matches to a particular search.

The system will be structured around a Microsoft Access database (in Office 2000 format). Figure 26.3 illustrates the current layout of the database.

FIGURE 26.3

The Access database holds various bits of information about 10 different imaginary people.

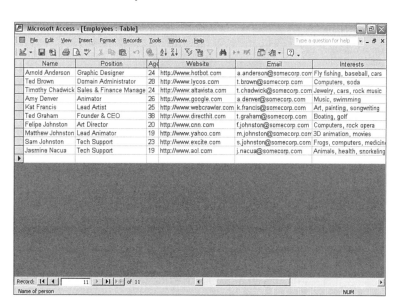

Now, in accordance with our development guidelines, let's get started creating our masterpiece.

Integration Project, Phase 1

Phase 1 of our project consists of database layout, script writing, and the layout of the profile page. Because this phase provides us with the entire foundation of the project, our design process will be slightly longer than the ones to follow. When analyzing the project, we will conceptualize the final product but specify the items relevant to Phase 1.

Analyze the Project

What are we trying to accomplish with this section of the project? Let's make our goals very clear so that we do not stray from the track. We should examine our planned approach and resources:

- The project involves one screen with dual functionality. It will list all employees of the company horizontally across the top of the movie in the form of buttons. The buttons are not generated dynamically, but the link info is loaded into them when the page is first called using the "one-shot" method. (It is, however, possible to have these buttons generated dynamically using duplicateMovieClip). Upon one of these buttons being clicked, the area in the center of the movie will display the user's profile. This will be accomplished using loadVariables. The layout of this page should be somewhat similar to Figure 26.4.

FIGURE 26.4

The Flash application will have 10 buttons across the top, used to load dynamic data into the center of the movie.

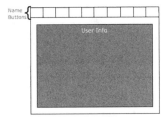

In the first section of the example, we will not dynamically generate or even display the navigation buttons, nor will we implement the search or login functions. This is to come in the later phases of this project.

- Because we are developing a corporate solution, we need to make sure that the destination server supports ASP. Furthermore, we need to decide about how long it will take to build this thing. Because we are not creating some extravagantly animated application, it might be something we can get done in one day. So, let's give an estimate of about 12 hours, to be safe. We also know that the content of the site is more important than the actual animation, so we know that we are going to put more effort into the code than the actual Flash movie.

Condense the Data

A large part of this step was completed when we created our Access database. The thought process in condensing the data should be structural and object oriented. When creating the database, we decide that our group of people can be safely referred to in one table called *Employees.* Each record in the Employees table represents one employee. Each has several fields, all of type Text. Each of these fields can change from employee to employee.

We need to consider exactly what to send to Flash in the different steps of data transferal:

- **Creating the Buttons**. When loading information into the buttons, we must send two pieces of data: the unique employee identifier (EmpID) and the employee name to display on the button. The employee identifier can be used to query the database for a certain employee record whenever we click that employee's button.

- **Loading the Employee Data**. This is the part where all employee data should be returned to the Flash movie. We will only be returning seven pieces of data to the Flash movie each time loadVariables is called, because we have a template in the Flash movie, which will update itself whenever we choose a new employee record.

Get the Backend Working

At this point, we have a clear outlook of where we are heading with this project. With that out of the way, let's start by creating our ASP code for the profile-display page. After this, we will add an entirely different script for the button-loading feature.

The code in ex4-1.asp will receive one parameter—EmpID—that tells ASP which employee record to look in. If no result is found, the script will write success=False to the Flash movie. The task of displaying "No record found" will be taken care of when we design the Flash front end.

> **Note**
>
> It is unnecessary to use a Do…While loop in ASP for this purpose, because the script receives a single unique identifier. When we implement the search engine, the Do…While construct will be used to build the VDS.

The following code should be very similar to what you have written for ex4-1.asp:

```
<%@Language="VBScript"%>
<%
    ' Declare recordset & connection objects,
    '    SQL string.
    Dim oRS, oConn, strSQL
    ' Declare VDS.
    Dim strVDS
```

```
' Get Employee ID from Request.
Dim EmpID
EmpID = Request("EmpID")
' Error checking for invalid EmpID
If EmpID > 10 Or EmpID < 1 Then
    EmpID = 0
End If
' Create recordset & connection objects.
Set oConn = Server.CreateObject("ADODB.Connection")
Set oRS = Server.CreateObject("ADODB.Recordset")
oConn.ConnectionString = "DRIVER={Microsoft Access Driver (*.mdb)};" & _
    "DBQ=" & Server.MapPath("ex4.mdb")
oConn.Open
strSQL = "SELECT * FROM Employees WHERE EmpID = " & EmpID
oRS.Open strSQL, oConn, 2, 3
' Check for invalid EmpID
If oRS.EOF Then
    strVDS = "success=False"
Else
    strVDS = "success=True"
    ' Build the VDS.
    strVDS = strVDS & "&EmpID=" & Server.URLEncode(oRS("EmpID")) & _
        "&Name=" & Server.URLEncode(oRS("Name")) & _
        "&Position=" & Server.URLEncode(oRS("Position")) & _
        "&Age=" & Server.URLEncode(oRS("Age")) & _
        "&Website=" & Server.URLEncode(oRS("Website")) & _
        "&Email=" & Server.URLEncode(oRS("Email")) & _
        "&Interests=" & Server.URLEncode(oRS("Interests"))
End If
Response.Write strVDS
oRS.Close
Set oRS = Nothing
oConn.Close
Set oConn = Nothing
%>
```

This code successfully writes a foolproof VDS to the Flash movie. To test the code, visit your ASP script and feed it an invalid EmpID for an error-handling message or a valid EmpID to see the complete VDS. You can feed it dummy variables by going to your browser and typing in something like this:

```
http://localhost/FlashUnleashed/ex4-1.asp?EmpID=3
```

Assuming all your files are in that particular folder, this URL will spit out a long and perfectly accurate VDS. If you leave off the question mark and the text beyond it, you will be rewarded with success=False. As noted earlier, some type of error message is crucial when integrating ASP with Flash, because if the ASP script is malfunctioning, Flash will never know (because ASP runs invisibly).

Now that we are sure our code works, we can begin designing our Flash interface.

Design the Flash Interface

As shown in Figure 26.5, we are creating a screen that does nothing more than load variables from ASP, using a hard-coded EmpID value. The six dynamic text boxes have variable names equal to the six fields in the database—that is, Name, Position, Age, and so on. Just for effect, I have made these fields unselectable and bordered. The Status field has the variable name LoadStatus, and it tells us if the script is loading or has been loaded. And, of course, this example is complete with our makeshift SomeCorp logo. Each item or group of items is logically layered, with a layer at the top to handle all ActionScript. After you create your version, call it ex4-1.fla.

FIGURE 26.5

The profile-viewing screen.

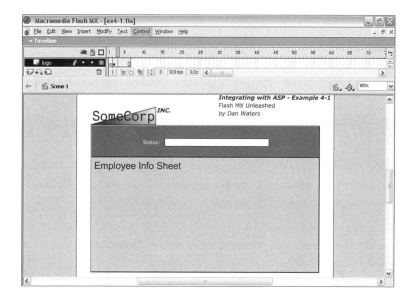

Apply the ActionScript

The timeline for this movie is somewhat complicated, because we haven't talked very much about loading loops yet. The first frame only has content in one layer: the Actions layer of this Flash movie. The sole action in that frame is

```
loadVariablesNum ("ex4-1.asp?EmpID=1", 0);
```

This command tells Flash to load variables from the script we just wrote. Using the question mark notation, it also sends an EmpID value of 1. Notice that we did not get or post any variables with this command. It was not necessary at this time, because we are only using the hard-coded EmpID value for testing purposes.

In frame 2, the interface is shown, minus the text boxes (to avoid embarrassing incidents of cached data if those variables are defined for some reason—you do not want people to see the results of previous queries). Also, _root.LoadStatus is set to "Loading" and the loading logic is performed:

```
if(_root.success eq "True")
{
    // Display data sheet
    gotoAndStop(5);
}
else if(_root.success eq "False")
{
    // Display Invalid Data screen
    gotoAndStop(6);
}
else
{
    // Continue to display loading message
    _root.LoadStatus = "Loading...";
}
```

The variable success is the first thing sent from the ASP script. It is also the only variable that is guaranteed to be written, whether a record is found or not. So, we must use it to determine the load status.

If it is true, we go to frame 5, which shows the interface and all the text boxes. The values of the text boxes are immediately set to their corresponding values.

If success is false, we go to frame 6, which is a message noting that no records were found. Otherwise, _root.LoadStatus is reset to "Loading..." and no redirection takes place.

The next frame (frame 3) is a copy of frame 2, but without actions. It is there to provide a small time window before frame 4.

Frame 4 has a simple Go To and Play command, which goes back to frame 2 to check for loaded variables again.

Frame 5 shows the full interface (with text boxes) and sports a single ActionScript command to set the value of _root.LoadStatus to "Loaded." This gives the user a visual cue that the data has been successfully transmitted.

Frame 6 is a copy of frame 5, only without the text boxes. In their place is a message notifying the user that their search has returned no results. The ActionScript in this frame is optional, but it sets the value of _root.LoadStatus to "Loaded, but with invalid data." This is, once again, for the purpose of giving a visual cue.

Figure 26.6 illustrates the timeline for this section.

FIGURE 26.6

The movie is composed of six frames. Frame 1 loads variables; frames 2 through 4 compose a loading loop; frames 5 and 6 are display frames.

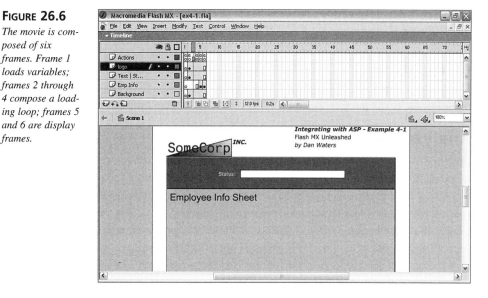

Testing Integration Project, Phase 1

Your Flash movie is now and complete. Use the Publish command to create the SWF and HTML files. Now, visit ex4-1.html via your Web server. Your output should show up fairly quickly and should appear similar to Figure 26.7.

FIGURE 26.7

The data is loaded successfully.

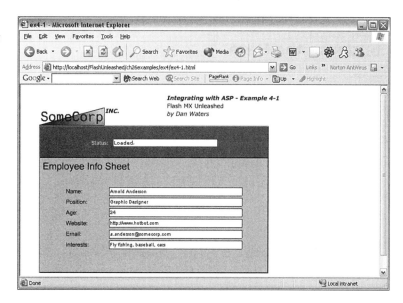

If the loop seems to continue forever, make sure the ASP file exists and is correctly referenced in your Flash movie. Also, make sure the ASP script returns a valid VDS.

Integration Project, Phase 2

In this phase of the project, we will create a series of 10 buttons across the top of the Flash movie. When clicked, they will reload all the data in the movie.

Analyze the Project

Now that we have laid down the backbone of the project, it's time to tie in the button functionality. This example uses the `duplicateMovieClip` function to produce the buttons and a short routine that determines even spacing for any number of buttons. We are going to need one single button inside one single movie clip. In that movie clip, we need a layer above the button to hold a text box, which will display the text. We need to make some flow changes to the program—when it opens up, the user should be confronted with the buttons and the input screen minus the boxes. That way, the user can choose which user profile to view immediately.

We will also need to build another script file that reads in all the employee IDs and names in order to populate the buttons. Let's call it `ex4-2.asp`, because this is Phase 2 of our project.

This new ASP file will also embed the new Flash movie, because it will use the one-shot method to initialize the button menu. We will still be making use of `ex4-1.asp` in order to reload variables based on a click.

Condense the Data

Because our database is complete, we do not need to condense data. However, we do know that we will be loading 10 records with two fields each into our ASP file, and eventually our Flash movie.

Get the Backend Working

The code for `ex4-2.asp` is shown here (note that there are a few changes from `ex4-1.asp`, especially in the SQL statement and VDS construction):

```
<%@Language="VBScript"%>
<%
    ' Declare recordset & connection objects,
    '    SQL string.
    Dim oRS, oConn, strSQL
    ' Declare VDS.
    Dim strVDS
    ' Get Employee ID from Request.
```

```
    ' Create recordset & connection objects.
    Set oConn = Server.CreateObject("ADODB.Connection")
    Set oRS = Server.CreateObject("ADODB.Recordset")
    oConn.ConnectionString = "DRIVER={Microsoft Access Driver (*.mdb)};" & _
        "DBQ=" & Server.MapPath("ex4.mdb")
    oConn.Open
    strSQL = "SELECT EmpID, Name FROM Employees"
    oRS.Open strSQL, oConn, 2, 3
    ' Check for invalid EmpID
    If oRS.EOF Then
        strVDS = "MenuLoaded=False"
    Else
        strVDS = "MenuLoaded=True"

        ' Looping variable
        Dim i
        i = 0

        ' Build the VDS.
        Do While Not oRS.EOF
            strVDS = strVDS & "&EmpID_" & i & "=" & _
                Server.URLEncode(oRS("EmpID")) & _
                "&Name_" & i & "=" & Server.URLEncode(oRS("Name"))
            i = i + 1
            oRS.MoveNext
        Loop

        strVDS = strVDS & "&count=" & i
    End If
    oRS.Close
    Set oRS = Nothing
    oConn.Close
    Set oConn = Nothing
%>
<HTML>
<HEAD>
 <TITLE>ex4-2</TITLE>
</HEAD>
<BODY>
<CENTER>
 <OBJECT classid="clsid:D27CDB6E-AE6D-11cf-96B8-444553540000"
codebase="http://download.macromedia.com/pub/shockwave/cabs/
flash/swflash.cab#version=5,0,0,0" WIDTH="550" HEIGHT="400">
  <PARAM NAME=movie VALUE="ex4-2.swf?<%=strVDS%>">
  <PARAM NAME=quality VALUE=high>
  <PARAM NAME=wmode VALUE="transparent">
<EMBED SRC="ex4-2.swf?<%=strVDS%>" QUALITY="high"
WIDTH="550" HEIGHT="400" TYPE="application/x-shockwave-flash"
PLUGINSPAGE="http://www.macromedia.com/shockwave/
download/index.cgi?P1_Prod_Version=ShockwaveFlash"
WMODE="transparent">
```

```
</EMBED>
 </OBJECT>
</CENTER>
</BODY>
</HTML>
```

Notice that this time, the VDS is generated wholly by a loop in the beginning of the file. Because it's rather large, it's easier to let ASP generate it and print it out in the movie parameter rather than print out individual parameters.

We return a success variable, but it is named differently. It could interfere with the other success variable, which is constantly loaded dynamically. Because this one is loaded once when the movie is loaded, give it a different name (MenuLoaded).

The database selects EmpID and Name from the database and loops until the recordset is empty. It also returns a count variable. Interesting, yes? Earlier in this chapter, I mentioned that returning your sentinel value to Flash can be very helpful; this phase explains why. We'll be using count to determine exactly how many people are in the database. We will build our menu based on that value.

Now, it's time to alter our Flash movie a little bit.

Design the Flash Interface and Apply ActionScript

Because we have already accomplished quite a bit, these steps go hand in hand at this phase.

Create a copy of ex4-1.fla and call it ex4-2.fla. The ActionScript can get a little tougher here, so you may need something to fall back on, just in case.

We only need one frame to handle the menu construction. Therefore, we must move all keyframes forward one frame. We also need to remove our loadVariables action in the second frame. We will be loading variables from the buttons themselves anyway. To rearrange the timeline, select all the frames and drag them forward one frame. Then, select frame 2 of the Actions layer and delete it. Then, simply adjust the other frames so that the last frame of each layer is in frame 6. In the first keyframe (which is now blank) of the Actions layer, which you have hopefully not removed, you need to add the actions that duplicate the movie clip dynamically and automatically position them:

```
// Move the button offscreen
_root.button._x = 700;
_root.button._y = 700;
// Looping, temp variables
var i;
var temp;
// Init temp x and y
```

```
var x, y = 10;
// Loop until count reached — works with any number of records.
for (i=0; i<count; i++) {
    // Duplicate the clip
    duplicateMovieClip (_root.button, "button"+i, i);
    temp = _root["button"+i];
    // Determine positioning
    if (i%10<5) {
        x = i*(temp._width)+(temp._width/2);
    } else {
        x = (i-5)*(temp._width)+(temp._width/2);
        if(i % 5 eq 0)
        {
            y = y+(temp._height);
        }
    }
    // Set positioning, values.
    temp._x = x;
    temp._y = y;
    temp.NameText = _root["Name_"+i];
    temp.EmpID = _root["EmpID_"+i];
}
stop();
```

This code uses the value of count, which is loaded by the one-shot method, to loop and duplicate movie clips. Each movie clip has a variable associated with a text box and a variable that is just associated with that clip. NameText will be shown in the text box, and EmpID will be used to reload the variables. The value 5 represents the number of 100×15 buttons that can fit in a 550×400 movie. The number 10 represents the base Y positioning.

In this same keyframe (the first), create a new layer called *menu*. Create a new movie clip called *Dup Button*. Create a new button of your choice called *Reload*. Drop a copy of Reload into Dup Button. Add a layer in Dup Button called *Text*. Place a dynamic text box roughly the size of the button on that layer and give it the variable name *NameText*. This is the box that will display the name of each person from the database.

Go to the button actions of the Reload button in the Dup Button clip. This is where you'll be reloading values in the Flash movie. You should have something like this:

```
on (release) {
    _root.success = "";
    loadVariables ("ex4-1.asp?EmpID=" + this.EmpID, "_root");
    _root.gotoAndPlay(2);
}
```

Setting _root.success to nothing essentially "clears" your search from the previous load and forces the ASP script to run again. The loadVariables call instructs our first ASP script to get the employee data for the employee specified in this current movie clip. This works because, when we duplicated all the movie clips, they were initialized with this value.

Drag a copy of Dup Button onto the stage in the first keyframe, on the Menu layer. Give it the instance name *button*. It doesn't matter where you put it, because if you notice the actions in the first frame, the source button (used for duplicating) is moved offstage.

Figure 26.8 shows our new, updated timeline.

FIGURE 26.8

Frame 1 of the Actions layer contains the duplication and positioning routine. Frames 2 through 4 contain the loading loop. Frame 5 contains the data display page, and Frame 6 contains the error page.

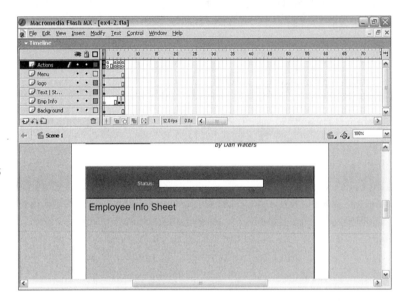

Testing Integration Project, Phase 2

Run ex4-2.asp. Now, you see the true potential of this method. Congratulations! You've made it this far. There's still even more to learn. In the next phase, we'll search these records using Flash.

Integration Project, Phase 3

Now, we'll implement a search feature in Flash. Flash will be used as the input screen, and ASP will handle *all* the search logic. Instead of displaying all fields of all search results, we will display the name, position, and hyperlinked e-mail address of each search result in a multiline HTML text box.

Analyze the Project

We'll be revamping the Flash movie and writing an entirely new ASP script to handle the search function. Search results will appear in a multiline text box, and e-mail addresses will be underlined and hyperlinked to open up your mail program when you click them.

So, back up your materials from Phase 2. Call the new script ex4-3.asp and do the same with the old FLA. The phase is composed of four files: the FLA, the SWF, the display page, and the search page.

Condense the Data

We will need to pull the names, positions, and e-mail addresses from the database in our ASP script. To match the user's query, we will build the SQL statement, step by step, for each piece of data possible.

Get the Backend Working

The script we use in this example is quite long, but only because we perform checks on all six possible search parameters (Name, Position, and so on). The code for ex4-search.asp is shown here:

```
<%@Language="VBScript"%>
<%
    ' Declare recordset & connection objects,
    ' SQL string.
    Dim oRS, oConn, strSQL
    ' Declare VDS.
    Dim strVDS
    ' Get Employee information from Request.
    Dim Name, Position, Age, Website, Email, Interests
    Name = Request("Name")
    Position = Request("Position")
    Age = Request("Age")
    Website = Request("Website")
    Email = Request("Email")
    Interests = Request("Interests")
    If Name = "" And Position = "" And Age = "" _
        And Website = "" And Email = "" _
        And Interests = "" Then
        strVDS = "FoundResult=False"
    Else
        ' Build SQL String
        strSQL = "SELECT * FROM Employees WHERE "
        If Name <> "" Then
            strSQL = strSQL & " NAME LIKE '%" & Name & "%'"
        End If
        If Position <> "" Then
            strSQL = strSQL & " AND Position LIKE '%" & Position & "%'"
        End If
```

```
        If Age <> "" Then
            strSQL = strSQL & " AND Age LIKE '%" & Age & "%'"
        End If
        If Website <> "" Then
            strSQL = strSQL & " AND Website LIKE '%" & Website & "%'"
        End If
        If Email <> "" Then
            strSQL = strSQL & " AND Email LIKE '%" & Email & "%'"
        End If
        If Interests <> "" Then
            strSQL = strSQL & " AND Interests LIKE '%" & Interests & "%'"
        End If
        ' Create recordset & connection objects.
        Set oConn = Server.CreateObject("ADODB.Connection")
        Set oRS = Server.CreateObject("ADODB.Recordset")
        oConn.ConnectionString = _
        "DRIVER={Microsoft Access Driver (*.mdb)};" & _
            "DBQ=" & Server.MapPath("ex4.mdb")
        oConn.Open
        oRS.Open strSQL, oConn, 2, 3
        ' Check for invalid EmpID
        If oRS.EOF Then
            strVDS = "FoundResult=False"
        Else
            strVDS = "FoundResult=True"
            ' Looping variable
            Dim i
            i = 0
            ' Build the VDS.
            strVDS = strVDS & "&ResultString="
            Do While Not oRS.EOF
                strVDS = strVDS & _
                Server.URLEncode("Name: " & oRS("Name") & vbCr & _
                    "Position: " & oRS("Position") & vbCr & _
                    "Email: <A HREF=" & Chr(34) & "mailto:" & _
                    oRS("Email") & Chr(34) & "><u>" & _
                    oRS("Email") & "</u></A>" & _
                    vbCrLf)
                i = i + 1
                oRS.MoveNext
            Loop
            strVDS = strVDS & "&numresults=" & i
        End If
        oRS.Close
        Set oRS = Nothing
        oConn.Close
        Set oConn = Nothing
    End If
    Response.Write strVDS
%>
```

The method for generating the VDS is slightly different than in previous examples. Because our destination is a text box, we only need one variable to display our information. In this script, we call it `ResultString`. To properly encode our data, we write `&ResultString=` to the VDS and then use `Server.URLEncode` to encode a string with line breaks in it. Each time the loop executes, it writes another chunk to the string. `VbCr` is a single linefeed, whereas `vbCrLf` is a linefeed and carriage return, which is like pressing Return twice in a Flash window.

Test this code to make sure it returns a VDS that seems valid. Once again, if your loading loop goes on forever, make sure this VDS is perfect.

Design the Flash Interface and Add ActionScript

Make a copy of `ex4-2.fla`. Call it `ex4-3.fla` and make these changes to it:

- The first frame should have the logo, background, and employee data fields (Name, Position, and so on). The text boxes themselves should be input text fields. If you like, write a message on this page instructing the users to input as much as they know about the employee. The actions for this frame should set every search parameter to a null value.

- The second frame needs to have a single action to load the variables:
  ```
  loadVariablesNum ("ex4-search.asp", 0, "POST");
  ```
  The `POST` command tells Flash to send its current variables—the entries for our search parameters—to the given script. Flash then loads a VDS from that script into level 0.

- The third frame, labeled TestSearch, contains the looping logic shown here:
  ```
  if(_root.FoundResult eq "True")
  {
      _root.SearchStatus = "Search successful.";
      gotoAndStop("DispSearchResults");
  }
  else if(_root.FoundResult eq "False")
  {
      _root.SearchStatus = "No results matching your query.";
      gotoAndStop("NoMatches");
  }
  else
  {
      _root.SearchStatus = "Searching...";
  }
  ```
  If there are matches, Flash goes to the frame labeled DispSearchResults and sets the status text to "Search Successful." If there are no matches, Flash goes to the NoMatches frame, which shows the message "Your search returned no matches." Otherwise, it continues to look for loaded variables. Your timeline should look similar to Figure 26.9.

Testing Integration Project, Phase 3

When you run the page, you should be confronted with a search input. Enter anything you want (but it's most impressive if you enter something in the database). If your search returns multiple results, it will be reflected in the text box.

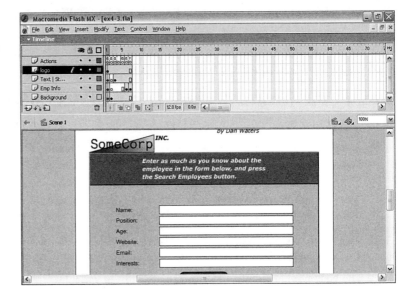

It is now safe to export your Flash movie as ex4-3.asp.

Working with Images and ASP

Prior to the release of Flash MX, it was nearly impossible to load JPEGs into your Flash movie on the fly. You either had to generate a SWF file and use loadMovie or had to create a movie clip containing several different JPEGs and control that clip to give the appearance of dynamicity. Those days are over. Now, it is possible to load JPEG and MP3 files dynamically using loadMovie in the same way you would load a SWF file, as shown here:

```
loadMovie("test.jpg", 0);
```

So, for example, if you load a variable into Flash called UserIcon, which has a value such as UserIcon_01.jpg, you could display that image dynamically using such a statement. This comes in very handy for making Web pages truly customizable.

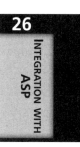

The Final Example

The last example is not something you will find in these pages. Because it is a sprawling project that integrates all the techniques I have shared with you over the course of this chapter, it is only available for download from www.danwaters.com/fmx or www.samspublishing.com.

This project manages a database in its full scope and extrapolates our current code for SomeCorp, Inc.'s profile page. It even utilizes dynamic image loading to display an icon representing a particular employee's personality.

To install the example, download the ZIP file, unzip it, and place all the items in the Launch folder somewhere in your Web server's file system (such as C:\Inetpub\www-root\SomeCorp\Launch). Then, navigate to that link via your Web browser (that is, http://localhost/SomeCorp/Launch). If the page is not found, go ahead and add default.asp to the end of that URL.

Summary of Concepts

Overall, you have learned quite a lot. You learned how to send data from ASP to Flash and from Flash to ASP. We covered some methods used to work with databases. Finally, you learned how to work with images. Here's a recap:

- **To send data from ASP to Flash.** You must always send a Variable Definition String to the HTTP Response for Flash to recognize variables. The variable names must not be URL encoded, but their values must be URL encoded. Loading an ASP script is very similar to loading a text file, because the ASP script simply generates text as it would appear in a text file.

    You can use two methods of data retrieval while playing the movie: getURL (if you want to open up a new window or generate code) and loadVariables (if you want to run an invisible script).

    It is also possible to initialize the movie with certain values by writing a query string after the *moviename*.swf occurrences in the <OBJECT> code.

- **To send data from Flash to ASP**. You can send data using loadVariables or getURL, as mentioned earlier, but you must specify a method (POST or GET). If you do not specify a method, you must call the script with a query string, such as the following loadVariables call:

    ```
    loadVariables("order.asp?OrderID=" + _root.OrderID, 0);
    ```

    Then, in ASP, use the Request collection to retrieve your data.

- **Working with databases**. Always structure your data logically. Map the database out before actually implementing it. Make sure that if you will ever need a particular piece of data, you either have a separate field for it or have a routine to extract it from another field. You can add records by using `oRS.AddNew`, followed by `oRS.Update`. You can delete records in the same way using `oRS.Delete`. Remember that ADO `Recordset` methods such as these may only be performed on a valid and open `Recordset` object. Otherwise, you must use `Connection.Execute(SQL)`.

- **Working with images**. Images can be dynamically loaded into Flash, with the release of Flash Player 6, in the same way that SWF files can be loaded. Here's an example:

```
loadMovie("somepicture.jpg", 0);
```

Troubleshooting

A lot of things can go wrong when so much data is changing hands. Here are a few very common problems and hints to help you alleviate them:

- **My ASP script does not run.** Make sure you are running the script via the HTTP protocol. If you do not, the server will try to have you download it.

  Make sure you are actually outputting something. Also, debug your VDS and SQL strings if you suspect there is something wrong with them. Use `Response.Write` to examine them after they have been built.

  Run the `SystemTest.asp` file from `SystemTest.zip`, provided with this example. If it notifies you that there is a problem, make sure you have a Web server installed and that it functions with Microsoft Access.

- **My Flash screen displays my Loading loop indefinitely.** This is usually a problem with the ASP script. Debug the SQL and Variable Definition Strings by printing them out and examining them directly.

  Make sure your frame labels are correct in your Flash movie, and that there are no duplicates. Furthermore, analyze your program flow in Flash to ensure that the user is directed to the right place no matter what.

- **My data looks like garbage.** Double-check that you are URL-encoding the correct portions of your VDS. Format it using ASP keywords such as `vbCr` and `vbCrLf`.

- **My data in Flash does not seem to refresh itself.** In the first call to `loadVariables`, set your test value (that is, `_root.Success` or `_root.FoundResults`) equal to nothing (`""`) and `loadVariables` using `POST` rather than not having a parameter there. This seems to solve problems involving the lack of refreshed data.

Hopefully, you have learned much from this chapter. The knowledge you have acquired can be applied to create one truly killer Web site by adding much-needed dynamics to an otherwise static graphical marvel. Here are some ideas to get you started on a project of your own: dynamic 3D, dynamic image masking, an MP3 player, a chat program the possibilities are only limited to what you can imagine.

Integration with PHP

By Brian Hoard

CHAPTER 27

PHP is a server-side scripting language. Some of its syntax was derived from C, Perl, and Java. You will notice many similarities between ActionScript syntax and PHP as well, which makes it easy to use the two languages together. PHP allows embedded Web content to be served to Web site visitors dynamically and quickly, and to both Windows and Unix servers.

PHP was originally conceived by Rasmus Lerdorf in 1994 for use on his personal home page. The name PHP originally derived from the initial letters of the phrase "personal home page." The current version of PHP, weighing in as another recursive acronym, stands for "PHP: Hypertext Preprocessor." PHP has been adopted by the Open Source development community, which has brought PHP to its current, mature form, now in version 4.

The PHP language was written specifically for the Web. This means it has built-in tools for Web developers as well as provides connectivity to powerful databases, including the following:

- dBASE
- DBM
- FilePro
- Hyperwave
- Informix
- InterBase
- Microsoft SQL Server
- mSQL
- MySQL
- ODBC
- Oracle
- Oracle8
- PostgreSQL
- Sybase

PHP is known for its speed and efficiency, causing little overhead on a server's resources. This allows it to run on even the most simple of hardware setups while handling millions of hits per day.

PHP is the scripting tool of choice for many Linux servers on the Web. A common setup uses Apache as the Web-serving software, PHP for scripting, and MySQL for database functions.

Besides Linux, PHP runs on other Unix flavors, such as Mac OS X and IRIX. It is also available on Windows servers running Windows Internet Information Server (IIS). PHP's design is native to Unix, so some functionality is not fully supported in a Windows environment.

PHP's incredible popularity can be attributed to its efficiency, reliability, ease of learning, connectivity to many databases, and its attractive pricing (pronounced *free*).

It serves over 7.5 million domains as of this writing, and over 1 million IP addresses. (To view the latest PHP statistics, along with other Web facts for geeks, see www.netcraft.com.)

PHP scripts are interpreted by the server, not the client, making them compatible with all browsers. This also has the benefit of adding a level of security to your code, because the final output is the only thing sent to the browser.

Often, the output of PHP is dynamically created HTML pages; however, it also can support XML, Java, SWF, PDF, and dynamically created JPEG and PNG images.

Why PHP and Flash?

Flash is a great interactive interface to the end user. Flash allows developers to work in a multimedia format that's presented consistently each time it is viewed, regardless of the visitor's computer or operating system.

Macromedia's ActionScript is becoming a powerful language that allows complicated functions to be done directly within the Flash player.

When the time comes to automate your site's updates, to add functionality not available in ActionScript, or to interact with external data on the server, it's time to use PHP.

PHP is analogous to a shoe salesman in a mall store. For example, a visitor puts his foot out, and PHP runs to the back room to open the MySQL database warehouse. PHP then retrieves the size and color of shoe the visitor requested and brings it back to the visitor and crams his foot in. PHP then rings up the sale, verifies the visitor's identification, offers the visitor a chance to sign up for notification of future sales, and hands the visitor a bag filled with colorful shoe paraphernalia.

PHP speaks to the server's securely guarded resources and retrieves information for the end user. These attributes, when coupled with the relational database, MySQL, result in you being two steps away from world domination (or at least some pretty good dynamic Web sites). Here are some things you can do using PHP and Flash:

- Externalize Flash content
- Create PHP scripts to update numerous Flash pages
- Read and store information in databases
- Load variables from dynamic sources outside of Flash
- Pass variables from Flash to PHP
- Run server-side scripts using information supplied by visitors
- Create e-commerce sites
- Create shopping carts
- Secure Web transactions
- Allow users to upload or download server files
- Launch e-mail scripts
- Generate dynamic images, PDFs, and SWF files
- Create calendars, time, and date outputs
- Run text-filtering scripts to process large amounts of data, outputting specific parts
- Set cookies
- Allow content to be updated from a browser, without the need to republish the SWF movie

PHP Scripting for Dynamic Content

Let's start with the opposite of dynamic, which is *static*. Static sites (or Web brochures) are the same each time they are visited. Updates to static pages are done manually.

Dynamic, on the other hand, refers to actions that take place at the moment they are needed, rather than in advance. For Web sites, this means that Web pages sent to the visitor's browser are created at the server, when they are needed.

Web sites, which use dynamic content, might ask the server to retrieve updated information or to run scripts to access other data before delivering the page to the visitor.

This process may take slightly longer than serving a static page, but the payoff for a few milliseconds delay is the ability to offer new, fresh content without constant Webmaster involvement. Therefore, a good PHP scripter is worth ten or twenty thousand static Webmasters (and should be compensated accordingly).

A search function is a good example of a dynamic Web page. The visitor inputs search terms into a form and submits the information to the server. A server-side script processes the input, retrieves information from a database, and the results are served to the visitor.

Figure 27.1 depicts a typical visit to a dynamic Web page using PHP. The Uber Scripter writes scripts and develops pages ahead of time that take advantage of dynamic content. Once these are in place, the server will deliver pages to visitors without the need for time-consuming manual page editing, as in static sites.

FIGURE 27.1

Roundtrip dynamic data flow using PHP.

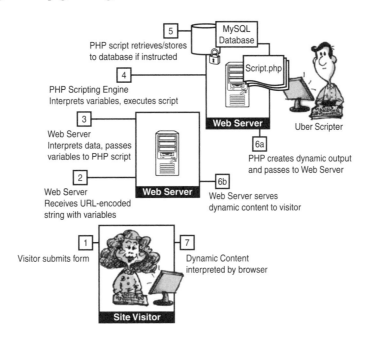

A dynamic data flow operates as follows:

1. A visitor fills in the entries on a Web form within an HTML or Flash site and submits the form.

2. The information is sent through the Internet by a URL-encoded query string. When the Uber Scripter uses the GET or POST option in a form, Flash takes care of the details to pass the data correctly. All the scripter has to do is set up the form correctly in Flash.

3. When the Web server receives the form data, it interprets the instructions and executes the proper PHP script. The server recognizes the characters, separating the variables and passing them to the PHP script.

4. The PHP script is executed.

> **Note**
>
> Although Figure 27.1 shows a separate Web server and PHP server, their functions are often performed by a single server. They are shown here as separate computers for clarity in their functions.

5. At the core of PHP is the Zend engine (`www.zend.com`), which processes the PHP script, substituting variable name pairs with the client-supplied data where they are called in the script.

6. The dynamic output of the script is passed back through the Internet and forwarded to the visitor.

7. The visitor's browser recognizes the returning data, just like any other Web page, and displays it. This is the magic of dynamic Web pages! On a remote paradise island, a scripter reads the site's visitor stats over his laptop and lets out the trademark PHP roar of victory.

Now that you've followed along the road a Web form takes, you should have a good understanding of what is taking place and what is handling the code throughout the process.

Your First PHP Script: Testing the Server

As the most popular scripting language on the Web, PHP is likely supported by your hosting server. If you are not sure whether your server is running PHP, this test will determine whether you have the power of PHP at your disposal.

If you have access to your own server, you can download the latest files to install PHP at `www.php.net`.

This first test script uses the PHP function `phpinfo`, which has the benefit of letting you look at the PHP server settings and see what modules and options are loaded.

The only requirement is that you have access to a Web server and the ability to upload files, because you will need to upload your PHP scripts in order to run them. PHP scripts are simple text files and don't need to be made executable by the operating system in order for them to work. The server's setup knows what to do when it receives PHP scripts.

> **Note**
>
> Be sure your PHP script's filename has the extension needed by your server's configuration. Some servers may be set up to recognize PHP files with the `.php` file extension (the default), whereas some servers may require an extension of `.php3`, `.php4`, or `.phtml`. If your script does not work initially, try renaming the script with one of the other possible extensions. If your server requires a `.php3` extension, that may mean it is only running PHP version 3, in which case it is in desperate need of an upgrade.

27

INTEGRATION WITH
PHP

Writing the Script

A PHP script is nothing more than a simple text file. It doesn't need to be compiled or made executable in order to work. Simply saving the script to your PHP-enabled server allows the script to be used immediately. Here are the steps to follow:

1. Using your favorite text editor, create a file with the following lines:

```
<?php
phpinfo();
?>
```

2. Save the file to your Web server and name it `phpinfo.php` (being sure to use the extension specified by your server's administrator). Here's an example:

   `http://www.YourDomain.com/php/phpinfo.php`

3. Execute the script by launching a browser and pointing it to the file you created. If everything is working correctly on the server, you should see a page like the one shown in Figure 27.2.

FIGURE 27.2
The PHP info screen.

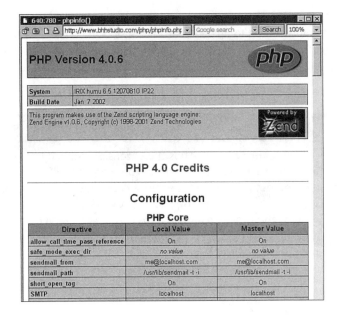

Troubleshooting the PHP Installation

If you don't get an output similar to Figure 27.2, here are some areas to check:

- Check for typing errors. Make sure the semicolon at the end of `phpinfo();` is present.

- Check the path where you loaded the file and try again.

- Your file extension needs to have the extension required by your server's configuration. Try renaming your file using one of the several possible extensions (`.php`, `.php3`, `.php4`, or `.phtml`). Also, if you are using a Windows system, check to make sure that Windows didn't sneak a `.txt` extension on the end of your file.

- The directory or file permissions are not correct. You need to have "read" access to the files from a browser.

  In UNIX, `chmod 0644` *filename* will give your file read/write access for the owner and read-only access for groups and others.

> **Warning**
>
> Be careful when changing permissions on files on your server connected to the Web or on your intranet. Be sure you understand the security implications of granting even read access to files. The ability for maliciously intended evildoers to exploit your code is a serious threat to your company's data and systems.

- Your server is not running PHP. In this case, you need to pull whatever strings are required to get it loaded or find a hosting company that supports PHP scripting.

If you get the PHP information screen, congratulations! You are knocking at the door of complete and total control of the world you live in (or at least some pretty snazzy, dynamic Web sites).

Take a few moments to look through the output of the PHP info screen. You should see many directives and settings specific to your server. Most of these will not make much sense at first, but you can see easily what your server is configured to do.

You will also see the command used when the software was compiled, bringing out excitement in any true, card-carrying geek.

Some of the settings will be very important if you want to make a specific database work or to perform image manipulation of certain file types. Some of the values may be baked into the software at compile time; others may be changeable within the server's `php.ini` configuration file, and still others may be set within your scripts. These are advanced topics you can find more information on in resources dedicated to PHP development as mentioned in "Further Reading," at the end of this chapter.

Exploring Optional Modules

PHP allows additional functionality to be specified during compiling. One of these functions is the ability to create dynamic images, such as JPEG, PNG, or WBMP images (not GIFs), from scripts through the GD Graphics Library, in addition to reading, modifying, and re-creating images.

Note

More information on the GD Library can be found at `www.boutell.com/gd`.

In the past, there have been other modules that increase the functionality of PHP. Development for some modules may come and go because they usually bridge a gap between what is available within PHP and what is desired. Therefore, it is always good to look at what the latest version of PHP is doing, as well as Flash, so you can plan sites that take advantage of your main tools first.

PHP Fundamentals

After getting the PHP info screen on your server, shown earlier in Figure 27.2, you are ready to start creating dynamic sites.

If you're new to scripting, this is a great way to introduce yourself to a powerful language.

Personalization

The rest of the examples in this chapter will use personalization and directory structures that have been built for simplicity and tested to run without error.

After going through these examples, you will most likely want to develop your own structures for your sites that work best for you.

Your PHP server may be different, depending on how it is configured. The examples in this chapter make use of the default PHP server settings.

Case Sensitivity

Except for keywords, ActionScript does not distinguish between upper- and lowercase letters. However, this will not allow you to name variables passed to PHP with reckless abandon. You should use a naming convention for your code that can be passed to and from Flash without problems.

PHP is case sensitive. This is important when you're passing data between Flash, PHP, and the server. MySQL, and Unix in general, are also case sensitive. Some people like to use all lowercase letters for variables, and other people prefer to use all capital letters. The examples in this chapter use capitalization for the first letter of each word. This lets us string many words together while making them easy to decipher. For example, we'll use variable names such as `MyVariable`.

Directory Structures

In this chapter's examples, we use the following directory structure:

- Site root: `www.YourSiteRoot/`
- Flash movies: `www.YourSiteRoot/flash/`
- PHP scripts: `www.YourSiteRoot/php/`

Published SWF movies are placed in the `flash` folder along with the HTML files that hold them. The PHP scripts are placed in the `php` directory.

Relative Paths

The scripts referenced in these examples use relative paths. Because our PHP scripts are in a separate directory from the HTML that launches the movie, we must tell `loadVariables` how to get to that directory. The HTML files are located in the same directory as the Flash SWF movie files they hold.

We want to keep our PHP scripts in their own directory to allow our root directory to remain uncluttered. By doing this, we will make it easy to remember where the scripts are located.

Because our Flash movie will eventually be viewed in a browser from an HTML page (when using PHP scripts within our ActionScript code), we have to tell the Flash player where to go get the script. Using `"../php/"` tells the Flash player that we are traveling up our directory tree one level, and then down again into the `php` directory.

The term *relative* here refers to where our Flash SWF file is being viewed from, which as far as the browser is concerned, is from the HTML file.

Why Not Absolute Paths?

You might be thinking, why not just use absolute paths, and not bother with the confusion, and just point to our scripts with `http://www.bhhstudio.com/php/simple.php`?

This might work for linking to other Web pages or launching other SWF movies, but for PHP scripts and interacting with the server, our Flash movies and scripts must reside within the same domain; otherwise, the Flash player will reject them.

By keeping our scripts relative to the Flash files, we also avoid problems associated with testing on local servers, where a browser may change the path

```
http://your_server/intranet-testing/
```

into this one:

```
file://E:/your_server/intranet-testing/.
```

If your ActionScript uses absolute paths, the latter address would reject your script as being from a different domain.

Domain Criteria for External Scripts

In order to prevent security problems and unauthorized use of data residing on sites outside of the requested URL, the Flash player will not accept data from outside addresses using `loadVariables`, `xml.load`, `xml.sendAndLoad`, or `xmlsocket.connect`.

To ensure your external data will not get rejected by the Flash player, your request for external data must meet the following criteria:

- Be a relative URL, such as `../php/MyOwnSweetFile.php`, or a file residing on a local disk, as in `file://D:/scripts/MyOwnLocalFile.php`.
- The Flash SWF movie and the requested external file must be on the same domain.

When developing dynamic content with PHP and Flash on a local server, you may run into the browser rejecting your external data, even though it is on the same subdomain. Your browser may try to resolve the addresses by using a path such as `file://local-host/E:/intranet/flash/simple.html`, which causes the Flash player to reject the external data.

Make sure, when viewing your content in your browser, that you use `http://` rather than `file://`, which will keep both your browser and Flash development on the same address.

Also, when previewing your Flash movies that use PHP scripts, you will only be able to run the scripts on a server running PHP. Some things may work within the Flash previewer, such as reading PHP scripts as text files. However, the best way to completely test your movies is to test them on the Web server and run them from within a browser.

Script Syntax for ActionScript and PHP

Both ActionScript and PHP use the semicolon character as the instruction terminator, which tells the script to follow the instructions preceding it. It is a good idea to use a syntax-highlighting text editor when writing scripts. As you edit your ActionScript code, you will see correctly formatted terms change colors in the Actions panel. Flash MX also has ActionScript code hinting, which helps you properly construct your scripts.

To activate the code hints, put your cursor between parentheses while entering scripts and select the Code Hint icon (see Figure 27.3).

For editing PHP, using a text editor that offers syntax highlighting makes it easy to avoid mistakes as you develop your scripts. UltraEdit at `www.ultraedit.com` has customizable syntax highlighting for PHP, HTML, and other languages, and provides a good way to work when simultaneously switching between PHP and other languages, such as HTML or XML.

Variables for ActionScript and PHP

PHP variables must begin with a letter or an underscore, not a number. Flash variables can be used directly within PHP by adding a $ symbol to the variable name.

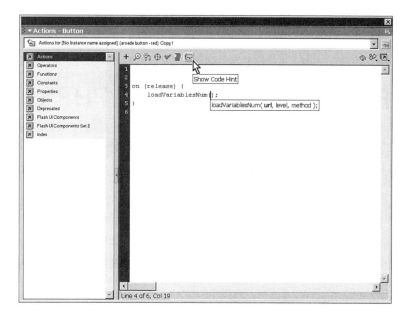

FIGURE 27.3

ActionScript syntax highlighting and code hinting.

When using the Flash variable called `MyVariable`, you would use the PHP variable `$Location` inside your PHP script (we discuss how to pass variables from Flash to PHP later).

Commenting Your Code

Both ActionScript and PHP use double-slash commenting. Consider the following examples:

```
//This is a comment in ActionScript.
//This is a comment in PHP (Look familiar?).
```

Escape Characters

Both ActionScript and PHP use the backslash to escape characters to prevent them from being interpreted as code. For example, the `\"quotes\"` in this line have been escaped by backslashes.

You may also see backslash escape characters in dynamic text output from a server. PHP has built-in functions to handle escape characters with `addslashes` and `stripslashes` commands. This is a security function of the Web server software to prevent malicious visitors from entering code within forms and executing horrible things on your server.

For instance, if a visitor tries to run the UNIX `ls` command in order to run a list of the server's files from a form by typing `'ls'`, the Web server escapes the single quotes with backslashes (`\'ls\'`), thus preventing it from being interpreted as a system command.

Receiving Data from PHP to Flash

The PHP script in this example passes information to Flash's variables, as seen in Figure 27.4. The following files are used from the companion Web site:

- `flash/simple.fla`. The Flash development file
- `flash/simple.swf`. The published Flash movie
- `flash/simple.html`. Holds the `simple.swf` movie
- `php/simple.php`. The external PHP file to be loaded

You will need to copy these files to a Web server running PHP in order to use the PHP scripts.

FIGURE 27.4
PHP to Flash.

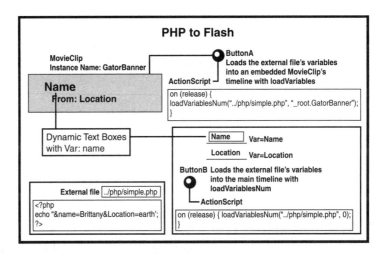

The ActionScript `loadVariables` is used to get information from PHP for a dynamic text box on the main (root) timeline:

```
loadVariables (url, target, method);
```

In this example, we aren't sending any variables, so the "method" is left out, making the ActionScript on Button A like this:

```
on (release) {
    loadVariables ( "../php/simple.php" , "_root.GatorBanner" );
}
```

Open `flash/simple.fla` and select Button B.

This button will load the information from PHP into the Flash movie at level 0 when released by using the following ActionScript:

```
on (release) {
    loadVariablesNum("../php/simple.php", 0);
}
```

Examining the PHP Script

Looking at the `php/simple.php` file, you can see that the contents are as follows:

```
<?php
echo "
&Name=Brittany&
&Location=Earth&
";
?>
```

First, the PHP open tag `<?php` tells the server that this is a PHP script. This is also the way PHP is embedded within the body of HTML code.

Several options are available for opening and closing your PHP scripts; some require customization on the PHP server to work. Besides the default tags, there are the following types of tags:

- **Short tags**. `<?` to open and `?>` to close
- **ASP tags**. `<%` to open and `%>` to close
- **Script tags**. Similar to JavaScript, which takes the form of `<SCRIPT LANGUAGE='php'>` to open and `</SCRIPT>` to close

For the examples in this chapter, we will use the `<?php` default tags, also known as *XML tags*, because they are easy to recognize as PHP. This is also the method you will need if you plan on integrating XML into your scripts later on.

Next, the variables are written one on each line, giving the variable `Name` a value of `Brittany` and the variable `Location` a value of `Earth`. The variables are placed one on each line in order to make the file easier to read and edit. We know that Brittany is not from Earth, but for the purposes of simplicity, we are using a planet most people can identify.

Ampersands are placed on both sides of each `Name=Variable` pair. We could call this technique *amper-sandwiching*, but we probably shouldn't.

The `echo` command is ended with double quotes, and the instructions are ended with a semicolon. Finally, we put a bow on it by using the default PHP close tag, `?>`.

The beauty of using external data like this is that by simply editing this PHP script, every Flash file that references this file will be updated automatically the next time someone visits it. Once again, everyone will bow to your greatness as geek-of-wonder, commander of external text files with ampersands.

Developing the Flash File

Open the file `flash/simple.fla` and select the dynamic text "Name." The first variable is called `Name`, as shown in the Flash Property Inspector in Figure 27.5.

FIGURE 27.5

Dynamic text variables.

Select the text box near Button B. The Var: box is where you enter your desired variable name for the text box you have selected. It is only available for dynamic text. Keep in mind that ActionScript variables are not case sensitive, but PHP is case sensitive. You should use a naming convention for your scripts that works with both languages. In this examples, we capitalize the first letter of each word.

The other dynamic text with a variable is "Location." All variables within the external file will be passed to Flash at once. Whether we use them all or not is up to us.

Next, we will tell Flash to replace the variables with the externally supplied data by using a button. A variable is a container for data. The data put into the variable could be from a user-input box from somewhere else in our script, or from an outside source. In this example, the variables (containers) are `Name` and `Location`. They will be filled with new data through the external PHP script.

You may want the external data to be available in the main timeline, on a particular level, or from within an embedded movie clip. Once we bring in the data with `loadVariables`, it will be available to us for all these methods. We only need to change our ActionScript in order to direct the variable's data to its correct location within our movie.

We have accomplished, with this example, the loading of externally created variables into Flash. This is exactly the same method you would use if the external data were a simple text (TXT) file. However, by using a properly formatted PHP file, you now have a good understanding of how to talk to PHP on the receiving end in Flash.

Sending Data from Flash to PHP (to Flash)

In this example, a PHP script will read variable data sent from Flash. PHP will read in the variables, use them within its script, then echo back to Flash using the variables within multiline text.

This example uses the following files from the companion Web site:

- `flash/Flash2PHP.fla`. The Flash development file
- `flash/Flash2PHP.swf`. The published Flash movie
- `flash/Flash2PHP.html`. Holds the `Flash2PHP.swf` movie
- `php/variables.php`. The PHP script

The functionality of this example shows how dynamic content can be used to generate interactive Flash pages. Open the file `Flash2PHP.fla` and refer to Figure 27.6.

FIGURE 27.6

Flash to PHP (to Flash) using `loadVariablesNum`.

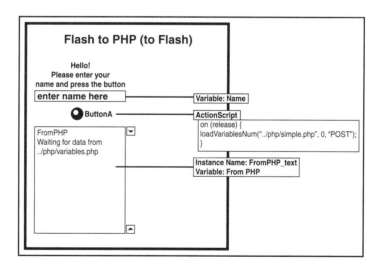

The variables defined in Flash are passed to the PHP script when Button A is released. Here's the ActionScript on Button A:

```
on (release) {
    loadVariablesNum("../php/variables.php", 0, "POST");
}
```

This example passes data directly from the main (root) timeline to PHP using POST. In practice, you will most likely want to limit the data being passed to PHP. You can do this by using movie clips in Flash. Passing data from individual movie clips lets you have more control of the variables being passed, as well as the ability to retrieve variables to different movie clips. To pass variables from a movie clip, you could use the following code on the first frame of the movie clip:

```
onClipEvent (enterFrame) {
this.loadVariables("../php/variables.php", "POST");
}
```

You would then put a button on the main timeline, which could be scripted to perform initial checking on the input data, and when ready, trigger the movie clip to send data to PHP.

Now back to our example, where we're using the main timeline. Refer to Figure 27.7 and the PHP script php/variables.php:

```
<?php
echo "
&FromPHP=Hello $Name, This is from the script.
Coming back at you live, all day, all night.
365 days a year, for all your day and night
comin' back at you live stuff, for as long
as you can stand it. Probably even longer.
And stand it you will, bla bla bla...&";
?>
```

FIGURE 27.7

Flash to PHP,
after visitor input.

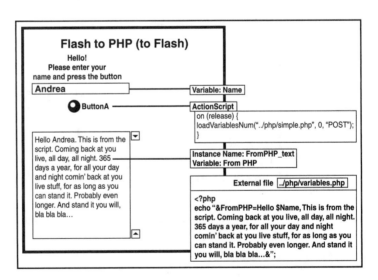

When the variables are passed to the PHP script from Flash, PHP can use them by you simply adding the dollar sign ($) symbol to the variable names in your PHP script. This allowed you to echo the Name variable back to Flash.

You can see that by communicating back and forth with a server's scripting engine, the possibilities are many. Developers who already use server-sided scripting but are new to Flash should see Flash as a way to integrate an attractive graphical front end to otherwise boring HTML-only database-driven sites.

Flash developers new to server-sided scripting should see solutions to some of their client-only development problems, such as the inability to store user information or the lack of dynamically created content.

"You can do that with PHP" will become a common phrase in your Web designing stages after learning its many uses. For example, when a client asks for the ability to update its Web pages without the assistance of a dedicated Webmaster, you could say, "You can do that with PHP." When a Flash designer needs to find a way to retrieve information from a database and tell Flash to load a specific frame based on the database's output, you might say, "You can do that with PHP."

By using Flash and PHP together, developers get the client-side power of ActionScript along with integrated server-side PHP tools. The ability to pass variables to and from Flash and PHP allows the two languages to communicate and act on each others' output.

Something else you may want to do with this capability is let Flash check for the script and provide gracious error checking in case the script can't be read. Also, for larger amounts of data, you can give the user a progress bar and signal to Flash when the script has been fully downloaded.

For these features, you may want to use the LoadVars object, which can perform error checking, progress information, and allow streaming of the data while it downloads.

The important thing to remember with interactive, dynamic pages like this is to make the most use of your scripts while keeping them manageable. Some of the scripting may be better left to ActionScript within each movie, whereas for other things, it make sense to create PHP scripts that update all your Flash movies.

With ActionScript becoming a more and more powerful language of its own with every incarnation, the art of combining the ActionScript and PHP languages, each doing what it does best, is key to great, interactive, and problem-free sites.

Echo Valley Becomes a Wishing Well

Storing information on the server and the ability to store information in such a way that a visitor is able to ask questions and retrieve answers from the server is what databases are all about. Information is stored in tables and organized in ways that queries can be sent to the server and the results given back.

A one-on-one interaction with the server, where a developer uses Flash as a front end for database management, is like Echo Valley. The server is pretty much giving back what the developer is putting in. But when you add the communication of the Internet, with people plugged into the same database, each inputting data, and the ability for any subscriber to retrieve data collected from everyone else, PHP at the core, driving this machine is less like Echo Valley and a lot more like a wishing well. You can throw a question to it and receive a new and unique answer based on the data stored within the database.

PHP acts as the middleware between Flash and a database. It translates Flash's queries in the format MySQL needs, and the output of MySQL is translated through PHP back to Flash.

Using MySQL

MySQL is a database management system. It is available to download through the GNU Public License (GPL) or through commercial licensing at a low cost through MySQL AB. MySQL AB is the company owned by the MySQL founders. More information can be found at `www.mysql.com`.

A database is where information is organized into tables, which are used on the Web to store information to support things such as e-commerce sites, shopping carts, address books, online catalogs, and so on. They all possess one common need: The ability to quickly search and retrieve information from a large amount of data.

Large amounts of data can be stored in flat files, which grow larger as more data is entered. Imagine a real-world situation such as printing a phone book for a large city. This single book grows larger and larger as the city grows. By the time the book gets to be about 4 inches thick, it becomes difficult to find information quickly. The book may be broken up into smaller books (by alphabet, for example), making the information within each book manageable.

In database terms, a single phone book could be stored in one flat file, but as it grows, the computer would take more time to sort through it in order to find answers. This is the job of a relational database management system (RDBMS). An RDBMS allows tables to relate to each other through common attributes, thus speeding up the searching and retrieving of data.

MySQL is one of the most widely used relational databases used on the Internet today. Like PHP, MySQL runs efficiently, making it very fast. It is easy to learn and is available on both Unix and Windows platforms.

This section explains how to use Flash, PHP, and MySQL together. Along the way, you'll learn some database basics.

Like PHP, MySQL must be run on your server. Depending on your situation, you may be using your own server or relying on a hosting company that supports MySQL databases. You may have privileges to create an unlimited amount of databases, or you may have a limit on the number of databases you can create.

Once you have access to a MySQL database, you're ready to begin using Flash as a front end. In order to allow Flash to talk to MySQL, we will use PHP as the translator (that is, the middleware).

Getting the `mysql>` command prompt will vary from system to system. Rather than discuss MySQL setups, we'll begin after you have made your way through your hosting company or system administrator in order to access the `mysql` command.

Once you have access to a database, you'll log in with something like the following:

```
mysql -u brian -p
    Enter password:******
Welcome to the MySQL monitor. Commands end with ; or \g.
Your MySQL connection is 258 to server version: 3.22.21
Type 'help' for help.
mysql>
```

Creating a Database in MySQL

The following command creates the new database called MyDatabase:

```
mysql> CREATE DATABASE MyDatabase;
Query OK, 1 row affected (0.01 sec)
```

Showing Databases

You can show databases in MySQL with the SHOW DATABASES command. A listing will appear as shown here:

```
mysql> show databases;
+ — — — — —·+
| Database |
+ — — — — —·+
| MyDatabase|
| mysql     |
| test      |
```

```
+ — — — — —·+
5 rows in set (0.00 sec)
```

MyDatabase is the database we have just created, and mysql and test are the MySQL default databases. The mysql database is the administrator's database.

Creating a New User

Your hosting company may have already set you up to use MySQL or may have granted you access to a database with a login name.

If you are running your own server, you will need to create a user using an administrator login. Once the new user is created, log out of the administrator account and log in as the new user.

In this example, we will create the user Nathan. Using an account with access to the administrator mysql database, create a new user:

```
mysql>use mysql
Database changed
```

The privilege system for MySQL allows critical data to be protected, and users may be granted or revoked privileges by administrators. Tables, columns, and databases all have permissions that users must be given access to work with. Understanding the MySQL privilege system will require some study.

We will create a monster of a user, with full privileges on the database. The syntax is GRANT privileges ON database TO username@host IDENTIFIED BY 'password' options. Here's the actual code:

```
mysql>GRANT all
    ->ON MyDatabase.*
    ->TO Nathan@localhost IDENTIFIED BY 'NaS&L';
    ->WITH GRANT OPTION
Query OK, 0 rows affected (0.01 sec)
```

Granting Database Privileges

The following command will grant permissions to Nathan for the MyDatabase database. Use this to add privileges to existing users. For this example, we are granting all privileges, but in the real world you will need to limit the privileges of users on your database by specifying only the necessary privileges needed by each user. Your methods will depend on the sensitivity of your data. Here's the code for granting the database privilege:

```
mysql> GRANT all
    -> on MyDatabase.*
```

```
    -> to Nathan;
Query OK, 0 rows affected (0.01 sec)
mysql> quit
Bye
```

Now, log in using the new user name:

```
    mysql -u Nathan -p
    Enter password: NaS&L
Welcome to the MySQL monitor. Commands end with ; or \g.
Your MySQL connection id is 36 to server version: 3.22.21
Type 'help' for help.
```

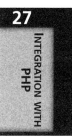

Column Types

Depending on the type of data to be stored within each table, you must define the data type to be used. MySQL supports many data types. The data types are grouped into three categories: numeric, date and time, and string (characters).

Table 27.1 details some of the more common data types used in typical databases. A complete list of types, along with detailed explanations, is available at www.mysql.com/doc/C/o/Column_types.html.

TABLE 27.1 Common Database Data Types

Data Type	Definition
Numeric	
INT	Integers
FLOAT	Floating-point numbers
DOUBLE	Double-precision floating-point numbers
Date and Time	
DEC	Decimals stored as a text string
DATE	Any date
YEAR	Years between 1900 and 2155
String	
CHAR	Fixed-length strings from 0 to 255 characters
VARCHAR	Variable-length strings from 0 to 255 characters
TEXT	Text fields from 0 to 65,535 bytes

Creating a Table

To create a new table, issue the CREATE TABLE command, followed by a comma-separated list of the new columns. Here's the syntax for this command:

```
CREATE TABLE TableName(Column1 Type(Length), Column2 Type(Length), etc;
```

Let's create a table for tracking information about the aliens we've captured. First, we need to make sure we are at the correct database:

```
    mysql> USE MyDatabase
    Database changed
mysql> CREATE TABLE Aliens (
    -> AlienID INT UNSIGNED NOT NULL AUTO_INCREMENT PRIMARY KEY,
    -> AlienName CHAR(30),
    -> LocationCaptured CHAR(50)
    -> );
Query OK, 0 rows affected (0.02 sec)
```

Showing the Tables

To see the tables in our database, issue the SHOW tables command. You should see a display like this one, showing our new Aliens table:

```
mysql> SHOW tables;
+--------------------+
| Tables in MyDatabase |
+--------------------+
| Aliens             |
+--------------------+
1 row in set (0.00 sec)
```

Describing the Tables

In order to see our columns, use the DESCRIBE command, followed by the name of the table:

```
mysql> DESCRIBE Aliens;
```

You should see a result similar to Figure 27.8.

Entering Information into Tables

Data can be entered into tables in several ways. Here's a common method:

```
INSERT INTO tablename VALUES(value1, value2);
```

Here's an example using this method:

```
INSERT INTO Aliens VALUES (NULL, "Brittany", "Earth");
```

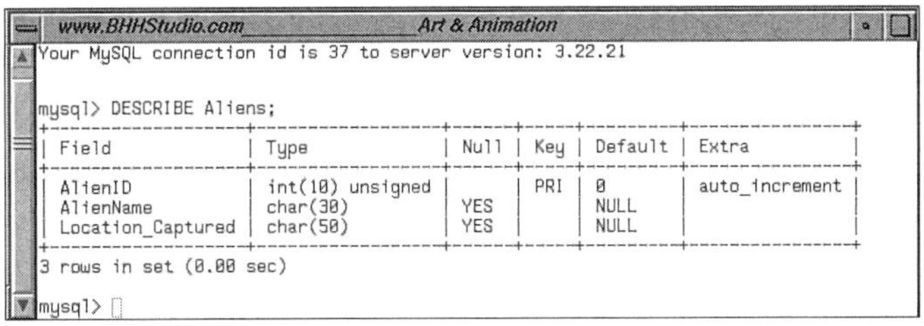

FIGURE 27.8

MySQL command-line output.

When entering text strings, wrap the string in single or double quotes. If you want to specify only certain columns within the table or enter data in a different order, you could use the following:

```
INSERT INTO tablename (column1, column2) VALUES ("YourData");
```

For example, enter this into the table to add the new alien named Henry from our last Mars expedition:

```
INSERT INTO Aliens (LocationCaptured, AlienName) VALUES ("Mars", "Henry");
```

Showing Table Contents

Now that we have a couple of entries in our table, let's see how it looks. Issue the SELECT command to view the table:

```
mysql> SELECT * from Aliens;
+--------+-----------+-----------------+
| AlienID | AlienName | LocationCaptured |
+--------+-----------+-----------------+
|      1 | Brittany  | Earth           |
|      2 | Henry     | Mars            |
+--------+-----------+-----------------+
2 rows in set (0.00 sec)
```

The wildcard character (*) tells SELECT to list everything in the table. Notice that the AlienID column is automatically filled in for us. Remember that when we created the table, we gave the AlienID column the following creation instructions:

```
AlienID INT UNSIGNED NOT NULL AUTO_INCREMENT PRIMARY KEY,
```

By creating the AUTO_INCREMENT column called AlienID, we have a running numerical list, which MySQL takes care of without our input.

Selecting Data from a Table

Once the table grows in size, the ability to selectively query the database for just the information that interests us at the time becomes important. It's also important to be able to sort data a certain way based on criteria we provide. We do this by using the SELECT command like this:

```
mysql> SELECT items
    -> FROM tables
    -> WHERE condition;
```

Notice the semicolon on the last line. MySQL waits for the semicolon/instruction terminator before executing the command. You could also write the same command in one line, like this:

```
mysql> SELECT items FROM tables WHERE condition;
```

The SELECT command has many more options, allowing for the sorting, grouping, and limiting of information. For our examples, we will be using simple conditions in order to blaze the trail for using Flash, and allow you to explore more advanced uses.

Before we ask the database for information, let's ask ourselves a regular question that makes sense to the humanoid in us: Where was Brittany captured?

Now, let's convert this question into a database query using the following syntax:

```
mysql> SELECT column
    -> FROM table
    -> WHERE condition;
```

Here's what we would write, along with the result of our query:

```
mysql> SELECT LocationCaptured
    -> FROM Aliens
    -> WHERE AlienName="Brittany";
+ — — — — — — — — —+
| LocationCaptured |
+ — — — — — — — — —+
| Earth            |
+ — — — — — — — — —+
1 row in set (0.00 sec)
```

We have successfully created a database, added a table, put data into the table, and now have the ability to ask questions to the database and receive formatted answers based on criteria we provide. Who's kicking sand in whose face now, on this dynamic cyber-beach of muscle? *You* are, and it's all because of the alphabet soup of acronyms known as PHP/MySQL-ville.

Connecting PHP to MySQL

In order to communicate with the database, we must open the door with a proper username and password as well as a host. This is done from PHP using the mysql_connect function. Here's the syntax for mysql_connect:

```
mysql_connect("servername", "user", "password");
```

For this example, we will be using the following files from the CD-ROM:

- `flash/Flash2MySQL.html`. The HTML file that holds our movie
- `flash/Flash2MySQL.fla`. The Flash development file
- `flash/Flash2MySQL.swf`. The published movie
- `php/AddAlien.php`. The PHP script

Refer to Figure 27.9 and the PHP script `php/AddAlien.php`.

FIGURE 27.9

Modifying the database from Flash.

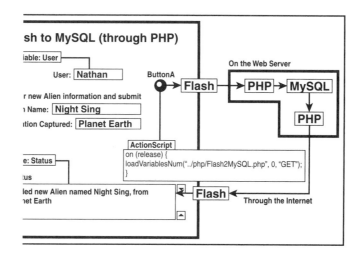

The `php/AddAlien.php` script allows Flash to communicate to the MySQL database through PHP and add an entry to the Alien table. The backslashes (\) in the following script are inserted for publication purposes; when typing in the code by hand, make sure these lines are continuous.

```php
<?php
//Set common variables
$Host="localhost";
// We'll get $User="Nathan"; from Flash2MySQL.swf
// This is Nathan's password on the MyDatabase Database on MySQL
$Passwd="NaS&L";
$FailMsg="Something's not right...";
$SuccessMsg="&Status=Added new Alien named \
$AlienName, from $LocationCaptured.";
$DBName="MyDatabase";
$TableName="Aliens";
$Column1="LocationCaptured";
$Column2="AlienName";
//Get busy...
```

```
//1: Connect to Database
$Connect=mysql_connect($Host, $User, $Passwd);
//2: Select Database
mysql_select_db($DBName, $Connect);
//3: Create MySQL command Query
$Query="INSERT INTO $TableName (LocationCaptured, AlienName) \
VALUES('$LocationCaptured', '$AlienName')";
//4: Send Query to MySQL, Adds new entry to database
mysql_query($Query, $Connect);
echo "$SuccessMsg";
?>
```

The Flash variable User is passed from Flash to PHP. Inside the AddAlien.php script, several variables are defined within PHP. By defining these at the beginning of the script, we'll find it easier to modify the script later while maintaining the integrity of the rest of the script.

This script is commented along the way, so it's quite self-explanatory. You can see that we get User from Flash and use it in several places. Also, when the user clicks Button A, the new column and value information is sent as well. PHP connects to the MySQL database using mysql_connect and selects the database to use with mysql_select_db. Also, the Flash dynamic text "Status" receives the output from PHP after the database has been updated.

Using these techniques, you can also add, delete, and modify MySQL databases from Flash. The possibilities are limited only by your imagination.

Further Reading

Integrating Flash with PHP brings about an entirely new dimension to the types of products you can create over using Flash alone.

If the idea of Open Source software appeals to you, PHP is a great start. The amazing generosity and sense of community that exists within the Open Source movement continues to amaze me. The benefits are better tools for everyone and an opportunity to learn and grow in developing valuable career skills in Web and interactive development.

PHP is a well-documented language. You will have no problem finding answers within the Open Source community. In order to complete your PHP training as Uber-Scripter/World Dominator, you should add the following books to your library:

- *PHP and MySQL Web Development*, by Luke Welling and Laura Thomson (ISBN: 0-672-31784-2)

- *Sams Teach Yourself PHP in 24 Hours*, by Matt Zandstra (ISBN: 0-672-32311-7)

- *PHP Developers Dictionary*, by R. Allen Wyke, Michael J. Walker, and Robert M. Cox (ISBN: 0-672-32029-0)

  Here's a list of online resources:

- An online reference is available along with everything else about PHP at `www.php.net`.

- PHP uses the Zend scripting language engine by Zend Technologies. More information can be found at `www.zend.com`.

27

INTEGRATION WITH PHP

Integration with Servers: An Overview

By James Smith

This chapter explains in general terms the issues involved in providing active data to a Flash movie embedded in a Web page. Perhaps the best place to start is to explain exactly what active Web content is, as opposed to static content. To understand either, some familiarity with the workings of the Web is needed.

To request a specific resource, a Web client uses a uniform resource locator, or *URL* for short. A URL contains everything that is needed to locate a file or resource. It starts with a protocol, followed by a colon and two forward slashes. Next is the hostname of the resource, usually a domain name. Then comes the absolute path to the resource itself. The slash that divides the host and absolute path is considered to belong to the latter. Take, for example, the following URL:

```
http://www.myhomepage.com/index.html
```

The protocol here is `http`, the hostname is `www.myhomepage.com`, and the absolute path is `index.html`. The IP address is obtained from the host using the Domain Name Service, or *DNS* for short. A Web server at this IP address will be configured to translate the absolute path into a path on its local file system.

In requesting a static resource then, a Web client sends the URL of that resource to a Web server. When responding, the Web server simply reads the requested file from disk and prints it out to a handle representing a data stream back to the Web client. Essentially, it's like copying a file from one place to another, albeit not very efficiently. Usually the Web client is a browser and the requested file is an HTML file, but not always.

As well as supplying static content in this manner, all Web servers provide containers in which active processes can run and supply content themselves. Containers are adjunct parts of Web servers and provide everything an active process needs to fulfill this role: namely, a handle to the client data stream, the actual request URL, and various server environment variables. These are all made available to the active process by one way or another. The most ubiquitous container is the Common Gateway Interface, or *CGI*, as it's widely known.

An active request URL can invoke an active process by naming the process file explicitly, in a similar manner to a static request. The Web server is configured, in this case, to "know" that the directory in which the file sits contains active processes to be run in a container rather than simply printed back to the Web client. This is commonly how CGI scripts are run. Alternatively, the relative URL of the request may correspond to a mapping describing the container for the active process and an alias for the process itself. This is commonly how server-side applets (servlets) are invoked.

To summarize then, *static content* is data served intact by the Web server itself, whereas *active content* is data served by a process running in a container. It may be that the active process does nothing more than read a file and pass it straight back to the Web client, but that's not the point. The point is that it's the active process that's doing this, not the Web server.

One further definition at this stage: The term *dynamic content* is often used to refer to active content as it's described in the preceding paragraph. I tend to use this term only for technologies running on the client side, however, such as JavaScript. Because these aren't the subject of this chapter, the term isn't used again. Furthermore, I'd go so far as to say that Flash has rendered most of these technologies obsolete anyway.

Embedded Flash Movies

Only Flash movies embedded in a Web page are dealt with in this chapter. Such movies can request data using only those URLs with the same subdomain as the page in which they are embedded. This is presumably a restriction placed on them by the Flash player, and it's similar to the concept of the "sandbox" in which Java applets run. What exactly is a subdomain then? Consider the following URL:

```
http://java.sun.com
```

The part of the hostname that is actually registered as a domain is just the `sun.com` part. The `java` bit isn't included in the registered domain name. This could be changed to the more familiar `www`, and strictly speaking the resulting URL would still be in the same registered domain. It's the `sun.com` part that qualifies this URL as belonging to Sun Microsystems, presumably. Of course, the name as a whole will be resolved to another server entirely. Therefore, according to the Flash documentation at least, `www.sun.com` and `java.sun.com` are both subdomains belonging to the same `sun.com` domain.

Flash movies embedded in Web pages only being able to connect to resources in the same subdomain is considerably less restrictive that you might think. According to a Macromedia techNote, a Flash movie loaded from `http://www.yourserver.com/flashmovie.swf` can access data residing at `http://www.yourserver.com/data.txt`. The text file is located within the same domain, `yourserver.com`, as the SWF. Data files within the same subdomain, for example, `dataserver.yourserver.com`, would also be accessible by this movie. However, the same movie's attempt to load data from `http://www.notmyserver.com/data.txt` will fail. Or, if the movie was running on the `java.sun.com` site, it would also be able to access resources on the `www.sun.com` site. Hardly a restriction, then.

Web Content: Format Versus Origin

A Web client, any Web client, is only "interested" in the type and format of the data it receives. It checks, more or less strictly, that this data matches certain criteria, enabling it to process the data correctly. In the case of a browser, for example, an HTML file is probably requested and it's validity checked against the document type definition (DTD) or schema that defines the format, pretty forgivingly, in order that some attempt to render it can be made.

Flash movies embedded in Web pages make a similar type of request but require data of a different format than HTML. The request and response mechanism, though, is essentially the same. A request for data from an embedded Flash movie passes through the parent browser, which may in fact cache the data in the same way it caches Web pages.

A most important point to emphasize, then, as mentioned earlier, is that it's the type and format of Web data that matters to any Web client—be it a browser, an embedded Flash movie, or whatever—and not the method of its generation. It simply doesn't matter whether the data is generated actively by a server process or read statically from a file by a Web server.

A concrete example might help. Consider a browser displaying information about your bank account (obviously data that one would hope is generated actively). However, viewing the HTML source from the browser gives a "static" page of numbers, tables, and formatting. There's no "activeness" in the plain HTML page itself. If this fact seems obvious to you, then fine, but it's a most important one, so it's stressed here: Actively generated content "looks" just like static content to any Web client.

Clearly then, active data can be served to Flash movies, too, as long as it fulfills the necessary type and format criteria. Then it's no different from static data, as far as the movie is concerned.

Furthermore, if active content "looks" just like static content, one method of actively generating it is just as good as another. Therefore, the choice of active process technology is essentially arbitrary, and to discuss Flash's interaction with one or another is to miss the bigger picture. That's why all the server code examples in this chapter are written in pseudo-code. It's an embedded movie's interaction with a supporting active process, together with the type and format of the data exchanged that's of interest here, not the implementation of the active processes per se.

What is meant by the *type* of the Web data, then? All Web content has a type or, specifically, a MIME type. This gives the Web client a broad hint as to how to handle the content. For example, HTML Web pages should have the MIME type "text/html." If you want to display a normal plain-text document in a browser, you could give it a MIME type of "text/plain." If you're sending binary data, (for example, a ZIP file), that you want people to be able to download, then you could set the MIME type to "application/octet-stream." A browser can be configured, on receipt of content with this MIME type, to display a download dialog box, rather than making an attempt to display it.

When a Web server serves your documents statically, the only way you have to set the MIME type is through its configuration, and then only if you know how to and have permission to do so. It is usually done by associating file extensions with their required MIME types. On the other hand, when you write an active server process, it's your job to set the MIME type. How this is done is explained in the next section.

Serving Active Content

Apart from interfacing with the required container then, writing active content entails specifying the correct MIME type, keeping to the correct format, and printing it all to a handle representing the data stream to the Web client. You normally just use a plain-old PRINT function. So, how do you specify the MIME type? You simply print it right at the beginning of the content, separated from the main body of the response by a blank line. For printing a simple HTML page, for example, you'd have this:

```
PRINT "Content-type: text/html\n\n";
PRINT "<HTML>";
PRINT "  <HEAD>Simple content</HEAD>";
PRINT "  <BODY>"
PRINT "Some simple content";
PRINT "  </BODY>"
PRINT "</HTML>";
```

Notice the two carriage returns after the content descriptor (the part that describes the MIME type, that is), ensuring a blank line between the header and body. The blank line in the pseudo-code is just for clarity. Some platforms may provide a method for setting the MIME type, but these just allow that it's not the first thing you have to do. They'll also provide a buffer to print to that won't be flushed until your function exits and the MIME type has been appended first.

Because the handle of the data stream is ubiquitous in many server-side implementations, it's omitted from the pseudo-code here. You might have to call a function to retrieve it, or it might be passed to the function that you have to implement, in which case you will have to explicitly reference it in your PRINT statement. It really depends on which active process container you're using. With CGI (still probably the most popular), neither is necessary, and the pseudo-code here pretty closely reflects what you'd actually write for a CGI program, in any language. A common misconception, by the way, is that CGI programs have to be written in Perl, but this isn't the case at all. You can write them in C, for example, or even Java.

The Data Format for Flash Movies

Before discussing the type and format of Flash data, let's quickly cover URL encoding. If you already know what this is, you can safely skip the next few paragraphs, but if you don't know, read on. Consider the Web address for Google:

```
http://www.google.com
```

This uses a colon, two forward slashes, and a couple of dots—all special characters. Characters are considered "special" if they make up part of the formatting of the URL. Usually this means splitting it up into its constituent parts, such as protocol, address, and form variables. Now consider submitting an incorrect GET request with a form variable set to "Hello, world!". A couple of further special characters are used in the URL here, specifically a question mark and an equal sign:

```
http://www.google.com?search=Hello, world!
```

Why is this incorrect? The variable name and values may well contain special characters themselves. What if the variable value was the pessimistic "Hello, world?". Given that the question mark is designated as a special character, used to separate the main URL from the form variable definitions, in fact, wouldn't its inclusion in the definition of a form variable effectively "break" the URL? Probably.

URL encoding fixes this problem by replacing instances of special characters that aren't meant to be treated as such with a different representation that can be safely ignored while the URL is examined. The rules for encoding are as follows:

- The ASCII characters "a" through "z", "A" through "Z", "0" through "9", and ".", "-", "*", and "_" remain the same.

- The space character " " is converted into a plus sign "+". The plus sign is encoded according to the third rule, next.

- All other characters are converted into the three-character string %*xy*, where *xy* is the two-digit hexadecimal representation of the lower 8-bits of the character.

Here's the correct request URL:

```
http://www.google.com?search=Hello%2C+world%21
```

In the case of appending form variables to a request URL, it's the browser's job to do the necessary encoding of form variable names and values before appending them to the main URL. In fact, if you type **Hello, world!** into the search field on Google, the preceding URL is pretty much what you'll see when the request is returned. Web content that has been encoded in this way is given the MIME type "application/x-www-form-urlencoded."

Content sent to an embedded Flash movie, statically or otherwise, should have this MIME type. In practice, however, text/plain works fine. In fact, if the movie has requested a URL statically, this is probably the MIME type that your Web server will assign to the file, especially if the file extension is `.txt`. To get the right MIME type, think up a unique file extension and configure your Web server to set the MIME type accordingly, if you can figure out how.

And the format of the content itself? Nothing so complicated as HTML. Data is presented as name/value pairs, URL encoded, and separated from one another by ampersands. This is an identical process to that of appending form variables to a URL, in fact. You have to do this encoding yourself, though, because it's not done by the server automatically.

in an embedded Flash movie, and you pass this cliché as the concatenation of two separate variables. Your data file would look like this:

```
var1=Hello%2C&var2=+world%21&
```

Your entire set of variable definitions must go on one line. Carriage returns are anathema to an embedded Flash movie. Note the extra, trailing ampersand, too. Even if your file appears to be all on one line, a carriage return may creep in at the end of it, and this will force the exclusion of the final variable on some platforms. Adding a trailing ampersand will protect the last variable definition, even if the trailing carriage return is present.

There are several limitations to this format, apart from the obvious ones of needing to put the whole lot on one line and having to encode everything yourself. You can't use arrays or dot syntax, for example. There are ways around these limitations, however, if you use an active process, and these are discussed later on.

How Flash Requests Data

Consider a movie that loads data from a static text file called `Template.txt`, for example, the contents of which are identical to the variable line in the preceding section. Assuming it contains a symbol formed from a dynamic text field with an associated dynamic variable, `value`, two event handlers in the object script associated with an instance of this symbol are needed in order to load the data.

The `onClipEvent ( load )` handler is called immediately on instantiation of the symbol, pretty much when the movie is first loaded (hence, the name). The body of the handler first sets the `value` variable to indicate that the data is being loaded. Notice how this variable is directly available in the object script because the dynamic text field itself doesn't have an instance. Let's take a look at the handler:

```
onClipEvent ( load ) {

    this.value = "loading...";
    this.loadVariables( "Template.txt" );
}
```

The `loadVariables(...)` function is a synchronous function that instructs the player to get variable definitions from a named file or network resource.

Synchronous functions return control immediately while working on in the background to fulfill their allotted task. If and when a synchronous function completes, it notifies the calling thread somehow, usually by calling an event handler. This contrasts with an asynchronous function, which doesn't return control to the main program until it has either completed or failed. Most functions are asynchronous, because they don't take long to execute their tasks or, at the very least, take a determinate amount of time to do so. `loadVariables(...)` is a synchronous function because it's often used to call remote resources over a network, which can take an indeterminate amount of time to respond, if they respond at all.

So, `loadVariables(...)` attempts to read the specified file or resource, loading variables into the movie based on definitions it finds. How are they loaded, and where are they made available? Different forms of the `loadVariables(...)` function allow the variables to be targeted at specific levels or symbol instances within the movie. In this example, the object-oriented form is used, with `this` prepended to the function call, instructing the variables to be loaded into the same symbol instance from which the function is called. The symbol into which the variables are loaded is commonly known as the *target symbol*.

How Flash Processes the Data It Receives

When `loadVariables(...)` has successfully loaded the last byte of information from the specified file, it signals that it has completed its task by calling the `onClipEvent ( data )` handler in the object script of the target symbol. It is a moot point whether some of the variables are available for use before this handler is called, because you should never use them. The data handler looks like this:

```
onClipEvent ( data ) {

    value = var1 + var2;
}
```

Here, the two variables are concatenated and assigned to the `value` variable of the text field, changing it from `loading...` to `Hello, world!`. The loading process should be almost instantaneous for local resources (that is, resources residing on the local file system). There's nothing specific you need to do in order to get hold of the variables. They appear as if by magic in the target symbol, once the data handler has been called, and they are immediately available for use thereafter. That's it.

In a "real" movie, the data handler would be the place to start off the movie proper, calling the required functions to handle the data once it has been loaded.

A note here about using long data sets: If arrays aren't allowed in variable definitions, how can we handle large amounts of linear data, or a multidimensional array? Naming the variables with the correct indexes is one answer, but how then do we get them into an array? Consider the following variable list:

```
count=4
var1=This
var2= is
var3= another
var4= example.
```

Now, assume that it has been loaded into a target symbol. You could associate the following code with the symbol in order to get these values into an array defined at the root level of the movie:

```
onClipEvent ( data ) {

    for ( i = 1; i <= count; i++ ) {
        _root.var[ i ] = eval( "var" + i );
    }
}
```

This breaks the rule that there's no need for any specific processing of variables in the data handler in order to make them available to the movie. It is up to you to decide whether this extra processing is necessary. Is the data more accessible in array form? Perhaps one motive for such a method is to move the data from one place to another. For example, you could associate the array with a different symbol or declare it in the frame script of the your root layer and assign it accordingly. Multidimensional arrays and dot syntax can also be handled in this manner.

An alternative to the eval(...) function is to use a notation that more closely reflects the nature of the data—namely, an array. Try the following in the preceding loop:

```
_root.var[ i ] = this[ "var" + i ];
```

Which method you choose is up to you. The former is considered outdated by many, and for object references at least, you should certainly follow convention and stick to the latter. The old method means, quite literally, "evaluate the following expression and return the result." In some languages, you can calculate whole expressions with it and even execute code.

Configuring a Movie to Load Network Data

You can use the loadVariables(...) function to query a resource across a network as well as on the local file system. In this case, the argument represents a URL, rather than just a reference on the local file system. In fact the most general definition of uniform resource locators does include file systems, so in a sense you can think of the argument as always being a URL. Without a leading forward slash, Template.txt becomes a relative URL and is evaluated within the context of the Web page in which the movie is embedded.

Consider hyperlinks in a Web page, for example. You don't need the fully qualified URL when referencing a resource with a hyperlink. The browser constructs the complete URL from the relative one given in the hyperlink, together with URL of the page itself. Browsers always request resources using a fully qualified URL, and certainly a Web server has no concept of relative URLs. The omission of the leading forward slash, in hyperlinks or the loadVariables(...) function, signifies a relative URL then, whereas its inclusion signifies an absolute one.

So, request URLs can be used instead of local filenames. Here are a few examples, all of which might respond with identical data:

```
this.loadVariables( "Template.txt" );

this.loadVariables( "/servlet/Template" );

this.loadVariables( "/cgi-bin/Template.cgi" );

this.loadVariables( "/Template.asp" );
```

Notice that the three requests for an active resource are all absolute, whereas the original static request is relative.

The only way a movie has to be configured, then, is in knowing what the correct request URL needs to be. We could use any of the server processes referenced in the preceding examples and never need to change a single line of the movie, if we could replace one of these calls with the line

```
this.loadVariables( requestURL );
```

and pass the `requestURL` parameter to the movie somehow. How do we get this variable into Flash reliably? You could use JavaScript, but it's badly supported, and even where it is supported, it's flaky. The answer is to append an encoded variable as a GET request to the movie URL in the OBJECT/EMBED tags. The movie URL is the reference to the Flash movie file itself, and it is indeed a URL, similar to a hyperlink. Consider the standard HTML code to embed a movie into a Web page:

```
<OBJECT          classid="..."
codebase="..."
        WIDTH="550"
                HEIGHT="400">
<PARAM NAME="movie" VALUE="Template.swf?requestURL=%2FTemplate%2Easp"
    <PARAM NAME="bgcolor" VALUE="#ffffff">
<EMBED src="Template.swf?requestURL=%2FTemplate%2Easp"
                bgcolor=#FFFFFF
                WIDTH=550
                HEIGHT=400
            TYPE="application/x-shockwave-flash"
                PLUGINSPAGE="...">
    </EMBED>
</OBJECT>
```

Here, a few attributes and elements have been left out or shortened for brevity, but the important bits (the movie URLs) contain a GET request with a `requestURL` form variable set to `/Template.asp`. There are two movie URLs here—one for the OBJECT tag and one for the EMBED tag. Notice that the form variable is URL encoded.

How is this form variable made available in the script of the movie itself? It appears at the lowest level in any script associated with the first frames on the main movie timeline. If you tend to use the lowest layer of the main movie timeline as the place to write general script and nothing else, you can declare the variable there as being defined by this mechanism, helping to avoid any naming conflicts:

```
///     Defined from without...
///
var requestURL;
```

Of course, you can append many variables to the movie URL in this manner to configure your movie, but the important one is the URL of the supporting server process. If the context in which the movie sits now changes (say it's moved from a development to production environment and hence the URL of the supporting active process changes), all you have to do is to change the encoded value of the query variable in the movie URL, and nothing else. Specifically, there's no need to change any script in the movie and recompile it.

One final note about how this variable is set: It can obviously be hard-coded into an HTML file, but usually the page in which the movie sits would also be actively generated. So, the request URL could be read from a configuration file and then encoded and placed in the HTML actively. With ASP and JSP, this is straightforward. With servlets, Perl scripts, and so on, you could use a custom tag library.

Sending Active Content to an Embedded Movie

Naturally, following the example of actively printing out an HTML file earlier, we could serve the data to the movie in the following manner:

```
PRINT "application/x-www-urlformencoded\n\n";
PRINT "var1=Hello%2C&";
PRINT "var2=+world%21&";
```

At the very least, though, your process could read the text file from the preceding static example, passing it to the movie when requested to do so. Here's what the pseudo-code for that might look like:

```
PRINT "application/x-www-urlformencoded\n\n";

/* process and print the data file */
WHILE ( there's another line ) {

        PRINT;
}
```

This is pretty much what the Web server does in response to a request for a static resource. It hardly seems a clever way to serve the data, though. For example, because the text file contains the variable definitions all in one line, this `while` loop should complete in one pass. And the text file is still just as unreadable.

If we have this freedom of reading a file before passing it on to the Web client, however, why not make the data file more readable by filtering it and doing some of the formatting on the fly? Surely a data file like the following would be far more maintainable:

```
var1=Hello,
var2= world!
```

We want an active process that reads a data file, making the straightforward conversions necessary to get it into a format acceptable to a Flash movie. This means reducing the output to a single line again, adding the required ampersands between variable definitions, and URL-encoding the variable names and values. Therefore, the pseudo-code will look something like this:

```
PRINT "application/x-www-urlformencoded\n\n";

/* process and print the list file */
WHILE ( there's another line ) {

    CHOP OFF THE TRAILING CARRIAGE RETURN;
    ENCODE THE NAME AND VALUE, APPEND AN AMPERSAND THEN PRINT;
}
```

The real code is hardly ever more complex than this. One important point to note about your choice of print function, though, is that if it automatically appends a carriage return to each line, you're in trouble. This doesn't matter with HTML files, because carriage returns and whitespace appearing outside HTML elements are ignored. This is not the case with data for Flash movies, though: The data must appear to be all on one line. Therefore, you should find a print command that doesn't automatically append carriage returns.

Technically speaking, the data has been abstracted from the program. This is incredibly useful—now nonprogrammers (Web developers) can change the list file as they wish; they don't even have to know about the existence of the active process in order to write content for Flash movies. This new data file is called a *list file*, to distinguish it from the previous raw data file and to highlight its main feature—namely, the spreading of variable definitions over several lines.

The use of comments and empty lines in a list file is possible with a minimum of changes to the process code, too. Consider the following:

```
#    A 'Hello, world!' example list file
#
var1=Hello,
var2= world!
```

This is stretching credibility perhaps a little far, but only because we are dealing with such a simple data set. The readability attained by not needing to encode the variable names and values, coupled with being able to space out variable definitions over several lines and add comments, constitutes a persuasive argument for the implementation of a simple active process.

Furthermore, adding custom tags allows for the inclusion of any type of data in the content stream for a movie. Custom tags can be picked up, parsed, and replaced with their true values as the active process reads through the list file. Consider the following:

```
#     The current date
#
currentDate=<<DATE.getCurrentDate.toString>>
#     The first product name and monthly volumes
#
label1=<<PRODUCT.1.name>>
amount1=<<PRODUCT.1.volume:ref[0]>>
...
amount12=<<PRODUCT.1.volume:ref[11]>>
```

Anything bounded by the double angle brackets is a custom tag. Here, there's a reference to a date object, as well as references to a products object. These objects could be taken from a database, the server environment, or just another text file. Implementation of these objects is not the issue here, however. Nor is the implementation of a simple tag library to reference them.

Is such a tag library necessary? Yes and no. If you're using a common server-side solution such as Perl or Java, the implementation of a small tag library could become a necessity, whether you decide to use your own or a third-party solution. Certainly you should consider adding the other list file functionality, though, even if you think custom tags are too much bother.

Active Process Models

If you choose to use an active server technology that doesn't support a tag library, you could use the same techniques outlined in the previous section to filter your HTML files, too. Some active method of setting the movie URL is usually needed at least, even if the remainder of the page remains unchanged. My preference is to go one stage further and use the same actual server process to service both the browser request for an HTML page containing an embedded movie and the request from the movie itself. In this case, how does active process know from where the request has come?

The easiest thing to do is to use a form variable to differentiate between the two types of request. If the request URL contains this variable, the active process knows that the request has come from the movie; if it doesn't, the request has come from the browser. Altering the request's URL to include a form variable is the easiest way to implement this model:

```
this.loadVariables( requestURL + "?" + "data=all" + "&" );
```

Here, the designated form variable is `data`. The value of the variable is unimportant with this model; its presence is all that's necessary. The outline of the active process to handle this model looks something like the following:

```
if ( "data" form variable exists ) {

    SEND CONTENT TO A MOVIE;
}
else {

    SEND CONTENT TO A BROWSER;
}
```

It may be that this convention is too restrictive. You may want just one server process to handle all the data requests from embedded movies, in which case the following model would be more suitable:

```
if ( "data" form variable exists ) {

    PROCESS AND PRINT THE FILE CALLED "data";
}
```

This process handles only list files; there's no mention of HTML pages. The value of the data form variable is now important and can be used to choose which list file to use. This model can also be used if generation of the HTML pages has nothing to do with the generation of content for the embedded movies.

Implementation Issues

There are two main solutions to generating active content for Web pages:

- Using a program or script that reads a file (usually HTML) and filters it (often by the detection of custom tags) before passing it on to the Web client. Visual Basic DLLs running in IIS, Perl scripts, and Java servlets all fall into this category.
- Using a scripting language based on code embedded in the HTML file itself. Microsoft's ASP and Sun's JSP technologies fall into this category. Special tags are used to discriminate between HTML and the embedded code.

The first of these naturally lends itself to the techniques described in this chapter—namely, filtering a list file before handing it back to the Web client. The first of the models outlined in the previous section works well in this scenario.

The second solution fits the mold a little less comfortably. Because of the problems outlined later in this section, some implementations don't necessarily make obsolete the use of a list file, nor the necessity of an active process to filter it. Specifically, you can't easily make your list file into a JSP or ASP page and request it directly from a movie.

Why not? Because the output generated by an ASP or JSP page reflects exactly the layout of the page itself, minus the custom tags. This includes formatting (namely, whitespace and carriage returns). Consider the following concrete example of a JSP page:

```
<%
String title = "Hello, world!";
%>
<html>
<head>
<title><%= title %></title>
</head>
<body bgcolor=white>
<h1><%= title %></h1>
</body>
</html>
```

You don't need to be familiar with this language to see immediately that a `title` variable is defined at the top of the page and inserted into the `<title/>` and `<h1/>` HTML elements later on. Clearly the funny `<%/>` element is used for code, and then the same tag with an equal sign in it allows the variable's value to be inserted into the page. Obviously, the result is going to be this:

```
<html>
<head>
<title>Hello, world!</title>
</head>
<body bgcolor=white>
<h1>Hello, world!</h1>
</body>
</html>
```

The custom tags are either removed completely, as in the case of the `title` variable definition, or replaced with their evaluated value. The important thing to notice here, though, is that the layout of the original file is kept intact. Whitespace and carriage returns are most definitely present.

Therefore, it becomes almost impossible to construct a data stream that Flash will accept without either further processing of the output or putting all your code on one line. Even this may not work, and certainly the following JSP code won't quite do the job:

```
<%
String var1 = "Hello, ";
String var2 = "world!";
%>var1=<%

out.print( java.net.URLEncoder.encode( var1 ) );
%>&var2=<%
out.print( java.net.URLEncoder.encode( var2 ) );
%>&
```

Of course, carriage returns and whitespace are ignored in the custom tags themselves. Compilers and interpreters don't take any notice of such things. But still, a carriage return is appended at the close of each <%/> element, even though an ampersand immediately follows the closing angle bracket. The output, then, is this:

```
var1=Hello%2C+
&var2=world%21
&
```

And Flash won't like it!

Therefore, if you choose to implement the techniques outlined in this chapter, you're stuck with the reading and processing of list files by an active process, rather than embedding the active parts in the list file itself. At a stretch, you could implement this model with code embedded in a vacuous holder file. Monitoring the trailing ampersand ensures that any stray carriage return appended to the data stream (by the closing of the elements in this vacuous file) won't adversely affect the loading of the data into the embedded movie.

There's nothing to stop you from using the ASP/JSP model for generating the page in which the Flash movie is embedded, of course, and using it to populate the movie URL based on configuration variables. Other languages are possible that perhaps suit Flash more closely, presumably by overcoming the hurdle of JSP's and ASP's insistence of mimicking carriage returns in the original file, but they're not the issue here.

To conclude, the main thrust of this chapter has been to describe a way of serving active data to an embedded Flash movie that doesn't get down to the specifics of implementation: One server technology is just as valid as another. They'll all produce exactly the same data, constrained by what the movie "expects" to receive.

Also, these constraints have been examined and solutions outlined that in some way work around them, allowing more freedom for the Web developer in specifying the content to be supplied to a movie. Again, this has been done with no mention of the underlying choice of server technology.

Perhaps the most important lesson to be learned from this chapter, then, is this: Often programming problems can be solved without recourse to a specific platform. Indeed, considering the details of implementation can often cloud one's reasoning. Never be quick to choose a "solution" to your requirements, if that "solution" is just a synonym for a vendor's product.

CHAPTER 29

ActionScript Reference

By David Vogeleer

This chapter covers many pieces of ActionScript in the same order the ActionScript panel has them listed. Because ActionScript has become an increasingly more powerful language, it has grown in size tremendously, encompassing well over 600 individual scripts, including properties, methods, actions, and objects. This chapter would be too large to go over every piece, so the objects covered are limited to only a few of the main ones, including sound, date, math, and object. Rest assured, however, that all nondepreciated actions are discussed, including actions, operators, functions, constants, and properties. Depreciated actions are those actions that are still legal to use, but now there are new ways of doing the same actions. Basically, depreciated actions are still allowed, but they might not be in the next release, so it is good practice to avoid using them. We will go over the details of these scripts, including availability, generic templates, and examples.

Remember, each example is not the limit of the script, but only the beginning.

Actions

Movie Control

gotoAndPlay

Availability: Flash Player 2

Generic Template: gotoAndPlay(*scene*, *frame*);

Constraints:

> *scene*—The scene where you would like to go
>
> *frame*—The frame where you would like to go

Description:

This script sends the playhead to a specific frame in the specified scene and then plays. If there is no scene specified, the playhead moves to the frame in the current scene.

Example:

This example moves the playhead to frame 10 and plays when the interpreter reads it:

gotoAndPlay(10);

gotoAndStop

Availability: Flash Player 2

Generic Template: gotoAndStop(*scene*, *frame*);

Constraints:

> *scene*—The scene where you would like to go
>
> *frame*—The frame where you would like to go

Description:

This script sends the playhead to a specific frame in the specified scene and stops there. If no scene is specified, the playhead moves to the frame in the current scene.

Example:

This example moves the playhead to the frame labeled myFrame and stops when the interpreter reads it:

```
gotoAndStop("myFrame");
```

nextFrame

Availability: Flash Player 2

Generic Template: nextFrame();

Constraints: None

Description:

Sends the playhead to the next frame and stops. This can also be used as a constraint for gotoAndPlay and gotoAndStop.

Example:

The first example moves the playhead to the next frame and stops when a mouse is clicked; the second example uses nextFrame in a gotoAndPlay action:

```
onClipEvent(mouseDown){
nextFrame();
}
gotoAndPlay(nextFrame());
```

nextScene

Availability: Flash Player 2

Generic Template: nextScene();

Constraints: None

Description:

Sends the playhead to the next scene and stops. This can also be used as a constraint for gotoAndPlay and gotoAndStop.

Example:

The first example moves the playhead to the next scene and stops when a mouse is clicked; the second example uses nextScene in a gotoAndStop action:

```
onClipEvent(mouseDown){
nextScene();
}
gotoAndPlay(nextScene());
```

on

Availability: Flash Player 2

Generic Template:

```
on(buttonEvent){
statement(s);
}
```

Constraints:

> *buttonEvent*
>
>> press—Occurs when the button is clicked (or *pressed*).
>>
>> release—Occurs when the button is released while the mouse is over it.
>>
>> releaseOutside—Occurs when the button is pressed and then released while the mouse is *not* over it.
>>
>> rollOut—Occurs when the mouse moves from being over the button to *not* being over the button.
>>
>> rollOver—Occurs when the mouse moves over the button.
>>
>> dragOut—Occurs when the button is pressed and the mouse moves outside the button without the button being released.
>>
>> dragOver—After a dragOut event, dragOver occurs if the mouse moves back over the button without the button being released.
>>
>> keyPress("*key*")—Unlike the other events, this one takes place when a key is pressed. Here, "*key*" can only be one key.
>>
>> *statement(s)*—Code to be executed when *buttonEvent* occurs.

Description:

An event handler that occurs within a button when a mouse event or keystroke occurs.

Example:

The first example runs a simple trace function when a button is pressed; the second example stops the dragging of a button:

```
//when the mouse clicks on the button, the statement will be traced
on(press) {
trace("This button has been pressed");
}

//this will stop an object from being dragged
on(release, releaseOutside){
stopDrag();
}
```

play

Availability: Flash Player 2

Generic Template: play();

Constraints: None

Description:

Moves the playhead forward.

Example:

This example moves the timeline forward when a button is pressed.

```
on(press){
play();
}
```

prevFrame

Availability: Flash Player 2

Generic Template: prevFrame();

Constraints: None

Description:

Sends the playhead to the previous frame and stops. This can also be used as a constraint for gotoAndPlay and gotoAndStop.

Example:

This example uses an on event handler to move the playhead back one frame:

```
on(press) {
prevFrame();
}
```

29

ACTIONSCRIPT
REFERENCE

prevScene

Availability: Flash Player 2

Generic Template: prevScene();

Constraints: None

Description:

Sends the playhead to the previous scene and stops. This can also be used as a constraint for gotoAndPlay and gotoAndStop.

Example:

The first example moves the playhead to the previous scene and stops when a button is pressed; the second example uses prevScene in a gotoAndStop action:

```
on(press){
prevScene();
}
gotoAndPlay(prevScene());
```

stop

Availability: Flash Player 2

Generic Template: stop();

Constraints: None

Description:

Stops the playhead from moving on the timeline.

Example:

This example stops the movie when a button is pressed:

```
on(press){
stop;
}
```

stopAllSounds

Availability: Flash Player 3

Generic Template: stopAllSounds();

Constraints: None

Description:

Stops all sounds that are playing without affecting the playhead. Sounds placed directly on the timeline will begin again as the playhead moves past the stopAllSounds action.

Example:

The following example stops all sounds when the loop variable reaches 3:

```
if(loop >=3){
stopAllSounds();
}
```

Browser/Network

fscommand

Availability: Flash Player 3

Generic Template: fscommand(*command*, *parameters*);

Constraints:

> *command*—A string passed for any purpose or as a command to the hosting application.
>
> *parameters*—Another string passed for any purpose or as a value.

Description:

This script allows the Flash movie to communicate with its host, including the Flash player. It can also be used to pass variables to other programs that can host ActiveX controls.

> **Note**
>
> When passing commands to the Flash Player, you must use the following predefined commands:
>
> - allowscale. Allows or disallows the ability to enlarge and shrink the content of the Flash movie. The parameters can be true or false.
> - fullscreen. Fills the user's entire screen when parameters are set to true. The parameters can be true or false.
> - showmenu. Can display or not display the controls in the context menu. The parameters can be true or false.

29

ACTIONSCRIPT
REFERENCE

- `trapallkeys`. Can allow or disallow the ability to pass keystrokes to the Flash Player. The parameters can be `true` or `false`.
- `quit`. Closes the standalone Flash player (will not close browser). No arguments.

Example:

These examples show how to use a couple of the predefined commands:

```
fscommand("fullscreen", "true");
fscommand("trapallkeys", "false");
fscommand("quit");
```

getURL

Availability: Flash Player 2

Generic Template: getURL(*url, window, variable*);

Constraints:

url—A string representing the exact URL for the document you wish to obtain.

window—An optional assignment that represents how to load the URL, including _blank, _self, _parent, and _top.

variable—Another optional command stating how to send variables associated with the Flash movie, such as GET and POST.

Description:

The getURL script can do much more than simply open another Web page; it can also execute code in HTML and initiate events in the Flash movie.

Example:

The first example loads a Web page into a new window; the second example triggers a javascript action to pop an alert:

```
getURL("http://samspublishing.com", "_blank");
getURL("javascript: alert ('Flash Unleashed');");
```

loadMovie

Availability: Flash Player 3

Generic Template: loadMovie(*url, level/target[, variable]*);

Constraints:

> *url*—A direct link to the SWF or JPG file you would like to load into the main Flash movie. When being used in the standalone player or in the testing environment, the loaded movie must be stored in the same folder.
>
> *level*—A numeric value representing the level in which to load the movie. In normal mode in the ActionScript panel, when you attempt to put a number in the loadMovie script, the panel will convert it to loadMovieNum. If you are in the expert mode, it will not be changed. Just something to remember.
>
> *target*—A target movie clip or level number representing where the movie will be loaded.
>
> *target movieclip*—A direct path to the movie clip where you would load the movie. When a loaded movie is placed within a movie clip, anything that currently resides in that movie clip will be replaced by the loaded movie.
>
> *variable*—An optional command stating how to send variables associated with the Flash movie, such as GET and POST.

Description:

This script loads a movie or JPEG into the main Flash movie either by using *target movieclip* or *level number* to represent where the movie is to be loaded. If the movie is loaded into a level, the script changes from loadMovie to loadMovieNum.

If a movie or picture is loaded into a movie clip, that file takes on the characteristics the movie clip already possesses, such as position, size, and alpha.

Example:

This example shows how to load a movie into a movie clip called myMovieclip.

```
loadMovie("theMovie.swf", "_root.myMovieclip");
```

loadMovieNum

Availability: Flash Player 4

Generic Template: loadMovieNum(*url, level, variable*);

Constraints:

> *url*—A direct link to the SWF or JPG file you would like to load into the main Flash movie. When being used in the standalone player or in the testing environment, the loaded movie must be stored in the same folder.
>
> *level*—A numeric value representing the level in which to load the movie.
>
> *variable*—An optional command stating how to send variables associated with the Flash movie, such as GET and POST.

29

ACTIONSCRIPT
REFERENCE

Description:

This script loads a movie or JPEG into the main Flash movie by level number to represent where the movie is to be loaded. If the movie is loaded into a level, the script changes from `loadMovie` to `loadMovieNum`.

If you load a movie into a level that already contains content, the loaded file will replace that content.

Levels provide a simple stacking method that Flash uses to separate different parts of the Flash movie. The levels start at 0. Once a movie is loaded into a Flash movie, you can refer to it as `_level` followed by the level you have loaded it into. For example, if you load a movie into the second level, refer to it as `_level2`.

Example:

This example loads a JPEG file called `myJpeg.jpg` into a specified level:

```
loadMovieNum("myJpeg.jpg", 1);
```

loadVariables

Availability: Flash Player 4

Generic Template: `loadVariables(url , level/"target"[, variable]);`

Constraints:

> `url`—A direct link to a file containing the variables you would like to load into the main Flash movie. When being used in the standalone player or in the testing environment, the loaded movie must be stored in the same folder.
>
> `level`—A numeric value representing the level in which to load the variables. In normal mode in the ActionScript panel, when you attempt to put a number in the `loadVariables` script, the panel will convert it to `LoadVariablesNum`. Just something to remember.
>
> `target`—A target movie clip or level number representing where the movie will be loaded.
>
> `variable`—An optional command stating how to send variables associated with the Flash movie, such as `GET` and `POST`.

Description:

This script loads variables from a text file or a file created by another script, such as CGI or ASP. The text must be in MIME format. Also, the file must be in the same folder as the Flash movie that is loading it.

You can only load these variables into a target movie clip or a level number. If you specify a level number when using loadVariables, the normal mode will convert the script to a loadVariablesNum script. If you're in expert mode, this must be done manually.

Standard MIME Format:

```
myVariable=Flash Unleashed&myName=David&myAge=22
```

Example:

This example loads a text file holding the variables into a movie clip:

```
loadVariables("myVariables.txt", "_root.myMovieclip");
```

loadVariablesNum

Availability: Flash Player 4

Generic Template: loadVariables(*url* , *level, variable*);

Constraints:

> *url*—A direct link to a file containing the variables you would like to load into the main Flash movie. When being used in the standalone player or in the testing environment, the loaded movie must be stored in the same folder.

> *level*—A numeric value representing the level to load the variables in. When using loadVariablesNum, you must signify the level in the movie in which to load the variables.

> *variable*—An optional command stating how to send variables associated with the Flash movie, such as GET and POST.

Description:

This script loads variables from a text file or a file created by another script, such as CGI or ASP. The text must be in MIME format. Also, the file must be in the same folder as the Flash movie that is loading it.

Standard MIME Format:

```
myVariable=Flash Unleashed&myName=David&myAge=22
```

Example:

This example loads variables into the root of a movie:

```
loadVariablesNum("myData.txt", 0);
```

unloadMovie

Availability: Flash Player 3

Generic Template: unloadMovie(*level*/*target*);

Constraints:

> *level*—A numeric value representing the level from which to unload the movie. In normal mode in the ActionScript panel, when you attempt to put a number in the unloadMovie script, the panel will convert it to unloadMovieNum. Just something to remember.

> *target*—A target movie clip or level number representing where the movie will be loaded from.

Description:

This script removes a loaded movie from a target movie clip or level (using unloadMovieNum).

Example:

This example unloads a movie from a movie clip:

```
unloadMovie("root.myMovie.myLoadedMovie");
```

unloadMovieNum

Availability: Flash Player 3

Generic Template: unloadMovieNum(*level*);

Constraint:

> *level*—The level where you are unloading the loaded movie from.

Description:

This script removes a loaded movie from a level in the main movie.

Example:

This example unloads a loaded movie from the _root level.

```
UnloadMovieNum(0);
```

Movie Clip Control

duplicateMovieClip

Availability: Flash Player 4

Generic Template: duplicateMovieClip(*target*, *newName*, *depth*);

Constraints:

> *target*—The path to the movie you would like to duplicate.
>
> *newName*—The name given to the duplicated movie clip. This name must be unique.
>
> *depth*—The amount of duplication to take place. This is also used for stacking so that multiple duplicated movies will not replace each other.

Description:

This script creates a new instance of the target movie clip. Each duplicated movie clip has its own unique name. The parent movie clip must remain for the duplicated movies to remain.

Example:

This example duplicates a movie five times using five unique instances of the original:

```
i = 0;
while(i < 5) {
duplicateMovieClip(myClip, "myClip"+i, i);
i++;
}
```

onClipEvent

Availability: Flash Player 5

Generic Template:

```
onClipEvent(movieEvent){
statements;
}
```

Constraints:

> *movieEvent*—An event that triggers any actions in between the curly brackets.
>
> > load—The first time the instance of the movie appears on the timeline.
> >
> > unload—This takes place when a movie clip has been removed from the timeline.

enterFrame—Actions are executed at the frame rate of the movie continuously.

mouseMove—Any time the _x or _y coordinate of the mouse changes within the borders of the root movie, code is executed.

mouseDown—Occurs when the left mouse button is pressed.

mouseUp—Occurs when the left mouse button is released.

keyDown—Occurs when a key on the keyboard is pressed.

keyUp—Occurs when a key on the keyboard is released.

data—When data is received from a loadVariables script, this event activates when the last piece of data is loaded. When a loadMovie script is run, the code runs continuously as each piece of the movie is loaded.

statements—The code to be executed when the clipEvent is true.

Description:

An event handler that focuses on movie events that can happen once or several times.

Example:

This example continually traces a string while the movie is on the stage:

```
onClipEvent(enterFrame){
trace("entering");
}
```

removeMovieClip

Availability: Flash Player 4

Generic Template: removeMovieClip(*target*);

Constraint:

target—The target path to a movie created by duplicateMovieClip or attachMovie.

Description:

This script removes a movie clip instance of movies created with either duplicateMovieClip or attachMovie.

Example:

This example removes a movie recently created with duplicateMovieClip:

```
duplicateMovieClip(myMovie, "myMovie1", 1);
removeMovieClip(myMovie1);
```

setProperty

Availability: Flash Player 4

Generic Template: setProperty(*target*, *property*, *value*/*expression*);

Constraints:

> *target*—A string literal representing the direct path to the movie you want to set the properties for.
>
> *property*—The property you want to set.
>
> *value*—The value you want to set the property to.
>
> *expression*— Any viable expression.

Description:

Changes the property of a movie during playback.

Example:

This example sets the alpha of a movie clip to 70:

```
setProperty("myMovie", _alpha, "70");
```

startDrag

Availability: Flash Player 4

Generic Template: startDrag(*target*, *lockCenter*, *left*, *top*, *right*, *bottom*);

Constraints:

> *target*—The direct path to the movie clip you would like to drag.
>
> *lockCenter*—If this is set to true, the mouse will lock to the center of the movie clip.
>
> *left*, *top*, *right*, *bottom*—You can set these boundaries so that the movie clip cannot drag outside of them.

Description:

This script allows a single movie clip to be draggable until a stopDrag script is executed or another movie clip is set to be draggable.

Example:

This example starts dragging a movie clip when it's pressed and stops dragging the movie clip when it's released:

```
on(press){
startDrag(this,true);
}
on(release){
stopDrag();
}
```

stopDrag

Availability: Flash Player 4

Generic Template: `stopDrag();`

Constraints: None

Description:

When this code is executed, any movie clip that is set to be draggable will be stopped at its current position until it's set to be draggable again.

Example:

This example starts dragging a movie clip when it's pressed and stops dragging the movie clip when it's released.

```
on(press){
startDrag(this,true);
}
on(release){
stopDrag();
}
```

updateAfterEvent

Availability: Flash Player 5

Generic Template: `updateAfterEvent();`

Constraints: None

Description:

This script updates a movie and is not dependent on frame rate speed. The `updateAfterEvent` script must be placed within a clip event handler.

Example:

This example moves a movie clip each time the user clicks the mouse. If the `updateAfterEvent` method were not present, it would be possible for the user to click faster than the frame rate, but with the `updateAfterEvent` method, it will update instantly.

```
onClipEvent(mouseDown){
    this._x++;
    updateAfterEvent();
}
```

Variables

delete

Availability: Flash Player 5

Generic Template: delete *object*;

Constraint:

object—The variable or object you want to delete.

Description:

This script deletes an object, variable, or even a user-defined property of an object in its entirety.

You cannot, however, delete a predefined object or property of Flash.

Example:

This example creates and traces a variable and then deletes the variable and traces again:

```
var myVariable = "Flash";
trace(myVariable);
delete myVariable;
trace(myVariable);
//output: Flash
//        undefined
```

set variable

Availability: Flash Player 4

Generic Template: set(*variable*, *value*);

Constraints:

variable—The name of the variable you want to set.

value—The value of the variable you want to set.

Description:

This script assigns a value to a variable. A variable is a storage device that can hold a string, number, or Boolean as well as other data types.

29

ACTIONSCRIPT
REFERENCE

Example:

This example sets a variable to the horizontal position of the mouse:

```
set(xMouse, _xmouse);
```

var

Availability: Flash Player 5

Generic Template: `var name = value;`

Constraints:

> `name`—The name of the variable.
>
> `value`—The value that will be set to the variable.

Description:

This script declares and assigns a value to a variable. It is possible to declare multiple variables on one line by separating the value from the next variable's name by a comma.

Example:

The first example declares a single variable and sets it to a string literal; the second example sets multiple variables:

```
//this will create a variable that will hold a string
var myVariable = "Flash";
//this will create multiple variables on a single line
var x = 10, y = 20, z = 30;
```

with

Availability: Flash Player 5

Generic Template:

```
with(object){
statements;
}
```

Constraints:

> `object`—A movie clip or user-defined object
>
> `statements`—The code to be run with the object associated with it

Description:

This script executes code with the given object.

Example:

This example sets the horizontal and vertical position of a movie clip:

```
with(myMovie){
_x = 125;
_y = 225;
}
```

Conditions/Loops

break

Availability: Flash Player 4

Generic Template: `break;`

Description:

This script is used for stopping infinite loop statements. When the interpreter reaches a break, it skips the rest of the statement and moves on to the code following the closing brackets.

Example:

This script stops an otherwise unstoppable loop:

```
for(var i=0; true; i++){
    if(i >=20){
        break;
    }
}
```

case

Availability: Flash Player 4

Generic Template: `case expression: statements`

Constraints:

> `expression`—Any viable expression
>
> `statements`—Code to be executed if the expression matches that of the `switch` action

Description:

This script is a keyword that represents a condition to be used in the `switch` action. The statements in the `case` script will execute if the expression in `case` matches the expression in the `switch` action.

Example:

This example checks to see which `case` matches the `switch` statement, similar to a conditional statement, and displays the results in the output window:

```
switch (1) {
case 1:
trace("It's Case 1");
break;
case 2:
trace("It's Case 2");
break;
default:
trace("None of the cases")
}
//output:  It's Case 1
```

continue

Availability: Flash Player 4

Generic Template: `continue;`

Description:

This script is used in many different ways, depending on what type of loop statement it's being placed in.

> `while/do while`—A `continue` statement will skip the rest of the statements and move back to the condition.

> `for…continue`—Skips the rest of the statements and goes back to the evaluation.

> `for in…continue`—Causes the interpreter to skip the rest of the statements and go back to the top and process the next incremental variable.

Example:

This example uses a `do while` loop with a `trace` statement that will be skipped every time:

```
do {
i++;
continue;
trace("this is skipped");
}while(i <=10);
```

default

Availability: Flash Player 6

Generic Template: `default: statements;`

Constraint:

> *statements*—The script to be executed if all cases in a switch statement evaluate to false.

Description:

This code is the default code to be executed if all cases in a switch statement do not evaluate to true.

Example:

This example goes through all the cases and uses the default because none of the cases will evaluate to true:

```
switch("Flash"){
    case "Unleashed":
        trace("Unleashed");
        break;
    case "MX":
        trace("MX");
        break;
    default:
        trace("Default works");
}
//output: Default works
```

do while

Availability: Flash Player 4

Generic Template:

```
do{
    statements;
}while(condition);
```

Constraints:

> *statements*—Code to be executed while *condition* is true.
>
> *condition*—The condition that must be evaluated.

Description:

This code executes its statements and then evaluates the condition. If the condition is true, it starts over; otherwise, it moves on.

Example:

This example traces the variable i until the condition evaluates to false:

```
i = 0;
do{
    trace(i);
}while(i<10);
```

else

Availability: Flash Player 4

Generic Template:

```
else{
statements;
}
```

Constraint:

> *statements*—Code to be executed if previous `if` and `else if` statements do not evaluate to `true`.

Description:

The `else` statement executes code when the `if` and `else if` statements evaluate to `false`.

Example:

This example uses an `else` statement similar to the way a `switch` statement would use a default statement:

```
var name = "David";
userName = "Admin";
if(name == userName){
    trace("Welcome");
}else{
    trace("No Entrance");
}
```

else if

Availability: Flash Player 4

Generic Template:

```
else if(condition){
    statements;
}
```

Constraints:

> *condition*—The condition that must be evaluated
>
> *statements*—Code to be run if *condition* evaluates to true

Description:

Another conditional statement that can be stacked if an `if` statement evaluates to `false`.

Example:

This example looks at several possibilities and narrows them down with conditional statements, including the `else if` statement:

```
age = 22;
if(age == 20){
    trace("20");
}else if(age == 21){
    trace("21");
}else if(age == 22){
    trace("22");
}else {
    trace("Older than 22");
}
```

for

Availability: Flash Player 5

Generic Template:

```
for(variable; condition; change){
    statements;
}
```

Constraints:

> *variable*—A variable is created to use in the condition.
>
> *condition*—The condition that must be evaluated.
>
> *change*—The change in the variable that will allow the loop to have an end.

Description:

A loop statement that uses its user-defined variable to control the amount of times it loops. The *change* constraint is used to eventually stop the loop statement.

Example:

This example uses a `for` loop to count down from 10:

```
for(var i = 11; i > 0; i--){
    trace(i);
}
```

29

ACTIONSCRIPT REFERENCE

for in

Availability: Flash Player 5

Generic Template:

```
for(variable in object){
    statements;
}
```

Constraints:

>*variable*—This variable represents a property in an object or element in an array.
>
>*object*—The object associated with the variable.
>
>*statements*—The statements to be run in regard to the object.

Description:

A loop statement that cycles through its statements involving each property of an object or each element of an array.

Not all properties of an object will be used. The built-in objects, such as _alpha and _xscale, are not used.

Example:

This example traces every property in the object (note that it will trace the property's name, not the value):

```
var myObject = new Object();
myObject.name = "David";
myObject.age = 22;
myObject.location = "Richmond";
for(myProp in myObject){
    trace(myProp);
}
```

if

Availability: Flash Player 4

Generic Template:

```
if(condition){
    statements;
}
```

Constraints:

>*condition*—The condition that needs to be evaluated
>
>*statements*—The statements to be run when the condition evaluates to true

Description:

A conditional statement that, if it evaluates to `true`, will run the associated statements contained between the curly brackets. If the condition evaluates to `false`, all content between the curly brackets will be skipped.

Example:

This example checks whether a user's age is high enough to enter a site:

```
var requiredAge = 21;
var inputAge;
if(inputAge >= requiredAge){
    gotoAndPlay("welcome");
}else{
    trace("Come back in " + (requiredAge-inputAge)+" years");
}
```

switch

Availability: Flash Player 4

Generic Template:

```
switch(expression){
    standardCase:
        statements;
    defaultCase:
        statements;
}
```

Constraints:

> `expression`—The expression that will be compared to the cases.
>
> `standardCase`—This is a case that compares another expression to the `switch` expression.
>
> `statements`—In `standardCase` the scripts are run if that particular case's expression is the same as the expression of `switch`; in `defaultCase` the scripts are run if none of the `standardCases` evaluate to `true`.
>
> `defaultCase`—The last case scenario. All scripts associated with it are run if this case is reached.

Description:

This script is a conditional statement similar to the `if` statement. It identifies an expression and, if any cases evaluate to `true`, the statements are run. If none of the cases evaluate to `true`, `defaultCase` is often used to run scripts automatically.

Example:

This example looks for a certain name in some of the cases and runs a script if this name is found:

```
var name = "David";
switch(name){
    case "Kevin":
        trace("Name is Kevin");
        break;
    case "Tanner":
        trace("Name is Tanner");
        break;
    case "David":
        trace("Name is David");
        break;
    default:
        trace("We don't know name");
}
```

while

Availability: Flash Player 4

Generic Template:

```
while(condition){
    statements;
}
```

Constraints:

> *condition*—A condition that must be evaluated
>
> *statements*—The script to be run while the condition is true

Description:

This script is a loop statement that runs its statements as long as the condition continues to evaluate to true. Unlike the do while loop statement, the while loop statement evaluates the condition before executing any code.

Remember when using loop statements to make sure the loop can come to an end to avoid errors.

Example:

This example increases a movie clip's horizontal position until it has reached or gone past a designated point:

```
while(myMovie._x<=100){
    myMovie._x+=5;
}
```

Printing

`print`

Availability: Flash Player 4.20

Generic Template: `print(target, boundaryBox);`

Constraints:

> *target*—A path to the movie clip to print. Unless otherwise assigned, the `print` action will print all frames. To specify which frames to print, assign a frame label of #p to them.

> *boundaryBox*—A modifier used to crop frames that are to be printed. Special values are used for this, and they are as follows:

>> `bmovie`—This will set the printable area of all frames in a movie clip to the printable area of a specific frame labeled #b.

>> `bmax`—All the printable frames are pooled to form one printable area for each box. This is useful if each frame changes size.

>> `bframe`—This will designate each frame's printable area based on the individual frame. This is useful if you want each frame to fill in as much space on a page as possible.

Description:

This script prints frames out of a movie clip. It prints all frames unless individual frames are labeled with #p. Boundaries can be set by using some of the keywords listed under *boundaryBox*.

Although the quality is higher with this script, you cannot print transparencies or certain special color effects. For those, you must use `printAsBitmap`.

All images must be loaded before they can be printed.

Example:

This example prints out of a movie and sets it so that each frame's print area is dependent on its individual area, instead of other frames' areas:

```
print("myMovie", "bframe");
```

29

ACTIONSCRIPT
REFERENCE

`printAsBitmap`

Availability: Flash Player 4.20

Generic Template: `printAsBitmap(target, boundaryBox);`

Constraints:

target—A path to the movie clip to print. Unless otherwise assigned, the `print` action will print all frames. To specify which frames to print, assign a frame label of #p to them.

boundaryBox—A modifier used to crop frames that are to be printed. Special values are used for this, and they are as follows:

`bmovie`—This will set the printable area of all frames in a movie clip to the printable area of a specific frame labeled #b.

`bmax`—All the printable frames are pooled to form one printable area for each box. This is useful if each frame changes size.

`bframe`—This will designate each frame's printable area based on the individual frame. This is useful if you want each frame to fill in as much space on a page as possible.

Description:

This script prints frames out of movies as bitmaps to maintain transparency and special coloring. The image will be printed at the highest quality the printer can handle to ensure the highest allowable quality.

If there are no transparencies in your movie, try using the `print` action instead for higher quality. All images must be loaded before they can be printed.

Example:

This example prints a specific movie that has frames labeled with #p when a button is pressed:

```
on(press){
    printAsBitmap("myPrint", "bmax");
}
```

printAsBitmapNum

Availability: Flash Player 5

Generic Template: `printAsBitmapNum(level, boundaryBox);`

Constraints:

level—The level of the Flash movie you would like to print.

boundaryBox—A modifier used to crop frames that are to be printed. Special values are for this, and they are as follows:

`bmovie`—This will set the printable area of all frames in a movie clip to the printable area of a specific frame labeled #b.

bmax—All the printable frames are pooled to form one printable area for each box. This is useful if each frame changes size.

bframe—This will designate each frame's printable area based on the individual frame. This is useful if you want each frame to fill in as much space on a page as possible.

Description:

This script prints frames out of levels as bitmaps to maintain transparency and special coloring. The image will be printed at the highest quality the printer can handle to ensure the highest allowable quality.

If there are no transparencies in your level, try using the printNum action instead for higher quality. All images must be loaded before they can be printed.

Example:

This example prints a frame labeled with #p when a button is pressed:

```
on(press){
    printAsBitmapNum(1,"bmovie");
}
```

printNum

Availability: Flash Player 5

Generic Template: printNum(*level, boundaryBox*);

Constraints:

level—The level of the Flash movie you would like to print.

boundaryBox—A modifier used to crop frames that are to be printed. Special values are used for this, and they are as follows:

bmovie—This will set the printable area of all frames in a movie clip to the printable area of a specific frame labeled #b.

bmax—All the printable frames are pooled to form one printable area for each box. This is useful if each frame changes size.

bframe—This will designate each frame's printable area based on the individual frame. This is useful if you want each frame to fill in as much space on a page as possible.

29

ACTIONSCRIPT
REFERENCE

Description:

This script prints frames out of a level in the player. It prints all frames unless individual frames are labeled with #p. Boundaries can be set by using some of the keywords listed under *boundaryBox*.

Although the quality is higher with this script, you cannot print transparencies or certain special color effects. For those you must use `printAsBitmapNum`. All images must be loaded before they can be printed.

Example:

This example print frames containing the label #p in a specified label when the playhead reaches the action:

```
printNum(2,"bmax");
```

User-Defined Functions

call

This script will be skipped because it is depreciated. It's only mentioned here because it is the first depreciated script listed in the Actions panel. Depreciated scripts are those scripts that can still be used, but their use is not recommended because they might be dropped completely in the next release of Flash.

See Instead: `function`

function

Availability: Flash Player 5

Generic Template:

```
function functionName(variables){
    statements;
}
```

Constraints:

>   *functionName*—Name of the function
>
>   *variables*—The variables to use in the function that can be set when the function is called
>
>   *statements*—The script to be run when the function is called

Description:

This script declares and sets functions that can be used to do almost any task inside the Flash player. You set variables to use in the function, and they can be set to anything when the function is called.

You can do two things with this script: First, you can create a function and use it later by calling it (you can even call it from anywhere in the Flash movie thanks to the new `global` function). Second, you can use it as an expression to create methods for objects.

Example:

This example declares a simple function:

```
function difference(x, y){
    trace(x-y);
}
difference(5,2);
```

This example adds a method to an object:

```
numbers.protoype.difference = function(){
    trace(this.x - this.y);
}
```

return

Availability: Flash Player 5

Generic Template: `return expression;`

Constraint:

> `expression`—Any data type or expression that can be evaluated

Description:

This script is used in a function to evaluate some of its statements. Once the `return` action is run, it stops and replaces the function with the value of the expression it ran.

Example:

This example uses a simple function and sets a variable to its return value; then the variable is traced:

```
function difference(x,y){
    return x-y;
}
myDif = difference(10,5);
trace(myDif);
```

Miscellaneous Actions

#endinitclip

Availability: Flash Player 6

Generic Template: `#endinitclip`

Description:

This script signifies the end of a block of components used in conjunction with `#init-clip`.

Example:

This example is just a generic statement showing how #initclip and #endinitclip are used in conjunction with components:

```
#initclip
    //all components that are to be initialized
#endinitclip
```

#include

Availability: N/A

Generic Template: #include "*file.as*";

Constraint:

> *file.as*—The exact path to the file that contains the code to add to the Actions panel. Note that .as is not the necessary extension, but it is recommended for consistency.

Description:

This script includes actions held outside the Flash movie and includes them upon testing, publishing, or exporting.

> **Note**
>
> If you adjust the code in the outside file after the Flash movie has been published, you will need to republish to gain access to the new version of the outside file.

Example:

This script loads actions from an outside file and uses them when it is published:

```
#include "myActions.as";
```

#initclip

Availability: Flash Player MX

Generic Template: #initclip *order*

Constraint:

> *order*—A number representing the order in which to execute the blocks. This is not a necessity.

Description:

This script starts the block of code to be initialized. If multiple clips are initialized at the same time, the *order* constraint can tell the interpreter which ones to do first. Component initialization takes place once the movie clip is defined.

When using this code, remember that all code initialized in the block is initialized only once.

Example:

This example is just a generic statement showing how #initclip and #endinitclip are used in conjunction with components:

```
#initclip
//all components that are to be initialized
#endinitclip
```

clearInterval

Availability: Flash Player MX

Generic Template: clearInterval(*interval*);

Constraint:

> *interval*—An object that has been returned using a call and is sent to a setInterval action

Description:

This script clears a call and sends it to the setInterval action.

Example:

This example sets an interval call and then clears it:

```
function myFunction() {
    trace("initialized interval");
}
var myInterval = setInterval(myFunction, 2000);
clearInterval( myInterval);
```

//comment

Availability: Flash Player 1

Generic Template: // *comments*

Constraint:

> *comments*—Any information you want to keep as a note

Description:

This script is solely for placing comments in the code itself. The interpreter will skip over these when it hits `//`, which initializes the comment.

Example:

Here are some examples of comments:

```
//name our variable
var myVar = "Flash";
//trace our variable
trace(myVar);
//and that's the end
```

/* comment delimiter */

Availability: Flash Player 5

Generic Template: `/* comments */`

Constraint:

> *comments*—Any information you want to keep as a note

Description:

This script is used to define the beginning of comments that will take up more than one line. Everything between `/*` and `*/` will be set as comments and will be skipped by the interpreter. If you do not use a closing comment delimiter, the player will return an error.

Example:

This example has several lines of code all contained between comment delimiters:

```
/*in this move, we will declare a variable, then change it,
and after that we will trace the new version
*/
var name = "Buster";
name = "David";
trace(name);
```

setInterval

Availability: Flash Player MX

Generic Template:

```
setInterval(function, interval, parameters);
setInterval(object, method, interval, parameters);
```

Constraints:

> *function*—The name of a function or a reference to an anonymous function.
>
> *interval*—The time in milliseconds between the function calling or method initialization.
>
> *parameters*—These are arguments that can be optionally passed to the function or method.
>
> *object*—Any object.
>
> *method*—A method to call in regard to the object.

Returns:

An interval that can be sent to `clearInterval` to cancel the specified `interval` itself.

Description:

This script calls a function, method, or object at periodic intervals. It can be used to update information from a remote file while the movie is playing.

The interval is a numeric value that represents how many milliseconds must occur until the script is run again.

Note

Use the `updateAfterEvent` action to make sure the screen refreshes fast enough if the interval is much faster than the frame rate.

29

ACTIONSCRIPT
REFERENCE

Example:

This example calls a simple function and passes the parameters in the interval statement; the script will be run about every second (1000 milliseconds):

```
function displayName(name){
    trace(name);
}
setInterval(displayName, 1000, "David");
```

This example calls a function that has no parameters every half a second:

```
function displayName(){
    trace("David");
}
setInterval(displayName, 500);
```

trace

Availability: Flash Player 4

Generic Template: trace(*expression*);

Constraint:

> *expression*—Any viable expression. It will be displayed in the output window when the movie is tested.

Description:

This script evaluates the expression and displays the result in the output window when the movie is tested. This script will not display anything except in the output window. You can use the Omit Trace option to remove the trace actions when exporting for file size.

Example:

This example traces a simple string:

```
trace("This was traced");
```

Operators

String Delimiter (" ")

Availability: Flash Player 4

Generic Template: "*string*"

Constraint:

> *string*—Any character or group of characters

Description:

These quotation marks are used to surround a group of characters, declaring it as a string.

Example:

This example sets a variable equal to a string:

```
var title = "Flash Unleashed";
trace(title);
```

Parentheses [()]

Availability: Flash Player 4

Generic Template: *(expression)*

Constraint:

> *expression*—Any viable expression

Description:

This operator groups expressions together.

Example:

This example shows different uses for grouping items together using parentheses:

```
x = 3;
y = 4;
z = (x+y);
function myFunction(myVar){
    trace(myVar);
}
```

Arithmetic Operators
Minus (-)

Availability: Flash Player 4

Generic Template: -

Constraints: None

Description:

This operator can be used in two ways: First, to turn an integer into a negative integer. Second, to subtract an integer from another.

Example:

Here are some examples of using the minus operator:

```
x = 2;
y = -3;
z = x - y;
```

Modulo (%)

Availability: Flash Player 4

Generic Template: *expression* % *expression*

Constraint:

> *expression*—Any viable number or an expression that can be converted to a number

Description:

This operator calculates the remainder of the first expression divided by the second expression.

Example:

This example uses the modulo to determine the remainder of apples when the bundle is split up:

```
bundle = 26;
people = 5;
remainder = bundle % people;
trace(remainder);
```

Multiplication (*)

Availability: Flash Player 4

Generic Template: *number* * *number*

Description:

This operator multiplies two numbers or expressions that evaluate to numbers.

Example:

Here is a simple example of using the multiplication operator:

```
var area = 10 * 10;
```

Division (/)

Availability: Flash Player 4

Generic Template: *number / number*

Description:

This operator divides two numbers or expressions that evaluate to numbers.

Example:

The following example uses the division operator to divide two variables:

```
var total = 100;
var attempts = 10;
var avg = total / attempts;
trace(avg);
```

Addition (+)

Availability: Flash Player 4

Generic Template: *expression + expression*

Constraint:

> *expression*—Any string or number

Description:

This operator adds two numbers together. It also combines two strings to form one string. If one of the expressions is a string, then all expressions are converted to strings and combined.

Example:

This example adds two numbers together:

```
var myVar = 1+2;
```

This next example combines two strings:

```
var fName = "Alex";
var lName = "Behr";
var fullName = fName +" "+ lName;
trace(fullName);
```

Finally, this example combines a string with a number to form a string:

```
var player = "Flash ";
var version = 6;
var fullVersion = player + version;
trace(fullVersion);
```

29

ACTIONSCRIPT
REFERENCE

Assignment

Subtraction Assignment (-=)

Availability: Flash Player 4

Generic Template: *expression -= expression*

Constraint:

> *expression*—Any viable number or an expression that can be converted to a number

Description:

This operator subtracts the second expression from the first and then sets the new value to the first expression. It is the same as setting the first expression equal to the value of the first expression minus the second.

Example:

This example sets a variable equal to itself minus another variable:

```
var x = 5;
var y = 10;
y-=x;
trace(y);
```

Modulo Assignment (%=)

Availability: Flash Player 4

Generic Template: *expression %= expression*

Constraint:

> *expression*—Any viable number or an expression that can be converted to a number

Description:

This operator performs a modulo operation with both expressions and then sets the new value to the first expression.

Example:

This example performs a modulo operation on two expressions and sets the value of the first expression to the new value:

```
var x = 20;
var y = 3;
```

```
x %= y;
trace(x);
```

Bitwise AND Assignment (&=)

Availability: Flash Player 5

Generic Template: *expression* &= *expression*

Constraint:

> *expression*—Any viable number or an expression that can be converted to a number

Description:

This operator performs a bitwise AND operation on expressions and assign the new value to the first expression.

Example:

Here is an example using the bitwise AND assignment operator:

```
var x = 6;
var y = 10;
x &= y;
trace(x);
//output: 2
```

Multiplication Assignment (*=)

Availability: Flash Player 4

Generic Template: *expression* *= *expression*

Constraint:

> *expression*—Any viable number or an expression that can be converted to a number

Description:

This operator multiplies two expressions and sets the value equal to the first expression.

Example:

This example multiplies two variables and sets the value equal to the first:

```
var x = 4;
var y = 3;
x *= y;
trace(x);
```

29

ACTIONSCRIPT
REFERENCE

Bitwise OR Assignment (|=)

Availability: Flash Player 5

Generic Template: *expression |= expression*

Constraint:

> *expression*—Any viable number or a variable holding a number

Description:

This operator performs a bitwise OR operation on expressions and sets the value of the first expression to the new value.

Example:

This example uses the bitwise OR assignment and sets the first variable equal to the result:

```
var x = 10;
var y = 12;
x |= y;
trace(x);
//output: 14
```

Division Assignment (/=)

Availability: Flash Player 4

Generic Template: *expression /= expression*

Constraint:

> *expression*—Any viable number or an expression that can be converted to a number

Description:

This operator divides the first expression by the second and then assigns the value to the first expression.

Example:

This example illustrates the use of the division assignment operator:

```
var x = 10;
var y = 5;
x /= y;
trace(x);
```

Bitwise XOR Assignment (^=)

Availability: Flash Player 5

Generic Template: *expression ^= expression*

Constraint:

>*expression*—Any viable number or a variable holding a number

Description:

This operator performs a bitwise XOR operation on expressions and assigns the value to the first expression.

Example:

This example illustrates the use of the bitwise XOR operator:

```
var x = 10;
var y = 6;
x ^= y;
trace(x);
//output: 12
```

Addition Assignment (+=)

Availability: Flash Player 4

Generic Template: *expression += expression*

Constraint:

>*expression*—Any number, string, or variable holding either a number or string

Description:

This operator adds numbers together and assigns the value to the first expression. It can also combine strings and assign the new string to the first expression.

Example:

This example uses the addition assignment to combine numbers:

```
var x = 10;
var y = 5;
x += y;
trace(x);
```

This example combines strings:

```
var name = "David";
var lName = "Vogeleer";
```

29

ACTIONSCRIPT
REFERENCE

```
name += lName;
trace(name);
```

Bitwise Left Shift and Assignment (<<=)

Availability: Flash Player 5

Generic Template: *expressionA <<= expressionB*

Constraints:

> *expressionA*—Any number or expression that can evaluate to a number
>
> *expression*—Any number or expression that can evaluate to an integer between 0 and 31

Description:

This operator performs a bitwise left shift on expressions and assigns the value to the first expression.

Example:

This example illustrates the use of the bitwise left shift and assignment operator:

```
var x = 10;
var y = 5;
x <<= y;
trace(x);
//output: 320
```

Assignment (=)

Availability: Flash Player 4

Generic Template: *expressionA = expressionB*

Constraints:

> *expressionA*—Any variable, property, or element of an array
>
> *expressionB*—A value being assigned to *expressionA*

Description:

This operator assigns a value (*expressionB*) to a named variable, property, or element (*expressionA*).

Example:

This example assigns a value to a variable and traces the variable to make sure it is there:

```
var title = "Flash Unleashed";
trace(title);
```

Bitwise Right Shift and Assignment (>>=)

Availability: >=) operator>>=)>>=)>Flash Player 5

Generic Template: *expressionA >>= expressionB*

Constraints:

> *expressionA*—Any number or expression that can evaluate to a number
>
> *expression*—Any number or expression that can evaluate to an integer between 0 and 31

Description:

This operator performs the bitwise right shift operation on expressions and then assigns the value to the first expression.

Example:

This example illustrates the use of the bitwise right shift and assignment operator:

```
var x = 10;
var y = 5;
x >>= y;
trace(x);
//output: 0
```

Bitwise Unsigned Right Shift and Assignment (>>>=)

Availability: >>=) (>>=) operator>>>=) (>>=)>>>=) (>>=)>Flash Player 5

Generic Template: *expressionA >>>= expressionB*

Constraints:

> *expressionA*—Any number or expression that can evaluate to a number
>
> *expression*—Any number or expression that can evaluate to an integer between 0 and 31

Description:

This operator performs the bitwise unsigned right shift operation on expressions and then assigns the value to the first expression.

Example:

This example illustrates the use of the bitwise unsigned right shift operator:

29

ACTIONSCRIPT
REFERENCE

```
var x = 10;
var y = 5;
x >>>= y;
trace(x);
//output: 0
```

Bitwise Operators

Bitwise AND (&)

Availability: Flash Player 5

Generic Template: *expression* & *expression*

Description:

This operator converts expressions to 32-bit unsigned integers and then runs a Boolean AND operation on each bit of the integer parameters, which returns a new 32-bit number.

Example:

This example shows the use of the bitwise AND operator:

```
var x = 5;
var y = 1;
var z = y & x;
trace (z);
//output: 1
```

Bitwise NOT (~)

Availability: Flash Player 5

Generic Template: ~ *expression*

Constraint:

> *expression*—Any viable number

Description:

This operator changes the positive/negative value of a number and then subtracts it by 1.

Example:

This example shows the use of the bitwise NOT operator:

```
var x = 10;
trace(~x);
//output: -11
```

Bitwise OR (|)

Availability: Flash Player 5

Generic Template: *expression | expression*

Constraint:

> *expression*—Any viable number

Description:

This operator converts expressions to 32-bit unsigned integers and sends back the number 1 in each bit position, where the corresponding bits of either expression are equal to 1.

Example:

This example shows the use of the bitwise OR operator:

```
var x = 10;
var y = 5;
var z = x | y;
trace(z);
//output: 15
```

Bitwise XOR (^)

Availability: Flash Player 5

Generic Template: *expression ^ expression*

Constraint:

> *expression*—Any viable number

Description:

This operator converts expressions to 32-bit unsigned integers and sends back the number 1 in each bit position, where the corresponding bits of either expression, but not both, are 1.

Example:

This example shows the use of the bitwise XOR operator:

```
var x = 10;
var y = 5;
var z = x ^ y;
trace(z);
//output: 15
```

29

ACTIONSCRIPT
REFERENCE

Bitwise Left Shift (<<)

Availability: Flash Player 5

Generic Template: *expressionA* << *expressionB*

Constraints:

> *expressionA*—Any number or expression that can evaluate to a number
>
> *expression*—Any number or expression that can evaluate to an integer between 0 and 31

Description:

This operator converts the expressions to 32-bit integers and shifts each bit in *expressionA* to the left by the number of places specified by the integer resulting from the conversion of *expressionB*. The empty bits are filled in with zeros. A shift to the left of an integer is equivalent to multiplying that integer by 2. In effect, here is what happens:

```
var i = 0;
while(i < expressionB){
    expressionA*=2;
i++;
}
trace(expressionA);
```

Example:

This example shows the use of the bitwise left shift operator:

```
var x = 10;
var y = 5;
var z = x << y;
trace(z);
//output: 320
```

Bitwise Right Shift (>>)

Availability: Flash Player 5

Generic Template: *expressionA* >> *expressionB*

Constraints:

> *expressionA*—Any number or expression that can evaluate to a number
>
> *expression*—Any number or expression that can evaluate to an integer between 0 and 31

Description:

This operator converts the expressions to 32-bit integers and then shifts the bits in *expressionA* to the right by the number of places specified by the integer resulting from the conversion of *expressionB*. All bits that are shifted to the right are useless. Extra bits that remain on the left are replaced with zeros. The result of this operator is *expressionA* being divided by 2 the number of times indicated in *expressionB*, and the remainder is left off. If expressionB is equal to 4, then expressionA would be divided by the number 2 four times.

Basically, it is equal to this:

```
var i = 0;
while(i<expressionB){
    expressionA = Math.floor(expressionA / 2);
    i++;
}
trace(expressionA);
```

Example:

This example shows the use of the bitwise right shift operator:

```
var x = 10;
var y = 2;
var z = x >> y;
trace(z);
//output: 2
```

Bitwise Unsigned Right Shift (>>>)

Availability: Flash Player 5

Generic Template: *expressionA >>> expressionB*

Constraints:

> *expressionA*—Any number or expression that can evaluate to a number
>
> *expression*—Any number or expression that can evaluate to an integer between 0 and 31

Description:

This operator acts the same as the bitwise right shift operator. The only difference in the two is that the bitwise unsigned right shift operator will not keep the sign of the original expression due to the fact that the left-side bits are continuously filled with zeros.

Example:

Here's an example of using the bitwise unsigned right shift operator:

```
var x = 10;
var y = 2;
var z = x >>> y;
trace(z);
//output: 2
```

Comparison Operators

Inequality (!=)

Availability: Flash Player 5

Generic Template: *value != value*

Description:

This operator evaluates two values, and if they are not equivalent, the expression evaluates to `true`. If the two values are equivalent, the expression evaluates to `false`.

Example:

Here are some examples using the inequality operator:

```
trace(10 != 5);
//output: true

trace(5 != 5);
//output: false

trace("David" != "david");
//output: true

trace("Alex" != "Alex");
//output: false
```

Strict Inequality (!==)

Availability: Flash Player MX

Generic Template: *value !== value*

Description:

This operator performs the same evaluation as the inequality operator, except that values of different data types are not converted and will automatically not be equivalent to each other. If the two values are not equivalent, the expression evaluates to `true`. If the two values are equivalent, the expression evaluates to `false`.

Example:

This example not only shows the use of the strict inequality operator but also compares its use to the inequality operator:

```
trace(5 !== 10);
//output: true

trace(5 !== 5);
//output: false

trace(5 != "5");
//output: false

trace(5 !== "5");
//output: true
```

Less Than (<)

Availability: Flash Player 4

Generic Template: *value < value*

Constraint:

> *value*—Any viable number or string

Description:

This operator compares two values, and if the first value is less than the second, the expression evaluates to `true`. If the first value is greater than or equal to the second value, the expression evaluates to `false`.

Example:

Here are a few example of using the less than operator:

```
trace(3<4);
//output: true

trace(4<3);
//output: false

trace(3<3);
//output: false

trace("a" < "b");
//output: true
```

Less Than Equal To (<=)

Availability: Flash Player 4

Generic Template: *value <= value*

Constraint:

    value—Any viable number or string

Description:

This operator compares two values, and if the first value is less than or equal to the second, the expression evaluates to `true`. If the first value is greater than the second value, the expression evaluates to `false`.

Example:

Here are a few examples using the less than equal to operator:

```
trace(3<=4);
//output: true

trace(4<=3);
//output: false

trace(3<=3);
//output: true

trace("a" <= "b");
//output: true
```

Equality (==)

Availability: Flash Player 5

Generic Template: *value* == *value*

Constraint:

    value—Any viable number, string, boolean, variable, object, array, or function

Description:

This operator compares two values. If the values are equal to one another, the expression evaluates to `true`. If the two values are not equal to each other, then the expression evaluates to `false`.

More than one data type can be evaluated, and they each evaluate differently. Let's take a look at them:

    Number and boolean. These two data types are compared by raw value.

    String. This data type is evaluated by the number of characters. If the characters match identically, remember that when you're comparing strings, the comparison *is case sensitive*.

    Variable, object, and function. Variables are considered equal or they refer to the identical object, function, or array.

Array. Arrays cannot be compared directly. This will always return a false evaluation. However, the elements in an array can be compared the same way variables are compared.

Example:

Here are a few examples using the equality operator:

```
trace(5==5);
//output: true

trace("David" == "david");
//output: false

var myArray = new Array();
var anotherArray = new Array();
trace(myArray == anotherArray);
//output: false

var myArray = new Array("David");
var anotherArray = new Array("David");
trace(myArray[0] == anotherArray[0]);
//output: true
```

Strict Equality (===)

Availability: Flash Player MX

Generic Template: *value* === *value*

Constraint:

> *value*—Any viable number, string, boolean, variable, object, array, or function

Description:

This operator compares two values just like the equality operator. However, unlike the equality operator, values are not converted for comparison. If the two values are of different data types, the expression automatically evaluates to `false`. That aside, if the values are equal to one another, the expression evaluates to `true`. If the two values are not equal to each other, the expression evaluates to `false`.

More than one data type can be evaluated, and they each evaluate differently. Let's take a look at them:

> **Number and Boolean**. These two data types are compared by raw value.
>
> **String**. This data type is evaluated by the number of characters. If the characters match identically, remember when you're comparing strings, the comparison *is case sensitive.*

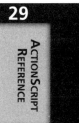

29

ACTIONSCRIPT
REFERENCE

Variable, object, and function. Variables are considered equal or they refer to the identical object, function, or array.

Array. Arrays cannot be compared directly. This will always return a false evaluation. However, the elements in an array can be compared the same way variables are compared.

Example:

Here are a few examples using the strict equality operator and a comparison to the equality operator:

```
trace(5 === 5);
//output: true

trace("Alex" === "Alex");
//output: true

trace(10 == "10");
//output: true

trace(10 === "10");
//output: false
```

Greater Than (>)

Availability: Flash Player 5

Generic Template: *value* > *value*

Constraint:

> *value*—Any viable number or string

Description:

This operator compares two values. If the first value is greater than the second, the expression evaluates to `true`. If the first value is less than or equivalent to the second value, the expression evaluates to `false`.

Example:

Here are a few examples using the greater than operator:

```
trace(4>3);
//output: true

trace(3>4);
//output: false

trace(3>3);
//output: false
```

```
trace("a" > "b");
//output: false
```

Greater Than Equal To (>=)

Availability: Flash Player 4

Generic Template: *value >= value*

Constraint:

> *value*—Any viable number or string

Description:

This operator compares the two values. If the first value is greater than or equal to the second, the expression evaluates to `true`. If the first value is less than the second value, the expression evaluates to `false`.

Example:

Here are a few examples using the greater than equal to operator:

```
trace(4>=3);
//output: true

trace(3>=4);
//output: false

trace(3>=3);
//output: true

trace("a" >= "a");
//output: true
```

Logical Operators

Logical NOT (!)

Availability: Flash Player 4

Generic Template: *!expression*

Description:

This operator inverts the boolean value of the expression. If the boolean value equals `true`, this operator converts it to `false`, and if the boolean value is `false`, the operator converts it to `true`.

Example:

The logical NOT operator is used in this example in an `if` statement:

29

ACTIONSCRIPT
REFERENCE

```
var myVar = false;
if(!myVar){
    trace("It converted the false to true");
}
```

Short-circuit AND (&&)

Availability: Flash Player 4

Generic Template: *expression && expression*

Description:

This operator connects two conditionals for evaluation. If the first condition evaluates to true, the second condition is evaluated. However, if the first condition evaluates to false, the second condition is never evaluated.

Example:

Here is an example using the short-circuit AND operator to link two conditionals in a looping statement:

```
var i = 0;
var j = 1;
while(i <10 && j <10){
    trace("i= " + i);
    trace("j= " + j);
    i++;
    j++;
}
```

Logical OR (||)

Availability: Flash Player 4

Generic Template: *condition || condition*

Description:

This operator connects two conditionals for evaluation. If the first condition evaluates to true, the second condition is skipped. However, if the first condition evaluates to false, the second condition is evaluated.

Example:

Here is an example of using the logical OR operator in a looping statement:

```
var i = 0;
var j = 1;
while(i <10 || j <10){
trace("i= " + i);
```

```
trace("j= " + j);
i++;
j++;
}
```

Miscellaneous Operators

Decrement (--)

Availability: Flash Player 4

Generic Template:

--number

number--

Constraint:

>   *number*—Any viable number, property of a movie clip, or variable holding a number

Description:

This operator has two uses. The first is the pre-number decrement (*--number*), which subtracts one from the number and returns that value. The second use it the post-number decrement (*number--*), which subtracts one from the number and returns the initial value.

The decrement operator is often used in loop statements to end them.

Example:

These examples show some uses of the decrement operator:

```
var x = 5;
var y = --x;
trace(y);
//output: 4

var x = 5;
var y = x--;
trace(y);
//output: 5

var i = 5;
while(i > 0){
    trace(i);
    i--;
}
```

Conditional (?:)

Availability: Flash Player 4

Generic Template: `condition? expressionA: expressionB`

Constraints:

> `condition`—A condition to be evaluated
>
> `expressionA`—The value returned if the condition is `true`
>
> `expressionB`—The value returned if the condition is `false`

Description:

This operator evaluates the condition; if it evaluates to `true`, `expressionA` is returned. If the condition evaluates to `false`, `expressionB` is returned.

Example:

This example uses the conditional operator:

```
var x = 10;
(x>5)? trace("X is greater"): trace("X is less than");
```

Increment (++)

Availability: Flash Player 4

Generic Template:

`++number`

`number++`

Constraint:

> `number`—Any viable number, property of a movie clip, or variable holding a number

Description:

This operator has two uses: The first is the pre-number increment (`++number`), which adds one to the number and returns that value. The second use is the post-number increment (`number++`), which adds one to the number and returns the initial value.

The increment operator is often used in loop statements to end them.

Example:

Here is an example of the increment operator:

```
var i = 0;
while(i <=10){
    trace("i = "+i);
    i++;
}
```

instanceof

Availability: Flash Player 6

Generic Template: *object* instanceof *class*

Constraints:

> *object*—Any viable ActionScript object
>
> *class*—Refers to an ActionScript constructor function

Returns:

If object is an instanceof class, the operator returns a value of true; otherwise, it returns a value of false.

Description:

This operator determines whether the object is part of the class. If it is, the value returned is true; otherwise, the value returned is false.

Example:

Here is an example using the instanceof operator:

```
trace(new Array (myArray) instanceof Array);
//output: true
```

typeof

Availability: Flash Player 5

Generic Template: typeof *value*

Constraint:

> *value*—Any viable type of string, movie clip, button, object, variable, or function

Description:

This operator, when placed before a value, evaluates the type of value.

Example:

This example uses the typeof operator to evaluate a variable to indicate what type it is:

```
var name = "David";
trace(typeof name);
//output: string
```

void

Availability: Flash Player 5

Generic Template: void (*expression*);

Description:

This operator evaluates an expression, disregards it, and returns a value of undefined.

Example:

This example shows the use of the void operator by using it on a simple expression of two variables:

```
var x = 10;
var y = 5;
var z = void(x+y);
trace(z);
//output: undefined
```

Functions

Conversion Functions

Availability:

Generic Template: *typeOfConversion* (*value*);

Constraints:

> *typeOfConversion*—The different types of conversions, including array, Boolean, number, object, and string.
>
> *value*—Any viable expression

Description:

Each type of conversion function converts the value to its data type.

Example:

Here are some basic examples of data-conversion functions:

```
var x = 5;
trace(typeof x);
//output: number
```

```
trace(typeof Array(x));
//output: object

trace(typeof Boolean(x));
//output: boolean

trace(typeof String(x));
//output: string
```

escape

Availability: Flash Player 5

Generic Template: `escape(expression)`

Constraint:

> *expression*—Will be converted to a string and encoded into a URL-encoded format

Description:

This function converts the expression to a string and then encodes it in a URL-encoded format.

Example:

Here is an example of the `escape` function:

```
var name = "David123";
trace(escape(name));
//output: David%20123
```

eval

Availability: Flash Player 4

Generic Template: `eval(expression);`

Constraint:

> *expression*—A string representing the name of a variable, property, object, or movie clip

Description:

This function is used to access an expression and return a value if the expression is a property or variable. Alternatively, it will return a reference if the expression is an object or movie clip. If the expression cannot be found, this function gives the value of undefined.

Example:

Here is an example of the `eval` function looking for a variable:

```
var myName = "David";
trace(eval("myName"));
//output: David
```

getProperty

Availability: Flash Player 4

Generic Template: `getProperty(name, property);`

Constraints:

> *name*—The name of the instance of a movie clip you're trying to access a property of
>
> *property*—The name of the property you're trying to access

Description:

This function retrieves the specific property of the specific instance being referred to.

Example:

This example attempts to retrieve the horizontal position of a movie clip:

```
trace(getProperty(myMovie, _x));
```

getTimer

Availability: Flash Player 4

Generic Template: `getTimer();`

Description:

This function gets the amount of milliseconds that have past since the movie began playing.

Example:

Here is an example of using the `getTimer` function:

```
onClipEvent(enterFrame){
    if(getTimer() >= 5000){
        trace("5 seconds has passed");
    }
}
```

getVersion

Availability: Flash Player 5

Generic Template: `getVersion();`

Description:

This function retrieves the Flash player version on the user's local computer at runtime.

> **Note**
>
> This will only work on Flash 5 players and above.

Example:

Here is a simple way to use the `getVersion` function:

```
trace(getVersion());
```

Mathematical Functions

isFinite

Availability: Flash Player 5

Generic Template: `isFinite(expression);`

Constraint:

    expression—A boolean, variable, or another expression that can be evaluated

Description:

This function evaluates an expression to see whether it is finite instead of infinity or negative infinity. If the expression is finite, it will evaluate to `true`; otherwise, it will evaluate to `false`.

Example:

Here is an example using the `isFinite` function:

```
var x = 10;
trace(isFinite(x));
//output: true
```

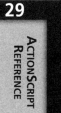

29

ACTIONSCRIPT
REFERENCE

isNaN

Availability: Flash Player 5

Generic Template: isNaN(*expression*);

Constraints: None

Description:

This function evaluates an expression, checking whether it is not a real number. If the expression is a real number, the function will evaluate it to `false`. Otherwise, it will evaluate to `true`.

Example:

Here are a couple of examples using the `isNaN` function:

```
trace(isNaN("David"));
//output: true

trace(isNaN(5));
//output: false
```

parseFloat

Availability: Flash Player 5

Generic Template: parseFloat(*string*);

Constraint:

> *string*—The string to convert into a floating-point integer

Description:

This function converts a string into a floating-point number if and only if the string starts with an integer. If the string does not start with an integer, the function will return NaN. When the parse reaches a nonnumeric value in the string, it stops converting.

Example:

Here are some examples of using the `parseFloat` function:

```
trace(parseFloat("5.5"));
//output: 5.5

trace(parseFloat("T1"));
//output: NaN

trace(parseFloat("1T"));
//output: 1
```

parseInt

Availability: Flash Player 5

Generic Template: parseInt(*string*, *radix*);

Constraints:

> *string*—The string to convert into a floating-point integer
>
> *radix*—A number representing the radix of the number to parse, which can be between 2 and 26, but it's not necessary

Description:

This function converts a string to a number. If the string cannot convert to a number, the function returns NaN.

Example:

Here are some examples of the parseInt function:

```
trace(parseInt("5"));
//output: 5

trace(parseInt("David"));
//output: NaN

trace(parseInt(0x123));
//output: 291
```

targetPath

Availability: Flash Player 5

Generic Template: targetPath(*movie*);

Constraint:

> *movie*—This is a reference to a movie clip.

Description:

This function returns the target path to a movie in dot syntax.

Example:

Here is an example of using the targetPath function to return a target path to a movie:

```
trace(targetPath(myMovie));
```

unescape

Availability: Flash Player 5

Generic Template: unescape(*hex*);

Constraint:

       hex—A string representing a hexadecimal sequence to escape

Description:

This function evaluates hex, decodes it from the URL-encoded format, and then returns a string.

Example:

Here is an example using the unescape function:

```
trace(unescape("David %7b%5bVogeleer%5D%7D"));
//output: David {[Vogeleer]}
```

Constants

false

Availability: Flash Player 5

Generic Template: false

Constraints: None

Description:

A boolean value representing the opposite of true.

Example:

This example sets the visibility of a movie clip to false, thus making it invisible:

```
myMovie._visible = false;
```

newline

Availability: Flash Player 4

Generic Template: newline

Constraints: None

Description:

This constant inserts a blank line into the code of the ActionScript panel.

null

Availability: Flash Player 5

Generic Template: null

Constraints: None

Description:

This constant is a keyword for representing the lack of data in variables.

Example:

This example sets a variable equal to null:

```
var myVariable = null;
```

true

Availability: Flash Player 5

Generic Template: true

Constraints: None

Description:

A boolean value representing the opposite of false.

Example:

This example sets the multiline property of a text field to true:

```
//First create the text field
_root.createTextField("myText",0,0,0,100,100);
myText.multiline = true;
```

undefined

Availability: Flash Player 5

Generic Template: undefined

Constraints: None

Description:

This constant is usually returned when you're looking for a variable that isn't identified yet.

Null and undefined are said to be equal to each other.

Example:

This example shows how undefined is used by setting a variable, but tracing a variable that has not been created instead. This will return undefined because the variable being looked for will not be created.

```
var x = 10;
trace(y);
//output: undefined
```

Properties

In the Actions panel, properties are not separated into subcategories. They are separated in this section, though. First, we will go over the general properties; then we will cover the movie clip properties.

General

_quality

Availability: Flash Player 5

Generic Template: _quality

Description:

This global property can be set or retrieved and represents the rendering quality used in the movie.

The different types of quality are as follows:

Low—Graphics are not antialiased; bitmaps are unsmooth.

Medium—Graphics are antialiased using a 2×2 grid, in pixels, but bitmaps are still unsmooth.

High—Graphics are antialiased using a 4×4 grid, in pixels, and bitmaps are smoothed. Note that this is Flash's default setting.

Best—Graphics are antialiased using a 4×4 grid, in pixels, and bitmaps are smooth.

Example:

This example turns the rendering quality to best:

```
_quality = "Best";
```

_soundbuftime

Availability: Flash Player 4

Generic Template: _soundbuftime = *number*;

Constraint:

> *number*—The number of seconds before a movie begins to stream

Description:

This property can be used to set a buffer before a movie or sound, in seconds, that will stop the playback until the indicated number of seconds has gone by (5 is the default value).

Example:

This example sets soundbuftime to 15 seconds so that the sound will not play for 15 seconds:

```
_soundbuftime = 15;
```

Movie Clip Properties

(e)_alpha

Availability: Flash Player 4

Generic Template: *movieClip*._alpha = *value;*

Constraints:

> *movieClip*—An instance of a movie clip on the timeline
>
> *value*—Any numeric value ranging from 0 to 100, where 0 is not visible and 100 is funny visible

Description:

This is the transparency of the movie clip, which can be set or retrieved. Values range from 0 (invisible) to 100 (no transparency).

29

ACTIONSCRIPT
REFERENCE

Note that even though an object has an _alpha of 0, it is still active. For instance, if a button has the _alpha of 0, it is not visible, but it can still be clicked. To make something invisible and not active, use the _visible property.

Example:

This example uses a movie clip event handler to fade a movie clip down to the value 0:

```
onClipEvent(enterFrame){
        if(this._alpha>0){
            this._alpha-=1;
        }
}
```

_currentFrame

Availability: Flash Player 4

Generic Template: *movieClip._currentFrame;*

Constraint:

> *movieClip*—An instance of a movie clip on the timeline

Description:

This read-only property is a number representing the exact frame in the movie clip's timeline where the playhead currently is.

Example:

This example checks to see whether the frame of a movie clip has reached the value 5 using a conditional statement in a movie clip event handler. If so, it will go back to frame 1.

```
onClipEvent(enterFrame){
    if(myMovie._currentFrame==5){
        myMovie.gotoAndPlay(1);
    }
}
```

_dropTarget

Availability: Flash Player 4

Generic Template: *movieClip._dropTarget*

Constraint:

> *movieClip*—An instance of a movie clip on the timeline

Description:

This read-only property returns the path in slash syntax of the movie clip instance on which the movie clip was dropped (released).

Example:

This example sees whether a movie clip has been dropped on another clip. If so, it will change the `stature` variable created for that movie; otherwise, it leaves this variable the same. Also, you use the `eval` statement to convert the `_dropTarget` path from slash syntax (its natural state) to dot syntax.

```
if(eval(fly._dropTarget)==_root.trap){
    flyStature = "caught";
}else {
    flyStature = "free";
}
```

_focusrect

Availability: Flash Player 6

Generic Template: *movieClip.*_focusrect = *value*;

Constraints:

> *movieClip*—An instance of a movie clip on the timeline
>
> *value*—A Boolean value (true/false)

Description:

This property returns a Boolean value if the movie clip has a yellow rectangle surrounding it when it has keyboard focus. It can be set to override the global property `_focusrect`.

Example:

This example checks a movie clip to see whether it has keyboard focus. If so, it displays a message in the output window:

```
if(myMovie._focusrect){
    trace(myMovie._name+" has keyboard focus");
}
```

_framesLoaded

Availability: Flash Player 4

Generic Template: *movieClip.*_framesloaded

Constraint:

> `movieClip`—An instance of a movie clip on the timeline

Description:

This read-only property is a number representing the amount of frames the playhead has loaded of the movie clip. When this is used in conjunction with `_totalframes`, you can create very functional preloaders.

Example:

This example uses the `_framesloaded` property in conjunction with the `_totalframes` property to control the playhead of the movie:

```
if(_root.framesloaded == _root.totalframes){
    gotoAndPlay("start");
}else{
    gotoAndPlay("loading");
}
```

_height

Availability: Flash Player 4

Generic Template: *movieClip._height = value;*

Constraints:

> *movieClip*—An instance of a movie clip on the timeline
>
> *value*—A numeric value representing the vertical size of an object

Description:

This read/write property represents the height of a movie clip in pixels.

Example:

This example sets the height of a movie clip to 100 if it is any height but 100:

```
if(myMovie._height!=100){
    myMovie._height=100;
}
```

_name

Availability: Flash Player 4

Generic Template: *movieClip._name = value;*

Constraints:

> *movieClip*—An instance of a movie clip on the timeline.
>
> *value*—A string representing the new name of the movie clip. Note that once the name is changed, you must call the movie clip by its new name for other properties.

Description:

This read/write property returns a string value representing the instance name of the movie clip.

Example:

This example traces the name of the movie clip when the movie clip is pressed:

```
onClipEvent(mouseDown){
    if(this.hitTest(_root._xmouse,_root._ymouse,true)){
        trace(this._name);
    }
}
```

_rotation

Availability: Flash Player 4

Generic Template: *movieClip._rotation = value;*

Constraints:

> movieClip—An instance of a movie clip on the timeline
>
> value—A numeric value representing the rotation of a movie clip

Description:

This read/write property is a number representing the rotation of a movie clip, in degrees.

Example:

This example uses an incremental variable to increase the speed of the rotation of the movie clip. It will appear to speed up, slow down, and change direction.

```
onClipEvent(enterFrame){
    i++;
    this._rotation = i;
}
```

_target

Availability: Flash Player 4

Generic Template: *movieClip.*_target

Constraint:

> *movieClip*—An instance of a movie clip on the timeline

Description:

This read-only property returns the target path to the movie clip instance.

Example:

This example traces the target path to a specific movie clip instance:

```
trace(myMovie._target);
```

_totalframes

Availability: Flash Player 4

Generic Template: *movieClip.*_totalframes

Constraint:

> *movieClip*—An instance of a movie clip on the timeline

Description:

This read-only property is a number representing the total frames in a movie clip. When this is used in conjunction with _framesloaded, you can create very functional preloaders.

Example:

This example uses the _framesloaded property with the _totalframes property to show the percentage of frames loaded:

```
onClipEvent(enterFrame){
    if(_root._totalframes != root._framesloaded){
    framePercent = root._framesloaded/root._totalframes;
    trace("Percentage of frames loaded is - "+framePercent);
    }
}
```

_url

Availability: Flash Player 4

Generic Template: *movieClip.*_url

Constraint:

> *movieClip*—An instance of a movie clip on the timeline

Description:

This read-only property returns the URL of the Shockwave file from where the movie clip was loaded.

Example:

This example retrieves the exact URL of where the movie clip was loaded from:

```
trace(myMovie._url);
```

_visible

Availability: Flash Player 4

Generic Template: *movieClip*._visible = *value*;

Constraints:

> *movieClip*—An instance of a movie clip on the timeline
>
> *value*—A boolean value that, if true, makes the movie clip visible. If false, the movie clip is not visible. Can also be a numeric value that can evaluate to a boolean value (zero for false and a number above zero to represent true).

Description:

This read/write property uses boolean values to set whether the movie clip is visible. False (or 0) will set the movie clip to zero visibility, and true (or 1) will set it to completely visible.

Example:

This example makes the movie clip invisible:

```
myMovie._visible = false;
```

> **Note**
>
> Buttons with zero visibility cannot be clicked, whereas buttons with zero alpha can still be clicked.

29

ACTIONSCRIPT REFERENCE

_width

Availability: Flash Player 4

Generic Template: *movieClip*._width = *value*;

Constraints:

> *movieClip*—An instance of a movie clip on the timeline
>
> *value*—A numeric value representing the horizontal size of a movie clip

Description:

This read/write property uses a number to specify the width of a movie clip, in pixels.

Example:

This example sets the horizontal size of the movie clip to 100:

```
myMovie._width = 100;
```

_x

Availability: Flash Player 3

Generic Template: *movieClip._x = value;*

Constraints:

> *movieClip*—An instance of a movie clip on the timeline
>
> *value*—A numeric value representing the horizontal position of a movie clip

Description:

This read/write property is a numerical representation of the horizontal position of the movie clip.

Example:

This example moves a movie clip to the right using a movie clip event handler:

```
onClipEvent(enterFrame){
    this._x++;
}
```

_xmouse

Availability: Flash Player 5

Generic Template: *movieClip._xmouse*

Constraint:

> *movieClip*—The direct path to a movie clip

Description:

This read-only property returns the horizontal position of the mouse.

Example:

This example constantly displays the horizontal position of the mouse on the main stage in the output window:

```
_root.onEnterFrame = function (){
    trace(_root._xmouse);
}
```

_xscale

Availability: Flash Player 4

Generic Template: *movieClip._xscale = value;*

Constraints:

> *movieClip*—An instance of a movie clip on the timeline
>
> *value*—A numeric value representing the horizontal scale of a movie clip

Description:

This read/write property controls the horizontal scale of the movie clip.

Example:

This example flips a movie clip horizontally:

```
flip = myMovie._xscale;
myMovie._xscale = -flip;
```

_y

Availability: Flash Player 3

Generic Template: *movieClip._y = value;*

Constraints:

> *movieClip*—An instance of a movie clip on the timeline
>
> *value*—A numeric value representing the vertical position of a movie clip

Description:

This read/write property is a number representing the vertical position of the movie clip.

Example:

This example moves a movie clip down, which is increasing its _root._x position because moving down on the main stage increases the _y value:

```
this._y+=5;
```

_ymouse

Availability: Flash Player 5

Generic Template: *movieClip._ymouse*

Constraint:

> *movieClip*—The direct path to a movie clip

Description:

This read-only property returns the vertical position of the mouse.

Example:

This example tells the user when the vertical position of the mouse has gone beyond a certain point:

```
_root.onEnterFrame = function (){
    if(_root._ymouse>200){
        trace("You have gone too far");
    }
}
```

_yscale

Availability: Flash Player 4

Generic Template: *movieClip._yscale = value;*

Constraints:

> *movieClip*—An instance of a movie clip on the timeline
>
> *value*—A numeric value representing the vertical scale of a movie clip

Description:

This read/write property controls the vertical scale of the movie clip.

Example:

This example flips a movie clip vertically:

```
vFlip = myMovie._yscale;
myMovie._yscale = -vFlip;
```

Objects

Again, not all objects are discussed in this section due to page-length considerations. However, here are the objects not covered and a brief description of each.

Core

arguments—This object is used for passing information to user-defined functions.

Array—This object assists in the use of arrays.

Boolean—This object aids in the use of boolean data types.

Function—This object is used in conjunction with functions.

_global—This object can create variables, objects, and classes available throughout the timelines of a movie.

Number—This object is used in representing and controlling numeric values.

String—This object is used with controlling and creating strings of text.

super—This object is used to create the superclass of a method.

this—This object is used inside a movie clip to represent the movie clip it is in without you having to type a direct path to the movie clip.

Movie

Accessibility—This object is used to improve the accessibility of a Flash movie using screen-reader programs.

Button—This object is used in conjunction with button instances.

Capabilities—This object is used to retrieve system characteristics from a user.

Color—This object is used for the coloring of movie clips.

Key—This object is used with a user input device (the keyboard).

_level—This object is used to retrieve or set the level depth of a movie clip.

Mouse—This object is used with another user input device, the mouse.

MovieClip—This object is used to represent a movie clip.

_parent—This object represents one level of hierarchy up from the current movie.

_root—This object represents the main stage or timeline.

Selection—This object is used to control text edits and focus.

Stage—This object is used to control properties of the stage itself.

System—This object is used to gather system information from the user.

TextField—This object is used in the creation and control of text fields.

TextFormat—This object is used for formatting the text of a text field.

Client Server

LoadVars—This is an object-oriented interface for loading variables.

XML—This object allows you to work with XML documents.

XML Socket—This object is used for an XML socket connection to a server.

Authoring

Custom Actions—This object is used to manage custom actions.

Live Preview—This object is used with the live preview of components.

Now that we have gone over the objects that are not covered in detail, let's move on to the ones that are covered in detail, starting with the Sound object.

Sound

new Sound Constructor

Availability: Flash Player 5

Generic Template: new Sound(target);

Constraint:

target—This optional constraint is the movie clip instance where the sound is operating.

Description:

This constructor creates a new Sound object with a target movie in mind. If no target is declared, the object controls all sounds in the movie.

Example:

This example shows a new Sound object being created and the volume being controlled:

```
mySound = new Sound();
mySound.setVolume(75);
```

Sound Methods

attachSound

Availability: Flash Player 5

Generic Template: Sound.attachSound(name);

Constraints:

Sound—A user-defined sound

name—Represents the identifier of an exported sound that can be found in the library

Description:

This method attaches the sound known as *name* to a Sound object. The sound being attached must be in the Library at runtime as well as specified for export in Symbol Linkage Properties.

Example:

This example attaches a sound from the Library to the Sound object:

```
mySound.attachSound("Disco");
```

getBytesLoaded

Availability: Flash Player 6

Generic Template: *Sound*.getBytesLoaded();

Constraint:

> *Sound*—A user-defined sound

Returns:

A numerical value representing the total bytes of the sound that have been loaded into the player.

Description:

This method retrieves the total bytes that have been loaded into the player. When it's used with getBytesTotal, you can create a functional loader.

Example:

This example loads a sound and shows the percentage of bytes loaded:

```
var mySound = new Sound();
//now load the audio file
mySound.loadSound("myMusic.mp3",false)
//Now we will get the bytes for the sound
_root.onEnterFrame = function (){
    trace(mySound.getBytesLoaded()/mySound.getBytesTotal());
}
```

getBytesTotal

Availability: Flash Player 6

Generic Template: *Sound*.getBytesTotal();

Constraint:

> *Sound*—A user-defined sound

Returns:

The total bytes of a specific `Sound` object.

Description:

This method returns the value of the total bytes of a given `Sound` object. When it's used with `getBytesLoaded`, you can create a functional loader.

Example:

This example displays the total bytes of a sound:

```
//First create the Sound object
var mySound = new Sound();
//now load the audio file
mySound.loadSound("test.mp3",false)
trace(mySound.getBytesTotal());
```

getPan

Availability: Flash Player 5

Generic Template: `Sound.getPan();`

Constraint:

> *Sound*—A user-defined sound

Description:

This method retrieves the pan of the `Sound` object in a numerical value. Pan is the balance of the sound from left to right, where –100 is left and 100 is right. When set at 0, the pan is balanced.

Example:

This example displays the pan value of a `Sound` object that has been loaded:

```
//First create the Sound object
var mySound = new Sound();
//now load the audio file
mySound.loadSound("test.mp3",false)
trace(mySound.getPan());
```

getTransform

Availability: Flash Player 5

Generic Template: *Sound*.getTransform();

Constraint:

> *Sound*—A user-defined sound

Description:

This method returns the sound transform information for our Sound object.

getVolume

Availability: Flash Player 5

Generic Template: *Sound*.getVolume();

Constraint:

> *Sound*—A user-defined sound

Description:

This method retrieves the volume of the Sound object in a numeric form, where 0 is no volume and 100 is full volume (100 is also the default setting for the volume).

Example:

This example loads a sound and displays the volume of that sound in the output window:

```
//First create the Sound object
var mySound = new Sound();
//now load the audio file
mySound.loadSound("myMusic.mp3",false)
trace(mySound.getVolume());
```

LoadSound

Availability: Flash Player 6

Generic Template: *Sound*.loadSound("*url*", *isStreaming*);

Constraints:

> *Sound*—A user-defined sound
>
> *URL*—A URL specifying the file location to get a sound file
>
> *isStreaming*—represents whether the sound takes place on an event or simply streams

Description:

This method loads an MP3 into the Sound object using the path of the URL. The *isStreaming* constraint sets whether the sound takes place on an event or just streams.

29

ACTIONSCRIPT
REFERENCE

The difference between sounds that take place on events and streaming sounds is that event sounds won't play until fully loaded. Streaming sounds play as they are being loaded.

Example:

This example creates a new Sound object and loads an MP3 into it:

```
mySound = new Sound();
mySound.loadSound("http://theURL/the file name");
```

setPan

Availability: Flash Player 5

Generic Template: `Sound.setPan(pan);`

Constraints:

> *Sound*—A user-defined sound
>
> *pan*—A numeric value between –100 and 100 that sets the pan of the Sound object, where –100 is the left side, 100 is the right side, and 0 is the center

Description:

In stereo, this method determines how much of the sound is played to one side or the other. In mono, it decides which speaker to play out of.

Example:

This example pans the sound from left to right on the speakers using a function:

```
//First create the Sound object
mySound = new Sound();
//Then load the sound
mySound.loadSound("myMusic.mp3",false);
//Start the sound
mySound.start();
//Create the variable
i = -100;
//Create the function
_root.onEnterFrame = function (){
    if (mySound.getPan()<100){
        mySound.setPan(i);
        i++;
    }
}
```

setTransform

Availability: Flash Player 5

Generic Template: `Sound.setTransform(soundObj);`

Constraints:

> *Sound*—A user-defined sound
>
> *soundObj*—This object is created with the constructor for the generic `Object` object for determining how the sound should be distributed.
>
> > `ll`—The percentage of left input to play in the left speaker
> >
> > `lr`—The percentage of right input in left speaker
> >
> > `rr`—The percentage of right input in the right speaker
> >
> > `rl`—The percentage of left input in the right speaker

Description:

This method sets the transform for the `Sound` object. The transform is used to set the balance (left to right) of the sound.

Example:

This example sets *soundObj* and implements it:

```
//create our sound transform object
mySoundObj = new Object;
mySoundObj.ll = 50;
mySoundObj.lr = 50;
mySoundObj.rr = 50;
mySoundObj.rl = 50;
//now create our sound object
mySound = new Sound();
//now implement it
mySound.setTransform(mySoundObj);
```

setVolume

Availability: Flash Player 5

Generic Template: `Sound.setVolume(vol);`

Constraints:

> *Sound*—A user-defined sound
>
> *vol*—A numerical value between 0 and 100 representing the volume

Description:

This method sets the volume of the `Sound` object.

Example:

This example creates a Sound object and sets the volume:

```
//create our sound object
mySound = new Sound();
mySound.setVolume(50);
```

start

Availability: Flash Player 5

Generic Template: *Sound*.start(*offset, loops*);

Constraints:

> *Sound*—A user-defined sound
>
> *offset*—The number of seconds to move into the sound. This becomes the starting point.
>
> *loops*—An optional parameter that sets how many times the sound will play through.

Description:

This method starts a Sound object playing, and you set the amount of times it will play with *loops*. Also, you can specify how far into the sound, in seconds, you want to start from.

Example:

This example creates a Sound object, loads a sound into it, and then starts to play it with a 50-second jump into the sound and at only one loop:

```
//First create the Sound object
mySound = new Sound();
//Then load the sound
mySound.loadSound("myMusic.mp3",false);
//Start the sound
mySound.start(50,1);
```

stop

Availability: Flash Player 5

Generic Template: *Sound*.stop(*name*);

Constraints:

> *Sound*—A user-defined sound.
>
> *name*—An optional constraint that can be used to stop a specific sound from playing instead of all the sounds at once.

Description:

This method stops the Sound object from playing (or a specific sound in that object).

Example:

This example create two Sound objects, load MP3s into them, and then starts them playing and, finally, stops one of them:

```
//First create the Sound objects
mySound = new Sound();
mySound2 = new Sound();
//Then load the MP3's
mySound.loadSound("myMusic.mp3",false);
mySound2.loadSound("diso.mp3",false);
//Start the sound
mySound.start();
mySound2.start();
//Now stop the first Sound object
mySound.stop();
```

Properties

duration

Availability: Flash Player 6

Generic Template: *Sound*.duration

Constraint:

> *Sound*—A user-defined sound

Description:

This is a read-only property of the Sound object that specifies the length of a sound, in milliseconds.

Example:

This example creates a Sound object, loads an MP3 into it, and views the length of it in milliseconds:

```
//First create the Sound object
mySound = new Sound();
//Then load the MP3
mySound.loadSound("myMusic.mp3",false);
//Now trace the length
trace(mySound.duration);
```

position

Availability: Flash Player 6

Generic Template: *Sound*.position

Constraint:

> *Sound*—A user-defined sound

Description:

This is a read-only property of the Sound object that specifies how long the sound has been playing, in milliseconds.

Example:

This example starts a sound playing and uses a onMouseDown event to trace the approximate second its at in the song:

```
//First create the Sound object
mySound = new Sound();
//Then load the MP3
mySound.loadSound("myMusic.mp3",false);
//Start the sound
mySound.start();
//Now trace the length
_root.onMouseDown = function (){
    trace(Math.round(mySound.position/1000));
}
```

Events

onLoad

Availability: Flash Player 6

Generic Template: *Sound*.onLoad = *function*

Constraints:

> *Sound*—A user-defined sound
>
> *function*—Any viable function

Description:

This event calls a function once the Sound object has loaded.

Example:

This example loads an MP3 into the Sound object and traces a message when it is complete:

```
//First create the function
function myTrace(){
    trace ("Success");
}
//Now create the Sound object
mySound = new Sound();
//Then load the MP3
mySound.loadSound("myMusic.mp3",false);
//Now call the function
mySound.onLoad = myTrace();
```

onSoundComplete

Availability: Flash Player 6

Generic Template: *Sound*.onSoundComplete = *function*

Constraints:

> *Sound*—A user-defined sound
>
> *function*—Any viable function

Description:

This event calls a function when the sound has completed playing.

Example:

This example displays a message when the sound has reached its end:

```
//First create the function
function myTrace(){
    trace ("All done");
}
//Now create the Sound object
mySound = new Sound();
//Then load the MP3
mySound.loadSound("myMusic.mp3",false);
//Now call the function
mySound.onSoundComplete = myTrace();
```

Date

new Date Constructor

Availability: Flash Player 5

Generic Template: new Date(*plus*);

Constraints:

> *plus*—In the `new` `Date` object, you can specify several pieces of information, separated by commas.
>
> > *year*—If you want the year to be between 1900 and 1999, you can specify a number between 0 and 99; otherwise, you must place the entire four digits.
> >
> > *month*—A numerical value between 0 and 11, with 0 being January and 11 being December.
> >
> > *date*—A number between 1 and 31 for specifying the day of the month.
> >
> > *hour*—A number between 0 and 23, where 0 is midnight and 23 is 11 p.m.
> >
> > *minute*—A number between 0 and 59.
> >
> > *second*—A number between 0 and 59.
> >
> > *millisecond*—A number between 0 and 999.

Description:

This constructor object creates a `new` `Date` object.

Example:

This example creates a `Date` object and then gets the time:

```
myDate = new Date();
myHour = myDate.getHours();
myMin = myDate.getMinutes();
myTime = (myHour+":"+myMin);
trace(myTime);
```

Methods

Three types of methods are associated with the `Date` object: general methods, `get` methods, and `set` methods. We will look at the methods in these groupings.

General Methods

toString
Availability: Flash Player 5

Generic Template: `myDate.toString();`

Returns:

This method returns a string.

Description:

This method converts the `Date` object to a string literal.

Example:

This example specifies a date and converts it to a string:

```
var bDay = new Date(80, 0, 9, 17, 30);
trace(bDay.toString());
//output: Wed Jan 9 17:30:00 GMT-0500 1980
```

UTC
Availability: Flash Player 5

Generic Template: `Date.UTC(year, month , date , hour , minute , second , millisecond)`

Constraints:

> *year*—A four-digit number representing the year
>
> *month*—A numerical value between 0 and 11, with 0 being January and 11 being December
>
> *date*—A number between 1 and 31 for specifying the day of the month
>
> *hour*—A number between 0 and 23, where 0 is midnight and 23 is 11 p.m.
>
> *minute*—A number between 0 and 59
>
> *second*—A number between 0 and 59
>
> *millisecond*—A number between 0 and 999

Example:

This example sets the `Date` object to a specific date:

```
merryChristmas = new Date(Date.UTC(2002, 11, 26));
```

get Methods

Because all `get` methods for the `Date` object have the same generic template, we will not go over each one in its own section but rather cover them all in this section.

getDate()
Availability: Flash Player 5

Generic Template: `Date.getDate();`

Constraint:

> *Date*—A user-defined `Date` object

Description:

This method gets the day of the month in a numeric form (1–31).

Example:

This example retrieves the current date off the user's system:

```
//Create the date object
myDate = new Date();
//Retrieve the information
theDate = myDate.getDate();
//Display the information
trace(theDate);
```

getDay()
Availability: Flash Player 5

Generic Template: `Date.getDay();`

Constraint:

> `Date`—A user-defined `Date` object

Description:

This method returns a numerical value representing the day of the week (0–6, where 0 is Sunday and 6 is Saturday).

Example:

This example retrieves the current day off the user's system:

```
//Create the date object
myDate = new Date();
//Retrieve the information
theDay = myDate.getDay();
//Display the information
trace(theDay);
```

getFullYear()
Availability: Flash Player 5

Generic Template: `Date.getFullYear();`

Constraint:

> `Date`—A user-defined `Date` object

Description:

This method returns the four-digit value of the current year.

Example:

This example retrieves the current full year off the user's system:

```
//Create the date object
myDate = new Date();
//Retrieve the information
theFullYear = myDate.getFullYear() ;
//Display the information
trace(theFullYear);
```

getHours()
Availability: Flash Player 5

Generic Template: *Date*.getHours();

Constraint:

> *Date*—A user-defined Date object

Description:

This method returns the current hour in a numeric form (between 0 and 23; 0 being midnight and 23 being 11:00 p.m.).

Example:

This example retrieves the current hour off the user's system:

```
//Create the date object
myDate = new Date();
//Retrieve the information
theHour = myDate.getHours()   ;
//Display the information
trace(theHour);
```

getMilliseconds()
Availability: Flash Player 5

Generic Template: *Date*.getMilliseconds();

Constraint:

> *Date*—A user-defined Date object

Description:

This method returns the current milliseconds in a numeric form (between 0 and 999).

Example:

This example retrieves the current millisecond off the user's system:

```
//Create the date object
myDate = new Date();
//Retrieve the information
theMillisecond = myDate.getMilliseconds()  ;
//Display the information
trace(theMillisecond);
```

getMinutes()

Availability: Flash Player 5

Generic Template: *Date*.getMinutes()   ;

Constraint:

> *Date*—A user-defined Date object

Description:

This method returns the current minutes in numerical form (between 0 and 59).

Example:

This example retrieves the current minute off the user's system:

```
//Create the date object
myDate = new Date();
//Retrieve the information
theMinute = myDate.getMinutes()  ;
//Display the information
trace(theMinute);
```

getMonth()

Availability: Flash Player 5

Generic Template: *Date*.getMonth()   ;

Constraint:

> *Date*—A user-defined Date object

Description:

This method returns a numerical value representing the current month (0–11, where 0 is January and 11 is December).

Example:

This example retrieves the current month off the user's system:

```
//Create the date object
myDate = new Date();
//Retrieve the information
```

```
theMonth = myDate.getMonth();
//Display the information
trace(theMonth);
```

getSeconds()
Availability: Flash Player 5

Generic Template: *Date*.getSeconds()   ;

Constraint:

> *Date*—A user-defined Date object

Description:

This method returns the current seconds in numerical form (between 0 and 59).

Example:

This example retrieves the current second off the user's system:

```
//Create the date object
myDate = new Date();
//Retrieve the information
theSecond = myDate.getSeconds()   ;
//Display the information
trace(theSecond);
```

getTime()
Availability: Flash Player 5

Generic Template: *Date*.getTime();

Constraint:

> *Date*—A user-defined Date object

Description:

This method returns the number of milliseconds in universal time, from January 1, 1970.

Example:

This example retrieves the current getTime() off the user's system:

```
//Create the date object
myDate = new Date();
//Retrieve the information
theTime = myDate.getTime()   ;
//Display the information
trace(theTime);
```

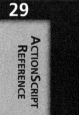

getTimezoneOffset()

Availability: Flash Player 5

Generic Template: *Date*.getTimezoneOffset();

Constraint:

> *Date*—A user-defined Date object

Description:

This method returns the difference, in minutes, between the operating system's local time and universal time.

Example:

This example retrieves the current time zone offset from the user's system:

```
//Create the date object
myDate = new Date();
//Retrieve the information
theTimeOffset = myDate.getTimezoneOffset()  ;
//Display the information
trace(theTimeOffset);
```

getUTCDate()

Availability: Flash Player 5

Generic Template: *Date*.getUTCDate();

Constraint:

> *Date*—A user-defined Date object

Description:

This method returns a specific day in the month, according to universal time.

Example:

This example retrieves the current UTC date from the user's system:

```
//Create the date object
myDate = new Date();
//Retrieve the information
theUTCDate = myDate.getUTCDate()  ;
//Display the information
trace(theUTCDate);
```

getUTCDay()
Availability: Flash Player 5

Generic Template: *Date*.getUTCDay();

Constraint:

> *Date*—A user-defined Date object

Description:

This method returns the day of the week, according to universal time.

Example:

This example retrieves the current UTC day from the user's system:

```
//Create the date object
myDate = new Date();
//Retrieve the information
theUTCDay = myDate.getUTCDay()  ;
//Display the information
trace(theUTCDay);
```

getUTCFullYear()
Availability: Flash Player 5

Generic Template: *Date*.getUTCFullYear();

Constraint:

> *Date*—A user-defined Date object

Description:

This method returns the four-digit year, according to universal time.

Example:

This example retrieves the current UTC full year from the user's system:

```
//Create the date object
myDate = new Date();
//Retrieve the information
theUTCFullYear = myDate.getUTCFullYear()  ;
//Display the information
trace(theUTCFullYear);
```

29

ACTIONSCRIPT
REFERENCE

getUTCHours()

Availability: Flash Player 5

Generic Template: *Date*.getUTCHours() ;

Constraints:

> *Date*—A user-defined Date object

Description:

This method returns the hours, according to universal time.

Example:

This example retrieves the current UTC hour from the user's system:

```
//Create the date object
myDate = new Date();
//Retrieve the information
theUTCHour = myDate.getUTCHours()    ;
//Display the information
trace(theUTCHour);
```

getUTCMilliseconds()

Availability: Flash Player 5

Generic Template: *Date*.getUTCMilliseconds() ;

Constraint:

> *Date*—A user-defined Date object

Description:

This method returns the milliseconds, according to universal time.

Example:

This example retrieves the current UTC millisecond from the user's system:

```
//Create the date object
myDate = new Date();
//Retrieve the information
theUTCMillisecond = myDate.getUTCMilliseconds()    ;
//Display the information
trace(theUTCMillisecond);
```

getUTCMinutes()

Availability: Flash Player 5

Generic Template: *Date*.getUTCMinutes() ;

Constraint:

> *Date*—A user-defined Date object

Description:

This method returns the minutes, according to universal time.

Example:

This example retrieves the current UTC minute from the user's system:

```
//Create the date object
myDate = new Date();
//Retrieve the information
theUTCMinute = myDate.getUTCMinutes()    ;
//Display the information
trace(theUTCMinute);
```

getUTCMonth()
Availability: Flash Player 5

Generic Template: *Date*.getUTCMonth()   ;

Constraint:

> *Date*—A user-defined Date object

Description:

This method returns the seconds, according to universal time.

Example:

This example retrieves the current UTC month from the user's system:

```
//Create the date object
myDate = new Date();
//Retrieve the information
theUTCMonth  = myDate.getUTCMonth()     ;
//Display the information
trace(theUTCMonth );
```

getUTCSeconds()
Availability: Flash Player 5

Generic Template: *Date*.getUTCSeconds()   ;

Constraint:

> *Date*—A user-defined Date object

29

ACTIONSCRIPT
REFERENCE

Description:

This method gets the day of the month in a numeric form (1–31).

Example:

This example retrieves the current UTC second from the user's system:

```
//Create the date object
myDate = new Date();
//Retrieve the information
theUTCSeconds  = myDate.getUTCSeconds()    ;
//Display the information
trace(theUTCSeconds );
```

getYear()
Availability: Flash Player 5

Generic Template: *Date*.getYear()   ;

Constraint:

> *Date*—A user-defined Date object

Description:

This method returns the full local year minus 1900 (in other words, the year 1998 would appear as 98).

Example:

This example retrieves the current year from the user's system:

```
//Create the date object
myDate = new Date();
//Retrieve the information
theYear  = myDate.getYear()     ;
//Display the information
trace(theYear );
```

set Methods

setDate()
Availability: Flash Player 5

Generic Template: *Date*.setDate(*value*);

Constraints:

> *Date*—A user-defined Date object
>
> *value*—A number between 1 and 31 for specifying the day of the month

Description:

This method sets the date of a `Date` object.

Example:

This example sets the date of the `Date` object:

```
myDate = new Date();
mySetDate = myDate.setDate(12);
```

setFullYear()
Availability: Flash Player 5

Generic Template: *Date.setFullYear(year [, month [, date]]);*

Constraints:

> *Date*—A user-defined `Date` object
>
> *year*—The year you would like to set
>
> *month*—The month you would like to set (0–11)
>
> *date*—The date you would like to set

Description:

This method sets the full year of a `Date` object.

Example:

This example sets the year of a `Date` object:

```
myDate = new Date();
mySetFullYear = myDate.setFullYear(2002);
```

setHours()
Availability: Flash Player 5

Generic Template: *Date.setHours(value);*

Constraints:

> *Date*—A user-defined `Date` object
>
> *value*—The hour you want to set the `Date` object to

Description:

This method sets the hour of a `Date` object.

Example:

This example sets the hour of a Date object:

```
myDate = new Date();
mySetHour = myDate.setHours(10);
```

setMilliseconds()
Availability: Flash Player 5

Generic Template: *Date.*setMilliseconds*(value)*;

Constraints:

> *Date*—A user-defined Date object

> *value*—The millisecond you want to set the Date object to

Description:

This method sets the millisecond of a Date object.

Example:

This example sets the millisecond of a Date object:

```
myDate = new Date();
mySetMilliseconds = myDate.setMilliseconds(30);
```

setMinutes()
Availability: Flash Player 5

Generic Template: *Date.*setMinutes*(value)*;

Constraints:

> *Date*—A user-defined Date object

> *value*—The minute you want to set the Date object to

Description:

This method sets the minute of a Date object.

Example:

This example sets the minute of a Date object:

```
myDate = new Date();
mySetMinutes = myDate.setMinutes(30);
```

setMonth()
Availability: Flash Player 5

Generic Template: `Date.setMonth(value);`

Constraints:

> `Date`—A user-defined `Date` object
>
> `value`—The month you want to set the `Date` object to (0–11)

Description:

This method sets the month of a `Date` object.

Example:

This example sets the month of a `Date` object to January:

```
myDate = new Date();
mySetMonth = myDate.setMonth(0);
```

setSeconds()
Availability: Flash Player 5

Generic Template: `Date.setSeconds(value);`

Constraints:

> `Date`—A user-defined `Date` object
> `value`—The second you want to set the `Date` object to

Description:

This method sets the second of a `Date` object.

Example:

This example sets the second of a `Date` object:

```
myDate = new Date();
mySetSeconds = myDate.setSeconds(30);
```

setTime()
Availability: Flash Player 5

Generic Template: `Date.setTime(value);`

Constraints:

> `Date`—A user-defined `Date` object
> `value`—The time, in milliseconds, you want to set the `Date` object to

Description:

This method sets the time, in milliseconds, of a `Date` object.

Example:

This example sets the time of a `Date` object:

```
myDate = new Date();
mySetTime = myDate.setTime(45);
```

setUTCDate()
Availability: Flash Player 5

Generic Template: `Date.setUTCDate(value);`

Constraints:

> `Date`—A user-defined `Date` object
>
> `value`—The date you want to set the `Date` object to (1–31)

Description:

This method sets the UTC date of a `Date` object.

Example:

This example sets the UTC date of a `Date` object:

```
myDate = new Date();
mySetUTCDate = myDate.setUTCDate(2);
```

setUTCFullYear()
Availability: Flash Player 5

Generic Template: `Date.setFullYear(year [, month [, date]]);`

Constraints:

> `Date`—A user-defined `Date` object
>
> `year`—The year you would like to set
>
> `month`—The month you would like to set (0–11)
>
> `date`—The date you would like to set

Description:

This method sets the UTC date of a `Date` object.

Example:

This example sets the UTC date of a Date object:

```
myDate = new Date();
mySetUTCFullYear = myDate.setUTCFullYear(2002);
```

setUTCHours()
Availability: Flash Player 5

Generic Template: *Date.*setUTCHours *(hour[, minute [, second [, millisecond]]])*

Constraints:

> *Date*—A user-defined Date object
>
> *hour*—The hour you want to set the Date object to
>
> *minute*—The minute you want to set the Date object to
>
> *second*—The second you want to set the Date object to
>
> *millisecond*—The millisecond you want to set the Date object to

Description:

This method sets the UTC hour of a Date object.

Example:

This example sets the UTC hour of a Date object:

```
myDate = new Date();
mySetUTCHours = myDate.setUTCHours(2);
```

setUTCMilliseconds()
Availability: Flash Player 5

Generic Template: *Date.*setUTCMilliseconds*(value)*;

Constraints:

> *Date*—A user-defined Date object
>
> *Value*—The number of milliseconds you want to set the Date object to

Description:

This method sets the UTC milliseconds of a Date object.

Example:

This example sets the UTC millisecond of a Date object:

29

ACTIONSCRIPT REFERENCE

```
myDate = new Date();
mySetUTCMilliseconds = myDate.setUTCMilliseconds(12);
```

setUTCMinutes()
Availability: Flash Player 5

Generic Template: *Date*.setUTCMinutes*(minute [, second [, millisecond]])*

Constraints:

> *Date*—A user-defined Date object
>
> *minute*—The minute you want to set the Date object to
>
> *second*—The second you want to set the Date object to
>
> *millisecond*—The millisecond you want to set the Date object to

Description:

This method sets the UTC minute of a Date object.

Example:

This example sets the UTC minute of the Date object:

```
myDate = new Date();
mySetUTCMinutes = myDate.setUTCMinutes(12);
```

setUTCMonth()
Availability: Flash Player 5

Generic Template: *Date*.setUTCMonth*(month [, date])*

Constraints:

> *Date*—A user-defined Date object
>
> *month*—The month you want to set the Date object to
>
> *date*—The date you want to set the Date object to

Description:

This method sets the UTC month of a Date object.

Example:

This example sets the UTC month of a Date object:

```
myDate = new Date();
mySetUTCMonth = myDate.setUTCMonth(10);
```

setUTCSeconds()
Availability: Flash Player 5

Generic Template: *Date*.setUTCSeconds*(second [, millisecond])*

Constraints:

> *Date*—A user-defined Date object
>
> *second*—The second you want to set the Date object to
>
> *millisecond*—The millisecond you want to set the Date object to

Description:

This method sets the UTC second of a Date object.

Example:

This example sets the UTC second of a Date object:

```
myDate = new Date();
mySetUTCSeconds = myDate.setUTCSeconds(12);
```

setYear()
Availability: Flash Player 5

Generic Template: *Date*.setYear*(value)*

Constraints:

> *Date*—A user-defined Date object.
>
> *value*—The year you would like to set your Date object to. Note that if this is a number between 0 and 99, the interpreter will set the date with the prefix "19" for 1900 instead of "20" for 2000.

Description:

This method sets the year of a Date object.

Example:

This example sets the year of a Date object:

```
myDate = new Date();
mySetYear = myDate.setYear(2002);
```

29

ACTIONSCRIPT
REFERENCE

Math

Methods

abs

Availability: Flash Player 5

Generic Template: `Math.abs(anyNumber);`

Returns: A number

Constraint:

anyNumber—Any viable number

Description:

This method evaluates and returns an absolute value of *anyNumber*. The absolute value of a number is the distance it is away from zero, whether it is a negative number, which is to the left of zero, or a positive number, which is to the right of zero. For example, the absolute values of 10 and –10 are equal because they have the same amount of numbers between them and zero.

Example:

This example displays the absolute value of negative 20:

```
trace(Math.abs(-10));
//output: 20
```

acos

Availability: Flash Player 5

Generic Template: `Math.acos(number);`

Returns: A number

Constraint:

number—Any viable number between 1 and –1

Description:

This method evaluates and returns the arccosine of *number* in radians.

Example:

This example displays the arccosine of the number 1:

```
trace(Math.acos(1));
//output: 0
```

asin

Availability: Flash Player 5

Generic Template: `Math.asin(number);`

Returns: A number

Constraint:

> *number*—Any viable number between 1 and –1

Description:

This method evaluates and returns the arcsine of *number* in radians.

Example:

This example displays the arcsine of the number 1 in the Output window:

```
trace(Math.asin(1));
//output: 1.5707963267949
```

atan

Availability: Flash Player 5

Generic Template: `Math.atan(anyNumber);`

Returns: A number

Constraint:

> *anyNumber*—Any viable number

Description:

This method evaluates and returns the arctangent of *anyNumber* (the value returned is between negative pi divided by 2 and pi divided by 2).

Example:

This example displays the arctangent of the number 1 in the Output window:

```
trace(Math.atan(1));
//output: 0.785398163397448
```

atan2

Availability: Flash Player 5

Generic Template: `Math.atan2(numA, numB);`

Returns: A number

Constraints:

> *numB*—A number that represents the x coordinate of a point
>
> *numA*—A number that represents the y coordinate of a point

Description:

This method evaluates and returns the arctangent of *numA*/*numB*.

Example:

This example displays the arctangent of the numbers 1 and 2:

```
trace(Math.atan2(1,2));
//output: 0.463647609000806
```

ceil

Availability: Flash Player 5

Generic Template: `Math.ceil(number);`

Returns: A number

Constraint:

> *number*—Any viable number or expression that evaluates to a viable number

Description:

Evaluates and returns the greatest whole number greater than or equal to *number*. In other words, `ceil` will constantly round up numbers to the nearest whole number.

Example:

This example shows how the `ceil` method works by automatically rounding up the number 5.2 and displaying the result in the Output window:

```
trace(Math.ceil(5.2));
//output: 6
```

cos

Availability: Flash Player 5

Generic Template: `Math.cos(angle);`

Returns: A number

Constraint:

> *angle*—Any angle represented in radians

Description:

This method evaluates and returns the cosine of *angle*, which is specified in radians. The result will be a floating-point number between -1 and 1.

Example:

This example displays the cosine of 1 in the Output window:

```
trace(Math.cos(1));
//output: 0.54030230586814
```

exp

Availability: Flash Player 5

Generic Template: `Math.exp(exponent);`

Returns: A number

Constraint:

>   *exponent*—Any viable number

Description:

Evaluates and returns the value of the base of the natural logarithm (e) to the power of *exponent*.

Example:

This example displays the natural logarithm (e) to the first power:

```
trace(Math.exp(1));
//output: 2.71828182845905
```

floor

Availability: Flash Player 5

Generic Template: `Math.floor(anyNumber);`

Returns: A number

Constraint:

>   *anyNumber*—Any viable number or expression that evaluates to a viable number

Description:

Evaluates and returns the nearest whole number that is less than or equal to *anyNumber*.

29

ACTIONSCRIPT REFERENCE

Example:

This example shows the `Math.floor` method in action:

```
trace(Math.floor(2.4));
//output: 2
```

log

Availability: Flash Player 5

Generic Template: `Math.log(number);`

Returns: A number

Constraint:

>   *number*—Any viable number greater than zero or an expression that evaluates to a number greater than zero

Description:

Evaluates and returns the natural logarithm of *number*.

Example:

This example displays the natural logarithm of the number 10:

```
trace(Math.log(10));
//output: 2.30258509299405
```

max

Availability: Flash Player 5

Generic Template: `Math.max(numA, numB);`

Returns: A number

Constraints:

>   *numA, numB*—Any viable number or expression that evaluates to a number

Description:

Evaluates and returns the larger number between *numA* and *numB*.

Example:

This example displays the larger of the two numbers 10 and 15:

```
trace(Math.max(10,15));
//output: 15
```

min

Availability: Flash Player 5

Generic Template: `Math.min(numA, numB);`

Returns: A number

Constraints:

> *numA, numB*—Any viable number or expression that evaluates to a number

Description:

Evaluates and returns the smaller number between *numA* and *numb*.

Example:

This example displays the smaller of the two numbers 10 and 15:

```
trace(Math.min(10,15));
//output: 10
```

pow

Availability: Flash Player 5

Generic Template: `Math.pow(number, exponent);`

Returns: A number

Constraints:

> *number*—Any viable number
>
> *exponent*—The number that represents the power two which *number* will be raised

Description:

This method evaluates and returns *number* to the power of *exponent*.

Example:

This example raises the number 2 to the fourth power:

```
trace(Math.pow(2,4));
//output: 16
```

random

Availability: Flash Player 5

Generic Template: `Math.random();`

29

ACTIONSCRIPT
REFERENCE

Returns: A number

Constraints: None

Description:

This method evaluates and returns any floating-point number between 0 and 1.

Example:

This example display a floating-point number between 0 and 1 in the Output window:

```
trace(Math.random());
//output: a random number between 0 and 1
```

round

Availability: Flash Player 5

Generic Template: `Math.round(anyNumber);`

Returns: A number

Constraint:

> *anyNumber*—Any viable number

Description:

Evaluates and returns *anyNumber* rounded up or down to the nearest whole number.

Example:

This example shows how the `Math.round` method is used:

```
trace(Math.round(2.4));
//output: 2
```

sin

Availability: Flash Player 5

Generic Template: `Math.sin(angle);`

Returns: A number

Constraint:

> *angle*—An angle represented in radians

Description:

Evaluates and returns the sine of *angle* in radians.

Example:

This example displays the sine of the number 1:

```
trace(Math.sin(1));
//output: 0.841470984807897
```

sqrt

Availability: Flash Player 5

Generic Template: `Math.sqrt(number);`

Returns: A number

Constraint:

> *number*—Any viable number greater than zero or an expression that evaluates to a number greater than zero

Example:

This example display the square root of the number 16 in the Output window:

```
trace(Math.sqrt(16));
//output: 4
```

tan

Availability: Flash Player 5

Generic Template: `Math.tan(angle);`

Returns: A number

Constraint:

> *angle*—An angle represented in radians

Description:

This method evaluates and returns the tangent of *angle* in radians.

Example:

This example displays the tangent of the number 1 in the Output window:

```
trace(Math.tan(1));
//output: 1.5574077246549
```

Constants

All `Math` constants have the same generic template and will be discussed in this section.

Availability: Flash Player 5

Generic Template: `Math.constant`

Constraints:

> `constant`—A numerical value that remains constant and can be called by using the `Math` object. Here are the `Math` constants:
>
> > `Math.E`—This constant is the base of natural logarithms, expressed as e, and is approximately equal to 2.71828.
> >
> > `Math.LN2`—This constant is the natural logarithm of 2, expressed as log2, and is approximately equal to 0.69314718055994528623.
> >
> > `Math.LN10`—This constant is the natural logarithm of 10, expressed as log10, and is approximately equal to 2.3025850929940459011.
> >
> > `Math.LOG2E`—This constant is the base-2 logarithm of `Math.E`, expressed as log2, and is approximately equal to 1.442695040888963387.
> >
> > `Math.LOG10E`—This constant is the base-10 logarithm of `Math.E`, expressed as log10, and is approximately equal to 0.43429448190325181667.
> >
> > `Math.PI`—This constant is the ratio of the circumference of a circle to its diameter (or half of its radius), expressed as pi. It's approximately equal to 3.14159265358979.
> >
> > `Math.SQRT1_2`—This constant is the reciprocal of the square root of one half and is approximately equal to 0.707106781186.
> >
> > `Math.SQRT2`—This constant is the square root of 2 and is approximately equal to 1.414213562373.

Object

new Object Constructor

Availability: Flash Player 5

Generic Template: `new Object(value);`

Constraint:

> `value`—Any viable expression that will be converted to an object. If this is left blank, an empty object is created.

Description:

This constructor creates an `Object` object.

Example:

This example creates a new object:

```
MyObj = new Object();
```

Methods

AddProperty

Availability: Flash Player 6

Generic Template: `myObject.addProperty(prop, get, set);`

Constraints:

> *prop*—A reference to the property being created.
>
> *get*—This is a function that gets the value of *prop*.
>
> *set*—This is a function that sets the value of *prop*. If it is set to `null`, *prop* is considered read-only.

Returns:

This method returns `true` if *prop* was created; otherwise, it returns `false`.

Description:

This method creates a GnS property (`get` and `set`). When the interpreter reaches a GnS property, it calls the `get` function, and the function's return value becomes a value of *prop*. When the interpreter writes a GnS property, it calls the `set` function and passes it the new value as a constraint. When the property is written, it overwrites any prior version of itself.

When the `get` function is called, it retrieves any type of data, even if the data does not match that of the previous *prop*.

The `set` function takes the data from the `get` function and sets it to *prop*, even if it means overwriting the existing data.

Example:

This example shows a use of the `Object.addProperty` method:

```
scrollBox.addProperty("scroll", scrollBox.getScroll, scrollBox.setScroll);
scrollBox.addProperty("maxscroll", scrollBox.getMaxScroll, null);
```

29

ACTIONSCRIPT
REFERENCE

registerClass

Availability: Flash Player 6

Generic Template: `Object.registerClass(symbol, class);`

Constraints:

    symbol—A reference to the identifier of the movie clip or ActionScript class.

    class—This is a reference to a constructor. To unregister the symbol, use `null`.

Returns:

This method returns `true` if the class registration was successful; it returns `false` otherwise.

Description:

This method associates an ActionScript class with a movie clip symbol. If the symbol is nonexistent, the interpreter will create a string identifier instead and link it to the class.

If the movie is on the timeline, it is registered to the new class instead of the `MovieClip` class. This happens to the movie clip if it is placed manually on the stage or with the `attachMovie` action. Also, if the movie clip identified uses the `duplicateMovieClip` action, this movie clip is placed in the class instead of the `MovieClip` class.

If the class is set to `null`, the `registerClass` method removes any remaining ActionScript definitions of the class, but the movies within the class remain intact.

Finally, if a movie clip is already in a class when it is invoked, the previous class is over written.

Example:

This example registers the `ballClass` class with the ball symbol:

```
Object.registerClass("ball" ,ballClass);
```

toString

Availability: Flash Player 5

Generic Template: `myObject.toString();`

Constraint:

    myObject—A user-defined object

Description:

This method returns converts an object to a string.

Example:

This example tests the toString method:

```
var myObj = new Object;
trace (typeof myObj);
//output: object
trace(typeof myObj.toString());
//output: string
```

unwatch

Availability: Flash Player 6

Generic Template: *myObject*.unwatch(*prop*);

Constraints:

> *myObject*—A user-defined object
>
> *prop*—Refers to the property of the object that should no longer be watched

Returns:

This method returns true if the watch was successfully removed; it returns false otherwise.

Description:

This method removes a watchpoint created by a watch method from an object.

Example:

This example will unwatch the property "value" in the CheckBox component:

```
CheckBox() {
    this.unwatch("value")
}
```

valueOf

Availability: Flash Player 5

Generic Template: *myObject*.valueOf();

Constraint:

> *myObject*—A user-defined object

Description:

This method returns a primitive value of an object unless the object does not contain one, in which case it will return the object itself.

Example:

This example sets the value of an object to the number 4 and traces the value of that new object:

```
var myObj = new Object(4);
trace (myObj.valueOf());
//output: 4
```

watch

Availability: Flash Player 6

Generic Template: *myObject*.watch(*prop, callback, data*);

Returns:

This method returns true if the watchpoint was created successfully; it returns false otherwise.

Constraints:

> *myObject*—A user-defined object.
>
> *prop*—A reference to the object property to watch.
>
> *callback*—This constraint is a function that will be invoked when the watched property changes. The callback form is callback(*prop, oldValue, newValue, data*).
>
> *data*—An optional piece of ActionScript data that is sent to the callback method. If the data parameter is not present, callback receives an undefined value.

Description:

This method defines a callback function that will be invoked when a property of an ActionScript object has changed.

Watchpoints are assigned to properties to "keep an eye on them" if *oldValue* and *newValue* do not match. If the property is removed, the watchpoint is not. The watchpoint must be cleared with an unwatch method. Only one watchpoint per property can be assigned.

Most ActionScript properties cannot be watched, including _x, _alpha, _height, and so on. This is because they are GnS properties already.

Example:

This example uses the RadioButton component to set and watch a defined property:

```
//Now make a constructor for and define the RadioButton class
function RadioButton() {
```

```
//then set the watch method
    this.watch ('value', function (id, oldval, newval)){
    }
}
```

Properties

__proto__

Availability: Flash Player 5

Generic Template: `myObject.__proto__`

Description:

This property is a reference to the prototype property of the constructor function that creates an `Object` object. The `__proto__` property is assigned automatically to all objects when they are created. The interpreter uses `__proto__` to access the prototype property to find out what properties and methods can be inherited from the class.

Example:

In this example, the `__proto__` property is used to declare the property "name":

```
//Create the class
function myObj (){
    this.__proto__.name="Ball";
}
//Now create a new object from the myObj
theObj = new myObj();
//Now trace the name of the new object you just created
trace(theObj.name);
```

Flash Alternatives

By George Gordon

CHAPTER 30

We have covered a lot of information about Flash MX in this book. I think you would agree that Flash MX is by far the most comprehensive tool for creating Flash on the planet. However, sometimes using Flash MX might be the equivalent of shooting a mosquito with a cannon. Many software tools are available that can be used to supplement your Flash development efforts. Refer to Appendix B, "SWF Software Tools," for a listing of many of these. This chapter covers a couple of the more popular general-purpose no-cost/low-cost SWF format development tools.

No-Cost Flash: FLASH*typer*

Flash for free? Yes, that's right. Our friends at FlashKit.com have provided us with a very easy-to-use online tool for creating simple SWF Flash files in a jiffy. Let's go to the Web site, `http://www.flashkit.com`, right now and take a look. FlashKit.com is a great developer community and resource site for Flash. You might want to check it out later for its many other features.

The name of the application is **FLASH***typer*. It can be found on the blue menu bar at the top of the FlashKit.com home page. Select **FLASH***typer* to go to the **FLASH***typer* Web page. **FLASH***typer* is an online text-effect generator and animation tool. Nothing fancy, but it's simple and fast. Once you master **FLASH***typer*, you can make a variety of text animation SWF files in a matter of minutes.

Sign Up and Log In

In order to use the **FLASH***typer* application, FlashKit requires you to be a member of the site. Underneath the application is what is known as the myFK engine. This allows you to individualize **FLASH***typer* to your own tastes by storing your selection of favorite fonts and text effects at the Web site. Membership is free. Select Sign Up Here! on the **FLASH***typer* Web page to sign up. Once you have signed up, you have the choice of taking a short tutorial or proceeding with the application.

After you have signed up for the first time, if you have cookies turned on in your computer, the Web site will take you directly into **FLASH***typer*. Just select Launch **FLASH***typer* Now from the **FLASH***typer* Web page. If you are away from your computer, you can log on from virtually any computer in the world that is connected to the Internet using your username and password, and you'll have access to your settings.

You may be asking yourself, why would I want to use an Internet-based application? Well, it just so happens that while I was getting comfortable at the beach in an unnamed location in the Caribbean for a *well-deserved* vacation, my cell phone shocked me back to the real world. You would think that I would leave it at home or at least turn it off, but what can I say? I am a workaholic. It's from Mr. Big—the top guy at the publishing house—and he has this grandiose idea that he wants to flood the Internet with a banner ad advertising this book. Thank goodness he doesn't want to spam everybody. (Editor, please note: Remove that last sentence. We do not want to give Mr. Big any more bright ideas.) He wants me to create the banner ad ASAP. He doesn't care that I am on vacation and that I didn't bring my notebook computer with me (at least I thought that would work—and, yes, choleric bosses are like that). Refer to the boss in the *Dilbert* comic strip. I now have two choices:

- Pack up and go home, where I have all my software tools on my computer to complete the assignment.

- Find a computer connected to the Internet, log on to **FLASH***typer*, quickly complete the assignment, and get back to the beach.

Tough decision. Can you guess my choice? I checked with the concierge at the hotel, and he directed me to the hotel's business center.

You can catch up with me in a bit while I let you get acquainted with **FLASH***typer*.

The FLASH*typer* Desktop Screen

You are now just six steps away from making your first **FLASH***typer* animation, but first let's take a tour of the main screen:

- **Text Box Attributes**. Indicates the offset of your text from the upper-left corner of the text box as well as the size of the text box in pixels.

- **Load Movie**. This menu allows you to enter the URL of your SWF file and put it right in the background to view how the text effect you are creating will look when it is imported into your SWF file.

- **High/Low**. This toggle allows to optimize **FLASH***typer* for your computer. The Low setting is for older computers.

- **Help**. Provides access to online tutorials for **FLASH***typer*. At the time of this writing, this and the other help links (labeled "?") throughout this application were not functioning. The tutorials, however, can be accessed through the **FLASH***typer* Web page.

- **Text Editor**. Enter the text you want for your text effect.

- **Color Editor**. Select the color to be used for your text.

- **BackColor Editor**. Select the background color for your text box.

- **FX Editor**. Select the special effect for your text.

- **Text Options Editor**. Select the font, size, kerning, and line spacing for your text.

- **0,0 Corner**. This is a reference point representing the upper-left corner of the text box.

- **Drag Me GENERATE**. This dialog box shows the current text contained in your text box and allows you to change the size of the box, change the offset of the text from the corner of the box, and launch the preview and generation of your SWF file.

- **Text Attributes**. This window is located on the right side of the screen and provides a glance at the current status of your text attributes.

From this main screen, you have a number of panels and menus at your disposal for creating your text animation and providing an at-a-glance view of your progress (see Figure 30.1).

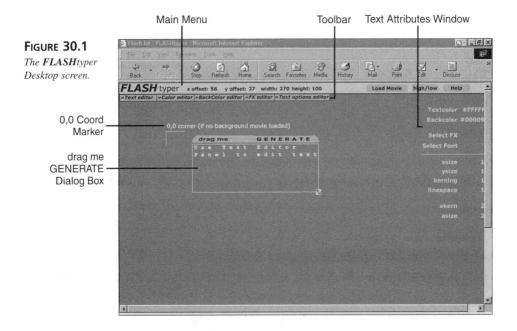

FIGURE 30.1

The FLASHtyper Desktop screen.

Before we get started on the project for Mr. Big, let's cover one item of note that we'll not be using for this project but that you might find useful on some other project—namely, the Load Movie menu.

Load Movie

From the main menu, select Load Movie. The Load Movie menu allows you to enter the URL of your SWF file and put it right in the background to view how the text effect you are creating will look when it is imported into your SWF file. Enter the URL of your SWF file in the URL field. Then enter the width and height and click Upload (see Figure 30.2).

FIGURE 30.2

The Load Movie menu.

Your SWF file will be brought to the background of the screen. If you don't have it loaded on the Internet yet or just want to check for relative size, then load the default, which will load a blue box for comparison (see Figure 30.3).

FIGURE 30.3

The default blue box, with custom height and width in pixels.

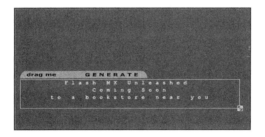

Drag Me GENERATE

Now let's get started on Mr. Big's project. The first thing we need to do is set the size of our workspace. Mr. Big wants a banner ad. We will make this banner ad 468 pixels wide by 60 pixels high. For this we will use the text box labeled Drag Me GENERATE, in the middle of the screen (see Figure 30.4).

Click and hold the small sizing box in the lower-right corner of the screen. As you move this box left and right or up and down, the text box will change its size. You'll also notice the width and height indicators in the Text Box Attributes area changing, as well, along with your movements. Continue adjusting the height and width until you have a reading of 468 wide by 60 high. Now we have created our text box.

FIGURE 30.4

*The Drag Me
GENERATE text
box's default set-
tings.*

Now let's orient the text in relation to the upper-left corner of the banner. Grab the Drag Me title bar and begin moving the text box over to the 0,0 corner. As you are doing this, you'll notice the x offset and y offset indicators in the Text Box Attributes area changing along with your movements. Keep adjusting until the x offset indicator reads 0 and the y offset indicator reads 8. Because I have done a few of these before, I have a feel for what it will take to center the text vertically. When you do some projects of your own, you may need to play with these settings until you get the placement of your text just right. Your screen should now look something like the one shown in Figure 30.5.

FIGURE 30.5

*The Drag Me
GENERATE text
box all set for our
project.*

Let's now proceed to enter the text.

Text Editor

From the toolbar, select Text Editor. The Text Editor allows you to enter the text you want for your text effect. Select it by clicking Text Editor on the toolbar. First, you'll need to clear the text. You can do this by either highlighting the text in the text box and pressing the Delete button on your keyboard or by simply clicking the Reset button. Now you can enter the text. For this exercise, enter the following text:

```
Flash MX Unleashed
Coming Soon
to a bookstore near you
```

You can use the Return (Mac) or Enter (Win) key to enter multiple lines of text. The text will not wrap in your text box, and it does not center. Therefore, if you wish to center the text, you'll need to adjust it by using the spacebar. Your text should look something like what's shown in Figure 30.6.

FIGURE 30.6
The Text Editor with your text entered.

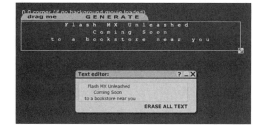

You can now close this editor. Before we proceed with choosing the font color, let's take a look at the Text Attributes window.

Text Attributes Window

The Text Attributes window is very similar to the Text Box Attributes area at the top of the screen. This window is located on the right side of the screen. It is always open and allows you to see the status of your project at a glance. All the information that you will enter through the next four menus will immediately appear on this summary window. The information is pretty self-evident as you review the contents of the window (see Figure 30.7).

FIGURE 30.7
The Text Attributes window.

Let's get back to the project now and proceed with the Color Editor.

Color Editor

From the toolbar, select Color Editor. The Color Editor allows you to select the color to be used for your text. You select it by clicking Color Editor on the toolbar. This editor is similar to many you may have used before. You can choose from one of the standard Internet-safe colors on the palette, or you can customize the color you want. Click the button at the bottom-right corner of the editor next to the color swatch, which shows the current selected color. This will toggle the red, blue, and green slider bars for precise selection of the amount of each color you want. These selections will automatically show in the R:, G:, and B: displays in the upper-right corner of the editor. The color is also displayed in HEX: in the middle-right side of the editor. For now, because Mr. Big didn't specify any color preferences, let's just choose his favorites—black and white. Therefore, leave the font color white. The settings should look like what's shown in Figure 30.8.

FIGURE 30.8

The Color Editor for selecting font color.

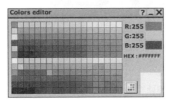 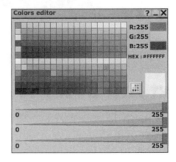

You can now close this editor, and we will proceed with choosing the background color.

BackColor Editor

From the toolbar, select BackColor Editor. The BackColor Editor allows you to select the background color for the text box. You can select it by clicking BackColor Editor on the toolbar. This editor is set up identical to the Color Editor. I'm going to keep this short because the beach awaits me. Again, with Mr. Big in mind, let's choose black by selecting the little square sample in the lower-left corner of the color display. The settings should look like what's shown in Figure 30.9.

FIGURE 30.9

The BackColor Editor for selecting background color.

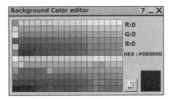 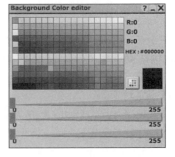

You can now close this editor, and we will proceed with selecting a special effect for our banner ad. Can you believe how simple this is? We're half way to completing our project for Mr. Big.

FX Editor

From the toolbar, select FX Editor. With the FX Editor, we can select the special effect for the text. Click the desired special effect, and it will preview on the screen. If you want to see a larger preview, click Big Preview. For this exercise, select Fold In and Out (see Figure 30.10). That's it. We are ready to go on to the next step.

FIGURE 30.10

The FX Editor for selecting text effects.

First, though, here are some other selections available in the FX Editor (we won't be using them for Mr. Big's project):

- **Edit button**. Allows you to reorder or delete effects from your myFK profile of favorites.

- **Add More button**. Allows you to select from a wide variety of categorized text effects from the ever-growing library of effects. As of this writing, the number is over 150. FlashKit occasionally has contests for designers to submit their newly designed effects. If you want to design your own effect for submission, FlashKit has a free design program called SDK available for download.

- **Refresh List button**. Once you have made your selection of the new effect you want to add and you return to the FX editor, this button refreshes your myFK profile with your new selection.

Close the FX editor and let's proceed with choosing the text options.

Text Options Editor

From the Toolbar select Text Options editor. The Text Options Editor allows you to select a TrueType font, the font size, kerning, and line spacing for your text. Because I have Mr. Big breathing down my neck, I vote for the "Biting My Nails" font. A sample of the font displays on the screen (see Figure 30.11). Perfect. You can change the size, kerning, and line spacing if you want; but for now, let's go with the defaults. We are ready to go on to the next step.

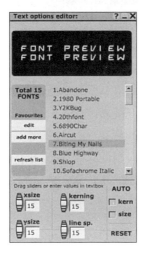

FIGURE 30.11

The Text Options Editor.

First, though, here are some other selections available in the Text Options Editor:

- **Edit button**. Allows you to reorder or delete TrueType fonts from your myFK profile of favorites.
- **Add More button**. Allows you to select from a wide variety of categorized TrueType fonts. As of this writing, the number is over 1,300.
- **Refresh List button**. Once you have made your selection of a new True Type font that you want to add and you have returned to the Text Options Editor, this button refreshes your myFK profile with your new selection.

Close the Text Options Editor and let's proceed with generating our banner ad.

Generate

At last, we are done. Everything has been tweaked and perfected. We are now ready to generate our banner ad. Click the Generate tab on the Drag Me GENERATE text box. You can click Play>> to test the text animation (see Figure 30.12).

FIGURE 30.12

*The Preview &
Download Effect
window.*

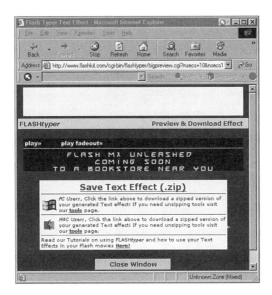

If you are satisfied, then click Save Text Effect (.zip) in the middle of the window. This
will open the Downloading Your Flash Typer Creation! window (see Figure 30.13).

FIGURE 30.13

*Downloading Your
Flash Typer
Creation! window.*

If it doesn't start downloading in a few seconds, press Click Here to download the movie
manually. On the File Download dialog box, select save (see Figure 30.14).

30

**FLASH
ALTERNATIVES**

FIGURE 30.14
*The File
Download dialog
box.*

In the Save As dialog box, choose a directory to save the file to and then click Save. This will save the file to your specified directory.

The file is now downloaded to your specified directory. It will have a very cryptic looking 16-character filename in ZIP format. When you unzip it, you'll have two files. The first one is `preview.html`. Open this file in your Web browser. This file provides you with a sample HTML Web page displaying the SWF file. If you are in Internet Explorer, you can review the source code for embedding your SWF file by selecting View, Source (see Figure 30.15).

FIGURE 30.15
*The **FLASH**typer
Text Effect
Preview window.*

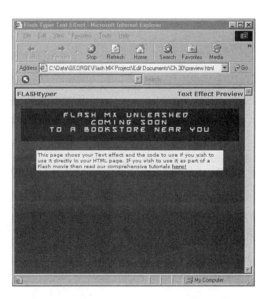

The second file is `FlashKitTE.swf`. This is your actual Flash file. Go ahead and click it. Flash Player will open and play this new Flash file for you (see Figure 30.16).

You can download this file, `FlashKitTE.swf`, from the Unleashed companion Web site, located at `http://www.flashmxunleashed.com`, by navigating to the Chapter 30 section.

FIGURE 30.16

The final product—our banner ad playing on Flash Player 6.

FLASH*typer* Conclusion

We finished the assignment. Mr. Big is happy, and I am back on the beach, umbrella drink in hand. **FLASH***typer* saved the day!

So that's all there is to it. For an online application, I think you will have to agree that **FLASH***typer* is a quite powerful and versatile tool. The only drawback to this application is that you can't save the equivalent of the FLA file of your work as you can in Flash, and you cannot store your SWF files. However, you can download them. Because creating a project takes only a minute or two, this is really only a minor inconvenience. After trying **FLASH***typer* a couple more times, you should be able to create a text animation SWF file for your Web site or Flash movie projects, from any Internet-connected computer, in just a minute or two.

Now that you know how to use **FLASH***typer*, I will just call you the next time Mr. Big gets another bright idea. I'm going to stay on the beach for just a little longer.

Low-Cost Flash: SWiSH

Many tools are available that are capable of producing SWF Flash files. A number of them can be purchased for a modest price. Some of the applications provide specific capabilities, such as creating 3D Flash files.

This portion of the chapter concentrates on one of the more popular general-purpose applications, called SWiSH, which can be purchased for under $50.

Like any application, SWiSH has both its detractors and loyal followers. The ratio for SWiSH is about the same as for Flash MX. Here are the main concerns some people have:

- It does not come in a version for Macintosh computers.
- It is too simple or lacks robustness.
- Issues with software protection, support, bugginess.

These kinds of issues will come up with virtually any kind of software product. You will see concerns running the full gamut, to both extremes. Even within a product line there

30

FLASH
ALTERNATIVES

are those who prefer the older version over the newer one, as is the case with Macromedia Flash 5 and MX.

Unlike Macromedia, however, DJJ Holdings Pty. Ltd., the developer of SWiSH, is currently keeping both versions available for its customers.

SWiSH 1.5

My first exposure to SWiSH was with version 1.5. Originally in version 1.0, it was a strictly a text animation tool similar to **FLASH***typer*, but then version 1.5 came out with significant new capabilities. It could do graphics and sound among other things, and a lot of people took notice, especially at the $30 price tag. The application came in two pieces: the Stage and the Application, as shown in Figure 30.17.

FIGURE 30.17
SWiSH version 1.5. The main screens.

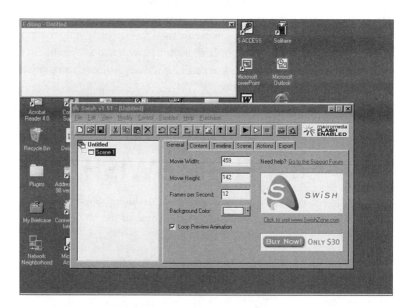

All this is just to make you aware of these two versions of SWiSH. In this chapter, however, we will concentrate on SWiSH version 2.0.

SWiSH 2.0

In version 2.0, SWiSH took on a whole new look. Everything is now accessible from one main screen. There are literally hundreds of new features. I won't go into detail here. Suffice it to say that several pages would be needed just to provide a high-level overview of the enhancements (see Figure 30.18).

FIGURE 30.18

SWiSH version 2.0. The main screen.

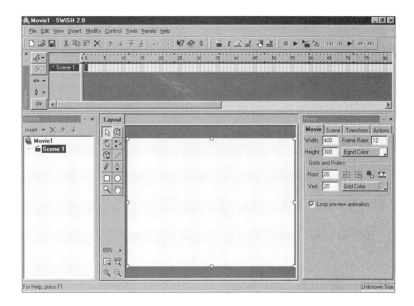

As I was getting comfortable at the beach *for the second time*, my cell phone went off again. You think I would learn to turn it off while I'm on vacation. It's Mr. Big—again —raving about how fast we were able to turn around that banner ad request for him. He's got the team back home scurrying around getting the banner ad placed all over the Internet. Also, he noticed that as he was using his computer, these annoying pop-up window ads kept appearing on his screen. This, of course, gave him the idea that "we" should create a pop-up window ad as well (*we* being you, me and, the team back home). Of course, this time he has more elaborate ideas. He wants more than just text; he wants graphics, sound—the whole enchilada. That rules out using **FLASH***typer*, which is great to a point but does have its limits. Therefore, I'm back to two choices:

- Pack up and go home, where I have all my software tools on my computer to complete the assignment.
- Find what's available here at the hotel.

So it's back to the business center. It just so happens that SWiSH is more popular than I thought. The hotel manager bought a copy and is using it. He agreed to let us use his computer to complete the assignment.

Because Mr. Big wants all the "bells and whistles" for this pop-up ad, I will go out to my FTP site and transfer some files we'll need for this project to the Unleashed companion Web site. While I do that, you can get acquainted with SWiSH 2.0.

Fundamentals

SWiSH animations are made up of a number of elements:

- **Movie**. A movie consists of one or more scenes.
- **Scene**. A scene has a timeline to apply effects.
- **Timeline**. Objects can be applied to a timeline. Timelines consist of one or more frames.
- **Frames**. A frame is the basic unit of a timeline.
- **Objects**. Objects consist of such elements as images, text, and so on.
- **Effects**. Effects span one or more frames. They are controlled by events and actions.
- **Events**. An event can release one or more actions.
- **Actions**. Actions consist of operations triggered by events.

These are the basic fundamental terms that make up SWiSH animations.

User Interface

The user interface allows you to control the SWiSH application. SWiSH's user interface contains the following components:

- **Main menu**. Located at the top of the SWiSH application screen. The main menu allows you to select commands and options.
- **Toolbars**. Toolbars generally appear below the main menu. They can be left open, moved about the screen, minimized, docked, or closed entirely. SWiSH has five toolbars: Standard, Insert, Control, Grouping, and Export.
- **Panels**. Panels control the various options and settings within the SWiSH environment.
- **Toolbox**. The toolbox contains tools that are modal commands, which determine what occurs during "click" and "drag mouse" commands in the workspace. The toolbox is located on the left of the Layout panel.
- **Status bar**. The status bar indicates the current status within the SWiSH application.

The layout of the application window is fairly straightforward (see Figure 30.19).

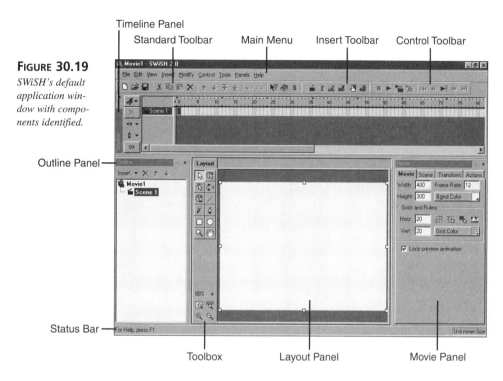

FIGURE 30.19
SWiSH's default application window with components identified.

Timeline Panel

Standard Toolbar   Main Menu   Insert Toolbar   Control Toolbar

Outline Panel

Status Bar

Toolbox   Layout Panel   Movie Panel

Movie Exercise

Now let's get on with Mr. Big's pop-up project. The first thing we want to do is create a new SWiSH SWI file (Ctrl+N) and save it as FMX_popup.swi (File, Save As). Check the Settings for the movie in the lower-right corner of the screen (see Figure 30.20). We want the width set to 400 and the height set to 300. The frame rate should be set at 24, and the background color should be white. The horizontal and vertical grids should be set to 20. Select the Show/Hide Grids button so that the grid lines will appear in the layout. We'll need these to set up our objects on the stage later. Check the Loop Preview Animation check box. Your screen should now look like Figure 30.20.

Adding Text

Next we want to put some text on the Layout panel. Click the Insert Text button on the Insert toolbar or select Insert, Text from the main menu. The panel in the lower-right side of the screen will change to the Text panel and the word *Text* will appear in the middle of the Layout panel. Type **FLASH** (Enter) **MX** (Enter) **Unleashed** in the text area of the Text panel. As you do this, the words will appear also on the Layout panel. You now need to adjust the settings for the text. Select Arial for the type font, set the font size to 48, and then select bold and center the text.

FIGURE 30.20

Movie panel settings and gridlines on the Layout panel.

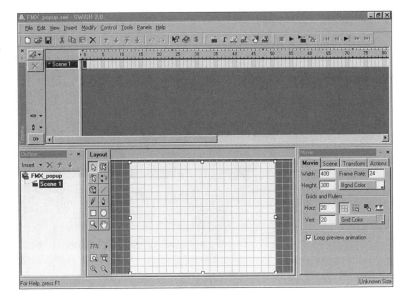

We will now add a special effect to the text. Click the text in the Layout panel to select it. Then right-click and select Effect, Blur. The Blur Settings panel will display. We'll leave the default settings, so select Close. Click the newly created blur effect on the timeline and move it one frame to the right (see Figure 30.21).

FIGURE 30.21

Layout panel with text and special effects added.

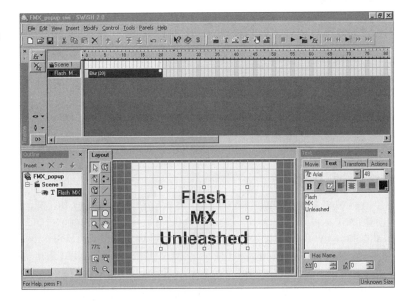

Note that the Outline panel at the lower-left side of the screen now has a text layer added to scene 1. Also note the text layer with the blur effect starting in frame 1 of the timeline.

Adding Images

We now want to add an image the movie pop-up. Download the file `FMX_book_cover.jpg` from the Unleashed companion Web Site, located at `http://www.flashmxunleashed.com`, by navigating to the Chapter 30 section.

Let's now add the image to the Layout panel. Click the Insert Image button on the Insert toolbar or select Insert, Image from the main menu. The panel at the lower-right side of the screen will change to the Shape panel, and an image of the *Flash MX Unleashed* book will appear in the middle of the Layout panel. Click the "book" in the middle of the Layout panel and drag it to the upper-left corner of the screen. Leave about a 5-pixel white border around it from the edge. Now place five more copies of the book image on the screen by repeating this process. We now have the screen filled with covers of the book. You will notice that you covered up the text with the books. We need the text to be on top. Therefore, click the Flash MX Unleashed text layer under scene 1 on the Outline panel. Now click the text box in the center of the Layout panel and then right-click and select Order, Bring to Front. This will bring the text back on top of the book covers. Your screen should now look like Figure 30.22.

FIGURE 30.22

Layout panel with book covers added and the text layer moved back on top.

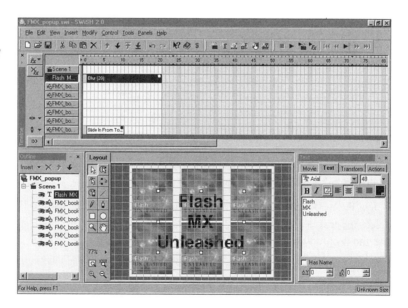

Notice that when you moved the text layer to the front, it also moved from the bottom of the stack of layers to the top of the stack of layers on the Outline panel.

Save this file by either clicking Save (Ctrl+S) on the main menu or selecting File, Save. Let's see what our movie looks like. Click Play on the Control toolbar or select Control, Play Movie from the main menu. It's easy to create text effects with SWiSH.

Adding Special Effects

You've already added a special effect to the text; now let's add some "action" to the book cover images. Click the book cover in the upper-left corner of the Layout panel, being careful not to select the text box. With this cover selected, right-click and select Effect, Slide In, From Top Left. The Slide In From Top Left Settings dialog box will display in the middle of the screen. Leave the default settings alone and click Close. Click the newly created special effect in the Timeline panel and drag it left to the first frame. Select the same book cover figure again and then right-click and select Effect, Move. This will open the Move Settings dialog box. Reset the duration to 20 frames. Click the X Position button and select Move Right By and set it to 135. Click the Y position button and select Move Down By 75 (see Figure 30.23).

FIGURE 30.23

The Move Settings dialog box with selections made.

Close this dialog box and move the newly created Move effect to the right so that the right side of the effect is in frame 42.

Select the next figure to the right in the top-center part of the screen. Be careful not to select the text box. Right-click the image and select Effect, 3D Spin. In the Name box, use the drop-down list to select 3D Spin, Out of Nowhere (see Figure 30.24).

FIGURE 30.24

*The 3D Spin
Settings dialog
box with the Name
drop-down setting
showing the selec-
tion 3D Spin, Out
of Nowhere.*

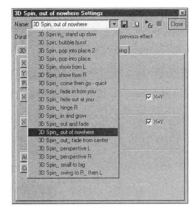

> **Note**
>
> Five other effects—Transform, Squeeze, Alternate, Snake, and Explode—offer
> an additional wide assortment of variations on the basic special effect theme.
> Buy using the many setting options available on the multiple menus in all the
> effects, you can customize these effects to your taste in an almost unlimited
> fashion.

Leave the default settings alone and click Close. Move the newly created 3D Spin, Out
of Nowhere effect to the left so that the right side of the effect is in frame 42.

Click the next book cover image in the upper-right corner of the Layout panel. Right-
click and select Effect, Explode. The Explode Settings dialog box will display in the
middle of the screen. Leave the default settings and click Close. Click the newly created
special effect in the Timeline panel and drag it to the left so that the right side of the
effect is in frame 38.

Click the next book cover image in the lower-left corner of the Layout panel. Right-click
and select Effect, Squeeze. The Squeezer Settings dialog box will display. In the Name
box, use the drop-down box to select Squeeze_Spin. Leave the default settings and click
Close. Click the newly created special effect in the Timeline panel and drag it to the left
so that the right side of the effect is in frame 31.

Click the same book cover image. Right-click and select Effect, Move. The Move
Settings dialog box will display. In the Name box, use the drop-down box to select
Squeeze_Spin. Leave the default settings alone and click Close. Click the newly created
special effect in the Timeline panel and drag it so that the right side of the effect is in
frame 42.

Click the next book cover image at the bottom-center area of the Layout Panel. Right-click and select Effect, Snake. The Snake Settings dialog box will display. Leave the default settings and click Close. Click the newly created special effect in the Timeline panel and drag it to the left so that the right side of the effect is in frame 42.

Click the next book cover image in the lower-right corner of the Layout panel. Right-click and select Effect, Vortex. The Vortex Settings dialog box will display. Leave the default settings and click Close. Click the newly created special effect in the Timeline panel and drag it to the left so that the right side of the effect is in frame 35. Let's take a look at what the screen should now look like (see Figure 30.25).

FIGURE 30.25

All the special effects loaded into the book cover images.

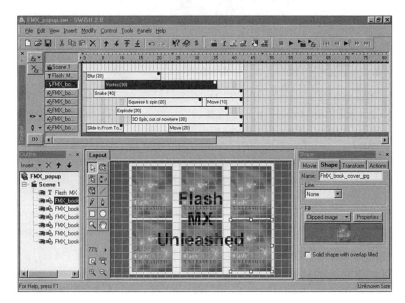

Wow! That was a lot of work. But notice how we were able to create a number of special effects in a relatively short period of time. Save this file again by either clicking Save (Ctrl+S) on the main menu or selecting File, Save. Now let's see what the movie looks like. Click Play on the Control toolbar or select Control, Play Movie from the main menu. Now you get to see a sampling of the eye-catching effects you can easily create with SWiSH.

Adding Sound

Let's continue on with the project for Mr. Big by adding some sound to the movie. For this I have created an MP3 file. You can download the file, New3.mp3, from the Unleashed companion Web site, located at http://www.flashmxunleashed.com, by navigating to the Chapter 30 section.

In the Timeline panel, click frame 1 in scene 1. Then right-click and select Play Sound. This will bring up the Actions panel in the lower-right corner of the screen. Click the Import button and find the New3.mp3 file you downloaded from the Web site (see Figure 30.26).

FIGURE 30.26

The New3.mp3
*sound file added
to the movie.*

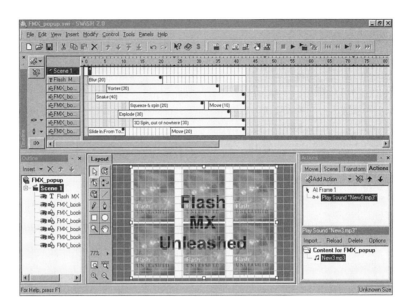

Notice that the New3.mp3 file is now attached to frame 1 in the Actions pane. Notice also the small speaker icon in frame 1 of scene 1 of the timeline.

Save this file again by either clicking Save (Ctrl+S) on the main menu or selecting File, Save. Now let's see what the movie "sounds" like. Click Play on the Control toolbar or select Control, Play Movie from the main menu. Sound effects are easily attached to a SWiSH movie and add an extra dimension.

The next thing we want to do is encourage the viewer of our pop-up ad to buy the book. Create a new scene for the movie by clicking FMX_popup in the Outline panel and then selecting Insert Scene from the Insert toolbar or selecting Insert, Scene from the main menu. Whoa, what happened? Everything disappeared. Don't worry, everything from the first scene is still intact. Click scene 1 in the Outline panel and you will see that everything is still as it should be. Now click scene 2 to start building the "buy" message.

First, we'll add some text on the Layout panel. Click the Insert Text button on the Insert toolbar or select Insert, Text from the main menu. The panel in the lower-right corner of the screen will change to the Text panel and the word *Text* will appear in the middle of

30

FLASH
ALTERNATIVES

the Layout panel. Type **BUY** (Enter) **NOW** (Enter) in the text area of the Text panel. Select Arial for the type font, set the font size to 72, an then select bold and center the text.

Click the text in the Layout panel to select it. Then right click and select Show. This effect will immediately display the text on the screen.

Next, we want to add another copy of the book cover to let the viewers know what we want them to buy. Let's now add the image to the Layout panel. Click the Insert Image button on the Insert toolbar or select Insert, Image from the main menu. The panel in the lower-right corner of the screen will change to the Shape panel, and an image of the *Flash MX Unleashed* book will appear in the middle of the Layout panel. Click the "book" in the middle of the Layout panel.

Click the Flash MX Unleashed text layer under scene 1 on the Outline panel. Now click the text box in the center of the Layout panel and then right-click the mouse and select Order, Bring to Front. This will bring the text back on top of the book covers.

Click the book cover image in the center of the Layout panel. Right-click and select Effect, Transform. The Transform Settings dialog box will display. Set the duration to 30 and click Close. Click the newly created special effect in the Timeline panel and drag it so that the left side of the effect is in frame 1.

Click the BUY NOW text layer under scene 2 on the Outline panel. Now click the text box in the center of the Layout panel and then right-click and select Order, Bring to Front. This will bring the text back on top of the book cover. Your screen should now look like Figure 30.27.

FIGURE 30.27

The text box is now back at the top.

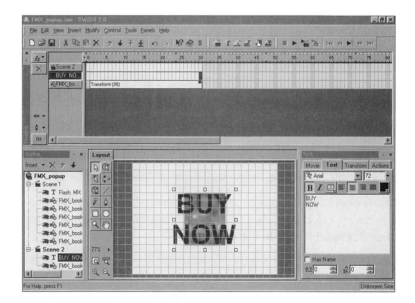

You will notice that the Outline panel shows your work in a truly easy-to-understand outline form. Let's see how the movie is coming along. Click Play on the Control toolbar or select Control, Play Movie from the main menu. Notice that although everything else from scene 1 is cleared when scene 2 begins, the sound file keeps on playing. You can stop the sound when you continue to another scene, but in this case we want it to continue, so leave it alone.

Save the file again by either clicking Save (Ctrl+S) on the main menu or selecting File, Save.

We now have our viewers ready to buy the book, but we offer no way to purchase it. We need to provide them with the means to go to the Sams Web site to buy the book. We'll do that by creating a button. It's easy to do in SWiSH.

Adding a Button

We can create an actual button on the screen or transform an area on the Layout panel into a button. Let's go with the latter option.

Select the BUY NOW text and right-click and select Convert, Convert to Button. You will notice in the Outline panel that all the button states have automatically been formed. Now go to the Actions panel and select the Actions menu. Click the Add Event button and select On Press. The button now converts to Add Action. Select Goto URL. The URL field opens up. Type `http://www.samspublishing.com` in the URL field and press Enter. The URL is added to our script. There you have it (see Figure 30.28)! We now have a link back to the Sams Web site where the viewer (now *shopper*) can go to the shopping area and buy the book. We need to add one more event. Click Add Event and select On Release. Then click Add Action and select Stop. This will stop the movie when it goes to the Web site. Otherwise, it will keep on playing.

FIGURE 30.28

The Actions panel with a URL link back to the Sams Publishing Web site.

Save this file again by either clicking Save (Ctrl+S) on the main menu or selecting File, Save.

Let's see how the finished movie looks. This time we will use Flash Player. Press File, Test, In Player. Our pop-up ad looks a little more impressive in Flash Player. You will notice now that when you place your cursor over the BUY NOW text, it changes to a select mode. Click it. If you are connected to the Internet, you'll be taken to the Sams Publishing Web site. Pretty slick. Figures 30.29 and 30.30 show what scenes 1 and 2 look like in the Flash Player.

FIGURE 30.29

Scene 1 shown in Flash Player 6.

FIGURE 30.30

Scene 2 shown in Flash Player 6.

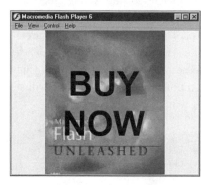

There are still a couple of things we need to do with our pop-up Flash movie project before we send it off to Mr. Big. We need to see how small the file is to ensure that it will not take too long to download. Select File, Test, Report. In the Details dialog box, click Maximize to view the report in full-screen mode. The report is shown here:

```
Filename: FMX_popup.swf
Version: SWF4
File length: 94848 bytes
Frame size: 400 x 300 pixels
```

```
Frame rate: 24.00 frames/sec
Total number of frames: 74 frames

- Entire Movie ----------------------
+     Header:                21 bytes
+     Shapes:        2        77 bytes
+     Images:        1      4749 bytes
+      Fonts:        2      1204 bytes
+      Texts:        2       125 bytes
+     Buttons:       1        89 bytes
+     Sounds:        1     82353 bytes
+     Actions:       1         5 bytes
+   PlaceTags:     325      6021 bytes
+ RemoveTags:      12        48 bytes
+ ShowFrames:      74       148 bytes
+     EndTag:        1         2 bytes
+     Others:        1         8 bytes
------------------------------------
      Total:       423     94850 bytes


- Preload Before Movie ---------------
+     Others:        1         8 bytes
------------------------------------
      Total:         1         8 bytes

- Scene #1 - Scene 1 ----------------
+     Shapes:        1        43 bytes
+     Images:        1      4749 bytes
+      Fonts:        2      1204 bytes
+      Texts:        1        78 bytes
+     Sounds:        1     82353 bytes
+     Actions:       1         5 bytes
+   PlaceTags:     294      5562 bytes
+ RemoveTags:      12        48 bytes
+ ShowFrames:      43        86 bytes
------------------------------------
      Total:       356     94128 bytes

- Scene #2 - Scene 2 ----------------
+     Shapes:        1        34 bytes
+      Texts:        1        47 bytes
+     Buttons:       1        89 bytes
+   PlaceTags:      31       459 bytes
+ ShowFrames:      31        62 bytes
------------------------------------
      Total:        65       691 bytes

- End -------------------------------
+     EndTag:        1         2 bytes
------------------------------------
      Total:         1         2 bytes
```

30

```
- Frame Lengths ---------------------

- Scene #1 - Scene 1 ----------------
     -Frame-      -Bytes-
         0         1206
         1        87374
         2          132
         3          144
         4          142
         5          141
         6          169
         7          167
         8          167
         9          194
        10          192
        11          183
        12          199
        13          221
        14          221
        15          223
        16          219
        17          223
        18          224
        19          224
        20          134
        21           99
        22          103
        23          117
        24          117
        25          117
        26          113
        27          117
        28          117
        29          118
        30          117
        31          108
        32           94
        33           98
        34           98
        35           77
        36           73
        37           73
        38           75
        39           47
        40           47
        41           47
        42           33

- Scene #2 - Scene 2 ----------------
     -Frame-      -Bytes-
         0          255
```

```
         1          19
         2          17
         3          17
         4          17
         5          17
         6          17
         7          17
         8          17
         9          17
        10          17
        11          17
        12          17
        13          17
        14          17
        15          17
        16          17
        17          17
        18          17
        19          17
        20          17
        21          17
        22          17
        23          17
        24          17
        25          17
        26          17
        27          17
        28          17
        29          17
        30          12
- End - - - - - - - - - - - - - - - - - - - - - - - - - - - - - -
                    2
- - - - - - - - - - - - - - - - - - - - - - - - - - - - - - - - -
```

Let's take a look at the report and see what it shows. The first six lines show the basic information about the movie: file ID, SWF version, speed, and so on. Notice that the file size is a little large. Let's investigate this a little further. It appears that the bulk of the size of the file is from the sound file. Everything else is relatively small in comparison. Notice that even though we inserted several instances of the cover image into the movie, it is only being counted once. SWiSH is automatically trying to keep the file size down. Scene 2 is really small, reusing virtually everything it needs from Scene 1. The number of bytes required in scenes 1 and 2 are also outlined. The majority of the load is placed on scene 1, frame 1, where both the sound and graphic image are loaded. You can experiment with the movie to see whether you can come up with a smaller MP3 file to use.

Now close the Details dialog box and select File, Export SWF (Ctrl+E). This will open the Export to SWF dialog box. If you wish to change the filename or save to a different

30

FLASH ALTERNATIVES

directory, then go ahead and do so. Otherwise, just click Save. You have now created the Flash pop-up ad for Mr. Big. Save the SWI file again by either clicking Save (Ctrl+S) on the main menu or selecting File, Save.

Interfacing SWiSH with Other Programs

The SWF files created in SWiSH can, with few exceptions, be used in other programs, such as Flash, FrontPage 2000, Dreamweaver, and PowerPoint. This topic won't be covered in depth here, other than to mention the possibility. However, you can find a tutorial in SWiSH that explores this topic in detail.

SWiSH Conclusion

Once again, we finished the assignment. Mr. Big is happy, and I am back on the beach, another umbrella drink in hand. This time SWiSH 2.0 saved the day!

A few SWI files (under File, SAMPLES) are supplied with SWiSH that show the versatility of the application. FlashKit.com also has quite a number of SWiSH files both in SWI and SWF formats for download and review. Go to
`http://www.flashkit.com/movies/Third_Party/Swish/index.shtml`.

SWiSH doesn't have the number of features that Macromedia Flash MX has, but it does allow you to put together a multimedia application in a jiffy. Once you have the opportunity to work with SWiSH a little more, you'll probably find a number of projects for which SWiSH is the ideal development tool.

SWF Links

By George Gordon

Due to the popularity of Flash, you'll find many Web sites dedicated to the software. These are developed and supported by everyone from individual fans to corporations. These Web sites supply books, chat rooms, communities, files, forums, help, links, news, e-zines, downloads, portals, resources, reviews, sample code, stores, tips, training, and tutorials. Quite frankly, some of the sites are totally indescribable—except to say that they are Flash. It's exhausting just thinking about all this stuff. A very expansive set of resources await you.

This appendix and Appendix B, "SWF Software Tools," provides you with an exhaustive collection of Flash sites on the Net. This list is multinational. A number of the Web sites are in foreign languages. If you need a Web page translated, you can go to the following Web page to translate it:

`http://world.altavista.com/tr/`

No affirmation is given as to the quality or usability of the materials on these Web sites. Every attempt has been made to provide as comprehensive a list as possible. Some sites may have been inadvertently omitted. By following the links listed on many of these sites, you will discover many more sites, because new sites spring up practically every day. Due to the nature of the Internet, some of these sites may be temporarily out of service or withdrawn at any time.

Here's a brief explanation of the information you'll find in Table A.1:

- **Site Name**. The Web site's name.
- **Web Site**. The URL for the Web site.
- **Description**. A brief description of the Web site's content.
- **Skill Level**. An estimate of the target audience of the Web site.
- **Language**. The native language for the site.

A lot of work has gone into these Web sites. Enjoy!

TABLE A.1 SWF Links

Site Name	Web Site	Description	Skill Level	Language
Actionscripts.org	www.actionscripts.org/	Community for Macromedia Flash developers at all skill levels. Offers resources, tutorials, and a means of contact between developers.	All	English
Action-Script.com	www.action-script.com/	News, tutorials, a store, events, a forum, a newsletter, and links.	All	German
Altermind	www.altermind.org/	Tutorials, newsletters, sites, and a forum.	Beg.	English
Asmussen Interactive	www.turtleshell.com/guide/	Tutorials and resource links.	All	English
Canfield Studios	www.canfieldstudios.com/flash3/	Samples and links.	All	English
CBT Cafe	www.cbtcafe.com/	Tutorials.	All	English
Chandesign.net	www.chandesign.net/	Tutorials, news, and links.	All	German
Colin Moock	www.moock.org	Colin Moock's Flash help site.	Adv.	English
Cool Home Pages	www.coolhomepages.com	You can search a database for the best home page designs on the Net. Offers a huge Flash section, as well as message boards and a bookstore.	All	English
Cybercollege	www.cyber-college.de	Tutorials, books, a forum, links, and more.	All	German
Dreamweaver Fever!	dreamweaverfever.com/	News	All	English
EchoEcho	www.echoecho.com/flash.htm	Tutorials, forums, an e-zine, tools, resources, and references.	All	English
eDevBoards	http://www.edevboards.com/forumdisplay.php?forumid=18	Flash and multimedia message boards.	All	English

TABLE A.1 SWF Links

Site Name	Web Site	Description	Skill Level	Language
Eflashy	www24.brinkster.com/eflashy/	All about Flash in Hebrew.	All	Hebrew
Evil Twin	www.eviltwin.co.uk/	News, links, FLA files, and misc.	All	English
Fast Files	www.geocities.com/thefastfiles/	Tutorials and ActionScripting.	Adv.	English
Fay Studios	www.webpagetogo.com/FS/WD/flashtutorials.html	Templates, images, art, and miscellaneous.	Beg.	English
FindTutorials.com	www.findtutorials.com	A list of Flash tutorials.	All	English
Flahoo	www.flahoo.com/	A Flash directory, store, and events.	All	English
Flash 4 All	www.flash4all.de/	Tutorials, sounds, links, and a forum/board.	All	English/German
Flash Official	www.flash.com	Forwards to www.macromedia.com/software/flash/.	All	English
Flasher.ru	flasher.ru/	A Russian site with sources, tutorials, and forums.	All	Russian
Flash Files	www.flashfiles.cjb.net/	Reference, tools, tutorials, tips, and miscellaneous links.	All	English
FlashFilez.com	www.w3source.net/	Book reviews, a forum, links, references, templates, and tutorials.	All	English
Flash Fruit	www.flashfruit.com/	News, ActionScripts, downloads, resources, tutorials, clipart, templates, sounds, freelance work, plug-ins, add-ons, third-party tools, games, a bookstore, software, magazines, forums, interviews, seminars, and miscellaneous.	All	English
Flashgeek	www.flashgeek.com/	News, a forum, a board, and tutorials.	All	English
FlashGuru	www.flashguru.co.uk	News, files, and tutorials.	All	English

TABLE A.1 SWF Links

Site Name	Web Site	Description	Skill Level	Language
Flash Kit	www.flashkit.com	The largest Flash community site on the Web.	All	English
Flashheaven	www.flashheaven.de/	Tutorials, movies, a forum, resources, games, a shop, sites, sounds, and fonts.	All	English/German
FlashLite	www.flashlite.net	News, tutorials, downloads, resources, a community, and a store.	All	English
FlashMaestro Mail List	www.flashmaestro.fm/	News, tutorials, and links.	All	Spanish
Flashmagazine	www.flashmagazine.com/	An e-zine on Flash. Offers articles, tutorials, applications, reviews, and resources.	All	English
FlashMove	www.flashmove.com	A Flash resource developer community. Offers a forum, links, products, books, tips, a calendar, news, newsletters, and events.	All	English
Flashplein	www.flashplein.nl/	Tutorials, FLAs, software, links, books, articles, a forum, sounds, and a gallery.	All	Dutch
FlashPro	www.flashpro.nl/	News, tutorials, FLAs, resources, books, cool sites, projects, a shop, and a forum.	All	English
Flashskills	www.flashskills.com/	A free directory of freelance Flash developers around the world. Searchable by city, province/state, country, current availability of members, and Flash skills.	All	English
FlashThief	www.flashthief.com/	Tutorials, FLA movies, downloads, fonts, sounds, games, news, a showcase, articles, a store, books, and newsletters.	All	English

Table A.1 SWF Links

Site Name	Web Site	Description	Skill Level	Language
Flazoom!	www.flazoom.com	A portal to the Web's coolest Flashers. This is a Web-based e-zine that covers issues relating to Flash, Live Motion, and SVG content on the Web. This site contains news, reviews, books, and more.	All	English
Help4Flash	http://www.help4flash.com/	News, forums, articles, links, contests, tutorials, movies, games, and sounds.	All	English
intelinfo.com	www.intelinfo.com/free_flash_training.html	Free Flash educational and tutorial Web resources.	All	English
ipopper.net	www.ipopper.net/	Movies, scripts, and source code.	All	English
Kirupa.com	www.kirupa.com/developer/index.htm	Tutorials, a gallery, forums, links, a shop, tips, and ActionScripts.	Beg.	English
Mano1	www.mano1.com/mano1_site.php?section=projects	Web site links and 3D Flash.	All	English
MM Flash Basics	www.webreference.com/dev/flash/	Tutorials	Beg.	English
mrhogg.com	www.mrhogg.com/	News, Flash downloads, newsletter.	Adv.	English
OpenSWF.org	www.openswf.org	The source for information on the Flash file format. Here you will find file format specifications, sample code, links to third-party tools, and more.	All	English
Partylogger	www.partylogger.de/	A portal, tutorials, and book reviews.	All	German
Pipey's Flash Resource	www.pipey.ndirect.co.uk/	Chat, forums, tutorials, and free stuff.	All	English
PontoFlash	www.pontoflash.com.br/	A Brazilian Flash site.	All	Portuguese

TABLE A.1 SWF Links

Site Name	Web Site	Description	Skill Level	Language
PopedeFlash	www.popedeflash.com/	Tutorials, a message board, reviews, sample code, newsletters, 3D Flash and models.	All	English
Proflasher	www.proflasher.com/	Links, newsletters, forums, news, articles, chat, and tutorials.	All	English
Quintus Index	www.quintus.org/	Links.	All	English
Shockzone.de	www.shock-zone.de/	Under construction.	All	German
Sousflash.com	www.sousflash.com/	Resources, tutorials, chat, links, and programs.	All	French
Spoono.com	www.spoono.com/	Tutorials, articles, links, a forum, newsletters, and scripts.	All	English
Stickman	www.the-stickman.com/	Flash tutorials and links.	All	English
The Digital Dude	www.xdude.com/	Flash movies/stories, newsletters, email, FAQS and book reviews.	All	English
theFlashAcademy	www.enetserve.com/tutorials	Flash tutorials, examples, templates, and links.	Adv.	English
thelinkz.com	www.thelinkz.com	Articles, links, and books.	All	English
The Flash Challenge	flashchallenge.com	Flash Web site review and comment.	All	English
Training Tools	www.trainingtools.com/	Tutorials, training, tips, products, and resources.	All	English
Treecity	www.treecity.co.uk/	Resources, book reviews, and a store.	All	English
Tutorials.it	www.tutorials.it/search.php?categoria=flash&offset=0	Tutorials.	All	Italian
UBB Developers Network	www.ubbdev.com/	Articles, news, a calendar, reviews, an e-zine, forums, a database, and tutorials.	All	English

TABLE A.1   SWF Links

Site Name	Web Site	Description	Skill Level	Language
Ultrashock	www.ultrashock.com/	Tips, tutorials, entertainment, FLAs, code, links, goodies, a shop, and forums.	All	English
Virtual F/X	www.virtual-fx.net	A Flash help site for developers dealing with effects.	All	English
Warp 9	www.warp9.it/	News, tutorials, a forum, links, newsletters, games, FLAs, and audio.	All	Italian
Webmonkey	hotwired.lycos.com/ webmonkey/multimedia/ shockwave_flash/ index.html	Tutorials and links.	All	English
We're Here	66.70.72.50	A Flash help site that includes tutorials, articles, FLAs, forums, games, links, resources, and sound loops.	All	English
Leogeo	leogeo.com/	Flash examples.	All	English

SWF Software Tools

By George Gordon

Many software tools are currently available on the market that create, convert, or use Flash (SWF) files. These tools may be able to provide certain capabilities as well as time and/or cost advantages you're looking for as a developer. This listing of software programs and utilities is provided as a convenient resource. No affirmation is given as to the quality or usability of these programs. Every attempt has been made to provide as comprehensive a list as possible. Some products may have been inadvertently omitted. Due to the nature of the software industry, some of these products may be withdrawn at any time.

Here is a brief explanation of the information provided in Table B.1:

- **Program**. The name of the product and the release level at its time of publication.
- **Vendor**. The name of the company that developed the product.
- **Web Site**. The Web site where you can find additional information and downloads as well as make purchases.
- **Description**. A brief description of the software or utility as it relates to Flash. Additional capabilities may also be available. Check the vendor's Web site for further details.

Some of these software tools were developed for certain releases of Flash, and their functions may have been incorporated in the more recent releases of Flash. Most of these software tools are available as shareware or demos or can be evaluated on a try-before-you-buy basis. It's recommended that you try out the software to make sure it meets your specific needs.

TABLE B.1 SWF Software Tools

Program	Vendor	Web Site	Description
FLASH EMBEDDER	NetKontoret	echoecho.com/toolflashembedder.htm	This online tool provides an easy alternative to using Aftershock for embedding Flash movies into HTML.
Flash Saver Maker 1.51	Zbsoft.net	www.zbsoft.net	Used to create a screensaver from any SWF file.
KoolMoves 3.0	KoolMoves.com	www.koolmoves.com	Web animation software for creating Flash-animated content.
Makaha 4.5	Brandyware Software	www.brandyware.com	A graphic viewer, graphic compressor, GIF animation program, video viewer, slide show, and graphic editor, all in one package.
SoundClick Designer Studio 1.0	SoundClick	www.soundclick.com	Used to create Flash animations for your favorite MP3 files.
Bundle 1	3rd Eye Solutions	www.flashjester.com	Bundle 1 contains Entertainor, JAvi, JEmail, JNetCheck, JPrintor, JSave, JShapor, JTools, JStart, Jugglor, JWeb, and Woof.
Bundle 2	3rd Eye Solutions	www.flashjester.com	Contains all of Bundle 1 plus Creator Pro.
Bundle 3	3rd Eye Solutions	www.flashjester.com	Contains all of Bundle 1 plus Creator Standard.
Creator Pro	3rd Eye Solutions	www.flashjester.com	Used to create screensavers from your Flash Projector files.

B

SWF SOFTWARE TOOLS

TABLE B.1 Continued

Program	Vendor	Web Site	Description
Creator Standard	3rd Eye Solutions	www.flashjester.com	Used to create screensavers from your Flash Projector files.
Entertainor	3rd Eye Solutions	www.flashjester.com	You can play any Projector files as screensavers and also have a MIDI file playing in the background.
JAvi	3rd Eye Solutions	www.flashjester.com	Used to launch AVIs from your Flash file.
JEmail	3rd Eye Solutions	www.flashjester.com	Starts up the user's default e-mail editor with the e-mail address you specify.
JNetCheck	3rd Eye Solutions	www.flashjester.com	Used to check whether a user is on the Internet.
JPrintor	3rd Eye Solutions	www.flashjester.com	Prints out a Flash screen.
JSave	3rd Eye Solutions	www.flashjester.com	Saves text entered into Flash to a text file on the hard drive.
JShapor	3rd Eye Solutions	www.flashjester.com	Shapes a Projector file in the exact shape you want it.
JTools/JStart	3rd Eye Solutions	www.flashjester.com	Provides nine add-ons for Projector files. Fscommand enhancer.
Jugglor	3rd Eye Solutions	www.flashjester.com	Used to customize and compress Projector files for optimum performance.

TABLE B.1 Continued

Program	Vendor	Web Site	Description
JWeb	3rd Eye Solutions	www.flashjester.com	Used to open different Web links from within your Flash file in the same browser window.
Woof	3rd Eye Solutions	www.flashjester.com	Used to save SWF files to view offline.
Adobe AfterEffects 5.5	Adobe Systems Inc.	www.adobe.com	Used to create motion graphics and visual effects and to import SWF files.
Adobe Illustrator 10	Adobe Systems Inc.	www.adobe.com	Vector graphics illustrator with enhanced SWF support.
Adobe LiveMotion 1.0	Adobe Systems Inc.	www.adobe.com	Used to create dynamic, interactive content in a variety of formats, including SWF.
Flash Typer 2.0	Andreas Hillberg	www.hillberg.nu/flash/	Converts FLA and SWF files generated on the PC platform to work on a Mac.
XML Tree	Basil28	www.basil28.com/tree/	Provides a very simple way to create a tree view in Flash and to administrate it.
e-Picture Pro 2.0.1	Beatware, Inc.	www.beatware.com	Advanced animation and custom video for the Web. Saved in SWF format.
eZ-Motion	Beatware, Inc.	www.beatware.com	Used to create Web animations and graphics and save them in SWF format.

B

SWF SOFTWARE
TOOLS

TABLE B.1 Continued

Program	Vendor	Web Site	Description
SoftwareASP Flash Turbine 5.0	Blue*Pacific Software	www.blue-pac.com/	Generates dynamic Flash content from ASP scripts. Uses Flash for the visuals, ASP scripting for the content access—a great combination.
Direct Flash Turbine 5.0	Blue*Pacific Software	www.blue-pac.com/	A high-performance, template-based version of Flash Turbine with easy-to-use dynamic Flash generation capabilities.
PHP Flash Turbine 5.0	Blue*Pacific Software	www.blue-pac.com/	A dynamic Flash solution designed for the powerful and fast PHP scripting platform.
Turbine Video Encoder v1.0	Blue*Pacific Software	www.blue-pac.com/	Used to create low bit-rate streaming Flash video.
Action Script Viewer v2.0	Burak KALAYCI & Manitu Group	buraks.com/	ASV lets you view the ActionScripts in SWF files. ASV decompiles the ActionScripts and presents text output that can be compiled. With ASV you can also browse the internals of a SWF file and see instance names, frame labels, and so on. Also, movie clips can be extracted as SWF files.

TABLE B.1 Continued

Program	Vendor	Web Site	Description
Swifty Utilities	Burak KALAYCI & Manitu Group	buraks.com/	Offers eight *free* utilities for SWF files, such as the ability to unprotect and extract movie clips, batch projector creation, and so on. Also, a free utility is available to extract SWF files from Flash projectors and extract DXR files from Director projectors.
URL Action Editor v2.0	Burak KALAYCI & Manitu Group	buraks.com/	UAE lets you edit getURL, LoadMovie, UnloadMovie, LoadVariables, and FScommand actions in SWF files. Also you can hide/swap any symbol in a SWF file.
Gypsee Pro 1.8	Casperlab Software	www.casperlab.com	An animated musical GIF and Flash SWF creator.
CoffeeCup Button Factory 6.0	CoffeeCup Software, Inc.	www.coffeecup.com	Used to make Flash buttons from GIF or JPG images.
CoffeeCup Firestarter 4.2	CoffeeCup Software, Inc.	www.coffeecup.com	Used to create Flash effects for your Web site.
CoffeeCup GIF Animator 6.1	CoffeeCup Software, Inc.	www.coffeecup.com	Used to create animated GIFs and save them as Flash SWFs.
CoffeeCup HTML Editor 9.1	CoffeeCup Software, Inc.	www.coffeecup.com	A Web utility with Flash Effects Wizard and Flash tag-insertion capabilities.

B

SWF SOFTWARE TOOLS

TABLE B.1   Continued

Program	Vendor	Web Site	Description
Fluition 1.52	Confluent Technologies, Inc.	www.fluition.com	Used to create dynamic media presentations.
Corel R.A.V.E.	Corel Corporation	www.corel.com	Part of the CorelDRAW 10 Graphics Suite.
CorelDRAW 10 Graphics Suite	Corel Corporation	www.corel.com	This application includes RAVE, a powerful vector-based animation program that allows for the importing and exporting of SWF files.
Flash Image Builder 3.2	Crazy Ivan Productions, Ltd.	www.gfx2swf.com/	Used to create Flash movie Web buttons, logos, banner ads, and slideshows for a Web site.
Gif2Swf 2.1	Crazy Ivan Productions, Ltd.	www.gfx2swf.com/	Used to convert animated or static GIF files to the SWF format.
SWiSH 2.0	DJJ Holdings Pty Ltd.	www.swishzone.com	Used to produce complex animations with text, images, graphics, and sound in no time and to save them in SWF format.
SWiSH Lite 1.5	DJJ Holdings Pty Ltd.	www.swishzone.com	A standalone Windows application designed to make animated text effects and to export them in SWF format.
Rain Editor 1.21	Editspeed Software, Inc.	www.editspeed.com/	You can make Flash movies with particle system fast and conveniently.

TABLE B.1 Continued

Program	Vendor	Web Site	Description
Swift 3D LW v1.00	Electric Rain, Inc.	www.swift3d.com	A vector-rendering plug-in for LightWave 3D.
Swift 3D MAX v1.00	Electric Rain, Inc.	www.swift3d.com	A plug-in for rendering 3D scenes directly to popular file formats, including SWF.
Swift 3D v2.00	Electric Rain, Inc.	www.swift3d.com	Used to create vector-based 3D animations.
Swift 3D XSI v1.00	Electric Rain, Inc.	www.swift3d.com	A powerful and versatile vector-rendering plug-in for Softimage XSI.
FLASHtyper	Flash Kit	www.flashkit.com	A text animation tool for creating SWF files.
FMPlayer 1.0	FLASHANTS, Inc.	www.flashants.com	Enables Flash to embed video. You can also play native video in Flash.
FMProjector 1.2	FLASHANTS, Inc.	www.flashants.com	Used to integrate Flash and video to create highly interactive, rich-media content.
SWF2Video Version 0.91	FLASHANTS, Inc.	www.flashants.com	Used to convert from Flash to AVI, including movie clips.
Windowless Flash Service	FLASHANTS, Inc.	www.flashants.com	Bring Flash out of the window! You can create a desktop agent and an application UI.
1 Cool Button Tool - Flash 1.5	Formula Software Pty Ltd.	www.buttontool.com	Used to make buttons, navigational tools, and menus in both Java and Flash.

B

SWF SOFTWARE TOOLS

TABLE B.1   Continued

Program	Vendor	Web Site	Description
Clipyard 0.84 Beta version	Goldshell Digital Media, Inc.	www.goldshell.com	A utility for combining multiple Shockwave effects into one bigger SWF file.
DirSaver Version 4.20	Goldshell Digital Media, Inc.	www.goldshell.com	Creates a screensaver and an installer out of your Macromedia Director projector.
FlashForge 5.41	Goldshell Digital Media, Inc.	www.goldshell.com	Creates screensavers from Macromedia Flash files.
FlaX 1.31	Goldshell Digital Media, Inc.	www.goldshell.com	A utility for creating text effects for Macromedia Flash.
FlareAnimation SWFlet 1.01	iMEDIA Builders	www.imediabuilders.com	Used to make GIF or JPG animations by sequencing images.
FlareBanner SWFlet 1.01	iMEDIA Builders	www.imediabuilders.com	Used to create banner ads.
FlareText SWFlet 1.01	iMEDIA Builders	www.imediabuilders.com	Used to create text effects.
FlareWorks Express 1.01	iMEDIA Builders	www.imediabuilders.com	Used to create Flash content from provided templates. You can modify object properties such as text, font, colors, and images.
iMB FlareWorks Professional 1.01	iMEDIA Builders	www.imediabuilders.com	Used to create interactive buttons, menus, banners, slideshows, presentations, animations, and Web sites in Flash.
iMB PageFlasher 1.0	iMEDIA Builders	www.imediabuilders.com	Used to create HTML documents for any Flash (SWF) file.

Table B.1 Continued

Program	Vendor	Web Site	Description
IncrediMail	IncrediMail Ltd.	www.incredimail.com	The new e-mail generation.
FlashDB v1.5	J. Kessels	www.kessels.com/	A small database for Flash 4 and 5 written in Perl. Counter and Chat examples are included in the download.
Form2Flash	J. Kessels	www.kessels.com/	Uses HTML forms to change Flash movies.
vid2flash Beta 1.3	Javakitty Media, Inc.	www.javakitty.com/	Used to convert video format files into Flash files.
FlashBlaster2	KRAM LLC.	www.screamdesign.com	Used to create screens, parts, banners, albums, and effects. Individual charges apply for each Flash file created.
AVI Decomposer v1	Live Tronix, Inc.	www.livetronix.com	Used to convert each frame of an AVI file to a JPG image and to convert the audio track from a movie to a WAV sound file. Offers multiple-stream support.
SWF Convert SE v1.1	Live Tronix, Inc.	www.livetronix.com	Used to convert an image to the SWF format in real time on your Web server.
SWF Convert Server Professional 1.2.3	Live Tronix, Inc.	www.livetronix.com	An ActiveX control for use in ASP/CFM Web pages. Provides an interface for converting image files to the SWF format.

B

SWF Software Tools

TABLE B.1 Continued

Program	Vendor	Web Site	Description
SWF Convert Server Standard 1.2.3	www.livetronix.com Live Tronix, Inc.		An ActiveX control for use in ASP/CFM Web pages. Provides an interface for converting image files to the SWF format.
SWF Convert v1.2.3	Live Tronix, Inc.	www.livetronix.com	Used to convert images, audio, and movie files straight to the SWF format.
SWF Scanner 2.6.3	Live Tronix, Inc.	www.livetronix.com	Used to extract sounds, ActionScript, and images. You can swap or exchange images within a SWF file without the need for the original FLA file.
Loris Vector Map Engine (LVME) 2.01	Loris Ltd.	lorissoft.com/index.htm	A Flash map engine (any maps can be loaded into it) and JavaScript bridge that connects static or dynamic (for example, from a database) outputs and Flash maps.
Director 8.5 Shockwave Studio	Macromedia, Inc.	www.macromedia.com	Used to create 3D entertainment, interactive product demonstrations, and online learning applications.
Fireworks MX	Macromedia, Inc.	www.macromedia.com	Used to create, optimize, and export interactive graphics in a single, Web-centric environment.

TABLE B.1 Continued

Program	Vendor	Web Site	Description
Flash Writer 4.0	Macromedia, Inc.	www.macromedia.com	This plug-in for Adobe Illustrator allows it to export Flash files.
FreeHand 10	Macromedia, Inc.	www.macromedia.com	Used to create illustrations, design and organize Web site storyboards, and lay out graphics-rich documents in a multipage workspace. You can produce Macromedia Flash movies and test them right inside of FreeHand with the new Flash Navigation Panel.
Macromedia eLearning Suite	Macromedia, Inc.	www.macromedia.com	Contains Macromedia Authorware 6, Flash MX, and Dreamweaver MX.
Macromedia Flash MX	Macromedia, Inc.	www.macromedia.com	You can use Flash MX to create rich Internet content and applications.
Macromedia Studio MX	Macromedia, Inc.	www.macromedia.com	This package is composed of Dreamweaver MX, Macromedia Flash MX, Fireworks MX, FreeHand 10, ColdFusion MX Developer Edition (Windows Only), and Macromedia Flash Player 6.
Magic Flare 1.0	MagicFlare, Epinoisis software	www.magicflare.com	Used to create text in Flash, without programming knowledge.

TABLE B.1 Continued

Program	Vendor	Web Site	Description
3D Flash Animator 3.5	Mofosoft Pty Ltd.	`www.insanetools.com`	Used to create Flash animations and games.
Flash Cam 1.66	Nexus Concepts	`www.nexusconcepts.com`	Used to record demonstration or training "movies" using screen captures and output to streaming Flash files.
SWF Studio 1.0 Build 1591	Northern Codeworks	`www.northcode.com`	Used to create standalone projectors and screensavers, with SWF support.
Flash Command Line Tools v5.0	Ophelus.com	`flashtools.net/`	Fully functional freeware tools available for Flash's Projector and/or the default viewer (`flash-pla.exe`) that allow Flash to manipulate windows.
Flash-O-Lizer 1.0	Rubberduck	`www.shareamp.com/content/download/`	A WinAmp (v.2.x) visualizer plug-in. Used to create visualizers for WinAmp.
Sothink Glanda 2001	SourceTec Software Co., Ltd.	`www.sothink.com`	A step-by-step wizard that provides a quick and easy way to add Flash animations to your Web site.
FAST! Flash ActionScript Tool, Public Beta 2	SwiffTOOLS BV Multimedia	`www.swifftools.com`	Aids you in creating, editing, organizing, and exchanging your ActionScripts, easier and faster.

TABLE B.1 Continued

Program	Vendor	Web Site	Description
Screenweaver 1.02 Freeware Edition	SwiffTOOLS BV Multimedia	screenweaver.com/index.htm	Used to create screensavers from Flash files.
Screenweaver v.2.05	SwiffTOOLS BV Multimedia	www.swifftools.com	Used to create screensavers from Flash files instantly.
SWF-Browser v.2.93	SwiffTOOLS BV Multimedia	www.swifftools.com	Used to browse through a SWF file's "guts." You can extract many parts from the file, including bitmaps, sounds, and movie clips.
SwiffCANVAS v.1.0, Final Release	SwiffTOOLS BV Multimedia	www.swifftools.com	A tool for preparing Flash Projector files for final distribution.
SwiffPEG SERVER, Private Beta	SwiffTOOLS BV Multimedia	www.swifftools.com	Does exactly what the regular version of SwiffPEG does—but now on the fly, at your NT server (account).
SwiffPEG v.1.0	SwiffTOOLS BV Multimedia	www.swifftools.com	Used to convert an MP3 file into a SWF file.
Swift Generator	Swift Tools	www.swift-tools.com	A content generator that aims at dynamically replacing text, fonts, sounds, images, and movie clips in either a template file or a standard Flash file. It can also dynamically change action parameters in either frames or buttons.

TABLE B.1   Continued

Program	Vendor	Web Site	Description
Swift-MP3 v2.1	Swift Tools	www.swift-tools.com	A utility that converts MP3 files into Flash files containing pure streaming audio data.
Bitbull v4.0	Wanpatan Software Lab	www.wanpatan.com	Turns Flash and Director projectors into screensavers.
Wildform Flix	Wildform, Inc.	www.wildform.com	This tool converts a wide variety of video, audio, and image formats to the SWF format.
Wildform SWfx	Wildform, Inc.	www.wildform.com	An easy-to-use SWF text animation tool.
Xara X 1.0c DL2	Xara Ltd.	www.xara.com	An advanced graphic illustration package for Windows.

INDEX

Debugger, *567-569*
mislabeled target paths, *571-573*
Output window, *559-560*
property values, *574-575*
variable values, *574-575*
variables, *564-566*
Watcher, *569-570*

built-in functions, 409-410

call, *410-411*
conversion, *412-413*
depreciated, *414*
chr, 414
int, 415
length, 415
mbchr, 415
mblength, 415
mbord, 416
mbsubstring, 416
ord, 416
random, 416
substring, 417
mathematical, *413-414*

Bundle 1 Web site, 939
Bundle 2 Web site, 939
Bundle 3 Web site, 939
Button class, 504
Button object, 855
button symbols, 108-110
buttons

Actions panel, *285-286*
Add Motion Guide, *215*
controlling movie clips with, *123-124, 126*
creating, *126-129, 484-486*
creating interactivity with, *119-122*
feedback, *367-371*
fire, creating, *630*
labels, creating, *460*
Render Text as HTML (Line Type menu), *528*
Selectable (Line Type menu), *528*
Show Border Around Text (Line Type menu), *528*

SWiSH movies, *923-928*
writing event handlers for, *484-486*

C

call function, 410-411
call script (User-Defined Functions), 806
calling functions, 256-258
Canfield Studios Web site, 931
Capabilities object, 855
carriage returns

embedded movies, *765*
HTML files, *771*

case script (Conditions/Loops), 795
case sensitivity, PHP, 738
case statement, 348-350
Category option (Save As dialog box), 9
CBT Cafe Web site, 931
Center Frame option, timeline, 88
CGI (Common Gateway Interface), 760
Chandesign.net Web site, 931
Change Handler parameter, 453

CheckBox component, *455*
ComboBox component, *456*
ListBox component, *458*
RadioButton component, *461*

CHAR data type, 751
charAt function, indexing string characters, 297
charCodeAt function, indexing string characters, 303-304
Check Syntax (expert mode only) button (Action panel), 286

Check Syntax option (Actions panel), 288
CheckBox component, 449, 455-456
chr function, 414
circles, drawing, 55
classes, 240-241, 504

ActionScript, *664*
Button, *504*
definition, *240*
methods, *504*
MovieClip, *504*
NetDebug, *675, 683*
NetServices, *675*
properties, *504*

clearInterval script (Miscellaneous Actions), 809
Click Accuracy option (Preferences dialog box Editing tab), 35
Click Handler parameter

passing component information to ActionScript, *467-471*
PushButton component, *459*

client/server objects, 504, 855
Clipboard tab (Preferences dialog box), 35-37
Clipyard 0.84 Beta version Web site, 946
Close Large option (Paint Bucket tool), 56
Close Medium option (Paint Bucket tool), 56
Close Panel option (Actions panel), 289
Close Small option (Paint Bucket tool), 56
CMYK Color Picker, 61
code

Account Management System example, *674-683*
comments. *See* comments
hinting (ActionSctip Editor), *17*

View menu
- *Antialias, 42*
- *Antialias Text, 42*
- *Fast, 42*
- *Go To, 41*
- *Grid, 42*
- *Guides, 43*
- *Hide Edges, 44*
- *Hide Panels, 44*
- *Magnification, 41*
- *Outlines, 42*
- *Rulers, 42*
- *Show All, 41*
- *Show Frame, 41*
- *Show Shape Hints, 44*
- *Show Streaming, 179, 600*
- *Snap to Objects, 44, 54, 158*
- *Snap to Pixels, 44*
- *Timeline, 42*
- *Work Area, 42*
- *Zoom In, 41*
- *Zoom Out, 41*

Window menu
- *Actions, 180, 231*
- *Align, 29, 594*
- *Components, 12, 448*
- *Info, 596*
- *Library, 230*
- *NetConnect, 683*
- *Save Panel Layout, 29*
- *Scene, 179*
- *Toolbars, 92*

comments, 331
- ActionScript, 741
- PHP, 741

Common Gateway Interface. *See* CGI

comparison operators, 277, 337-338
- equality operator (==), 338, 828
- greater than (>), 339, 830

greater than equal to(>=), 339, 831
- inequality (!=), 826
- inequality operator (!=), 338
- less than (<), 338, 827
- less than equal to (<=), 339, 827
- strict equality (===) operator, 339, 829
- strict inequality (!==) operator, 340, 826

comparison variables, 316-318

compatibility, 10-11

Component Definition dialog box, 477

Component Parameters panel, 452-453

components, 11, 448-449, 454, 665-667
- adding to movies, 449-450
  - *with ActionScript, 450-451*
  - *manually, 450*
- appearance, 471
  - *changing manually, 471-472*
  - *changing with ActionScript, 472-474*
  - *registerSkinElement method, 474-476*
- Change Handler parameter, 453
- CheckBox, 449, 455-456
- ComboBox, 449, 456-457
  - *creating color lists, 457*
  - *keystrokes, 456*
  - *parameters, 456*
- creating, 11-13, 476-478
- disadvantages of, 478
- Initial Value parameter, 453
- Label parameter, 453
- Label Placement parameter, 453
- ListBox, 449, 457-459

passing information to ActionScript, 467
- *Click Handler parameter, 467-471*
- *get methods, 468-471*
- PushButton, 449, 459-460
- RadioButton, 449, 460-462
- resources, 478-479
- ScrollBar, 449, 463
  - *creating dynamic text boxes, 464*
  - *parameters, 463*
- ScrollPane, 449, 464-466
- setting parameters, 452
  - *ActionScript, 454*
  - *manually, 452-453*

Components command (Window menu), 12, 448

Components panel, 665-667

compound animation, 126-129

Compress Movie option (Publish Settings Flash tab), 193

compression files, 141
- AIFF, 145
- MP3, 145
- sound, 141-143
- WAV, 145

Compression menu commands
- ADPCM, 142
- Default, 141
- MP3, 142
- Raw, 141
- Speech, 142

concat function, joining strings, 296

concat method, 430-431

Conditional (?:) operator, 834

D

Dashed option (Stroke Style dialog box), 51
data
changing in variables, 313
interfacing with text, 543-544
external text format, 544-545
HTML, 548-550
JavaScript, 550-553
scrolling, 545-548
management
ASP integration, 688-691, 704-706
condensing data, 707, 710-711, 716, 721
Flash/ASP hybrid environments, 700-702
sending data from Flash to ASP, 691-694
sending data to Flash from ASP, 694-700
processing, 767-768
requests, 766
retrieval, ASP, 704-706
data form variable, 773
data format (Flash movies), 764-765
Data parameter
ComboBox component, 456
ListBox component, 458
RadioButton component, 461
data types, 258, 292
arrays. *See* arrays
Boolean, 292, 309-310
MovieClip, 292, 310-311
MySQL, 751
Null, 292
numbers, 292, 305-306
creating, 306
math constants, 308-309
MAX VALUE, 307-308
MIN_VALUE, 307-308
NaN, 307

NEGATIVE_INFINITY, 308
POSITIVE_INFINITY, 308
repeating decimal points, 306-307
Object, 292, 311
strings, 292-293
creating, 293
empty, 293
indexing characters in, 296-304
joining, 295-296
length property, 297-298
literal, 293-294, 304-305
undefined, 310
data variable, 678
databases, 702-703
Access, integration with ASP, 708-716
Account Management System application, 671
ADO, 703-704
Connection object, 703-704
data management in ASP, 704-706
data retrieval in ASP, 704-706
Recordset object, 703-704
MySQL
columns, 751
connecting PHP to, 754-756
creating, 749
creating new users, 750
creating tables, 752
data types, 751
describing tables, 752-753
entering information into tables, 752-753
granting permissions, 750-751
PHP, 748-756
selecting data from tables, 753-754

showing, 749-750
showing table contents, 753
showing tables, 752
PHP storage, 747
RDBMS (relational database management system), 748
DATE data type, 751
date objects, 507-511
methods, 866
general, 866
get, 867-876
set, 876-883
new Date Constructor, 865-866
Debug menu, modem speeds, 182
Debug options (Actions panel), 286
Debugger, 567-569
debugging. *See also* **troubleshooting**
Account Management System example, 683
ActionScript, 556
naming conventions, 557-559
trace action, 557
identifying bugs, 559
Bandwidth Profiler, 561-564
Debugger, 567-569
mislabeled target paths, 571-573
Output window, 559-560
property values, 574-575
variable values, 574-575
variables, 564-566
Watcher, 569-570
remote locations, 575
enabling remote debugging, 576
from servers, 577-578
Debugging Permitted option (Publish Settings Flash tab), 192

Guides, 43-44
Import Video, 229, 235
Import Video Settings, 229-230
Insert Target Path, 125, 174, 231
Layer Properties, 153, 159
Linkage Properties, 495, 517-518
Move Settings, 918-919
New Symbol, 173, 229, 601
PNG import settings, 235
Preferences, 33
  ActionScript Editor tab, 37
  Clipboard tab, 35-37
  Editing tab, 35
  General tab, 33-34
  Warnings tab, 37
Publish Settings, 9, 141-143, 204, 236, 576, 612
Rectangle Settings, 230
Remote Debug, 577-578
Round Rectangle Radius, 54
Save As, 11, 910
Save As Template, 9-10
Select External Editor, 13
Slide In From Top Left Settings, 918
Snake Settings, 920
Sound Properties, 141-142, 144
Squeezer Settings, 919
Stroke Style, 50-51
Trace Bitmap, 82
Transform Settings, 922
Dictionary Reference Guide (Actions panel), 283
Diffusion option (Publish Settings dialog box GIF tab), 197
Digital Dude Web site, 935
digital video. *See* **video**
digital videos, 228, 234, 229-232

Dimensions option
  Document Properties dialog box, 26
  Publish Settings dialog box GIF tab, 195-196, 201, 206
Direct Flash Turbine 5.0 Web site, 942
Director 8.5 Shockwave Studio Web site, 948
directories
  Account Management System application, 670-671
  PHP, 738
DirSaver Version 4.20 Web site, 946
Display Menu option (Publish Settings dialog box HTML tab), 202
displaying time with Date object, 507-509, 511
Distort option (Free Transform tool), 69-70
Distribute button (Align panel), 30
Distribute to Layers feature, 5-6
distributive tweening, 95
Dither option (Publish Settings dialog box GIF tab), 197
Dither Solids option (Publish Settings dialog box GIF tab), 197
division (/) operator, 814-815
division assignment (/=) operator, 818
DLLs, Visual Basic, 773
do loops, 277
do while loop, 354-355
do while loops, 277, 279
do while script (Conditions/Loops), 797
Document command (Modify menu), 25, 225, 235, 594
Document Properties command (Modify menu), 368

Document Properties dialog box, 26, 174, 225, 235
document type definition. *See* **DTDs**
documents, saving as templates, 9-10
domains, PHP scripts, 739-740
dot (.) operator, 259
dot syntax, 259-260, 324
Dotted option (Stroke Style dialog box), 51
DOUBLE data type, 751
Down arrow keystroke
  ComboBox component, 456
  ListBox component, 458
Drag Content parameter (ScrollPane component), 465
Drag Me GENERATE dialog box, 902-904, 908-910
drag-and-drop interactions, creating, 583-589, 593
draggable objects
  creating, 580-582-589, 593
  masks, creating, 602-603, 605
drawing
  primitive objects, 75
  rectangles, 54-55, 75
  squares, 54-55
  stars, 75
Drawing Settings area (Preferences dialog box Editing tab), 35
Dreamweaver Fever Web site, 931
drop-down menus (Actions panel), 281
Dropper tool, 51
dropTarget property, 846
DTDs (document type definition), 762
duplicateMovieClip action, 384
duplicateMovieClip script (Movie Clip Control), 789

gradients

applying to objects, 56

creating, 62-63

modifying, 62-63

Transform Fill tool, 63-64

Gradients area (Preferences dialog box Clipboard tab), 36

Gradients drop-down menu (Preferences dialog box Clipboard tab), 36

graphics, 48

Arrow tool, 49

ASP, 724

bitmap

importing, 80

Lasso tool, 80-81

Swap Bitmap feature, 83

trace, 82-83

bitmaps, 81-82

Brush tool, 65-66

drawing primitive items, 75

Dropper tool, 51

effects, 79

Eraser tool, 66-67

Faucet tool, 67

Fireworks, integration with Flash MX, 13-15

Ink Bottle tool, 51

Line tool, 49-50

moving primitive items, 75

objects, 244

Oval tool, 55

Paint Bucket tool, 55-56

Pen tool. *See* Pen tool

Pencil tool, 52-53

placing primitive items on top of each other, 76

Rectangle tool, 53-54

drawing rectangles, 54-55

drawing squares, 54-55

rectangles. *See* rectangles

squares. *See* squares

Subselection tool, 49

symbols, 104-105

creating, 105-108

instances, 106

Library panel, 107

Transform Fill tool, 63-64

vector, 22

gravity effect, easing technique, 219-221

greater than equal to operator (>=), 339, 831

greater than operator (>), 339, 830

Grid command (View menu), 42

Grid dialog box, 43

Group Name parameter (RadioButton component), 461

groups, objects, 77-79

Guides command (View menu), 43

Guides dialog box, 43-44

Gypsee Pro 1.8 Web site, 943

H

Hairline option (Stroke Style dialog box), 50

Hand tool, 74

handlers, 482-483

actions

buttons, 484-486

movie clips, 487-488

ActionScript, 483-484

creating buttons, 484-486

methods, 484-485, 487-488, 492

attachMovie action, 494-496

buttons, 484-486

movie clips, 487-488

writing, 492-493

movie clips, 487-489, 491-492

onClipEvent, 484, 488-489, 766-767

onEnterFrame, 489

onLoad, 489

onMouseMove, 490

onUnload, 489

Prototype object, 496-501

trace actions, 485-487

user-controlled, 490

writing, 483

buttons, 484-486

movie clips, 484, 488-490

Hatched option (Stroke Style dialog box), 51

Heads Up Display (HUD) layer, 635

Height option (Grid dialog box), 43

height property, 848

Help (FLASH*typer*), 901

Help option (Actions panel), 289

Help4Flash Web site, 934

Hide Edges command (View menu), 44

Hide Panels command (View menu), 44

High/Low toggle (FLASH*typer*), 901

Highlight Color option (Preferences dialog box General tab), 34

hinting feature (ActionScript editor), 364

hit detection (games)

code, 632

updates, 636-637

hitCheck(thisEnemy) function, 633

Home keystroke

ComboBox component, 456

ListBox component, 458

Horizontal parameter (ScrollBar component), 463

Horizontal Scroll parameter (ScrollPane component), 465

horizontal scrolling, 546-548

N

Component Parameters, setting component parameters, 452-453
Components, 665-667
FS commands, 205
Info, 31-32, 596
Layers, 79
layouts, 29
Library, 129-131
Macintoshes, 27
Properties
 setting component parameters, 452-453
 Text tool, 526
Reference, 17
SWiSH, 914
timeline. *See* timeline
Transform, 32
Windows, 27
parameters, 392-393
Align panel, 29-30
Click Handler, passing component information to AcrionScript, 467-471
components
 Change Handler parameter, 453
 CheckBox, 455
 ComboxBox, 456
 Initial Value parameter, 453
 Label parameter, 453
 Label Placement parameter, 453
 setting, 452-454
ListBox component, 458
PushButton component, 459
RadioButton component, 460-462
ScrollBar component, 463
ScrollPane component, 464-465
Parent keyword, 264-265
Parent object, 855
Parent tag, 325
parentheses [()] operator, 813

parseFloat function, 321, 413, 840
parseInt function, 321, 414, 841
Partylogger Web site, 934
passing, HTML values to Flash, 696-699
password-verification example, variable comparison, 316-318
Path option (Publish Settings PNG tab), 199
Paused at Start option (Publish Settings dialog box HTML tab), 201
Pen Tool (Preferences dialog box Editing tab), 35, 67-68
Pencil tool (Properties Inspector), 27, 52-53
Perl scripts, 773
permissions, MySQL, 750-751
personalization, PHP, 738
Photoshop, integration with Flash MX, 13
PHP, 730-731, 738
absolute paths, 739
case sensitivity, 738
comments, 741
database storage, 747
directory structures, 738
dynamic content, 732-734
escape chracters, 741-742
functions, phpinfo, 734
installation, troubleshooting, 736-737
integration with Flash, 731-732
MySQL, 748-749
 columns, 751
 connecting PHP to, 754-756
 creating databases, 749
 creating new users, 750
 creating tables, 752
 describing tables, 752-753

 entering information into tables, 752-753
 granting permissions, 750-751
 resources, 756-757
 selecting data from tables, 753-754
 showing databases, 749-750
 showing table contents, 753
 showing tables, 752
optional modules, 737
personalization, 738
receiving data to Flash, 742
 Flash file development, 744
 loadVariables ActionScript, 742-743
 php/simple.php file, 743-744
 tags, 743
relative paths, 739
scripts, 743-744
 ActionScript, 740
 domain criteria, 739-740
sending data from Flash to PHP, 745-748
tags, 743
 ASP, 743
 script, 743
 short, 743
testing script, 734-736
PHP Flash Turbine 5.0 Web site, 942
php/simple.php file, 743-744
phpinfo function, 734
PICT area (Preferences dialog box Clipboard tab), 36
Pipey's Flash Resource Web site, 934
Pixels option (Lasso tool), 81
play and stop controls, digital videos, 229-232